LETTERS OF ANTON CHEKHOV

ANTON CHEKHOV
1890

Letters of

Translated from the Russian

Selection, Commentary

NEW YORK, EVANSTON, SAN FRANCISCO, LONDON

ANTON CHEKHOV

by Michael Henry Heim

in collaboration with Simon Karlinsky

and Introduction by Simon Karlinsky

HARPER & ROW, PUBLISHERS

 For information address Harper & Row, Publishers, Inc., 10 East 53rd Street, New York, N.Y. 10022. Published simultaneously in Canada by Fitzhenry & Whiteside Limited, Toronto.

FIRST EDITION

STANDARD BOOK NUMBER: 06-012263-3

LIBRARY OF CONGRESS CATALOG CARD NUMBER: 72-9098

Designed by Sidney Feinberg

CONTENTS

FOREWORD

To our knowledge there have been four previous publications of Anton Chekhov's letters in English. Constance Garnett's two volumes (*Letters of Anton Chekhov to His Family and Friends* and *Letters of Anton Chekhov to Olga Knipper*), Louis S. Friedland's *Anton Chekhov's Letters on the Short Story, the Drama and Other Literary Topics*, and *The Life and Letters of Anton Tchekhov*, translated and edited by S. S. Koteliansky and Philip Tomlinson, all appeared in the early twenties. They were followed thirty years later by *The Selected Letters of Anton Chekhov*, edited by Lillian Hellman and translated by Sidonie Lederer, which is now, in paperback, the most readily available source of Chekhov's letters for the general reader.

A comparison of these editions with Chekhov's Russian originals has left us with a lasting sense of admiration for Constance Garnett's talent as a translator. Despite occasional misreadings she manages to convey both the tone and spirit of the letters with a resourcefulness and fidelity no one else has matched. Unfortunately, she did her translations at a time when fewer than half the letters presently available in Russian had been published; moreover, her prunings and abridgments frequently reduced the text to a mere skeleton of the original. In contrast to Garnett, the Koteliansky-Tomlinson translation often misses the mark stylistically; its excessive adherence to the letter of the original makes many of its passages needlessly ambiguous or simply incomprehensible. Louis Friedland's 1924 volume, recently reissued with a new introduction by Ernest J. Simmons, is a not very coherent patchwork of snippets accompanied by a regrettably uninformed commentary (which among other blunders places the heroes of the most famous comedies of Gogol and Griboyedov in a melodrama by Alexei Suvorin and confuses Thoreau with the Russian woman novelist Yevgenia Tur). The Hellman-Lederer volume, which is widely quoted in studies of modern drama, abounds in mistranslations and arbitrary cuts of crucial passages. These are the factors which convinced us of the need for a new, enlarged edition of Chekhov's letters in English.

Out of the more than four thousand published letters of Anton Chekhov we have tried to select those that give a comprehensive picture of his literary, social and scientific interests and views. To put together a coherent intellectual portrait, we have found it necessary to sacrifice several groups of letters emphasized by our predecessors: the vituperative, painfully humorous letters to Chekhov's older brother Alexander; the letters to his sister Maria from the Ukraine and Siberia (the latter are mostly identical in content to his series of articles "Across Siberia," which is available in English in a fine translation by Avrahm Yarmolinsky in the collection *The Unknown Chekhov*); and the flirtatious letters to various women who were of no real importance in his life. On the other hand, letters dealing with medical and biological topics, usually omitted in non-Russian editions of Chekhov's letters, receive their full due.

D. S. Mirsky, the noted Russian literary historian, justly calls Chekhov one of the three finest letter writers in the Russian language (Mirsky's other two paragons are Alexander Pushkin and the philosopher Vladimir Solovyov). We have accordingly decided to print every letter we have selected in its entirety, preferring the practice of elucidating occasional trivial detail in footnotes to that of making the whimsical and often distorting cuts which all our predecessors have allowed themselves. And because maximal comprehension of the letters requires that the reader have some idea of the people to whom and about whom Chekhov is writing, we have provided more detailed annotations than the usual "X was a writer who lived in St. Petersburg" sort of thing.

We have taken particular pains to identify the frequent quotations which Chekhov liked to incorporate into his letters. His principal sources are the Bible, Alexander Griboyedov's verse comedy *The Misfortune of Being Clever* (1828), the fables of the Russian neoclassical poet Ivan Krylov (1769–1844) and the plays of William Shakespeare (in early nineteenth-century Russian translations, usually those of Nikolai Polevoy). The biblical quotations, cited by Chekhov in Russianized Old Church Slavic, are given in their standard King James equivalents, the Griboyedov and Krylov lines in our own translation.

The letters are arranged in sections, each of which is preceded by an introduction outlining the literary and biographical background for that particular group. For the most part, they appear in chronological order, but in a few instances, when their contents so dictated, we have taken them out of sequence. These instances are indicated in the annotations.

In line with our principle of presenting complete and undoctored texts, we have aimed at producing a translation that respects the original. When Chekhov repeats a word, we do not make him more eloquent by casting about for synonyms. When he uses an ambiguous phrase, we do not make up his mind for him by smoothing it over. When he writes a long or convoluted sentence, we do not explicate him by breaking it up into easily digestible morsels. Repetition, ambiguity and sentence structure combine to form a writer's style, and though style is commonly associated with talent, it may also be influenced by such external factors as haste (the bugaboo of Chekhov's early period) and illness (which plagued him from the late nineties on).

For the sake of accuracy and authenticity we have retained the Julian calendar (to calculate the date of any letter according to the Gregorian calendar, now in use throughout the world, add twelve days to nineteenth-century dates and thirteen days to twentieth-century dates); the centigrade temperature scale (according to which 36.6 degrees is normal body temperature); Russian weights and measures (one pood equals about 40 pounds, one verst equals 3,500 feet, one arshin equals 28 inches, one sazhen equals three arshins, one dessiatine equals 2.7 acres) and monetary units (the ruble was worth slightly more in purchasing power than the American dollar was at that time; a common laborer was paid twelve rubles a month and a qualified factory worker got thirty). We have converted the typographical term *pechatny list*, which corresponds to the English signature in octavo and consists of sixteen printed pages, to the actual number of pages involved. When an addressee is known by a name other than his real name, we give his real name and then his pseudonym in parentheses. Finally, we have tried to be especially precise in our renditions of plant and animal nomenclature—another area in which previous translators have been notoriously lax—because Chekhov's involvement in medicine and the natural sciences clearly warrants it (for an example of Chekhov's concern over the correct name of a plant, see Letter 161).

No complete, unexpurgated edition of Chekhov's letters is available in any language. To obtain maximally complete texts, however, we have collated the versions presented by the three most complete collections to appear in his native country:

1. The pre-revolutionary six-volume edition published by his sister Maria between 1912 and 1916.
2. Volumes XIII-XX of the twenty-volume edition of Chekhov's complete works published between 1944 and 1951 by special decree of the

Soviet government to commemorate the fiftieth anniversary of his death.
3. Volumes XI and XII of the twelve-volume edition of collected works published in 1963 and 1964.

We have also taken several letters from Volume 68 of *Literary Heritage* (Moscow, 1960), a regularly appearing miscellany specializing in literary documents and documentary studies.

Passages considered censorable vary considerably from one edition to the next, with the mode and extent of variation reflecting the development of Russian cultural attitudes. Chekhov's sister brought out her edition during the period after the abortive 1905 revolution, when Russian censors interfered less with literature than in almost any other period of recent history. She could accordingly include passages of political and religious commentary that would have had a hard time passing the censor in Chekhov's own lifetime. For many of the most important letters her edition remains the least-impaired source.

But Maria Chekhova was handicapped by the fact that most of the people Chekhov discussed in his letters were still alive when her edition appeared. Some of them were personal friends or members of the family. To spare their feelings, she found it desirable to eliminate numerous passages.

By the 1940s, however, there was no longer any need for such delicacy, and many of the passages Maria Chekhova had deleted were restored in the 1944–51 edition. In addition, the editors gathered together several thousand previously unpublished letters and provided the entire corpus with a scholarly apparatus of astounding scope and thoroughness. Theoretically, then, the eight volumes of letters in this edition are the fullest and most complete collection of Chekhov's letters ever published.

At the same time, however, they are a monument to the ruthlessness of Stalinist censors, to their mania for tampering with texts and rewriting history—even, as in Chekhov's case, when dealing with an officially approved national classic. There is no other instance on record of a comparable procedure being applied to a major nineteenth-century Russian writer on such a scale, which of itself speaks for the deeply felt, if unacknowledged, subversive potential of Chekhov's views within the Soviet context.

Literally hundreds of deletions come to light when the 1944–51 Soviet edition is set beside the 1912–16 Maria Chekhova edition. There are cuts made for political and nationalistic considerations, as when Chekhov makes too much of life in Western Europe or fails to sound patriotic enough to suit the Stalinist censor. There are cuts of passages that mention Jews, because the word he uses for "Jew" is *zhid*. Though ugly and highly pejorative when used by a present-day anti-Semite, this happened to be the normal word for Jew in the South Russian dialect Chekhov grew up speaking. (When Chekhov does in fact wish to use an anti-Jewish epithet, he chooses a different word, *shmul*, which was also carefully deleted throughout the edition.) Even a passage that compares newly hatched nightingale fledglings to naked Jewish children was not allowed to appear in print. Also excluded were all passages that might have seemed offensive to the Soviet Union's allies in the late 1940s—the Chinese and Yugoslavs, for example; occasional derogatory references to the Germans and French, on the other hand, were allowed to stand.

Since Soviet neo-Victorian prudery abhors all references not only to sex but to many other normal bodily functions such as childbirth and digestion, many letters underwent extensive bowdlerizing. Here is one example from several dozen, the postscript to a letter Chekhov wrote to his friend Ivan Shcheglov from a village in the Ukraine on May 10, 1888.

> *Maria Chekhova's 1912 edition:*
> P.S. There is no outdoor privy here. You have to answer the call of nature in nature's very presence, in ravines and under bushes. My entire [. . .] is covered with mosquito bites.

The grammatical agreement of the verb and of the adjective in the last sentence makes it clear to a speaker of Russian that the omitted word is "backside."

> *Volume XIV of the twenty-volume edition, 1949:*
> P.S. [. . .]

The extent of the license the censors took with Chekhov's letters was documented in 1954 and 1955 when Professor Gleb Struve published a series of articles on the subject in Russian émigré, British and French journals. Partly in response to the shock caused in international scholarly circles by Struve's disclosures, many (but by no means all) of the passages deleted by the censors in the 1944–51 edition were reinstated in the 1963–64 edition, which was published, we might recall, at the height of the de-Stalinization campaign. In the postscript from the letter to Shcheglov quoted above, for example, the first two sentences are printed in full, though the third sentence was apparently still too colorful to appear in print in the Soviet Union—even in the 1960s.

While undoing some of the damage done by the censors of the 1940s, however, the more recent edition has introduced a more subtle form of censorship. It includes more than eight hundred letters, yet omits some of the most significant: letters dealing with personal freedom, the rights of the writer and of literature, and unfavorable comparisons of life in Russia with life in Western Europe. The commentary to the present volume will point out some of the more blatant of these omissions. We have reinstated the censored words and passages wherever possible; when there was no way to re-establish them, the deletion is indicated in the text of the letter as follows: [. . .].

With all the shortcomings imposed from without by the censors, there is nonetheless no doubt that both the 1944–51 and 1963–64 Soviet editions of Chekhov's letters were put together by able and knowledgeable scholars. Our collection owes a deep debt of gratitude to their efforts for a large portion of our commentary. We would also like to acknowledge the help of friends and colleagues who were kind enough to share with us their competence in special fields: Dr. Roy Leeper of San Francisco on medical history and medical terminology; Professor Francis J. Whitfield on Slavic biblical texts; Dr. Erica Brendel on ornithology; and Professor Olga Raevsky Hughes, whose profound knowledge of Russian culture and Russian religious lore repeatedly saved the day after all other sources failed us. We are grateful to Father Leonid Kishkovsky of St. Innocent's Orthodox Church, San Francisco, and to Mr. Dennis Powers of the American Conservatory Theater for supplying particularly hard-to-find bits of information. Mr. Barry Jordan served as the research assistant for the project, typing numerous drafts, checking sources in at least four languages, and looking up more books, writers, plants, animals and minerals than any of us cares to remember (but none is likely to forget). His help is deeply appreciated.

M. H. H.

S. K.

LETTERS OF ANTON CHEKHOV

INTRODUCTION:

THE GENTLE SUBVERSIVE

To Vladimir Nabokov

MOST PEOPLE can visualize him easily enough: the dour, sickly man in a long black overcoat buttoned to the top, a black hat pulled low over his eyes, leaning wearily on his cane in a flowering Yalta garden. That photograph, taken shortly before Chekhov's death, is reproduced on the cover of Ernest J. Simmons's popular biography sold at all paperback stands. It also served David Levine as the model for his widely reproduced caricature, which appears in the *New York Review of Books* jigsaw puzzle and which shows Chekhov as an elongated gloomy black tapeworm. The other best-known image of Chekhov is that of the morose consumptive in an armchair, glaring balefully at the world through his pince-nez, all shaggy tweeds and shaggy gray beard. This one comes from a portrait painted in oil toward the end of Chekhov's life by a mediocre painter named Iosif Braz. An earlier portrait by Braz for which Chekhov sat looked so little like him that it was destroyed. The second try, not much more successful, ended up at the Tretiakov Gallery in Moscow, and it is to this day the most widely reproduced portrait of Chekhov. It is the one most likely to grace the jacket of a collection of his stories or plays, or to be appended to one of the numerous biographies that have been appearing in Western languages with increasing frequency. Chekhov himself disliked the Braz portrait, thought that it made him look as if he'd been sniffing grated horseradish, and would refuse to autograph reproductions of it; those who knew Chekhov believed that this portrait falsified his appearance.

The multivolume Russian editions of Chekhov's collected writings and of his letters reproduce dozens of photographs and paintings where he looks quite different. There is the broad-shouldered, open-faced young giant of the early 1880s, who wrote hundreds of humorous stories, frequented Moscow night clubs, studied medicine and suddenly realized, at the age of twenty-six, that he was becoming an important and admired writer. There is the strikingly handsome, elegantly dressed Chekhov of thirty (a trim goatee, but still no pince-nez), who had already written some of his major masterpieces—"The Steppe," "The Duel," "A Dreary Story"—and had witnessed successful productions of his play *Ivanov*. This Chekhov was celebrated throughout Russia. He had traveled to Sakhalin, to Ceylon, to France and Italy, had climbed Vesuvius and gone swimming in the Indian Ocean. There is the Chekhov of the mid-1890s, the author of *The Seagull*, the builder of schools, the famine fighter, the bed partner of celebrated actresses and stylish literary ladies. All these different Chekhovs are there in the photographs, and in his letters, and they are all equally essential for understanding the man and his work.

The shaggy beard, the pince-nez, the funereal clothes, the exhausted look are not falsifications. They also existed, but they belonged to the last three years of Chekhov's life, when his lungs were ravaged by tuberculosis and when it was plain to everyone except himself that he was about to die. This was the Chekhov who wrote "The Bishop" and *The Cherry Orchard*, and this seems to be the Chekhov that the world prefers to remember. The pictures of the dying invalid of Yalta go well with the widely held view that Chekhov was a man who wrote gloomy stories and plays about unhappy, spineless people leading frustrated and melancholy lives.

This legend, like most legends, contains a small grain of truth. Chekhov *was* capable of being frustrated and bored, as his letters show; and he was very good at depicting these states of mind in his work. But to reduce the entire man and the content of his work to this particular dimension is like hearing a full symphony orchestra perform a Beethoven symphony and deliberately ignoring all the instruments except the cellos. The view of Chekhov as *The Voice of Twilight Russia* (the title of Princess Nina Andronikova Toumanova's platitudinous, cliché-filled book in English which is still widely read), as the "poet of twilight moods," was created by Russian critics at the turn of the century, when Chekhov was still alive. He hated it, thought it stupid, and made a point of leaving the room if anyone brought it up. But many people close to him were receptive to this view, including his wife Olga Knipper, who in 1901 wrote to him: "My heart aches when I think of the quiet sadness that seems to be so deeply entrenched in your heart." To which Chekhov replied: "But, darling, that is utter nonsense! There is no sadness in me, there never was; most of the time life is bearable and when you are with me, things are really fine." (Letter to Olga Knipper, August 24, 1901.)

None of the major literary figures of his time who were Chekhov's friends and who loved him as a writer ever accepted this reductionist concept—not Lev Tolstoy, not Nikolai Leskov, not Ivan Bunin. But Konstantin Stanislavsky was certainly influenced by it in everything he wrote about Chekhov, and so were some of Chekhov's close personal friends, whose reminiscences occasionally reflect the prevailing critical views at the turn of the century, rather than their own memories and observations. Basically, the image of Chekhov as the melancholy bard of a vanishing Russia represents the final success of Russian nineteenth-century critics in their determined effort to label and pigeonhole a major writer who did not fit their traditional and simplistic recipes for classifying writers. And, of course, Stanislavsky's drawn-out, elegiac productions of Chekhov's plays, with which Chekhov disagreed and which he disliked but which set the pattern for later generations, also served to contribute to that particular image.

Chekhov's quarrel with the critical establishment of his time is one of the central facts of his literary biography. The issues debated and the positions taken are enormously important, and they touch the very mainsprings of Russian cultural life both in nineteenth-century Russia and in the present-day U.S.S.R. The circumstances of Chekhov's advent as a serious writer have almost no precedent in Russian or any other literature. His acclaim by the reading public of the 1880s and '90s, the recognition of his talent by the finest older writers of his time were accompanied by a steady stream of jeremiads by leading literary critics, lamenting Chekhov's lack of human concern and of moral principles, warning their readers that this writer was dangerous and that by writing the way he did he was betraying the humanitarian traditions of his native literature. When fifteen years of this sort of attack failed to halt the spread of Chekhov's reputation, a new generation of critics managed to reduce the complexities of Chekhovian concern and compassion to their own moaning and melancholy level and thus at last to co-opt him into the very tradition to which he was so alien and so opposed. His second co-optation came in the 1930s and '40s, when orthodox Stalinist Soviet critics like Vladimir Yermilov created the even more false and fraudulent image of the optimistic, quasi-revolutionary Chekhov, whose main aim in writing what he wrote was to indict the bourgeoisie and the ruling classes. To understand the causes for all this requires at least a minimal glance at the Russian cultural history of the past century and a half.

The epoch of the Great Reforms of the 1860s looms particularly large in forming Chekhov's attitudes and the attitudes of his detractors, and it frequently comes up in his correspondence. Chekhov was a small child when the reforms took place, but their impact on his life was crucial. Most of the important Russian writers of the nineteenth century were born into families which, whether affluent or impoverished, belonged to the nobility. Anton Chekhov, on the other hand, was born into a family of emancipated serfs. His grandfather, his father, his uncles had all known existence as human chattels owned by other men. The future writer was slightly more than one year old when Emperor Alexander II, reacting to Russian defeat in the Crimean War, initiated the most sweeping of his several major reforms, the emancipation of all serfs. With one stroke of the tsar's pen, some fifty-two million slaves became free human beings. Other reforms, almost as momentous, followed. Trials by jury replaced the horrors of the archaic judicial system based on written procedures kept secret from the parties to the case and under which the court was not even required to inform the accused of the exact nature of the charges. A network of semi-autonomous, elective local administrative units called *zemstvos* was instituted and given considerable powers to establish schools and hospitals, to build roads and to provide veterinary and insurance services at the local level. Under the *zemstvo* system, tsarist Russia was one of the first countries in the world to offer its citizens free medical, dental and surgical care in its village hospitals. Anton Chekhov was frequently involved in the *zemstvo* system and its hospitals in one capacity or another, and many of his stories and private letters contain fascinating insights into the workings of this often-forgotten institution.

There was a great deal that went wrong with the implementation of the reforms of Alexander II, and it has become customary in the West to dismiss them as partial solutions that did not change the basically oppressive system. But their results on the local level, as seen and described by Chekhov, brought an increase in freedom to millions of formerly enslaved human beings and provided them with better education and medical care and with a chance of getting a fair trial in the courts. Chekhov was not one to dismiss or to ridicule this kind of achievement.

But the epoch of the sixties left Russia with another legacy, one that directly affected literature. For all his reforming, Alexander II did not authorize anything resembling real freedom of the press or any sort of open criticism of the government, even when it came from a loyal opposition, such as had by then become customary in most Western European monarchies. And, as most of the literate segment of society realized, many aspects of life in post-reform Russia deserved to be criticized. Many articulate people wanted to express their disapproval in something more durable and widely disseminated than an illegal anti-government leaflet. In the liberalized atmosphere of the 1860s a very special kind of literary criticism was developed to deal with this predicament.

The precedent for this sort of criticism and for many of its basic methods had already been established in the 1840s by the fiery Romantic critic Vissarion Belinsky. To outwit the censor, Belinsky was the first to exploit the device of pretending to criticize the reality depicted in a work of fiction while actually telling his readers what he thought of the state of affairs in the country. It was also Belinsky who began the practice of distorting the content and the meaning of a work of literature or even the stated social views of a given writer when he felt it necessary for the purpose of his political sermon. Thus, in his influential series of articles on Gogol, Belinsky turned that most fantastic and surrealistic of Russian writers into a photographic realist, because such an approach enabled him to use Gogol's work for an indictment of existing Russian customs; furthermore, Belinsky managed to read into Gogol's stories and plays a subversive, anti-government message, which the politically conservative Gogol had never intended and which horrified him. All objective facts notwithstanding, Belinsky's image of Gogol prevailed in Russian criticism until the end of the nineteenth century, and although the Symbolist and Formalist critics of the first three decades of our century did brilliant work in establishing and asserting the full complexity and uniqueness of Gogol's genius, the simplistic Belinskian view has been forcibly revived in the Soviet Union in recent decades and has remained compulsory there ever since.

Despite Belinsky's excesses and his ruthless hounding of several fine writers who to this day have lesser reputations than they deserve merely because Belinsky could not find suitable texts for sermons in their work, his love for literature was genuine, and it earned him the friendship and respect of such men as Turgenev, Herzen and the young Dostoyevsky. His successors of the 1860s, the men who set the tone for all Russian literary criticism in Chekhov's time—Nikolai Chernyshevsky and his two young disciples, Nikolai Dobrolyubov and Dmitry Pisarev—were social critics who were forced to write about literature and art because that was the only way they could get around the censor.

Nikolai Chernyshevsky's battle against tsarist tyranny was a beautiful and courageous thing to behold. His notions of literature, however, were primitive, oppressive and ultimately irrational. Literature and the other arts were for Chernyshevsky inferior substitutes for real life. Their only useful aspect was their hypnotic power to show people the desirable directions for society to take and to warn them against taking wrong paths by providing cautionary examples. Once these aims had been accomplished, art itself could be safely discarded. Chernyshevsky also postulated a peculiarly quantitative criterion for judging artistic quality: a large edition of a book by Gogol was artistically superior to Gogol's original manuscript of the same work and a full-dress production of an opera (*any* opera, presumably) was on an artistically higher level than a performance of a string quartet.

It was Lenin himself who best described the critical method of Chernyshevsky's disciple Dobrolyubov. "He turned his discussion of *Oblomov* into a battle-cry, into a call to activism and revolutionary struggle," Lenin wrote admiringly, "and he turned his analysis of *On the Eve* into a genuine revolutionary manifesto, written in such a way that it remains unforgotten to this day." Of course even Lenin knew that these novels by Goncharov and Turgenev did not contain the ideas that Dobrolyubov read into them or derived from them.

The third member of the critical trinity of the 1860s, Pisarev, Chekhov's particular *bête noire*, but actually the most readable and, in the long run, the most logical of the three, took the basic attitudes of his age to their ultimate conclusion and indicted all imaginative literature as frivolous and superfluous.

"Never, it would seem, was more scorn heaped upon literature generally, nor were people more eager to put literature in its place, to puncture its illusions, if not destroy it altogether," wrote Hugh McLean of this period in his masterful examination of the development of modern Russian literature. McLean summarizes the respective attitudes of the critics of the 1840s and 1860s as follows: "Belinsky had said that art should be a textbook of life; Chernyshevsky would make it a second-rate surrogate for reality; Pisarev would abolish it."

Dobrolyubov and Pisarev both died very young. The government managed to make a national martyr out of Chernyshevsky by putting him on trial on insufficient evidence, framing him with false testimony and banishing him to Siberia. But for most Russian critics of the last quarter of the nineteenth century and for their readers, Belinsky and Chernyshevsky were literary figures as important as Gogol, Turgenev and Tolstoy. Their prestige was unassailable, their opinions and pronouncements not to be questioned, and they managed to change the literary outlook of many generations of Russians. During the more repressive decades of the seventies and the eighties, literary criticism remained in the hands of their successors and erstwhile associates. These men could not match the by then canonized radical saints of the sixties in their revolutionary fervor, but they reiterated the demand that literature express simplistic political and sociological clichés, and above all they continued the tradition of negating and vilifying all literature that did not conform to their insistence on easy didacticism.

The available histories of Russian literature usually overlook one basic fact of late-nineteenth-century intellectual life, with which Chekhov, like all Russian writers from the 1860s on, had to contend: the existence of two separate but equally repressive systems of censorship in the country. The *de jure* censorship of the tsarist government still had considerable powers in the 1880s. Its job was to weed out all expression of anti-government sentiments and to watch out for any excessive liberties in the religious and sexual areas. The government censors could temporarily bar the publication of Tolstoy's *The Kreutzer Sonata,* and one of them managed to ban outright Chekhov's early play *On the High Road* because it was to his way of thinking "gloomy and filthy." But the censors' powers were visibly dwindling throughout the course of Chekhov's writing career, and if he could still worry in 1891 about the feasibility of making an ex-revolutionary the hero of a short story (Letter 63), a few years later sympathetic portrayals of active revolutionaries became quite acceptable, as the publication of Tolstoy's *Resurrection* in 1899 eloquently demonstrated.

Far more powerful and, in the long run, even more oppressive was the *de facto* unofficial censorship by the anti-government literary critics, who not only ceaselessly demanded that all writers be topical, obviously relevant and socially critical, but also prescribed rigid formal and aesthetic criteria to which all literature was supposed to conform. Because a soberly realistic depiction of Russian life had been assumed since the days of Belinsky to be the most effective way of exposing social shortcomings, the critics of the 1860s, '70s and '80s fought an unending battle against fantasy, imagination, poetry, mysticism, against excessive depth in psychological perception, against all joy and humor that was not topical or satirical, and above all against any formal or stylistic innovations in literature and literary craftsmanship in general. Their rationale was that all these things could detract from the ideological message which was the sole aim of literature. The radical utilitarians would also have liked to attack religion and the Orthodox Church, but in this one area government censorship remained adamant and rigid. In matters of sex, however, the anti-government utilitarians were even more puritanical than the official censors. Pisarev was outraged and revolted by the character of Lensky in Pushkin's *Eugene Onegin* because he mentions his fiancée's shoulders and bosom to a close friend, and Saltykov-Shchedrin was so shocked by the gynecological and sexual aspects of Tolstoy's *Anna Karenina* that he ridiculed the work as a "genito-urinary novel." The power of these critics to enforce their prejudices and taboos was awesome, and they used this power ruthlessly and often vindictively. There is no doubt that recognition of Dostoyevsky's true stature was delayed for decades because of Belinsky's disappointment in him after *The Double* and by the asininities that Dobrolyubov and Pisarev wrote about his later novels. Literary hacks like Zlatovratsky and second-raters like Gleb Uspensky enjoyed great and undeserved reputations as a result of the efforts of their utilitarian champions, while a writer of the stature of Nikolai Leskov was read out of Russian literature for the rest of the nineteenth century because of an early novel in which he had satirized a socialist commune. Afanasy Fet, one of the greatest Russian poets of the century, was treated as a criminal and a public enemy by several generations of

Russian critics because he openly declared that he was neither willing nor able to discuss social issues in his poetry. And, of course, the sad decline of Russian poetry in the 1870s and '80s is directly attributable to the savage hounding and ridicule with which the critical fraternity of the period greeted the appearance of any poet of originality or technical ability.

One of the best fictional reflections of the effect that decades of utilitarian brainwashing had on many intelligent and socially aware Russian readers is to be found in Chekhov's short novel "Three Years" (1895), which contains the following literary discussion at the home of a wealthy intellectual of merchant-class origin:

> "A work of literature cannot be significant or useful unless its basic idea contains some meaningful social task," Konstantin was saying, looking at Yartsev angrily. "If the book protests against serfdom or if the author indicts high society and its trivial ways, then it is a significant and useful piece of writing. But as for those novels and tales where it's oh and ah and why she fell in love with him, but he fell out of love with her,—such books, I say, are meaningless and to hell with them."
>
> "I quite agree with you, Konstantin Ivanych," said Yulia Sergeyevna. "One writer describes a lovers' tryst, another describes infidelity, a third one —a reunion after separation. Can't they find any other subjects? There are, after all, many people who are ill, unhappy, worn out by poverty, who must be disgusted to have to read about such things."
>
> Laptev was disturbed to hear his wife, a young woman of not quite twenty-two, speak of love so seriously and coldly. He could guess why this was so.
>
> "If poetry does not solve the problems that you consider important," said Yartsev, "why don't you try books on technology, on police and financial law or read scientific essays? Why should *Romeo and Juliet* have to deal with academic freedom or with sanitary conditions in prisons, instead of with love, when you can find any number of articles and handbooks on these other subjects?"
>
> "But look here, you exaggerate!" Konstantin interrupted him. "We are not speaking of such giants as Shakespeare or Goethe. We speak of scores of talented and average writers who would be of much more use were they to leave love alone and take up indoctrinating the masses with knowledge and humanitarian ideas."

Some of the central issues of Russian intellectual history are encapsulated in this brief dialogue. Konstantin's views on the uses of literature are a minute summary of one of the basic theses of Peter Lavrov's *Historical Letters* (1870, final version 1891), which is perhaps the most representative, influential and widely read single document of Russian nineteenth-century anti-government dissent (it is available in English in a brilliantly idiomatic translation by James P. Scanlan, who has also contributed an illuminating introductory essay). Yulia's reasons for rejecting literature that deals with love (and, by implication, with other personal and psychological themes) are a simple-minded paraphrase of the reasons advanced by the Populist critics of Chekhov's time when they dismissed Tolstoy's *Anna Karenina* as socially irrelevant. Yartsev's mention of Shakespeare is a dodge, used repeatedly since Belinsky's time, to appeal to the prestige of recognized foreign classics in order to secure some freedom of expression for Russian literature. This dodge never worked, however: it was all very well for E. T. A. Hoffmann to write fantasies, because he was a foreign writer acknowledged throughout Western Europe, but a Russian writer, Vladimir Odoyevsky, who tried treating subjects similar to Hoffmann's, was condemned to literary death on the spot by Belinsky. Later on, in the 1870s, the defenders of Alexander Ostrovsky's play *The Snow Maiden* (it was attacked not for its insipid and mawkish poetry, but for bringing mythological creatures to the stage, which was contrary to the principles of realism) unsuccessfully cited the precedents of Shakespeare's *The Tempest* and *Midsummer Night's Dream*, but were told by the utilitarians that a man of Shakespeare's stature could permit himself a few aberrations; Shakespeare, after all, did not have the obligation to help the downtrodden Russian people which every Russian writer automatically had.

It was easy enough to see that the literary views of Russian radical utilitarians were primitive and simplistic. Turgenev, Tolstoy and Dostoyevsky all saw and said as much. But Chekhov saw more. He saw that the men whom most of his contemporaries considered champions of freedom and giants of literary criticism were not any kind of *literary* critics at all, and that this whole critical dynasty, with the possible exception of Belinsky, neither liked nor understood literature. While the entire Russian intelligentsia, save for its most reactionary segment, worshiped these critics and their tradition because of their opposition to the tsarist regime, Chekhov almost alone seemed to realize that men who fight tyranny and oppression by using tyrannical and oppressive means and who pursue their goals with ruthless and single-minded fanaticism are not likely to further the cause of freedom and bring about democracy in literature or in any other area. It took both courage and vision to discern this oppressive strain in the mainstream of Russian radical dissent, although even Chekhov could not foresee the catastrophic effect on twentieth-century Russian literature and its writers of the officially imposed revival of radical-utilitarian criteria and literary ethics in Soviet times (backed by state-supported judicial enforcement of these views).

Chekhov's quarrel with the presuppositions of his epoch was fought in subdued and civilized tones, without ranting and without proselytizing. He preferred his literary work to speak for itself and reserved his polemics for his private correspondence and for an occasional editorial article, published, as a rule, anonymously. His natural mode of expression was understatement rather than diatribe. In fact, he would again and again overestimate the perceptive powers of his reading audience and even of close personal friends and have to explain his views and intentions all over after having stated them precisely and clearly in a story or in a personal letter. The total misunderstanding of the meaning of the play *Ivanov* by many people closely associated with its production is only the most spectacular example of this sort of thing in Chekhov's correspondence. Chekhov's letters of the late 1880s are particularly rich in intellectual drama because he has to articulate his private ideas on the rights of the individual and of literature and on personal freedom to friends who in literary matters live and breathe the utilitarian traditions of their age, regardless of their social position or political orientation. The wealthy and mystical-minded society lady Maria Kiselyova, in objecting to "Mire" (Letter 9) used the same didactic-utilitarian approach that the liberal editor Vukol Lavrov was to take a few years later in condemning Chekhov's "lack of principles." Indeed, for all the political polarization in nineteenth-century Russian society, by Chekhov's time the demand that all literature be didactic and contain some instantly obvious and certifiably relevant social idea became the norm for everyone, moderates and conservatives included. In Chekhov's story "In the Landau," a snobbish aristocratic young army officer, who moves in circles close to the imperial court, offhandedly condemns Turgenev for not having written about "freedom of the press or about social consciousness." And, in real life, a committee of three liberal professors of literature who were asked in 1899 by the management of the government-owned Imperial Theaters to judge the suitability of Chekhov's *Uncle Vanya* for presentation in official theaters turned the play down, among other reasons, for its lack of social relevance.

As long as Chekhov published his humorous and satirical early stories in humor magazines, serious and influential critics could afford to ignore him. But in 1886–88, when his startlingly original, seriously conceived mature stories began to appear in the leading literary journals, an alarm was sounded. The structural originality of "Heartache," "Anyuta" and "The Steppe" was seen as an affront to Russian realism, a betrayal of the most cherished traditions of Turgenev, Grigorovich and the simplistically understood Gogol. Above all, Chekhov's eschewing of all easily paraphrasable social tendentiousness, his preference for dealing with social realities rather than with social theories, was seen as subversive to their cause by the entrenched utilitarians.

The principal keepers of the Belinskian-Chernyshevskian flame in the 1880s were the facile and prolific Populist hack Alexander Skabichevsky (1838–1910) and the more serious political thinker and journalist Nikolai Mikhailovsky (1842–1904). Because of their doctrinaire differences with the Russian Marxists and with Lenin, these men are styled "Populist critics" in Soviet literary histories and reference books and are denied the adulation accorded their predecessors of the 1860s, who are now described as "Revolutionary Democrats." But in actual fact, Skabichevsky and, to a lesser degree, Mikhailovsky form an important bridge between the utilitarians of the sixties and Russian Marxist criticism, both before and after the October Revolution. Reading Skabichevsky's sarcastic articles on *War and Peace* and *Anna Karenina,* with their sneers at Tolstoy's lack of social awareness and purpose and their insistence that a few changes in the political system could instantly solve all of Anna's and Vronsky's emotional problems, today's Soviet readers should have an overwhelming sense of *déjà vu*: this is exactly the tone, the method and the literary ethics of all those denunciatory articles that they have been reading for the last five decades about Anna Akhmatova, Boris Pasternak, Alexander Solzhenitsyn and so many others. And, since the main source of Soviet-Marxist aesthetics is Chernyshevsky and his various successors rather than anything Marx or Engels ever wrote, the similarities have logical and obvious causes.

Skabichevsky's initial comment on Chekhov's more serious work was that this writer was a mindless literary clown who would eventually die in the gutter, forgotten by everyone. Skabichevsky lived long enough to witness Chekhov's later popularity and the general acceptance of his work; he accordingly toned down his hostility, especially when the impact of Chekhov's views had been neutralized by his being represented by the reductionist critics as the elegiac bard of a vanishing social order. But Mikhailovsky, the most popular and influential critic of the period, staked his entire literary reputation on discrediting Chekhov in the eyes of enlightened and liberal readers; his failure to achieve this goal was the most momentous failure of the entire tradition he represented, and it was this failure that probably opened the door for the eventual liberation of Russian literature from utilitarian dictatorship during the Symbolist and Futurist periods. It is typical of Chekhov's personality that he managed to maintain cordial personal relations with Mikhailovsky and even nominated him for election to the Russian Imperial Academy. In an age when the views of Nikolai Mikhailovsky represented for the majority of thinking Russians the ultimate in literary wisdom (this is perceptively stressed by Alexander Solzhenitsyn in several episodes in *August 1914*) it was Chekhov who, in the course of a conversation with a young radical student, formulated the truest possible characterization of this critic: "Mikhailovsky is an important sociologist and a failed critic; by his very nature he is incapable of understanding what imaginative literature is."

Mikhailovsky's stubborn rejection of Chekhov, his refusal to recognize that there was a humanitarian side to Chekhov's literary art, is usually regarded in Chekhov scholarship as a grotesque failure of literary taste, especially since Mikhailovsky was later to acclaim Maxim Gorky and Leonid Andreyev as being socially aware in ways that Chekhov for him was not. Yet perhaps in sticking to his guns to the last Mikhailovsky showed more honesty and more perception of Chekhov's true significance than did his successors of the turn of the century, who preferred to love a mournful and despondent Chekhov created in their own image rather than face the full implications of what Chekhov actually represented. For, in his own quiet and gentle way, Chekhov is one of the most profoundly subversive writers who ever lived. He is as subversive of the sociological presuppositions of a Russian Populist such as Mikhailovsky as of the Christian mysticism of a Lev Shestov, whose widely circulated essay on Chekhov draws heavily on Mikhailovsky's earlier articles and cites some of the same examples to indict Chekhov from a position of Christian metaphysics.

The letters in the present volume provide numerous examples of the ways in which Chekhov's adherence to his "holy of holies . . . the most absolute freedom imaginable, freedom from violence and from lies" (Letter 23) could undercut the fundamental assumptions of the Russian Empire, its dissident critics and, in fact, the very basis of Western Judeo-Christian civilization. In this respect the letters themselves are eloquent enough. However, in order to point out the essential affinity between the views expressed in the letters and Chekhov's stories and plays, it might be worthwhile to concentrate for a moment on the reflection in his creative writing of the three spheres of human activity which have always supposedly been safer to practice than to discuss: religion, politics and sex. Twentieth-century thinkers, such as Aldous Huxley in *The Devils of Loudun* and H. Rattray Taylor in *Sex and History*, have convincingly demonstrated that the basic human impulse from which religious, political and sexual activities all spring is often one and the same, and they have gone a long way toward explaining why repression in any one of these areas inevitably leads to repression in the other two. A study of the various forms of censorship exercised over Russian literature for the past two centuries should convince anyone that every curtailment of political expression and every liberalization is sure to be followed or accompanied by a corresponding increase or decrease of freedom in dealing with religious and sexual topics as well.

"Between the statements 'God exists' and 'There is no God' lies a whole vast field, which a true sage crosses with difficulty. But a Russian usually knows only one of these two extremes; what lies between them is of no interest to him and he usually knows nothing or very little." This maxim is to be found in Anton Chekhov's private notebooks not once, but several times. The tyrannical and pharisaic religious upbringing which Chekhov's father forced on his children resulted in a loss of faith by every single one of them once they became adults. While Anton did not turn into the kind of militant atheist that his older brother Alexander eventually became, there is no doubt that he was a nonbeliever in the last decades of his life. But his early religious upbringing never quite left him and it is very much in evidence both in his correspondence (with its frequent quotations from the Bible and from Orthodox prayers and its lapses into an ecclesiastical Old Church Slavic style for purposes of either solemnity or irony) and in the religious themes of many of his short stories. The Russian clergy appear in Chekhov's stories as frequently as do other social groups. In this Chekhov differs markedly from Tolstoy and Dostoyevsky, who, for all their preoccupation with religion, never thought of making an Orthodox priest, deacon or monk a central character in a work of fiction as Chekhov did in "The Bishop," "On Easter Eve," "Saintly Simplicity," "A Nightmare" and so many other stories. Most of these men of the Church are presented as full-blooded human beings with their own joys and problems; but we also find in Chekhov an occasional mean, dehumanized cleric, such as the heartless priest who appears briefly toward the end of "In the Ravine" or the nasty and vicious one who provides the comic element in "It Was Not Fated."

Chekhov's own favorite among the hundreds of stories he wrote was "The Student," a very brief story that, in moving and utterly simple terms, states the case for the importance of religious traditions and religious experience for the continuation of civilization. In Chekhov's last prose masterpiece, "The Bishop," the churchman-hero, sustained by his faith, faces the prospect of his own death with understanding and dignity, whereas a man much closer to Chekhov's own spiritual outlook, the professor of medicine in "A Dreary Story," who has no faith to lean on, deteriorates and withdraws from the life around him. The religious solace sought and found by Sonya in *Uncle Vanya* and by Yulia in "Three Years" are depicted by Chekhov with the utmost sympathy and understanding. And it was the nonbeliever Chekhov who, in the character of Lipa in "In the Ravine," created one of the most persuasive portraits of a meek Christian saint in Russian literature, comparable only to the similar creation of another nonbeliever, Turgenev's Lukeria in "The Living Relic."

Yet, for all these examples, religion, Christianity and the Church in Chekhov's work are totally divorced from the very things they are traditionally supposed to promote in Western civilization: morality, kindness and ethical treatment of fellow human beings. There are people in Chekhov's stories who are naturally good and kind, and religious belief or going to church are not shown to affect their natural goodness in one way or the other. But the unkind and the uncharitable in Chekhov's work, the exploiters and the manipulators, can and do use religion self-righteously and with impunity to further their selfish ends. The closest we come to an out-and-out villain in Chekhov's writings is the pious, churchgoing peasant Matvei in "Peasant Women," who uses religious teachings and prayers to rid himself of the woman he has seduced, to betray her, to frame her for a crime she probably did not commit and, after her death, to exploit and terrorize her small son. Another churchgoing Christian, the shopkeeper Andrei in "The Requiem," condemns his actress daughter as a harlot and is enabled by his religious beliefs to persist in this condemnation even after his priest explains to him how wrong he is. A whole gallery of cultivated upper-class ladies in Chekhov's stories use their church-sanctioned positions as Christian wives and mothers to humiliate other human beings (the professor's wife in "A Dreary Story"), to assert their own smug superiority (Maria Konstantinovna in "The Duel") or to bludgeon another person into submission (the wife in "The Chorus Girl"). The wise old professor in "A Dreary Story" drives this point home when he remarks that "virtue and purity are little different from vice when they are practiced in the spirit of unkindness."

While Tolstoy and Dostoyevsky both believed that Christian faith was the main source of moral strength for the impoverished and ignorant Russian peasants, Chekhov's much more closely observed and genuinely experienced picture of peasant life shows nothing of the sort. In the poverty-ridden world of "The Peasants," religion and the Church do nothing whatsoever to raise the moral or ethical level of the benighted peasantry, whose religious expression takes the form of superstition or of empty and meaningless ritual (this story so contradicted everything Tolstoy believed about Russian peasant religiosity that he called it a "sin against the Russian people"). In Chekhov's most brutal and violent story, "The Murder," a family of peasant religious fanatics are led by their search for God to hate and brutalize each other and to commit a religiously motivated murder.

In a literature that had produced Gogol, Tolstoy, Dostoyevsky and Leskov, the view that Christianity and religion in general are morally neutral is startling enough. This view is clearly subversive from the point of view of all established churches, but Chekhov's simultaneous insistence that religious experience can be tremendously enriching and rewarding when it brings consolation and spiritual profundity into people's lives sits very badly with his Soviet commentators and annotators, who are duty-bound to represent all religion as exploitative and reactionary. Chekhov's view of sex, however, is even more startling, coming as it does from a writer raised in the second half of the nineteenth century. For Chekhov, sex, like religion, is also a morally neutral quantity, whose moral and ethical implications depend on the circumstances and the attitudes of the people involved. Had Chekhov stated such a view openly and militantly in the midst of the Victorian age in which he was living, he would have been dismissed as a crackpot by almost everyone. Because of his usual gentle and subdued mode of presentation, he was able to make his point without shocking too many people—but it was at the cost of having his views in this area almost overlooked.

In the eighteenth century, and especially during the reign of Catherine the Great, Russian literature enjoyed considerable freedom in treating sexual themes. Alexander Pushkin, who was the last nineteenth-century Russian writer to have profound ties with eighteenth-century traditions, was also the last to write openly and without guilt about the joys of sexual love. Pushkin's remarkably free treatment of sexual themes (including an early poem about female masturbation and a verse epistle addressed to a homosexual friend whom Pushkin invited for a visit, with the assurance that, although he himself was not available, he would be happy to introduce the visitor to some like-minded young men) was no longer possible when the long night of Victorian repression of all sexuality descended on Russia, as it did on other European countries. The change of sexual attitudes is reflected in Pushkin's outlook as compared with that of Nikolai Gogol, who was only ten years younger. When the young Pushkin contracted gonorrhea, he informed some of his friends of the fact in a tone of puckish humor and with a touch of pride about having thus confirmed his full manhood. But when Gogol's mother, less than two decades later, mistook a skin rash described in one of his letters for a venereal disease symptom, Gogol replied in a hysterical letter that if he had had such a loathsome disease he would have banished himself from the company of all decent men and never dared to see his mother again. It is highly instructive to compare Chekhov's nonjudgmental, matter-of-fact discussion of syphilis in Letter 91 to the just-cited letters of Pushkin and Gogol. Gogol might well be a special case, obsessed as he was by fear of the exposure of his homosexuality and by his terror of sexually available women. Because of all this, he shrouded the considerable sexual content of his work in such a mist of symbols and surrealist fantasies that it took the twentieth-century sensibility to discern it at all.

By mid-century, Victorian sexual taboos were fully operative in Russian literature and in Russian culture in general. For Dostoyevsky, the whole of the sexual sphere was sinful, depraved and threatening, albeit secretly attractive and fascinating, especially in its possibilities for mutual humiliation of the partners. It was clearly the sado-masochistic aspects of sex, its potential for human degradation, that interested Dostoyevsky most of all; and also its paradoxical role as a steppingstone toward redemption, as the ordeal of Sonya Marmeladova in *Crime and Punishment* was meant to demonstrate. For Tolstoy, on the other hand, sexuality, and especially female sexuality, was a sin pure and simple. If at the time of *War and Peace* sexual relations could be justified for Tolstoy by procreation and by building up a family, for the post-conversion Tolstoy, who wrote *The Kreutzer Sonata* and *Resurrection*, all sexuality, including sex within marriage, was an abomination that could lead only to total perdition. Against this background of fear, guilt and sexual repression, Chekhov's attitudes toward sex come as a refreshing breath of sanity.

Of course, Anton Chekhov was a man of his time. He did not try to write of sexual love with the same freedom that Pushkin enjoyed and that he himself occasionally displayed in his private letters (making some of them unpublishable in Russian to this day). Nor could he permit himself the open treatment of the less-usual forms of sexuality which had been possible in the eighteenth century and became briefly possible again in the first two decades of the twentieth for certain Russian writers of the Symbolist period. But his ideal of the utmost literary objectivity prevented him from overlooking this basic human drive, from substituting the subjectively desirable in this sphere for that which actually exists, and from imposing moralizing sanctions and inflicting morally motivated penalties on his "transgressing" (i.e., sexually liberated) characters, as had been the custom in the literature of his time.

In 1886, the year that marks Chekhov's attainment of full literary maturity, he wrote four masterful stories that show young women of various social strata in out-of-wedlock sexual involvements. In "Agafya," the young peasant wife of a railroad switchman is caught by her husband when she fails to return in time from a tryst with her lover; "Anyuta" is about an urban proletarian girl, who cohabits with a succession of university students; "The Chorus Girl" is another lower-class woman, active as a call girl in addition to her job as an entertainer; and in "A Calamity," the wife of a well-to-do lawyer discovers hitherto unsuspected sexual desires within herself when an old family friend suddenly starts pursuing her with his attentions. What interested Chekhov in these stories is not that his heroines are having sexual experiences not sanctioned by the morality of the times, but rather what is done to them by others and what they do to themselves in connection with these experiences. Agafya comes to grief not because she has betrayed her husband, but because she needs her lover more than he needs her and because he refuses to take an interest in the consequences for her of their involvement. Anyuta is shown as an appealing, almost saintly creature, whose educated temporary lover is too tied down by social prejudices and cultural stereotypes to appreciate her selfless kindness. The same prejudices and stereotypes, mechanically accepted by everyone involved, enable the client and his self-dramatizing, bitchy wife to subject the heroine of "The Chorus Girl" to undeserved humiliation and actually to rob her, with her own guilty compliance, of her few pieces of jewelry. And, while Sofya in "A Calamity" finds her newly discovered sexuality alarming and distasteful, it is because her discovery brings out the discrepancy between the bourgeois wife and mother she thinks herself to be and her true self, and also because her sexual drive becomes obsessive, robbing her of the ability to decide freely on a course of action.

The very concepts of "adultery," "adultress," "the fallen woman," so very important in Russian literature of the Victorian age, simply do not exist as far as Chekhov is concerned. The fact that a man and a woman not married to each other may sleep together has no moral or immoral dimensions or value in his stories and plays. When sex is degrading in Chekhov (as it is in "A Calamity" or in "Ariadne"), it is because the people involved have degraded it, not because degradation is intrinsic to it as it so often is in Dostoyevsky. Nor does Chekhov accept the facile notion, made popular by Dobrolyubov in his celebrated essay on Ostrovsky's play *The Thunderstorm,* that in tsarist Russia marital infidelity could be a form of social protest. Even though the educated heroines of "The Duel" and "An Unknown Man's Story" tend to regard themselves as socially and politically liberated because they have left their husbands and are openly living with their lovers, Chekhov gently exposes their attitudes as wishful illusions, stemming from the same set of taboos and prohibitions that would have branded them "adultresses" or "fallen women" in the work of most of his contemporaries. Where a reader of *Anna Karenina* or of *Resurrection* cannot forget for one moment that out-of-wedlock sex was the main cause of the troubles and sufferings of their heroines, the last and greatest of Chekhov's plays, *The Seagull, Three Sisters* and *The Cherry Orchard,* make a point of depicting attractive, believable women whose unconventional sex lives have no bearing on his or our evaluation of their ethics and morals.

Nor is there even a vestige of the double sexual standard in the mature Chekhov. The courtship of the married Yelena by both Uncle Vanya and Dr. Astrov (which so outraged Tolstoy that he insulted one of the actors after a performance of *Uncle Vanya*) is presented in the same objective, nonjudgmental manner as the fact that Lyubov Ranevskaya is about to return to her kept lover at the end of *The Cherry Orchard* (which caused Vladimir Korolenko to protest that Chekhov should have exposed her as an "aristocratic slut" instead of enveloping her in a romantic aura). The husband in Tolstoy's *Family Happiness* puts his wife into a purgatory because for a brief moment she *considered* the possibility of betraying him. Prince Andrei in *War and Peace* is unable even to imagine the possibility of forgiving the cheated and repentant Natasha, who had planned to betray him but actually did not. In contrast, Chekhov's Layevsky in "The Duel" is able to rise to the realization that it was his own selfish and callous behavior that drove his mistress into other men's arms and to beg for *her* forgiveness; his Kulygin in *Three Sisters* is unimaginative and faintly ridiculous, but kind and magnanimous in his understanding and forgiveness of his wife's extramarital love affair; above all, his generous and appealing Dr. Dymov in "The Grasshopper" is not in the least concerned with his own hurt pride as he tries to alleviate his wife's pain and suffering over her break with her lover. It is this kind of realization, common to eighteenth- and twentieth-century thinking, but rarely found in the nineteenth, that women are as subject to sexual desires, obsessions and whims as men and should be judged by the same standards, that made the motivations of Layevsky in "The Duel" incomprehensible to Chekhov's elderly poet-friend Pleshcheyev. A similar thesis, embodied in Lorenzo da Ponte's libretto for Mozart's *Così fan tutte*, outraged the nineteenth-century minds of both Beethoven and Wagner and, despite all the glories of Mozart's music, made that masterpiece the least performed of his operas throughout the nineteenth century.

In *The Second Sex*, Simone de Beauvoir singled out Stendhal as the only major writer who understood the particular situation of women in a male-dominated world. Twenty years later, Kate Millett was to proclaim that Jean Genet's special vantage point as a homosexual, outcast and criminal enabled him to perceive the specific situation of women better than male writers blinded by their *machismo*. But had the work of Anton Chekhov been read in the West as it is written, rather than through the prism of inherited Russian critical distortions, many of his stories would surely be in the canon of the women's liberation movement. What other writer so habitually showed his female characters robbed of their individuality by the traditional roles society forces upon them? What better image of a woman reduced to the level of an inanimate object is there in literature than the self-abnegating Anyuta, shivering from cold at the beginning of the story, while her lover, a medical student, uses her as an anatomical aid in studying for an exam, and later allows a friend to borrow her for a few hours, despite her objections, to serve without pay as a nude model? Chekhov's stories dealing with similar themes are too many to enumerate, but a few can be cited to demonstrate the nature of his concern and its depth. In "Big Volodya and Little Volodya" we are shown in the space of a few pages the plight of an intelligent young woman, recently married to a high-ranking army officer much older than herself, trying to share her religious and intellectual interests with her husband and, getting no response, turning to a young literary scholar who was her childhood friend. But the younger man (he has the same first name as her husband) refuses to take her genuine intellectual and spiritual hunger seriously and utilizes her despair to effect an easy sexual conquest. The military husband and the academic-intellectual lover both see the heroine's dissatisfaction as a symptom of hysteria and make no effort to understand it. The hopelessness of her situation is further emphasized by the two other female characters in the story, her closest friends, one of whom becomes an acid-tongued, disillusioned old maid loathing herself for her failure to find a husband, while the other gives up all worldly ambitions and withdraws to a convent.

A somewhat similar constellation of characters appears in another story from Chekhov's last period, "A Visit with Friends," which also depicts an upper-class group of three women and two men. There is an older sister, a beautiful and intelligent woman, who allows her own and her younger sister's property to be squandered by her husband, a fraud, a poseur and a wastrel, adored and pampered by all the women in the story. The visiting bachelor lawyer, from whose vantage point the story is told, wonders at this woman's uncritical devotion to her husband and her two little daughters and at her total absorption in her homemaking:

> . . . he found it strange that this healthy, young, by no means stupid woman, who was in fact such a powerful and complex organism, should expend all of her energy, all of her life forces on such primitive, petty work as the building of this particular nest, which in any case had already been built.
>
> "Perhaps this is how it should be," he thought, "but it is neither interesting nor intelligent."

The younger sister spends all her time yearning for the kind of domestic arrangements in which her older sister is caught. She longs for a marriage proposal from the visiting lawyer, not, Chekhov carefully makes clear, because she loves him or feels close to him, but because his proposal would enable her to fulfill what she has been brought up to believe is her biological destiny. An alternative to the situation of these two sisters is represented by their friend, a woman doctor who is independent and self-supporting, but crushed by loneliness and poverty. At the end of the story, the lawyer, bored by the matrimonial moonings of the younger sister, dreams of another kind of woman, the kind who could tell him "something fascinating and new, not related to either love or happiness, or else if she should speak of love, that it would be a call for a new way of life, lofty and rational, on the brink of which we might be living, the advent of which we might perhaps sense now and then."

The heroine of "Ariadne" has been brought up on the notion that the aim of a girl's life is to please men and to appeal to their sexual appetites. She grows into a calculating, cold-blooded predator, unable to enjoy any human relationship or even sex, preoccupied solely with the material advantages her victims can provide. But, because of the naked selfishness and pettiness of her approach to life, Ariadne fails to make it as a big-time *femme fatale*. At the end of the story she seems to be headed for marriage with a dull, aged lecher. In an outburst of moral preaching, unique in the mature Chekhov, the author allows one of Ariadne's male victims to blame it all on the education that women get in Western societies:

> "Yes, sir, it is all the fault of our education, my good man. In the cities the entire upbringing and education of a woman comes down essentially to converting her into a human animal, that is, to have her please the male and to teach her how to conquer this male. Yes, sir," Shamokhin sighed. "What is needed is to have the girls brought up and educated together with the boys, to have both of them together at all times. A woman should be brought up to realize when she is wrong, just as a man is, because otherwise she is sure that she is always right. Convince a little girl from the cradle on that a man is not primarily a suitor, a prospective bridegroom, but a fellow human being equal to her in every way. Get her accustomed to think logically, to generalize, and stop assuring her that her brain weighs less than a man's and that therefore she may remain indifferent to the sciences, the arts, to cultural tasks in general. A young boy who is an apprentice shoemaker or housepainter also has a smaller-sized brain than an adult man, but he nevertheless takes part in the general struggle for survival, he works, he suffers. And we'd better drop this manner of blaming everything on physiology, pregnancy and childbirth, because first of all, a woman does not give birth every month, secondly not all women give birth, and thirdly a normal peasant woman works in the fields right up to the day before she gives birth, and is not harmed in any way. Also, we should achieve the most complete equality imaginable in our daily life. If a man offers the lady a chair or picks up the handkerchief she has dropped,—why, let her repay him in kind. I would not object if a girl of good family were to help me put on my overcoat or bring me a glass of water."

The inability of even educated and well-to-do women to attain personal freedom and independence without a man's help is a major theme of Chekhov's, recurring constantly in his work. It is present, in a muted and subdued form, in *Three Sisters*, but it is given a much more overt and eloquent treatment in such stories as "Lights," "A Woman's Kingdom" and "Anna on the Neck." In "The Darling," we are shown a woman who by choice gives up all her individual qualities and derives whatever existence or dimensions she may possess from the males in her life. Chekhov intended her as a humorous creation, but Lev Tolstoy saw in her the embodiment of some of his own most cherished notions about what a woman should be. In a very significant little critical article on "The Darling," Tolstoy argued that Chekhov accomplished the very opposite of what he had intended in this story, depicting, instead of the laughable creature he had in mind, a beautiful, saintly and totally fulfilled woman.

An instance of a woman genuinely liberating herself from the compulsory biological and social roles which society and her family relentlessly impose on her and achieving an independent existence as an inwardly free individual is described in the very last story Chekhov wrote, "The Bride" (also known in English as "The Betrothed"). This story has become the traditional prize exhibit of orthodox Soviet critics, who are out to prove that at the end of his life Chekhov was moving toward espousing the cause of violent revolution. Although the text of the story does not state the exact future path that the heroine of "The Bride," Nadya, will follow, it is invariably assumed by the commentators in Soviet editions of Chekhov that in Nadya he has portrayed an upper-class girl who is about to become a revolutionary. This is the reasoning that underlies the commentary to "The Bride" in the twelve-volume Soviet edition of Chekhov's complete works, which states that this story is the most important thing Chekhov ever wrote. It must also explain why a recent American translator of "The Bride" renders the key phrase "to change the course of your life" (*perevernut' zhizn'*) as "to revolutionize your life" every time it occurs in the story.

But to reduce "The Bride" to the clichés and platitudes that are compulsory in Soviet criticism is to deprive a unique and remarkable story of its particular and profound meaning. As was the case with Misail Poloznev in Chekhov's "My Life" (in some ways Misail is Nadya's male counterpart), Nadya's first step toward her personal liberation is taken when she begins to question the values of her family—her mother and her grandmother in this case. Her distant cousin Sasha, a consumptive young revolutionary, adds fuel to her resolve to escape by preaching the imminence of a social revolution which will instantly change men into demigods and cover the face of the earth with beautiful buildings and fountains. A further degree of freedom is achieved by Nadya when she rejects the comfortable marriage into which her entire culture is pushing her. When she escapes to St. Petersburg, her liberation from the small town where she was raised is complete. At this point the Soviet commentators prefer to stop; but in the text itself Chekhov takes his heroine still further in her quest for inner freedom. After living independently in St. Petersburg for a year, Nadya has another encounter with the revolutionary Sasha. She is still attached to him and grateful for his help in her escape, but she has by now traveled beyond the stage of sloganeering, where he still remains: ". . . and now there was about Sasha, about his smile, about his entire figure something outmoded, old-fashioned, something that had had its day and had perhaps already gone to its grave." A revolution based on the promise of material affluence and on humanity reduced to a standardized common denominator rather than on freedom of thought and universal equality now holds as little attraction for Nadya as it did for Chekhov himself. "The Bride" is certainly as subversive of Soviet society today as it was of the society of Chekhov's day; hence the orthodox Leninist glosses in the Soviet commentaries and hence the hypnotic reiteration of the word "revolutionary" and the avoidance of all mention of Nadya's achievement of an intensely personal inner liberation.

The principal implications of "The Bride" pertain not only to sexual politics, but to politics pure and simple. It is Chekhov's socio-political views, such as they are, that many of his Russian commentators have tried hardest to overlook or to distort. If Chekhov undercuts the traditional views on religion and sexuality by denying that these two areas have any inherent ethical or moral dimensions, politically the most subversive aspect of his thinking is his systematic demonstration of the illusory nature of all labels, categories and divisions of human beings into social groups and social classes, which are the starting point of all political theories of his time and ours. Chekhov's repeated insistence that "labels and trademarks" such as "liberal," "conservative," "Populist" or "neurotic," when used as a total description of any one person, are nothing but superstitions which keep people from perceiving the deeper moral and human realities implies a reasoned rejection of the political thinking that has been one of the mainstays of Russian literature and literary criticism from the 1840s on.

It is hard for foreign audiences to realize the determined audacity, bordering on insolence, with which Chekhov flies in the face of the cherished stereotypes of the Russian intelligentsia when he makes the progressive and enlightened Dr. Lvov the villain of *Ivanov*, and yet shows the professional soldier Lieutenant Colonel Vershinin in *Three Sisters* as a socially aware idealist and the rising capitalist Yermolai Lopakhin in *The Cherry Orchard* (who takes over the heroine's estate) as a complex and appealing human being, who is, furthermore, on friendly and affectionate terms with the revolutionary-minded Petya Trofimov. It is this same kind of Chekhov-inspired rejection of stereotypes that makes the confrontation between the perceptive tsarist officer Colonel Vorotyntsev and the frightened, young radical Sasha Lenartovich in Solzhenitsyn's novel *August*

1914 so startling and convincing. In the Soviet Union, where the labeling and compartmentalizing of groups of people is the basis of an entire culture, this aspect of Chekhov would be explosive indeed if anyone dared to bring it out into the open. The parable of litigation between the tavern keeper and the poor peasant, in which the jury of enlightened intellectuals decides in favor of the peasant solely because their culture assumes every tavern keeper to be an exploiter and every poor peasant a hero, appears in Chekhov's notebooks and is used in his story "The Name-Day Party." This parable is a beautiful illustration of the politically induced disregard of facts and the impairment of moral judgment that arise in any deeply polarized society. A recognizable present-day parallel would be a shootout between a white policeman and a black militant: regardless of how or why it happened, large groups of people would instantly want to believe that it must have been the black militant's fault, while other large groups, equally predictably, would want to blame it on the policeman. This is precisely what Chekhov's objection to labels and trademarks is all about.

Chekhov was almost as good as Tolstoy at puncturing the prevailing political illusions of the nineteenth century. He took on the illusion that industrialization is always beneficial in "A Woman's Kingdom" and "A Case from a Doctor's Practice"; the illusion that Russian peasants were a breed of Rousseauist saints in "The Phonies" (*Svistuny* in Russian), "The Village Elder" and "The Peasants"; and the Dostoyevskian notion of Russian messianism in "Three Years." But, unlike Tolstoy, he was not given to creating his own social myths and illusions. The principal document on Chekhov's socio-political views is of course his magnificent letter to Pleshcheyev (Letter 23), which expresses his basic credo better than a whole volume of commentary could. Numerous insights into his political views and their evolution are to be found in other letters included in the present volume. However, since he did occasionally indulge in politically oriented polemics in his stories and plays, it may be worthwhile to point out a few such instances in his imaginative writing which may enhance and amplify the material found in the letters.

While Chekhov had little interest in political theories, programs and parties, he was tremendously sensitive to and aware of the human and moral realities that might underlie them. In his immature early stories, written for a quick ruble, he would occasionally serve up the kind of social and political satire for which the editors of humor magazines, general readers and the leading critics of the time all had a limitless appetite. As well as anyone, he could go through the motions of indicting corrupt high officials, hypocritical and groveling civil servants, harebrained society ladies, dishonest merchants and bribe-taking policemen. But, while still in his humor-magazine period, Chekhov managed to create one of the most profound political archetypes in all Russian literature, the figure of Sergeant Prishibeyev in the story of that name (1885). Prishibeyev is the quintessential authoritarian, an almost biologically depicted representative of the elderly human male, who is naturally convinced that people do not know what is good for them and need constant supervision if they are not to cause trouble, while he, the sergeant, knows what is right and has a God-given mission to tell everyone else what to do. Thirteen years later Chekhov provided Sergeant Prishibeyev with a companion figure in the person of the schoolteacher Belikov (in the story "The Man in a Shell"), the quintessential conformist, who is both the reverse of Prishibeyev's coin and his Siamese twin in the universal political landscape. Where Prishibeyev needs to run other people's lives, Belikov requires to be guided by rules and regulations devised by others. Not only does he require it for himself, but he needs to force everyone around him to conform to restrictions imposed from the outside, no matter how useless or nonsensical these restrictions may be.

It is easy to regard Prishibeyev and Belikov as satirical representations of political types peculiar to the tsarist Russia of Chekhov's time. But to do so is to miss the entire point of these two archetypes, both of which became instantly proverbial in Russia. Prishibeyev represents the embodiment of a widespread, recognizable human instinct (in Chekhov's story, he is actually put on trial for exercising unlawful authority), while Belikov, embodying an equally recognizable opposite instinct, complements Prishibeyev the way a masochist complements a sadist and a criminal in Jean Genet's novels complements a policeman. Both types are observable in every kind of society, democratic as well as totalitarian. Both types are traditionally involved in political activity and, in fact, the more oppressive a given society, the more scope it affords its Prishibeyevs and Belikovs. But it took Chekhov's particular insight to detect them in their embryonic stage and to show that they were present not only in the official regime of his country, but in its revolutionary movement as well. The character of the idealistic, ideologically committed Dr. Yevgeny Lvov in *Ivanov* is a case in point. Moved by the most decent and humanitarian motivations imaginable, Lvov ends up treating those around him cruelly and unfairly because he insists on seeing everyone as a reflection of his ideological stereotypes instead of as an individual and fallible human being (see Letter 14 for Chekhov's own commentary on Dr. Lvov's character).

Even more telling is the character of the socially and politically active young girl, Lida Volchaninova, who appears in one of the most poetic stories of Chekhov's maturity, "The House with a Mansard." In his book on Chekhov, Kornei Chukovsky, a perceptive and knowledgeable Soviet critic, pretended to be puzzled why the do-gooder Chekhov depicted Lida so harshly and her idle younger sister with so much kindness and sympathy. "Hypnotized by Chekhov's magical craftsmanship, all of Russia fell poetically in love with this spineless, weak girl and came to despise her older sister for the very deeds and actions which *not in literature,* but in real life were so dear to Chekhov," Chukovsky wrote (the italics are his). "The Chekhov we know from innumerable memoirs and letters,—the district physician, the founder of libraries, the builder of schools—had he met Lida not in literature, but in life, would undoubtedly have become her faithful ally; but in literature he is her indicter and enemy."

In a book published in the Soviet Union, this is as far as Chukovsky could go in making his point, but the story itself tells us more. Yes, there is no doubt that Lida's social-improvement program parallels Chekhov's own. But this outwardly civilized partisan of civil rights is in her private life an authoritarian who keeps her mother and sister in fear and subjugation. She is also a political fanatic. When her political convictions are brought into question and challenged by the artist-narrator with whom her sister is in love, Lida steps in and brutally breaks up their love affair. The very act of questioning her cherished political views is seen by Lida as a threat to her dominant position in the family—and she strikes out at her opponent with every ethical and unethical means she can muster. In this story, political fanaticism is as inhuman and as destructive as religious fanaticism was in "Peasant Women" and "The Murder."

Unlike Lida and Dr. Lvov, other Chekhovian characters who are committed to revolutionary change are not necessarily dehumanized by rigid fanaticism and the dogmatic classification of all mankind into "us" and "them." There is the appealing Sasha in "The Bride," the naïvely idealistic Petya Trofimov in *The Cherry Orchard* and Vladimir, the intellectual would-be terrorist who narrates "An Unknown Man's Story" ("An Anonymous Story" in Constance Garnett's English version). Vladimir could agree to commit a political assassination in principle, but he was unable to bring it off once he came to see his intended victim as an individual human being rather than an abstract political cipher. With the hindsight of the second half of the twentieth century, it is not difficult to imagine this entire group of dedicated, revolutionary-minded young people succeeding in their efforts to overthrow the old regime and to redress its wrongs. But the next step would inevitably be for Dr. Lvov and Lida Volchaninova to purge the individualistic Sasha, the excessively idealistic Petya Trofimov and the ideologically unstable hero of "An Unknown Man's Story" to impose their own simple-minded dogmatism on everyone else and call the results the ultimate liberation. Yes, perhaps stubborn old Nikolai Mikhailovsky, who so persistently accused Chekhov of slandering the ideals of the Russian revolutionary movement, was more perceptive and honest than the official

Soviet criticism of our day, with its compulsory eulogies of the progressive Chekhov.

While Chekhov valued and appreciated the many genuinely liberating and democratic trends that the enlightened anti-government intelligentsia of his time was helping to further, his idea of social involvement and of activism was basically different from theirs. For Chekhov's contemporaries, as for many Western commentators on Russian literature today, the standard examples of socially involved turn-of-the-century writers are Tolstoy with his defiance of the government, his excommunication from the Orthodox Church and defense of persecuted religious sects, and the young Maxim Gorky, with his support of the revolutionary movement and his fund-raising campaigns for outlawed political parties. Such actions are remembered because they are dramatic; their effect depends on dramatizing current political issues by deliberately attracting public attention to them. But in its own way Anton Chekhov's life was probably more filled with direct involvement in valid social and humanitarian activity than that of any other writer one could name. His life was one continuous round of alleviating famine, fighting epidemics, building schools and public roads, endowing libraries, helping organize marine-biology laboratories, giving thousands of needy peasants free medical treatment, planting gardens, helping fledgling writers get published, raising funds for worthwhile causes, and hundreds of other pursuits designed to help his fellow man and improve the general quality of life around him. If Chekhov's foreign admirers usually think of his trip to the penal colony on the island of Sakhalin as the one exceptional humanitarian act of his life, it is because this trip has been misrepresented by commentators to look like an act of open political defiance, such as Western readers have traditionally come to expect of Russian writers.

There are two main reasons why Chekhov's social activism has not been sufficiently stressed by his commentators and biographers (Kornei Chukovsky's book is the only one that emphasizes this aspect of Chekhov and does it ably and forcefully). One reason is that the genuinely modest Chekhov avoided personal publicity and would select causes not likely to attract sensation-seeking journalists. But the more important reason is that the basic outlook of the Russian liberal intelligentsia was derived from the field of the social sciences, humanities and, in some important instances, religion, while Chekhov's continuous commitment to medicine and the biological sciences in general gave him an entirely different set of priorities, both in his life and in literature. For his Russian contemporaries, Chekhov's efforts to prevent a cholera epidemic, his involvement in census taking both on Sakhalin and at his own estate of Melikhovo, his concern for the mistreatment of the Tatars, Gilyaks and Ainus, his alarm over the disappearance of wildlife were simply not as interesting as Tolstoy's or Gorky's open defiance of the tsarist government. This attitude is still evident in various Western biographies, television programs and biographical plays, which project the same tired stereotypes of the dynamic activist Gorky contrasted with the withdrawn, sad and resigned Anton Pavlovich Chekhov. But perhaps we are at long last ready to perceive the true value of Chekhov's wider-ranging and, in the long run, more realistic humanitarian concerns, which are focused on the physical and biological realities of man's existence and future rather than on the topical political passions of a particular decade.

Chekhov himself was well aware of the paramount importance of his training in the biological sciences for his general outlook and for his formation as a literary artist (Letter 130). This training and his constant reading of Darwin, of books by travelers and explorers such as Nevelskoy and Przhevalsky, and of Russian biological scientists enabled him to bring to Russian literature dimensions and methods that were very much at odds with most of its previous assumptions. Instead of starting from a preconceived moral, sociological or religious position, Chekhov begins with scrupulously unbiased observations of the life around him, and he refrains from deriving sweeping social generalizations from an insufficient body of observable facts. Whereas the attempts of Chekhov's French contemporaries, especially Zola and Maupassant, to apply the methodology of the biological sciences to literary art sometimes reduced their peasant and proletarian characters to the level of laboratory animals subjected to vivisection, Chekhov's unfailing humanity and compassion led him to an approach closer to that of a doctor observing his patients for symptoms. However, Chekhov refrained from prescribing a cure—his vocation as a writer did not entitle him to prescribe panaceas for humanity's ills, something that all too many Russian novelists and especially critics have had no qualms about doing.

Chekhov's very profound involvement with biology and its role as a key to much of his art have been noted by two Soviet critics of the Formalist generation, Boris Eichenbaum and Leonid Grossman (their articles are included in the fine collection of Chekhov criticism in English edited by Robert Louis Jackson for the Twentieth Century Views series). But, by and large, this important topic has not received the critical attention it requires and neither has the problem of the stylistic affinity of Chekhov's writing with the books of Russian nineteenth-century explorers and biologists, to whom he felt so close and from whom he learned so much. The orientation of Chekhov's literary art toward the empirical sciences rather than toward intuitively grasped social theories, moral preaching or religious revelation presaged the later appearance of such similarly oriented twentieth-century Russian writers as Vladimir Nabokov, equally well grounded in biology, and Alexander Solzhenitsyn, whose training in physics and mathematics brings to his art a precision and objectivity that make his indignation and passion all the more persuasive.

Teaching courses on Chekhov at American universities in the second half of the 1960s was a particularly rewarding experience, because during those years the intellectual life of the Western world was gradually catching up with many of Chekhov's insights and preoccupations which his contemporaries had chosen to overlook. His views on the situation of women provides one of the more spectacular examples of this. Another is his constant theme of the threatened environment and industrial pollution, with which he was concerned as early as the 1880s. This theme appears in "The Steppe" in the character of the cart driver Vasya, who is almost uncannily attuned to nature and to all living creatures (he goes into sentimental ecstasies on observing a fox and is morally hurt when one of his colleagues wantonly kills a snake) and whose jaw is hideously swollen from the chemical poisoning resulting from his work at a match factory. In "The Reed Flute" (*Svirel'* in Russian), one of the most crucial earlier stories, unaccountably omitted from most English-language collections of his work, Chekhov describes, in the highly poetic form of a colloquy between an aged village shepherd and the steward of a nearby estate, the effect of the poor management of natural resources and laments the pollution of rivers and lakes and the predictable disappearance of wild animals and birds. Two years later, in 1889, he made this topic one of the central themes of the most openly polemical of his full-length plays, *The Wood Demon*. The attractive, positive hero of this play (the only instance of a character in Chekhov's plays who clearly expresses the author's views and has the author's full support) is the young landowner with a medical degree, Mikhail Khrushchev, whose main passion is saving the local forests and wildlife from senseless destruction. Khrushchev's conservationist efforts and his selfless medical aid to the surrounding peasants are regarded with suspicion by the other characters in the play because they cannot find a reductionist political or sociological label to pin on his activities. The most hostile attitude of all is taken by Alexander Serebryakov, a professor of literature, whose catch phrase for socially useful action is "*delo delat' nado*," which can mean both "you must do something useful" and, in the context of Chekhov's time, "you must do something for the cause." Coming from Serebryakov, the implication of the phrase is that writing articles of literary pseudo-criticism in the radical-utilitarian tradition is of more value for the Russian people than Khrushchev's program of medical and conservationist action. Serebryakov's daughter Sonya (a character vastly different in *The Wood Demon* from the Sonya of *Uncle Vanya*) loves Khrushchev and dramatically liberates herself at the end of the play from her father's cliché-ridden thinking, resolving to consider her loved one's actions on their own merits only.

The Wood Demon was an artistically unsatisfactory play in many ways, and Chekhov later discarded it, salvaging many of its characters, themes and portions of its actual text for his later and much more nearly perfect play, *Uncle Vanya*. The somewhat idealized Mikhail Khrushchev was replaced by the hard-drinking and cynical Dr. Astrov. But Astrov retained his prototype's conservationist interests and he is made to repeat verbatim Khrushchev's impassioned speech about the destruction of forests:

> "Yes, I can see it when you cut down forests out of need, but why exterminate them? The forests of Russia are groaning under the ax, billions of trees perish, the dwellings of animals and birds are laid waste, rivers run shallow and dry up, marvelous landscapes disappear forever and all because the lazy man doesn't have the sense to pick his fuel up from the ground [the use of peat is meant]. (Turning to Yelena) Isn't that true, madam? One has to be a mindless barbarian to burn this beauty in one' stove, to destroy what we cannot create. Man was granted reason and creative abilities to increase that which was given him, but until now he has not created, but destroyed. There are fewer and fewer forests, the rivers dry up, wild animals are dying out, the climate is ruined and with each passing day the earth is becoming poorer and uglier."

This theme is given additional focus in the third-act scene between Astrov and Yelena (there was no corresponding scene in *The Wood Demon*) in which he shows her colored maps documenting the land spoliation and systematic disappearance of various species of wildlife. And yet the contrast between the reality and value of nature conservation on the one hand and the sterility of simplistic social theorizing on the other, which is one of the main themes of *Uncle Vanya*, usually goes unperceived during the frequent productions of this play in Western countries. So does the irony of Professor Serebryakov's exit line, "You must all do something useful."

Chekhov returned to the ecological theme in one of his very last stories, "In the Ravine," which, because of the complexity and profundity of the questions it raises and the perfection of its technical realization, may well be the most impressive story he ever wrote. Here, the vivid picture of unchecked industrial pollution that poisons and disfigures the countryside, described in the opening pages, sets the scene for the examination of human greed, venality and corruption which are the subject of the story.

Chekhov's ideas on various topics that were subversive within the culture of his time and which might remain so in our day are not what made him the very great writer he is. His greatness lies more in the radically new ways he had discovered of perceiving and expressing the human predicament and in the dazzlingly original literary forms he devised for conveying his perceptions. These facets of Chekhov will not be found in his letters and neither will his great personal leitmotifs that flow from story to story and from play to play: the semantic tragedy that arises from the inability or unwillingness of human beings to communicate fully and from the inadequacy of language itself as a means of communication; and the changes in the texture of time's fabric which cause every attained goal to be different from what it was at the planning stage and which make a teleological approach to any undertaking or any personal relationship an absurdity. But a good understanding of the ideological underpinnings of his creative writing should enhance the understanding of his letters, just as the letters provide an essential key to the unstated implications of many of his stories and plays. In terms of illustrating Chekhov's views and attitudes, the artistically inferior plays of the middle period, such as *Ivanov* and *The Wood Demon*, are more revealing than the dramatic masterpieces of his last years, which he no longer bothered to infuse with his current ideological preoccupations.

Chekhov's libertarian views, his moral relativism, his recognition that there could be a variety of acceptable and valid approaches to many fundamental issues, his hatred and resentment of dividing people into categories and pinning simplistic labels on them were clearly at variance with much of the Russian culture of his day and would be most unwelcome, were they to be openly recognized, in the Soviet Union. The uniqueness of his views within the Russian intellectual tradition has led to much distortion, both deliberate and unconscious, of Chekhov's attitudes by modern Russian commentators. Remarkably few Russians who have written on Chekhov have shown the perception and acceptance of his modes of thinking that we can find in the better discussions of his work by the more understanding foreign critics. There is nothing in Russian critical literature that for empathy and penetration could be placed next to the journals of the French critic Charles Du Bos (who understood Chekhov better than any other critic who ever lived, but who refrained from writing a book on him for fear that he didn't understand him enough), "The Russian Point of View" by Virginia Woolf or "Seeing Chekhov Plain" by Edmund Wilson. Creative Russian *writers* and Russian *poets*, on the other hand, have been able to see into Chekhov with a freshness and spontaneity that seem beyond the grasp of Russian critics. So, by way of summary, three views of Chekhov by three of Russia's most outstanding twentieth-century poets are hereby offered.

In 1914, the twenty-one-year-old Vladimir Mayakovsky commemorated the tenth anniversary of Chekhov's death with a jaunty, irreverent little essay called "The Two Chekhovs." Written at a time when Mayakovsky was one of the leaders of Russian Futurism, the essay, for all its youthful desire to shock, remains to this day one of the most intelligent appraisals of Chekhov's role in Russian literature. In its level-headed insistence that Chekhov is important as an innovative literary artist rather than as a sociological phenomenon, Mayakovsky's Chekhov essay was the signal for the soon-to-develop Formalist school of Russian criticism (which was closely allied with Mayakovsky and his Futurists). Its concluding passages read:

> Chekhov's language is as precise as "Hello!" and as simple as "Give me a glass of tea." In his method of expressing the idea of a compact little story, the urgent cry of the future is felt: "Economy!"
>
> It is these new forms of expressing an idea, this true approach to art's real tasks, that give us the right to speak of Chekhov as a master of verbal art.
>
> Behind the familiar Chekhovian image created by the philistines, that of a grumbler displeased with everything, the defender of "ridiculous people" against society, behind Chekhov the twilight bard we discern the outlines of the other Chekhov: the joyous and powerful master of the art of literature.

In 1929, Boris Poplavsky, one of the finest poets of the Russian emigration, the author of brilliant surrealist and at times mystical poems, made this entry in his personal journal:

> Dostoeysky cannot help us live, he can only help us when we quarrel, separate, die. Tolstoy perhaps could, but how revolting is his eulogizing of bourgeois prosperity,—the Levins, the end of W. and P. Now Chekhov—yes, Chekhov can help us live, he and Lermontov.

A few pages later we read:

> Chekhov teaches me to endure in my own special way, not to give up, to keep hoping, for there is much in Chekhov that is Roman, there is much of some kind of "no matter what happens," of *quand même*.

And still further:

> Chekhov is the most [Russian] Orthodox of Russian writers or more correctly the only Orthodox Russian writer. For what is Russian Orthodoxy if not absolute forgiveness, absolute refusal to condemn.

And in the early 1950s, Boris Pasternak's hero in *Doctor Zhivago*, who, like Chekhov, combined literature with medicine, wrote the lines that could not help but be the expression of the author's view as well:

> Of things Russian, I love now most of all the Russian childlike quality of Pushkin and Chekhov, their shy lack of concern over such momentous

> matters as the ultimate aims of mankind and their own salvation. They understood all that very well, but they were far too modest and considered such things beyond their rank and position. Gogol, Tolstoy, Dostoyevsky prepared for death, worried, searched for meaning, drew final conclusions, but those two were to the end distracted by the current private interests of their artistic calling and in this preoccupation lived out their lives also as a private matter of no concern to anyone else. And now, this private matter turns out to be of general concern and, like apples removed from the tree to ripen, keeps filling of itself in posterity with ever greater sweetness and meaning.

No, these three major Russian poets did not see Chekhov as a prophet of despair, as that jigsaw puzzle's ugly and morose tapeworm. All three would have agreed with Charles Du Bos, who wondered why so many people found depressing instead of bracing Chekhov's combination of an unflinching look at life's realities with a deep compassion. Perhaps the readers of Anton Chekhov's letters selected for this volume will also come to see this supreme realist in life and in literature as Mayakovsky, Poplavsky, Pasternak and Du Bos were able to see him, rather than as that hazy twilight creature of created legend who has been usurping the real Chekhov's place for so long.

SIMON KARLINSKY

I

THE TAGANROG METAMORPHOSIS

The most decisive development in the spiritual and intellectual formation of Anton Chekhov took place during the least well-documented period of his life, between the ages of sixteen and nineteen. Left alone in his native city of Taganrog after his father's bankruptcy forced the rest of the family to move to Moscow, supporting himself by tutoring younger students at the school he attended, reading voraciously at the Taganrog public library, the young Anton gradually replaced the patriarchal peasant and merchant-class values in which he had been brought up with their very opposite, the intellectual and ethical values of the liberal nineteenth-century intelligentsia. Chekhov's two older brothers, Alexander and Nikolai, had gone through similar transformations somewhat earlier when they went off to study in Moscow, but Anton's spiritual metamorphosis was both less violent in its expression and more thoroughgoing than that of his brothers. Typically, Chekhov's liberation from the traditions and values of his parents did not take the form of a violent rebellion against his parents and against the entire social structure of his country, as had been the case with so many young Russians of his time. The actual process was later described by Chekhov with exemplary objectivity and precision in the much-quoted passage from his letter to Suvorin (Letter 15 in the present collection) about the young man, son of a serf, a former grocer, who rids himself of the servile thinking instilled by his upbringing, and by squeezing the slave out of himself, drop by drop, awakes one fine morning feeling that the blood flowing in his veins is no longer that of a slave but that of a real human being.

The earliest set of Chekhov letters we have are the ones he wrote from

Taganrog to his Moscow cousin Mikhail Chekhov. Anton's initial reply to Cousin Mikhail's offer to correspond provides us with a glimpse of the pre-transformation Chekhov. The servile and self-deprecating tone is most uncharacteristic of Chekhov as we know him: "You were the first to hint at the possibility of a fraternal friendship between us. It was an impertinence on my part to have allowed this. The younger person is duty-bound to beg for friendship first, not the older one. Therefore I beg you to forgive me" (Letter to Mikhail Mikhailovich Chekhov, December 6, 1876). This tone disappears in the letters written to the same addressee in 1877. By the time Chekhov came to write to his brother Mikhail in the spring of 1879 on the subject of personal dignity and of his literary preferences, his metamorphosis was complete. Letter 2 is the earliest authentically Chekhovian document we have: neither the tone nor the ideas of that letter would be imaginable in the milieu of Chekhov's father, uncles and cousins. At nineteen, Chekhov had already gained that freedom of thought and independence of spirit that were later to cause the young Maxim Gorky to remark after meeting the famous writer that Anton Chekhov was the first genuinely free human being he had ever encountered.

1. To Mikhail (Mikhailovich) Chekhov[1]

Taganrog, May 10, 1877

Dearest Cousin Misha,

Not having had the fortune of seeing you again, I take up my pen. First, let me give you a fraternal vote of thanks for everything you did for me throughout my stay in Moscow.[2] Second, I am delighted we parted such intimate friends and brothers, and therefore dare to hope and trust that the twelve hundred versts that may long stand between two letter-writing brothers who have come to know each other well will prove but a trifling distance for the long-term maintenance of our good relations. Now I have a request which I imagine you will carry out because it is so insignificant: if I send my mother letters through you, will you give them to her secretly, when there's no one else around? There are certain things in life that can be said to only one trustworthy individual. It is for this reason that I am forced to write Mother in secret from the others, whom my secrets (I have a special kind of secrets, and I don't know if you're interested in them or not; if you like, I'll reveal them to you) do not interest in the least or rather do not concern. My second and last request will be somewhat more serious. Could you continue to comfort my mother? She is physically and morally crushed and has found in you much more than merely a nephew. My mother's nature is such that she has a very strong positive reaction to any kind of moral support coming from another person. A ridiculous request, isn't it? But you'll come to understand it, especially since I've asked for your "moral," in other words, spiritual support. In this archmalicious world there is nothing dearer to us than our mother, and therefore you will much oblige your humble servant by comforting his half-moribund mother. We will carry on a good, steady correspondence, won't we? And let me assure you in passing that you won't be sorry for having told me all those things. All I can do is thank you for your confidence in me. I want you to know that I value it highly. Good-bye and best wishes. My regards to Liza and Grisha[3] and to your friends.

Your cousin,
A. Chekhov

1. Mikhail Mikhailovich Chekhov (1851–1909) was the son of Pavel Yegorovich Chekhov's older brother Mikhail. He was apprenticed at the age of twelve at a warehouse owned by a wealthy Moscow merchant and he worked there as a clerk for the rest of his life. While much can be said against Pavel Chekhov's ideas of upbringing, it is to his everlasting credit that his insistence on as much education as possible for every one of his children enabled them to become literary figures and educators. The children of his less stern brothers Mikhail and Mitrofan never rose beyond the station of salesmen, seamstresses and warehouse attendants. The young Chekhov was quite attached to his cousin Misha and corresponded with him during his school years. In the early 1880s Misha succeeded in obtaining a job for Chekhov's father at the warehouse where he worked. By that time, the contact between Anton and Cousin Misha had dwindled. The warehouse where Misha worked and its employees served as the models for the warehouse and employees in Chekhov's "Three Years"; Misha himself appears in that novel, slightly caricatured, as the warehouse clerk Pochatkin.

2. During the Easter recess in March, 1877, Chekhov visited his family in Moscow and met his cousin Misha in person after exchanging several sentimental letters with him.

3. Cousin Misha's younger sister and brother.

2. To Mikhail (Pavlovich) Chekhov[1]

Taganrog,
between April 6 and 8, 1879

Dear Brother Misha,

I got your letter while sitting around yawning by the gate at the height of a horrible fit of boredom, so you can imagine how perfectly timed it seemed—and so enormous too. You have a good handwriting, and I didn't find a single grammatical error anywhere in the letter. There is one thing I don't like, though. Why do you refer to yourself as my "worthless, insignificant little brother"? So you are aware of your worthlessness, are you? Not all Mishas have to be identical, you know. Do you know where you should be aware of your worthlessness? Before God, perhaps, or before human intelligence, before beauty or nature. But not before people. Among people you should be aware of your worth. You're no cheat, you're an honest man, aren't you? Well then, respect yourself for being a good honest fellow. Don't confuse "humility" with "an awareness of your own worthlessness." Georgy[2] has grown. He's a nice boy. I often play knucklebones with him. He's received your packages. You do well to read books. Get into the habit of reading. You'll come to appreciate it in time. So Madame Beecher Stowe brought tears to your eyes? I thumbed through her once and read her straight through for scholarly purposes six months ago, and when I was done I experienced that unpleasant sensation that mortals are wont to feel when they've eaten too many raisins or dried currants.[3] The hawfinch[4] I promised you has escaped, and little is known of his present place of residence. I'll figure out something else to bring you. Take a look at the following books: *Don Quixote* (complete, in all seven or eight parts). It's a fine work written by Cervantes, who is placed on just about the level of Shakespeare. I recommend Turgenev's "Hamlet and Don Quixote" to our brothers if they haven't read it already. As for you, you wouldn't understand it. If you feel like reading an entertaining travelogue, try Goncharov's *Frigate Pallada,*[5] etc. I send Masha special regards. Don't all of you feel bad that I'm coming late. Time flies no matter how bored you brag you are. I'm bringing a lodger along who will pay twenty rubles a month and be under our personal supervision. I'll soon be off for a bargaining session with his mother. Pray for my success![6] However, even twenty rubles is not much, considering Moscow prices and Mother's character—she'll give him good honest food. Our teachers get three hundred fifty rubles a head, and they feed the poor boys on the blood drippings from their roasts, like dogs.

A. Chekhov

1. Mikhail Pavlovich Chekhov (1865–1936) was Anton Chekhov's youngest brother. He grew up to be a writer, magazine publisher and literary translator (of Jack London's work, among others). His most durable contribution, however, was as his brother's biographer. His biographical essays that were appended to his sister Maria's edition of Chekhov's letters and his book *Around Chekhov. Encounters and Impressions* (first published in 1933) are basic and indispensable sources for all students of Chekhov.

2. Chekhov's Taganrog cousin, the son of his Uncle Mitrofan.

3. Harriet Beecher Stowe's *Uncle Tom's Cabin* enjoyed tremendous prestige in Russia. In Turgenev's novel *Smoke,* the reputation of an exiled Russian radical among his fellow dissidents is instantly ruined when his enemies spread the rumor that he had been slapped in the face by Mrs. Beecher Stowe—no one even bothers to ask why she did it; the man is simply ostracized. Tolstoy could think of no higher praise for his favorite Dostoyevsky novel, *Notes from the House of the Dead,* than to compare it to *Uncle Tom's Cabin.* The similarity of the book's abolitionist message to the theme of such classics of Russian anti-serfdom literature as Turgenev's *Sportsman's Sketches* made any questioning of its literary value unthinkable. No respectable Russian critic of the period would have dared point out in print the book's melodramatic sentimentality, as the nineteen-year-old Chekhov is doing here, for fear of being thought obscurantist and reactionary.

4. This bird (*dubanos* in Russian) for some reason proved to be a stumbling block for the earlier translators of Chekhov's letters into English. Mrs. Garnett preferred to omit this entire passage, while Koteliansky decided that *dubanos* must be a dog.

5. Chekhov's interest in Ivan Goncharov's book of travel impressions, which records among other things his visits to China, Japan and Eastern Siberia, is the earliest instance of his preoccupation with the Far East. This interest was to be echoed sporadically in his later reading and correspondence and to find its climax in his voyage to Sakhalin.

6. In the spring of 1879, while preparing for a set of elaborate examinations that were required for graduation from the Taganrog school and arranging to be accepted by the Medical School of Moscow University, Chekhov showed remarkable resourcefulness in trying to help alleviate his mother's financial burdens. He persuaded the parents of two of his fellow students, also headed for Moscow University, to let his mother take them in as paid lodgers. Also, without any help from his relatives or teachers, he got himself nominated for the newly instituted twenty-five-ruble-a-month fellowship that the city administration of Taganrog decided to award to one of the city's natives interested in continuing his education.

II

THE MEDICAL STUDENT WHO WROTE FOR HUMOR MAGAZINES

When Anton Chekhov came to Moscow from Taganrog in order to enroll at the university, he almost immediately found himself in the role of head of the family. His two elder brothers led independent lives and his once-authoritarian father had a job away from home and saw his family only on Sundays. Mikhail Chekhov's book *Around Chekhov* gives a vivid account of the changes which the practical-minded and energetic young Anton instituted in the lives of his mother and younger siblings upon arrival. He made them move from the tenement basement apartment where he found them to more wholesome quarters; he made his mother buy only the groceries she immediately needed for cash, instead of in bulk and on credit, and thus freed her from constant and humiliating indebtedness at the corner grocery store; and he set about re-educating his younger brothers, Ivan and Mikhail, and his sister Maria in his newly found ways of personal dignity and inner freedom. He rapidly became a father figure for these three and established a personal closeness with them that was to last for the rest of his life. His older brothers, however, proved beyond his educational reach, which explains the bitterness, rancor and sermonizing that we find in his letters to Alexander and to Nikolai. (The letter to Nikolai, from Chekhov's student period, is presented in this section, in violation of the chronological sequence.)

Chekhov began his studies at medical school in September of 1879. In his first year, which corresponded to premedical studies, he took courses in physics, inorganic chemistry, botany, zoology, mineralogy, anatomy and religion. In the next four years, he followed this with a solid program of specifically medical subjects. Some of Russia's finest biological scientists and medical specialists were among his teachers. He remained on cordial terms with some of them after leaving the university, and he kept track of their scholarly publications. In his later years, Chekhov was to renew some of the friendships he had formed with a few fellow medical students at the university. During his university years, however, he seems to have been on closer terms with the fellow students of his brother Nikolai, who was studying at the Moscow School of Painting, Sculpture and Architecture. Among Chekhov's closest personal friends of this period, Isaak Levitan and Konstantin Korovin were later to become celebrated painters and Franz Schechtel a renowned architect. Korovin, who is known in the West mostly for the sets and costumes he designed for the Sergei Diaghilev and Anna Pavlova ballet companies, wrote two delightful memoirs about his early friendship with Chekhov, which are also the most vivid record we have of Chekhov's university years (these memoirs have been mostly ignored by Chekhov's Western biographers). One of them contains an account of the young Chekhov's encounter with several dogmatic activist students, full of quotations from Chernyshevsky and Mikhailovsky, who berated him for writing nonideological humorous stories and publishing them under a comical pen name. As Korovin tells it, Chekhov's amused and tolerant reaction to all this was: "These students will make excellent doctors. They are lovely people and I envy them having their heads full of ideas."

Chekhov's publications in humor magazines initially came about for reasons that had nothing to do with the art of literature. While he was still at school in Taganrog, his brothers Alexander and Nikolai had stumbled upon the possibility of augmenting their income by selling stories and, in Nikolai's case, cartoons to the numerous lowbrow publications which proliferated in Moscow and bore names like *Dragonfly*, *Spectator* and *Alarm Clock*. Within months after coming to Moscow, Anton was submitting sketches and stories to several of these magazines, and on December 24, 1879, he made his debut in print when *Dragonfly* published his short piece "Letter to a Learned Neighbor," a remarkably old-fashioned piece of writing that imitated the form and standard devices of Russian eighteenth-century satirical journals. In the next five years Chekhov published several hundred pieces in these magazines under at least a half-dozen different pen names (the best known of these—Antosha Chekhonte—was originally a humorous nickname given Chekhov by his teacher of religion back in Taganrog) and ranging in size from one-line cartoon captions to his two early full-length novels. The first of these novels, *Useless Victory* (1882), was written on a bet and was intended to parody the melodramatic clichés of the popular high-society novels of the Hungarian novelist Mor Jókai; it was eventually made into two Russian silent films, one before and one right after the Revolution. The other novel of Chekhov's student years, the somewhat Dostoyevskian murder mystery *The Shooting Party* (the original Russian title was *Drama During a Hunt*) of 1884, had an even more distinguished career; its basic narrative structure was borrowed by none other than Agatha Christie for one of her novels and after World War II it was made into a Hollywood movie called *Summer Storm.* Even though scholarly studies have been written about these two works, the truth of the matter is that they both were frank potboilers, hastily written for money by a bright medical student, and that no one would have ever heard of them again had they not been written by Chekhov.

Throughout the period of his medical studies, Chekhov kept regarding his writing as nothing more than an additional source of money needed to support his family and put himself through medical school. And yet it was in the course of these five years that he gradually learned his craft as a writer. There is a world of difference between the melodramatic and moralizing productions of 1880–82, such as "For Little Apples" or "The Lady of the Manor," with their total reliance on secondhand traditions and second-rate devices and the concise, masterful little stories Chekhov could write by 1885, such as "The Malefactor" or "Sergeant Prishibeyev," with their unhackneyed observation of life and their taut economy of form. The size limitations and requirements imposed by various humor magazines were particularly important in training Chekhov to rely on careful organization rather than on the traditional eventful plot for producing the impact he wanted.

With his full program of medical studies combined with a full-time literary career, Chekhov had understandably little time for personal correspondence during his university years. Some of his more informative letters for that period were addressed to Nikolai Leykin, publisher of the St. Petersburg–based humor magazine *Fragments,* for which Chekhov worked as a columnist and in which many of his stories of 1883–85 appeared. Author of numerous novels and stories about life among Russian merchant families (their wide popularity with less-literate readers rapidly dwindled at the beginning of the twentieth century), owner of his own publishing firm, Leykin was of considerable help to the young Chekhov and to his two older brothers, both editorially and financially. In subsequent years, with the spread of Chekhov's fame, Leykin repeatedly claimed to have been the first to discern his talent. But, as his published diaries demonstrate, he was actually incapable of appreciating Chekhov's mature work and, like many Russians to this day, admired the early humorous sketches, such as "Surgery" and "A Horsy Name," while being quite baffled by *The Seagull* and "The Lady with the Dog."

Chekhov completed his medical studies in the spring of 1884. In the fall of that year he was awarded the title of District Physician, which entitled him to practice medicine in the Russian provinces. To complete the requirements for his M.D. degree he still had to produce a dissertation. A year earlier he had tried to get his brother Alexander interested in a joint research project on the subject of "Sexual Authority," which was designed to prove, on the basis of wide reading in zoology and anthropology, that the inequality in strength and intelligence that is observable between the males and the females of certain species is attributable to their breeding and brooding methods and that this inequality is likely to disappear in species which will evolve in the future, since "nature abhors inequality" (Letter to Alexander Chekhov, April 17–18, 1883). But this teleological, Herbert Spencer–inspired project failed to interest Alexander and all that remains of it is Chekhov's initial outline of research. After the termination of his studies, Anton chose as his dissertation topic "The History of Medicine in Russia," and embarked on his research all alone. In 1885 and 1886 he read a number of medieval Russian chronicles and some memoirs dating from the beginning of the seventeenth century, looking for evidence of medical practices in these documents. But, as the years advanced, he found his time more and more occupied by creative literary work, for which from 1886 on there was considerable demand.

3. To Nikolai Leykin

Moscow,
between August 21 and 24, 1883

Dear Nikolai Alexandrovich,

This batch is one of the less successful. The column is pallid, and the story rough and awfully shallow.[1] I have a better topic and would gladly have written and earned more, but fate is against me this time. I'm writing under abominable conditions. Before me sits my nonliterary work pummeling mercilessly away at my conscience,[2] the fledgling of a visiting kinsman is screaming in the room next door,[3] and in another room my father is reading "The Sealed Angel"[4] aloud to my mother. . . . Someone has wound up the music box, and I can hear *La Belle Hélène*. . . . It makes me want to slip off to the country, but it's already one in the morning. It would be hard to think up a more abominable setting for a writer. My bed is occupied by the visiting kinsman, who comes up to me now and then and starts discussing medicine. "My daughter must have colic. That's what's making her yell. . . ." I have the misfortune of being a medic, and there isn't a man alive who doesn't think it necessary to "have a little chat" with me about medicine. And if they get tired chatting about medicine, they change the subject to literature.

The surroundings are matchless. I keep kicking myself for not having sneaked off to the country where I could probably have had a good night's sleep, written a story for you, and above all pursued medicine and literature in peace.

In September I'm going to sneak off to Voskresensk,[5] weather permitting. I was utterly delighted by your last story.

The fledgling is howling away!! I promise myself never to have children. . . . The reason the French have so few children is probably that they spend all their time in their studies writing stories for *L'Amusant.* I hear they're trying to get them to have more children, a cartoon subject for *L'Amusant* and *Fragments*: "The Situation in France." A police commissioner enters a home and demands that the parents start making children.

Good-bye. I'm trying to figure out how and where to catch a few winks.

I have the honor of remaining

Respectfully yours,
A. Chekhov

1. At that time Chekhov supplied Leykin's magazine *Fragments* with a monthly column "Fragments of Moscow Life," in which he reported recent trials, financial scandals, new stage productions, etc. The story in question is Chekhov's "Intercession" (*Protektsiya*) (1883).

2. Reference to Chekhov's medical studies.

3. Alexander Chekhov, the writer's older brother, came for a visit from St. Petersburg, bringing his current mistress and their baby daughter.

4. A short story by Nikolai Leskov.

5. A town near Moscow, where Chekhov's younger brother Ivan had a spacious house that went with his job as schoolmaster and where Chekhov was to begin practicing medicine after his graduation.

4. To Nikolai Leykin

Moscow, May 20, 1884

Dear Nikolai Alexandrovich,

I received both your letter and the enclosure.[1] I've read the letter and this is my answer. As for the enclosure, I have passed it on to the party in question with your advice to write about life among customs officials.

A trip to Petersburg is one of my oldest dreams. I gave my word to myself that I would visit your imperial city in early June, but now I'm taking my word back. The reason is financial, damn it. The trip requires a hundred to a hundred fifty rubles, and the other day I had the pleasure of running all my holdings through the wringer of life. I had to cough up fifty rubles for the summer cottage, paid twenty-five for my tuition and as much again for my sister's and so on and so forth. Add to that the paucity of my recent earnings, and you'll understand the state of my pockets. By the first of June I should have a free fifty rubles, but you can't get very far on that. The trip will have to be postponed indefinitely, and I'll have to be content with the journey to the summer place and back. Wild Palmin[2] was planning to go with me. He and I agreed to leave on the second or third of June, but . . . he came over a few days ago shaking his head and announcing he wouldn't be able to go to Petersburg. He is tormented by something murky which finds expression in the form of extremely vague and undecipherable memories that come out as "My childhood . . . my youth." You'd think he'd committed a murder back in Petersburg.

He gave me a long exposition of the reasons for his antipathy toward his native city, but I didn't understand a word of it. Either he's trying to wiggle out of it to avoid the expense (between you and me, he's something of a tightwad) or there is actually something peculiar about his Petersburg past. He's coming for dinner on Friday. . . . We'll have some drinks, and toward nightfall we'll go to his summer cottage in Petrovsko-Razumovskoye, and maybe have a bit of a spree. Just as he is about to raise his wiry finger and talk to me of "riberty, equarity, and fraternity," when his emotion is reaching its acme, I'll start telling him about the charms of a trip to Valaam[3] and trying to convince him to go. . . . I just might succeed. If we go together, we'll probably need no more than a hundred rubles apiece. That's a good argument too. And he really needs to be aired out a bit. Even if his fine talent doesn't require it, hygiene very definitely does. He drinks much too much; in that respect he's incurable. But there are so many other things that can be cured. What a hell of a way to live! He's always shabbily dressed and he never sees sunlight or people. I've never seen what he eats, but I'd be willing to bet it's real junk. (His wife doesn't give the impression of being a wise housekeeper.) All in all, I have the feeling he's going to die soon. His system is so run down that it is a wonder that such a versifying mind can be lodged in such a sick body. The man definitely needs to be aired out. He told me he was going to take a trip down the Volga, but that's hard to believe. He won't get any farther than his shed of a summer cottage. I'll let you know how Friday's conversation turns out. If I don't go myself, at least I'll get him going.

Tomorrow I have my last exam, and the day after my person will represent what the crowd honors with the title of "doctor" (provided, of course, I pass the exam tomorrow). I am ordering a "doctor" shingle with a pointing finger, not so much for my medical practice as for putting the fear of God in janitors, mailmen and the tailor. When the inhabitants of Yeletsky's house call me—a writer of comic piffle—doctor, I am so unused to it that it grates on my ears. My parents, on the other hand, enjoy it. My parents are noble plebeians who have always looked on Aesculapians as something grimly arrogant and official, something that doesn't receive you without being announced and then charges you five rubles. They can't believe their eyes. Am I an impostor, a mirage, or an honest-to-goodness doctor? They are showing me the sort of respect they'd show me if I had become a police captain. They imagine that thousands of rubles will pass through my hands in the very first year. Fyodor Glebych, my patient tailor, is of the same opinion. They all have to be disillusioned, the poor things.

Exams are over, so there's nothing left to hold me back from applying for admission to the select few. I'll be sending you something every issue. I haven't quite settled down into my new routine yet, but in four or five days I'll be lifting my eyes heavenward and starting to think up new subjects. I'm going to spend the summer at the New Jerusalem monastery[4] writing on and off. The only thing that scares me is high-minded passion; I find it worse than any exam. Enclosed you will find "Vacation Hygiene," a seasonal piece. If you like it, I'll work up a few more along the same lines: "A Hunter's Rules and Regulations," "A Forester's Rules and Regulations" and so on. I want to write a *Fragments* statistical survey: population, death rate, occupations and so on. It will be a little long, but if it works, it will be quite lively. (I got the idea from cramming for medical statistics recently.) I would now enjoy writing a satirical medical text in two or three volumes. First of all, I'd get my patients into a laughing mood, and only then would I begin to treat them. Moscow is having rainy weather: it's too cold for a summer coat and too hot for a winter one. The state of my health is not dazzling; at times I'm fine, but at times I'm in pain. I drink and then stop drinking. . . . As yet there's nothing definite in sight.

I'm sitting down to read. Good-bye.

Your respectful contributor,
A. Chekhov

Is it true that *The Cause*[5] is on its way out? If so, then good riddance! I never liked that journal, sinner that I am. It irritated me. Of course, even *The Cause* could have served a purpose, considering the present paucity of journals.

1. The enclosure consisted of a story by Alexander Chekhov, which Leykin rejected and returned to Anton Chekhov with the suggestion that Alexander, who had obtained a temporary job as a customs official, describe his new surroundings in his next story.

2. Iliodor (or Lyodor) Palmin (1841–91) made a certain name for himself as a writer of civic and political verse during the politically permissive period of the 1860s. By the beginning of the twentieth century, Palmin's doggerel had been deservedly forgotten and his name remained in literary history only because of his friendship with the young Chekhov, whom he introduced to Leykin (it was at Palmin's urging that Leykin first invited the three Chekhov brothers—Alexander, Nikolai and Anton—to become contributors to *Fragments*). Since the 1930s, in line with the officially imposed revival of all nineteenth-century civic poetry regardless of its quality, Palmin's verse has been repeatedly reissued and anthologized in the Soviet Union.

3. A well-known monastery, which was also a popular excursion site.

4. In the town of Voskresensk, where Chekhov began his medical practice that summer.

5. A liberal political journal that was temporarily closed down due to censorship troubles, but which was able to resume publication soon afterward.

5. To Viktor Bilibin[1]

Moscow,
February 1, 1886

Kindest of humorists and law clerks and least
bribable of secretaries,* Viktor Viktorovich,

Five times I've begun to write you and five times I've been interrupted. I've finally nailed myself to the chair and am writing [several words are crossed out in the original] which offended you and me and which with your permission I now declare closed, though it hasn't begun yet in Moscow. I wrote Leykin about it and received an explanation. I've just returned from a visit to the well-known poet Palmin. When I read him the lines from your letters that pertain to him, he said, "I respect this man. He is very talented." Upon which His Inspiration raised the longest of his fingers and deigned to add, with an air of profundity of course, "But *Fragments* will ruin him! Have some spiced vodka."

We talked for a long time and about many things. Palmin is a typical poet, if you admit the existence of such a type. He is a poetical

* *An idea: consistory secretaries probably don't envy editorial secretaries [Chekhov's own footnote].*

individual, easily carried away and packed from head to toe with subject matter and ideologies. Talking with him is not tiring. True, while talking with him, you have to drink a lot, but then you can be certain that during an entire three- or four-hour talk with him you won't hear a single lying word or trite phrase, and that's worth sacrificing your sobriety.

By the way, he and I tried to think up a title for my book. After racking our brains for hours, all we could come up with was *Cats and Carps* and *Flowers and Dogs*.[2] I was willing to settle for *Buy This Book or You'll Get a Punch in the Mouth* or *Are You Being Helped, Sir?*, but after some thought the poet pronounced them hackneyed and cliché. Why don't you think up a title for me? As far as I'm concerned, all titles with a (grammatically) collective meaning belong in a saloon. I would prefer what Leykin wants, to wit: *A. Chekhonte. Stories and Sketches* and nothing else, even though that kind of title is suited only to celebrities, not $-\infty$'s like me. *Varicolored Stories* would also do. There you have two titles. Choose one of them and let Leykin know. I am relying on your taste, though I realize that by placing demands on your taste, I'm placing demands on you too. But don't be annoyed. When, God willing, your house is on fire, I'll send you my fire hose.[3]

Many thanks for the trouble you took to have the original clipped and sent to me. So as not to be in your debt (monetarily), I am sending you for the postage a thirty-five-kopeck stamp that you once sent me with a fee and that I have never been able to get rid of. Now you can be stuck with it.

And now a few words about my fiancée and Hymen. With your permission I will postpone these two items until next time when I am free from the inspiration communicated to me by my talk with Palmin. I'm afraid of saying too much—too much nonsense, that is. When I speak of women I like, I tend to draw out what I say until it reaches the *ne plus* ultra, the Pillars of Hercules—a trait that has remained with me since my school days. Thank your fiancée for remembering me and tell her that my wedding will most likely—alas and alack! The censor has cut out the rest. . . . My one and only is Jewish.[4] If the rich young Jewess has enough courage to convert to Orthodoxy with all that this entails, fine. If not, that's fine too. Besides, we've already had a quarrel. We'll make up tomorrow, but in a week we'll quarrel again. She breaks pencils and the photographs on my desk because of her annoyance at being held back by religion. That's the way she is. . . .[5] She has a terrible temper. There is no doubt whatsoever that I will divorce her a year or two after the wedding. But . . . *finis*.

Your gloating over the censors' prohibiting my "Attack on Husbands"[6] does you honor. Let me shake your hand. But it would have been more pleasant just the same to have earned sixty-five rather than fifty-five rubles. To take revenge on the censors and all those who gloated over my misfortune, my friends and I are forming a Cuckolding Society. The constitution has already been submitted for approval. I was elected chairman by a majority of fourteen to three.

There is an article called "Humor Magazines" in the first issue of *Ears of Grain*.[7] What's going on? And speaking of that . . . once when you, your fiancée and I were talking about young writers, I brought up Korolenko. Remember? If you want to get to know him, get hold of the fourth or fifth issue of the *Northern Herald* and read his article "The Vagabonds." I recommend it.

Give my regards to Roman Romanych.[8] My ambassador, Schechtel,[9] the artist and Moscow celebrity, visited him the other day and told him more than the longest letter could possibly have told him.

I have to write, but there are no suitable topics. What should I write about?

But it's time for bed. I send you my regards and a handshake. Every day I go out into the country for my medical practice. What ravines, what views!

Yours,
A. Chekhov

Why haven't you said anything about the summer cottage? You complain of bad health and then don't give a thought to the summer. . . . Why, you'd have to be a pretty dry, wiry, immobile crocodile to spend all summer in the city! Two or three good months of tranquillity are certainly worth giving up your work or anything else for that matter.

By this seal and signachur[10] I do certify that I have received in full the sum of fifty-five rubles, seventy-two kopecks.

A. Chekhov,
Nongovernment doctor

1. Bilibin was the editorial secretary of *Fragments*, a prolific contributor to humor magazines and a mediocre playwright.

2. A possible gibe at the collection of stories by Bilibin's employer Leykin, entitled *Carps and Pikes*.

3. Bilibin's letter, to which this is the reply, described a fire that was going on next door to Bilibin's house.

4. According to the very plausible guess of the editors of Volume 68 of *Literary Heritage*, who first published this letter in 1960, Chekhov's Jewish fiancée must have been Yevdokia (Dunya) Èfros, a school friend of his

tuals, to fit in and not find their presence burdensome, you have to have a certain amount of breeding. Your talent has brought you into their midst. You belong there, but . . . you seem to yearn to escape and feel compelled to waver between the cultured set and your next-door neighbors. It's the bourgeois side of you coming out, the side raised on birch thrashings beside the wine cellar and handouts, and it's hard to overcome, terribly hard.

To my mind, well-bred people ought to satisfy the following conditions:

1. They respect the individual and are therefore always indulgent, gentle, polite and compliant. They do not throw a tantrum over a hammer or a lost eraser. When they move in with somebody, they do not act as if they were doing him a favor, and when they move out, they do not say, "How can anyone live with you!" They excuse noise and cold and overdone meat and witticisms and the presence of others in their homes.

2. Their compassion extends beyond beggars and cats. They are hurt even by things the naked eye can't see. If for instance, Pyotr knows that his father and mother are turning gray and losing sleep over seeing their Pyotr so rarely (and seeing him drunk when he does turn up), then he rushes home to them and sends his vodka to the devil. They do not sleep nights the better to help the Polevayevs,[8] help pay their brothers' tuition, and keep their mother decently dressed.

3. They respect the property of others and therefore pay their debts.

4. They are candid and fear lies like the plague. They do not lie even about the most trivial matters. A lie insults the listener and debases him in the liar's eyes. They don't put on airs, they behave in the street as they do at home, and they do not try to dazzle their inferiors. They know how to keep their mouths shut and they do not force uninvited confidences on people. Out of respect for the ears of others they are more often silent than not.

5. They do not belittle themselves merely to arouse sympathy. They do not play on people's heartstrings to get them to sigh and fuss over them. They do not say, "No one understands me!" or "I've squandered my talent on trifles! I am [. . .]" because this smacks of a cheap effect and is vulgar, false and out-of-date.

6. They are not preoccupied with vain things. They are not taken in by such false jewels as friendships with celebrities, handshakes with drunken Plevako,[9] ecstasy over the first person they happen to meet at the Salon de Variétés,[10] popularity among the tavern crowd. They laugh when they hear, "I represent the press," a phrase befitting only Rodzeviches and Levenbergs.[11] When they have done a penny's worth of

work, they don't try to make a hundred rubles out of it, and they don't boast over being admitted to places closed to others. True talents always seek obscurity. They try to merge with the crowd and shun all ostentation. Krylov himself said that an empty barrel has more chance of being heard than a full one.[12]

7. If they have talent, they respect it. They sacrifice comfort, women, wine and vanity to it. They are proud of their talent, and so they do not go out carousing with trade-school employees or Skvortsov's[13] guests, realizing that their calling lies in exerting an uplifting influence on them, not in living with them. What is more, they are fastidious.

8. They cultivate their aesthetic sensibilities. They cannot stand to fall asleep fully dressed, see a slit in the wall teeming with bedbugs, breathe rotten air, walk on a spittle-laden floor or eat off a kerosene stove. They try their best to tame and ennoble their sexual instinct . . . [. . .] to endure her logic and never stray from her. What's the point of it all? People with good breeding are not as coarse as that. What they look for in a woman is not a bed partner or horse sweat, [. . .] not the kind of intelligence that expresses itself in the ability to stage a fake pregnancy and tirelessly reel off lies. They—and especially the artists among them—require spontaneity, elegance, compassion, a woman who will be a mother, not a [. . .]. They don't guzzle vodka on any old occasion, nor do they go around sniffing cupboards, for they know they are not swine. They drink only when they are free, if the opportunity happens to present itself. For they require a *mens sana in corpore sano*.

And so on. That's how well-bred people act. If you want to be well-bred and not fall below the level of the milieu you belong to, it is not enough to read *The Pickwick Papers* and memorize a soliloquy from *Faust*. It is not enough to hail a cab and drive off to Yakimanka Street if all you're going to do is bolt out again a week later.

You must work at it constantly, day and night. You must never stop reading, studying in depth, exercising your will. Every hour is precious.

Trips back and forth to Yakimanka Street won't help. You've got to drop your old way of life and make a clean break. Come home. Smash your vodka bottle, lie down on the couch and pick up a book. You might even give Turgenev a try. You've never read him.

You must swallow your [. . .] pride. You're no longer a child. You'll be thirty soon. It's high time!

I'm waiting. . . . We're all waiting. . . .

Yours,
A. Chekhov

1. Nikolai Pavlovich Chekhov (1858–89) was the second son of Pavel and Yevgenia Chekhov. As a child he showed talents for both art and music and was considered the most gifted of the Chekhov children. He was later a student at the Moscow School of Painting, Sculpture and Architecture, where he associated with some of the most promising young Russian artists of the time. However, he never completed his studies owing to chronic alcoholism and a fatal attraction for the Moscow equivalent of skid row, where he would disappear for weeks on end. Nikolai died at thirty-one of tuberculosis aggravated by alcoholism.

2. Zabelin was the name of the Zvenigorod town drunk.

3. The flutist Alexander Ivanenko was for many years a close friend of the entire Chekhov family; Mishka is Chekhov's brother Mikhail, according to whose memoirs Nelly (her full name was Yelena Markova) was a pretty girl with whom Nikolai was once involved romantically, the niece of a hospitable lady to whose villa in the city of Zvenigorod all Chekhov brothers were frequently invited.

4. Nicholas Voutsina was an ex-pirate who operated a Greek school in Taganrog which Nikolai and Anton attended for one year in their childhood, with rather disastrous results.

5. The pianist Niktopoleon Dolgov was Ivanenko's usual accompanist.

6. A Moscow journalist.

7. The Chekhov family resided on Yakimanka Street at the time; "the man who bolts" from there is Nikolai Chekhov.

8. At the time of publication of the twenty-volume edition of Chekhov's works in 1944–51, Maria Chekhov informed the editors that she remembered the Polevayevs as a family which had "played a negative role" in the lives of her brothers Alexander and Nikolai.

9. Fyodor Plevako was a celebrated trial lawyer of the period.

10. A Moscow night club, which also functioned as a pickup point for ladies of the night. Chekhov described it in a memorable piece of journalism that appeared in *Spectator* in October of 1881 with illustrations by Nikolai Chekhov.

11. Two minor Moscow journalists.

12. In his fable "The Two Barrels," where a barrel filled with fine wine rolls sedately and quietly down the street, while an empty one rattles noisily over the cobblestones, attracting everyone's attention.

13. The name of one of Nikolai's trade-school employee friends.

III

SERIOUS LITERATURE

After Chekhov became famous, a number of literary celebrities either claimed or were given the credit for having first discovered the magnitude of his talent. By any objective criteria, this honor should go to Nikolai Leskov, who from the vantage point of today, was, after Tolstoy, the most important living Russian writer at the time Chekhov began his literary activity. One drunken night in October of 1883, after he and Chekhov had made a tour of Moscow night clubs and possibly brothels, Leskov anointed the younger writer "the way Samuel anointed David" and predicted a great future for him. But Leskov was at the time at the very nadir of his literary reputation, following almost two decades of vilification by the utilitarian critics. Chekhov may have been pleased by his words and by being offered inscribed copies of Leskov's finest novel, *Cathedral Folk*, and of his now famous experimental story "The Left-Handed Blacksmith," but in his letter to his brother Alexander (Letter of October 15–20, 1883) he treated the whole thing as a joke, referring to Leskov as "my favorite scribbler" (and not *writer*, as the Western biographers of Chekhov inevitably mistranslate his term *pisaka*).

Chekhov's joyous reaction to the letter of acclaim he received three years later from Dmitry Grigorovich, on the other hand, shows that even he, for all the independence of his judgment, was not entirely immune to the reputation-making powers of literary criticism. Grigorovich, who is little read and rarely reprinted even in the Soviet Union, was undeservedly overpraised by Belinsky for his philanthropic stories of peasant life originally published in the 1840s, and from that time until the end of the nineteenth century he was regarded as the equal of Turgenev and Tolstoy by the majority of literate Russians, a view that can only raise eyebrows today. Still, the renown that the name of Grigorovich enjoyed at the time makes Chekhov's response understandable, even though the very existence of Grigorovich elicited the somewhat comical disbelief of Thomas Mann in the oddly out-of-focus essay on Chekhov he wrote at the end of his life.

And yet, gracious as Leskov's statement and Grigorovich's letter may have been, they were no more than private gestures. The man, however, who backed his recognition of Chekhov's talent with concrete action and who did more than anyone else to launch him on a major career in serious literature was the writer and publisher Alexei Suvorin. It was Suvorin's publication of Chekhov's stories in his newspaper *New Times* and his subsequent securing of Chekhov's nomination for the Pushkin Prize that gained Chekhov entry into serious literary journals and brought him to the attention of important editors, of Lev Tolstoy, and of the literate reading public. Chekhov's friendship with Suvorin was one of the most significant and intimate relationships in his entire life. His letters to Suvorin are the frankest and most revealing letters Chekhov ever wrote to anyone and they provide us with indispensable insights into the mind of this frequently reticent writer. And yet, for peculiarly Russian reasons, unimaginable in any other literature, Chekhov's relationship with Suvorin has been systematically downgraded, obscured and distorted by Chekhov's Russian biographers and commentators.

When Chekhov began to contribute stories to *New Times*, it was generally regarded as a conservative, pro-government publication. By the turn of the century, the newspaper's stand on the Dreyfus affair and on Russian students' uprisings and its chauvinistic baiting of Poles, Finns and Jews made Suvorin's name and that of his newspaper odious to most liberal Russians. The view of Suvorin that was formed at the beginning of the twentieth century has been summed up by Lenin in a statement that is inevitably brought up in Soviet criticism and historiography whenever Suvorin's name is mentioned: "A poor man, a liberal and even a democrat at the beginning of his life's road, a millionaire and a smug, shameless eulogizer of the bourgeoisie, groveling before every change of official policy at the end of that road." The existence of this Lenin text on Suvorin has made it mandatory for Chekhov's Soviet biographers to minimize the closeness of the relationship and to ascribe dishonest or devious motives to all of Suvorin's dealings with Chekhov. Writing in 1933, Mikhail Chekhov was still able to give Suvorin a modicum of credit for the things he had done for his brother. But Maria Chekhova's book of memoirs, which she dictated in the early 1950s, had to bow to the general trend and to depict Suvorin as a crafty hypocrite, subtly luring the gullible Anton Pavlovich into his reactionary nets.

Chekhov disagreed with Suvorin strongly on many issues, both before and after the Dreyfus case, which is usually represented as the breaking point in their friendship, and he was eventually to come to see many of the older man's shortcomings and unattractive qualities. But he valued Suvorin's literary advice and he never forgot Suvorin's early help. Chekhov's typical disregard for labels and categories enabled him to form a friendship with the revolutionary writer Vladimir Korolenko shortly after beginning his association with Suvorin, and to see and appreciate the good things each of these men had to offer.

The first appearance of Chekhov's work in *New Times* coincided with a major breakthrough in the development of his talent. Eighteen eighty-six and early 1887 brought a whole stream of stories, unprecedented in Russian literature for the originality of their form and subject matter and for their compression and concision: "The Requiem," "Heartache," "The Witch," "The Chorus Girl," "Agafya," "A Calamity" and numerous others. One of the most controversial of them was "Mire," to this day one of Chekhov's least-understood works. Because the story featured a Jewish seductress and because it appeared in *New Times*, the prominent anti-government journalist Vukol Lavrov proclaimed it reactionary and racist. A recent American book on Chekhov described "Mire" as a study of an amoral nymphomaniac. But a closer reading of this story within the context of Chekhov's writing of 1886–88 shows that it was one of several works written during that period which examined, possibly under the impact of his broken engagement to Dunya Èfros, the reactions of sensitive Russian Jews to the discrimination and repression with which they had to live. Sarah in *Ivanov* is crushed by the non-Jewish world into which she has married and which does not want her. Solomon, in the Jewish inn episode in "The Steppe," expresses his resentment of the stereotype of the money-mad Jew in which society has cast him by burning his share of the family inheritance and by incoherent harangues which no one around him can understand, including his brother Moses (who gets along as best he can by playing the comical role of an obsequious Jewish Uncle Tom). The wealthy and educated Susannah in "Mire," unlike Sarah and Solomon, does not have to contend with overt and crude anti-Semitism. But she constantly expects it just the same and her resentment finds its expression in a series of sexual conquests of young Russian noblemen; her promiscuity is the only way she has of asserting her own worth and of defying the hostility of the neighboring Russian gentry. Ironically, the two brothers who are involved with her in the course of the story are not at all anti-Jewish, but they are nevertheless victimized by Susannah's neurotic response to her predicament, which Chekhov depicted with remarkable understanding.

Among the numerous readers and scholars who misunderstood or misread "Mire" was Chekhov's friend and frequent hostess, the amateur writer Maria Kiselyova. The spirited and detailed letter Chekhov sent her in defense of "Mire" is another basic Chekhovian document, with its clear statement of his views on the uses and limitations of literature and on the dangers of subjective censorship.

7. To Alexei Suvorin[1]

Moscow,
February 21, 1886

Dear Sir,

I have received your letter. Thank you for writing such flattering words about my work and printing my story so promptly.[2] You can judge for yourself what a refreshing and even inspiring effect the kind attentions of as experienced and talented a person as you have had on my ambitions as a writer.

I agree with your opinion that I threw away the end of my story, and I thank you for this useful piece of advice. I've been writing for six years now, and you are the first person who ever took the trouble to give me suggestions and then motivate them.

The pen name A. Chekhonte probably sounds odd and recherché. But it was thought up at the dawn of my misty youth,[3] and I've grown accustomed to it. That's why I don't notice how odd it is.

I write comparatively little: no more than two or three brief stories a week. I can find the time to work for *New Times*, but I'm glad nonetheless that you didn't make deadlines a condition for my becoming a contributor. Deadlines lead to haste and the feeling of having a weight around your neck. Both of these together make it hard for me to work. For me personally a deadline is inconvenient if only because I'm a physician and practice medicine. I can never guarantee that I won't be torn away from my desk for a whole day on any given day. The risk of my being late and not finishing a story by the deadline is always there.

The fee you have proposed is fully satisfactory for the present. If you could arrange to have the newspaper sent to me regularly—I rarely get a chance to see it—I will be very grateful.

This time I'm sending you a story that is exactly twice as long as the previous one, and, I fear, twice as bad.[4]

I remain

Yours truly,
A. Chekhov

1. Alexei Suvorin (1834–1912) was, like Chekhov himself, of peasant origin. He began his career as a village schoolmaster. During the reform era of the 1860s, he became a popular muckraking journalist and earned a six-month prison sentence for one of his anti-government exposés. At the time of the Russian-Turkish War of 1878 he purchased the newspaper *New Times*, which until then owed its circulation primarily to its domestic-help advertisements. Because of his friendly relations with Prince Milan of Serbia, Suvorin was able to send detailed dispatches from the front to *New Times*, and the newspaper quickly became the favorite reading of the Russian military, who were often kept in the dark by their own command about the progress of the war in which they were engaged. This made Suvorin's fortune, and it also determined the subsequent conservative orientation of the newspaper, since in later years army officers and civil servants, both active and retired, formed a large segment of its subscribers.

Suvorin later branched out into book publishing (he was the first publisher to put out cheap editions of Russian classics) and book selling (he held a monopoly on book stands at all Russian railroad stations). He was a millionaire by the time Chekhov met him. He was also a novelist and something of a literary scholar (his essay on Griboyedov was much admired by Alexander Blok), and he wrote a series of flashy plays, which, although devoid of literary merit, were popular with actresses for providing them with showy starring roles. After the turn of the century, Suvorin's energies were mainly devoted to the theater which he privately organized and operated in St. Petersburg and for which he engaged some of the biggest acting names of the period.

The excerpts from Suvorin's private journal which were published after the Revolution in 1923 with the avowed purpose of exposing his hypocrisy and corruption show a man of broad culture, with access to the centers of political power, who is helping to prop up the regime which he sees as neither honest nor just. In addition to numerous chunks of back-stairs gossip, Suvorin's journal contains fascinating accounts of his dealings and encounters with Dostoyevsky, Tolstoy, Émile Zola, Alphonse Daudet, Tchaikovsky, Nekrasov, Chernyshevsky and a number of other literary and political figures of the last forty years of the nineteenth century. In contrast to the often gossipy and cynical tone of the journal, Suvorin writes of his encounters with Chekhov in tones of warmth and friendship that seem otherwise untypical of this hardheaded, powerful and frequently lonely man.

2. "The Requiem," which was submitted by Chekhov on February 10, and which appeared on February 15. This was his first work to appear in *New Times* and also the first to be published under his real name instead of one of his pen names.

3. "At the dawn of my misty youth" is the first line of a popular song by the peasant poet of the Romantic period, Alexei Koltsov. For Chekhov's high opinion of this poet, see Letter 17.

4. "The Witch."

8. To Dmitry Grigorovich[1]

Moscow,
March 28, 1886

Your letter,[2] my kind and dearly beloved bearer of glad tidings, struck me like a thunderbolt. I was so overwhelmed it brought me to the brink of tears, and even now I feel it has left a deep imprint on my innermost being. May God comfort your old age as you have befriended my youth; I can find neither words nor deeds to thank you enough. You know how ordinary people look upon the favored few such as yourself, and so you can imagine what your letter does for my pride. It is worth more than the highest diploma, and for the neophyte writer it is tantamount to royalties for his present and future. I've been walking about in a daze. I lack the acumen to judge whether or not I deserve this great reward. I can only repeat that I am thunderstruck.

If I do have a gift that warrants respect, I must confess before the purity of your heart that I have as yet failed to respect it. I felt I had one, but slipped into the habit of considering it worthless. Purely external factors are sufficient to cause an organism to treat itself with excessive mistrust and suspicion. I've had my share of such factors, now that I think of it. All my friends and relatives have looked down on my work as an author, and they never stop giving me friendly advice against giving up my real life's work for my scrawling. I have hundreds of friends in Moscow, about twenty of whom are writers, and I can't remember even one of them ever reading my things or considering me an artist. There exists in Moscow a so-called "literary circle"; talents and mediocrities of all ilks and ages gather once a week in a specially reserved restaurant dining room to air their tongues. If I were to go there and read the least snippet from your letter, they would laugh in my face. In the five years I've spent hanging around newspaper offices, I've become resigned to the general view of my literary insignificance, soon took to looking down on my work, and kept plowing right on. That's the first factor. The second is that I am a doctor and up to my ears in medicine. The saying about chasing two hares at once has never robbed anybody of more sleep than it has me.

The only reason I am writing all this is to justify my grievous sin in your eyes to some small degree. Until now I treated my literary work extremely frivolously, casually, nonchalantly, I can't remember working on *a single* story for more than a day, and "The Huntsman," which you so enjoyed, I wrote while I was out swimming.[3] I wrote my stories the way reporters write up fires: mechanically, only half-consciously, without the least concern for the reader or myself. While writing, I would do my best not to waste images and scenes I liked on the story at hand. Heaven knows why, but I would carefully put them away and save them for later.

What impelled me to take a critical look at my works was Suvorin's[4] very gracious and, as far as I can tell, sincere letter. I began making plans to write something worthwhile, yet I still had no faith in my own literary worth.

But there out of the blue was your letter. Please forgive the comparison, but it had the same effect on me as a governor's order to leave town within twenty-four hours, that is, I suddenly felt an uncontrollable urge to hurry and extricate myself from the spot where I was stuck.

I agree with you on all points. I myself felt the improprieties you point out when I saw "The Witch" in print. If I had taken three or four days to write the story instead of one, they wouldn't be there.

I will try to stop writing for a deadline, but this cannot be done at once. There's no way for me to get myself out of the rut I've fallen into. I have nothing against going hungry as I have in the past, but I'm not the only one involved. I write in my spare time, two or three hours a day and a small chunk of the night, that is, stretches suitable only for minor production. During the summer when I have more spare time and expenses are down, I'll undertake something more serious.

I can't put my real name on the book because it's too late: the cover design is ready and the book has already been printed. Even before you, many people in Petersburg advised me not to spoil the book with a pen name, but I wouldn't listen to them, perhaps out of pride.[5] I am very dissatisfied with the book. It's a hodgepodge, an indiscriminate conglomeration of the tripe I wrote as a student, plucked bare by the censors and humor-sheet editors. I'm sure that many people will be disappointed once they've read it. Had I known that I was being read and that you were keeping track of me, I would never have let it be published.

All my hope lies in the future. I'm still only twenty-six. I may still manage to accomplish something yet, though time is flying.

Please forgive this long letter and don't hold it against a man for daring the first time in his life to indulge himself in the pleasure of writing a letter to Grigorovich.

If possible, send me a photograph of yourself. You have shown me such kindness and so exhilarated me that I feel I could write you a whole ream instead of just a page. May God grant you health and happiness. Please trust the sincerity of your deeply respectful and grateful

A. Chekhov

1. The leonine and sociable Grigorovich (1822–99) was one of the major Russian literary celebrities in the second half of the nineteenth century. Today, he is remembered not for his own writings, but because of the providential role he happened to play in the biographies of two great Russian writers. In 1844, the young Grigorovich shared an apartment with an engineering student named Fyodor Dostoyevsky. With his encouragement, Dostoyevsky wrote his first novel, *Poor Folk,* which Grigorovich then brought to the attention of the poet-publisher Nekrasov and the celebrated critic Belinsky. Belinsky's acclamation of Dostoyevsky as "the new Gogol" inaugurated the great novelist's literary career. Now, forty-two years later, Grigorovich's recognition of Chekhov's talent had almost as momentous an impact on the literary evolution of the young man who in many ways became Dostoyevsky's very antipode in the Russian literary tradition.

2. On March 25, Grigorovich wrote Chekhov a long letter telling him that he had the most outstanding talent of all the writers of the younger generation and predicted for him a great literary future, if he learned to work slowly, carefully and conscientiously. Grigorovich also advised Chekhov to avoid excessively naturalistic detail and warned him against "pornographic subjects," which he believed he had discerned in some of Chekhov's stories.

3. *V kupal'ne* was translated as "in a bathing-shed" by Koteliansky and by Garnett and appears as "in a bath house" in the Hellman-Lederer volume. Actually it is a wooden-fenced enclosure on a river or a lake, built to allow nude swimming (usually segregated by sex).

4. Grigorovich claimed in his letter that he was the one who brought Chekhov to Suvorin's attention in the first place.

5. Like Suvorin, Viktor Bilibin and several of Chekhov's other literary friends, Grigorovich advised Chekhov to drop his humor-magazine pen name of Antosha Chekhonte and to publish his forthcoming book of short stories under his own name. Because the book was already typeset, Chekhov could not follow this advice. For his work that appeared in serious "thick" journals, Chekhov dropped his earlier pen names, but he reverted to them occasionally in his humor-magazine publications until the end of his life.

9. To Maria Kiselyova[1]

Moscow,
January 14, 1887

Your "Larka"[2] is quite charming, dear Maria Vladimirovna. It has its bumpy spots, but its brevity and virile style make up for everything. Not wishing to be the sole judge of your creation, however, I am sending it to Suvorin, a true connoisseur in such matters. I will let you know what he has to say in due course. And now allow me to take a snarl at your criticism. Even your praise of "On the Road" has failed to mellow my auctorial wrath, and I am eager to take my revenge for

"Mire."[3] Careful, now. And hold fast to the back of your chair so you won't fall into a faint. Well, here I go. . . .

Critical articles, even the unjust, abusive kind, are usually met with a silent bow. Such is literary etiquette. Answering back goes against custom, and anyone who indulges in it is justly accused of excessive vanity. But since your criticism has an "evening talks on the Babkino wing-porch or the main-house terrace in the presence of Ma-Pa, the Counterfeiter and Levitan"[4] sort of flavor to it, and since it passes over the story's literary aspects to concentrate on more general ground, I will not be violating the laws of etiquette if I permit myself to continue our talk.

First of all, I have no more love for literature of the school we have been discussing than you do. As a reader and man in the street I try to stay clear of it. But if you ask me my sincere and honest opinion about it, I must say that the issue of whether it has a right to exist or not is still open and unresolved by anyone, even though Olga Andreyevna[5] thinks she has settled it. Neither you nor I nor all the critics in the world have any hard evidence in favor of denying this literature a right to exist. I don't know who is right: Homer, Shakespeare, Lope de Vega and the ancients as a group, who, while not afraid of digging around in the "manure pile," were morally much more stable than we are, or our contemporary writers, prudish on paper, but cold and cynical down deep and in life. I don't know who is in bad taste: the Greeks, who were not ashamed to celebrate love as it actually exists in all its natural beauty, or the readers of Gaboriau, Marlitt and Pierre Bobo.[6] Just like the problems of nonresistance to evil, free will and so on, this problem can only be settled in the future. All we can do is bring it up; any attempt at resolving it would involve us in spheres outside the realm of our competence. Your reference to the fact that Turgenev and Tolstoy avoid the "manure pile" throws no light on the matter. Their squeamishness proves nothing; after all, the generation of writers that came before them condemned the description of peasants and civil servants beneath the rank of titular councilor as filth, to say nothing of your "villains and villainesses." And anyway, one period, no matter how glorious it is, does not give us the right to draw conclusions in favor of one or another school. Your reference to the corrupting influence of the school under discussion does not solve the problem either. Everything in this world is relative and approximate. There are people who can be corrupted even by children's literature, who take special pleasure in reading all the little piquant passages in the Psalter and the Book of Proverbs. And there are people who become purer and purer the more they come into contact with the filth of life. Journalists, lawyers and doctors, who are initiated into all the mysteries of human sin, are not known to be particularly immoral, and realist writers are more often than not of a higher moral caliber than Orthodox churchmen. And anyway no literature can outdo real life when it comes to cynicism. You're not going to get a person drunk with a jigger when he's just polished off a barrel.

2. Your statement that the world is "teeming with villains and villainesses" is true. Human nature is imperfect, so it would be odd to perceive none but the righteous. Requiring literature to dig up a "pearl" from the pack of villains is tantamount to negating literature altogether. Literature is accepted as an art because it depicts life as it actually is. Its aim is the truth, unconditional and honest. Limiting its functions to as narrow a field as extracting "pearls" would be as deadly for art as requiring Levitan to draw a tree without any dirty bark or yellowed leaves. A "pearl" is a fine thing, I agree. But the writer is not a pastry chef, he is not a cosmetician and not an entertainer. He is a man bound by contract to his sense of duty and to his conscience. Once he undertakes this task, it is too late for excuses, and no matter how horrified, he must do battle with his squeamishness and sully his imagination with the grime of life. He is just like any ordinary reporter. What would you say if a newspaper reporter as a result of squeamishness or a desire to please his readers were to limit his descriptions to honest city fathers, high-minded ladies, and virtuous railroadmen?

To a chemist there is nothing impure on earth. The writer should be just as objective as the chemist; he should liberate himself from everyday subjectivity and acknowledge that manure piles play a highly respectable role in the landscape and that evil passions are every bit as much a part of life as good ones.

3. Writers are men of their time, and so, like the rest of the public, they must submit to the external conditions of life in society. There is therefore no question but what they must keep within the bounds of decency. That is all we have a right to demand of the realists. But since you have nothing to say against the execution or form of "Mire," I must have remained within the bounds.

4. I must admit I rarely consult my conscience as I write. This is due to habit and the trivial nature of my work. Consequently, whenever I expound one or another view of literature, I always leave myself out of consideration.

5. You write that if you were my editor you would return the story to me for my own good. Why not go even further? Why not put the editors on the carpet for publishing this kind of story? Why not address a strongly worded reprimand to the Bureau of Press Affairs for not banning immoral newspapers?

The fate of literature (both major and minor) would be a pitiful one if it were at the mercy of personal opinions. Point number one. And number two, there is no police force in existence that can consider itself competent in matters of literature. I agree that we can't do without the muzzle or the stick, because sharpers ooze their way into literature just as anywhere else. But no matter how hard you try, you won't come up with a better police force for literature than criticism and the author's own conscience. People have been at it since the beginning of creation, but they've invented nothing better.

Now you would have me lose 115 rubles and give an editor a chance to embarrass me. Others, including your own father, are delighted with the story. And still others are sending Suvorin vituperative letters, rabidly denouncing both the newspaper and me, etc. Well, who is right? Who is the true judge?

6. You also write I should leave such stories for hacks like Okreyts, Pince-nez and Aloe,[7] who are poor in spirit and have been short-changed by fate. Allah forgive you if you mean those lines sincerely! To write in such scornful, condescending accents about little people just because they're little does the human heart scant honor. The lower ranks are just as indispensable in literature as they are in the army; that's what your head tells you, and your heart should tell you even more.

Now I've gone and worn you out with my long and drawn-out taffy. . . . If I had known my criticism would go on for so long, I wouldn't have started in the first place. . . . Please forgive me!

We are coming. We wanted to leave on the fifth, but . . . we were held up by a medical congress. Then came St. Tatyana's Day,[8] and on the seventeenth we're having a party: it's "his"[9] name day!! It will be a dazzling ball with all sorts of Jewesses, roast turkeys and Yashenkas.[10] After the seventeenth we'll fix a date for the Babkino trip.

So you've read my "On the Road" . . . Well, how do you like my audacity? I'm no longer afraid to write about things intellectual. In Petersburg it caused quite a raucous uproar. When I dealt with nonresistance to evil a short while ago, I also surprised my public.[11] The New Year's editions of all the papers ran complimentary remarks, and the December issue of *Russian Wealth*, the journal Lev Tolstoy publishes in, is carrying an article by Obolensky[12] (thirty-two pages) entitled "Chekhov and Korolenko." The good fellow goes into ecstasies over me and sets out to prove that I'm more of an artist than Korolenko. He's probably wrong, but I'm nevertheless beginning to feel I've earned one distinction: of all those who write only newspaper trash and don't publish in thick journals I'm the only one who has won the attention of the long-eared critics—this is the first time that's ever happened. The *Observer* reviled me—and did they catch it! As 1886 came to end, I felt like a bone that had been tossed to the dogs.

Vladimir Petrovich's[13] play is being published by *Theater Library*, and will be sent around to all major cities by them.

I've written a four-page play.[14] It will take fifteen to twenty minutes to perform, the shortest drama on earth. Korsh's famous actor Davydov will act in it. It will be published in *The Season* and will therefore make the rounds. It's much better as a rule to write short works than long ones: fewer pretensions and more success. . . . What else could you ask for? My play took me an hour and five minutes to write. I started another one, but I didn't finish it, because I had no time.

I'll write Alexei Sergeyevich[15] when he gets back from Volokolamsk. My sincere regards to everyone. You'll forgive me, won't you, for having written such a long letter? My hand ran away with me.

Happy New Year to Sasha and Seryozha.[16]

Does Seryozha receive *Around the World*?[17]

Your devoted and respectful
A. Chekhov

1. Maria Kiselyova, a writer of stories for children, was the daughter of the director of the Imperial Theaters in Moscow. She and her husband, Alexei, owned an elegant estate called Babkino, situated near the city of Voskresensk. The Chekhov and Kiselyov families formed a close friendship during his Voskresensk period, and it was at Babkino that Chekhov made the acquaintance of some prominent writers and musicians of the time. Mikhail Chekhov's *Around Chekhov* contains an obviously improbable and spurious statement that Maria Kiselyova was the great love of the composer Tchaikovsky, who supposedly lost her by proposing too late, after she was already engaged to Kiselyov.

2. A story she wrote for a children's magazine and submitted to Chekhov for criticism. Maria Kiselyova was the first in a long string of literary ladies, later to include Yelena Shavrova and Lydia Avilova, for whom Chekhov acted as a literary doctor-*cum*-agent.

3. At the end of December, 1886, Maria Kiselyova sent Chekhov a letter in which she praised his story "On the Road" and severely criticized "Mire." In it she wrote, "I am personally chagrined that a writer of *your* caliber, i.e., not short-changed by God, shows me nothing but a 'manure pile.' The world is teeming with villains and villainesses and the impression they produce is not new; therefore, one is all the more grateful to a writer who, having led you through all the stench of a manure pile, will suddenly extract a pearl from it [this imagery and vocabulary refer to Ivan Krylov's translation of La Fontaine's fable "Le coq et la perle," in which a rooster finds a pearl in a manure pile and wishes it were edible]. You are not myopic, you are perfectly

capable of finding this pearl, so why do we get only a manure pile? Give me that pearl, so that the filth of the surroundings may be effaced from my memory; I have a right to demand this of you. As for the others, the ones who are unable to find and to defend a human being among the quadruped animals—I'd just as soon not read them. Perhaps it might have been better to remain silent, but I could not resist an overpowering desire to give a piece of my mind to you and to your vile editors who allow you to wreck your talent with such equanimity. If I were your editor, I would have returned the story to you for your own good. No matter what you may say, the story is utterly disgusting! Leave such stories (such subjects!) to hacks like Okreyts, Prince-nez, Aloe and *tutti quanti* mediocrities, who are poor in spirit and have been short-changed by fate."

4. Ma-Pa is Chekhov's sister Maria Pavlovna. Counterfeiter was the name of Maria Kiselyova's dog. The painter Isaak Levitan, a close friend of Chekhov's, was a frequent guest at Babkino.

5. The amateur playwright Olga Golokhvastova, a friend of the addressee.

6. Some forgettable literary lights of the time. Émile Gaboriau was a French writer of popular detective novels, Marlitt was a pen name of a German lady who wrote pulp fiction, and Pierre Bobo was the nickname of the prolific and facile Russian novelist Pyotr Boborykin.

7. Stanislav Okreyts was a rabidly anti-Semitic journalist and publisher, whom Chekhov satirized several times in humor magazines; Pince-nez was a pen name of Maria Kiselyova herself and Aloe that of Chekhov's brother Alexander.

8. St. Tatyana was the patron saint of Moscow University, designated as such by its founder Ivan Shuvalov in honor of his mother, whose name was Tatyana. The feast day of this saint was traditionally celebrated by all the loyal alumni of Moscow University (cf. also Letter 17).

9. I.e., Anton Chekhov's own name day.

10. This was Chekhov's nickname for the two surviving sisters of the painter and stage designer Alexander Yanov. Shortly after Chekhov began to practice medicine, Yanov's mother and three sisters all came down with typhus. Yanov, who was a classmate of Nikolai Chekhov's at the art school, was unable to pay a doctor and Anton Chekhov volunteered to look after the stricken family. Despite his efforts, the mother and one of the sisters died. According to Mikhail Chekhov, the experience of losing two patients so early in his medical practice prompted Anton Chekhov to reduce his medical activities to a minimum and to concentrate on literature. The two Yanov sisters whose lives he managed to save became good friends of the entire Chekhov family; an album on the cover of which one of them embroidered in gold thread the legend "In Remembrance of Saving Me from Typhus" is now on display at the Chekhov Museum in Yalta.

11. Reference to the story originally published in *New Times* as "The Sister," but subsequently renamed "Good People" by Chekhov.

12. The critic Leonid Obolensky managed within the same year (1886) to compare Chekhov favorably to Korolenko in a signed article in *Russian*

Wealth and to pan Chekhov's collection *Varicolored Stories* in an unsigned review he published in the *Observer*, which Chekhov mentions below.

13. The play by the addressee's father, Vladimir Begichev, which was called *Firebird*.

14. Chekhov's one-act play *Calchas*, also known as *The Swan Song*.

15. The addressee's husband.

16. Maria Kiselyova's children. Chekhov wrote some delightful nonsense poetry for the amusement of Sasha Kiselyova, whom he had for some reason nicknamed Vasilisa.

17. A "Journal of Travel and Adventure on Land and Sea," published in Moscow and popular with juvenile readers.

10. To Vladimir Korolenko[1]

Moscow,
October 17, 1887

Many thanks, dear Vladimir Galaktionovich, for your book, which I have received and am now in the process of rereading. Since you already have my books, it looks as though I'll have to limit the present shipment to a thank-you note.

By the way—to keep the letter from being too short—I might tell you how glad I am to have gotten to know you. I say this sincerely and with all my heart. In the first place, I deeply respect and admire your talent; it is precious to me for many reasons. In the second place, I have the feeling that if you and I make it through another ten or twenty years, we will inevitably encounter further points of contact. Of all the currently prosperous Russian writers[2] I'm the least serious and most frivolous. I am on probation. In the language of poetry: I loved my pure muse, but lacked the proper respect, betrayed her, and all too often led her into realms unbefitting her. But you are serious, strong and true. As you can see, there are a great many differences between us, but nonetheless, when I read your work, especially now that I've made your acquaintance, I get the feeling that we're not such strangers after all. I don't know if I'm right or not, but I'd like to think so.

Oh and by the way again, I've enclosed a clipping from the *New Times*. This Thoreau[3] fellow, whom you'll find out about in the article, sounds quite promising, the first chapter at least, and I'll keep clipping him out and save him for you. He's got ideas and a certain freshness and originality about him, but he's hard to read. The architectonics and construction are impossible. He piles attractive and unattractive, slight and weighty ideas one on top of the other in such a way that they crowd each other out, squeeze the juice out of one another, and before you know it, they'll all be squealing from the crush.

I'll give you the Thoreau when you get to Moscow. In the meantime, good-bye and keep well.

Korsh will probably put on my play.[4] If so, I'll let you know the date of the performance. It may coincide with the period of your stay here. I hope you'll do me the honor if it does.

Yours,
A. Chekhov

1. Like Chekhov, Vladimir Korolenko (1853–1921) made his literary debut in 1879. Of all the writers of the "generation of the eighties" whom Chekhov considered to be his contemporaries and with whom he corresponded, Korolenko is the only one whose work is still remembered, reprinted and read. Unlike Chekhov, Korolenko was a political activist by temperament, and both his life and his writings were largely devoted to organized political protest and to efforts to secure a greater degree of freedom for the Russian people. He lived long enough to see the Revolution for which he had been waiting all his life and to witness the abrogation of the very rights and freedoms which this Revolution was meant to achieve. His writings of 1919–1921, which are never reprinted in the Soviet Union (in contrast to the rest of his work, which is regularly reissued), vehemently express the revulsion of the old freedom fighter against the betrayal and perversion of the ideals to which he had devoted his life.

There was no real spiritual affinity between Chekhov and Korolenko, as is witnessed by Korolenko's qualification of *Ivanov* as a "socially harmful play," his failure to understand *The Cherry Orchard* and his oddly colorless memoir about Chekhov. But there was a great deal of mutual sympathy and warmth, which continued for many years even in the absence of much personal contact. After a few friendly encounters in the late 1880s, the two writers lost contact until their joint resignation from the Academy over the cancellation of Maxim Gorky's election in 1902 (see Letters 153, 154 and 158).

2. The wording here seems to paraphrase the title of Nikolai Kushchevsky's political novel *Nikolai Negorev, or the Prosperous Russian* (1871).

3. In 1887, a Russian translation of Henry David Thoreau's *Walden, or Life in the Woods* was serialized in *New Times*. Annotating this passage in his edition of fragments from Chekhov's letters, Louis S. Friedland transcribed Thoreau's name from the Cyrillic as "Toro," and, disregarding both grammar and logic, suggested that Chekhov probably had in mind Yevgenia Tur, a Russian lady novelist of the nineteenth century.

4. *Ivanov*.

IV

SUCCESS AS A PLAYWRIGHT: "IVANOV"

ANTON CHEKHOV'S EARLIEST ATTEMPTS to write plays go back to his school years in Taganrog. As a medical student in 1880–81, he wrote a sprawling, interminable monster of a play in which he managed to combine the more obvious situations and devices of nineteenth-century melodrama with some original departures which in retrospect seem to presage a number of themes and characters from his later mature plays. He took this play to the celebrated actress Maria Yermolova to ask her advice about the feasibility of its being produced. What she told him is not known, but whatever it was, it made Chekhov put the manuscript away in a file, where it was discovered in the 1920s. It is usually published (the manuscript lacked a title page) as either *Play Without a Title* or, after the name of the principal character, as *Platonov*. It has become in recent decades a favorite of adapters and abridgers, who are wont to give the results of their efforts their own titles, such as *A Country Scandal* or *Don Juan in the Russian Manner,* and then get them produced as a new play by Chekhov. In fact, whenever one hears of a play by Chekhov one cannot quite place, it is a sure sign that somebody else has tried to trim down his untitled 1881 play to manageable size. The manuscript young Chekhov once discarded is thus gradually becoming an inexhaustible source of new Chekhov plays.

Chekhov's next serious playwriting effort, the one-act *On the High Road* of 1885, which he adapted from his story "In Autumn," ran afoul of a drama censor with the resoundingly Germanic name Kaiser von Nilckheim, who found it filthy and morbid and arranged to get it banned. The situation and the mood of this play, which showed a group of derelicts in a sleazy inn on a stormy night, were eventually reincarnated in Gorky's

Lower Depths and still later Americanized in Eugene O'Neill's *The Iceman Cometh.*

In September of 1887, at the request of the impresario Fyodor Korsh, Chekhov undertook to write a full-length play for Korsh's theater and within less than two weeks completed the first version of *Ivanov*. In this play Chekhov had hoped finally to put to rest that tired old commonplace of the Russian critical tradition (still with us today, alas): the superfluous man, that sensitive and bright nobleman, unable to find the proper use for his talents. Unimaginative critics have been discovering this prototype for decades in Lermontov's Pechorin, Turgenev's Rudin, Goncharov's Oblomov and the heroes of innumerable other books. With his habit of breaking through stereotypes, Chekhov wanted to show that for men of this ilk disappointment and frustration spring not so much from immutable social reality as from their own inability to translate their idealism into a meaningful program of action because their interest in any project or undertaking fades so quickly. With all his faults and shortcomings, the weak and ineffectual Ivanov (his ordinary name was meant to be symbolic) was contrasted in the play on the one hand with a group of provincial bores and gossips, every one of them far less attractive than he, and on the other hand with the humorless radical fanatic Dr. Lvov, who passes judgment on him for all the wrong reasons and reduces Ivanov's complex predicament to simple-minded sociological clichés.

The play was produced first by Korsh in Moscow and then by several provincial companies and, despite Nikolai Mikhailovsky's denunciations, enjoyed a considerable success, placing Chekhov in the front rank of Russian playwrights of the period. It was not until the preparations for a St. Petersburg production of *Ivanov* were under way one year after its initial production that Chekhov finally realized to what extent his play had been generally misunderstood. Conditioned by the conventions of the nineteenth-century well-made play, the director and the actors of the St. Petersburg production, as well as Chekhov's friend Suvorin, all saw Ivanov himself as either a sly fortune hunter or as the old familiar superfluous man. The idealistic verbiage of Dr. Lvov, furthermore, led them to take him for the play's attractive hero and caused them to overlook or to minimize his heartlessness and cruelty. The realization of the misunderstanding hit Chekhov hard; he reworked the play drastically in order to clarify its meaning and he wrote Suvorin a long and detailed letter, explaining the play and its characters with utmost precision. This letter to Suvorin is of course a basic key to Chekhov's intentions in *Ivanov;* but, despite its wide availability, this key has remained unused to this day. In the Soviet Union, a production that would realize Chekhov's intentions as he spells them out would offend some of that society's most cherished beliefs about itself and its past; in the West, directors who put on this play are usually not aware of the Russian social and intellectual realities with which Chekhov is dealing. Sir John Gielgud's widely acclaimed London and New York production of *Ivanov* a few years ago is a good case in point. Just how thoroughly Gielgud missed the meaning of the play was made clear in his article on *Ivanov* in the *New York Times* of May 1, 1966: "One feels that Chekhov must have seen something of himself both in the character of Ivanov and that of Doctor Lvov, the two most intelligent men in the play, whose attempts to understand each other and win each other's confidence result in such violent mutual destruction." In line with this totally erroneous conception of the play and of its principal characters, Gielgud played Ivanov as an aging Russian Hamlet and allowed the actor who played the fanatical Dr. Lvov to turn him into a sort of languid romantic poet.

Yet there surely must be a way of making the polemical aspects of *Ivanov* clear and comprehensible to a contemporary Western audience. A production that would bring them out in an imaginative way could generate considerable excitement; and it would also tell the non-Russian public for practically the first time just what Chekhov's first important play is really about.

11. To Nikolai Leykin

Moscow,
November 15, 1887

Forgive me, kind Nikolai Alexandrovich, for not sending you a story this time round. Wait a bit. My play is opening on Thursday, and as soon as that is over with, I'll sit myself down and hack away. Your lines about production of plays puzzle me. You write that the author only gets in the production's way, makes the actors uncomfortable, and more often than not contributes only the most inane comments. Let me answer you thusly: (1) the play is the author's property, not the actors'; (2) where the author is present, casting the play is his responsibility; (3) *all* my comments to date have improved the production, and they have all been put into practice, as I indicated; (4) the actors themselves ask for my comments; (5) there is a new Shpazhinsky[1] play presently in rehearsal at the Maly; Shpazhinsky has changed the furniture *three* times and gotten the authorities to lay out money for new props on *three* occasions. And so on. If you reduce author participation to a naught, what the hell will you come up with? Remember how Gogol raged when they put on his play![2]

And wasn't he right?

You write that Suvorin agrees with you. I'm surprised. Suvorin wrote me not long ago that I should "take my actors in hand" and advised me how to go about the in-hand-taking process.

In any case, thank you for bringing up the subject. I'll write Suvorin and raise the question of the limits of an author's competence in such matters.

You also write, "Why the blazes don't you forget about your play?" An eye for an eye: "Why the hell don't you forget about your shareholding operations?" Dropping the play means dropping my hopes for a profitable deal.

But since all this whining of mine must be getting on your nerves, let's move on to more timely affairs.

All the *Innocent Talk*[3] stories are printed on one type of paper.

I'll be in Petersburg by December.

We have a lot to talk about.

I don't know what to say to your remark about Davydov.[4] Maybe you're right. My opinion of him is based not so much on my personal impression as on Suvorin's recommendation. "You can trust Davydov," he writes.

My regards to Praskovya Nikiforovna and St. Fyodor.[5] Each time I write, my family sends its regards, but, forgive me, I always forget to include them.

When will we have dinner at Testov's?[6] Come pay us a visit.

Yours,
A. Chekhov

1. Ippolit Shpazhinsky was a popular and widely performed playwright of the period. His plays combined the well-made-play kind of craftsmanship typical of Ostrovsky with certain unmistakable Dostoyevskian overtones. The play Chekhov mentions is his historical drama *Princess Kurakina*, which ended up being one of the biggest successes of the season.

2. Reference to Gogol's detailed criticism of the first production of *The Inspector General*, which displeased him in many respects. Gogol appended his critique to the second edition of the play, published five years after the première.

3. The title of a collection of Chekhov's stories.

4. The famous actor Vladimir Davydov created the role of Ivanov. He and Chekhov became good personal friends after that production. In the midst of the rehearsals, the pathologically suspicious Leykin wrote Chekhov, warning him against Davydov: "He is the most perfidious man I've ever known."

5. Leykin's wife and son.

6. One of the best-known restaurants in Moscow.

12. To Alexander Chekhov

Moscow,
November 20, 1887

Well, the play has opened. . . . Let me take it point by point. To begin with, Korsh promised me ten rehearsals and gave me only four, of which only two can be called rehearsals, because the other two were more like tournaments for the actors to display their skills of disputation and invective. Only Davydov and Glama[1] knew their parts; the rest of them relied on the prompter and inner conviction.

First Act. I'm backstage in a tiny box that looks like a prisoner's cell. The family is in an orchestra box—and trembling. Contrary to my expectations, I feel calm and collected. The actors are keyed up and tense; they keep crossing themselves. Curtain. Enter the celebrant,[2] unsure of himself, unfamiliar with his lines. He is then presented with a wreath, with the result that from the very first lines I don't recognize my play. Kiselevsky,[3] on whom I had staked such high hopes, does not get a single line right. Literally not a single one. He says whatever comes into his head. Despite all this and the director's blunders, the first act is quite successful. Many curtain calls.

Second Act. A crowd on stage. Guests. Not knowing their lines, they fumble and talk nonsense. Every word is like a knife in my back. But—O Muse!—this act is successful too. The entire cast gets a curtain call. Even I am called twice. Everyone congratulates me on my success.

Third Act. The acting doesn't go too badly. An enormous success. I get three curtain calls. Davydov shakes my hand during one of them and Glama presses my other hand to her heart à la Manilov.[4] Talent and virtue reign triumphant.

Act Four, Scene One. Everything goes all right. Curtain calls. Then a long, tedious intermission. Not in the habit of getting up and moving out to the buffet between scenes, the audience grumbles. The curtain goes up. A beautiful set: dinner table (wedding) seen behind an arch. The orchestra plays a fanfare, and out come the men of the wedding party. They are drunk, you see, and therefore feel obliged to clown around and cut up. A circus, a drunken brawl. I am horrified. Thereupon Kiselevsky's grand entrance. A heart-rendingly poetic passage. But, because my Kiselevsky doesn't know his lines and is drunk as a lord, the short poetic dialogue comes out long-winded and vile. The audience is perturbed. The hero dies at the end of the play because he cannot stand to live after being insulted. By this time the audience has grown so tired and so indifferent that they are unable to understand why he must die. (The actors insisted on this ending; I have an alternate one.) Both the actors and I take our curtain calls. During one of them I detect a clear hissing, though it is drowned out by applause and stamping feet.

On the whole I feel exhausted and chagrined. I am disgusted even though the play was a big success (which fact is denied only by Kicheyev[5] and Co.). Theater lovers say they've never seen so much ferment, so much universal applause-*cum*-hissing, or heard so many arguments as they saw and heard at my play. And Korsh has never had an author take a curtain call after the second act.

The play will be performed for the second time on the twenty-third—with the alternate ending and several other changes: I'm getting rid of the wedding-party men.

Details when we get together.

Yours,
A. Chekhov

Tell Burenin[6] that I've fallen back into my routine, now that the play is out of the way, and am hard at work on my contribution for the Saturday issue.

1. Vladimir Davydov and Alexandra Glama-Meshcherskaya were two of the brightest names in the impressive all-star cast that Korsh assembled for the first performance of *Ivanov*. She appeared in the role of Sarah.

2. The opening night was also the occasion of a benefit performance honoring the actor Nikolai Svetlov, who played the role of Misha Borkin. In accordance with the quaint custom, his first entrance was interrupted by the ceremonial presentation of a wreath.

3. Ivan Kiselevsky, a highly popular actor of the time, played Count Shabelsky.

4. A sentimental character in Gogol's *Dead Souls*.

5. The critic Pyotr Kicheyev's review of *Ivanov* qualified the play as "profoundly immoral," accused it of an "insolent and cynical confusion of ideas" and described its form as "incoherent."

6. The arch-reactionary critic and playwright Viktor Burenin was at the time one of the editors of *New Times*, where Alexander Chekhov was also employed.

13. To Alexander Chekhov

Moscow,
November 24, 1887

Well, dearest Gusev,[1] the dust has finally settled and everything has calmed down. Here I am as usual, sitting at my desk and placidly writing stories. You can't possibly imagine what it was like! The devil only knows what they've made out of so insignificant a piece of junk as my miserable little play. (I've sent a copy to Maslov.)[2] As I wrote you, the première caused more excitement in the audience and backstage than the prompter had seen in all his thirty-two years with the theater. People were screaming and yelling and clapping and hissing, there was almost a brawl in the buffet, some students in the gallery tried to throw someone out and two people were ejected by the police. The excitement affected everybody. Masha almost fainted, Dyukovsky,[3] whose heart started palpitating, ran out of the theater, and Kiselyov[4] for no earthly reason grabbed himself by the head and wailed in all seriousness, "What am I going to do now?"

The actors were in a state of nervous tension. Everything I've written you and Maslov about their acting and their attitudes must of course be held in strict confidence. A great deal can be explained and justified. It turns out that the actress who played the leading role has a daughter who was on her deathbed. How could she keep her mind on the stage? Kurepin[5] did well to praise the actors.

The day after the performance the *Moscow Press* published a review by Pyotr Kicheyev calling my play insolently cynical and immoral claptrap. The *Moscow News* praised it.

The second performance went well, though it did have its surprises. Without any rehearsals, a new actress took over for the one with the sick daughter. Again we had curtain calls after the third act (two of them) and the fourth, but this time no one hissed.

There you have it. My *Ivanov* will go on again this Wednesday. Now everyone's quieted down and fallen back in their rut. We've marked off November 19th on the calendar and will celebrate it every year with a drunken spree; it will be a day long remembered by our family.

I won't be writing you any more about the play. If you feel like getting an idea of what it's like, ask Maslov to let you have a look at his copy. Reading the play won't tell you what all the excitement was about; you won't find anything special in it. Nikolai, Schechtel and Levitan—all of them painters—assure me that it's so original on stage that watching it is a strange experience. None of this comes through when you read it.

If you notice anyone at *New Times* about to come down on actors in my play, ask them to refrain from calumny. At the second performance they were splendid.

Well, in a few days, I'll be leaving for Petersburg. I hope to get away by December 1st. We'll celebrate your eldest puppy's name day together at any rate. . . . Warn him there won't be any cake.

Congratulations on your promotion. If you really are a secretary now, then insert a notice in the paper saying that "*Ivanov* had its second performance on November 23rd at the Korsh Theater. The actors, especially Davydov, Kiselevsky, Gradov-Sokolov and Kosheva,[6] earned many curtain calls. The author was called to the stage after the third and fourth acts." Something along those lines . . . A notice like that will make them do the play again, and I'll get an extra fifty or a hundred rubles. But if it's inconvenient for you, then forget about it.

How's Anna Petrovna[7] doing? *Allah Kerim*[8] . . . The Petersburg climate doesn't agree with her.

I've received the forty rubles. Thank you.

Have I been getting on your nerves? I've felt like a psychopath all November. Gilyarovsky[9] is leaving for Petersburg today.

Keep well and forgive the psychopathy. I'm over it now. Today I'm normal.

I've sent Maslov a thank-you note for his telegram.

Yours,
Schiller Shakespearovich Goethe

1. Chekhov used this name for many years as an affectionate nickname in his correspondence with his older brother before he gave it to the principal character (a dying peasant soldier, returning from Sakhalin to Russia) in the story "Gusev," which he wrote during his visit to Ceylon in 1890.

2. Writer and playwright Alexei Maslov (Bezhetsky) was a fellow employee of Alexander's at the St. Petersburg offices of *New Times*. See also Letter 27, note 11.

3. A schoolteacher who was a friend of the Chekhov family.

4. The husband of Maria Kiselyova.

5. The drama reviewer of *New Times*.

6. Leonid Gradov-Sokolov appeared as Kosykh and Bronislava Kosheva played Babakina.

7. Alexei Suvorin's wife.

8. This originally Arabic phrase meaning "God is merciful" was an expletive commonly used by various Moslem peoples of the Caucasus and the Crimea; it was also popularized in the Oriental tales of Russian romantic writers.

9. Vladimir Gilyarovsky was a colorful adventurer, circus performer and writer, a friend of Chekhov's who frequently appears in various memoirs connected with Chekhov.

14. To Alexei Suvorin

Moscow,
December 30, 1888[1]

Nikulina thanks you for the corrections. Gorev is playing Sabinin. Rehearsals have not yet begun. I am certain the play will be successful because the actors' eyes are clear and their faces do not look treacherous; that means they like the play and believe in its success themselves. Nikulina has had me to dinner. Thank you.[2]

The director sees Ivanov as a superfluous man in the Turgenev manner. Savina[3] asks why Ivanov is such a blackguard. You write that "Ivanov must be given something that makes it clear why two women throw themselves at him and why he is a blackguard while the doctor is a great man." If all three of you have understood me this way, it means my *Ivanov* is a failure. I must have lost my mind and written something entirely different from what I had intended. If my Ivanov comes across as a blackguard or superfluous man and the doctor as a great man, if no one understands why Sarah and Sasha love Ivanov, then my play has evidently failed to pan out, and there can be no question of having it produced.

Here is how I understand my protagonists. Ivanov is a nobleman who has been to the university and is in no way remarkable. He is easily excitable, hot-headed, strongly inclined to be carried away, honest and straightforward—like most educated noblemen. He lived on his estate and served in the *zemstvo*. His words to the doctor (Act I, Scene 5) indicate what he did, how he behaved, what occupied and what fascinated him: "Don't marry Jewesses or psychopaths or blue stockings . . . don't take on thousands of foes all by yourself, don't do battle with windmills, don't knock your head against the wall. May God protect you from all sorts of scientific farming methods, unusual schools and hot-headed speeches. . . ." That's what his past is like. Sarah, who has seen his scientific farming methods and other projects, describes him to the doctor as follows: "He's a remarkable person, doctor, and I'm sorry you didn't know him two or three years ago. He's despondent now; he doesn't say or do anything. But the way he used to be . . . oh, lovely!" (Act I, Scene 7). His past, like that of most Russian intellectuals, is wonderful. Russian gentlemen or university graduates who do not boast of their past are few and far between. The present is always worse than the past. Why? Because Russian excitability has one specific property: it quickly turns into weariness. As soon as he leaves the school bench, the Russian recklessly takes on a burden beyond his endurance. He simultaneously becomes involved with the schools, the peasants, scientific farming and the *Herald of Europe*;[4] he makes speeches; he writes to cabinet ministers; he fights evil and applauds good; instead of loving simply or haphazardly, he must love blue stockings, or psychopaths, or Jewesses, or even the prostitutes he tries to save, and so on and so forth. But no sooner does he reach the age of thirty or thirty-five than he starts feeling weary and bored. He doesn't even have a respectable mustache yet, but he says "Don't get married, old boy. . . . Take it from me" with great authority. Or "What is liberalism essentially? Between you and me, Katkov[5] was often right." He is already willing to reject the *zemstvo* and scientific farming and science and love. My Ivanov tells the doctor (Act I, Scene 5), "You, dear friend, graduated only last year. You are still young and vigorous, and I am thirty-five. I have the right to give you some advice. . . ." That's the way those prematurely weary people speak. Then, with an authoritative sigh they'll say, "Don't get married to this one or that one (see one of the categories above). Choose someone ordinary and colorless, someone who is neither striking nor has anything much to say. Structure your entire life according to accepted patterns. The more colorless and monotonous the surroundings, the better. And the life I've been through, it's been wearisome. Lord, how wearisome it's been!"

Since he feels physically weary and bored, he doesn't understand what he is undergoing now or what has taken place. In horror he tells the doctor (Act I, Scene 3), "You say she's going to die soon, and I feel no love or pity. All I feel is a sort of emptiness and weariness. . . . To someone looking at me from outside it probably looks horrible, but I myself can't understand what's going on in my soul. . . ." When narrow-minded, dishonest people get into a situation like this, they usually place all the blame on their environment or join the ranks of the Hamlets and superfluous men, and let it go at that. The straightforward Ivanov, however, openly admits to the doctor and the audience that he doesn't understand himself: "I don't understand, I don't understand. . . ." That he genuinely does not understand himself is clear from his long third-act soliloquy when, left alone to converse with the audience and make his confession to them, he even weeps.

The change that has taken place within him offends his sense of decency. He seeks its causes from without and fails to find them, and when he starts seeking them within himself all he finds is an indefinable feeling of guilt. This feeling is a Russian feeling. If someone in his house has died or fallen ill, or if he owes or has lent someone money, a Russian always feels guilty. Ivanov is constantly holding forth about a guilty feeling he has, and this feeling of guilt grows within him from every jolt. In Act I he says, "I must be terribly guilty, but my thoughts are confused, I am chained down by a sort of indolence, and I am powerless to understand myself. . . ." In Act II he tells Sasha, "My conscience pains me day and night. I feel that I'm profoundly guilty, but I can't understand of what."

To weariness, boredom and guilt feelings add another enemy: loneliness. Had Ivanov been a government official, an actor, a priest, or a professor, he would have resigned himself to his situation. But he lives on his estate. He is in the provinces. People are either drunkards or card players or like the doctor. None of them are concerned with his feelings or the change within him. He is lonely. Long winters, long evenings, a barren garden, barren rooms, a grumbling count, a sick wife. . . . And there's nowhere for him to go. That's why he is constantly tormented by the problem of what to do with himself.

And now a fifth enemy. Ivanov is weary, he doesn't understand himself, but life doesn't care. It presents him with its legitimate demands and, whether he likes it or not, he must solve its problems. His sick wife is a problem, his pile of debts is a problem, Sasha hanging on his neck is a problem. How he goes about solving all these problems should be evident from his third-act soliloquy and the contents of the last two acts. People like Ivanov don't solve problems; they fall under their burden. They become flustered, they feel helpless and nervous, they complain and make fools out of themselves, and in the end give free rein to their frazzled and undisciplined nerves, lose the ground from under their feet and enter the ranks of the "broken" and "misunderstood."

Disappointment, apathy, frayed nerves and weariness are the inevitable consequences of excessive excitability, and this excitability is to a great degree characteristic of our young people. Take literature. Take the present. Socialism is one form of excitement. But where is it? It's in Tikhomirov's[6] letter to the tsar. The socialists have gotten married and are criticizing the *zemstvo*. Where is liberalism? Even Mikhailovsky says the sides are no longer clearcut. And what is all this Russian enthusiasm worth? We're weary of the war, we've so wearied of Bulgaria[7] it's ironic, we've wearied of Zucchi[8] and even of operettas.

This susceptibility to weariness (as Doctor Bertenson[9] will confirm) finds expression in more than merely whining or feeling bored. The life of the weary man cannot be represented like this: It is not particularly even. The weary do not lose their ability to work up a high pitch of excitement, but their excitement lasts for a very short time and is followed by an even greater sense of apathy. Graphically we can represent this as follows:

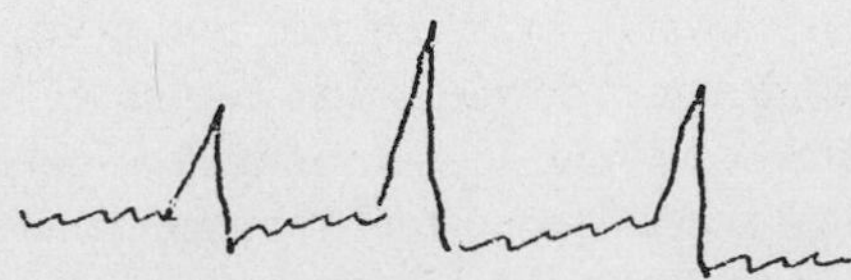

As you can see, the descent forms something rather different from a gradual inclined plane. Sasha declares her love. Ivanov shouts in ecstasy: "A new life!" But the next morning he has as much faith in that life as he does in ghosts (see his third-act soliloquy). When his wife insults him, he loses control, gets excited and flings a cruel insult at her. He is called a blackguard to his face. If this doesn't finish off his frazzled brain, it does make him excited and forces him to pass sentence on himself.

So as not to weary you to exhaustion, I will turn now to Doctor Lvov. Lvov is the model of an honest, straightforward, hot-headed, but narrow-minded and limited man. It is about his kind that intelligent people say: "He's stupid, but his heart is in the right place." Everything resembling breadth of vision or spontaneity of feeling is alien to Lvov. He's a stereotype personified, a walking ideology. He looks at every phenomenon and person through a narrow frame and judges everything by his prejudices. He's ready to worship anyone who shouts, "Make way for honest labor!"[10] and anyone who doesn't is a blackguard and kulak. There is nothing in between. He grew up on the novels of Mikhailov[11] and on the stage saw the "new people," namely kulaks and sons of this age as depicted by the new playwrights, such "money grubbers" as Proporyev, Okhlyabyev, Navarygin[12] and so on. He mastered what they had to teach, mastered it so well that while reading *Rudin* he never fails to wonder whether Rudin is or is not a blackguard. Literature and the stage have brought him up to approach every individual in life and in literature with this question. If he'd had the chance to see your play, he would have taken you to task for not making it clear whether Messrs. Kotelnikov, Sabinin, Adashev and Matveyev[13] are or are not blackguards. This is an important matter for him. He is not satisfied that all men are sinful. He wants either saints or blackguards.

He was prejudiced before he ever arrived in the district. He immediately saw a kulak in every well-to-do peasant and a blackguard in Ivanov, whom he couldn't understand. If a man's wife is ill and he is off visiting the rich woman on the neighboring estate, can he be anything but a blackguard? It's quite clear he's murdering his wife to marry the rich woman.

Lvov is honest and straightforward, and he calls a spade a spade whatever the consequences. If necessary, he'll throw a bomb under a carriage, punch an official in the face, call anyone a blackguard. He'll stop at nothing. He never feels any pangs of conscience: what should an "honest laborer" do but exterminate "the powers of darkness"?

Such people are necessary and for the most part likeable. It would be dishonest to caricature them for purposes of stage effect, and anyway, there is no reason for it. True, caricatures are more pointed and therefore more comprehensible, but it's better to leave out a few strokes than to overdo it.

And now a word about the women. What makes them love him? Sarah loves Ivanov because he's a good man, because he's passionate and brilliant and speaks with as much ardor as Lvov (Act I, Scene 7). She loves him as long as he is excited and interesting; as soon as he grows nebulous in her eyes and loses his well-defined personality, she ceases to understand him and at the end of the third act speaks her mind plainly and pointedly.

Sasha is a damsel of the latest vintage. She is well educated, intelligent, honest, etc. In the land of the blind, the one-eyed man is king, so she singles out thirty-five-year-old Ivanov. He is better than all the rest. She knew him when she was a little girl and saw him in action at close range before he wearied of everything. He is a friend of her father's.

She is a female whom males win over not by the brilliance of their plumage, or their versatility, or courage, but by complaints, whining and failures. She is a woman who loves men on their way down. No sooner does Ivanov lose heart than up pops the damsel. That's all she was waiting for. What else! Now she has a noble and sacred mission. She will revive her fallen man, set him on his feet, give him happiness. She doesn't love Ivanov; she loves her mission. Daudet's Argenton said, "Life is not a novel."[14] Sasha doesn't realize this. She doesn't realize that for Ivanov love is merely an additional complication, another stab in the back. And what happens? Sasha works on him for a whole year, yet instead of reviving he sinks lower and lower.

My fingers hurt. I'm coming to the end. . . . If nothing I've described above is in the play, there can be no question of having it produced. It must mean I didn't write what I intended. Have the play withdrawn. I don't mean to preach heresy from the stage. If the audience leaves the theater thinking all Ivanovs are blackguards and Doctor Lvovs great men, I might as well go into retirement and give up my pen. Corrections and insertions won't help. No corrections can bring a great man down from his pedestal, and no insertions are capable of turning a blackguard into an ordinary sinner. I could bring Sasha in at the end, but I can't add a thing to Ivanov and Lvov. I haven't the skill. And even if I were to add something, I have a feeling I'd only make it worse. Have faith in my feelings. After all, they belong to the author.

My apologies to Potekhin and Yurkovsky[15] for putting them through all this needless trouble. I hope they forgive me. Frankly speaking, it was neither fame nor Savina that tempted me to have the play produced. I was counting on earning about a thousand rubles from it. But I'd rather borrow the thousand than risk making a fool of myself. Don't try to tempt me with success. Unless I die, success is still ahead.

Want to bet that sooner or later I'll soak the management for six or seven thousand? How about it?

I wouldn't let Kiselevsky play the count for anything! My play caused him quite a bit of chagrin in Moscow. He went around complaining to everyone about being forced to play my son of a bitch of a count. Why chagrin him again?

People say it will be awkward to refuse because he's already had the part. Then why isn't it awkward to let Sazonov or Dalmatov[16] play Ivanov? After all, Davydov had the part of Ivanov!

How weary I must have made you with this letter. Enough, *basta*!

Happy New Year! Hurra-a-ah!

Lucky you! You'll be drinking or have already been drinking real champagne, and all I have is the dregs.

My sister is ill. Her joints ache, she has a high temperature, a headache, etc. Our cook has the same thing. Both are bedridden. I fear it may be typhus.

Do forgive me for this desperately long, tiresome letter. My regards to your family. I kiss Anna Ivanovna's hand. Keep well.

Yours,
A. Chekhov

If the public can't understand "iron in the blood," then to hell with it, the blood, I mean, the blood without iron.[17]

I've read through this letter. The word "Russian" often crops up in my characterization of Ivanov. Don't be angry. As I wrote the play, I had in mind only what I needed, only typical Russian traits. And excessive excitability, guilt feelings, and weariness are all purely Russian. Germans never get excited. That's why Germany has no disillusioned, superfluous, or weary people. The Frenchman's excitability constantly remains on one and the same plane; it never takes any sharp rises or falls. That's why the Frenchman's normal state is one of excitement and why it stays with him well into decrepit old age. In other words, the French don't spend their energy on excessive excitement; they spend their energy sensibly and therefore never go bankrupt.

Of course I don't use terms like Russian, excitability, weariness, etc., in the play; I'd hoped that the reader and the spectator would be attentive and not need a sign saying, "This is a plum, not a pumpkin."[18] I have tried to express myself simply. I have not resorted to tricks and was far from suspecting that my readers and spectators would be out to trip up my characters on a phrase or lay special emphasis on the dowry talks, etc.

I failed in my attempt to write a play. It's a pity, of course.

Ivanov and Lvov seemed so alive in my imagination. I'm telling you the whole truth when I say that they weren't born in my head out of sea foam or preconceived notions or intellectual pretensions or by accident. They are the result of observing and studying life. They are still there in my mind, and I feel I haven't lied a bit or exaggerated an iota. And if they came out lifeless and blurred on paper, the fault lies not in them, but in my inability to convey my thoughts. Apparently it's too early for me to undertake playwriting.

1. This letter and the next one, written on the occasion of the first St. Petersburg production of *Ivanov,* are removed from their proper chronological sequence and included in this section for obvious thematic reasons.

2. While Suvorin was supervising the St. Petersburg production of *Ivanov,* Chekhov in Moscow was reciprocating by helping with the casting arrangements for the first Moscow production of Suvorin's play *Tatyana Repina,* a lurid melodrama about a famous actress who is abandoned by her lover and is driven by the intrigues of a Jewish banker and an evil Jewish confidante to take poison onstage during a performance. Blinded by his affection for Suvorin, Chekhov managed to overlook the shoddy literary quality of *Tatyana Repina* (and its explicit and ugly racist overtones) and he paid it the tribute of writing a one-act sequel for it, also called *Tatyana Repina,* which he had printed in an edition of three copies and presented to Suvorin as a private gesture of friendship. After Chekhov's death, this sequel was occasionally published and translated into other languages as an original dramatic work of Chekhov's, although it makes no sense whatsoever when it is read outside the context of Suvorin's play.

During the preparations for the Moscow production of *Tatyana Repina* at the famous Maly Theater, Chekhov's contribution was to carry out negotiations with various actors and actresses whom Suvorin wanted to appear in his play. Chekhov's letters to Suvorin during that period give a vivid and not very flattering account of backstage mores at the Maly Theater. His particular feat was to talk the actress Nadezhda Nikulina (of whom he wrote in another letter to Suvorin: "Actresses are cows who imagine themselves to be goddesses") into accepting a smaller role in the production and relinquishing the lead, for which the celebrated Maria Yermolova unexpectedly became available. The actor Fyodor Gorev was cast in the role of the heroine's lover.

3. Maria Savina (1854–1915) was one of the biggest names in Russian theater in the last quarter of the nineteenth century, celebrated both as an actress and for her intimate friendship with Ivan Turgenev (there was a book published after her death about her relationship with him). Her consenting to appear in *Ivanov* was felt as a great honor by Chekhov; later on, his opinion of her acting abilities was not as high as that of most of his contemporaries (see note 4 to Letter 50).

4. A generally respected, moderately liberal literary and political journal that was published in Moscow from 1866 to 1918.

5. Mikhail Katkov was a right-wing journalist and publisher who opposed and criticized the reforms of the 1860s, the *zemstvo* system and any kind of liberalization in general.

6. The former revolutionary Lev Tikhomirov, who had earlier helped organize several attempts to assassinate the tsar, published in 1888 a brochure called "Why I Stopped Being a Revolutionary." His abject repentance and his appeal for the tsar's mercy eventually secured for Tikhomirov a full pardon and permission to return to Russia from abroad.

7. Another big news story of 1888 was the diplomatic conflict between Russia and Bulgaria, caused by Russian objections to the invitation extended to the German Prince Ferdinand of Coburg to occupy the Bulgarian throne.

8. The third press sensation of the year to which Chekhov here alludes had to do with the failure of the Imperial Ballet management to renew the contract of the Italian *prima ballerina* Virginia Zucchi after her three years of successful appearances with their company. Instead of leaving Russia upon the expiration of her contract, Zucchi chose to form her own ballet company in Moscow.

9. The popular St. Petersburg physician Lev Bertenson, with whom Chekhov was later to correspond about the nomenclature of Sakhalin plants (see Letter 161).

10. A hackneyed slogan of anti-government dissent.

11. The numerous didactic novels of Alexander Sheller-Mikhailov (1838–1900), artistically hopeless but ideologically progressive, were widely read by socially aware young people in Chekhov's time.

12. Evil capitalist villains in popular melodramas by Alexander Palm and Alexander Yuzhin (pseudonym of Prince Sumbatov, who was later to become Chekhov's good friend).

13. Characters in Suvorin's *Tatyana Repina.*

14. In Alphonse Daudet's novel *Jack.*

15. Alexei Potekhin, a playwright of some distinction, whose skillfully written realistic dramas have been unfairly forgotten, was at the time in charge of repertory for the government-owned theaters in St. Petersburg, and was thus instrumental in selecting *Ivanov* for production; Fyodor Fyodorov, whose real surname was Yurkovsky, was the stage director of the St. Petersburg production.

16. St. Petersburg actors Nikolai Sazonov and Vasily Dalmatov were proposed for the role of Ivanov; in the end, Vladimir Davydov came from Moscow to repeat his original role.

17. A not entirely clear reference to something in Suvorin's letter which Chekhov is answering. Like all Suvorin's letters to Chekhov, it was either destroyed or lost.

18. A Ukrainian saying, which Chekhov quotes in Ukrainian. Earlier translators of this letter into English have confused the Ukrainian *hàrbuz* (pumpkin) with the Russian *arbùz* (watermelon) and rendered it as either "melon" or "watermelon."

15. To Alexei Suvorin

Moscow,
January 7, 1889

I am enclosing a document which I ask you to countersign and send back to me. You may consider yourself a member of the Society from January 7th until exactly fifty years after your death. And this pleasure costs a mere fifteen rubles.[1]

I sent you two variants for my *Ivanov* today.[2] If Ivanov were to be played by an agile, energetic actor, I would have added and altered many things. I'm in fine writing form. But Ivanov, alas, is being played by Davydov, which means that I have to write as succinctly and grayly as possible, keeping in mind that all my niceties and nuances will be fused into one gray blot and make a dreary impression. You can't expect Davydov to switch back and forth between gentleness and rage, can you? Whenever he plays serious parts, a muffled, monotonous little gristmill sits in his throat and does his acting for him. I'm sorry for poor Savina; I'm sorry she's stuck with that lifeless Sasha. I'd be glad to do something for Savina, but if Ivanov mumbles his lines, there's not much point in polishing up Sasha's role. It's a hell of a part to give Savina, and I'm ashamed of doing it to her. Had I known way back when that she would be playing Sasha and Davydov Ivanov, I would have called my play *Sasha* and centered everything around her role; and as for Ivanov, I would have brought him in as nothing more than a sidelight, but then, who could have known?

Ivanov has two long monologues which are decisive for the fate of the play: one in the third act and one at the end of the fourth. The first must be sung, the second recited with ferocity. Davydov can't do either. He'll recite both monologues "with intelligence," in other words, with infinite lethargy.

What is Fyodorov's[3] full name?

I would very much have enjoyed delivering a paper to the Literary Society on where I found the idea for writing *Ivanov*. I would have publicly admitted my guilt. I cherished the audacious dream of summing up everything written thus far about whining, despondent people and of having my *Ivanov* put a stop to this sort of writing. It seemed to me that all Russian novelists and playwrights feel a need to portray dejected men and that they all write by instinct, without a clearcut picture or position on the matter. My basic conception of the work came close to the mark, but the realization isn't worth a damn. I should have waited!

I'm glad I didn't listen to Grigorovich two or three years ago when he advised me to write a novel. I can just imagine how much good material I would have wasted if I had listened to him. "Talent and spontaneity will win out in the end," he said. Talent and spontaneity can cause a great deal of waste is closer to the truth. There are other things no less necessary than talent and an abundance of material. Maturity, to begin with. Then, *a sense of personal freedom* is also quite indispensable. And this sense didn't begin growing inside me until very recently. I had never had it before, replacing it quite successfully with frivolity, carelessness and a lack of respect for my work.

What aristocratic writers take from nature gratis, the less privileged must pay for with their youth. Try and write a story about a young man—the son of a serf, a former grocer, choirboy, schoolboy and university student, raised on respect for rank, kissing the priests' hands, worshiping the ideas of others, and giving thanks for every piece of bread, receiving frequent whippings, making the rounds as a tutor without galoshes, brawling, torturing animals, enjoying dinners at the houses of rich relatives, needlessly hypocritical before God and man merely to acknowledge his own insignificance—write about how this young man squeezes the slave out of himself drop by drop and how, on waking up one fine morning, he finds that the blood coursing through his veins is no longer the blood of a slave, but that of a real human being.[4]

There's a poet named Palmin in Moscow, a very miserly man. He recently cracked his head open, and I treated him. Today, when he came to have his bandage redone, he brought me a bottle of real ilang-ilang, costing three rubles fifty. I was touched.

Keep well, now, and forgive the long letters.

Yours,
A. Chekhov

1. Chekhov is recruiting Suvorin for membership in the Society of Russian Playwrights and Opera Composers, in which he was active.

2. After Chekhov became aware how widely misunderstood his play was, he rewrote it in an effort to clarify the characterizations. The second version, which he sent to Suvorin, was the one that was produced in St. Petersburg, despite the objections of Vladimir Davydov that he found the role of Ivanov harder to understand after the revision. The second version is the one that is usually performed today.

3. The director of the St. Petersburg production of *Ivanov,* referred to as Yurkovsky in the previous letter.

4. The Soviet songwriter and underground poet Alexander Galich, who was expelled early in 1972 from the Soviet Writers' Union for writing and

recording songs that extol personal freedom, incorporated a passage from this paragraph into his best-known song, "I Choose Freedom":

I choose freedom
Even if she's pockmarked and crude.
And you go ahead and squeeze
The slave out, drop by drop.

V

A SENSE OF LITERARY FREEDOM

In 1883, Anton Chekhov advised his brother Alexander on how to write a story that would sell to Leykin's *Fragments*: "1. The shorter, the better; 2. A bit of ideology and being up to date is most *à propos*; 3. Caricature is just fine, but ignorance of civil service ranks and of the seasons is strictly prohibited" (Letter of April 17, 1883). But only three years later, on May 10, 1886, Alexander was sent a drastically different recipe for a successful short story: "1. Absence of lengthy verbiage of political-social-economic nature; 2. total objectivity; 3. truthful descriptions of persons and objects; 4. extreme brevity; 5. audacity and originality: flee the stereotype; 6. compassion." Instead of a set of humorous rules on production of marketable topical pieces that Antosha Chekhonte knew so well how to peddle, we now get a capsule description of an authentic Chekhovian short story.

By 1888, after the recognition of his talent by Grigorovich and Suvorin and the successful performances of *Ivanov*, Chekhov was no longer satisfied with the brief, seemingly plotless kind of story which he pioneered and which he had brought to such a high level of perfection. For the next two years he deliberately tried his hand at larger narrative forms. Among his fictional work of that time we find some of the most highly experimental longer stories he ever wrote. "The Steppe" is an account of a journey through the south of Russia told from the vantage point of a nine-year-old boy, whose impressions and perceptions are subtly mingled with the ever-present voice of an omniscient adult narrator. In "A Dreary Story," Chekhov, who had earlier in a story called "Grisha" depicted the world as it is seen by a two-year-old child, takes the reader inside the mind of a dying intellectual in his sixties, who has behind him a rich and rewarding life which he now finds meaningless in the face of his impending death. The narrative viewpoint is even more daringly original in "The Name-Day Party," one of Chekhov's most overtly political stories, where the marriage of a liberal heiress and her conservative poseur of a husband is endangered and the life of their baby is lost because of excessive adherence to social amenities and because of passions aroused by meaningless political stereotyping. Chekhov's tour de force of making the reader continuously aware that the heroine's perception of people and events in "The Name-Day Party" is constantly affected by her physical discomfort (her advanced stage of pregnancy and the corset which social convention forces her to wear to hide her condition) is something that could have only been brought off by a writer with Chekhov's knowledge of medicine and physiology. In "An Attack of Nerves" he took up the nearly taboo subject of houses of prostitution and made his presentation of it both more objective and more poignant by showing it through the eyes of an inexperienced and painfully sensitive young university student.

The years 1888–90 were a period during which Chekhov was more exclusively involved with literature, literary theories and literary politics than he would ever again be in his life. In the stories he wrote in that period, in his long, detailed letters to his St. Petersburg friends we see Chekhov gaining in literature that same sense of personal freedom of which he wrote to Suvorin after revising the script of *Ivanov* and which in his personal life he had already won by the time he was nineteen. His quiet discarding of hitherto accepted forms of fictional narrative in "The Steppe" and "The Name-Day Party" caused one of the critics to complain of Chekhov's "inability or unwillingness to write as required by literary theories." And this was indeed the time when Chekhov came to a reasoned and eloquently stated rejection of all the critics and critical theories of his period. It was probably the critics' own campaign against his work that made him take a closer look at their assumptions and premises; and although he took their railings and barbs with seeming equanimity, his emotional letter to Vukol Lavrov, written on the eve of his departure for Sakhalin (Letter 43), shows that he could be hurt by some of their unfair accusations.

Despite his literary success, despite the acceptance of his work in the respected "thick" journals, his socially busy winters in Moscow, and the two memorable and productive summers he spent at the Lintvaryov estate in the Ukraine, by the end of 1889 Chekhov was faced with the two most momentous failures of his entire literary career. The long novel that had as its provisional title *Stories from the Lives of My Friends*, on which he had worked with great enthusiasm for two years, refused to pan out. Chekhov judged that both its theme and its presentation (of which we know almost nothing) could never pass the censor and therefore decided to destroy the manuscript. His play *The Wood Demon,* in which he expressed his innermost convictions about nature conservation and the intellectual bankruptcy of Russian literary criticism, was performed in Moscow at the end of 1889 and met with general indifference, its ideas and views totally unperceived by the press and public. In his letters to friends, Chekhov frequently compared his medical and biological interests to his lawful wedded wife and his literary work to a mistress. The failure of his novel and his play and his depression over the death of his brother Nikolai caused Chekhov to terminate his two-year honeymoon with the "mistress" and to cast about for a project that would take him back to the "wife." He found one in the research trip to Sakhalin.

16. To Vladimir Korolenko

Moscow,
January 9, 1888

I have unwittingly cheated you, my most kind Vladimir Galaktionovich, by not having rescued a copy of my play for you.[1] I'll send you one when it comes out in print or give it to you when I see you. In the meantime don't be angry. Yesterday I received a letter from old man Grigorovich, and it occurred to me it would be nice to have it copied and to send it to you. There are many reasons why it's worth more than its weight in gold to me, and I have avoided reading it a second time for fear of losing my first impression. It will show you that a literary reputation and good royalties provide no salvation from such humdrum prose as sickness, cold and loneliness: the old man's life is coming to an end. His letter will also make it clear that you were not the only one who made an honest attempt to set me on the true path, and you'll understand how ashamed I feel.[2]

After reading Grigorovich's letter, I thought of you, and my conscience started bothering me. I began to see how wrong I am. I'm writing this specifically to you because I have no one around me with a need for or a right to my sincerity, and because, although I've never asked you for permission, I've formed a union with you deep in my heart.

On your friendly advice I have begun a short novelette for the *Northern Herald.*[3] For a start I have undertaken to describe the steppe, the people of the steppe and the things I experienced in the steppe. It's a good theme, and I'm enjoying writing about it, but unfortunately, since I'm not used to writing anything long and am afraid of writing to excess, I've gone to the other extreme: every page comes out as compact as a little story, and the scenes keep piling up, crowding each other, getting in each other's way, and ruining the general impression. Instead of a scene in which all the particulars merge into the whole like stars in the sky, I end up with an outline, a dry list of impressions. A writer, you for instance, will understand me, but the reader will get bored and drop the whole thing.

I spent two and a half weeks in Petersburg and saw a lot of people. The general impression I came away with can be summed up as follows: "Put not your trust in princes, ye sons of men. . . ."[4] I saw a lot of nice people, but no judges. However, that may be all for the best.

I'm looking forward to reading your "Going the Same Way" in the February issue of the *Northern Herald.* Pleshcheyev says the censors have nipped you badly.[5] Happy New Year! Keep well and happy.

Your sincerely devoted,
A. Chekhov

P.S. I find your "Escapee from Sakhalin"[6] the most outstanding work that has appeared of late. It is written like a good musical composition in accordance with all the rules an artist's instinct suggests to him. Throughout the book you show yourself to be such a powerful artist, such a powerhouse, that even your biggest faults, which would be the death of any other writer, pass by unnoticed. Women, for instance, are stubbornly absent from the entire book, and I have only just managed to detect it.

1. *Ivanov.* Korolenko had visited Chekhov's home in the fall of 1887 while the play was being written and Chekhov had promised to show him a draft of it.

2. Both Korolenko and Grigorovich had urged Chekhov not to devote himself entirely to short stories and to try writing a book-length work of fiction.

3. This was one of the most prestigious literary journals of the time. Its fiction editor was the poet Alexei Pleshcheyev; Nikolai Mikhailovsky himself was in charge of its literary-criticism section. Korolenko was a member of the journal's editorial board and it was on his recommendation that Pleshcheyev, disregarding Mikhailovsky's hostility to Chekhov's work and the objections of some other contributors who considered Chekhov politically compromised because he was a regular contributor to Suvorin's *New Times,* invited Chekhov to submit a story to *Northern Herald.* The result was "The Steppe," which Chekhov wrote slowly, carefully and with great deliberation, because he had never before written for a publication of comparable stature. He considered the occasion his debut in a major literary journal.

4. Somewhat garbled partial citation of verse 3 from Psalm 146 ("Put not your trust in princes, nor in the son of man, in whom there is no help").

5. On February 4, 1888, Korolenko wrote to Chekhov from St. Petersburg that the government censors had not only abridged his story "Going the Same Way" (*Po puti*), but scrambled the sequence of its sections, so that when he

read it in *Northern Herald* he found his own story incomprehensible. Korolenko later reworked this story and it now appears in collections of his work as "Fyodor the Homeless."

6. "Escapee from Sakhalin" (*Sokolinets*), like "Going the Same Way," belongs to the group of Korolenko's stories about convicts in Siberia, which he based on the experiences of his own four-year Siberian exile and which made his literary reputation. The story describes, in grim and gory detail, the escape of a group of convicts from the penal colony on Sakhalin. Chekhov's enthusiasm for this story consolidated his interest in Eastern Siberia, which began with his reading of Goncharov's *Frigate Pallada* while still at school and culminated in his famous voyage to Sakhalin.

17. To Dmitry Grigorovich

Moscow,
January 12, 1888
Saint Tatyana's Day.
University Anniversary

I won't try to explain to you, dear Dmitry Vasilyevich, how precious and meaningful I found your splendid last letter. I must admit I couldn't keep it to myself and sent a copy to Korolenko, who by the way is a very fine man. Reading the letter did not put me to any particular shame, because it came while I was already at work on a thick-journal[1] project. Here is my answer to the essence of your letter: I've undertaken something big. I've already written slightly more than fifty pages, and I'll probably be writing another seventy-five. For my thick-journal debut I've selected the steppe, which no one has described for some time now. I describe the plain, its lilac vistas, the sheep breeders, the Jews, the priests, the nocturnal storms, the inns, the wagon trains, the steppe birds and so on. Each chapter is a separate story, but all the chapters are as interconnected and closely related as the five figures of a quadrille. I'm trying to give them a common aroma and a common tone, and the better to accomplish this I follow one character through all the chapters. I feel I've made a lot of headway and that there are passages that smell of hay, but on the whole I'm ending up with something rather odd and much too original. Since I'm not used to writing anything long and am constantly, as is my wont, afraid of writing too much, I've gone to the other extreme. All the pages come out compact, as if they had been condensed, and impressions keep crowding each other, piling up, and pushing one another out of the way. The short scenes, or as you call them, spangles, are squeezed tightly together; they move in an unbroken chain and are therefore fatiguing. Instead of a scene, I end up with a dry, detailed list of impressions, very much like an outline; instead of an artistically integrated depiction of the steppe, I offer the reader an encyclopedia of the steppe. Nothing works right the first time around. But that doesn't discourage me. Who knows, maybe even an encyclopedia can have its uses. Perhaps it will open the eyes of my contemporaries and show them what splendor and rich veins of beauty remain untapped, and how much leeway the Russian artist still has. If my novelette reminds my colleagues of the steppe they've forgotten, if even one of the motifs I have so lightly and dryly touched upon gives food for thought to some insignificant little poet, then that will be my reward. You will understand my steppe, I know, and you will pardon my unwitting sins for its sake. As it now turns out, the reason I have sinned unwittingly is that *I do not yet know how* to write long pieces.

This summer I will go back to my interrupted novel.[2] It encompasses an entire district (the local gentry and administration) and the domestic life of several families. The steppe is a rather exceptional and specialized topic; if you depict it for its own sake and not in passing, its monotony and rural character tend to become boring. But the novel deals with ordinary people, members of the intelligentsia, women, love, marriage, children—and it all makes you feel almost at home and you don't tire so easily.

The suicide of a seventeen-year-old boy is a very promising and tempting theme, but a frightening one to undertake.[3] An issue so painful to us all calls for a painfully forceful response, and do we young writers have the inner resources for it? No. When you guarantee the success of this theme, you are judging by your own standards. But then, in addition to talent, the men of your generation had erudition, schooling, iron and phosphorus, while contemporary talents have nothing of the sort. Frankly speaking, there is reason to rejoice that they keep away from serious problems. Let them have a go at your seventeen-year-old, and I am certain that X, completely unaware of what he is doing, will slander him and pile lie upon blasphemy with the purest of intentions; Y will give him a shot of pallid and petty tendentiousness; while Z will explain away the suicide as a psychosis. Your boy is of a good, pure nature. He seeks after God. He is loving, sensitive and deeply hurt. To handle a figure like that, an author has to be capable of suffering, while all our contemporary authors can do is whine and snivel. As for me, in addition to everything I've said above, I happen to be sluggish and lazy.

Vladimir Davydov came to see me a few days ago. He was in my *Ivanov*, and we have become friends. When he learned I was going to write you, he took heart, sat down at my desk and wrote you the letter I have enclosed.

Have you been reading Korolenko and Shcheglov?[4] People are talking a lot about Shcheglov, who in my opinion is talented and original. Korolenko is still the favorite of both public and critics; his book is selling splendidly. Fofanov is beginning to make a name for himself among the poets. He is genuinely talented; the others are worthless as artists. Our prose writers are still more or less acceptable, but the poets are very weak. As a group they are illiterate and lack education and a world view.[5] Koltsov the cattle dealer, who couldn't write literate Russian, was much more genuine, intelligent and educated than all our young contemporary poets put together.[6]

My "Steppe" will be published in the *Northern Herald*. I'll write Pleshcheyev to have a copy reserved for you.

I'm very glad your pains have left you. They are the crux of your illness; the rest is not so important. There's nothing serious about your cough, nothing with any connection to your illness. It doubtless comes from a cold and will go away as soon as the weather turns warmer. We'll be drinking a lot of toasts tonight to the people who taught me to cut up corpses and write prescriptions. We'll probably be drinking a toast to you too, because on every single Tatyana's Day we drink to Turgenev, Tolstoy and you. Writers and critics drink to Chernyshevsky, Saltykov and Gleb Uspensky, but the crowd (students, doctors, mathematicians and so on) to which my Aesculapian background binds me, still holds fast to the good old days and refuses to betray the old and much beloved stand-bys. I am firmly convinced that as long as Russia still has forests, ravines and summer nights, and as long as snipes still call and lapwings wail, neither you, nor Turgenev, nor Tolstoy—like Gogol—will ever be forgotten. The people you have portrayed may die off and be forgotten, but you will remain whole and unscathed. Such is your power, and such your fortune.[7]

Forgive me for having exhausted you with such a long letter, but what can I do? My hand ran away with me, and I felt like having a good long talk with you.

I hope this letter will find you in a warm spell, sprightly and well. Come to Russia this summer. The Crimea, they say, is just as pleasant as Nice.

Once again I thank you for the letter and send you all my best. I remain your truly, sincerely devoted

A. Chekhov

1. Both Grigorovich and Korolenko considered Chekhov's talent too important to be wasted on ephemeral humor magazines and the daily newspapers, where all his work had until then appeared. They urged him to write

longer works and to publish them in the "thick" literary journals which were read by more cultivated readers and reviewed by prominent critics.

2. *Stories from the Lives of My Friends* was the working title of this novel, to which Chekhov was to devote two years of enthusiastic work.

3. In the letter from Grigorovich, which he is here answering, Chekhov was urged to write a novel dealing with the suicide of a teen-aged boy; Grigorovich considered this subject highly topical and predicted Chekhov a huge success if he would undertake it.

4. On Shcheglov, see Letter 20.

5. An astoundingly correct appraisal of the sorry state of Russian poetry in the 1880s. After two decades of radical-utilitarian tyranny in criticism, the understanding and appreciation of all poetry fell so low that the verbose and bathetic Semyon Nadson, the most popular poet of the eighties, could be acclaimed as a new incarnation of Pushkin merely because his main topics were the evils of oppression and tyranny. Konstantin Fofanov (1862–1911), minor and uneven as his poetry was, almost single-handedly created a sort of native Russian poetic Impressionism, occasionally reminiscent of French Impressionist paintings, and kept a tiny spark of poetic feeling glowing until the brilliant poetic revival of Russian Symbolism began in the early nineties.

6. Alexei Koltsov (1809–42), sometimes called the Robert Burns of Russia, was indeed a cattle dealer by trade. He wrote charming imitation folk songs, many of which ended up as folklore and became genuine folk songs.

7. The lumping together of Grigorovich's name with those of Gogol and Tolstoy may be attributed to Chekhov's fondness for the old man and to the inflated reputation Grigorovich still enjoyed at the time. But the crucial point of this paragraph, the opposition of Gogol's, Turgenev's and Tolstoy's names (note the absence of Dostoyevsky) to those of Chernyshevsky, Saltykov-Shchedrin (valued at that time not for his great novel *The Golovlyov Family* but for his savage, satirical lampoons of government officials and the post-reform gentry) and the muckraking Gleb Uspensky, implies a principled and reasoned preference of literary quality and depth to topical relevance in literature. This juxtaposition would have puzzled the typical literary critic of the time (for whom Tolstoy and Chernyshevsky were national classics of equal magnitude) and would have seemed intolerably reactionary to a typical radicalized university student.

18. To Alexei Pleshcheyev[1]

Moscow,
February 5, 1888

Thank you so much, dear Alexei Nikolayevich! Yesterday I received the seventy-five rubles and took them to Putyata.[2] The money came just in time, because though Putyata is lying in bed, he is at the same time rapidly marching toward his grave.

Have you received my "Steppe"? Has the *Northern Herald*

rejected it or accepted it into the fold? Instead of sending it parcel post as I had originally intended, I sent it registered mail yesterday. That way it will get there faster. I hope it did not come too late.

I'm very anxious to read Korolenko's story. He's my favorite contemporary writer. His colors are rich and vivid, his language impeccable—though a bit recherché in places—his images noble. Leontyev[3] is also good. Though he does not write as boldly or beautifully, he is warmer than Korolenko, more restful and feminine. But—*Allah Kerim*—why must they both specialize so? Korolenko refuses to forsake his convicts, and Leontyev feeds his readers on a steady diet of army officers. I can understand specialization in art when it comes to genres: landscapes, history and the like, and I understand type casting and training instrumentalists, but I cannot reconcile myself to specializations in convicts, officers or priests. That's not specialization; that's predilection. You in St. Petersburg don't care for Korolenko, and here in Moscow we don't read Shcheglov, but I firmly believe in both their futures. Oh, if only we had decent critics!

Mardi gras is upon us. You've practically promised to come, and I'm expecting you.

Tonight is Davydov's benefit performance. He's doing the *Bourgeois gentilhomme*. It will be stuffy, crowded and noisy, and I'll spend the whole night after the performance coughing. I've gotten out of the habit of attending theaters.

If my "Steppe" has not been rejected, would you drop a word on my behalf at the *Northern Herald* when you get a chance and ask them to send me a subscription? I'm looking forward to Korolenko's "Going the Same Way."

I've bored you with my letters.

Good-bye. My regards to all your family.

Yours sincerely,
A. Chekhov

1. Alexei Pleshcheyev (1825–93) belonged in his youth, together with Fyodor Dostoyevsky, to the Petrashevsky political club and like Dostoyevsky he was sent to Siberia because of this, and spent ten years there. Upon his return to St. Petersburg, Pleshcheyev built for himself a reputation as a lyric and civic-protest poet. One of his songs, "Forward Without Fear or Doubt!", became something of an anthem of Russian anti-government dissent (Chekhov's comment on this song was: "If you call people to march forward, the least you can do is to indicate the goal, the path and the means"). Like the more famous civic poet Nekrasov, Pleshcheyev possessed considerable literary taste and was a discerning editor. His opening of the pages of *Northern Herald* to Chekhov was an important event in Chekhov's literary

biography. From 1887 to 1889, Pleshcheyev was one of Chekhov's most sympathetic and perceptive readers, as his letters to Chekhov printed in *Literary Heritage,* vol. 68, demonstrate. But he showed himself incapable of understanding "The Duel" (possibly because Chekhov chose to publish it in *New Times* rather than in *Northern Herald*) and he refused to publish the text of *The Wood Demon,* finding the conservationist views of its hero incomprehensible (". . . what sort of an idealist is he if he likes the forest and not the people?"). Pleshcheyev's surname has three syllables, incidentally (it rhymes with Nureyev), even though some of Chekhov's biographies in English reduce it to only two.

2. Chekhov was active in the Literary Fund, an organization devoted to aiding needy writers. He is here thanking Pleshcheyev for his contribution sent in response to an appeal to help the Moscow journalist Nikolai Putyata, who was destitute and ill.

3. I.e., Ivan Shcheglov. See Letter 20.

19. To Alexei Pleshcheyev

Moscow,
March 6, 1888

Today, dear Alexei Nikolayevich, I read two critiques of my "Steppe": Burenin's[1] article and Pyotr Ostrovsky's[2] letter. The latter is very congenial, sympathetic and intelligent. Besides the warm concern that constitutes its essence and purpose, it has many virtues, some that are even purely external: (1) If you look at it as a review, it is written with feeling, understanding and deliberation,[3] and it reads like a good, solid report. I haven't found it to contain a single heartrending word,[4] which clearly distinguishes it from run-of-the-mill critical articles, which are as overgrown with forewords and heartrending words as a neglected pond with algae. (2) It is eminently comprehensible; you can tell at once what he's driving at. (3) It is free from philosophizing about atavism, reincarnation and the like, keeps as plainly and cold-bloodedly to elementary matters as a good textbook, tries to be precise, etc., etc. And many more things too numerous to mention. I read Pyotr Nikolayevich's letter three times through, and I'm sorry he hides himself from the public. He would make a worthwhile addition to our corps of journalists. It's not that he has definite views and convictions or a clear-cut world view—nowadays everyone does; the important thing is that he has a *method.* For the analyst, be he scientist or critic, method constitutes one half of talent.

Tomorrow I'm going to pay Pyotr Nikolayevich a visit; I have a proposal for him. I'm going to remind him of 1812 and guerrilla warfare when anyone who so desired could attack the French without donning a uniform.[5] Maybe he'll like my idea that in our time, when literature has fallen prisoner to a thousand score false doctrines,[6] a guerrilla corps of critic irregulars would be far from superfluous. If he wishes to bypass journals and newspapers, break ambush, and charge forward into the foe Cossack-style, he can do so with the aid of the pamphlet. Pamphlets are the rage; they are so inexpensive and easy to read. With this in mind our priests bombard the public daily with their pharisaical eructations. Pyotr Nikolayevich stands nothing to lose.

Now—how is your health? Do you ever get out into the fresh air? Judging by Burenin's criticism of Merezhkovsky, it must be freezing in St. Petersburg now, somewhere between 15° and 20° below zero.[7] And even though it's still damned cold, the poor birds are already on their way back to Russia. They are driven on by homesickness, by love for their native land. If poets only knew how many millions of birds fall victim to love and longing for their homes, how many freeze on the way, what tortures they endure in March and early April when they come home to roost, they would long ago have written about it. Put yourself in the place of a rail who walks all the way instead of flying,[8] or the wild goose who is willing to surrender himself to man rather than freeze to death. . . . It's a hard world to live in.

I'll be going to Petersburg at the beginning of Lent, two or three days after I receive my *Northern Herald* payment. If you happen to be at the office on Tuesday, could you remind the cashier when you see her of my existence and lack of funds?

I didn't publish a line all February, so my budget's in a state of havoc.

I hope you haven't forgotten about the Volga.[9]

Keep well. I wish you a good appetite, sound sleep, and as much money as possible.

Good-bye.

Yours,
A. Chekhov

1. On Burenin, see Letter 12, note 6. Burenin's review of "The Steppe" was quite favorable.

2. Pyotr Ostrovsky, the younger brother of the famous playwright Alexander Ostrovsky. His abilities as a critic were admired in literary circles, but he preferred to couch his criticism in the form of private letters to various writers and was averse to having them published. The letter he sent to Chekhov concerning "The Steppe" was highly critical and pointed out a number of supposed deficiencies in the story.

3. A verse from Alexander Griboyedov's *The Misfortune of Being Clever* (also known in English as *Woe from Wit*), a brilliant and totally untrans-

latable neoclassical verse comedy, which is a marvel of verbal richness and precision in the original Russian. The line Chekhov quotes comes from Act II, Scene I, where an important government official asks that his appointment book be read to him "with feeling, understanding and deliberation."

4. "Heartrending words" (*zhalkie slova*) is a phrase repeatedly used by the hero's valet in Ivan Goncharov's novel *Oblomov* to describe his master's gentle remonstrances.

5. The guerrilla-warfare imagery here and later in this paragraph seems to be derived, at least in part, from Book III of Tolstoy's *War and Peace*.

6. The idea that Russian literature in the second half of the nineteenth century was a prisoner not only of the government censors but also of the anti-government ideologues was frequently expressed at the beginning of the twentieth century by such Symbolist writers as Merezhkovsky, Bryusov and Blok. It must have seemed startlingly original at the time this letter was written. This concept is utterly sacrilegious in the Soviet Union and commentators there have to pretend that Chekhov can't possibly be saying what he does in fact say in this passage and numerous others like it.

7. Centigrade, of course. In his review of Chekhov's "The Steppe," Burenin ridiculed a recent poem by Merezhkovsky hailing the onset of spring, quoting the recent freezing temperatures in St. Petersburg. On Merezhkovsky, see Letter 27.

8. The rail's migrations on foot were mentioned by Chekhov two years earlier in his story "Agafya."

9. In his letter to Chekhov of February 5, 1888, Pleshcheyev informed him that he and Korolenko were planning to take a trip along the Volga that summer and asked whether Chekhov would care to join them.

20. To Ivan Leontyev (Shcheglov)[1]

Moscow,
May 3, 1888

Dear Alba,[2]

You can finally congratulate me: the day after tomorrow, May 5th, I'm off for *dahin*. . . . Because of which fact you shall address your answer to this letter thusly: The Estate of A. V. Lintvaryova, Sumy, Kharkov Province. Pleshcheyev is coming to stay with me some time after the tenth. Why don't you come too? How about it? At any rate I'll be expecting you all summer. Who knows? You might just decide to come after all! I won't expect you in June, though; I'll be traveling around all month. If you do come, bring along three pounds of good ham sausage, the most expensive kind (I'll foot the bill).

I've sent the *Northern Herald* a story.[3] I'm a little ashamed of it. It's awfully boring and cloyingly full of philowisdomizing.[4] I feel bad about it, but there's nothing I can do: I need money as much as air.

Tomorrow I'm finishing a story for *New Times*.[5] This summer I won't be writing anything but trifles.

I received a letter from Lehmann[6] informing me that "we (that is, everyone in Petersburg) have agreed to print advertisements for one another in our books," asking me to comply, and warning me that "only those authors who are more or less in solidarity with us may be included" among the elect. I responded by sending my consent and asking him how he knew with whom I am or am not in solidarity? How all of you in Petersburg enjoy being stifled! Aren't you stifled by expressions like solidarity, the unity of young writers, a community of interests and so on? Solidarity and the like I can understand on the stock exchange, in politics, in religious affairs (sects), etc., but solidarity among young writers is impossible and unnecessary. We can't all think and feel in the same way. We have different goals or no goals at all; we know one another slightly or not at all. As a result there's nothing to which solidarity can firmly attach itself. And is it necessary? No. To help a colleague, to respect his person and his work, to refrain from gossiping about him and envying him, lying to him and acting hypocritical toward him, all this requires that one be not so much a young writer as simply a human being. Let us be ordinary people, let us treat everybody alike and there won't be any need for artificially blown-up solidarity. The insistent efforts toward achieving the sort of private, professional, cliquish solidarity that you in Petersburg want will inevitably lead to spying, suspiciousness and controls, and without meaning to we will each turn into something like a Jesuit socius of the other. I am not in solidarity with you, dear Jean, but I promise you to the grave complete freedom as a writer, that is, you may write wherever and however you please, think like Koreysha[7] if you like, go back on your convictions and ideas a thousand times and so on and so forth, and my attitude toward you as a person won't change an iota and I'll always print advertisements for your books on my book jackets. I can promise the same to many other of my colleagues and would like them to do the same for me. As I see it, this sort of relationship is only normal. It is the only way we can have respect and even friendship and sympathy during life's difficult moments.[8]

Now I've let my tongue run away with me again. May the heavens keep you!

Yours,
A. Chekhov

1. Captain Ivan Leontyev (1856–1911) was an army officer who in the early 1880s embarked on a promising career as a playwright and novelist,

publishing his work under the pen name of Ivan Shcheglov. When this letter was written, Chekhov considered Shcheglov (to whom he alternately refers in his correspondence by his real name and his pen name) to be the most interesting new writer of the decade, on a par with Korolenko and Vsevolod Garshin. In a long letter to Shcheglov of February 22, 1888, Chekhov characterized him as a writer of the bourgeoisie, able to depict that class in a manner comparable to that of Alphonse Daudet. But Shcheglov's promisingly inaugurated literary career petered out by the mid-nineties, and by the turn of the century both he and his writings were generally forgotten. His private diary entries made after Chekhov's death, when Shcheglov realized that posterity would remember his name only because he had once corresponded with Chekhov, make heartbreaking reading. Shcheglov published a memoir about his encounters with Chekhov.

2. Chekhov and Shcheglov were given to using nicknames in their correspondence. One set of nicknames originated when one of Pleshcheyev's daughters, upon seeing a photograph of Chekhov in Shcheglov's presence, declared that he would be an ideal choice to play the title role in Goethe's *Egmont*. This led Shcheglov to address his letters to Chekhov as "Dear Egmont" and Chekhov reciprocated by calling Shcheglov "Dear Alba," after another character in Goethe's tragedy. The other set of nicknames they used involved substituting the French versions of their first names, Jean and Antoine, for Ivan and Anton.

3. "Lights."

4. In the original, the word is *filosomudrie*, which combines the first part of the Greek word for "philosophy" with the second part of its Russian calque, *lyubomudrie*.

5. "An Unpleasantness."

6. Anatoly Lehmann wrote mainly manuals on plucked-string instruments and on how to play billiards. He was exceedingly active in literary politics of the day, trying repeatedly to organize writers into various groups or clubs which he hoped to direct. In Pleshcheyev's letters to Chekhov, Lehmann is referred to as "the woodlouse."

7. Ivan Yakovlevich Koreysha (1790–1861) was nineteenth-century Russia's most famous holy idiot. He was confined in a Moscow mental institution, where he regularly held court for his admirers. A profound occult meaning was read by his followers into his most trivial utterances, such as "More sugar, please!" Wives of millionaire merchants were known to consult him about business ventures and arranging marriages for their children.

8. In the Soviet Union, where all writers are presumed to be in full solidarity with each other and with the state at all times and where they demonstrate this solidarity by voting unanimously to denounce Pasternak's *Doctor Zhivago* (which none of them had read at the time) or to expel Solzhenitsyn from the Writers' Union, this letter makes embarrassing reading. It was printed, uncut, in the 1944–51 edition of Chekhov, but omitted from the 1963–64 collection of his letters for obvious reasons.

21. To Alexei Suvorin

Sumy,[1]
May 30, 1888

Dear Alexei Sergeyevich,

This is in answer to your letter which I received only yesterday. The envelope was torn, crumpled and soiled, which my hosts and kinsmen have interpreted as having profound political overtones.

I'm living on the banks of the Psyol in a wing of an old mansion. I rented it at random, sight unseen, and have as yet had no cause to regret it. The river is wide and deep with an abundance of islands, fish and crayfish. The banks are beautiful, and there is greenery everywhere. But, best of all, it is so spacious here that I have the feeling that my hundred rubles have earned me the right to live on a boundless expanse. Here, nature and life follow a pattern that has so gone out of style that it gets rejected in editorial offices. To say nothing of the nightingales singing day and night, the dogs barking in the distance, the old overgrown gardens, the very poetic and melancholy boarded-up manors where souls of beautiful women dwell; to say nothing of the ancient, moribund butlers who look back fondly on their serf days and of young ladies pining for the most stereotyped kind of love. Not far from here there is even as overworked a cliché as a sixteen-wheel water mill complete with a miller and his daughter, who is always sitting at the window, apparently waiting for something.[2] Everything I see and hear around me seems long since familiar from ancient tales and legends. The only new thing I have come across is a mysterious bird, "the water bittern," that sits somewhere off in the reeds and day and night utters a cry that sounds partly like someone whacking an empty barrel and partly like a bellowing cow shut up in the barn. Every Ukrainian has seen this bird in the course of his life, but each one describes it differently. In other words, no one has seen it. There are other new things around, but since they aren't native to the area, they're not entirely new.

Every day I take a boat to the mill, and in the evening I row over to the islands to fish with the fishing addicts from the Kharitonenko factory. Our conversations are often interesting. On Whitsunday Eve the addicts are going to spend all night fishing on the islands, and so will I. There are some splendid types among them.

My hosts have turned out to be very nice, hospitable people, a family worthy of study and consisting of six members. The mother is a kind, plump old woman who has known her share of suffering. She reads Schopenhauer and goes to church but only to services honoring her favorite saints. She conscientiously pores over each issue of the

Herald of Europe and the *Northern Herald* and knows of writers I've never dreamed existed. It means a lot to her that the painter Makovsky[3] once stayed in the wing of her mansion and that a young writer is staying there now. When she talks with Pleshcheyev, she feels a tremor of awe throughout her body, and she is constantly rejoicing over "having been granted the grace" of seeing the great poet.

Her eldest daughter, a physician, the pride of the family, and—as the peasants reverently call her—a saint, is truly an extraordinary phenomenon. A brain tumor has rendered her totally blind, and she suffers from epilepsy and constant headaches. She knows what awaits her and speaks stoically and with remarkable sang-froid about her approaching death. As a doctor I have grown used to seeing people who are going to die soon, and I've always felt somehow strange when people close to death talked, smiled, or cried in my presence. But here, when I see this blind woman out on the terrace laughing, joking or listening to my *Twilight*[4] being read to her, I get the feeling that what's strange is not that she is about to die, but that instead of feeling the approach of our own deaths we write *Twilights* as though we were never going to die.

The second daughter, also a physician, is an old maid, a quiet, shy, infinitely kind and loving, homely creature. Patients are sheer torture for her, and she is anxious to the point of psychosis over them. At our medical consultations we always disagree: I bear glad tidings where she sees death; and I double the doses she prescribes. But, where death is obvious and inevitable, my doctor friend reacts quite unprofessionally. Once she and I were seeing patients at the local clinic. One of them was a young Ukrainian woman with a malignant tumor of the glands on her neck and the back of her head. The malignancy had spread so far that any treatment was unthinkable. And because the woman was experiencing no pain then, but would die six months later in terrible agony, the lady doctor looked at her with a profoundly guilt-ridden expression as if to apologize for her own good health and to show her shame for the helplessness of medical science. She takes an active interest in running the household and understands it down to the last detail. She even understands horses. When for instance the side horse won't pull or starts to get restless, she knows just what to do and issues the coachman instructions. She dearly loves family life, and though fate has denied her one of her own, she nonetheless seems to yearn for it. In the evening when there's music and singing in the main house, she strides briskly and nervously up and down the dark tree-lined path like a caged-in animal. I can't imagine she has ever done anyone any harm, and I have the feeling she has never been and never will be happy for a single moment.

The third daughter, a graduate of the Bestuzhev courses,[5] is a young girl of masculine build—strong, as bony as a bream, muscular, suntanned and raucous. When she laughs, you can hear her a mile away. She is a passionate Ukrainophile. She's built a school on the estate at her own expense and teaches Krylov's fables in Ukrainian translation to the little Ukrainians. She visits Shevchenko's[6] grave the way a Turk goes to Mecca. She doesn't cut her hair, wears a corset and a bustle, and takes an active interest in running the household. She loves to sing and laugh and wouldn't turn down even the most banal love affair even though she has read Marx's *Das Kapital*, but there's not much chance of her getting married, she's so homely.

The elder son, a quiet, modest, bright, untalented and hardworking young man, is completely without pretensions and appears to be content with his lot. He was expelled from the university in his fourth year there, but doesn't brag about it. He talks very little. He loves farming and the land and lives in harmony with the Ukrainians.

The second son is a young man obsessed with the idea that Tchaikovsky is a genius. He is a pianist, and yearns for a Tolstoyan life.

There you have a brief description of the people among whom I now live. As for the Ukrainians, the women remind me of Zankovetskaya, and all the men of Panas Sadovsky.[7] There are always many guests around.

Pleshcheyev has come to visit me. Everyone looks upon him as a demigod and they consider it a stroke of fortune if he deigns to honor their yogurt with his attention. People offer him bouquets, invite him everywhere, etc. A Poltava schoolgirl named Vata, a guest of my hosts, is particularly zealous in looking after him. And he "listens and goes on eating" and smoking his cigars, which gives the admiring ladies headaches. He is sluggish and lazy, the way old men tend to be, but that doesn't prevent the fair sex from taking him out for boat rides or visits to neighboring estates and singing him songs. He is the same sort of symbol here as in Petersburg, that is, an icon people pray to because it's old and hung once upon a time beside the wonder-working icons.[8] I, for my part, regard him as a vessel full of tradition, interesting reminiscences and pleasant platitudes, though of course he is also a good, warm, sincere person.

I have written a story and sent it off to *New Times*.[9]

What you say about "Lights" is perfectly just. The "Nikolai and Masha"[10] situation runs glaringly through it, but what can be done about it? Not being in the habit of writing long stories, I am over-anxious. Each time I start writing, I am frightened by the thought that my story has no right to be as long as it is, and so I try to make it as short as possible. The final scene between Kisochka[11] and the engineer seemed to me like an insignificant detail that only weighed down the story, so I threw it out and had no choice but to put "Nikolai and Masha" in its place.

You write that neither the conversation about pessimism nor Kisochka's story help to solve the problem of pessimism. In my opinion it is not the writer's job to solve such problems as God, pessimism, etc.; his job is merely to record who, under what conditions, said or thought what about God or pessimism. The artist is not meant to be a judge of his characters and what they say; his only job is to be an impartial witness. I heard two Russians in a muddled conversation about pessimism, a conversation that solved nothing; all I am bound to do is reproduce that conversation exactly as I heard it. Drawing conclusions is up to the jury, that is, the readers. My only job is to be talented, that is, to know how to distinguish important testimony from unimportant, to place my characters in the proper light and speak their language. Shcheglov-Leontyev criticizes me for finishing the story with "You can't figure anything out in this world!"[12] To his mind, the artist who is a psychologist *must* figure things out because otherwise, why is he a psychologist? But I don't agree with him. It's about time that everyone who writes—especially genuine literary artists—admitted that in this world you can't figure anything out. Socrates admitted it once upon a time, and Voltaire was wont to admit it. The crowd thinks it knows and understands everything; the stupider it is, the broader it imagines its outlook. But, if a writer whom the crowd believes takes it upon himself to declare he understands nothing of what he sees, that alone will constitute a major gain in the realm of thought and a major step forward.

As for your play,[13] you are wrong to run it down. Its shortcomings are not due to a lack of talent or observation; they are due to the nature of your creative ability. You are more inclined toward an austere sort of writing, the sort that love for and frequent readings of classical models has inculcated in you. Try to picture your *Tatyana* written in verse, and you'll see how its shortcomings take on a different physiognomy. If it were written in verse, no one would notice that all the characters speak the same language, no one would reproach them for philosophizing and editorializing instead of talking—in a classical form, a verse form, all this would merge into the general background, like smoke into the air—and no one would feel the lack of vulgar language and other petty vulgarities in which contemporary comedy and drama must abound and which your *Tatyana* completely lacks. Give your heroes Latin names, dress them in togas, and the result will be the same. . . . The shortcomings in your play are irremediable because they are organic. Console yourself with the thought that they are the product of your positive traits and that if you were to make a gift of them to other playwrights, Krylov or Tikhonov[14] for example, their plays would become more interesting and more intelligent.

Now a word about the future. In late June or early July I am going to Kiev. From there I will follow the Dnieper down to Yekaterinoslav, then to Alexandrovsk and on to the Black Sea. I'll be stopping in Feodosia. If you really do go to Constantinople, might I go with you? We could visit Father Paisy,[15] who would demonstrate to us that Tolstoy's teachings come from the devil. I'll spend all of June writing, and so in all likelihood I'll have enough money for the trip. From the Crimea I will go to Poti, from Poti to Tiflis, from Tiflis to the Don, and from the Don to the Psyol. . . . In the Crimea I'm going to start work on a lyric play.

That's quite a long letter I've written! I'll have to close now. Give my regards to Anna Ivanovna, Nastya and Borya.[16] Alexei Nikolayevich[17] sends you his greetings. He's slightly ill today: he's having trouble breathing and his pulse is limping along like Leykin. I'll have to start treating him. Good-bye, keep well, and God grant you all the best.

Your sincerely devoted,
A. Chekhov

1. Sumy is a town in the Ukraine situated on the river Psyol. Chekhov and his family rented a summer cottage there on the estate called Luka, belonging to Alexandra Lintvaryova, with whose entire family the Chekhovs became close friends. Chekhov spent the summers of 1888 and 1889 at Luka. The family described in this letter is, of course, the Lintvaryovs.

2. Alexander Pushkin's unfinished play *The Water Nymph* is evoked in this sentence (or, possibly, Alexander Dargomyzhsky's popular opera based on this play).

3. Russian commentators disagree as to which of the three academic painters of that name had stayed at Luka.

4. A collection of Chekhov's short stories, actually called *In the Twilight*.

5. Government-owned Russian universities were not open to women in the nineteenth century (admission of women was a recurrent demand of the male students during the periodic student disturbances). However, some of the major universities offered special courses for women, taught by their regular professors. The authorities did not object, provided that these women's colleges were called "courses" and not "universities." The Bestuzhev "courses" were the women's branch of the St. Petersburg University.

6. Taras Shevchenko (1814–61) is the national poet of the Ukraine.

7. Maria Zankovetskaya (1860–1934) was the most famous Ukrainian actress of all time. Chekhov corresponded with her and intended to write a play that would contain a role for her to be spoken entirely in Ukrainian. The

male name cited is an amalgam consisting of the first name of one popular Ukrainian actor combined with the last name of another.

8. The liberal Lintvaryovs were awed by Pleshcheyev's one-time association with Chernyshevsky, Dobrolyubov, Nekrasov and other radical saints of the 1860s. His earlier friendship and correspondence with Dostoyevsky, on the other hand, probably meant very little to them. The phrase "listens and goes on eating" applied to Pleshcheyev in this paragraph is quoted from Ivan Krylov's fable "The Cat and the Cook," where it describes a cat helping itself to a variety of foods.

9. "An Unpleasantness."

10. "Nikolai and Masha" refers to some unidentified work of literature mentioned in Suvorin's letter (now lost) which Chekhov is answering. There are certainly no such characters in Chekhov's "Lights," as the translator of Lillian Hellman's edition of his letters had assumed.

11. Kisochka ("Kitten") is the nickname of Natalia, the heroine of Chekhov's "Lights," one of his more memorable depictions of educated women taken advantage of by callous males. After the engineer who is the narrator-villain of the story tells how he seduced and betrayed her in a particularly heartless way, Chekhov concludes his narrative with the words: "You can't figure out anything in this world."

12. On May 29, 1888, Shcheglov wrote to Chekhov: "I was not entirely satisfied with your latest story 'Lights.' Of course I swallowed it in one gulp, there is no question about that, because everything you write is so appetizing and real that it can be easily and pleasantly swallowed. But that finale 'You can't figure out anything in this world . . .' is abrupt; it is certainly the writer's job to figure out what goes on in the heart of his hero, otherwise his psychology will remain unclear."

On June 9, Chekhov answered Shcheglov as follows: "I permit myself not to agree with you about my 'Lights.' It is not the psychologist's job to understand things that he in fact does not understand. Let us not be charlatans and let us state openly that you can't figure out anything in this world. Only fools and charlatans know and understand everything."

13. Suvorin's *Tatyana Repina.*

14. Viktor Krylov was a prolific and popular hack of a playwright; on Vladimir Tikhonov, see Letter 30.

15. A minor provincial Rasputin of the 1880s, who was at one time a friend of Chekhov's uncle Mitrofan in Taganrog.

16. Suvorin's second wife and their two children.

17. Pleshcheyev.

22. To Alexei Suvorin

Moscow,
September 11, 1888

I hope this letter will find you still in Feodosia, dear Alexei Sergeyevich.

I will be glad to undertake to proofread the directory of Moscow doctors for your yearbook and I'll be happy if you are satisfied with my work. The proofs haven't been sent to me yet, but most likely they will be sent out soon. I expect to take certain liberties with them and will do what I can, but I'm afraid that it won't resemble the Petersburg directory when I'm done, that is, it will be fatter or leaner. If you find my apprehensions well founded, send the printers a telegram and ask them to send along the Petersburg proofs for guidance. It's not right to make Petersburg a lean cow and Moscow a fat one or vice versa within the same section. Both capitals should be treated with equal respect; if anything, Moscow should have less.

I'd like to take this opportunity to include an "Insane Asylums in Russia." It's an up-and-coming issue and one of great interest to doctors and land administrators. I'll merely provide a brief list. Next year with your permission I will take over the entire medical section of your yearbook. All I'm doing now is pouring new wine into old bottles, and I won't be able to do anything more, because for the time being I don't have any material available or any plan.

You advise me not to chase after two hares at once and to forget about practicing medicine. I don't see what's so impossible about chasing two hares at once even in the literal sense. Provided you have the hounds, the chase is feasible. In all likelihood I am lacking in hounds (in the figurative sense now), but I feel more alert and more satisfied with myself when I think of myself as having two occupations instead of one. Medicine is my lawful wedded wife, and literature my mistress. When one gets on my nerves, I spend the night with the other. This may be somewhat disorganized, but then again it's not as boring, and anyway, neither one loses anything by my duplicity. If I didn't have medicine, I'd never devote my spare time and thoughts to literature. I lack discipline.

The last letter I wrote you was full of incongruities (I was in the dumps), but I give you my word that when I spoke of my relations with you I had only myself in mind, not you.[1] I have always interpreted your advance payments, your kind disposition toward me and so on at face value. A person would have to know you very poorly and at the same time be a twenty-two-carat psychopath to suspect a stone in the bread you offer. While I was going on about my apprehensiveness, all I had in mind was my own charming trait of shying away from publishing a second story in a paper where I've just had a story published because I fear that people as decent as myself might get the idea that I'm publishing so often only for the sake of lucre. Please, please forgive me for inaugurating this ridiculous and useless "polemic" for no earthly reason.

I received a letter from Alexei Alexeyevich[2] today. Pass on the following advice to him (it is based on experience): never let illustrators get away with anything, and never trust them, no matter how sweet and eloquent they are. Tell him—and Borya too, now that I think of it —that I know Godefroy[3] the bareback rider. She's not at all pretty. She had nothing to offer but advanced training in horsemanship and fine muscles; everything else about her is ordinary and vulgar. Judging by her face, though, she must be a nice woman.

The young lady from Sumy[4] who tried to stop me from going to see you was thinking in terms of "tendentiousness" and "spirit," not of the sort of corruption you write about. She feared your political influence over my person. Yes, she is a good, pure soul, but when I asked her where she knew Suvorin from and whether she read *New Times*, she faltered, wiggled her fingers, and said, "In a word, I don't advise you to go." Yes, our young ladies and their political beaux are pure souls, but nine-tenths of their pure souls isn't worth a damn. All their inactive sanctity and purity are based on hazy and naïve sympathies and antipathies to individuals and labels, not to facts. It's easy to be pure when you can hate the Devil you don't know and love the God you wouldn't have brains enough to doubt.[5]

Regards to everyone.

Yours,
A. Chekhov

1. In his previous letter to Suvorin (August 29, 1888), Chekhov complained of financial worries and expressed the fear that his financial dependence on *New Times* might cast a shadow over their friendship.

2. Suvorin's oldest son by his first marriage. He was a co-editor of *New Times* and a well-known journalist in his own right.

3. Suvorin's sons Alexei and Boris (Borya) were enthusiastic fans of the bareback rider Maria Godefroy. Chekhov later used her name as the nickname of the hero's bride in his story "The Teacher of Literature."

4. Natalia Lintvaryova, the third daughter of the Lintvaryov family, described in Letter 21 as the bony and raucous Ukrainophile. The Lintvaryovs, who were overjoyed about Pleshcheyev's visit to Luka, boycotted the Chekhovs when Suvorin came to stay with them a little later during the same summer and they refused to meet him because of his widespread reputation as a reactionary (not realizing, apparently, that Pleshcheyev and Suvorin were on friendly terms personally and carried on a correspondence). Natalia Lintvaryova was trying to dissuade Chekhov from visiting Suvorin and his wife in the Crimea where he went in July of 1888.

5. This paragraph was deleted by Maria Chekhova in her edition of the letters in order to spare the feelings of Natalia Lintvaryova, who remained a friend and correspondent of Chekhov for the rest of his life. The entire letter is omitted from the 1963–64 edition.

23. To Alexei Pleshcheyev

Moscow,
October 4, 1888

I had barely mailed you a letter, dear Alexei Nikolayevich, when I received the news from you. Svetlov will be quite displeased. I will advise him of your answer immediately and will strongly recommend *A Bad Man* to him as a suitable replacement.[1]

If your letter had arrived two hours earlier, I would have mailed my story directly to you. As it is, it's now on its way to Baskov Lane.

I'd be happy to read what Merezhkovsky[2] had to say. Good-bye for now. Write me once you've read my story. You won't like it, but I'm not afraid of you and Anna Mikhailovna.[3] The people I am afraid of are the ones who look for tendentiousness between the lines and are determined to see me as either liberal or conservative. I am neither liberal, nor conservative, nor gradualist, nor monk, nor indifferentist. I would like to be a free artist and nothing else, and I regret God has not given me the strength to be one. I hate lies and violence in all of their forms, and consistory secretaries are just as odious to me as Notovich and Gradovsky.[4] Pharisaism, dullwittedness and tyranny reign not only in merchants' homes and police stations. I see them in science, in literature, among the younger generation. That is why I cultivate no particular predilection for policemen, butchers, scientists, writers or the younger generation. I look upon tags and labels as prejudices. My holy of holies is the human body, health, intelligence, talent, inspiration, love and the most absolute freedom imaginable, freedom from violence and lies, no matter what form the latter two take. Such is the program I would adhere to if I were a major artist.

But I've gone on too much as it is. Keep well.

Yours,
A. Chekhov

1. Pleshcheyev had translated Émile Augier's play *Les Effrontés*, and the Moscow actor Nikolai Svetlov, who the previous year had presented Chekhov's *Ivanov* on the occasion of his benefit performance, used Chekhov as an intermediary in order to secure the rights to this translation for his 1888 benefit. But Augier's play was already promised elsewhere and Pleshcheyev offered Svetlov *A Bad Man*, a comedy he had translated from the German, as a replacement. It was after apprising Pleshcheyev of the state of negotiations (and possibly in order to prepare him for the startling content of "The Name-Day Party" which he had just sent to *Northern Herald*) that Chekhov added, almost as a postscript, the great credo that forms the bulk of this letter,

certainly the most personal and revealing statement in the entire corpus of his correspondence. Kornei Chukovsky called this letter "a gauntlet flung in the face of an entire age, a rebellion against everything it held sacred."

A more typical Soviet commentator, Maria Semanova, mentioning this letter in her book *Chekhov and Soviet Literature* (1966), hastens to assure her readers that Chekhov's desire to be a free artist and his defense of the most absolute freedom "had nothing whatsoever to do with that 'freedom of the arts' that was militantly preached by the bourgeois writers and was so resolutely condemned by V. I. Lenin in his essay 'Party Organization and Party Literature' " (p. 19).

2. Pleshcheyev's letter which Chekhov is here answering contained an enthusiastic account of Merezhkovsky's recent essay on Chekhov, which Chekhov had not yet seen. On Merezhkovsky, see Letter 27.

3. Anna Mikhailovna Yevreinova was the owner and publisher of *Northern Herald*. Despite Chekhov's apprehensions both she and Pleshcheyev liked "The Name-Day Party" very much.

4. Osip Notovich and Grigory Gradovsky were two unscrupulous left-liberal journalists.

24. To Alexei Pleshcheyev

Moscow,
October 9, 1888

Forgive me for writing on plain paper, Alexei Nikolayevich. There's not a single sheet of letter paper left, and I have neither the time nor the inclination to wait for some to be brought from the store.

Many thanks for reading my story and for your last letter. I value your opinions. I have no one to talk to in Moscow, and I'm glad I have good people in Petersburg who don't find corresponding with me boring. Yes, my dear critic, you are right! The middle part of my story is boring, gray and monotonous.[1] I was lazy and careless when I wrote it. Because I'm used to writing short stories having only a beginning and an end, I get bored and start dragging things out when I realize I'm writing a middle. You're also right to come straight out with your suspicion that I might be afraid of people thinking me a liberal. It gives me an opportunity to take a good deep look into myself. The way I see it, I can be accused of gluttony, drunkenness, frivolity, coldness—of anything at all rather than wishing to seem or not to seem. I've never been secretive. If I am fond of you or Suvorin or Mikhailovsky,[2] I don't ever hide it. If I find my heroine Olga Mikhailovna, a liberal and a former university student, likable, I don't hide it in my story. Everyone should be able to see that. Nor do I hide my respect for the *zemstvo* system, which I like, nor for the practice of trial by jury. What is suspicious in the story is my attempt at balancing off the pluses with the minuses. But it's not conservatism I'm balancing off with liberalism —they're not at the heart of the matter, as far as I'm concerned—it's the lies of my heroes with their truths. Pyotr Dmitrich[3] lies and clowns around in court, he is heavy-handed and a hopeless case, but I can't hide that he is a nice, gentle person by nature. Every other word Olga Mikhailovna utters is a lie, but there is no need to hide that telling lies causes her pain. The Ukrainophile cannot serve as evidence. I did not have Pavel Lintvaryov[4] in mind. Good heavens! Pavel Mikhailovich is an intelligent, modest fellow who can think for himself and never tries to force his ideas on anyone. The Lintvaryovs' Ukrainophilia is love for the warmth, the costumes, the language and their native land. It is appealing and moving. What I had in mind was those idiot pseudo-intellectuals who denigrate Gogol for not having written in Ukrainian and who try to seem better than the average and to play an important role—when in fact they are pale, untalented, wooden ignoramuses with nothing in their heads or hearts—by sticking labels on their foreheads. As for the man of the sixties,[5] I tried to be cautious and brief in depicting him and though he actually deserves an entire sketch to himself, I spared him. He's the sort of faded, inert mediocrity who usurps the sixties. In his last year at the gymnasium he picked up five or six of someone else's ideas, stuffed and mounted them, and will keep mumbling them doggedly until he dies. He's no charlatan; he's a little ninny who believes in what he's mumbling, but has little or no comprehension of what he's mumbling about. He's dense, deaf and heartless. You ought to hear how in the name of the sixties, which he does not understand, he crabs about the present, which he does not see. He vilifies students, schoolgirls, women, writers and everything modern. This for him is the essence of being a man of the sixties. He is as dull as a hole in the ground and as harmful as a gopher for those who believe him. The sixties were a sacred period, and letting those dumb gophers usurp it means vulgarizing it. No, I will not cross out the Ukrainophile or that fake of whom I've had enough! He began to get on my nerves way back in school and he hasn't let up yet. When I write or talk about people like him, it's stupidity and pretension I have in mind, not conservatism and liberalism.

Now a few words about minor matters. When a student at the Academy of Military Medicine is asked what department he's in, he answers simply, "The school of medicine." Only a student who finds the academy-university distinction interesting and isn't bored by it will take the trouble to explain it in normal colloquial language to the general public.[6] You're right about the conversation with the pregnant peasant woman smacking of something in Tolstoy. I realize it now. But that conversation is unimportant; I wedged it in only so the miscarriage wouldn't seem *ex abrupto*. I'm a doctor, and so as not to disgrace myself, I must motivate everything in my stories that has to do with medicine. You're right about the back of the head too. I felt it while I was writing, but I lacked the courage to drop it; it seemed a shame.[7]

You are likewise correct in pointing out that a person who has just wept cannot tell a lie.[8] But you're only partly correct. Lying is like alcoholism. A liar will lie with his dying breath. The other day an officer—an aristocrat and the fiancé of a girl who is a friend of our family—tried to shoot himself to death. The fiancé's father, a general, hasn't gone to the hospital to visit his son and won't go until he learns how society has reacted to the attempted suicide.

I've received the Pushkin Prize![9] Oh, how I wish I could have gotten those five hundred rubles in the summer when I could enjoy them. In the winter they'll only go to waste.

Tomorrow I'll sit myself down and get to work on the story for the Garshin anthology.[10] I'll do my best. As soon as it starts taking shape, I'll let you know and make it definite. It probably won't be ready before next Sunday. I'm still excited and haven't been working well.

Put down the Lintvaryovs for one copy of the book, and Lensky the actor for another. But I'll be sending you a list of my subscribers anyway. How much will the book cost?

The answer to Svetlov was mailed out long ago.

Sumbatov's *Chains* is quite good. Lensky does a superb job in the role of Proporyev.[11] Keep well and happy. The prize has upset my routine. My thoughts are in more of a whirl than ever. All my family sends you its best and I send my best to yours. It's cold.

Yours,
A. Chekhov

Is there really no "ideology" in the last story? You once told me that my stories lack an element of protest, that they have neither sympathies nor antipathies. But doesn't the story protest against lying from start to finish? Isn't that an ideology? It isn't? Well, I guess that means either I don't know how to bite or I'm a flea.

I'm afraid of the censors. They'll cross out the parts where I describe how Pyotr Dmitrich presides at court. But that's how all courts are chaired these days.

Oh, how sick you must be of me!

1. Chekhov is replying to a detailed critique of "The Name-Day Party" which Pleshcheyev sent him after accepting the story for *Northern Herald*.

2. When Chekhov's work first began appearing in *Northern Herald*, Korolenko made a determined effort to effect a rapprochement between Chekhov on the one hand and the journal's leading literary critic Mikhailovsky and its star fiction writer Gleb Uspensky on the other. But Korolenko's plan did not work. Uspensky was clearly resentful and jealous of Chekhov's success, while Mikhailovsky attempted to convert Chekhov to his own mode of thinking. After the publication of "The Steppe," Mikhailovsky wrote to Chekhov, recognizing his tremendous talent but calling his new work shapeless and comparing it to the stroll of a mindless young giant who has no idea where he is going or why. Mikhailovsky urged Chekhov to devote his talent to "worthwhile" causes and ideals and demanded that he break his "disgraceful" association with Suvorin and *New Times*. It was after Chekhov failed to comply with any of this advice that Mikhailovsky's most virulent attacks on his work began to appear in the press.

3. The husband of the heroine in "The Name-Day Party."

4. The elder son of the Lintvaryov family, whom Pleshcheyev met when he visited Chekhov in Luka that summer. In the original version of "The Name-Day Party" there was a satirical vignette of a morose, fanatical Ukrainophile whom Pleshcheyev thought Chekhov had modeled on Pavel Lintvaryov. In the final version of the story, prepared for publication in book form, Chekhov removed this character.

5. Another satirical figure in the story, a man who believes himself to be the keeper of the flame of the age of the great reforms and therefore "yearns for the beautiful past and rejects the present." He was also deleted by Chekhov in the final version of the story, apparently in response to Pleshcheyev's criticism.

6. A student from St. Petersburg who appears episodically in the story tells the heroine that he attends medical school. Pleshcheyev objected that there was no medical school at St. Petersburg University and suggested that Chekhov have him say, "I attend the Medical Academy in St. Petersburg."

7. Another part of Pleshcheyev's critique concerned the similarity of the heroine's discussion of childbirth with a peasant woman and her sudden focusing of attention on the back of her husband's head to certain episodes in Tolstoy's *Anna Karenina*.

8. Pleshcheyev had referred to Pyotr's "posturings and clowning" after his wife's miscarriage.

9. Two days earlier, a four-man jury (one of whom was Grigorovich) convened by the Imperial Academy of Sciences voted to award Chekhov's collection *In the Twilight* one-half of the Pushkin Prize for literature, cutting the amount of the award from 1,000 rubles to 500. Three years before, in 1885, the maudlin poetaster Nadson was awarded the full amount, to the acclaim of the entire Russian press.

As Alexander Chekhov's letters to his brother of October 18 and 22, 1887, make clear, it was Suvorin who did all the work and lobbying to secure Chekhov's nomination for the prize.

10. The young writer Vsevolod Garshin, a fervent admirer and champion

of Chekhov's work, committed suicide early in 1888. Chekhov was asked to contribute a story to an anthology honoring Garshin's memory. Because guilt and pain were among Garshin's principal themes, Chekhov chose as his subject a painful encounter of a compassionate young man with the evils of prostitution. The result was "An Attack of Nerves."

11. The actor Alexander Lensky, with whom Chekhov soon established friendly relations, scored a great success in the role of the villain Proporyev in Prince Sumbatov's melodrama *Chains*. The play and the character are also alluded to in Letter 14 as having helped to form the world view of Dr. Lvov in *Ivanov*.

25. To Dmitry Grigorovich

Moscow,
October 9, 1888

It gave me great joy, dear Dmitry Vasilyevich, to hear that you've finally recovered and returned to Russia. People who have seen you write me that you're entirely well and as vigorous as ever, that you have even given a reading of your new novel, and that you now have a long beard.

If the pains in your chest have disappeared, they probably won't come back, but the bronchitis is probably still giving you trouble; it may die down in the summer and then flare up again in the winter if you at all neglect it. Bronchitis isn't dangerous in and of itself, but it keeps you from sleeping, wears you out and upsets you. Smoke as little as you can, avoid quass and beer, stay away from smoking rooms, dress warmly in damp weather, don't read aloud and don't walk as fast as you usually do. These minor precautions are just as irritating and confining as the bronchitis itself, but what can you do?

I'm also happy to have received a letter from you. Your letters are brief, like good poems. I don't see you very often, yet I have the feeling, I'm even quite certain, that if you and Suvorin were not around and about in Petersburg I would lose my equilibrium and write terrible drivel.

Of course I was very lucky to get the prize. If I were to say it didn't excite me, I'd be lying. I feel as if I had just graduated, not only from the gymnasium and the university, but from some additional third place as well. I spent yesterday and today pacing back and forth like a lovesick boy, doing nothing but thinking, and getting no work done.

Of course—and of this there can be no doubt—I do not owe the prize to myself. There are young writers who are better and more needed than I am, Korolenko, for example, who is quite a good writer and an honorable man, and would have been awarded the prize if he had submitted his book. It was Polonsky[1] who first thought of nominating me for the prize, and Suvorin backed him up and sent my book to the Academy. And then you, being a member of the Academy, stood up for me there.

You must admit that if it hadn't been for you three I wouldn't have had any more chance of seeing that prize than I do of seeing my own ears. I'm not going to be modest and assure you that you three were biased or that I do not deserve the prize, and so on. To say that would have been old hat and a bore. I only want to say that I do not owe this good fortune to myself. I offer my infinite thanks, and I will continue being grateful the rest of my life.

I haven't done any work at all for minor journals this year. I publish my shorter stories in *New Times*, and the longer ones I give to the *Northern Herald*, which pays me a hundred fifty rubles for sixteen pages of text. I won't abandon *New Times*, though, because I feel attached to Suvorin; and anyway, *New Times* is not a minor newspaper. I don't have any definite plans for the future. I feel an urge to write a novel, and I have a marvelous theme. At times I'm overcome by a passionate desire to sit down and start work, but I don't seem to have the energy. I have already begun and I'm afraid to go on. I've decided to take my time, to write only during the best hours, to revise and polish. I'm going to spend several years on it; I don't dare write it out all at once in one year, I'm terrified of my impotence, and anyway there's no need to hurry. I have a talent for disliking this year what I wrote last year, and I have the feeling that I'll be stronger next year than I am now. And that's why I'm in no hurry to risk a definitive decision at this point. After all, if the novel turns out to be bad, it could mean that my cause is lost forever. All the ideas, women, men and nature scenes I have amassed for the novel will remain whole and unharmed. I won't squander them on trivia, I promise. The novel encompasses several families and an entire district—its forests, rivers, ferries and railroad. Two figures, one male and one female, form the district's focal point, and the pawns group themselves around them. I still lack a political, religious and philosophical world view—I change it every month—and so I'll have to limit myself to descriptions of how my heroes love, marry, give birth, die, and how they speak.[2]

Until the novel's hour strikes, I'll go on writing what I like, namely stories of sixteen to twenty-four pages—and shorter. Stretching insignificant themes to cover large canvases is boring, though profitable. Touching on major themes and wasting precious images on urgent piecework is a pity. I'll just have to wait for a more suitable time.

I have no right to forbid my brother to sign his own name. Before he began signing his stories, he asked my permission, and I told him I had nothing against it.[3]

I had a wonderful summer. I lived in Kharkov, in Poltava Province, and went to the Crimea, Batum, Baku, and experienced the Georgian military road. I have many impressions. If I lived in the Caucasus, I'd write fairy tales there. An amazing country!

I won't get to Petersburg before November, but I'll report to you the day I arrive. In the meantime, let me thank you once again with all my heart and wish you health and happiness.

Your sincerely devoted,
A. Chekhov

1. Yakov Polonsky (1820–98) was the author of some of the more attractive lyrics written in Russia in the middle of the nineteenth century. His poems were highly regarded by Turgenev and Alexander Blok and some of them were set to music by Tchaikovsky. Polonsky is also the poet of whom Solzhenitsyn wrote in his prose poem "The Poet's Grave." An early admirer of Chekhov, he dedicated a poem to him and Chekhov reciprocated by dedicating to Polonsky his story "Happiness."

2. This was the subsequently destroyed *Stories from the Lives of My Friends.*

3. Grigorovich had expressed objections to the publication of Alexander Chekhov's articles under the signature "A. Chekhov."

26. To Alexei Suvorin

Moscow,
October 27, 1888

Yezhov[1] is no sparrow; he's more like a puppy who (to use the elegant language of the hunt) has not yet reached doghood. All he does is run around sniffing and pouncing upon birds and frogs indiscriminately. I'm still having trouble figuring out his breed and capabilities. His youth, decency and unspoiled nature (in the Moscow-newspaper sense) speak strongly in his favor.

I sometimes preach heresies, but I haven't once gone so far as to deny that problematic questions have a place in art. In conversations with my fellow writers I always insist that it is not the artist's job to try to answer narrowly specialized questions. It is bad for the artist to take on something he doesn't understand. We have specialists for dealing with special questions; it is their job to make judgments about the peasant communes, the fate of capitalism, the evils of intemperance, and about boots[2] and female complaints. The artist must pass judgment only on what he understands; his range is as limited as that of any other specialist—that's what I keep repeating and insisting upon. Anyone who says the artist's field is all answers and no questions has never done any writing or had any dealings with imagery. The artist observes, selects, guesses and synthesizes. The very fact of these actions presupposes a question; if he hadn't asked himself a question at the start, he would have nothing to guess and nothing to select. To put it briefly, I will conclude with some psychiatry: if you deny that creativity involves questions and intent, you have to admit that the artist creates without premeditation or purpose, in a state of unthinking emotionality. And so if any author were to boast to me that he'd written a story from pure inspiration without first having thought over his intentions, I'd call him a madman.

You are right to demand that an author take conscious stock of what he is doing, but you are confusing two concepts: *answering the questions* and *formulating them correctly.* Only the latter is required of an author. There's not a single question answered in *Anna Karenina* or *Eugene Onegin*, but they are still fully satisfying works because the questions they raise are all formulated correctly. It is the duty of the court to formulate the questions correctly, but it is up to each member of the jury to answer them according to his own preference.

Yezhov is not yet fully grown. Another writer I've recommended to your attention, Gruzinsky (Lazarev),[3] is more talented, intelligent and strong.

I saw off Alexei Alexeyevich[4] with an injunction to go to bed no later than midnight. Spending whole nights in work and conversation is just as harmful as staying out all night carousing. He looked more cheerful in Moscow than he did in Feodosia. We had a good time together, each according to his means: he treated me to operas, I treated him to bad meals.

My *Bear* is playing at Korsh's tomorrow. I've written another farce, too; it has two male roles and one female.[5]

You write that the hero of my "Name-Day Party" is a figure worth developing. Good Lord, I'm not an insentient brute, I realize that. I realize I hack up my characters, ruin them, and I waste good material. To tell you the truth, I would have been only too glad to spend half a year on "The Name-Day Party." I like taking my own good time about things, and see nothing attractive about slapdash publication. I would gladly describe *all* of my hero, describe him with feeling, understanding and deliberation,[6] I'd describe his emotions while his wife was in labor, the trial, his sense of disgust after being acquitted, I'd describe the midwife and doctors having tea in the middle of the night, I'd describe the rain. . . . It would be sheer pleasure for me, because I love digging deep and rummaging. But what can I do? I began the story on September

10th with the thought that I have to finish it by October 5th at the latest; if I miss the deadline I'll be going back on my word and will be left without any money. I write the beginning calmly and don't hold myself back, but by the middle I start feeling uneasy and apprehensive that the story will come out too long. I have to keep in mind that the *Northern Herald* is low in funds and that I am one of its more expensive contributors. That's why my beginning always seems as promising as if I'd started a novel, the middle is crumpled together and timid, and the end is all fireworks, like the end of a brief sketch. Whether you like it or not, the first thing you have to worry about when you're working up a story is its framework. From your mass of heroes and semi-heroes you choose one individual, a wife or a husband, place him against the background, and portray only that person and emphasize only him. The others you scatter in the background like so much small change. The result is something like the firmament: one large moon surrounded by a mass of tiny stars. But the moon doesn't work, because it can only be understood once the other stars are understandable, and the stars are not sufficiently delineated. So instead of literature I get a patchwork quilt.[7] What can I do? I don't know. I have no idea. I'll just have to trust to all-healing time.

To tell the whole truth, even though I did receive the prize, I still have not begun my literary career. The plots for five stories and two novels are languishing away in my head. One of the novels I conceived so long ago that some of the characters have grown out of date before my ever getting them down on paper. I have a whole army of people in my head begging to be let out and ordered what to do. Everything I've written to date is nonsense compared with what I would like to have written and would be overjoyed to be writing. It doesn't make any difference to me whether I'm writing "The Name-Day Party," or "Lights," or a farce, or a letter to a friend—it's all boring, mechanical and vapid and at times I feel chagrined on behalf of some critic who ascribes great significance to, say, my "Lights," I feel as if I'm deceiving him with my writings, just as I deceive many people with my now serious, now inordinately cheerful face. I don't like being a success. The themes sitting around in my head are irritated by and jealous of what I've already written. It annoys me to think that all the nonsense has already been written, while all the good things lie abandoned in a stockroom like unsold books. Of course a great deal of my lament is exaggerated; much of it is only *my imagination*, but it does contain a measure of truth, a large measure. What do I call good? The images that I feel are best, that I love and jealously hold on to so as not to waste and mangle them on short-order "Name-Day Parties." If my love errs, then I am wrong, but it's also possible that it does not. I am either a conceited fool or an organism genuinely capable of being a fine writer. Everything now being written leaves me cold and indifferent, whereas everything stored in my head interests, moves and excites me, from which I conclude that everyone is on the wrong track and I alone know the secret of what needs to be done. That's most likely what all writers think. But the devil himself would break his neck over these problems.

Money won't help me figure out what I should do. An extra thousand rubles won't settle my problem, and a hundred thousand is a castle in the air. Besides, whenever I do have money (maybe because I'm so unused to it, I don't know), I become extremely carefree and lazy; I feel as if I could wade across the seas. I need privacy and time.

Forgive me for monopolizing your attention with my own person. My pen got the better of me. For some reason I can't get down to work these days.

Thank you for agreeing to print those little articles of mine.[8] For God's sake, don't stand on ceremony; shorten them, lengthen them, change them around, throw them out, do whatever you like. As Korsh says, I give you *carte blanche*. I'll be glad if they don't take up someone else's place.

Look up the section on sending money through the mails in your yearbook. Your Alexei Alexeyevich has been making up his own regulations. His medical section is beneath all criticism—you can pass that on to him as the opinion of a specialist![9]

Write me the Latin name for Anna Ivanovna's eye ailment, and I'll write you back whether it's serious or not. If atropine has been prescribed, it's serious, though not absolutely. And what's wrong with Nastya? If you're thinking of curing your boredom in Moscow, you're wrong: the boredom here is something terrible. Many writers and critics have been arrested, including that busybody Goltsev, author of "The Ninth Symphony."[10] Mamyshev,[11] who visited me today, is trying to get one of them out.

Regards to all.

Yours,
A. Chekhov

There's a mosquito flying around my room. Where did it come from? Thanks for the eye-catching advertisements of my books.

1. Chekhov's spectacular ascent as a serious writer after he began publishing in *Northern Herald* occasionally brought forth the envy and resentment of his erstwhile associates from his humor-magazine days. Nikolai Yezhov (1862–1942), a very minor writer and journalist, is a particularly striking example of this. Helped and befriended by Chekhov, who recommended him

to Suvorin and other publishers, Yezhov maintained an outwardly friendly relationship with him while conducting a low-key campaign of gossip and slander behind his back (as the memoirs and journals of their mutual acquaintances have subsequently revealed). After Chekhov's death, Yezhov published in 1909 a scurrilous essay in which he endeavored to prove that Chekhov was a petty and dishonest man and an inept writer.

2. "To make judgments . . . about boots" paraphrases the ending of Pushkin's poem "The Bootmaker," in which the Greek painter Apelles advises a presumptuous bootmaker to pass judgment only on things he can understand.

3. Alexander Lazarev (1861–1927), whose pen name was A. Gruzinsky, was a now-forgotten minor writer whom Chekhov knew in his humor-magazine period and whom he helped to gain access to publication in *New Times* and other major newspapers and journals. Lazarev wrote a whole series of affectionate memoirs about his association with Chekhov (the only portion of his writings that keeps his name alive today), in some of which he polemicized against the allegations of his one-time friend and colleague Yezhov.

4. Suvorin's son, who had visited Chekhov in Moscow.

5. Chekhov's farce *The Bear* was performed for the first time on October 28, 1888. Berated by the critics, it immediately became his most popular work with actors, audiences and, above all, with amateurs. It remained a major source of income for the rest of his life ("I live off the labors of my bear" he was to write on several occasions). The other farce mentioned is *The Proposal.*

6. The same Griboyedov quotation that appeared in Letter 19.

7. "Patchwork quilt" is our replacement for "Trishka's Coat" of the original. Chekhov is referring to a fable by Krylov in which a peasant ruins a good coat by cutting parts out of it to patch the elbows.

8. In October of 1888, *New Times* published two of Chekhov's most significant editorial articles (both appeared anonymously). "Moscow Hypocrites" was a denunciation of that city's municipal administration for having abrogated the recently passed piece of labor legislation that cut Sunday working hours of salesmen in Moscow stores to three (instead of ten to twelve hours on Sundays as well as on all the other days, as was the practice previously). Chekhov's particular indignation was aroused by the rationale that, with a shortened working day, the younger salesmen were sure to go carousing instead of attending church. His other editorial was a paean to explorers such as Przhevalsky and Livingstone and to the moral uplift implicit in their lives.

9. This despite Chekhov's own assistance with the medical portions of the yearbook (something like a Russian version of the *World Almanac*).

10. The liberal editor Viktor Goltsev, subsequently a friend and correspondent of Chekhov's, was placed under arrest for three weeks for harboring a political prisoner escaped from Siberia.

11. Vasily Mamyshev was a criminal investigator in Zvenigorod and Suvorin's brother-in-law.

27. To Alexei Suvorin

Moscow,
November 3, 1888

Greetings, Alexei Sergeyevich. I am presently donning my tails to go to the opening of the Society for Arts and Literature, to which I've been invited as a guest. There's going to be a formal ball. I don't know what sort of goals or resources the Society has or who its members are, and so on. All I do know is that it is headed by Fedotov,[1] an author of many plays. I am glad not to have been elected a member, because I have no desire to lay down twenty-five rubles in dues for the right to be bored. If anything interesting or amusing happens, I'll write you about it. Lensky's going to give a reading of my stories.

There's an article about yours truly in the *Northern Herald* (for November) by the poet Merezhkovsky.[2] It's a long article, but I commend the conclusion to your attention; it is typical. Merezhkovsky is still very young; he's a student—in science, possibly.[3] Anyone who has mastered the wisdom of the scientific method and therefore knows how to think scientifically undergoes any number of delightful temptations. Archimedes wanted to turn the earth upside-down, and present-day hotheads want to embrace the scientifically unembraceable: they want to discover physical laws for creativity, they want to grasp the general law and the formulae by which the artist, who feels them instinctively, creates landscapes, novels, pieces of music and so on. These formulae probably do exist in nature. We know that nature has a, b, c, d, do, re, mi, fa, sol, and curves, straight lines, circles, squares, green, red, blue. . . . We know that all this in a given combination will yield a melody or a poem or a picture, just as simple chemical elements in a given combination yield a tree or a stone or the sea, but all we know is that they are combined; yet the principle according to which they are combined is concealed from us. Anyone who is at home with the scientific method senses intuitively that a piece of music and a tree have something in common and that both one and the other are created in accordance with identically regular and simple laws. Hence the question of what these laws are. Hence the temptation to write a physiology of creativity (Boborykin) and among the younger and more diffident to make reference to science and the laws of nature (Merezhkovsky). A physiology of creativity probably does exist in nature, but all dreams of it must be abandoned at the outset. No good will come of critics taking a scientific stance: they'll waste ten years, they'll write a lot of ballast and confuse the issue still further—and that's all they'll do. It's always good to think scientifically; the trouble is that thinking scientifically about art will inevitably end up by degenerating into a search for the "cells" or "centers" in charge of creative ability, whereupon some dull-witted German will discover them somewhere in the temporal lobes, another will disagree, a third German will agree, and a Russian will skim through an article on cells and dash off a study for the *Northern Herald*, and the *Herald of Europe* will take to analyzing the study, and for three years an epidemic of utter nonsense will hover in the Russian air, providing dullards with earnings and popularity and engendering nothing but irritation among intelligent people.

For those who are haunted by the scientific method and whom God has granted the rare talent of thinking scientifically, there is in my opinion only one way out: the philosophy of creativity. By gathering together all the best creations of artists through the ages and applying the scientific method, we can grasp the common denominator that causes them to resemble one another and lies at the root of their value. That common denominator will then be law. Works usually called immortal have a great deal in common; remove the element they have in common, and the work loses its value and charm. That element is therefore indispensable and constitutes the *conditio sine qua non* for every work aspiring to immortality.

Writing criticism is more useful to the younger generation than writing poetry. Merezhkovsky writes smoothly and youthfully, but on every page he loses his nerve and makes reservations and concessions—a sure sign he himself isn't quite clear on where he stands. He honors me with the name of a poet, my stories he calls novellas, and my heroes failures—all the old clichés. It's high time we gave up these failures, superfluous men and so on, and thought up something on our own. Merezhkovsky calls my monk, the one who composes Orthodox hymns, a failure.[4] How is he a failure? God grant everyone a life like his: he believed in God, he had enough to eat and he was creatively gifted. Classifying people as successes and failures is looking at human nature from a narrow, biased vantage point. Are you a success or not? Am I? What about Napoleon? And your Vasily?[5] Where is the criterion? You have to be a god to distinguish the successes from the failures without making a mistake. I'm off to the ball.

I'm back from the ball. The Society's goal is "unity." A learned German once taught a cat, a mouse, a hawk and a sparrow to eat out of the same plate. That German had a system; this Society has none. It was deadly dull. Everyone wandered from room to room pretending not to be bored. A young lady sang, Lensky read my story (someone in the audience said, "A pretty weak story!" and Levinsky[6] was stupid and cruel enough to interrupt him with "Why, there's the author! Let me introduce you to him" whereupon the man nearly sank through the floor with embarrassment), there was some dancing, we had a miserable supper, the waiters short-changed us. If indeed actors, painters, writers and critics do in fact constitute the elite of society, it's too bad. A fine society that must be where the elite is so poor in color, desire and intention, so poor in taste, beautiful women and initiative. By putting up some Japanese figure in the vestibule, sticking a Chinese parasol in the corner and draping a rug over the banister, they think they're being artistic. They've got Chinese parasols, but no newspapers. If when an artist decorates his apartment he can't do any better than a museum-piece with a halberd or shield, and fans on the walls, if that's really the way he wants it, if he deliberately plans it that way, then he's no artist, he's a sanctimonious ape.[7]

I received a letter from Leykin today. He writes he's been to see you. He's a kindhearted and harmless person, but bourgeois to the marrow of his bones. Whenever he visits anyone or says anything, he always has an ulterior motive. He carefully thinks out his every word, and stores away your every word for future reference, no matter how casually you may have meant it, in the firm conviction that he, Leykin, has to have things this way, because otherwise his books won't sell, his enemies will triumph, his friends will abandon him and his shareholders will disown him. A fox fears every minute for his skin and so does Leykin. A subtle diplomat he is! If he talks about me, it means he wants to take a jab at the "nihilists" (Mikhailovsky), who have spoiled me, and at my brother Alexander, whom he hates. His letters to me are full of warnings, caveats, advice and confidences. That miserable, lame martyr! He could live out his life in peace and quiet, but a demon keeps getting in his way.

A slight *calamity* has befallen my family. I'll tell you about it when we get together. A thunderbolt has descended on the head of one of my brothers, and it prevents me from working and robs me of peace and quiet.[8] What a job it is, O Creator, to head a household![9]

French women put atropine in their eyes to be coquettish and make their pupils bigger, and there are no side effects.[10]

Petipa is reading Maslov's play.[11] Korsh's theater is in an uproar. The steam coffeepot exploded and scalded Rybchinskaya's face, Glama-Meshcherskaya has gone to Petersburg, Solovtsov's lifelong friend Glebova is ill, etc.[12] There's no one left to act, nobody listens to anybody else, all they do is scream and argue. . . . A lavish costume play will apparently be turned down in horror, and I would so like to have seen them stage *The Seducer of Seville*. Not only for Maslov's sake, but because I have an attachment to the stage and a certain amount of self-esteem. We've got to do whatever we can to see that the theater passes from the hands of the grocers into the hands of writers and critics. Otherwise it is doomed.

The coffeepot has slaughtered my *Bear*. With Rybchinskaya sick, there's no one to play in it.

We all send our best. My warmest regards to Anna Ivanovna, Nastya and Borya.

Yours,
A. Chekhov

It's best to publish one-acters in the summer; winter is bad for them. In the summer I will supply a one-acter a month, and in the winter I'll have to do without the pleasure.[13]

Enroll me as a member in the Literary Society. I'll go to their meetings when I'm in Petersburg.[14]

1. Alexander Fedotov, the husband of the actress Glykeria Fedotova, was mainly known as the head of a drama school and a stage director, although he also wrote plays.

2. Although Dmitry Merezhkovsky (1866–1941) is remembered in the West, if he is at all, for the historical novels he wrote at the turn of the century (his *Romance of Leonardo da Vinci* was recently shown to have served as a basic source for Sigmund Freud's psychoanalysis of Leonardo), his most durable contribution to Russian literature lies not in his novels or in his facile and voluminous verse, but in his literary criticism. His articles on Chekhov, published in *Northern Herald* over Mikhailovsky's objections and at the insistence of the journal's publisher Anna Yevreinova, are not particularly perceptive or original, but they are the beginning of the evolution which enabled Merezhkovsky by the turn of the century to write his book on Tolstoy and Dostoyevsky, which is the beginning of all meaningful modern Dostoyevsky criticism, and his very imaginative study of Gogol, which put an end to the short-sighted view that Gogol was an ethnographic realist. It was Merezhkovsky who more than anyone else brought back into Russian criticism the understanding that literature has philosophical, psychological and aesthetic dimensions in addition to social ones and that the erotic and mystical aspects of the human spirit, as reflected in literature, deserve to be studied and understood rather than shunned and ignored. Because of Merezhkovsky's anti-materialistic views and his emigation after the Revolution, his significance is systematically downgraded and minimized in Soviet literary studies.

3. Merezhkovsky had actually majored in history and philology at St. Petersburg University, not in natural sciences as Chekhov had believed.

4. The monk Ieronim, who appears in Chekhov's story "On Easter Eve."

5. Suvorin's manservant.

6. The publisher of the humor magazine *The Alarm Clock*, where some of Chekhov's earliest published work appeared.

7. Chekhov later moved some of the décor mentioned in this paragraph into the apartment of the heroine of his story "The Grasshopper."

8. Chekhov's brother Nikolai, through sheer carelessness, failed for five consecutive years to get his identity card (which everyone in Russia was required to have by law) renewed. This was a grave offense punishable by imprisonment or forcible drafting into the army. It took considerable effort on the part of Chekhov and his influential friends to extricate Nikolai from his predicament.

9. A paraphrase of the last two lines of Act I of Griboyedov's *The Misfortune of Being Clever*, which read:

> What a job it is, O Creator,
> To be the father of a grown-up daughter!

10. In his previous letter, Chekhov had told Suvorin that the atropine prescribed for Anna Suvorina's eye ailment might indicate that the condition was a serious one. This alarmed Suvorin and now Chekhov is trying to reassure him.

11. Alexei Maslov (who published articles under the pen name of Bezhetsky) was regularly employed by Suvorin at the St. Petersburg office of *New Times*. He had asked Chekhov to offer his play (*The Seducer of Seville*) to the Moscow impresario Fyodor Korsh. Maslov was also a close friend of the composer Tchaikovsky; Suvorin's journal contains some rather intimate details about Tchaikovsky's affair with the poet Alexei Apukhtin, as told to Suvorin by Maslov. The Russian actor Marius Petipa was the son of the famous French choreographer Marius Petipa.

12. Nikolai Solovtsov and Natalia Rybchinskaya played the leading roles during the original run of *The Bear*. After Rybchinskaya's accident, Alexandra Glama-Meshcherskaya and Maria Glebova (Solovtsov's wife) were proposed as replacements but neither was available. Solovtsov was the actor for whom *The Bear* was written and to whom it was dedicated.

13. Since Suvorin's letters are missing, it is not clear for just what Chekhov proposed to supply these one-acters.

14. The St. Petersburg branch of the Literary Society. Chekhov's application for membership was almost blackballed because of his supposed "lack of views and principles."

28. To Alexei Suvorin

Moscow,
between November 20 and 25, 1888[1]

. . . Oh what a story I've started! I'll bring it along and ask you to read it. The subject is love. I've chosen the form of a fictionalized sketch. A decent man runs off with another decent man's wife and writes position papers about it: one when he lives with her and another when he breaks up with her. In passing I mention the theater, the prejudices involved in "ideological incompatibility," the Georgian Military Road, family life, the contemporary intellectual's inability to cope with family life, Pechorin, Onegin, Mount Kazbek[2] . . . Good heavens, what a hodgepodge! My brain is flapping its wings, but I don't know where to fly.

You write that writers are God's chosen people. I won't argue. Shcheglov calls me the Potyomkin[3] of literature, so I'm not the one to speak of the thorny path and disappointments and the like. I don't know if I've ever suffered more than shoemakers, mathematicians or train conductors; I don't know who is making pronouncements through my lips, God or someone slightly worse. Let me bring up just one minor irritating point which I have experienced and you probably have too. Here is what I mean. You and I like ordinary people; they like us because they regard us as out of the ordinary. I, for instance, am forever being invited out and wined and dined like the general at the wedding. My sister is indignant at being invited everywhere merely because she's the writer's sister. No one wants to like the ordinary people in us. Consequently, if tomorrow we were to appear as ordinary mortals in the eyes of our acquaintances, they'd stop liking us and pity us instead. Now that's bad. And what's just as bad is that the things they like in us are often the things we neither like nor respect in ourselves. It's bad that I was right when I wrote the discussion on being famous between the engineer and the professor in my "First-Class Passenger."[4]

I'm going to retire to a farm. The hell with them. You have your Feodosia.

And speaking about Feodosia and the Tatars, the Tatars have had their land stolen from them, but no one gives a thought to their welfare. There is a need for Tatar schools. Why don't you write an article suggesting that the Ministry turn over the money they spend on Dorpat Wurst University where Useless Germans study to schools for the Tatars, who are useful to Russia? I'd write about this myself, but I don't know how.[5]

Leykin has sent me another one of those hilarious farces of his own making. He is really one of a kind.

Keep well and happy.

Yours,
A. Chekhov

Tell Maslov that the fate of his play is being decided and that it could go either way. The one Spanish play[6] they put on was a flop, so they're hesitant about putting on another one.

1. The beginning of this letter is missing; it has been dated on the basis of internal evidence.

2. This is the earliest draft of "The Duel," which Chekhov was to complete three years later. Pechorin and Onegin are the heroes of Lermontov's *A Hero of Our Time* and Pushkin's *Eugene Onegin,* respectively. Mount Kazbek in the Caucasus has appeared prominently in works of Russian writers, ranging from Lermontov (*The Demon*) to Nabokov (*Ada*).

3. The invidious comparison of Chekhov to the favorite of Catherine the Great (often spelled Potemkin) was made by Shcheglov and several other younger writers of the eighties. The implication is that Chekhov owed his success to good luck rather than to ability.

4. Each of these two men in Chekhov's story, who share a compartment on a train, believes himself to be a celebrity in his own field and each is surprised to learn that the other man has never heard of him.

5. Chekhov's fondness for the Tatars was expressed in the appealingly depicted Tatar characters in the two stories he wrote after his return from Sakhalin, "The Duel" and "In Exile." It ripened into a systematic championing of Tatar causes after Chekhov established his residence in the Crimea (cf. Letter 128, note 3).

6. The Spanish playwright José Echegaray's *The Great Galeoto* was a flop when presented by Korsh's company. Maslov's play was "Spanish" in terms of its setting only.

29. To Alexander Chekhov[1]

Moscow,
January 2, 1889

O Most Wise Secretary,

I wish your radiant person and your progeny a very happy new year. I hope you win two hundred thousand and become a state councilor on active duty, but most of all that you remain healthy and supplied with our daily bread in sufficient quantity for a glutton like you.

The last time I was in Petersburg we met and parted as if we had had some sort of misunderstanding. I'll be back soon, and to put an end to the misunderstanding I feel I must in all conscience make the following sincere statement. I was seriously angry at you and left in anger, and this I will confess. During my very first visit I was repelled by your *shocking*, completely unprecedented treatment of Natalia Alexandrovna[2] and the cook. Forgive me please, but treating women like that, no matter who they are, is unworthy of a decent, loving human being. What heavenly or earthly power has given you the right to make them your slaves? Constant profanity of the most vile variety, a raised voice, reproaches, sudden whims at breakfast and dinner, eternal complaints about a life of forced and loathsome labor—isn't all that an expression of blatant despotism? No matter how insignificant or guilty a woman may be, no matter how close she is to you, you have no right to sit around without pants in her presence, be drunk in her presence, utter words even factory workers don't use when they see women nearby. You think of decency and good breeding as prejudices, but you have to draw the line somewhere—at feminine frailty perhaps, or the children, or the poetry of life if there's no prose left. No decent husband or lover will permit himself to talk [. . .] with a woman, or coarsely, for the sake of a joke, to treat the marital bed with irony, [. . .]. That corrupts a woman and takes her away from the God she believes in. A man who respects a woman, a man who is well bred and really loving will not permit himself to be seen without his pants by the maid or yell, "Katka, let me have the pisspot!" at the top of his lungs. When men sleep with their wives at night, they behave decently; in the morning they rush to put on a tie so as not to offend the woman by their improper appearance, to wit, their careless dress. This point may be pedantic, but it is based on something you'll understand if you think about what a terrifying educational role the environment and all sorts of trifles play in man's life. The difference between a woman who sleeps between clean sheets and the woman who sacks out on filthy ones and roars with laughter when her lover [. . .] is like the difference between a salon and a low dive.

Children are sacred and pure. Even thieves and crocodiles place them among the ranks of the angels. Whatever pit we may be crawling into, we must surround them with an atmosphere befitting their rank. You cannot with impunity use filthy language in their presence, insult your servants, or snarl at Natalia Alexandrovna: "Will you get the hell away from me! I'm not holding you here!" You must not make them the plaything of your moods, tenderly kissing them one minute and frenziedly stamping at them the next. It's better not to love at all than to love with a despotic love. Hate is much more honest than the love of a Nasr-ed-Din, who sometimes makes his dearly beloved Persians satraps and other times impales them on stakes. You shouldn't take the names of your children in vain, and you have the habit of calling every kopeck you give or want to give to someone "money taken from the children." Taking money away from someone implies that *you've given* some in the first place, and talking about your own charity and handouts is not particularly becoming. It's like begrudging somebody something. Most people live for their families, but rare is the person who dares to think himself praiseworthy for doing so, and it would be hard to find anyone courageous enough to say as you do: "I'm taking it away from my children," whenever he lends anyone a ruble. You really have to lack respect for your children or their sanctity to be able to say—when you are well fed, well dressed and tipsy every day—that *all* your salary goes for the children. Stop it.

Let me ask you to recall that it was despotism and lying that ruined your mother's youth. Despotism and lying so mutilated our childhood that it's sickening and frightening to think about it. Remember the horror and disgust we felt in those times when Father threw a tantrum at dinner over too much salt in the soup and called Mother a fool. There is no way Father can forgive himself all that now.

Despotism is three times criminal. If the Day of Judgment is not a fantasy, you will get worse treatment at the hands of the Sanhedrin than Chokhov and Gavrilov.[3] It's no secret to you that the heavens have given you something ninety-nine out of a hundred men lack: you are by nature infinitely magnanimous and gentle. That's why a hundred times more is demanded of you. Besides, you've been to the university and are considered a journalist.

Your difficult situation, the bad disposition of the women it falls to your lot to live with, the idiocy of your cooks, your forced and loathsome labor and all the rest cannot serve to justify your despotism. It's better to be the victim than the hangman.

Natalia Alexandrovna, the cook and the children are weak and defenseless. They have no rights over you, while you have the right to throw them out the door at any moment and have a good laugh at their weakness if you so desire. Don't let them feel that right of yours.

I have interceded to the best of my ability, and my conscience is clear. Try to be magnanimous and consider the misunderstanding settled. If you are a direct and not a devious person, you won't say that this letter has any bad motives, that for instance I wrote it to insult you or was inspired by rancor. All I'm looking for in our relationship is sincerity. I have no desire for anything more. We have nothing else to contest.

Write me that you too have stopped being angry and that our bone of contention no longer exists.

The whole family sends its regards.

Yours,
A. Chekhov

1. Alexander Chekhov (1855–1913), Chekhov's oldest brother, was the first of the family to hit on the idea of writing and publishing for money. However, for all of Alexander's activities as a fiction writer, journalist and trade-journal editor, he was rapidly overtaken in literary ability not only by Anton but by their younger brother Mikhail as well. He spent most of his

life in St. Petersburg, where he was regularly employed at *New Times*. His sense of unrealized ambition was aggravated by alcoholism and by a series of unfortunate common-law marriages, all of which combined to make him an embittered man. Alexander's memoirs about Anton Chekhov's childhood, written after his famous brother's death, reflect his bitterness and his desire for revenge against his father, whom Alexander blamed for his wrecked life. Non-Russian biographers of Chekhov have been extremely gullible about Alexander's sensational disclosures (the biography by Ernest J. Simmons uncritically paraphrases pages and pages of Alexander's memoirs), even though Mikhail Chekhov and Maria repeatedly pointed out the mistakes and fabrications their older brother's memoirs contain. Alexander's letters to Anton Chekhov, rather painful in their self-conscious buffoonery, were published in a separate volume in Moscow in 1939. They are highly informative on the literary life of Chekhov's time.

2. Natalia Golden, Alexander's second common-law wife.

3. "Chokhov" was Anton's humorous nickname for his cousin Mikhail (see Letter 1); Ivan Gavrilov was the merchant in whose warehouse Mikhail and Chekhov's father Pavel were employed. The point is that Alexander, who has had the benefit of a university education and who works as a writer, has a greater obligation to behave in a civilized manner than their unlettered cousin and his employer.

30. To Vladimir Tikhonov[1]

Moscow,
March 7, 1889

Dearest benefriend[2] Vladimir Alexeyevich,

I was a bit surprised at your review.[3] I had no idea you were so at home in journalistic style. It is all extremely articulate and polished, well reasoned and matter of fact. It even made me envious, because I've never quite gotten the hang of the journalistic style.

Thank you for your kind words and warm sympathy. I had so little kind treatment as a child that now that I'm an adult I look on it as something out of the ordinary, something that is still a new experience for me. That's why I would like to treat others kindly but I don't know how, I've grown hardened and lazy even though I know that we writers can't get along without kindness.

I haven't heard any news about Korsh's theater lately. All I know is that Solovtsov has left and that old man Poltavtsev is apparently also leaving. Agramov is the new stage director.[4]

God grant that you successfully complete the comedy you are now gestating and that it give you everything you desire. The greater its success, the better off our entire generation of writers will be. I, as opposed to Wagner,[5] believe that none of us will be an "elephant" or any other beast among writers and that we can prevail only through the efforts of our entire generation, and not otherwise. Instead of being known as Chekhov, Tikhonov, Korolenko, Shcheglov, Barantsevich or Bezhetsky, we will be called "the eighties" or "the end of the nineteenth century." A guild, so to speak.[6]

I have nothing new to report. I'm planning to write a novel of sorts and have already begun. I'm not writing any plays and won't write any in the near future because I have neither the subject matter nor the desire. To write for the theater, you must love it; without love, nothing worthwhile will come of it. Without love even success has no appeal. Next season I'll start going to the theater regularly and try to educate myself in matters of the stage.

Give my regards to your brother. My entire family sends you their best. I send you a friendly handshake and my most cordial wishes. Write.

Yours,
A. Chekhov

1. For a brief period in the 1880s the comedies of Vladimir Tikhonov (1857–1914) enjoyed a temporary renown. Chekhov described Tikhonov as "something of a drunk and something of a liar," but he seemed to like his company and he corresponded with him over a period of years. The entries from Tikhonov's personal journal that pertain to his encounters with and his opinions of Chekhov were published in the Chekhov volume of *Literary Heritage*. They are a primary source for documenting the widespread envy and resentment that Chekhov's success aroused among his fellow writers and journalists. Tikhonov records their statements and feelings, but he himself is quite admirably free of any rancor; having decided quite early that he was fated to remain a minor figure, he could take a selfless pleasure in Chekhov's ascent.

2. The Russian has a hybrid word that combines parts of "benefactor" and "friend."

3. Tikhonov published a highly favorable review of the St. Petersburg production of *Ivanov*.

4. Actor-director Nikolai Solovtsov had left the Korsh company for a new theater headed by the impresario Maria Abramova, taking with him Yevgeny Poltavtsev and some of the other actors and actresses. Mikhail Agramov took over Solovtsov's job as the stage director of the Korsh theater. It was Maria Abramova's company that put on the original stage production of Chekhov's *The Wood Demon*.

5. Nikolai Wagner, a professional zoologist and writer of books for children, had applied to Chekhov (according to the letter from Tikhonov which Chekhov is answering) Turgenev's words about Tolstoy: "He is an elephant

among us." Nikolai Wagner should not be confused with another zoologist, also named Wagner (first name Vladimir) who in 1891 collaborated with Chekhov on an exposé of the inhuman treatment of animals at the Moscow zoo published in *New Times* under the title "The Charlatans" and who served in part as the model for the character of von Koren in "The Duel."

6. Contrary to Chekhov's prediction, only his own name and that of Korolenko survive today on their own merits. The other four have long since become footnotes to Chekhov's biography and letters. Kazimir Barantsevich (or Kazimierz Barancewicz) was a Pole who wrote in Russian and was widely published in the last two decades of the nineteenth century. Chekhov was later to compare Barantsevich's writings to a stale, unappetizing fried fish left over at a railway station buffet.

31. To Anna Yevreinova[1]

Moscow,
March 10, 1889

Dear Anna Mikhailovna,

I have received the payment.[2] Thank you. I received more than expected, and I'm afraid you didn't subtract my debt. I do owe the office a bit, you know.

Yesterday I finished and made a clean copy of a story, but it's for my novel, the project that is presently taking up all my time. Oh, what a novel! If it weren't for the accursed censorship situation, I'd promise it to you for November. There's nothing in the novel inciting anyone to revolution, but the censors will ruin it anyway. Half the characters say, "I don't believe in God," it has a father whose son has been sent to life-long forced labor for armed resistance, a police chief who is ashamed of his uniform, a marshal of the nobility whom everybody hates, etc.[3] There's a wealth of material for the red pencil.

I have plenty of money now, enough to get me through September. Nor am I bound by any commitments. This is the ideal time to work on the novel.[4] If I don't write it now, when will I? That's how I see it, though I'm almost certain that I'll grow tired of the novel within two or three weeks and that I'll lay it aside again.

I have an idea for a brief story. I'll try to have the story done in time for the May or June issue. But if it could wait until July or August, my novel would say "Many thanks" to you.

Get the censors off your back, for heaven's sake.[5] Even though they haven't crossed out anything of mine so far, I still fear and dislike them. Even Turkey should have no censorship for thick journals and newspapers.[6] The theater is another matter.

Just you wait! I'll buy up all the thick journals and close them down, except the *Northern Herald*. Then we'll install electric lighting and our own private printing presses, hire a majestic doorman, purchase rubber-tired carriages for the editorial board, invite Milan of Serbia[7] to be our colleague (for the Foreign Bureau), take on Ashinov[8] as doorman . . . and we'll have forty thousand subscribers. Though, of course, I still haven't seen my rich fiancée even once.[9] Nor has she seen me. I'll touch her by writing, "Don't love me, love my cause. . . ."[10]

I am anxiously awaiting my copies of *Ivanov*. Shall I challenge Mr. Demakov[11] to a duel?

I'll be staying in Moscow until May and writing. An urge to write has come over me. I keep writing and writing and never leave the house.

My regards to Maria Dmitrievna[12] and Alexei Nikolayevich.[13]

My family sends you their greetings, and I wish you good health and all my best.

Your sincerely devoted,
A. Chekhov

You have Gilyarovsky's story about rafts floating down river. This is the very time to run it.[14]

1. Anna Yevreinova (1844–1919), the publisher of *Northern Herald*, was the first Russian woman to be awarded an LL.D. (from the University of Leipzig). Zinaida Gippius described her as follows: "Inseparable from her pugdog, her gray hair closely cropped, a maroon velvet jacket thrown over her shoulders, she was constantly in three simultaneous but different kinds of excitement." Chekhov carried on an affectionately humorous correspondence with Yevreinova and occasionally tried to advise her on editorial matters. Thus, on November 7, 1889, after Nikolai Mikhailovsky's demonstrative resignation from *Northern Herald* (according to Pleshcheyev's letter to Chekhov about this incident, Mikhailovsky left because the government censors failed to delete anything from several of his reviews, which made Mikhailovsky feel he was losing his touch by writing for *Northern Herald*), Chekhov sent Yevreinova a list of medical, agricultural and other natural-science experts, recommending them as literate men who could contribute interesting articles to her journal. "Go ahead and invite genuine scholars and genuine practical men and stop regretting the departure of fake philosophers addicted to sociologizing," Chekhov wrote.

2. For the right to publish *Ivanov*.

3. This is the closest we can ever come to learning what *Stories from the Lives of My Friends* was like.

4. In Russian, there is an untranslatable pun on the meanings of the word *roman*, which means both "novel" and "love affair."

5. *Northern Herald* was classed as a publication that had to undergo pre-publication censorship. Other journals and newspapers (e.g., *New Times*) were free of all preliminary censorship, it being understood that the editor would be held responsible for any objectionable material. Chekhov is urging Yevreinova to petition for release from pre-publication censorship ("Get the censors off your back").

6. In the period between 1905 and *ca.* 1921, Russian literature and the press were to all intents and purposes freed from pre-publication censorship. It was reinstated a few years after the October Revolution; after the 1930s, when the government became the sole publisher and banned all private publishers and publications, pre-publication censorship attained a degree of stringency unimaginable in Chekhov's time.

7. He had been forced to abdicate his throne a few days earlier.

8. He was a Russian adventurer who had tried to occupy a portion of the Abyssinian coast to start a Russian colony and was very much in the news at the time.

9. There was a running gag in Chekhov's correspondence with Yevreinova about her finding a millionairess he could marry so as to be able to write without financial worries.

10. A line from a "Socialist Song" quoted in Turgenev's novel *Virgin Soil.*

11. The owner of the printing plant where *Northern Herald* was printed.

12. Maria Fyodorova, the editorial secretary of *Northen Herald* and Anna Yevreinova's long-time intimate friend and companion.

13. Pleshcheyev.

14. According to Pleshcheyev's letter to Chekhov, the jolly and athletic Gilyarovsky so charmed Yevreinova that she talked Pleshcheyev into accepting the manuscript against his own better judgment.

32. To Alexei Suvorin

Moscow,
March 11, 1889

When you were enumerating the charms of the Kharkov estate, you didn't mention any river. There's no getting along without a river. If it's near the Donets, then buy it, but if it's the Lopan or just some ponds, then don't.[1] There's a professor of surgery here, a little man with short-cropped hair, with ears that stick out and with eyes like Yuzefovich's,[2] who owns a nearby estate. He invites everyone he likes to buy the estate next to his. He usually places both hands on the waist of the person he has taken a fancy to, looks him sentimentally in the eyes, and says with a sigh, "What good times we would have together!" I too am looking at you sentimentally and saying what good times we would have together! You're doing me great harm by not buying the estate.

All I need is your photograph, I don't need photographs of myself, but there are people who make believe they very much need my photograph. Since even I have my admirers, there must be a shoe to fit everyone.[3]

Guess what! I'm writing a novel!! I keep writing and writing and there's no end in sight. I started it, the novel, I mean, by making major revisions and cuts in what I'd already done. I already have nine clearly delineated characters. And what an intricate plot! I've called it *Stories from the Lives of My Friends* and am writing it in the form of separate stories that are complete within themselves and closely linked by a common plot, idea and characters. Each story will have its own title. Don't go thinking the novel will be made up of shreds and tatters. No, it will be a genuine novel, a whole body, in which every character will be organically indispensable. Grigorovich, to whom you relayed the content of the first chapter, was alarmed at my using a student who dies and thus does not last through the entire novel, and will therefore seem superfluous. But that student is a nail from a large boot as far as I'm concerned. He's a mere detail.

I can barely manage the technique. I'm still weak in that area, and I have the feeling I'm making scores of bad mistakes. Some passages will ramble on and others will be silly. I'll try to avoid faithful wives, suicides, kulaks, virtuous peasants, devoted slaves, moralizing old ladies, kindly nannies, provincial wits, red-nosed captains and the "new people," though in places I come awfully close to clichés.[4]

I've just received the proofs of "The Princess"[5] and will mail them directly to the printers tomorrow.

For dessert, here's a classified ad from *Russian News*:

MATURE PERSON WANTED

to help with housework and education of children in a family on estate near Moscow. Must be acquainted with views on life and education set forth by our writers: Dr. Pokrovsky, Goltsev, Sikorsky and Lev Tolstoy.[6] Imbued with the beliefs of those writers and convinced of the importance of physical labor and the harm of excessive mental exertion, she must direct her educational activities toward instilling strict truth, goodness and love for one's neighbor in the children.

Address all inquiries in writing to No. 2183 of the "V. Miller" Employment Agency, Kabanov House, Petrovka, Moscow.

That's what they call freedom of conscience. For room and board a young lady is obliged to be imbued with the views of Goltsev and Co., while the children, apparently to show their gratitude for having such liberal, intelligent parents, are obliged to watch after themselves day and night to make sure they love their neighbor and don't overexert themselves mentally.

It's odd how people fear freedom.

By the way, *New Times* carried a quote not long ago in the "Other Newspapers and Journals" column from a newspaper praising German maids for working *all day* like forced laborers and receiving only two or three rubles a month for it. *New Times* endorses this praise and adds of its own accord that our trouble is that we keep more servants than we need. To my mind Germans are scoundrels and poor political economists. In the first place, it is wrong to equate servants with prisoners. Second, servants have legal rights and are made from the same flesh and blood as Bismarck; they are free employees, not slaves. Third, the higher the recompense labor receives, the more fortunate the state, and we should all do everything in our power to see that labor is as well recompensed as possible. To say nothing of the Christian point of view. As far as having too many servants is concerned, they are kept on only where there is a lot of money and they receive more than civil service department heads. They should not be taken into account because they represent a chance phenomenon, not an essential one.

Why aren't you coming to Moscow? What good times we would have together!

Yours,
A. Chekhov

1. Suvorin was apparently so charmed by the Lintvaryov estate, where he had visited Chekhov the previous summer, that he began to consider buying an estate for himself in the Ukraine.

2. A Ukrainian newspaper editor.

3. Our rendition of the last sentence replaces the untranslatable Russian folk saying Chekhov quotes in the original but conveys its meaning very closely.

4. One of the earliest pieces of prose Chekhov ever published was called "Things Most Frequently Encountered in Novels, Stories and Other Such Things" (1880). It consisted of a one-page list of stock characters and situations found in the popular fiction of his time.

5. "The Princess" is one of Chekhov's few stories that unequivocally indict the Russian aristocracy and the ruling classes. He himself described this story as written "in a tone of protest." As if to stump Chekhov's future commentators, the story was written at Suvorin's request and it was first published in *New Times*.

6. The combination of the names of Tolstoy and the liberal editor and journalist Viktor Goltsev (Chekhov's future friend) on the one hand with

the unknown and unidentifiable Pokrovsky and Sikorsky on the other (all of them considered the highest authorities on life and education) must have produced a grotesque effect even in Chekhov's day.

33. To Alexei Suvorin

Sumy,
early May, 1889[1]

I can't believe my eyes. Only recently it was snowy and cold, and now I'm sitting at an open window and listening to the continuous screams of the nightingales, hoopoes, orioles and other beasties in a green garden. The Psyol is majestically affectionate, the hues of the sky and the horizon warm. The apple and cherry trees are in bloom. The geese are walking their goslings. In short, it's spring with all the trimmings.

Stiva[2] never sent the boats, so there is nothing for us to go rowing in. The Lintvaryovs' boats are out in the woods somewhere with the woodsman. I am therefore limited to walks up and down the shore and to keen envy of the fishermen darting around the Psyol in their light craft. I get up early, go to bed early, eat a lot, write and read. The painter[3] is coughing and being irritable. He's in a bad way. Since I don't have any new books, I'm going back over the rudiments and reading things I've already read. By the way, I'm reading Goncharov and am amazed. I'm amazed at myself: what made me think Goncharov a first-rate writer all these years? His *Oblomov* is a pretty shoddy piece of work. Ilya Ilyich himself[4] is far-fetched and not imposing enough to have a whole book written about him. He is an obese loafer like many others, with a simple, unexceptional, petty character. To raise this sort of person to a social type is far more than he deserves. I ask myself: if Oblomov hadn't been a loafer, what would he have been? And I answer: nothing. And if so, then let him go on snoring. The other characters are petty too; they reek of Leykinism, they were chosen carelessly and are half contrived. They are not typical of their time and have nothing new to add. Stoltz does not engender any confidence in me. The author says he's a fine fellow, but I don't believe him. He's a slippery rascal who thinks highly of himself and is extremely smug. He's half contrived and three-quarters stilted. Olga is contrived and has been dragged in for no reason. And, worst of all, the entire novel is freezing, freezing cold. I am crossing Goncharov off my list of demigods.

But how spontaneous, how powerful Gogol is in comparison! What an artist he is! His "Carriage"[5] alone is worth two hundred thousand rubles. Sheer delight, nothing more or less. He is the greatest

Russian writer. The best part of *The Inspector General* is the first act; the worst part of *The Marriage* is Act Three.[6] I'm going to read him aloud to the family.

When are you off? How happy I would be to go to some Biarritz or other, where there's music and lots of women. If it weren't for the painter, I'd rush out after you. The money would turn up somewhere. I give you my word that next year if I'm still alive and well I will go to Europe without fail. If I could only wangle about three thousand from the theater management and finish the novel.

Your bookstand at the Sumy station is out of both *In the Twilight* and *Stories* and has been out of them *for a long time*. And I'm a fashionable writer in Sumy, because I live nearby. If Mikhail Alexeyevich[7] were to send another fifty or so copies, they'd all be sold.

The dogs howl hideously at night. They keep me awake.

My *Wood Demon* is shaping up.[8]

My cordial regards to Anna Ivanovna, Nastya and Borya. I dreamt of Mlle. Émilie[9] last night. Why? I don't know.

Be happy and don't forget me in your orisons.[10]

Yours,
Akaky Tarantulov[11]

1. Written at the Lintvaryov estate, where Chekhov had returned for his second summer in the Ukraine, this letter lacks a date in the original. It could be dated approximately, because of the mention of Nikolai Chekhov's illness.

2. Dr. Nikolai Obolonsky, a mutual acquaintance of Chekhov and Suvorin, had on his estate some rowboats belonging to Suvorin, who had asked that they be sent to Luka for the use of the Chekhov family. Chekhov had nicknamed Dr. Obolonsky "Stiva Oblonsky," after the brother of the heroine of Tolstoy's *Anna Karenina*.

3. Nikolai Chekhov, who was gravely ill with tuberculosis. He died one month later.

4. Ilya Ilyich is the first name and patronymic of the hero of Goncharov's *Oblomov*. Stoltz and Olga, mentioned later, are the two other principal characters of the novel.

5. The unique originality of Gogol's story "The Carriage" (also translated as "The Calash") was not generally appreciated until the twentieth century.

6. This is either a slip of the pen or a particularly elaborate compliment to Gogol's second play. *The Marriage* has only two acts.

7. Suvorin's second-eldest son, who was in charge of the family's railroad bookstand operations.

8. *The Wood Demon* began as a joint writing project of Chekhov and Suvorin. After sketching one scene, Suvorin lost interest in the collaboration and by now Chekhov is referring to it as his own play.

9. The French governess of Suvorin's two youngest children.

10. The formula "Remember me in your holy prayers" existed in Russia as an acceptable form of salutation when writing to church dignitaries. But in his 1837 translation of *Hamlet,* Nikolai Polevoy utilized it to render Hamlet's words to Ophelia, "Nymph, in thy orisons/Be all my sins remember'd." Chekhov used this Shakespearean quotation parodistically in *The Cherry Orchard* (Lopakhin's teasing of Varya in Act II), but for many years, long before he wrote that play, he was wont to use an assortment of free variations on this quotation as a humorous concluding salutation in many of his letters.

11. Akaky Tarantulov appears in a brief satirical skit "A Forced Declaration," which Chekhov published anonymously in *New Times* in April of 1889. In the space of a few lines, the skit parodies popular melodramas, indicts the mistreatment of horses by Russian cabbies (a theme treated along similar lines but at greater length by both Dostoyevsky and Mayakovsky) and pokes fun at authoritarian nonwriters who join literary associations and then try to control them.

34. To Alexei Suvorin

Sumy,
May 4, 1889

I am writing this, Alexei Sergeyevich, just after getting back from the hunt: I was out catching crayfish. The weather is marvelous. Everything is singing, blooming and sparkling with beauty. By now the garden is all green, and even the oaks are covered with leaves. The trunks of the apple, pear, cherry and plum trees have been painted white to protect them from worms.[1] All of these trees have white blossoms, making them look strikingly like brides during the wedding ceremony: white dresses, white flowers and so innocent an appearance that they seem to be ashamed of being looked at. Myriads of beings are born every day. Nightingales, bitterns, cuckoos and other feathered creatures keep up a ceaseless din day and night, and the frogs accompany them. Every hour of the day and night has its own specialty: during the hour between eight and nine in the evening, for instance, the garden is filled with what is literally the roar of maybugs. The nights are moonlit, the days bright. As a result, I'm in a good mood, and if it weren't for the coughing painter and the mosquitoes—even Elpe's[2] formula is no protection against them—I'd be a perfect Potyomkin. Nature is a very good sedative. It makes you reconciled, that is, it gives a person equanimity. And you need equanimity in this world. Only people with equanimity can see things clearly, be fair and work. This, of course, applies only to intelligent and honorable people; selfish and shallow people have enough equanimity as it is.

You write I've grown lazy. This doesn't mean I've gotten any lazier than I was. I'm working now as much as I did three to five years ago. Working and looking as if I am working from nine in the morning until the midday meal and from evening tea until I go to sleep has become a habit with me, and in this respect I am like a government official. So if my work does not produce two stories a month or a yearly income of ten thousand, it's the fault of my psycho-organic makeup, not my laziness. I don't love money enough for medicine, and I lack the necessary passion—and therefore talent—for literature. The fire in me burns with an even, lethargic flame; it never flares up or roars, which is why I never find myself writing fifty or sixty pages in one night or getting so involved in my work that I force myself to stay up when I feel sleepy; I therefore never do anything outstandingly stupid or anything notably intelligent. I fear that in this respect I am very similar to Goncharov, whom I don't like and who is ten heads above me in talent. I have very little passion. Add to that the following psychopathic trait: for two years now, seeing my works in print has for some reason given me no pleasure. I've grown indifferent to reviews, conversations about literature, gossip, successes, failures, high royalties—in short, I've become a damn fool. My soul seems to be stagnating. I explain this by the stagnation in my personal life. It's not that I'm disappointed or exhausted or cranky; it's just that everything has somehow grown less interesting. I'll have to light a fire underneath myself.

Can you believe it? I've got the first act of *The Wood Demon* ready. It's turned out all right, though a bit long. I have a greater sense of my own strength than when I was writing *Ivanov*. The play will be ready by the beginning of June. Watch out, theater management! That's five thousand in my pocket. It's an awfully strange play; I'm amazed to see such strange things emerging from my pen. My only fear is that the censors won't pass it. I'm also writing a novel that appeals to me more and lies closer to my heart than *The Wood Demon*, where I have to be devious and put up a false front. Last night I remembered I'd promised Varlamov to write a farce for him. Today I wrote it, and I've already sent it off.[3] You see how fast I turn things out! And you write I've grown lazy.

So you've finally taken notice of King Solomon. When I first talked to you about him, all you ever did was nod indifferently. In my opinion, it was Ecclesiastes that gave Goethe the idea to write his *Faust*.[4]

I was extremely pleased with the tone of your letter to the editor about Likhachov. I feel that this letter could serve as a model for polemics of all kinds.[5]

I went to theater in Sumy and saw *Second Youth*.[6] The trousers the actors wore and the living rooms they acted in turned the play into *The Servants' Quarters*.[7] During the last act there was a drum beaten offstage. They are going to put on *Tatyana Repina* and *Ivanov*. I'm going to attend. I can just imagine what the Adashev[8] will be like!

Send me my copy of *Tatyana Repina* if it's out.

My brother writes me he's having a terrible time with his play.[9] I'm very glad. Let him. He looked down his nose at *Tatyana Repina* and my *Ivanov* when he saw them performed, drank cognac during the intermissions, and deigned to offer his criticism. Everyone passes judgment on plays as though they were very easy to write. What they don't know is that it is difficult to write a good play and twice as difficult—and terrifying, besides—to write a bad play. I would like to see the entire public merge into one person and write a play. Then you and I would sit in Box I and hiss it off the stage.

Alexander suffers from too many rewrites. He is very inexperienced. I'm afraid he uses a lot of false effects, spends all his time fighting them, and wears himself out in the fruitless battle.

Bring me some banned books and newspapers from abroad.[10] If if weren't for the painter, I'd go with you.

God knows what He is doing. He took Tolstoy and Saltykov[11] unto Himself and thereby reconciled what appeared to us irreconcilable. Now both are rotting, and both are equally indifferent. I hear that people are rejoicing over Tolstoy's death; their joy seems quite bestial to me. I don't believe in the future of Christians who hate the police yet at the same time welcome someone's death and see death as an angel of deliverance. You can't imagine how disgusting it is to see women rejoice in this death.

When will you be back from abroad? Where will you go then?

Will I really sit it out until autumn on the banks of the Psyol? Why, that's horrible! After all, spring won't last that long.

Lensky has invited me to accompany him on tour to Tiflis. I'd go if not for the painter, who's not doing any too brilliantly.

Tell Anna Ivanovna that from the bottom of my heart I wish her a most cheerful journey.

If you happen to play the roulette, bet twenty-five francs for me to test my luck.

Well, God grant you health and all the best.

Yours,
A. Chekhov

1. In the translation of this passage that appears in the Lillian Hellman edition of his letters, Chekhov is sent to catch crabs, rather than crayfish, in

the inland river Psyol, oaks are said to be covered with blossoms, and the fruit trees have been given "a white coat" by "the busy worms." Elsewhere in that volume, gobies (a species of fish) are confused with bulls, cod becomes "a fish from the Caspian," a siskin (a free bird) is rendered as "bird in a cage," and chanterelles as "various kinds of mushrooms." In the English translation of Chekhov's biography by Daniel Gillès, almost every animal Chekhov mentions is replaced by another, vaguely similar one: a cockroach becomes a beetle, dachshunds become bassets, and a woodcock is taken for a quail. All this is particularly regrettable because Chekhov is not the hazy writer some of his translators take him to be, but a very precise and observant one.

2. "Elpe" was the pen name of Lazar Popov (a phonetic transcription of his initials), who wrote a popular science column for *New Times*.

3. Chekhov's farce *A Tragedian in Spite of Himself*, which was written at the request of the actor Konstantin Varlamov.

4. Chekhov was fascinated by King Solomon and Ecclesiastes for several years. His notebooks contain indications that he contemplated writing a play about Solomon at one point.

5. Suvorin had published a letter to the editor in his own newspaper, asserting the right of *New Times* to criticize the St. Petersburg municipal administration and its mayor, Likhachov, despite certain favors the newspaper had owed to the mayor in the past.

6. A melodrama by Pyotr Nevezhin about the breakup of an upper-class family, first performed in 1887 and enormously popular for about a decade after that.

7. A fragment from Gogol's unfinished comedy *The Order of St. Vladimir*, which was occasionally performed as a separate little play.

8. A character in Suvorin's *Tatyana Repina*.

9. Encouraged by the success of his brother's *Ivanov*, Alexander Chekhov also decided to try his hand at playwriting. In his letters written in the spring of 1889, Anton repeatedly offered his brother advice on how to write a play. Thus, on April 11, he wrote Alexander: "My advice is to try to be original in your play and as intelligent as possible; but also, have no fear of appearing stupid. Freethinking is what's needed and only he who is not afraid of writing stupid things is a real freethinker. Don't smooth things over, don't polish them, be clumsy and daring. Brevity is the sister of talent. Keep in mind that declarations of love, infidelities of husbands and wives, the tears of widows and orphans and all other kinds of tears have long since been described. But the main thing: Mommy and Daddy gotta eat. So write!"

And on May 11: "A great deal of rewriting should not disturb you, because the more mosaiclike the results, the better. The characters in your play only stand to gain from this. The main thing is to avoid the personal element. Your play won't be worth a thing if all of its characters resemble you [. . .] Is there no life outside yourself? And who cares about my life and your life, my thoughts and your thoughts? People should be shown people, not your own self."

Despite all this advice and a great deal of encouragement from his employer, Suvorin, Alexander never completed his play. Ten years later he published a one-act farce which was given a few performances.

10. Throughout the years of their friendship, Suvorin regularly supplied Chekhov with illegal, anti-government Russian publications that were printed abroad. (See also Letter 170, note 5.)

11. The widely disliked ultra-reactionary minister of education, Count Dmitry Tolstoy, and the popular anti-government satirist Mikhail Saltykov-Shchedrin died within a few days of each other.

35. To Alexei Suvorin

Sumy,
May 7, 1889

I've read Bourget's *Disciple*[1] in your paraphrase and in Russian translation (*Northern Herald*). This is the way I see it. Bourget is a talented, very intelligent and well-educated man. He is thoroughly familiar with the scientific method and is as imbued with it as if he had studied science or medicine. He is no stranger to the field he has chosen to handle—a merit unknown by past or present Russian writers. As for his bookish, learned psychology, he knows about it as little as the best of psychologists. Knowing it is just about the same as not knowing it, since it is more a fiction than a science, a kind of alchemy, and it is high time for it to be filed away in the archives. And so I don't intend to say anything about whether Bourget is a good or bad psychologist. The novel is interesting. Once I had read it, I understood why you were so taken by it. It's intelligent, interesting, witty in places and somewhat fantastic. As for its faults, the main one among them is his pretentious crusade against materialist doctrine. Forgive me, but I just can't understand that sort of crusade. It never leads anywhere and does nothing but introduce needless confusion in the sphere of ideas. Against whom is he crusading and why? Where is the enemy and what is so dangerous about him? To begin with, materialism is not a school or doctrine in the narrow journalistic sense. It is neither chance occurrence nor passing fancy; it is something indispensable and inevitable and beyond human power. Everything that lives on earth is necessarily materialistic. In animals, in savages and in Moscow merchants everything that is elevated and non-animal is conditioned by unconscious instinct; everything else in them is materialistic—and not by their own choosing, certainly. Creatures of a higher order, thinking humans, are also necessarily materialists. They search for truth in matter because there is nowhere else for them to search: all they can see, hear and feel is matter. They can necessarily seek out truth only where their microscopes, probes and knives are effective. Prohibiting materialist doctrine is tantamount to preventing man from seeking out the truth. Outside of matter there is no experience or knowledge, and consequently no truth. Is it perhaps bad that Monsieur Sixte, as it seems, pokes his nose into areas outside his field and is insolent enough to study the inner man on the basis of cell theory? But is it his fault that psychic phenomena are so strikingly similar to physical ones that it is almost impossible to figure out where the former start and the latter end? It seems to me that, when a corpse is being dissected, even the most inveterate spiritualist must *necessarily* come up against the question of where the soul is. And if you know how great the similarity is between mental and physical illnesses and when you know that both one and the other are treated with the very same remedies, you can't help but refuse to separate soul from body.

As for the "psychological experiments," instilling vices in children and the figure of Sixte himself, all this is exaggerated beyond belief.

The title of spiritualist is honorary, not scholarly. As scientists they are unnecessary. And anyway, in everything they do and try to accomplish they are just as necessarily materialist as Sixte himself. If they win out over the materialists and wipe them off the face of the earth (which is impossible), their very victory will prove them the greatest of materialists, for they will have destroyed an entire cult, nearly a religion.

Talking about the harm and dangers of materialist doctrine and even more so fighting it is premature, to say the least. We lack sufficient evidence to put together a case against it. There are many theories and suppositions, but no facts; all our antipathy goes no further than a fantastic bogeyman. Merchants' wives are horrified by the bogeyman. And why? No one knows. Priests make reference to lack of faith, profligacy and the like. There's no lack of faith. Everyone believes in something, even Sixte, for that matter. And as for profligacy, it's not Sixtes and Mendeleyevs who have a reputation for being the most refined profligates, lechers and drunkards; it's the poets, abbots and persons diligently attending Embassy churches.

In short, Bourget's crusade is beyond my comprehension. If when setting off for the crusade Bourget had also taken the trouble to point out to the materialists the incorporeal God in heaven and point him out in such a way that they would see Him, that would have been another question; in that case I would have understood his excursus.[2]

Forgive the philosophy. I'm off for the post office. Regards to you all, and keep well.

Yours,
A. Chekhov

1. Paul Bourget's anti-materialistic novel *Le Disciple* was the literary sensation of 1889 throughout Europe. A Russian translation was serialized in *Northern Herald* and Suvorin devoted to it several enthusiastic articles in *New Times*. The hero of Bourget's novel is the atheistic philosopher Adrien Sixte. Sixte's disciple Robert Greslou, under the influence of Sixte's deterministic materialism, drives a young girl to suicide by way of a psychological experiment. Greslou is in turn killed by the brother of his victim, and the penitent Sixte shows that he is cured of his atheism at the end of the novel by reciting the Lord's Prayer.

2. The materialistic component in Chekhov's philosophical outlook and his repeated insistence on its validity was what caused some of the leading thinkers of Russian Symbolism, such as Zinaida Gippius and Lev Shestov, to dislike his work and to minimize its importance. As for Suvorin, his anti-materialistic philosophical bias was to find a full response in Vasily Rozanov, a writer he discovered and helped popularize after his contacts with Chekhov dwindled.

36. To Alexei Suvorin

Sumy,
May 15, 1889

If you still haven't gone abroad, let me answer your letter about Bourget. I'll be brief. You write among other things, "Let the science of matter pursue its course, but at the same time let some place remain where one can hide from endless matter." The science of matter is indeed pursuing its course, and places where you can hide from endless matter do exist, and no one seems to be encroaching on them. If anyone is taking a beating, it's the sciences, not the holy shrines where you can hide away from science. My letter formulates the problem more correctly and inoffensively than yours, and I am closer to the "life of the spirit" than you are. You are talking about the right of one or another type of knowledge to exist, whereas I'm talking about peace, not rights. I want people not to see war where there isn't any. Different branches of knowledge have always lived together in peace. Both anatomy and belles-lettres are of equally noble descent; they have identical goals and an identical enemy—the devil—and there is absolutely no reason for them to fight. There is no struggle for existence going on between them. If a man knows the theory of the circulatory system, he is rich. If he learns the history of religion and the song "I remember a Marvelous Moment"[1] in addition, he is the richer, not the poorer, for it. We are consequently dealing entirely in pluses. It is for this reason that geniuses have never fought among themselves and Goethe the poet coexisted splendidly with Goethe the naturalist.

It is not branches of knowledge that war with one another, not poetry with anatomy; it is delusions, that is, people. When a person doesn't understand something, he feels discord within. Instead of looking for the causes of this discord within himself as he should, he looks outside. Hence the war with what he does not understand. Gradually, following its own natural peaceful course throughout the Middle Ages, alchemy evolved into chemistry; astrology into astronomy. The monks didn't understand; they saw war and took to arms. Our Pisarev[2] was just such a militant Spanish monk during the sixties.

Bourget is also at war. You say he's not, but I say he is. Imagine what will happen if his novel falls into the hands of a man whose children are studying natural sciences or of a bishop who is looking around for a topic for his Sunday sermon. Will the resultant effect bear any resemblance to peace? No. Imagine what will happen if the book catches the eye of an anatomist or physiologist, etc. It will not breathe peace into any man's breast; it will irritate the well informed and reward the not so well informed with false notions—nothing more.

You may object that he is warring with deviations from the norm rather than with the essence. I agree that every writer must war with deviations from the norm. But why compromise the essence itself? Sixte is regal, but Bourget has turned him into a caricature. His "psychological experiments" are a libel of man and science. Supposing I wrote a novel in which my anatomist dissects his wife and infant children alive for the sake of science, or a learned woman doctor goes to the Nile to copulate with a crocodile and a rattlesnake for scientific ends, would that novel be a libel or would it not? And I could doubtless write that sort of thing and make it interesting and clever.

That Bourget is as attractive to the Russian reader as a thundershower after a drought is understandable. The novel shows the reader an author and heroes smarter than himself and a life richer than his own. Russian writers are duller than their readers, their heroes are pallid and insignificant, and the life they portray meager and uninteresting. The Russian writer lives in the drainpipe, eats sowbugs and has love affairs with hussies and laundresses; he knows nothing of history or geography or science or the religion of his country or its administration or its legal procedures . . . in short, he doesn't know a goddamn thing. In comparison with Bourget he's nothing but a brazen fake. I can understand why Bourget is popular, but it still doesn't follow that Sixte is right or honest when he recites the Lord's Prayer.

Well, I won't pester you any more with Bourget. You have a talent for conveying the plots of novels like *Le Disciple* in concise form. I was happy for you as I read. Very well done. You handled the philosophical and scientific part of the novel very well, I didn't know you had it in you. I would have gotten everything confused and ended up with something longer than Bourget's original.

I'm bored. Pleshcheyev isn't coming and I wish he would. He's a fine old man.

I'll be sending you a letter written in French and German soon.[3] Regards to Anna Ivanovna, Nastya and Borya.

Have a good trip.

Yours,
A. Chekhov

1. An art song by Mikhail Glinka, which is a setting of one of Alexander Pushkin's most popular lyrics.

2. On Pisarev and Chekhov, see Letter 69.

3. Chekhov began an intensive study of French and German at that time.

37. To Peter Tchaikovsky[1]

Moscow,
October 12, 1889

Dear Pyotr Ilyich,

I'm preparing a new book of my stories for publication this month. The stories are as dull and dreary as autumn and monotonous in style, and the artistic element in them is thickly interlarded with the medical, but that still doesn't prevent me from making bold to address you a humble request: may I dedicate the book to you?[2] I am very anxious to receive an affirmative answer from you because, first, the dedication would give me great pleasure and, second, it would serve in some small way to satisfy the profound feeling of respect that impels me to think of you daily. I became determined to dedicate my book to you as far back as the day we had lunch together at Modest Ilyich's[3] and I learned from you that you had read my stories.

If you include a photograph together with your authorization, I will have received more than I am worth and will be grateful to the end of time. Forgive me for bothering you, and allow me to wish you all the best.

With sincere devotion,
A. Chekhov

1. Tchaikovsky became a fervent admirer of Chekhov after reading his story "The Letter" in 1887. After that time, Chekhov and his stories are frequently mentioned in the composer's correspondence. For his part, Chekhov

knew and loved Tchaikovsky's music. After receiving this letter, Tchaikovsky paid Chekhov a personal visit and proposed that they collaborate on an opera libretto (which, according to Mikhail Chekhov, was to be based on one of the episodes from Lermontov's *A Hero of Our Time*). The project never materialized. For all their mutual admiration, the contacts between the two men were neither frequent nor particularly intimate.

Because of the aura of melancholy that surrounds the art of both in the minds of many Russians, one occasionally encounters the view that Tchaikovsky is Chekhov's counterpart in music. The obvious superficiality of this view does not detract from the beauty of its expression in one of Boris Pasternak's most perfect poems, "Winter Is Approaching" (1943), with its concluding lines:

> The autumnal twilight of Chekhov,
> Tchaikovsky and Levitan.

2. Tchaikovsky's consenting to the dedication was accompanied by his photograph bearing the inscription: "To A. P. Chekhov, from his ardent admirer P. Tchaikovsky, October 14, 1889." Chekhov's collection of stories *Morose People* was published in 1890, with a dedication to Tchaikovsky.

3. Tchaikovsky's playwright brother Modest, whom Chekhov got to know considerably better than the composer. In one of his letters to Modest, Chekhov assigned to Tchaikovsky the second place in the entire pantheon of Russian arts, second only to that of Tolstoy, "who took the first a long time ago."

38. To Alexei Suvorin

Moscow,
October 17, 1889

I wrote you yesterday about the yearbook's medical section. Today Ostrovsky, of whom I've also written you before, dragged over a whole bale of his sister's stories.[1]

Everyone is tearing Goreva[2] to pieces—unfairly, of course, because tearing people to pieces should be done in public only when ill intent is involved, and even then judiciously. But Goreva is miserably bad. I went to her theater once and almost died of boredom. Her actors are drab and their pretentiousness depressing.

Don't rejoice over becoming a character in my play. Your joy is premature; your turn is still to come. If I live long enough, I'll describe the Feodosia nights we spent together in conversation and the time we went fishing and you walked along the piles of the Lintvaryovs' windmill—that's all I need from you for the time being. You're not in the play, you can't be in the play, even though Grigorovich with his usual perspicacity manages to see otherwise.[3] The play deals with a dull, self-satisfied, wooden man who has lectured on art for twenty-five years without understanding anything about it, a man who makes everyone despondent and bored, who allows no laughter or music around him, and so on and so forth, and nonetheless is extraordinarily happy. For heaven's sake, don't go believing all those people who look first of all for what's bad in everything, measure everyone else by their own standards, and attribute their own fox and badger traits to others. Oh how pleased this has made Grigorovich! And how they would all rejoice if I were to slip some arsenic in your tea and turn out to be a Third Department spy.[4] Of course you may say that all this is trifling. Well, it isn't. If my play were being performed, the entire audience, following the example of a bunch of perjured good-for-nothings, would look at the stage and say, "So that's what Suvorin is like! And that's what his wife is like! Hm . . . what do you know! We had no idea."

It's all trivia, I agree. But this is the sort of trivia that makes the world fall apart. The other day I met a Petersburg writer at the theater. We struck up a conversation. When he learned from me that Plescheyev, Barantsevich, you, Svobodin[5] and others had visited me at various times during the summer, he sighed sympathetically and said, "You're wrong to think that's good publicity. You're making a big mistake to count on them."

In other words, I invited you in order to have someone write me up and I tried to get Svobodin to come so as to palm off my play on him. Ever since my conversation with that writer I've had the sort of aftertaste in my mouth I'd get if, instead of vodka, I'd had a shot of ink mixed with flies. It may be trivia and of no importance, but without those trivia all human life would be sheer joy—and now it's half disgusting.

If someone serves you coffee, don't try to look for beer in it. If I present you with the professor's ideas, have confidence in me and don't look for Chekhovian ideas in them.[6] No, thank you. In the whole story there is only one idea that I share, the idea that obsesses the professor's son-in-law, that swindler Gnekker, namely, "The old man's losing his mind!" Everything else I've made up and invented. Where do you see the polemics? Do you so value opinions—any opinions—that you conceive them alone as the center of gravity rather than the manner in which they're expressed or their origins, and such? Would you say that Bourget's *Disciple* is also polemics? The substance of all these opinions is of no value to me as an author. Their substance is not the point; it is variable and lacks novelty. The crux of the matter lies in the nature of the opinions, in their dependence on external influences, and so on.

They must be examined like objects, like symptoms, with perfect objectivity and without any attempt to agree with them or call them in question. If I had described St. Vitus's dance, you wouldn't have considered it from the point of view of a choreographer, would you? The same must be done with opinions. I had no intention at all of astounding you with my amazing views on the theater, literature and so on. All I meant to do was make use of my knowledge to depict the vicious circle that causes even a kind and intelligent man who enters it—despite his resolve to accept life from God as it is and think of everyone according to Christian precepts—to mumble and grumble like a slave whether he means to or not and speak ill of people even when he is forcing himself to say nice things about them. He wishes to stand up for his students, but all that comes out is hypocrisy and Resident-style[7] abuse. But that's a long story.

Your sons are certainly very promising. They've raised the price of the *Yearbook* and cut back on the size. They promised me a keg of wine for my stories and didn't come across with it, and to keep me from getting angry they put my portrait opposite the Shah of Persia's.[8] Speaking of the Shah, I recently read the poem "A Political Concert," which speaks about the Shah in more or less the following terms: "And the Persian Shah, the East's finest flower, went to Paris to compare his [. . .] with the Eiffel Tower." Come to Moscow. We'll go to the theater together.

Yours,
A. Chekhov

1. The dramatic tradition that Chekhov revolted against and overthrew in his last great plays was that of the well-made social drama of Alexander Ostrovsky. It is ironic, therefore, that Chekhov, who had never met his famous predecessor, was frequently involved in the affairs of Ostrovsky's surviving siblings. The Ostrovsky mentioned here is the unpublished critic of whom Chekhov wrote to Pleshcheyev in Letter 19. Chekhov acted as an intermediary between Pyotr Ostrovsky and Suvorin, helping to arrange the publication of some stories for children written by Ostrovsky's sister Nadezhda.

2. The provincial actress Yelizaveta Goreva organized her own company and brought it to Moscow for one season. The critical reception given her company by the press was disastrous.

3. Early in October, an "unofficial theatrical committee" met in St. Petersburg to consider the suitability of *The Wood Demon* for presentation at Imperial Theaters. Under the chairmanship of Grigorovich, the committee ruled that the work was a "beautiful dramatized novel, unsuitable for the stage." Furthermore, Grigorovich hastened to inform Suvorin that the figures of Professor Serebryakov and his young wife, Yelena (these characters are

nearly identical with their descendants in *Uncle Vanya*), were patterned by Chekhov after Suvorin and his much younger second wife, Anna. The duplicity and tactlessness that Grigorovich displayed in this entire affair considerably diminished the respect and admiration that Chekhov previously felt for him.

Suvorin never served as a prototype for any character in Chekhov's work; however, he was to make a veiled, thoroughly disguised appearance in "Goosefoot" (*Lebeda*), a story Vladimir Nabokov wrote in 1932. As the Russian version of Nabokov's autobiography (*Other Shores*, 1954) makes clear, this story of a young boy's agonizing over his father's involvement in a duel was based on an analogous episode in the writer's own childhood, when his father, the leader of the Constitutional-Democratic party, was slandered by an article published in *New Times* and challenged Suvorin to a duel. This would make Suvorin the real-life prototype of the fictional Count Tumansky of the story. But the character's similarity to Suvorin does not extend beyond this initial point of departure: in the story, Tumansky is supposedly a dangerous adversary and it is by a lucky chance that the boy's father is not killed; the real-life Suvorin was nearly eighty at the time of the challenge (*ca.* 1912) and the duel never did take place.

4. The political police in tsarist Russia.

5. The actor Pavel Svobodin, who was trying to arrange a St. Petersburg production of *The Wood Demon*.

6. Chekhov's "A Dreary Story" had just been published and its publication gave rise to numerous discussions and misinterpretations. Everyone admired it, but even such men as Suvorin, Grigorovich and Pleshcheyev managed to read into it things that Chekhov never intended to say. His irritation with the widespread misunderstanding of his story may have contributed to his ripening decision to move away from literature for a while.

The first-person form of narration used in the story leads commentators to this day to identify the twenty-nine-year-old Chekhov with the aged and dying professor who narrates "A Dreary Story." Even though Chekhov here explicitly denies this identity, it has served as a point of departure for a number of later essays on Chekhov, and especially for Lev Shestov's "Creation Out of the Void."

7. "The Resident" (*Zhitel*) was the pen name of Alexander Dyakov, whose vitriolic columns in *New Times* Chekhov strongly disliked.

8. Suvorin's *Yearbook* for 1890 contained Chekhov's story "Champagne," an essay about him, and his portrait, which was printed facing a portrait of Shah Nasr-ed-Din of Persia.

VI

THE JOURNEY TO SAKHALIN

Chekhov, probably as devoted to the purity of art as Ralph Ellison, dragged himself from a sick-bed to visit the penal colony at Sakhalin Island and speak to the conscience of his country about the tormented prisoners. Other writers have done similar deeds, for they have felt obliged to live not merely as writers but also as men engaged with the problems and passions of their time. Was Chekhov "right" in doing what he did? I don't know. All I would like to say is that his trip to Sakhalin was, for him, necessary and, in my view of things, noble.

—IRVING HOWE, "A Reply to Ralph Ellison"

I like your part about Chekhov arising from the sick bed to visit the penal colony at Sakhalin Island. It was, as you say, a noble act. But shouldn't we remember that it was significant only because Chekhov was *Chekhov*, the great writer?

—RALPH ELLISON, "A Rejoinder"

(Both in *The New Leader*, February 3, 1964)

NO OTHER EVENT in Chekhov's life is more surrounded by myths, more misunderstood and more frequently misinterpreted than his Sakhalin journey. There are two principal interpretations of this journey that are widespread in the West, both of them simplistic and essentially wrong. The first interpretation is political: the mortally ill Chekhov traveled to Sakhalin in order to write an exposé of the mistreatment of political prisoners by the tsarist authorities. This view, partially embodied in Irving Howe's statement quoted above, assumes that Chekhov's motives for the trip are obvious to everyone and are generally known. The second, opposing interpretation, as expressed in Lillian Hellman's commentary to her edition of Chekhov's letters and, significantly enough, by the annotators of the 1944–51 Soviet edition of Chekhov, assumes that Chekhov had some mysterious private motive for going to Sakhalin which he for some reason failed to state to anyone in the vast body of letters he wrote during the trip and in his subsequently written book about it.

The assumptions about Chekhov's health are wrong to begin with. Although he undoubtedly had incipient tuberculosis in 1890, he was in no sense a sick or dying man. For all the hardships of the journey and the backbreaking work of census taking, the fresh air, regular hours and wholesome food he enjoyed in Siberia and Sakhalin, followed by a leisurely sea voyage through the warm Indian Ocean, must have been a tremendous improvement as far as his health was concerned over his hectic Moscow social life, long nights of drinking with other writers in smoke-filled nightclub rooms and his general hyperactive pace in the period immediately preceding his departure. His swimming exploits in the Indian Ocean, his amorous exploits in Siberia and on Ceylon, his healthy and suntanned appearance upon his return and the energy with which he undertook the extended journey through Western Europe very soon thereafter all easily demolish the myth that the Sakhalin journey was detrimental to Chekhov's health.

As for the assertion that the journey was a subversive act or an act of political defiance, its proponents should be told that Sakhalin was not any kind of political prison to begin with. It was a recently acquired territory, bleak and inhospitable, which the Russian government was trying to colonize with convicted murderers, swindlers, thieves and embezzlers. It was a penal colony in the original sense of the term, the sort of colony that the British and French governments maintained on the East Coast of North America in the eighteenth century and to which Abbé Prévost's Manon Lescaut and Daniel Defoe's Moll Flanders were sent, the kind of colony that was used to get Australia settled. There were very few political prisoners on Sakhalin (they were usually kept on the mainland in Siberia, where the government could keep a better eye on them), and the only restriction that the Sakhalin authorities imposed on Chekhov upon his arrival was that he stay away from those few. But, as Letter 49 shows, even this condition was not always met. Otherwise, Chekhov traveled to Sakhalin with the full approval of the authorities, both those in St. Petersburg and those on the island. He went as an accredited correspondent of Suvorin's pro-government newspaper, and he paid for the journey by writing his six-part cycle of travel pieces for *New Times*, "Across Siberia." The authorities on Sakhalin, for all the mismanagement and blunders which Chekhov points out in his book, had hoped that publicizing the wretched conditions in the penal settlements would move the central government to do something to improve them. They therefore gave Chekhov a free hand, delegating some of the convict-settlers to assist him with the medical-statistical census that was the main purpose of his trip to the island.

The notion that there was some unfathomable ulterior motive that caused Chekhov to undertake the journey has been devised by people who see him solely as a short-story writer and playwright and who refuse to allow for the equally important part played by medicine and biology in his life. He had not done any work on his dissertation on "The History of Medicine in Russia" since 1887, and it bothered him that the requirements for his doctoral degree were still incomplete. He had hoped to do a medical-statistical survey of the Sakhalin settlements that would be acceptable for his degree requirements in lieu of a dissertation. Chekhov's physician friends who later wrote memoirs about him, such men as Grigory Rossolimo and Isaak Altschuller, were never in any doubt that research for a thesis was one of the primary reasons for his Sakhalin journey. But this reason is too dull for popular biographies and so we get legends about political protest or even an unfortunate love affair that caused Chekhov to flee to Sakhalin.

Of course there was also a humanitarian motive involved, as the impassioned letter to Suvorin, defending the importance of Sakhalin as a research topic, makes abundantly evident (Letter 41). But, even here, the nature of Chekhov's concern and its objectives are all too often distorted or misunderstood. Most of the educated Russians of his day knew about the grim physical conditions under which the convict-settlers on Sakhalin lived—Korolenko's "Escapee from Sakhalin" and numerous other publications that were available had already informed the public on that score. What Chekhov discovered and later described in the book which took him several years to write added completely new dimensions to the previously known picture: the neglect of the orphaned children of the settlers, the widespread teen-age prostitution, the forcing of women convicts into concubinage, and the wanton and stupid mismanagement of the few available natural resources of the island. But the most harrowing passages of his book on Sakhalin do not deal with convicts or settlers at all. They describe instead the genocidal policies of both the Sakhalin authorities and the convict-settlers toward the indigenous populations, the Gilyaks and the Ainus. The heartless colonial policies that were leading to the extermination of these peoples are reflected in pages that were written in Chekhov's heart's blood; like so many other things that he tried to tell his countrymen and the world, these pages have remained mostly unread and unnoticed to this day.

39. To Mikhail Galkin-Vrasky[1]

Your Excellency
Mikhail Nikolayevich,

Planning as I am to leave for Eastern Siberia in the spring of this year on a journey with scientific and literary goals and desiring as part of this journey to visit the island of Sakhalin, both its central and southern areas, I am taking the liberty of most humbly asking Your Excellency to extend to me all possible assistance in achieving the goals stated above.[2]

With sincere respect and devotion I have the honor to remain Your Excellency's most humble servant,

Anton Chekhov

20 January, 1890
Malaya Italyanskaya 18, c/o A. S. Suvorin

1. The chief administrator of all the prisons and penal institutions of the Russian Empire. This letter is the first written record of Chekhov's intention to go to Sakhalin.

2. Chekhov personally took this letter to the office of the Central Prison Administration in St. Petersburg and was at that time received by Galkin-Vrasky, who promised him every kind of assistance in carrying out his project. But that promise proved illusory and it was only because of the cooperation of the two highest officials on the local level, Baron Korf and General Kononovich, that Chekhov was able to accomplish what he did on the island.

The "secret order" that Galkin-Vrasky dispatched to Sakhalin, instructing the authorities there to bar Chekhov from contact "with certain categories of political prisoners and exiles," discovered in the archives after the October Revolution, of which so much is made in the commentary to the 1944–51 edition of the letters (a part of that commentary is quoted in a footnote to this letter in the Lillian Hellman volume in English), was not in the least secret, since Chekhov was informed upon his arrival on Sakhalin that he had to stay away from *all* categories of political prisoners there.

40. To Alexei Pleshcheyev[1]

Moscow,
February 15, 1890

I just received your letter, dear Alexei Nikolayevich, and I am answering it at once. So you've had a name day, have you? And I forgot!! Please forgive me and accept my belated best wishes.[2]

Do you mean you really don't care for *The Kreutzer Sonata*?[3] I won't say it's an immortal work or a work of genius—I'm no judge of that—but in my opinion, among the mass of what is presently being written here and abroad, you won't find anything to match it in importance of conception or beauty of execution. Even without mentioning its artistic achievements, which are in certain passages astounding, you must be grateful if only because the work is extremely thought-provoking. As you read it, you can barely keep from shouting, "That's true!" or "That's ridiculous!" True, it has some very irritating faults. Besides the ones you listed, there is one that I am unwilling to pardon the author, namely the audacity with which Tolstoy treats topics about which he knows nothing and which out of obstinacy he does not wish to understand. For example, his opinions on syphilis, foundling homes, women's revulsion for sexual intercourse and so on are not only debatable; they expose him as an ignorant man who has never at any point in his long life taken the trouble to read two or three books written by specialists. Nevertheless, these faults are as easily dispersed as feathers in the wind; the worth of the work is such that they simply pass unnoticed. And, if you do notice them, the only result is that you find yourself annoyed it has not escaped the fate of all human works, all of which are imperfect and tainted.

So my Petersburg friends and acquaintances are angry at me?[4] What for? Because I annoyed them too little with my presence, which has long since become annoying to myself! Set their minds at rest. Tell them that while in Petersburg I had many dinners and many suppers, *I didn't capture the heart of a single lady*, that every day I was certain I'd be leaving on the evening express, that I was held back by friends and the *Marine Almanac*, which I had to go through page by page, beginning with 1852. While I was in Petersburg, I got more done in a month than my young friends could possibly do in a whole year. Well let them be angry.

Young Suvorin wired my family as a joke that Shcheglov and I had left for Moscow in a troika, and they believed it.[5] As for the 35,000 couriers galloping after me from the ministries[6] to invite me to become governor general of the Island of Sakhalin, it is simply nonsense. My brother Misha wrote the Lintvaryovs that I was going through the procedure necessary to get to Sakhalin, and they must have misunderstood him. If you see Galkin-Vrasky, tell him not to bother trying to get his report reviewed in the press. I will devote a great amount of space to his reports in my book and immortalize his name. The reports could have been better: the material is fine and rich, but its authors—civil service officials—were unable to do it justice.[7]

I've been sitting here all day reading and taking notes. I have nothing but Sakhalin in my head or on paper. Mental derangement. *Mania Sachalinosa*.[8]

I recently had dinner at Yermolova's. When a wildflower is placed in a bouquet of carnations, the good company adds to its fragrance. Two days after dining with a star, I can still feel the halo around my head.

I've just read Modest Tchaikovsky's *Symphony*.[9] I liked it. Reading it leaves a very clear-cut impression. The play ought to be a success.

Good-bye for now. Come visit us. Regards to your family. My sister and mother send their best.

Yours,
A. Chekhov

1. This letter is a detailed, point-by-point reply to Pleshcheyev's letter of February 13, 1890, which was first published in volume 68 of *Literary Heritage* in 1960. To facilitate the reader's comprehension of the letter's content, pertinent passages from Pleshcheyev's letter are cited, in quotation marks, at the beginning of some of the notes.

2. "Your letter came as a nice present for my name day, which was the day on which I received it."

3. "I've read *The Kreutzer Sonata* and I cannot say that it produced a particularly strong impression on me. [. . .] The first half of it, especially, contains much that is paradoxical, one-sided, extraordinary and possibly even false. Of course you dare not open your mouth about any of this in front of his admirers."

Because of its sexual content, this novel of Tolstoy's was banned by the censors. It was published clandestinely in an edition of three hundred copies, which were passed around from hand to hand. It was in this edition that both Chekhov and Pleshcheyev read it. Eventually, it took a personal visit by Countess Tolstoy to Emperor Alexander III to secure the authorization for a general publication of *The Kreutzer Sonata*.

4. ". . . had you lived here [i.e., in St. Petersburg] permanently, you would most likely write nothing, but only have dinners, suppers, and capture the hearts of ladies. [. . .] Some of your friends in St. Petersburg are displeased with you (I don't mean the ones associated with the *New Times*) and, I must say, not without reason. In a sense, I could include myself among them. None of us managed to have a proper conversation with you. You dropped in on everyone for only a moment, you were always in a hurry to leave, as if you had paid a call out of a sense of duty, and, finally, you bid everyone good-bye, saying to some you were departing on that very day and to others that it was on the next one. And then you remained in St. Petersburg for another two weeks. Translated into ordinary human speech this could only mean: will all of you please leave me alone."

Chekhov spent most of January of 1890 in St. Petersburg, arranging the authorization and financial backing for his trip and doing extensive research in various libraries on the history, geography, geology and fauna of Sakhalin. At first, he found it difficult to convince even such good friends as Suvorin and Pleshcheyev of the seriousness of his intentions and the depth of his commitment to the project. Hence the complaints about his supposed aloofness and unsociability.

5. "Georges Lintvaryov told me that your brother Mikhail wrote to the

Lintvaryov family that you and Shcheglov departed from St. Petersburg for Moscow not by train but by troika and that you are being sent to Sakhalin by the Ministry of the Interior to inspect something or other. Why this mystification?"

6. Reference to Khlestakov's drunken bragging in Gogol's *The Inspector General.*

7. "Last Sunday Galkin-Vrasky paid me a visit, although he usually comes to see me very rarely. I was not in and he left his calling card. Apparently there was something he needed from me. I have not gotten around to repaying his call; this might incur his wrath, which, however, is no concern of mine. I will have to tell him that you took the copy of the Report on Prisons from the editorial office, otherwise he might expect us [i.e., *Northern Herald*] to review it."

8. During his research in St. Petersburg, Chekhov compiled a basic bibliography on Sakhalin, comprising sixty-five titles. Works on penology (which is always assumed to have been his sole concern during his trip to Sakhalin) are only a small portion of this total. He was equally interested in a large number of additional topics: the island's native inhabitants, the history of its colonization, the memoirs of travelers who had been there (he found a large number of these unreliable), and he paid considerable attention to the island's wildlife and natural resources.

When he returned to Moscow early in February, his sister Maria and a group of her fellow students at the teachers' college for women she was attending were organized into a voluntary corps of research assistants. They looked up the various items he needed in old periodicals and translated for him references published in languages he could not read. In addition, Mikhail Chekhov, who was at law school, had to supply his brother with materials pertaining to criminal law, and Alexander Chekhov in St. Petersburg kept getting requests for library materials not available in Moscow. By the time Chekhov left for Sakhalin late in April of the same year, he had amassed enough research material on the subject for a whole thick volume.

9. A play by Modest Tchaikovsky, set in a musicians' milieu, which had a considerable success in Russian theaters during the next few years.

41. To Alexei Suvorin

Moscow,
March 9, 1890
Forty Martyrs and 10,000 larks[1]

We are both mistaken about Sakhalin, but you are probably more mistaken than I am. I am going there absolutely secure in the thought that my journey will not make any valuable contributions to literature or science: I have neither the knowledge, time nor pretensions for that. My plans are neither Humboldtian nor even Kennanian.[2] I want to write at least one or two hundred pages to pay off some of my debt to medicine, toward which, as you know, I've behaved like a pig.[3] I may not be able to write anything at all, but the journey still retains its charm for me. By reading, looking around and listening, I'll discover and learn a great deal. I haven't even left yet, but thanks to the books I've had to read, I've learned about things that everyone should know on pain of forty lashes and that I had the ignorance not to know before. Besides, the journey as I see it means six months' continuous physical and mental labor, something I absolutely need, because I'm a Southerner and have already begun to grow lazy. I've got to discipline myself. Granted, my journey may be trifling, hardheaded, capricious, but think a while and tell me what I stand to lose by going. Time? Money? Will I suffer hardships? My time is worth nothing and I never have any money anyway. As for hardships, the horse-drawn part of the trip won't last more than twenty-five or thirty days; the rest of the time I'll be sitting on the deck of a steamer or in my room and constantly bombarding you with letters. Granted, I may get nothing out of it, but there are sure to be two or three days out of the whole trip that I'll remember all my life with rapture or bitterness. And so on and so forth. There you have it, kind sir. All this may be unconvincing, but what you write is just as unconvincing. You write, for instance, that Sakhalin is of no use or interest to anyone. Is that really so? Sakhalin could be of no use or interest only to a society that doesn't deport thousands of people to it and doesn't spend millions on it. Except for Australia in the past and Cayenne, Sakhalin is the only place where the use of convicts for colonization can be studied. All Europe is interested in it, and we don't find it of any use? Not more than twenty-five to thirty years ago our own Russians performed astounding feats in the exploration of Sakhalin, feats that are enough to make you want to deify man, but we have no use for it, we don't even know who those people were,[4] and all we do is sit within our four walls and complain what a mess God has made of creating man. Sakhalin is a place of unbearable suffering, the sort of suffering only man, whether free or subjugated, is capable of. The people who work near it or on it have been trying to solve problems involving frightening responsibility; they are still trying. I'm sorry I'm not sentimental or I'd say that we ought to make pilgrimages to places like Sakhalin the way the Turks go to Mecca. Moreover, sailors and penologists ought to regard Sakhalin the way the military regards Sevastopol. From the books I've read and am now reading, it is evident that we have let *millions* of people rot in jails, we have let them rot to no purpose, unthinkingly and barbarously. We have driven people through the cold, in chains, across tens of thousands of versts, we have infected them with syphilis, debauched them, bred criminals and blamed it all on red-nosed prison wardens. Now all educated Europe knows that all of us, not the wardens, are to blame, but it's still none of our business; it's of no interest to us. The much-glorified sixties[5] did *nothing* for the sick and the people in prison and thereby violated the chief commandment of Christian civilization. In our time a few things are being done for the sick, but nothing at all for the prisoners; prison management holds absolutely no interest for our jurists. No, I assure you, Sakhalin is of great use and interest, and the only sad part of it all is that I'm the one who's going and not someone more conversant with the problems and capable of arousing public interest. I myself am going there on a trivial pretext.

Concerning my letter about Pleshcheyev, I wrote you that my young friends had become dissatisfied with my idleness and to justify myself I wrote you that, my idleness notwithstanding, I still accomplished more than my friends who never do anything at all. At least I read *Marine Almanac* and went to see Galkin, whereas they didn't do a thing.[6] That's all there is to it, I guess.

We've been having some grandiose student disorders. It all began with the Academy of Peter the Great when the administration prohibited students from taking girls to official dormitory rooms, suspecting the girls not only of prostitution, but of politics as well. From the Academy it spread to the University, where students, surrounded by heavily armed Hectors and Achilleses, mounted and bearing lances, are now demanding the following:

1. Complete autonomy for universities.
2. Complete academic freedom.
3. Free admission to the university without regard to religion, nationality, sex or social status.
4. Admission of Jews to the university without any restrictions, in addition to granting them rights equal to those of other students.
5. Freedom of assembly and recognition of student associations.
6. Establishment of a university and student tribunal.
7. Abolition of school inspectors' police functions.
8. Lowering of tuition.

I copied this with a few abridgments from a leaflet. I think the flames are being fanned most vehemently by a bunch of young Jews and by the sex that is dying to get into the university, though five times worse prepared than the men, while even the men are miserably prepared and with rare exceptions make abominable students.[7]

I've sent you Krasheninnikov, Khvostov and Davydov, *Russian Archives* (III, 1879) and *Proceedings of the Archeological Society* (1 and 2, 1875).

Please send the sequel to Khvostov and Davydov if there is one, and I need volume five of the 1879 *Russian Archives*, not volume three. I'll mail out the rest of the books either tomorrow or the day after.[8]

I deeply sympathize with Gey,[9] but he is torturing himself without cause. There are excellent treatments for syphilis these days; it can be cured beyond any doubt.

Send me my farce *The Wedding* along with the books. Nothing else. Come and see Maslov's play.[10]

Keep well and content. I am as willing to believe in your old age as in the fourth dimension. In the first place, you're not an old man yet; you think and work enough for ten people and the way you use your mind is far from senile. In the second place, you have no illnesses besides migraine headaches; I will swear to it. In the third place, old age is bad only for bad old people and difficult only for the difficult, and you're a good person who is not difficult. And in the fourth place, the difference between youth and age is quite relative and dependent on convention. And with this, out of respect for you, allow me to fling myself into a deep gorge and smash my skull to smithereens.

Yours,
A. Chekhov

A while ago I wrote you about Ostrovsky.[11] He's paid me another visit. What shall I say to him?

You ought to go to Feodosia! The weather is marvelous.

1. The Feast of the Forty Martyrs of Sebastia was celebrated on the day of the vernal equinox (March 9 on the Julian calendar corresponded to March 21 on the Gregorian one in the nineteenth century). The day was traditionally marked in Russia by eating sweet rolls shaped to resemble birds, with cloves for eyes, which were called "larks" (*zhavoronki*).

2. The German scientist Friedrich Heinrich Alexander von Humboldt explored the Far Eastern areas of the Russian Empire at the invitation of the Russian government in 1829. The American traveler and journalist George Kennan visited the Siberian prisons in 1886 and described his impressions of them in a series of articles which appeared in a magazine, the title of which is cited in the 1944–51 edition of Chekhov's letters as *The contrari Monthey Magasine* (i.e., *The Century Illustrated Monthly Magazine*). Kennan's exposés of the conditions in Siberia were banned in Russia, but they were printed abroad in Russian-language editions, which were clandestinely imported into Russia. After the abolition of preliminary censorship in 1905, collections of Kennan's articles appeared in Russia in several simultaneous editions.

3. As clear a statement of Chekhov's true motive for going to Sakhalin as one could wish—in addition to the humanitarian ones expressed in this

letter—but apparently not clear enough for the partisans of the "secret, undiscoverable motive" theory.

4. Chekhov had in mind the explorations of Sakhalin described in Gennady Nevelskoy's book *The Exploits of Russian Naval Officers in the Russian Far East 1849–55,* which he read in the course of his preparatory research and which he cites in his book on Sakhalin.

5. I.e., the period of the reforms of the 1860s.

6. Reference to the widespread complaints by Chekhov's St. Petersburg friends about his unavailability to them during his Sakhalin research.

7. Free admission of women and Jews provided the main issue for the student disturbances on this occasion as it did on so many others at the end of the nineteenth century. There is a striking difference in Chekhov's tone and attitude toward the student disturbances in this letter and in the letters he was to write to Suvorin on the same subject in 1899, with their understanding and sympathy for the students' demands and position.

8. Books and scholarly journals that Suvorin lent Chekhov for his research out of his own personal library and from the library of *New Times.* Stepan Krasheninnikov's book was a compilation of Russian scientific explorations of the early nineteenth century. Khvostov and Davydov were two Russian naval officers who sailed to America and published a book about their voyage in 1810.

9. Gey was the pen name of Bogdan Heymann, who wrote for *New Times* on foreign affairs.

10. Maslov's *The Seducer of Seville* was, despite Chekhov's intercession, turned down by Korsh's company. It was, however, accepted by the Maly Theater, where it had its première on April 9, 1890. It did not last beyond the end of its first season there and was quickly forgotten.

11. Pyotr Ostrovsky was apparently still pestering Chekhov to get Suvorin to publish his sister's stories.

42. To Ivan Leontyev (Schcheglov)

Moscow,
March 22, 1890

Greetings, dear Jeanchik,[1]

Thank you for your long letter and the good will that fills it from top to bottom. I'll be glad to read your military story. Will it come out in the Easter issue? It's been a long time since I've read anything of yours or anything of my own.

You write that you feel like giving me a harsh scolding, "particularly for my views on moral and artistic problems," you talk vaguely of some crimes of mine as deserving of friendly reproach, and even threaten me with "influential newspaper critics." If we cross out the word "artistic," the entire phrase in quotation marks becomes clearer, but takes on a meaning which I must say disturbs me quite a bit. What's going on, Jean? How shall I take it? Can my ideas of morality differ so greatly from the ideas of people like you that I am deserving of reproach and the special attention of influential critics? I can't accept the possibility that you have some complex, lofty morality in mind, because there is no such thing as low, high or medium morality; there is only one, the one which in days of old gave us Jesus Christ[2] and which now prevents you, me and Barantsevich from stealing, calling names, lying, etc. As for me, if I can trust my clear conscience, never in my life have I ever in word, deed or thought, in my stories or farces coveted my neighbor's wife, nor his manservant, nor his ox, nor any of his cattle,[3] nor have I ever stolen, or played the hypocrite, or flattered the strong, or sought any advantage from them, or engaged in blackmail, or lived at another's expense. True, I have wasted my life in idleness, laughed mindlessly, made a glutton of myself and indulged in drunkenness and fornication,[4] but all that is my own personal affair and doesn't deprive me of the right to think that as far as morality is concerned I am distinguished from the ranks by neither pluses nor minuses, neither feats nor infamies: I am just like the majority. I have committed many sins, but I am quits with morality: I more than pay for my sins with the discomforts they entail. And if you want to give me a harsh scolding for not being a hero, you'd do better to throw your harshness out the window and substitute your charming tragic laugh for the scolding.

As to the word "artistic," it frightens me the way brimstone frightens merchants' wives. When people speak to me of what is artistic and what anti-artistic, of what is dramatically effective, of tendentiousness and realism and the like, I am at an utter loss, I nod to everything uncertainly, and answer in banal half truths that aren't worth a brass farthing. I divide all works into two categories: those I like and those I don't. I have no other criterion. And if you were to ask me why I like Shakespeare and do not like Zlatovratsky,[5] I would be unable to answer. Maybe with time, when I grow wiser, I'll acquire a criterion, but in the meanwhile all discussions on what is and is not artistic wear me out. I see them as a continuation of the same scholastic discourses that people used in the Middle Ages for purposes of wearing themselves out.

If the critics to whose authority you refer know something you and I do not know, then why have they kept it to themselves for so long? Why don't they reveal their truths and immutable laws to us? If they did know some such thing, then believe me they would have long since showed us the way and we would know what to do, Fofanov wouldn't be locked up in an insane asylum, Garshin would still be alive,

Barantsevich would not be in the doldrums, and we wouldn't be as absolutely and utterly bored as we are now, and you wouldn't feel drawn to the theater, nor I to Sakhalin.[6] But the critics maintain a dignified silence or talk their way out with idle blather. If they seem influential to you, it is only because they are nothing more than an empty barrel you can't help hearing.[7]

But let's drop all that and change the subject. Please don't place great literary hopes on my Sakhalin trip. I'm not going for observations or impressions; all I want to do is live six months differently from the way I've lived so far. Don't get your hopes up, old boy. If I have the time and ability to get something done, so much the better, if not, accept my humble apologies. I'll be setting out after Easter Week. I'll send you my Sakhalin address and detailed instructions as soon as I can. My family sends their regards, and I send mine to your wife.

Dear mustachioed junior captain,[8] stay well and happy.

Yours,
A. Chekhov

1. The Russian diminutive suffix *-chik* is added to the French version of Shcheglov's first name.

2. The meaning of the Russian is quite unequivocal here. Nevertheless, both Constance Garnett and the translator of the Lillian Hellman edition have disregarded the Russian syntax, the active participle and case governance, and translated this phrase as "only one which Jesus Christ gave us" and "only one, namely, that given us in his day by Jesus Christ," respectively. In terms of determining Chekhov's attitude to both morality and religion, it is surely important to know that he says morality gave Christ to the world and not vice versa.

3. Paraphrase of either Exodus 20:17 or Deuteronomy 5:21.

4. The elevated Church Slavic grammar and vocabulary of the original quotes and paraphrases a passage from an Orthodox Lenten prayer.

5. Nikolai Zlatovratsky, author of Populist novels that were for several generations the favorite reading of Russian radical university students.

6. An eloquent expression of Chekhov's disgust with literary circles and literary politics at the time of his departure for Sakhalin. This passage is a reply to the following statement in Shcheglov's letter to Chekhov of March 20: "Fofanov is in a mental institution. Gleb Uspensky is suffering from hallucinations. Albov recently buried his wife, to whom he had been married for only eight months, while Barantsevich is yearning to challenge some scoundrel to a duel and to die the death of Lermontov." On Mikhail Albov, see Letter 63.

7. Reference to Krylov's "The Two Barrels" which Chekhov already referred to in Letter 6.

8. Shcheglov's army rank.

43. To Vukol Lavrov[1]

Moscow,
April 10, 1890

Vukol Mikhailovich,[2]

In the March issue of *Russian Thought*, on page 147 of the book review section I happened to read the following sentence: "Only yesterday the high priests of unprincipled writing, like Messrs. Yasinsky[3] and Chekhov, whose names" etc. Criticism usually goes unanswered, but in this instance, it seems to be a question not of criticism, but of libel, plain and simple. I might have let even libel go by, except that in a few days I will be leaving Russia for an extended period, perhaps never to return,[4] and I lack the strength to refrain from responding.

I have never been an unprincipled writer or, what amounts to the same thing, a scoundrel.

True, my literary career has consisted of an uninterrupted series of errors, sometimes flagrant errors, but that can be explained by the dimensions of my talent, not by whether I am a good or bad person. I have never gone in for blackmail, I have never written lampoons or denunciations, I have never toadied, nor lied, nor insulted. In short, I have written many stories and editorials that I would be only too glad to throw out because of their worthlessness, but I have never written a single line I am ashamed of today. If we assume that what you mean by a lack of principles is the sad situation that I, an educated man whose work frequently sees print, have done nothing for those I love and that my writing career has left no trace on, say, the *zemstvo*, the new courts, freedom of the press, freedom in general and so on, then in this respect *Russian Thought* should in all fairness think of me as a comrade instead of leveling accusations against me, because so far it has gone no farther than I in this direction—but you and I are not the ones to blame for this situation.

Even when judged externally as a writer, I certainly do not deserve to be publicly accused of a lack of principles. To date I have led a secluded life, shut up within four walls. You and I meet once every two years, and I have never even seen Mr. Machtet,[5] for instance, and you can judge by that how often I get out of the house. I have always made a point of avoiding literary soirées, parties, conferences, etc. I never show my face in editorial offices without an invitation, I've always tried to have my friends think of me more as a doctor than a writer—in short, I was a modest writer, and the letter I am writing you now is my first immodest act in the ten years of my career as a writer. I am on excellent terms with my colleagues; I have never taken it upon myself to judge them or the journals and newspapers they work for, considering it beyond my competence and realizing that, given the present dependent state of the press, every word against a journal or a writer is not only merciless and tactless, but nothing less than criminal. Until now I have made a policy of refusing my services only to journals and newspapers whose shoddy quality was obvious and well proven, but when forced to choose among them, I gave preference to those who needed my services most of all, whether for material or other reasons. That is why I have worked for the *Northern Herald* and not for you or for the *Herald of Europe*, and that is why I have earned half as much as I could have earned if I had had a different view of my duties.

Your accusation is a libel. I cannot ask you to take it back, since the damage has already been done and cannot be chopped out with an ax. Nor can I explain it as an imprudence or an act of thoughtlessness or something else along those lines, since I am aware that the people who work in your editorial office are unquestionably decent and well brought up and, I hope, do not merely read and write articles, but exercise a feeling of responsibility for their every word. The only thing left for me to do is point out your error to you and ask you to believe in the sincerity of the oppressive feeling that led me to write you this letter. It goes without saying that after your accusation all business relations between us and even conventional social relations have become impossible.[6]

A. Chekhov

1. Lavrov was a member of a wealthy Moscow merchant family, whose fortune he inherited. He invested a part of it in the left-liberal literary journal *Russian Thought*, of which he was owner, publisher and editor. He translated Polish writers (especially Henryk Sienkiewicz) into Russian and was noted for giving large and lavish literary dinner parties. Lavrov's son Mikhail was one of the leaders of the 1899 student strike at St. Petersburg University and was responsible for getting Chekhov interested in the students' side of the strike (see Letter 120).

2. The address by first name and patronymic alone, not preceded by any adjective, is deliberately abrupt to the point of rudeness. This letter and the preceding one to Shcheglov represent Chekhov's cumulative reaction to four years of critical baiting and endless accusations of "indifference," "lack of involvement" and "absence of principles." This psychologically significant flareup on the eve of his departure for Sakhalin was to remain the only one of its kind and was not repeated in Chekhov's later life.

3. Ieronim Yasinsky was a very minor writer who in the course of his long life (1850–1930) indeed changed his convictions and positions numerous times. A sort of radical in his youth (the exiled Chernyshevsky hailed the young Yasinsky as the finest Russian writer since Turgenev and Tolstoy), he moved toward the positions of extreme reaction in the 1890s and was the first Russian writer to align himself with Lenin after the October takeover. Ostensibly a personal friend of Chekhov's, Yasinsky also led the critical pack at the time of the initial failure of *The Seagull,* penning a poisonous, but unfortunately untranslatable epigram about the play, which is his only utterance that is still remembered.

4. A unique instance in which Chekhov's emotion has led him to tell an outright lie.

5. Grigory Machtet was a revolutionary writer and journalist who spent several years in the United States in the early 1870s (and wrote voluminously about his experiences there) and also a number of years in exile in Siberia. He was a valued contributor to *Russian Thought.*

6. This letter occasioned a two-year break in relations between Lavrov and Chekhov, after which they made up and became rather close friends (Lavrov eventually came to be one of Chekhov's very few literary friends with whom he was on a first-name basis).

44. To Alexei Suvorin

Blagoveshchensk,[1]
June 27, 1890

Greetings, dearest friend. The Amur is a very fine river; it has given me much more than I ever expected. I've been meaning to share my raptures with you for a long time now, but the damn boat vibrated seven days straight and kept me from writing. Besides, I lack the skill to describe anything as beautiful as the banks of the Amur; I am at a loss and concede my impoverishment. How can it be described? Think of the Suram Pass forced into being a river bank—and there you have the Amur. Cliffs, crags, forests, thousands of ducks, herons and all sorts of long-beaked rascals, and utter wilderness. The Russian bank is on the left, the Chinese on the right. If I feel like it, I can look at Russia, and if I feel like it, I can look at China. China is just as barren and savage as Russia: villages and sentinel huts are few and far between. Everything in my head has jumbled up and turned to dust. And no wonder, Your Excellency! I've sailed more than a thousand versts down the Amur and seen millions of landscapes. And before the Amur, mind you, there was Lake Baikal and the Transbaikal region. I can truly state that after seeing such riches and experiencing so many delights I am now not afraid of dying. People on the Amur are out of the ordinary; the life is interesting and quite unlike ours. The only subject of conversation is gold. Gold, gold, and nothing but gold. I'm in a silly mood. I don't feel like writing. I'm writing much too little, and even that like a pig. Today I mailed you four pages about the Yenisey and the taiga, and I will be sending you material about Baikal, the Transbaikal region, and the Amur. Don't throw them away. I will collect them and use them as a sort of musical score to tell you about what I can't get down on paper. I've just changed boats and am now on the steamship *Muravyov,* which is said not to vibrate. Maybe I'll be able to write now.

I've fallen in love with the Amur. I'd be only too happy to live here a year or two. It's beautiful and spacious and free and warm. Switzerland and France have never known such freedom. The lowliest convict on the Amur breathes more freely than the highest-placed general in Russia. If you were to live here for a while, you'd write many good things and captivate the public, but as for me, I don't have the skill.

Once you get to Irkutsk, you start running across the Chinese and they're as thick as flies. They are a most good-natured people. If Nastya and Borya got to know the Chinese, they'd stop playing with their donkeys and transfer their sympathies to the Chinese. They'd make delightful pets.[2]

Once you get to Blagoveshchensk, you start seeing the Japanese, or to be more exact, Japanese women, petite brunettes with large, complicated hairdos, beautiful torsos, and, as I had occasion to observe, low-slung hips. They dress beautifully. Their language is dominated by the sound "ts" [. . .]. The Japanese girl's room was neat, asiatically sentimental, and cluttered with bric-a-brac. [. . .].[3]

When I invited a Chinese to have a vodka with me at the buffet, he kept offering his glass to me, the bartender, and the waiters and saying, "Taste, taste," before taking a drink himself. It's the Chinese ceremonial. Instead of drinking it all down at once the way we do, he took little gulps, had a bite of something to eat after each gulp, and then, to express his gratitude, gave me a few Chinese coins. They're an awfully polite people. They dress austerely, but beautifully. They eat delicious food with great ceremony.[4]

The Chinese will take the Amur away from us, of that there is no doubt. They won't take it themselves; others will hand it to them, the English, for example, who are acting like provincial governors in China and building a fortress. The people living along the Amur are great scoffers. They all laugh about how Russia is fretting and fuming over Bulgaria, which isn't worth a brass farthing, and has completely forgotten about the Amur. This is neither far-sighted nor clever. But I'll save the politics for when we get together.

I got your wire suggesting I return via America. I've thought of that myself. But people have been scaring me with tales of how expensive it will be. Money can be transferred to Vladivostok, not only to New York. It goes via Irkutsk, the Bank of Siberia, where I was received with extreme kindness. I still haven't run out of money, though I'm spending it shamelessly. I sustained more than a hundred-sixty-ruble loss on the carriage,[5] and the officers who have been traveling with me have taken more than a hundred from me. But even so it's hardly likely a transfer of funds will be needed. But should the need arise I'll contact you well ahead of time. I am in perfect health. How could it be otherwise when for more than two months I've been out in the open, day and night. And what a lot of exercise!

I'm writing in a hurry because the *Yermak* is leaving with mail for Russia in an hour. You should get this letter in August. I kiss Anna Ivanovna's hand and pray to the heavens for her health and well-being. Has Ivan Pavlovich Kazansky,[6] the young student whose well-ironed trousers are so depressing, been to see you?

I've been keeping up my medical practice along the way. In the village of Reynovo on the Amur, inhabited entirely by gold prospectors, a man asked me to take a look at his pregnant wife. As I was leaving, he slipped a wad of bills into my hand. I was embarrassed and tried to refuse, assuring the patient's husband I was very wealthy and in no need of money. He then took to assuring me that he too was very wealthy. It finally ended by my slipping him back part of the wad, though fifteen rubles stayed behind in my hand.

Yesterday I treated a boy and declined the six rubles his mommy tried to slip me. Now I'm sorry I declined.

Keep well and happy. Forgive me for writing so poorly and with so few details. Have you written me a letter addressed to Sakhalin yet?

I've been going swimming in the Amur. Swimming in the Amur and chatting and dining with gold smugglers—what could be more interesting? I'm off for the *Yermak*. Good-bye! Thanks for the news about my family.

Yours,
A. Chekhov

1. A city in Eastern Siberia, where Chekhov had arrived by river boat the day before, after traveling continuously since April 21 by railroad, horse-drawn carriage and boat (and occasionally a few miles on foot), experiencing spring floods, carriage collision and shipwreck along the way.

2. The last two sentences were deleted by censors in both Soviet editions.

3. This censored version is from Maria Chekhova's pre-revolutionary

edition. But the maidenly modesty of Chekhov's sister is wildly permissive when compared to the more delicate sensibilities of the Soviet censors, both Stalinist and post-Stalinist. They were so shocked by the idea that Chekhov actually went into the room of the Japanese girl with the low-slung hips that they cut the passage off after the sound "ts" in both editions. This was apparently one of Chekhov's exotic conquests during his Sakhalin trip of which he was later to brag, rather uncharacteristically, to such friends as Grigorovich and Shcheglov.

4. Chekhov's amiable curiosity about members of other nationalities and his delight in getting to know them are a prominent feature of his entire journey. In Siberia, he had friendly encounters with some Polish exiles, banished for participation in the 1863 rebellion against the Russians. He treated a Jewish patient at one relay and accepted the family's invitation to stay for a Sabbath supper of gefilte fish, which he pronounced the best meal of his entire trip. On Sakhalin he spent almost as much time studying the Gilyaks and the Ainus as he did the convict-settlers. This is all very much at variance with the chauvinistic, anti-foreign attitude common to many nineteenth-century Russian writers.

5. Instead of depending on the postal relay coaches, Chekhov purchased a carriage in the course of his trip. This proved an ill-advised move, for the carriage kept breaking down, involving Chekhov in frequent delays and costly repairs.

6. This unfortunate student struck up a conversation with Suvorin and Chekhov during Chekhov's visit to Feodosia in 1888 and bored them both to such an unbelievable extent that he became the epitome of everything dull and boring in their subsequent correspondence.

45. To Alexei Suvorin

Tatar Strait, S.S. *Baikal*[1]
September 11, 1890

Greetings! I'm sailing through the Tatar Strait from North to South Sakhalin. I write this letter without knowing when it will reach you. I'm well, though cholera has set a trap for me and its green eyes are staring at me from all sides. Cholera is everywhere: in Vladivostok, Japan, Shanghai, Chefoo, Suez and apparently even on the moon. Quarantines and fear are everywhere. They're expecting cholera on Sakhalin too and are holding all vessels in quarantine. In short, things are out of kilter. Europeans have been dying in Vladivostok, a general's wife among them.

I spent exactly two months on North Sakhalin. I was received extremely cordially by the local administration, though Galkin never wrote a word about me. Neither Galkin, nor Baroness Uxküll,[2] nor any of the other genii I was silly enough to turn to for help gave me any help whatsoever. I've had to act entirely on my own.

Kononovich,[3] the commanding general of Sakhalin, is an intelligent and decent person. We hit it off well together, and everything went smoothly. I'll be bringing back some documents that will show you that the conditions I worked under were from the outset as favorable as could be. I saw everything, so the problem now is not *what* I saw, but *how* I saw it.

I don't know what I'll end up with, but I've gotten a good deal accomplished. I have enough for three dissertations.[4] I got up every day at five in the morning, went to bed late, and spent all my days worrying about how much I had yet to do. Now that I'm done with the penal colony, I have the feeling I've seen it all, but missed the elephant.[5]

By the way, I had the patience to take a census of the entire population of Sakhalin. I went around to each of the settlements, stopped at each hut and talked with each person. I used a filing-card system for purposes of the census, and have records of about ten thousand convicts and settlers by now.[6] In other words, there's not a single convict or settler on Sakhalin who hasn't talked with me. I was particularly successful in the children's census and I place great hopes in it.

I've had dinner at Landsberg's and sat in the kitchen of the former Baroness Heimbruck.[7] I've visited all the celebrities. I attended a flogging session, and for three or four nights thereafter dreamed of the hangman and the repulsive flogging bench. I had conversations with convicts handcuffed to wheelbarrows. Once when I was having tea in a mine, Borodavkin, the former Petersburg merchant who was sent here for arson, took a teaspoon out of his pocket and offered it to me, and as a result of all this my nerves took such a beating that I resolved never to return to Sakhalin.

I'd write you more, but there's a lady in the cabin who is constantly chattering and laughing. I don't have the strength to write. She has been laughing and jabbering since last night.[8]

This letter will go via America, but it looks as if I won't. Everyone says the American route is more expensive and more boring.

Tomorrow I'll be seeing Japan—the Island of Matsmai—in the distance. It's past eleven at night. It's dark out on the sea and the wind is blowing. I can't understand how this ship can move on and keep its bearings in the pitch darkness and in such savage, little-known waters as the Tatar Strait to boot.

When I stop and think that I am separated from the world by ten thousand versts, I am overcome with apathy. I get the feeling it will take me a hundred years to get home.

My most humble respects and cordial greetings to Anna Ivanovna and your entire family. God grant you happiness and all the best.

Yours,
A. Chekhov

I'm bored.

1. Having completed his medical census in the settlements of North Sakhalin, Chekhov was traveling by ship to the southern part of the island to continue his census-taking activities there.

2. Baroness Varvara Uxküll (1850–1929) was a member of a noted Baltic family and a widely known philanthropist, equally at home at the imperial court, with Tolstoy and Chekhov and, in the early twentieth century, with some of the best Symbolist and Acmeist poets, whose friend she was. Zinaida Gippius described her as a woman everyone instantly loved upon first meeting her. The poet Vladislav Khodasevich encountered her after the Revolution, when she lived in penury, relying on the kindness of writers whom she had once so generously helped. Chekhov was in contact with her before his departure for Sakhalin because her son, a naval officer, was stationed there.

3. In his book on Sakhalin, Chekhov wrote of General Vladimir Kononovich with tremendous warmth and respect.

4. The trip to Sakhalin was to result not only in the book about it, but also in two extremely important stories, "In Exile" and "Gusev."

5. Quotation from Krylov's fable "The Inquisitive Man," in which a visitor to a museum gets so absorbed in examining tiny insects mounted in display cases that he fails to notice that there is a stuffed elephant in the room.

6. The census data were recorded on questionnaires printed to Chekhov's specifications by the Sakhalin administration. Chekhov and his assistants filled these questionnaires with personal and medical information on every man, woman and child who lived in the penal settlements on the island at the time of his visit.

7. Karl Landsberg and Baroness Olga Heimbruck were the two best-known convicts on Sakhalin. Each had been banished there after a widely publicized criminal trial. Landsberg induced a wealthy moneylender to name him his heir and then murdered him. Olga Heimbruck was convicted of arson, which she had committed at her lover's instigation. The invitation to dinner that Landsberg sent Chekhov has been preserved in the writer's archive.

8. In *The Island of Sakhalin* this lady was described somewhat more charitably. There, her laughter was said to have been so infectious that it could make a passing whale burst out laughing. She was the wife of a naval officer stationed in Vladivostok, who left her husband behind and went to Sakhalin to escape from the cholera epidemic on the mainland.

46. To Alexei Suvorin

Moscow,
December 9, 1890
Viergang House,
Malaya Dmitrovka Street

Greetings, dearest friend! Hurrah! Well, here I am at last, sitting at my desk, praying to my slightly faded penates, and writing to you. I feel good inside, almost as if I had never left home. I am well and content to the marrow of my bones. Here is a very brief report, I spent three months plus two days on Sakhalin, not two months as was reported in your paper. My work was strenuous; I took a complete and detailed census of the entire Sakhalin population and saw *everything* except an execution. When we get together, I'll show you a trunkful of odds and ends pertaining to convict life that are extremely valuable as raw material. I now know a great deal, but have brought back unpleasant feelings. While I was living on Sakhalin, I felt nothing more than a certain bitterness in my innards, the sort that comes from rancid butter, but now, when I think back on it, Sakhalin seems to me like hell itself. For two months I worked strenuously, giving myself no rest, and during the third the bitterness I've just spoken of became more than I could stand, the bitterness and boredom and the thought that cholera was on its way to Sakhalin from Vladivostok and that I might therefore risk spending the winter quarantined in the penal colony. But thank heavens the cholera epidemic ended, and on October 13th the steamer bore me away from Sakhalin. I stopped in Vladivostok. Of the Maritime Region and of our eastern coast in general with its fleets, problems, and dreams of the Pacific all I can say is: what crying poverty! The poverty, ignorance and pettiness are enough to drive you to despair. For every honest man there are ninety-nine thieves who are a disgrace to the Russian people. We bypassed Japan because of the cholera there; as a result I didn't get to buy you anything Japanese, spending the five hundred rubles you gave me for purchases on my own needs, which gives you the legal right to have me deported to a Siberian settlement. The first foreign port on our route was Hong Kong. The bay is marvelous, and the activity on the water was like nothing I'd ever seen before, even in pictures. They have excellent roads, horse-drawn streetcars, a funicular railway, museums, botanical gardens; wherever you turn you see how solicitous the English are for their employees; there is even a sailors' club. I rode in a jinrickshaw, that is, on people, bought all sorts of baubles from the Chinese, and became outraged when I heard my fellow travelers, Russians, vilifying the English for exploiting the natives. Yes, the Englishman exploits the Chinese, the Sepoys and the Hindus, I thought, but in return he gives them roads, water mains, museums, Christianity. You do your own exploiting, but what do you give in return?[1]

Once we left Hong Kong, the ship started to roll. It was empty and made thirty-eight-degree dips, and we were afraid it would capsize. The discovery that I am not susceptible to sea sickness was a pleasant surprise. On the way to Singapore we threw overboard two men who had died. When you see a dead man wrapped in sailcloth flying head over heels into the water and when you think that there are several versts down to the bottom, you grow frightened and somehow start thinking that you are going to die too and that you too will be thrown into the sea.[2] Our horned cattle fell ill, and they were slaughtered and thrown overboard in accordance with the sentence passed by Dr. Shcherbak and yours truly.

I don't remember Singapore any too well because while driving around it I was for some reason depressed, almost in tears. Then came Ceylon, the place where I found paradise. Here in paradise I traveled more than a hundred versts by train and had my fill of palm groves and bronze women. When I have children, I'll say to them, not without pride: "Why, you sons of bitches, I've had relations in my day with a black-eyed Hindu girl, and guess where? In a coconut grove, on a moonlit night!"[3] From Ceylon we sailed thirteen days without a stop and nearly went out of our minds with boredom. I can take extreme heat quite well. The Red Sea looks dismal. Seeing Mount Sinai was a moving experience.

God's world is good. Only one thing in it is bad: we ourselves. How little justice and humility there is in us, and how poorly we understand patriotism! A drunken, frazzled, dissolute husband may love his wife and children, but what good is his love? The newspapers tell us we love our great homeland, but how do we express our love? Instead of knowledge we have insolence and arrogance beyond measure, instead of work—indolence and swinishness; we have no sense of justice, our conception of honor goes no farther than honor for one's uniform, a uniform that usually adorns the prisoner's dock in court. What is needed is work, and the hell with everything else. We must above all be just, and all the rest will be added unto us.[4]

I have a passionate desire to have a talk with you. I'm seething inside. You're the only one I want because you're the only one I can talk to. The hell with Pleshcheyev. The hell with the actors too.

Your telegrams arrived in an unbelievable state. Everything was garbled.

I traveled from Vladivostok to Moscow with the son of Baroness Uxküll (the desman[5] I wrote you about) who is a naval officer. His mother is staying at the Slavic Bazaar Hotel. I'm on my way to see her now; she's called for me for some reason. She's a good woman. At any rate her son goes into raptures over her, and he is a pure and honest boy.

How happy I am to have done without Galkin-Vrasky! He didn't write a single line about me, and when I made my appearance on Sakhalin, I was a total stranger.

When will I see you and Anna Ivanovna? How is Anna Ivanovna? Write me about everything in detail, because it's not likely that I'll get to see you before the holidays. Regards to Nastya and Borya. To prove I've been to the penal colony I'll pounce on them with a knife and scream in a savage voice when I visit you, set Anna Ivanovna's room on fire, and preach subversive ideas to poor Kostya, the public prosecutor.[6]

I embrace you all and your entire household with the exception of the Resident and Burenin,[7] to whom I ask you merely to send my regards and who should long ago have been sent off to Sakhalin.

I had many opportunities to speak about Maslov with Shcherbak.[8] I find Maslov very likable.

May the heavens keep you.

Yours,
A. Chekhov

1. After witnessing the abject misery to which Russian genocidal policies were reducing the Ainus and the Gilyaks on Sakhalin, Chekhov could hardly be expected to wax indignant over British colonial exploitation. This unfavorable comparison of Russian colonialism to its British variety was more than the nationalistic hearts of Soviet censors could take. They deleted the entire text after the words "like nothing I've ever seen before, even in pictures" from the 1944–51 edition. Of all their deletions this particular cut was the one most widely noticed by Western scholars, and because of the wide publicity it was given, the passage was reinstated in the 1963–64 edition.

2. This burial at sea was later depicted by Chekhov in the magnificently poetic closing passages of "Gusev." The provenance of the shark and the pilot fish which appear in the same portion of that story has been described by Mikhail Chekhov on the basis of his brother's account: "In the Indian Ocean, while the ship was moving full speed ahead, he would jump into the water from the prow and grab a towline thrown to him from the stern. This was his way of taking a swim. During one such swim he saw not far from him a shark and a school of pilot fish which he later described in his story 'Gusev.' "

3. Deleted by censors in both 1944–51 and 1963–64 editions. Ivan Shcheglov's journal records that at Chekhov's name-day dinner, which was

celebrated at an elegant St. Petersburg restaurant on January 17, 1891, Chekhov told the all-male group of guests (consisting of Shcheglov, Pleshcheyev and his son, the actor Svobodin and the writers Barantsevich and Modest Tchaikovsky) that "he had [. . .] a bronze woman under a palm tree" in Ceylon. He also advised Shcheglov to get himself a dusky-skinned mistress, as it would be most stimulating for his writing.

4. A formulation from the Russian version of Luke 12:31 is quoted here (the English equivalent is: "But rather seek ye the kingdom of God; and all these things shall be added unto you").

5. Baroness Uxküll's Baltic name reminded Chekhov of the Russian word *vykhukhol*, which means a desman, an aquatic insectivore, valued for its fur. Lucette in Nabokov's *Ada* wears a desman fur, identified as such in both English and Russian, when she attempts to seduce her half-brother Van.

6. Konstantin Vinogradov, the deputy chief prosecutor of the Russian navy, was a St. Petersburg friend of Suvorin's who had offered Chekhov the use of his extensive private library for preliminary research on Sakhalin.

7. The Resident (Alexander Dyakov) and Burenin were the most scurrilous and overtly reactionary members of the *New Times* staff. Shortly after Chekhov's return from Sakhalin, Burenin published a few nasty innuendoes about his trip in Suvorin's paper.

8. Dr. Alexei Shcherbak, mentioned earlier in this letter in connection with the slaughtering of sick cattle, was a naval physician who regularly traveled to Sakhalin as a part of his duties. He later published some articles about his Sakhalin experiences.

47. To Alexei Suvorin

Moscow,
December 24, 1890

We wish you and your esteemed family a happy holiday season and we wish your home many happy returns in good health and well-being.[1]

I believe in both Koch and spermine, and I praise the Lord. Kochines, spermines, etc. all appear to the public to be some sort of miracle that has sprung unexpectedly from someone's head like Pallas Athene, but people on the inside see it as nothing more than the natural result of everything that has been done for the last twenty years. Much has been done, my dear friend. Surgery alone has done so much it's dumfounding. The situation twenty years ago appears simply pitiful to today's medical student. Dear Alexei Sergeyevich, if I were offered a choice between the "ideals" of the celebrated sixties and today's poorest *zemstvo* hospital, I'd take the latter without the least hesitation.

Does the kochine cure syphilis? Possibly. But as far as cancer is concerned, you'll have to permit me to have my doubts. Cancer is not a microbe; it is a tissue that grows in the wrong place and like a weed overgrows all the neighboring tissues. If Gey's uncle has experienced some relief, it only means that erysipelatous fungus,[2] that is, the elements that produce erysipelas, is an integral part of the kochine. It has long been observed that the growth of malignant tumors is temporarily halted during erysipelas.

I hate your Trésor. I've brought some highly interesting animals back from India with me. They are mongooses, and are known for waging war on rattlesnakes. They are very inquisitive, love humans and break dishes. If it weren't for Trésor, I'd take one for a stay in Petersburg. He'd sniff out all your books and inspect the pockets of everyone who came to call. During the day he roams all over the room and follows people around, and at night he sleeps on someone's bed and purrs like a cat. He might well tear out Trésor's throat or Trésor his. He can't stand other animals.[3]

Send me stories to be polished the way you used to. I enjoy doing it.

It's really strange. On my way to Sakhalin and back, I felt perfectly healthy, and now that I'm home I don't know what the hell is going on inside me. I have a constant headache, my whole body feels lethargic, I tire quickly, I'm indifferent to everything, and most important—my heartbeat is irregular. Every minute my heart stops a few seconds and refuses to beat.

Misha has had a Rank Six uniform made and is going to make a round of official visits in it tomorrow.[4] Mother and Father look at him with tender emotion. "Lord, now lettest thou thy servant depart in peace" is written on both their faces as it was on the face of Simeon who received Our Lord at the Temple.[5]

The Baroness Uxküll (the desman) is publishing books for the peasants. The motto "Truth" adorns each book; truth costs between three and five kopecks a copy. She publishes Uspensky and Korolenko and Potapenko, and other greats. She asked me for advice on what to publish. I was unable to give her any, but recommended in passing that she rummage around in old journals, yearly miscellanies and the like. I've also advised her to read Grebenka.[6] When she complained of having trouble getting books, I promised to intercede with you on her behalf. If she does make a request, don't turn her down. The Baroness is an honest lady and won't swipe any books. Besides returning them, she'll reward you with a bewitching smile.

Alexei Alexeyevich has sent me some splendid wine.[7] Everyone who has tasted it agrees the wine is so good that you have every right to be proud of your son. He also sent me a letter in Latin. Splendid.

Yesterday I mailed you a story.[8] I'm afraid I missed the deadline. The story is on the short side, but what the hell.

In Moscow medical circles Koch is regarded with extreme caution and nine-tenths of the doctors don't believe in him.

Well, God grant you all the best and, most important of all, good health.

Yours,
A. Chekhov

1. In Russian, this sentence imitates the diction of a semiliterate person trying to sound cultured and elegant.

2. Apparently a slip of the pen for "erysipelatous organism" or "bacillus."

3. Trésor was Suvorin's dog. The mongooses Chekhov brought from India are frequently mentioned in his correspondence during the next year; decades later his sister Maria and his brother Mikhail were to recollect these animals with great fondness in their respective memoirs. The two male mongooses adjusted nicely to life in Chekhov's household. In the summer they were taken to the country, where they killed snakes and where one of them became lost in the woods and was recovered by a searching party many days later. During the winter, one of the males fell ill and was nursed back to health by Chekhov with great solicitude. The female mongoose, which was smaller and looked somewhat different from the males, was a surly little animal that spent her time hiding under the furniture, from where she would dash out now and then to sink her teeth into people's ankles. After one year it was no longer convenient to keep the mongooses about the house and Chekhov decided to donate his pets to the Moscow Zoo. It was only when Maria took them there that it was discovered that the animal sold to Chekhov in India as a female mongoose was actually a palm civet, a fierce little Asian carnivore, totally unsuited to be a domestic pet.

Chekhov's involvement with the mongooses (and his subsequent involvements with dachshunds and with his pet crane) point to a basic trait in his psychological makeup that sets him off once more from other great nineteenth-century Russian writers. To ask a possibly unfair question, could anyone ever imagine Gogol or Dostoyevsky noticing that such a thing as a mongoose existed in this world?

As for the rattlesnakes (*gremuchie zmei*), which are actually restricted to the American continent, where mongooses are not likely to get at them, this might be a slip of the pen for *ochkovye zmei* (cobras). However, all Russian nineteenth- and twentieth-century dictionaries, from Dahl to the present-day Academy of Sciences dictionary, state that rattlesnakes live "in the tropics" and do not restrict them to any particular continent. As Letter 36 suggests, Chekhov believed that rattlesnakes could be found on the banks of the Nile.

4. After finishing law school, Mikhail Chekhov, lacking confidence in his ability to become a practicing lawyer, accepted a civil service job with the Ministry of Finance and was appointed a tax inspector.

5. Quotation of Luke 2:29 and reference to the surrounding context of that verse.

6. Yevgeny Grebenka (1812–48), a Ukrainian writer who wrote both in

Ukrainian and in Russian. Chekhov recommended his folksy stories and fables to Baroness Uxküll as being of possible interest for the peasant and factory-worker readers for whom her publications were intended.

7. Suvorin's eldest son Alexei sent the wine to Chekhov in payment for reprinting his story "Champagne" in the yearbook published by Suvorin (cf. the end of Letter 38).

8. "Gusev."

48. To Anatoly Koni[1]

Petersburg,
January 26, 1891

Dear Anatoly Fyodorovich,

I have taken my time answering your letter because I won't be leaving Petersburg before Saturday.

I am sorry I didn't go to see Madame Naryshkina,[2] but I think it best to postpone a visit to her until my book comes out and until I am more at home in my material. My brief Sakhalin past seems so enormously long to me that when I wish to speak about it I don't know where to begin, and I always seem to be saying the wrong thing.

I will try to describe the situation of Sakhalin's children and adolescents in great detail. It is quite extraordinary. I saw starving children, I saw thirteen-year-old kept women, and pregnant fifteen-year-olds. Girls start practicing prostitution at the age of twelve, sometimes before the onset of menstruation. Churches and schools exist only on paper; children are educated by their milieu and the penal colony environment. I have a record, by the way, of a conversation between a ten-year-old boy and myself during my census taking in the settlement of Upper Armudan. The settlers are uniformly destitute and have a reputation for being passionate stuss players. I entered one of the huts. No one was at home but a towheaded, stoop-shouldered barefoot little boy sitting on a bench and lost in thought. We started up a conversation.

I: What is your father's patronymic?
He: I don't know.
I: You live with your father and you don't know his name? Shame on you.
He: He's not my real father.
I: What do you mean, "not real"?
He: He's just living with ma.
I: Is your mother married or widowed?
He: She's a widow. She came here for her husband.
I: What is "for her husband" supposed to mean?

He: For killing him.
I: Do you remember your father?
He: No, I don't. I'm a bastard. Ma gave birth to me on the Kara.

On the Amur steamer with me there was a prisoner in foot shackles who was going to Sakhalin for having murdered his wife. He had his six-year-old daughter with him. I noticed that whenever the father went below to the lavatory from the upper deck, his escort and his daughter followed him, and while he sat in the lavatory, his daughter and a soldier with a gun stood outside the door. When he made his way back up the ladder, his daughter clambered up behind him holding onto the shackles. At night the girl slept in a pile with the prisoners and soldiers. I remember once attending a funeral on Sakhalin. The wife of a settler who was away in Nikolayevsk was being buried. Four *ex officio* convict pallbearers; the paymaster and I, in the capacity of Hamlet and Horatio wandering around the cemetery; a Circassian, who had been a boarder of the deceased and who came out of idle curiosity; and a woman convict who came out of pity were all standing around the newly dug grave. The woman had brought along the two children of the deceased, an infant and a four-year-old boy named Alyoshka who was wearing a woman's jacket and blue pants with bright patches on the knees. It was cold and damp, the grave had water in it, and the convicts were laughing. We were in sight of the ocean. Alyoshka peered into the grave with curiosity. He tried to wipe his chilled nose, but the jacket's long sleeves got in the way. While the grave was being filled in, I asked him, "Alyoshka, where's your mother?" He made the gesture of a landowner who has been wiped out at cards, laughed, and said, "Buried!" The convicts laughed. The Circassian turned to us and asked what he was supposed to do with the children, since he's not obliged to feed them.

I met with no infectious diseases on Sakhalin, and there is very little congenital syphilis, but I did see blind children, children who were filthy and covered with rashes, the sorts of diseases that give evidence of neglect.

Of course I can't solve the child question. I don't know what needs to be done. But it seems to me that charity and the surplus left from prison and various other funds will never get anything done; to my mind, it is harmful to leave the solution up to private charity—which in Russia is very much a matter of chance—and surpluses that don't exist. I would prefer it if governmental funds were involved.[3]

My Moscow address is:

Viergang House
Malaya Dmitrovka

Allow me to thank you for your hospitality and your promise to come visit me and remain your sincerely respectful and devoted

A. Chekhov

1. Anatoly Koni (1844–1927) was one of the most prominent Russian jurists of the period, and at various times held some of the highest positions in the Russian judiciary. A great connoisseur of literature, he was a friend or associate of almost all the important Russian writers of the second half of the nineteenth century and he wrote about all of them in his fascinating memoirs, which were reissued in the Soviet Union in 1965. His memoir on Chekhov, in particular, contains one of the most sober and factual appraisals of the impact of *The Island of Sakhalin* on Russian penology and on Russian society.

2. Yelizaveta Naryshkina was a lady in waiting to the Empress Maria Fyodorovna, the wife of Alexander III. On January 18, 1891, Chekhov wrote to his sister: "I went to see Koni yesterday and we discussed Sakhalin; we've agreed to go to see Naryshkina next week to ask her to bring the Sakhalin children to the attention of the Empress and to suggest arranging an orphanage for them." In addition to her position at the court, Madame Naryshkina was also the president of two important charitable organizations concerned with aiding the families of convicts and deportees. Koni's memoirs describe her as a highly energetic, resourceful and efficient person. After Koni showed her the present letter, she started a campaign to get the authorities interested in the plight of Sakhalin children, as a result of which three children's homes were built and operated on the island by the organization she headed, with the authorities' full support.

3. Portions of this letter were later incorporated by Chekhov into the text of *The Island of Sakhalin.*

49. To David Manucharov[1]

Lopasnya,
March 21, 1896

Most Honored David Lvovich,

Let me answer your questions:

1. Baron Korf, former governor-general of the Amur region, granted me permission to visit the prisons and settlements on the condition that I avoid all contact with political prisoners—I was obliged to give him my word. I had very little occasion to speak with political prisoners, and then only in the presence of witnesses—officials (several of whom were meant to spy on me), and I know very little about their lives. Political prisoners on Sakhalin dress as they like and do not live in prisons. They serve as clerks, overseers (in the kitchen and the like),

weather station observers. While I was there, one was a church elder, another an assistant prison warder (unofficially), and yet another ran the police department library, and so on.[2] While I was there, none of them were subjected to corporal punishment. It was rumored that their morale was very low. It was also rumored that there had been cases of suicide.

2. If you have technical training, you can occupy the post of senior overseer in the local workshop, where in my time there was an extremely great need for experienced managers. Senior overseers receive fifty to sixty[3] rubles a month and even more. The way to go about securing a position is to apply to the commander of the island or visit the Main Prison Department in Petersburg. It seems to me that if you take your case to the head of the department, show him your documents, explain to him that you wish to live and work on Sakhalin for family reasons, he will deal with your request most favorably.

I wish you the best of luck and remain at your service.

A. Chekhov

1. David Manucharov was a railroad mechanic, whose younger brother had been earlier sentenced to ten years of solitary confinement at the Schlüsselburg Fortress on political charges. The sentence was later commuted to deportation to Sakhalin, and David Manucharov wrote to Chekhov, asking whether political prisoners on Sakhalin were subject to corporal punishment and whether it would be possible for him to move voluntarily to Sakhalin so as to be near his brother. Chekhov's reply, first published in 1960, is placed here in violation of the chronological sequence, since it obviously belongs with the Sakhalin letters.

2. The custom of allowing the better-educated political prisoners to occupy the more comfortable jobs in the tsarist penal colonies is the very opposite of the current practice in Soviet labor camps (as illustrated in Solzhenitsyn's *One Day in the Life of Ivan Denisovich* and *The Love Girl and the Innocent*), where the common criminals are given the privileged jobs and the political offenders are restricted to menial work.

3. The amount Alexander Chekhov was paid for his editorial job on the staff of *New Times* in St. Petersburg. High salaries, used as an enticement to get a free labor force to move voluntarily to the inhospitable regions of the Far East, remain a part of Russian reality today, eighty years after Chekhov's Sakhalin trip.

VII

WESTERN EUROPE

"GUSEV" WAS PUBLISHED in *New Times* a few weeks after Chekhov's return to Russia from Sakhalin. This story of an encounter between a dying peasant soldier and a dying radical intellectual in the sick bay of a military transport passing through the Indian Ocean was an instant and durable success. The inability of the two principal characters to communicate because of the cultural gap that separates them epitomizes the great Chekhovian theme of mutual incomprehension; the device of subtly intermingling the soldier's speech patterns and his stream of consciousness with the authorial voice, which Chekhov utilized in this story, was later to be developed to striking effect by Solzhenitsyn in *One Day in the Life of Ivan Denisovich*.

Early in January of 1891, Chekhov went to St. Petersburg for a reunion with Suvorin and other friends. It did not turn out well. "I am surrounded by a dense atmosphere of unwarranted, undefinable ill will," Chekhov wrote to his sister on January 14.

> They feed me dinners and praise me in trite eulogies, but at the same time they'd like to eat me alive. Why is that? The devil alone knows. Were I to shoot myself, it would afford great pleasure to nine-tenths of my friends and admirers. And in what petty ways they express their petty feelings! Burenin berated me in his article, even though berating your own contributors is simply not done; Maslov (Bezhetsky) keeps turning down Suvorin's invitation to come to dinner; Shcheglov collects and repeats all the gossip that circulates about me and so on. All this is horribly stupid and dreary. They are not people, they're some kind of walking mildew.

He returned to Moscow, collected and shipped several crates of books for Sakhalin schools and libraries and resumed work on "The Duel." But somehow Chekhov just could not get settled and early in March, when Suvorin suggested that he accompany him on a tour of Italy and France, he jumped at the chance. The tour lasted for a little over a month and had to be cut short because of persistent rainy weather. But, for all its brevity, Chekhov's first personal contact with the Western world resulted in a crop of highly significant letters, important for our understanding of his views and his character.

Ever since Denis Fonvizin, the finest Russian playwright of the eighteenth century, toured Western Europe on the eve of the French Revolution and declared upon his return, "We are beginning, but they are finished," the traditional outlook of Russian literary travelers in the West had been set. Ilya Ehrenburg unwittingly summed up this outlook when he explained during a visit to the United States in the late 1940s that he was not interested in seeing American theaters, universities or health clinics—all he wished to see was the slums. No matter how critical a Russian writer might be of the institutions of his own country, no matter how flawed or grim Russian reality might appear in his writings, he inevitably becomes a superpatriot once he sets foot outside Russia, ever on the lookout for proof that things are worse abroad than at home, drawing sweeping generalizations from incidental or trivial occurrences and vociferously yearning for the comforts of the familiar Russian reality he has left behind. Fonvizin on his grand tour in the eighteenth century, Dostoyevsky in Paris and London in the middle of the nineteenth, Maxim Gorky in New York at the beginning of the twentieth, Boris Pilnyak in Hollywood in the 1920s all conform to this pattern with remarkable consistency and with almost no variations.

Chekhov's independence from this chauvinist tradition is quite astounding. It does not even occur to him that unbiased observations and independent thinking might be incompatible with patriotism. He loves freedom and he loves culture and in his letters he is happy when he sees that people abroad can enjoy them. When he is jostled by a policeman during the dispersal of a demonstration in Paris, he does not see in this one incident the key to Western culture and political systems. If some aspect of foreign life is superior to something in Russia, he sees no reason for not saying so. And he does notice the things that really matter: the freedom to publish and read books on any subject in Vienna, the free and open discussion in the French Parliament of the mistreatment of striking workers by the police.

During Chekhov's subsequent visits to Western Europe, the glowing enthusiasm expressed in some of the letters in this section came to be tempered by his closer acquaintance with Western realities. But the obvious pleasure of his first encounter with European countries is a source of acute embarrassment for his Soviet biographers and annotators. The attitude he expresses is clearly the one that in Stalin's time was branded as "cosmopolitan" (this word meant the same thing in Russian that it means in other European languages until some time after World War II, when its meaning was arbitrarily changed and it came to indicate the opposite of "patriotic"). Maria Chekhova, dictating her memoirs shortly after one of the anti-cosmopolitan campaigns, when she was past ninety, made a desperate attempt to prove that her brother had liked Italy so much only because of its art and that he yearned to return to Russia every moment of his stay abroad. The 1963–64 State Publishing House edition of Chekhov's collected works solved this problem in a simpler way. Except for letters 52 and 54, all the other letters included in this section were omitted from the two thick volumes of Chekhov's letters in that edition.

50. To Maria Chekhova

Petersburg,
March 16, 1891[1]

I've just seen Duse,[2] the Italian actress, in Shakespeare's *Cleopatra.* I don't understand Italian, but she played so beautifully that I had the feeling I understood every word. A remarkable actress. I've never seen anything like it.[3] Watching Duse, I was overcome by depression from the thought that we have to form our reactions and taste on such wooden actresses as X[4] and those like her whom we call great only because we've never seen better. Looking at Duse, I realized why the Russian theater is such a bore.

I sent you a money order for three hundred rubles today. Have you received it?

After Duse it was amusing to read the enclosed address.[5] Good God, what a decline in taste and justice! And these are supposed to be students, damn their hides! It does not matter to them whether it's Solovtsov or Salvini:[6] both enjoy the same "fervid popularity in the hearts of the younger generation." Hearts of this kind aren't worth a brass farthing.

We're leaving for Warsaw tomorrow at one-thirty. Stay alive and well, all of you. I send my regards to all of you, to everyone, even the lady mongoose, who doesn't deserve regards.

I'll be keeping in touch.

With all my heart,
A. Chekhov

1. The original is dated March 16, but the annotators to the 1944–51 edition maintain that it had to have been written on the seventeenth, apparently because Chekhov wrote it after returning past midnight from the theater, where he had witnessed Duse's performance on the sixteenth.

2. It is fitting to have Chekhov's homage to the acting genius of Eleonora Duse serve as a prelude to his Italian journey. His unreserved delight at her performance in *Anthony and Cleopatra* makes an interesting contrast to his reactions to the acting of the other most celebrated actress of the period, Sarah Bernhardt, whose Moscow appearances he covered ten years earlier for several humor magazines. While Russian critics and audiences went delirious with admiration, the twenty-one-year-old Chekhov denied that the Divine Sarah had any true acting ability at all, praising her instead for her hard work. Her performance of *La Dame aux Camélias* was for Chekhov a triumph of meticulously and intelligently planned stage effects, lacking in any true depth or meaning.

3. The rest of the paragraph from this point on was deleted by the censors in the 1944–51 edition. The entire letter was omitted in the 1963–64 one.

4. Only three Russian actresses could be called "great" when this letter was written: Maria Savina, Maria Yermolova and Glykeria Fedotova. All three were alive when Maria Chekhova published her edition of the letters, the only one in which this passage appears, and since all three were on friendly terms with Chekhov, the replacement of the name with an X seems understandable. Chekhov venerated Yermolova both as an actress and as a person and he described Fedotova as a "genuine, authentic actress." His opinion of the celebrated Savina, however, is known to have deteriorated after she played Sasha in his *Ivanov.* Ivan Bunin remembered Chekhov's saying to him: "No matter how much people might admire her, Savina is to acting what Viktor Krylov is to writing drama" (Krylov was a hack of a playwright whose work Chekhov held in contempt). It seems plausible, therefore, that the name replaced by the X is that of Maria Savina.

5. A newspaper clipping was enclosed in this letter, which cited the address sent to Nikolai Solovtsov by the students of the Kharkov Technological Institute on the occasion of his guest appearance in that city. Chekhov was revolted by the trite and platitudinous wording of the address.

6. The Italian tragedian Tommaso Salvini, who made a tour of Russia and was greeted by similarly worded addresses.

51. To Maria Chekhova[1]

Vienna,
March 20, 1891

Dear Czech[2] friends,

I'm writing you from Vienna. I arrived yesterday at four in the afternoon. The trip went very well. From Warsaw to Vienna I traveled like a railroad Nana in a luxurious car of the "International Society of Sleeping Cars": beds, mirrors, gigantic windows, carpets and so on.

O my Tungus[3] friends! If you only knew how lovely Vienna is! It is not to be compared with any city I have seen in my entire life. The streets are broad and elegantly paved, there are a lot of boulevards and public gardens, six- and seven-story houses, and stores—stores that are sheer vertigo, sheer mirage! The store windows have billions of neckties alone! And what amazing bronze, china and leather objects! The churches are gigantic, but their size is not oppressive; it caresses the eyes because it seems as though they are spun of lace. St. Stefan's Cathedral and the Votiv-Kirche are especially lovely. They are more like pastries than buildings. The parliament, the town hall, the university are all magnificent. Everything is magnificent, and it wasn't until yesterday and today that I fully realized that architecture is indeed an art. And here that art is not scattered in bits and pieces as it is in our country; it extends for verst after verst. There are many monuments. No side street is without its own bookshop. Some of the bookshops even display Russian books, but alas, they are the works of all sorts of anonymous writers who write and publish abroad, not of Albov, Barantsevich or Chekhov. I've seen Renan, *Secrets of the Winter Palace*,[4] etc. It's odd that here you may read anything you like and say whatever you please.

Harken, O ye nations, unto what the goddamn cabbies here are like.[5] Instead of droshkies they have stunning, brand-new carriages with one, or more often, two horses. The horses are excellent. The driver's seats are occupied by dandies in jackets and top hats, reading newspapers. They are courteous and obliging.

The dinners are fine. There's no vodka; they drink beer and fairly good wine instead. There's only one bad point: they charge for bread. When they bring you the check, they ask you, "Wieviel Brötchen?" that is, how many rolls did you polish off? And they charge you for each roll.

The women are beautiful and elegant. When you get down to it, everything is pretty damn elegant.

I haven't completely forgotten my German. I understand them, and they understand me.

It was snowing as we crossed the border, and though there's no snow in Vienna, it's cold all the same.

I'm homesick and miss you all, and besides I feel guilty for having abandoned you again. It's no great tragedy, though. When I get back, I won't set foot out of the house for a year. My regards to everybody, everyone. Papa, do me a favor and buy me a copy of the folk print of St. Varlaam riding in a sleigh with the bishop standing on a balcony in the distance and the text of the life of St. Varlaam written out underneath. You can get it at Sytin's or wherever you like. Leave it on my desk when you get it.

We probably won't be going to Spain. We'll visit Bukhara.[6]

Semashko, have you written Ivanenko?[7] Have you spoken with Lika[8] about the city-hall job?

I wish you all the best. Don't forget me, sinner that I am. I send you all my most humble respects, I embrace you, bless you, and remain

Your loving
A. Chekhov

Everyone we meet recognizes us as Russians. No one looks me in the face; they all stare at my grizzled cap. Looking at my cap probably makes them think I'm a very rich Russian count.

Have I written you about Alexander's children? They are both well and making an excellent impression.

My regards to handsome Levitan.

1. The letter is actually addressed to the entire Chekhov family and to some of their friends as well.

2. The name Chekhov is a possessive form of the Russian word for "Czech." There is a theory that the original form of the name was Chokhov, in which case it would refer to charms and magic spells.

3. Chekhov jokingly addressed his family by the name of this Siberian tribe in the letters he wrote them from Siberia.

4. Ernest Renan's books on the history of Christianity, written from the position of scientific positivism, were banned in Russia by ecclesiastic censorship as sacrilegious. Paul Grimm's lurid German novel *Secrets of the Winter Palace*, a sensationalist exposé of the Romanov dynasty, was frequently smuggled into Russia by returning tourists.

5. An amusing mixture of biblical and vulgar diction in the original.

6. Obviously, a joke.

7. The Polish cellist Marian Semashko and the flutist Alexander Ivanenko had been close and faithful friends of the entire Chekhov family since Chekhov's student days.

8. Lydia (Lika) Mizinova was a colleague of Maria Chekhova's at the school where the latter taught after finishing teachers' college. Chekhov carried on a humorous correspondence with her, but, as her published letters to him show, rejected her attempts to establish a serious emotional relationship. But because of her rather tenuous connection with the character of Nina in *The Seagull* (always denied by Chekhov himself), because she saved and published all the letters Chekhov wrote her and because she was a great favorite of Maria Chekhova, who in subsequent years was likely to exaggerate

the importance of her brother's involvement with Lika, this rather casual friend was given a position of quite unwarranted prominence in Chekhov's popular biographies and in his legend. It is odd indeed that Lika, whom Chekhov rejected, whom he tried to hand over to Levitan and did succeed in passing on to Ignaty Potapenko, should be considered as one of his major loves, while women with whom he had deep and meaningful involvements, such as Dunya Èfros, Olga Kundasova and Lydia Yavorskaya, remain mere footnotes in his biography only because they did not choose to publish the letters he wrote them or to publicize their affairs with him.

52. To Ivan Chekhov[1]

Venice,
March 24, 1891

I am now in Venice. I arrived from Vienna the day before yesterday. All I can say is never in my life have I seen a city more remarkable than Venice. Such fascination, such glitter, such exuberance. For streets and alleyways it has canals, for cabs, gondolas, the architecture is amazing, and there's not the least corner anywhere that is unworthy of historical or artistic interest. Gliding along in a gondola, you see palaces of the doges, the house where Desdemona lived, the homes of famous artists, churches. And the churches have paintings and sculpture that surpass our wildest dreams. In a word, it's enchanting.

All day from morning till night I sit in my gondola and glide from street to street. Or else I wander all over famous St. Mark's Square. The square is as smooth and clean as parquet flooring. This is where St. Mark's Cathedral is—something that eludes description. And the Palace of the Doges and all the other buildings made me feel the way I do when I hear part singing: I feel overwhelming beauty, and revel in it.

And the evenings! Good Lord in Heaven! I could die from the novelty of it all. There you are gliding along in your gondola. It's warm, it's quiet, the stars are out. There are no horses in Venice, so it's as quiet here as in the fields. Gondolas are darting about on all sides. Then up floats a gondola strung with lanterns carrying a double bass, some violins, a guitar, a mandolin, a cornet-à-pistons, two or three ladies, several men—and you hear singing and music, operatic music. What voices! You move on a bit, and there's another boat with singers, and still another. Until midnight the air is filled with a mixture of tenors, violins and all sorts of sounds that tear at your heartstrings.

Merezhkovsky, whom I met here, has gone wild with ecstasy.[2] A Russian, poor and humbled, can very easily go out of his mind in this world of beauty, wealth and freedom. You feel like staying here forever, and when you stand in church listening to the organ, you feel like converting to Catholicism.

The burial chambers of Canova and Titian are magnificent. Great artists here are buried in church like kings. Art is not looked down upon as in our country. Churches give refuge to statues and paintings, no matter how naked they are.

There's a painting in the Palace of the Doges showing about ten thousand human figures.

Today is Sunday. There will be a band playing in St. Mark's Square.

Keep well, now. I send you all my best wishes. If you ever happen to spend a few days in Venice, they will be the best of your life. If you could only see the local glass production! Compared with local bottles, your bottles are so ugly that they make my stomach turn.[3]

I'll be keeping in touch, but good-bye for now.

Yours,
A. Chekhov

1. Chekhov's brother Ivan (1861–1922) was the only member of the family devoid of writing talent or any other artistic gift. He lived out his life as a modest schoolmaster in Moscow and in the provinces.

2. Merezhkovsky's wife, Zinaida Gippius, has described her and her husband's encounter with Chekhov and Suvorin "in the varicolored twilight of Piazza San Marco" on two occasions: in her memoir *Living Portraits* (1924) and in the biography of her husband that she wrote in Paris in 1943 shortly before her own death. Chekhov's presence made it possible for the Merezhkovskys to meet the dreaded, awesome Suvorin, whom under other circumstances this liberal-minded young couple would have refused to meet. Merezhkovsky was actually charmed by Suvorin's personality and culture and his work began appearing in Suvorin's publications as a result of this encounter.

Zinaida Gippius (more correctly, Hippius, 1869–1945) was, as we can now see, a far more talented and important writer than her more famous husband. A religious and metaphysical poet of depth and brilliance, she was a very able playwright as well. (Her play about the younger generation's revolt against the materialism of their parents, *The Green Ring,* directed by Meyerhold, and with Maria Savina, who came out of retirement to play one of the lesser roles, was a memorable success of the 1916 season.) Gippius was also a prolific but remarkably insensitive literary critic. Of her numerous critical blind spots the biggest one was Chekhov. Considered from the vantage point of her subtle mysticism, Chekhov appeared as a dull, normal, prematurely aged doctor, incapable of perceiving the deeper spiritual realities and devoid of all understanding of women (Gippius was a spectacular early advocate and practitioner of psychological unisex and of abandoning the traditional sexual roles). This provincial dullard was somehow granted a magnificent writing talent, but was prevented by his essential shallowness from writing anything of lasting importance. This is the view of Chekhov that Gippius developed in her numerous critical articles and this is the Chekhov who appears in her memoirs. She lived long enough to read the Russian novels of Vladimir Nabokov and to dismiss him on rather similar grounds as a writer who "has nothing to say."

According to her recollections, Chekhov became so accustomed to census taking on Sakhalin that he could not resist carrying out a sort of census in Venice, asking all the streetwalkers he met "Quanto?" in order to establish the going rate. Because of Zinaida Gippius's obvious animosity toward Chekhov, this anecdote should be taken with a grain of salt.

3. Ivan Chekhov's hobby was glass blowing.

53. To Maria Chekhova

Florence,
March 29 or 30, 1891

I'm in Florence. I'm worn out with racing through museums and churches. After seeing the Venus dei Medici I can only say that if she were dressed in modern clothes she would look hideous, especially around the waist. I'm well. The sky is overcast, and Italy without the sun is like a face hidden under a mask. Keep well.

Yours,
Antonio

The Dante monument is beautiful.

54. To Maria Kiselyova

Rome,
April 1, 1891

The Pope has commissioned me to congratulate you on your saint's day and wish you as much money as he has rooms. And he has eleven thousand rooms! Sauntering around the Vatican, I wilted from exhaustion, and when I got home, my legs felt as if they were made out of cotton.

I take my meals at the common table. Can you imagine? There are two sweet little Dutch girls sitting opposite me, one of whom makes me think of Pushkin's Tatyana and the other of her sister Olga.[1] I look at both of them all through the meal, and picture a neat little white turreted house, excellent butter, superb Dutch cheese, Dutch herring, a dignified pastor, a staid schoolmaster . . . and it makes me want to marry a sweet little Dutch girl and have her and me and our neat little house become a picture on a tray.

I've seen everything and dragged myself everywhere I was ordered. When I was offered something to sniff, I sniffed. But all I feel is exhaustion and a craving for a bowl of cabbage soup and buckwheat kasha. Venice fascinated me and drove me wild, but ever since I left, Baedecker and bad weather have set in.

Good-bye, Maria Vladimirovna. May the good Lord keep you. The Pope and I send our most humble respects to His Excellency, Vasilisa and Yelizaveta Alexandrovna.[2]

Neckties are amazingly cheap here, so terribly cheap that I may even take to eating them. A franc a pair.

Tomorrow I'm going to Naples. Pray that I meet a beautiful Russian lady there, a widow or divorcee if possible.

The guidebooks say that a love affair is a must for any tour of Italy. Well, what the hell, I'm game for anything. An affair would be fine with me.

Don't forget the miserable sinner who regards you highly and is devoted to you.

A. Chekhov

P.S. My respects to the starlings.

1. In *Eugene Onegin*.

2. "His Excellency" is Kiselyova's husband Alexei, who was a land captain; "Vasilisa" is Chekhov's private nickname for her daughter Sasha; the last-named lady is the governess of the Kiselyov children. Chekhov spent a week with the Kiselyovs at Babkino shortly before his departure for Italy.

55. To Maria Chekhova

Rome,
April 1, 1891

When I arrived in Rome, I went to the post office and didn't find a single letter. The Suvorins got several letters apiece. I decided to pay you back in kind, that is, to stop writing, but then, why bother? I'm not especially fond of letters, but there's nothing worse than a lack of news when you're on a trip. Where did you decide to stay for the summer? Is the mongoose still alive? And so on and so forth.

I've been to St. Peter's, the Capitol, the Colosseum and the Forum, I've even been to a *café chantant*, but I haven't enjoyed it the way

I thought I would. The weather has been getting in the way. It's raining. I'm hot in my fall coat and cold in my summer one.

Traveling is very cheap. You can take a trip to Italy on only four hundred rubles and return home with souvenirs. If I had gone on my own or, say, with Ivan, I would have come home with the conviction that it's much cheaper to take a trip to Italy than to the Caucasus. But, alas, I'm with Suvorin. In Venice we stayed at the best hotel and lived like doges; here in Rome we are living like cardinals because we're occupying a suite in the former palace of Cardinal Conti, presently the Hotel Minerva. We have two large drawing rooms, chandeliers, carpets, fireplaces and all kinds of other needless nonsense, and it costs us forty francs a day.

My back is aching and the soles of my feet are burning from doing so much walking. The amount of walking we do is unbelievable.

I can't understand why Levitan didn't like Italy. It's a fascinating country. If I were an artist entirely on my own and had the money, I would spend my winters here. After all, even apart from its natural beauty and warm clime, Italy is the only country where you realize that art indeed reigns over everything, and this conviction is very encouraging.

I am well. You keep well too. My regards to everybody.

Yours,
A. Chekhov

56. To Maria Chekhova

Naples,
April 4, 1891

When I arrived in Naples, I went to the post office and found five letters from you. I'm very grateful to you for them. My, what nice relatives I have! Even Vesuvius was so moved it stopped erupting.

Vesuvius hides its summit in the clouds and is clearly visible only in the evening. By day the sky is overcast. Our hotel is on the waterfront, and we have a view of everything: the sea, Vesuvius, Capri, Sorrento. During the day we drove up to the monastery of St. Martini. I have never seen a view like the view from up there. The panorama is remarkable, something like what I saw in Hong Kong riding up the mountain on the funicular railway.

Naples has a magnificent shopping gallery. And the stores!! The stores make me dizzy. What glitter! You, Masha, and you, Lika, would have gone wild with delight.

Tell Semashko I wasn't able to get him the catalogue. Every store carries its *own* catalogue only, and for a great maestro like Semashko I assume that's not sufficient.[1]

There is an amazing aquarium in Naples that even has sharks and octopi. It's disgusting to watch an octopus devouring some animal.

I went to a barbershop and watched a young man having his beard trimmed for a whole hour. He must have been either a bridegroom or a card shark. The ceiling and all four walls of the barbershop are lined with mirrors, so you're reminded more of the Vatican, where they have eleven thousand rooms, than of a barbershop. They give an amazing haircut.

I'm not going to bring you any souvenirs, because you refuse to write me about your summer plans and the mongoose. I almost bought you a watch, Masha, but decided the hell with it. But then again, God will pardon you. Keep well. Regards to all, and to Aunt Fedosya and Alyosha.[2]

Yours,
A. Chekhov

I'll be back by Easter. Come and meet me at the station.

1. Semashko had requested a general catalogue of all music available in Italy.

2. Chekhov's maternal aunt Fedosya Dolzhenko and her son Alexei.

57. To Maria Chekhova

Naples,
April 7, 1891

Yesterday I went to have a look around Pompeii. As you know, it's a Roman city buried by the lava and ashes of Vesuvius in 79 A.D. I walked through the streets of the city and saw its houses, temples, theaters and squares. I saw and marveled at the Romans' ability to combine simplicity with convenience and beauty.

After having a look around Pompeii, I had lunch in a restaurant and decided to move on to Vesuvius. This decision was strongly influenced by the excellent red wine I had drunk. I had to ride horseback to the foot of Vesuvius. Today, as a result of that ride, several parts of my earthly frame feel as if I'd been to the Third Department and gotten flogged. What a torture it is to climb Vesuvius! Ashes, mountains of lava, congealed waves of molten minerals, mounds and all sorts of nasty things. You take one step forward and fall a half step back.

The soles of your feet hurt; you have trouble breathing. You keep going and going and going, and the summit is still far off. You start thinking you ought to turn back, but you're ashamed to for fear of ridicule. The ascent began at two-thirty and ended at six. Vesuvius's crater is several sazhens in diameter. I stood at its edge and looked down into it as if I were looking into a teacup. The earth surrounding it is covered with a thin coating of sulphur and gives off a dense vapor. A noxious white smoke pours out of the crater, sparks and red-hot rocks fly everywhere, while Satan lies snoring beneath the smoke. There is quite a mixture of sounds: you hear breakers beating, thunder clapping, railroad trains pounding, boards falling. It is all quite terrifying, and at the same time makes you want to jump right down into the maw. I now believe in Hell. The lava is of such high temperature that a copper coin will melt in it.

Coming down is just as bad as going up. You sink into ashes up to your knees. I was terribly tired. I returned on horseback through tiny villages and past summer villas; the fragrance was magnificent, and the moon was shining. I breathed in the fragrance, gazed at the moon, and thought of *her,* that is, Lika Lenskaya.[1]

All of us, dear noblemen, will have no money this summer, and the mere thought of it ruins my appetite. For a trip I could have done *solo* for three hundred rubles I've contracted a thousand-ruble debt. My only hope is those fool amateurs who will be putting on my *Bear.*

Have you decided where we're going for the summer, signori? You're behaving like pigs by not writing. I don't know what's going on at home at all.

My humble regards to everyone. Take care of yourselves and don't completely forget your

Antoine

1. The wife of the actor Alexander Lensky. This is a teasing jab intended for Lika Mizinova.

58. To Mikhail Chekhov

Nice,
April 15, 1891
The Monday of Easter Week

Papa's postcard was forwarded to me from Rome yesterday. It told me that you've rented a place for the summer. Well, thank God. I'm very happy for you and for myself. Take your time moving. Subscribe to *Russian News* and *News of the Day* and notify *New Times* and

Fragments of our change of address. I'll write to the *Historical Herald* and the *Northern Herald* myself.

We are staying on the waterfront in Nice. The sun is shining, the weather is warm, everything is green and fragrant, but it's windy. Famous Monaco is about an hour's ride from Nice. That's where Monte Carlo is, the town where they play roulette. Picture the rooms of the Hall of Nobles[1]—as beautiful and high-ceilinged, but broader. The rooms are furnished with large tables, and the tables have roulette wheels on them, which I'll describe to you when I get home. The day before yesterday I went there and lost. It's a terribly absorbing game. When I lost, Suvorin-*fils*[2] and I set to thinking, and I thought up a system that couldn't lose. We went back yesterday with five hundred francs apiece. On my first bet I won a few gold pieces, then more and more. My vest pockets bulged with gold. The money passing through my hands included French coins from as far back as 1808, as well as Belgian, Italian, Greek and Austrian coins. Never before had I seen so much gold and silver. I started playing at five, and by ten I didn't have a single franc left in my pocket. All I did have left was the satisfaction of knowing that I had already bought my ticket back to Nice. How do you like that, ladies and gentlemen! Of course you'll say, "What baseness! We're living in poverty and he plays roulette." That's perfectly just, and I give you my permission to slit my throat. But personally I'm quite pleased with myself. At least I can now tell my grandchildren that I played roulette and experienced the sensation the game arouses.

Next to the casino with the roulette wheels there is another sort of roulette—the restaurants. They fleece you terribly and feed you magnificently. Every serving is a complex production that you should venerate on bended knee rather than dare to eat it. Every morsel is garnished abundantly with artichokes, truffles and all sorts of nightingale tongues. And yet, good Lord in Heaven, how contemptible and loathsome that life is—with all its artichokes, palms and orange-blossom fragrance! I love luxury and opulence, but this sort of roulette luxury gives me the impression of a luxurious lavatory.[3] There's something in the air that offends one's sense of decency and cheapens nature, the sound of the waves, the moon.

Yesterday, Sunday, I went to the local Russian church. Peculiarities: palm branches instead of willow; ladies singing in the choir instead of boys, which gives the music an operatic tinge; foreign money on the plate; French-speaking church elders. The choir did a magnificent job with Bortnyansky's[4] "Cherubimic Hymn No. 7" and the plain version of the Lord's Prayer.

Of all the places I've been so far, Venice has left me with the brightest memories. Rome is more or less like Kharkov, and Naples is filthy. The sea has no hold over me; I tired of it back in November and December. Now that I think about it, damn it all, it turns out I've been traveling around all year. No sooner did I get back from Sakhalin than I went off to Petersburg. Then I went back to Petersburg and on to Italy.

If I don't get back in time for Easter, remember me in your prayers when you break the fast, accept my best wishes in absentia and rest assured that I'll miss you all terribly on Easter night.

Are you saving newspapers for me?

My regards to everyone: Alexei and Aunt Fedosya, Semashko, handsome Levitan, Lika the golden-tressed, the old lady,[5] and everyone else. Stay well. May the heavens keep you. I beg permission to take your leave and to remain your homesick

Antonio

Regards to Olga Petrovna.[6]

1. A concert hall and ballroom in Moscow, often mentioned in Russian literature.

2. Suvorin's eldest son, Alexei, joined his father and Chekhov in Nice.

3. In her memoirs dictated in 1954 (she was no longer physically capable of writing), Maria Chekhova singled out these last two sentences and quoted them as her brother's typical reaction to everything foreign and Western. It was obviously a desperate effort to create for Chekhov posthumously the kind of nationalistic pride that the Soviet government demands from any writer it honors.

4. Dmitry Bortnyansky, a Russian composer of the end of the eighteenth century, who wrote some charmingly rococo operas and instrumental pieces, but who is mainly remembered today for his church music.

5. The family cook.

6. Olga Kundasova. For a number of years, the women in Chekhov's life were almost inevitably chosen from among his sister's fellow students and colleagues. Among them, he had light flirtations with Darya Musina-Pushkina, Lika Mizinova and Alexandra Khotyaintseva; the more serious involvements were those with Dunya Èfros and Olga Kundasova. Olga Kundasova held a degree in mathematics and was at one time employed at an astronomical observatory and therefore Chekhov often referred to her as "the astronomer." Thoroughly unconventional in dress, radical in her politics, given to fits of uproarious laughter, Olga Kundasova was a true eccentric and a real intellectual. It is impossible to say now if her involvement with Chekhov was a close friendship only or had more intimate aspects.

Their period of greatest closeness seems to have been just prior to his departure for Sakhalin. It was actually arranged that she accompany him for the earlier stages of the journey. Chekhov sent a humorous letter to his sister expressing surprise that Olga had come with him and pleading ignorance of her destination which seems to have been a ruse aimed at placating the family's sensibilities. Chekhov was not the man to allow any woman to force herself on him against his will, and his letter to Maria made it clear that he was most happy to have Olga along.

But he eventually grew tired of her, as he inevitably did of all his involvements with women up to the time of his marriage. For several years she remained on friendly terms with Chekhov and his family, visiting them at Melikhovo, seeing Chekhov in Moscow on occasion. Then, in 1895, came the publication of "Three Years," in which Olga and all of her friends easily recognized her portrait in the character of the hero's former mistress, the radicalized bluestocking music teacher Polina Rassudina. It was not a very flattering portrait—an intellectual, not too attractive woman hysterically refusing to understand why her lover leaves her for a young girl who cannot share his interests, but is physically more desirable. It is highly tempting to see in Polina's reactions a faithful reflection of Chekhov's break with Olga Kundasova, but there is not enough factual basis for it at the present time (her letters to Chekhov, known to be in the Soviet archives, have not been published and are seldom cited in the annotations to his correspondence).

Whatever the facts may have been, Olga refused to allow Maria Chekhova to publish Chekhov's letters to her, refused even to show them to her and later had them destroyed. She chose not to appear in Chekhov's biography and was so successful that today no one knows where, when and how she died. A careful reading of all the available Chekhov correspondence, of Suvorin's journal (he and Kundasova became good friends in the 1890s) and of the more reliable memoirs leaves one with the impression that Chekhov's relationship with this woman was something significant and lasting.

59. To Maria Chekhova

Paris,
April 21, 1891

Today is Easter. Very well, then, Christ is risen! This is the first Easter I've ever spent away from home.

I arrived in Paris on Friday morning and went straight to the Exposition.[1] Yes, the Eiffel Tower is very, very high. The rest of the Exposition buildings I saw from the outside only, because the cavalry was stationed inside in case of disturbances. Riots were expected for Friday.[2] Crowds of highly agitated people walked up and down the streets yelling and whistling, and the police kept dispersing them. About ten policemen are enough here to break up a big crowd. The police all attack together, and the crowd runs like crazy. I was deemed worthy of being caught in one of the attacks: a policeman grabbed me by the shoulder and began shoving me in front of him.

The city is very crowded. The streets swarm and seethe with

people. Every street is like a turbulent Terek.[3] The noise and hubbub are constant. The sidewalks are filled with tables; at every table there sit Frenchmen who feel completely at home on the street. They're a wonderful people. But Paris is indescribable, so I'll put off describing it until I get home.

I went to midnight mass at the Embassy Church.

We've been joined by a retired diplomat by the name of Tatishchev. Paris correspondent Ivan Yakovlev-Pavlovsky[4] follows us everywhere in the capacity of aide. He lived in the Moiseyev House[5] at the same time we did; he lived with the Fronshteyns. Pleshcheyev and his daughters and son are here too.[6] In brief, there are many people I know here, a whole Russian colony.

Tomorrow or the day after we leave for Russia. I'll be in Moscow on Friday or Saturday. I'll be arriving via Smolensk, so if you should have a desire to meet me, come to Smolensk Station.

If they don't let me go on Tuesday or even Wednesday, I'll still return to Moscow no later than Monday, so ask Ivan to put off his departure and wait for me.

I fear that you may be out of money.

Misha, get my pince-nez fixed and God will repay you. Put in the same lenses that you have. It's a torture for me to be without glasses. I didn't see half the pictures at the picture exhibition (*Le Salon*) thanks to my nearsightedness. By the way, Russian painters are far more solid than French ones. Compared to the French landscape painters I saw yesterday, Levitan is a king.[7]

This is my last letter. Good-bye. I left with an empty suitcase and I'm returning with a full one. Each of you will receive his just deserts.

I wish you all good health.

Yours,
A. Chekhov

1. The site of the Paris World Exposition of 1889, for which the Eiffel Tower was built.

2. On May 1, 1891 (Gregorian calendar), there were major workers' demonstrations throughout France. In the city of Fourmies, the clash between the demonstrators and the police led to a number of casualties (see next letter).

3. A turbulent stream in the Caucasus, described by numerous Russian poets ranging from Pushkin to Mayakovsky.

4. The Paris correspondent of *New Times* turned out to be Chekhov's former neighbor from Taganrog.

5. A small apartment house in Taganrog, where Chekhov's parents lived before they moved into their own house in 1873.

6. The formerly impoverished Pleshcheyev suddenly received an inherit-

ance of two million rubles from a distant relative and was taking his family on a tour of Europe in grand style.

7. Soviet commentators and Maria Chekhova in her memoirs cite this passage as proof of Chekhov's outstanding Russian patriotism. It is not clear from the letter which of the three Salons that were open at the time of his visit Chekhov attended. Sophie Laffitte in her book *Chekhov par lui-même* assumed that it was the Salon des Indépendants and that Chekhov is therefore preferring Levitan to Degas, Renoir, Monet and Pissarro in their prime. Given the parochial and provincial state to which Russian tastes in painting at the end of the nineteenth century were reduced by dogmatic utilitarianism and demands for didactic storytelling art (it was some eight years later that Sergei Diaghilev's journal *The World of Art* and other similar publications initiated the dazzling revival of taste and creativity in Russian visual arts that distinguish the first two decades of our century), such an attitude on Chekhov's part is a distinct possibility. However, it would seem more likely that Suvorin took him to the far more prestigious (at the time) and better-known Salon des Artistes Français, which by 1891 was a refuge of the safely traditionalist nineteenth-century art, untouched by the winds of Impressionism. If this is the case, then Chekhov merely compares Russian academic painting to its French equivalent and finds the French variety inferior.

60. To Maria Chekhova

Paris,
April 24, 1891

Another change has come up. One of the Russian sculptors living in Paris has agreed to make a bust of Suvorin, and it will keep us here until Saturday. We'll definitely leave on Saturday, and on Wednesday I'll be in Moscow.

How are you getting along without money? Hold on until Thursday.

Imagine how pleased I was to visit the Chamber of Deputies during the very session at which the Minister of Internal Affairs was being called to account for the violence the government resorted to while putting down the workers in revolt at Fourmies (many people were killed and wounded). It was a stormy and highly interesting session.

Anthropi girdling themselves with boa constrictors, ladies kicking their legs up to the ceiling, flying people, lions, *cafés chantants*, dinners and lunches are beginning to disgust me. It's time to go home. I feel like working.

My regards to everyone, everybody. Keep well.

Yours,
Antoine

VIII

THE BUSY YEARS

Indeed, it was in a queer world of silvery twilight and dark shadows that the gentle soul of Chekhov took refuge in a desperate fear of life.

—PRINCESS NINA ANDRONIKOVA TOUMANOVA,
Anton Chekhov, The Voice of Twilight Russia

THE TENUOUS LINE THAT DIVIDES a long short story from a short novel makes the classification of Chekhov's fiction difficult in English (in Russian, the term *povest'*, meaning a genre halfway between the story and the novel, does the job nicely). By the complexity of the ideas it treats, by its large number of clearly delineated important characters, by the author's deep penetration into the dialectic of their interaction, if not by its actual length, "The Duel" should certainly qualify as an important novel. The weak-willed hero Layevsky (a younger version of Ivanov, but far better realized); his opponent von Koren, a dedicated zoologist who tries to transfer Darwinism into the social and moral sphere and ends up preaching genocidal theories that foreshadow Hitler; Layevsky's pathetic mistress Nadezhda who sought freedom and found promiscuity; the virtuous matron Maria Konstantinovna, outwardly sympathetic but inwardly bitchy; the gruff and yet compassionate military doctor Samoilenko; the giggly, lovable young deacon Pobedov—all these fully realized complex human beings and the problems their lives and actions raise shatter the framework of the conventional short story and raise "The Duel" to the level of a complex novel of ideas. At least three of Chekhov's subsequent works of fiction—"Three Years," "My Life" and "In the Ravine"—could by the same token also be considered novels, certainly with far greater justification than his earlier *Useless Victory* or *The Shooting Party*, which on the basis of length alone are true and undoubted novels.

After traveling almost continuously for more than a year, Chekhov plunged into writing with renewed energy. Throughout the summer of 1891 he worked on *The Island of Sakhalin* three days a week, and on "The Duel" another three and devoted his Sundays to what he called "the lesser stories." In the midst of it all, he found time to write "Peasant Women" (also called "Peasant Wives" in some English translations), a somewhat Leskovian tale of a peasant lecher and hypocrite who finds in the Christian religion and its moral teachings the perfect justification for his cruelty and self-indulgence. The stories written in the next eighteen months are among Chekhov's most serious and profound: "The Wife"; "The Grasshopper"; "In Exile," with its evenly balanced debate on the value of involvement and noninvolvement carried on by deportees on the shore of an icy Siberian river; "An Unknown Man's Story," in which Chekhov confronts the issue of revolutionary violence; and the most grimly prophetic story he ever wrote, "Ward Number Six," which casts doubts on the conventional division between madness and sanity, advances the notion that doing nothing at all and looking the other way can on occasion be criminal, and predicts the post-Stalinist Russian practice of incarcerating in psychiatric clinics those who question the political system.

But the habit of humanitarian involvement which Chekhov acquired on Sakhalin remained with him after he returned. Because of the disastrous harvest of the previous summer, much of Russia was famine-stricken in the winter of 1891–92. Inspired by the example of his friend Yevgraf Yegorov, Chekhov devoted much of that winter to famine relief work, concentrating, with characteristic practicality, not on charity handouts, but on an organized campaign to prevent the peasants from slaughtering their horses for food, a practice that perpetuated the famine cycle, since it left no horses for next year's spring plowing.

In the spring of 1892, the Chekhov family realized their long-standing dream of acquiring their own permanent home when Chekhov purchased the rural estate of Melikhovo, near the city of Serpukhov, a few hours by train from Moscow. Chekhov, his parents and his sister, occasionally aided by Mikhail, plunged into the work of renovating the house, planting vegetable gardens and tending livestock. But the famine was followed by a cholera epidemic, which by summer was threatening the area where Melikhovo was located. For several months in the summer and fall of 1892, Chekhov gave up writing and took the unpaid job of local medical inspector in charge of containing the cholera epidemic. To follow a day-by-day account of Chekhov's activities during this period in *A Chronicle of Chekhov's Life and Writings* (compiled by Nina Gitovich and published in Moscow in 1955) is to marvel at the energy and endurance of this man, who risked his life and health (as seriously as at any point on his trip to Sakhalin), getting lost in the frozen fields in the winter, trudging on foot through muddy fields in the spring, giving free medical treatment to over a thousand peasants at his Melikhovo clinic, building a comfortable home for himself and his family, planting a park and an orchard, and writing some of the greatest masterpieces of Russian prose ever written—all in the span of some sixteen months.

61. To Alexei Suvorin

Moscow,
September 8, 1891

I've already moved back to Moscow and haven't set foot outside the house. The family has been looking around for a new apartment, but I don't say a word because I'm too lazy to budge. They want to move to somewhere near Devichie Pole for economy's sake.

"The Lie," the title you recommended for my story, won't do.[1] It would be suitable only if a conscious lie were involved. An unconscious lie is an error rather than a lie. Tolstoy calls our having money and eating meat a lie; that's going too far.

I was informed yesterday that Kurepin[2] is hopelessly ill. He has cancer of the neck. By the time he dies, the cancer will devour half his head and torment him with neuralgic pains. I have heard that Kurepin's wife has written you.

Death plucks off people one by one. It knows its business. Write a play about an old chemist who has invented an elixir of immortality (you take fifteen drops and live forever) but has broken the phial with the elixir for fear that scum like himself and his wife would live forever. Tolstoy denies mankind immortality, but good God, how much personal animosity there is in his attitude! I was reading his "Afterword"[3] the day before yesterday, and I'll be damned if it isn't sillier and more stultifying than "The Letters to a Governor's Wife,"[4] which I despise. To hell with the philosophy of the great men of this world! All great wise men are as despotic as generals and as impolite and insensitive as generals because they are confident of their impunity. Diogenes spat in people's beards knowing that he would not be called to account; Tolstoy calls doctors scoundrels and flaunts his ignorance of important issues because he is another Diogenes whom no one will report to the police or denounce in the papers. So to hell with the philosophy of the great men of this world. With all its half-wit afterwords and letters to governors' wives, it's worth less than the filly in "Kholstomer."[5]

Send my regards to my schoolfellow Alexei Petrovich[6] and wish him good health, a playful disposition and seductive dreams. May he dream of a naked Spanish girl with a guitar.

My most humble respects to Anna Ivanovna and Alexei Alexeyevich and his progeny.

Keep well and don't forget me, sinner that I am. I'm very bored.

Yours,
A. Chekhov

1. After accepting "The Duel" for serialization in *New Times*, Suvorin suggested that Chekhov change its title to "The Lie."

2. Alexander Kurepin was the editor of the humor magazine *The Alarm Clock* in the early eighties, when Chekhov was a regular contributor. At the time of this letter he was employed by Suvorin. He died before the end of 1891.

3. Chekhov read Tolstoy's anti-sex novel *The Kreutzer Sonata* prior to his departure for Sakhalin and, despite certain reservations, found it highly impressive as a work of literature (see Letter 40). After returning from his journey he wrote to Suvorin: "Before my trip, *The Kreutzer Sonata* seemed a major event, but now I find it ridiculous and confused. Either the trip has matured me or I've taken leave of my senses—the devil alone knows which" (Letter of December 17, 1890).

For the 1890 edition of his collected works, Tolstoy wrote an "Afterword" to *The Kreutzer Sonata*, in which, in response to many anxious inquiries from his readers, he spelled out in full the puritanical message he wished to express in the novel. Not only was illicit sex sinful, but sex within marriage, except for the specific purpose of procreation, was unchristian. The whole notion of romantic love between men and women was now seen as wasteful and useless by Tolstoy, since it made them expend effort on looking attractive, rather than concentrating on their relationship with God and on the welfare of their fellow man.

4. The scholarly-looking footnote appended to this passage in the Lillian Hellman edition of Chekhov's letters identifies this work as Gogol's *Letters to a Governor's Wife*. There is, of course, no such work by Gogol. Chekhov is referring to the section entitled "What Is a Governor's Wife?" in Gogol's book *Selected Passages from Correspondence with Friends*, a volume of social and moral sermons intermingled with passages of literary criticism. After the critics and the readers of his time saw in *The Inspector General* and *Dead Souls* an indictment of the social system, Gogol decided to produce a work that would embody his positive and constructive program for Russian society. As outlined in *Selected Passages* that program turned out to be simplicity itself: the existing social order is divinely ordained and to change it in any way or to aspire to a position higher than your own in the social hierarchy is an offense against God and religion. "What Is a Governor's Wife?," in particular, advises the addressee (she was Pushkin's one-time friend, the beautiful Alexandra Rossetti, whom Gogol knew and who was married to

the governor of Kaluga) on how to support the status quo by discreet spying, collecting useful gossip and forming alliances with local clergymen. Gogol's program of ostentatious display of modesty and frugality ("Do not miss a single reception or ball, go especially so that you can be seen wearing the very same dress. Appear in the same dress three, four, five, six times. Praise the attire of others only when it is cheap and simple") finds its echo in the passages of Tolstoy's "Afterword" which condemn all interest in attractive and becoming clothes as sinful and frivolous.

5. "Kholstomer" (sometimes translated into English as "Strider. The Story of a Horse") is Tolstoy's somewhat Swiftian story in which human institutions and customs are exposed in all their absurdity and cruelty when shown through the eyes of an intelligent horse. Chekhov's choice of the filly from that story as a contrast to both Tolstoy's "Afterword" and Gogol's "What Is a Governor's Wife?" is by no means accidental, since that filly is the embodiment of healthy and normal female sexuality.

6. Alexei Kolomnin, Suvorin's brother-in-law, who in his childhood attended the same school in Taganrog that Chekhov went to some years later.

62. To Yelena Shavrova[1]

Moscow,
September 16, 1891

So we old bachelors smell like dogs, do we? Maybe so, but allow me to take exception to your statement that doctors specializing in female complaints are skirt chasers and cynics at heart. Gynecologists deal with the sort of violent prose you've never dreamed of; if you were acquainted with it, the ferocity peculiar to your imagination might lead you to attribute to it a smell worse than that of dogs. Anyone who constantly sails the seas loves dry land; anyone who is forever submerged in prose passionately longs for poetry. All gynecologists are idealists. Your doctor reads verse; here your instinct proved true. I would have added that he's a great liberal, something of a mystic, and that he dreams of a wife along the lines of Nekrasov's Russian woman.[2] The well-known Professor Snegiryov can't talk about the "Russian woman" without a quiver in his voice. Another gynecologist I know is in love with a veiled mystery woman whom he has only seen from a distance. A third attends every opening night, and then goes into loud tirades in the cloakroom about how authors ought to portray only ideal women, etc. You disregard the fact that a stupid or mediocre person can't be a good gynecologist. Intelligence, even seminary-trained intelligence, shines brighter than a bald pate, but what you've done is to observe and accentuate the pate and throw intelligence overboard. You have also observed and accentuated the fact that a fat man—ugh!—exudes a kind of grease, but you've completely disregarded the fact that he's a professor, that for some years he thought and did things that placed him above millions of people, above all the Verochkas and Greek girls of Taganrog, above all dinners and wines. Noah had three sons: Shem, Ham, and—was it Aphet?[3] All Ham could see was that his father was a drunkard; he completely disregarded the fact that Noah was a genius, that he had built the Ark and saved the world. Writers must avoid imitating Ham. Mull that one over for a while. I don't dare ask you to love the gynecologist and the professor, but I do dare remind you of justice, which is more precious for an objective writer than air.

The girl of merchant background is excellently done. The part of the doctor's speech where he talks about his lack of faith in medicine is also good, but there's no reason to have him take a drink after every sentence. The fondness for corpses you attribute to doctors comes from your irritation with your own captive thinking. You've never so much as seen a corpse.

Next, from the particular to the general. Here I'm duty bound to sound a general alarm. What you have written is not a story or a novel or a work of art; it is a long row of gloomy, oppressive barracks.

Where is the architecture that so fascinated yours truly at first? Where is the lightness, the freshness, the grace? Read your story through: a description of a dinner, followed by a description of a series of ladies and girls walking by, then a description of the people at the dinner table, then the description of the dinner, and so on without end. Descriptions, descriptions, descriptions . . . and not a bit of action. You've got to start right off with the merchant's daughter and then concentrate entirely on her. Throw out Verochka, throw out the Greek girls, throw them all out except the doctor and the merchant's offspring.

We need to have a talk. So you're not moving to Petersburg. I was counting on seeing you in Petersburg; Misha assured me you were going to move there. Anyway, keep well. May the heavenly hosts protect you. Your imagination is becoming interesting.

Forgive the long letter.

Yours,
A. Chekhov

1. Chekhov met Yelena Shavrova (1874–1937) at a picnic in the Crimea when she was fifteen. She handed him a story she had written, and after editing it, he submitted it to *New Times*, where it was accepted and published. In subsequent years, she became his literary protégée, sending her work to him for approval and publishing it after obtaining his advice. By the early

nineties, she was a member of a whole horde of young literary hopefuls who constantly sent Chekhov their efforts for advice and approval. Another such beginner was Ivan Bunin, who in 1891 wrote Chekhov asking him to read a manuscript. Chekhov read astounding quantities of these manuscripts, edited many, and managed to get a number of them placed with various publications. But not all of the applicants were Bunins or even Yelena Shavrovas (who with Chekhov's consistent aid managed to have a minor literary career). More typical were the two would-be writers Chekhov described in his letter to Suvorin of December 3, 1891:

> Yesterday an apparently very young man from Voronezh sent me a manuscript of some 640 pp. in minuscule handwriting. A novel. The title is quite new: *The Poor in Spirit.* The youthful author implores me to read it and to write him my opinion. Can you imagine my horror? Late last night, I started leafing through the novel and it was all about how honest the past was, about serving the people, about the community of interests, the setting sun . . . Another, not so young writer, actually a retired colonel, brought me two manuscripts: *The Unbidden Civilizers, or the Fruits of Ignorance* and *The Famous Cabby.* The second manuscript describes an ideological young man whom need has forced to become a cabby (a reproach addressed to the indifferent society which reduces its finest representatives to such a horrible situation). Well, then, the cabby sits in his driver's seat and discusses Marx, Buckle and the logic of [John Stuart] Mill with his fares.

2. Reference to Nikolai Nekrasov's narrative poem "Russian Women," which is about the wives of the aristocratic participants in the Decembrist uprising of 1825, who voluntarily followed their husbands into Siberian exile.
3. Chekhov's misspelling retained.

63. To Mikhail Albov[1]

Moscow,
September 30, 1891

Dear Mikhail Nilovich,

I have a short novel for you that is almost ready. It's sketched out, but not finished, nor has a clean copy been made. It needs another week or two of work, not more. It is called "The Story of My Patient."[2] But I am possessed by very grave doubts as to whether the censor will pass it. After all, the *Northern Herald* is one of the publications subject to censorship, and although it is true that my story doesn't preach any harmful doctrines, its cast of characters might not please the censors.

The narrator is a former socialist, while the son of a Deputy Minister of Internal Affairs plays the role of protagonist number one. Both my socialist and the son of the deputy minister are peaceful fellows who indulge in no political action in the story, but I still have my fears about announcing the story to the public, or at least I consider it premature. Let me send you the story, and once you've read it, you can decide what to do. If you feel the censors will pass it, have it set and announce its publication, but if when you've read it you find my doubts well founded, please return it to me without having it set or read by the censors, because if the censors reject it, it will be awkward for me to send it to a censorship-free publication: once a publisher finds out the story has already failed to pass, he'll be afraid to publish it.

Send my regards to Kazimir Stanislavovich[3] and tell him I wish him all the best.

Stay well.

Sincerely and respectfully yours,
A. Chekhov

1. Mikhail Albov (1851–1911), considered a highly promising writer in the 1880s, described at great length, as D. S. Mirsky put it, the morbid states of mind experienced by priests and clerics. Among Chekhov's and Korolenko's lesser contemporaries, Albov was almost the only one on whom the work of Dostoyevsky made a discernible impact (it was not until Russian Symbolism that Dostoyevsky became a major literary influence). Albov replaced Pleshcheyev as the literary editor of *Northern Herald* when the latter inherited his huge fortune and retired. It is in his editorial capacity that Chekhov is writing to Albov here.

2. As early as 1887 Chekhov first sketched out a story about a revolutionary who engages in conspiratorial work and gradually realizes that the moral and ethical implications of his activities are more important to him than the ideological ones. At that time he had no hopes of publishing anywhere a work containing an objective, unprejudiced portrayal of revolutionary violence. In the fall of 1891 he returned to this story, which he now called "The Story of My Patient" and in the present letter he is offering it to Albov for publication in *Northern Herald*. A few weeks after this letter was written, Chekhov read the story to Suvorin, who after listening to its first twenty lines declared that he would never dare publish it in *New Times* and that he doubted the advisability of publishing it anywhere. Chekhov thereupon informed Albov that the story was not available. In the fall of 1892, he revised the manuscript again and submitted it to Vukol Lavrov's *Russian Thought*. It passed the censorship without a single change and was published in *Russian Thought* in February of 1893 as "An Unknown Man's Story."

3. Barantsevich.

64. To Yevgraf Yegorov[1]

Moscow,
December 11, 1891

Dear Yevgraf Petrovich,

Here is the story of why my trip to see you did not materialize. It was not as a newspaper correspondent that I planned to visit you; it was on behalf of or rather by agreement with a small group of people who wished to do something for the famine victims. The problem is that because the public has no confidence in the administration it is holding back its contributions. A thousand fantastic tales and fables about embezzlement, brazen thievery, etc. are making the rounds. People keep their distance from the governmental Department of Church Affairs and are indignant with the Red Cross. The owner of unforgettable Babkino, a land captain,[2] snapped plainly and categorically at me: "There's thievery afoot at the Moscow Red Cross." With this as the prevailing mood the administration can scarcely expect to receive earnest assistance from society. And yet the populace does want to help, and its conscience is uneasy. In September the Moscow intelligentsia and plutocracy got together in groups, thought, talked, puttered around and invited experts in for consultation. Everybody discussed how to bypass the administration and go about organizing aid independently. They decided to send their own agents to the famine-stricken provinces to acquaint themselves with the situation at first hand, set up relief kitchens, and so on. Several of the group leaders, highly influential people, went to see Durnovo[3] for permission, but Durnovo refused, declaring that the right to organize aid belonged exclusively to the Department of Church Affairs and the Red Cross. In short, private initiative was nipped in the bud. Everyone fell into the doldrums and lost heart; some became incensed, others simply washed their hands of the whole affair. It takes the courage and authority of a Tolstoy[4] to act in defiance of all prohibitions and prevailing moods and do what duty commands.

Now a few words about myself. I was in complete sympathy with private initiative, because everyone is free to do good as he sees fit. But all the discussion about the administration, the Red Cross and so on seemed inopportune and impractical to me. I felt that with a modicum of composure and a kind disposition we could bypass everything fearful and ticklish and that to do so there was no need to go see the Cabinet minister. I went to Sakhalin without a single letter of recommendation, yet I accomplished everything I needed to do. Why then can't I go to the famine-stricken provinces? I also thought of administrators like yourself, Kiselyov and all the land captains and tax inspectors I know—people who are eminently decent and deserving of the utmost confidence. And I decided to try to coordinate the efforts of both the administration and private initiative, if only over a small area. I wanted to see you as quickly as possible and ask your advice. The public has confidence in me and would have confidence in you too, so I was sure I could count on success. If you'll recall, I sent you a letter. Then Suvorin came to Moscow; I complained to him of not knowing your address. He sent Baranov[5] a telegram and Baranov was kind enough to send me your address. Suvorin had influenza. Whenever he comes to Moscow we are inseparable for days on end; we discuss literature, which he knows so well. It happened this time too, with the result that I caught influenza from him, took to bed, and went into a frenzy of coughing. Korolenko came to Moscow and found me stricken. Lung complications dragged it out for an entire month; I lay around the house doing absolutely nothing. I've begun to get over it now, but I'm still coughing and losing weight. There's the whole story for you. If it hadn't been for the influenza, the two of us might have been able to wrench two to three thousand more from the public, depending on the circumstances.

Your exasperation with the press is fully comprehensible. You, who are familiar with the actual situation, are as exasperated by the disquisitions of newsmen as I, a doctor, am exasperated by an ignoramus's disquisitions on diphtheria. But what are we supposed to do? You tell me. Russia is neither England nor France. Our newspapers are not wealthy and have very few people at their disposal. It costs money for them to send an Engelhardt[6] or a professor from the Academy of Peter the Great to the Volga; nor can they send a knowledgeable, talented reporter: they need him at home. The *Times* would have organized a census of the famine-stricken provinces at its own expense; it would have placed a Kennan[7] in each district, paid him forty rubles a day, and gotten results. But what can *Russian News* or *New Times* do when a hundred thousand seems like Croesus's fortune to them? As for the correspondents themselves, you must keep in mind that they're city-bred and all they know about the countryside comes from Gleb Uspensky. They are in an extremely false position. They rush into a district, sniff around, write a few lines, and off they go. They lack material resources, freedom and authority. For two hundred rubles a month they are continually on the run, and their only prayer is that no one will get angry at them for their involuntary and unavoidable lies. They feel guilty, but it is Russian benightedness, not they, that is guilty. In the West, a correspondent has excellent maps, encyclopedias and statistical studies at his disposal. In the West you can write your reports in your own home. And here in Russia? Our correspondent has only conversations and hearsay to draw upon. Why, in all Russia only three districts have as yet been investigated: Cherepov, Tambov and one more. And that's all, out of the whole country! The papers lie, the correspondents are young whippersnappers, but what can be done about it? *You can't just stop writing.* If the press were to remain silent, you must admit that the situation would be even worse.

Your letter and your project of buying up cattle from the peasants have set me in motion. I am willing to follow you and do whatever you say with all my heart and everything in my power. I've given the problem much thought, and here is my opinion. We can't count on the rich. It's too late. The rich have all forked out whatever thousands they were predestined to fork out. Now everything depends on the average citizen, the man who gives by the ruble and half ruble. The people who were discoursing about private initiative in September have found shelter in various sorts of commissions and committees and are already at work. It follows that only the average citizen is left. Let's set up a donation list. You write a letter to the editor, and I'll have it published in *Russian News* and *New Times.* To combine the two elements mentioned above, we might both sign the letter. If your official position makes this inconvenient for you, we can write a report signed by some third person, saying that in the fifth constituency of the province of Nizhny Novgorod such and such has been organized and is fortunately having great success, and that contributions may be sent to Land Captain Y. P. Yegorov, followed by your address, or A. P. Chekhov, or the editor's offices. The main thing is that the letter be comprehensive. Write it up in great detail, I'll add a thing or two, and it's in the bag. We must ask for contributions, not loans. No one is going to come up with a loan: it'll scare them off. Giving is hard enough; taking back is even harder.

I have only one rich friend in Moscow—Varvara Morozova, the well-known philanthropist, and I went to see her yesterday with your letter. I talked and had dinner with her. At the moment she is involved in the Committee for Literacy, which sets up relief kitchens for schoolchildren, and she is giving her all to it. Since literacy and horses are incommensurable values, Morozova promised me the assistance of her committee if you wish to set up relief kitchens for schoolchildren and send her detailed information. I felt *uneasy* about asking her for money right away because people never stop taking her money and pouncing on her like a fox at bay. All I did was ask her not to forget about us if she has any contact with commissions or committees, and she promised me she wouldn't. Sobolevsky,[8] the editor of *Russian Bulletin*, has been informed of your letter and your idea—just in case. Everywhere I go, I've been shouting from the rooftops that the project is already organized.

If any rubles and half rubles do come in, I'll send them on to you without delay. And please dispose of me as you see fit. You can rest assured I will be truly happy to do what little I can, because to date I have done absolutely nothing for the famine victims or the people who are helping them.

All of us are well except for Nikolai, who died of consumption in 1889 and Aunt Fedosya Yakovlevna (remember, she came to visit Ivan at school), who died last October, also of consumption. Ivan is teaching in Moscow. Misha is working as a tax inspector.

Keep well.

Yours,
A. Chekhov

1. In 1883–84, Yevgraf Yegorov was an army lieutenant stationed in the city of Voskresensk, where Ivan Chekhov was the schoolmaster and Anton Chekhov began his medical practice at the *zemstvo* hospital. The group of officers to which Yegorov belonged became friendly with the entire Chekhov family, and some of them eventually served as prototypes for the characters in Chekhov's stories "The Kiss" and "The Teacher of Literature" and in his play *Three Sisters*. Yegorov fell in love with Chekhov's sister, who was eighteen at the time, and wrote her asking her to marry him. The proposal frightened Maria and she asked Chekhov to convey her refusal, which he must have done with tact, since Yegorov remained on good terms with the Chekhovs. By 1891, Yegorov was out of the army. After settling on his estate in the Nizhny Novgorod Province, he was appointed as the local land captain (see next note). Chekhov learned from the newspapers of Yegorov's project to salvage the peasants' horses. He wrote to him, offering his help.

2. Alexei Kiselyov. The office of land captain (*zemsky nachalnik*) was established in 1889 by the imperial government in an obvious effort to curb the liberalizing effects of the *zemstvo* system and to undo some of the results of the emancipation of the serfs. A local landowner was appointed to this office by the Ministry of the Interior and given considerable administrative and even judicial powers over peasant affairs. The reactionary motivation for establishing this office was unmistakable, and land captains quickly became a target for the satirical literature of the period. As Chekhov's correspondence documents again and again, however, humane and enlightened members of the Russian intelligentsia, such as Kiselyov and Yegorov, were on occasion appointed land captains and were able in such cases to do a great deal of good both for the peasants and for the local *zemstvo* they were supposed to curb and counteract.

3. Ivan Durnovo, the Minister of Interior.

4. Disregarding government interference, Tolstoy and his followers sponsored a network of relief kitchens for famine victims in Samara Province.

5. The governor of Nizhny Novgorod Province.

6. Nikolai Engelhardt, a crack reporter for *New Times.*

7. George Kennan (see Letter 41, note 2). The word *Times* is in English in the original to indicate the *Times* of London.

8. The editor Vasily Sobolevsky was married to the wealthy philanthropist Varvara Morozova, mentioned in this paragraph.

65. To Alexander Smagin[1]

Moscow,
December 11, 1891

Greetings again, Your Excellency,

Thanks for the telegram. We are anxiously awaiting an answer because the twentieth is almost upon us. The day I get the telegram from Masha I'll arrange for the power of attorney to be issued and the money sent.[2]

And now, a few words about something else, kind sir. While I am still confined to Moscow, my Nizhny Novgorod project is in full swing! A friend of mine and I—he's the most wonderful person, a land captain in the most backwoods constituency of Nizhny Novgorod Province, where there are no landowners or doctors or even educated young ladies, of whom even hell has a great many nowadays—have undertaken a little venture that we figure will bring in somewhere around a hundred thousand for each of us. In addition to various famine problems, we are mainly interested in saving next year's harvest. Because peasants are selling their horses for practically nothing, for a pittance, there is grave danger that the fields won't get plowed in the spring and that the whole famine cycle will therefore be repeated. So what we're going to do is buy up the horses, feed them and return them to their owners in the spring. By now the project is firmly on its feet, and in January I'm going there to behold its fruits. Here is why I'm writing you all this. Just in case you or anyone else should happen during some raucous feast[3] or other to scrape up so much as a half ruble for the benefit of the famine victims or if some Korobochka[4] should bequeath a ruble toward the same cause or if you yourself win a hundred rubles at cards, then please remember us sinners in your orisons and share a fraction of the bounties with us! It doesn't have to be right away, but it should not be later than spring. In the spring the horses will no longer be ours. All contributors will receive a most detailed account of how each kopeck was spent, in verse if they like, which I will commission

Gilyarovsky to write. We'll advertise in the papers in January. Address your bounty either to me or straight to the field of battle:

Land Captain Yevgraf Petrovich Yegorov,
Bogoyavlennoe Station,
Nizhny Novgorod Province.

Where did you get the idea we had grown cool toward Sumbatov? It's not true. We are as ecstatic about his talents as we ever were.

Will I really be living in Sorochintsy or nearby? I somehow can't believe it, but it would be fine if I could. I would fish for gudgeons in the summer and fall, and in the winter I'd whip off to Petersburg and Moscow. . . .

Write.

Devotedly yours,
A. Chekhov

1. It is an odd coincidence that our information about Chekhov's famine relief work should come from letters he wrote to two of his sister's suitors. Alexander Smagin's family owned an estate in the Ukraine and was related to the Lintvaryovs, through whom he met the Chekhovs. Maria Chekhova (1865–1957, although by now she needs no introduction) worked as a schoolteacher and studied art, but after her other brothers were married, her primary task in life was to be her work as a secretary and general factotum to Chekhov. There was something in their relationship akin to that of a father and a devoted daughter. She was attracted to Alexander Smagin, and when he followed her to Moscow after the Luka summers of 1888–89, she accepted his proposal. When she announced her decision to Anton, she heard (or thought she heard) a tinge of disappointment in his reply. This was enough to make her break off her engagement to Smagin. Forty years later, he wrote to her that he never married because she was the only love of his life.

2. Maria (Masha) was in the Ukraine, staying with Smagin's family and inspecting an estate which Chekhov hoped to buy as a permanent home for his family.

3. A burlesqued paraphrase of the first line of Tchaikovsky's song "At the Ball," Opus 38, No. 3, which is a setting of a poem by Alexei Tolstoy.

4. A parsimonious landowning widow in Gogol's *Dead Souls*.

66. To Alexei Suvorin

Moscow,
January 22, 1892

Well, I'm back from Nizhny Novgorod Province. Since I hope we'll soon be seeing one another and since I'll be writing about the famine tomorrow or the day after, I'll keep it short: the famine is *not* being exaggerated by the newspapers. Things are in a bad way. The government is not behaving poorly, it is helping where it can; the *zemstvo* is either unable to do anything or is misrepresenting the situation, while private charity amounts to almost nothing. In my presence, fifty-four poods of dried bread arrived from Petersburg for twenty thousand people. The philanthropists would feed five thousand people with five loaves—as in the Gospel.

I had quite a trip. During a fierce snowstorm one evening, I lost my way and was nearly buried under the snow. It was a vile sensation. I went to see Baranov. I had lunch and dinner with him and was driven to the station by the governor's own horses.

Generally speaking, at least in Nizhny Novgorod Province, the administration is not putting any obstacles in the way of private initiative; in fact, the opposite is true. You can do whatever you like.[1] When I got home, I found the proofs for "Kashtanka."[2] Allah, what illustrations! Dear Alexei Sergeyevich, I'm willing to give the artist fifty rubles out of my own pocket to get rid of those illustrations. Good grief! Stools, a goose laying an egg, a bulldog instead of a dachshund . . .

If there were as much talk and action about the famine in Petersburg and Moscow as there is in Nizhny, there wouldn't be any famine.

What wonderful people they have in Nizhny Novgorod Province. The peasants are robust, vigorous, and one more handsome than the next. Each one could pose for a painting of the merchant Kalashnikov.[3] And they're intelligent to boot.

Shelaputin, the Moscow magnate, has anthrax, I've just been told.

Well, I'm waiting for your arrival, so that we can travel to Bobrov together.[4] Write and let me know when you'll be in Moscow.

All my best.

Yours,
A. Chekhov

Ask Alexei Alexeyevich to send me posthaste the article on petroleum by Batsevich, the mining engineer. While I was in Petersburg I forgot to read it.

1. This picture of governmental permissiveness must be the cause for the omission of this particular letter from the 1963–64 edition, which otherwise includes all the letters dealing with the famine.

2. Chekhov's most popular animal story, describing the adventures of a

cobbler's dog which joins a circus. It is regularly reissued to this day in illustrated editions intended for children. The "goose laying an egg" was meant to depict the trained gander Ivan Ivanych, which appears in the story.

3. The athletic and dashing hero of Lermontov's narrative poem set in the period of Ivan the Terrible.

4. Chekhov invited Suvorin to accompany him on a famine relief field trip to Bobrov and other cities. Because of Suvorin's influential position as the most important publisher in the country, local authorities in the cities they visited found it necessary to entertain him, and instead of working for famine relief, Chekhov found himself involved in a series of dinners, receptions and amateur theatricals honoring Suvorin. Suvorin never got to see the actual famine victims, while Chekhov was highly irritated at being forced to waste his time and at all the conspicuous consumption amidst the surrounding misery (Letter to Maria Chekhova of February 9, 1892).

67. To Yevgraf Yegorov

Voronezh,
February 6, 1892

My most kind Yevgraf Petrovich,

I am writing this from Voronezh Province. The same thing has happened as in Nizhny: the governor invited me to dinner, and I had to talk a lot and hear about the famine. Here is how the horse project is being handled in this area: following your method, Governor Kurovsky is buying up horses wherever he can. He has already bought up about four hundred. The prices are the same as in Nizhny. If you import horses from the Don area, each horse will cost fifty to sixty rubles, not counting feeding. Kurovsky doesn't keep the horses himself; he distributes them among the peasants as quickly as he buys them.

He sends for horseless peasants from famine-stricken districts and says to them, "Here's a horse. You will now transport grain." By transporting grain, the peasant earns his own and his horse's keep. In the spring he will be told, "You have earned so much; the horse cost so much. Therefore, you still owe so much (or you have so much coming to you)." In short, the horse constitutes a loan and the loan is already being paid off gradually.

Voronezh is seething with action. Famine relief here has been set up on a much more solid base than in Nizhny Novgorod Province. Besides grain they are handing out portable ovens and coal. They've organized workshops and many relief kitchens. Yesterday there was a benefit performance for the famine victims at a local theater, and the house was full. Kurovsky is an intelligent, sincere person; he works as hard as Baranov. He's not an army man, and for a governor that is a great convenience: he can act with greater freedom. But we'll talk about that when we get together.

I saw Sofya Alexandrovna Davydova[1] and gave her your address. She's a kind, capable, modest woman. There are many things she can do.

My report on the Nizhny Novgorod and Voronezh provinces will be published in *Russian News*.[2] Regards to your family. Keep well. Write. I'll be in Moscow sometime between the tenth and twelfth.

Yours,
A. Chekhov

1. A local Voronezh civic leader and philanthropist.

2. Chekhov's experiences with famine fighting were also reflected in "The Wife," a story of a failed marriage which is unexpectedly saved when the authoritarian, self-centered husband learns to value his wife as an individual after observing her efficient and imaginative work in helping the famine-stricken peasants. Published in February of 1892, "The Wife" incurred the wrath of most critics for using the famine as a background for the private marital drama of an upper-class couple instead of depicting the suffering of the peasants or indicting the system for allowing the famine to happen.

68. To Ivan Leontyev (Shcheglov)

Melikhovo,[1]
March 9, 1892

My dear Jean,

Your wish is going to come true: I'm sending a story to *The Week*.[2] And I'm all the more willing to do so because I find the journal congenial. Tell the helmsman[3] to reserve me a cabin on his ship for no later than April.

Yes, there are very few people in the world like Rachinsky.[4] I can certainly understand your enthusiasm. After the stifling atmosphere one feels in the company of our Burenins and Averkievs[5]—and the world is full of them—the high-minded, humane and pure Rachinsky is like a spring breeze. I am willing to lay down my life for Rachinsky, but, dear friend . . . allow me this "but" without getting angry—I would never send my children to his school. Why? In my childhood, I received a religious education and the same sort of upbringing—choir singing, reading the epistles and psalms in church, regular attendance at matins, altar boy and bell-ringing duty. And the result? When I think back on my childhood it all seems quite gloomy to me. I have no religion now.

You know, when my two brothers and I would sing the "Let my prayer arise" trio or the "Archangel's voice,"[6] everyone looked at us and was moved. They envied my parents, while we felt like little convicts. Yes, dear Jean. I understand Rachinsky, but I don't know the children who study with him. What they have in their hearts is a mystery to me. If there is joy in their hearts, they are more fortunate than my brothers and I; for us childhood was sheer suffering.[7]

Being lord of the manor is quite nice. There's lots of room, it's warm, and the doorbell is not in continual operation. But it is an easy fall from lordship to conciergeship or doormanship. The estate cost thirteen thousand, dear sir, and I've paid off only a third. The rest is a debt that will keep me on a chain for many years to come.

Here is my address: Melikhovo Village, Lopasnya Station, Moscow-Kursk Line. It will serve for ordinary letters and telegrams.

Come visit me along with Suvorin, Jean. Arrange it with him. What an orchard I have! What a naïve barnyard! What geese!

Write more often.

Regards and greetings to your hospitable wife. Keep well and cheerful.

Yours,
A. Chekhov

Send me a copy of your latest story.

1. Chekhov's own estate, to which he had moved a few days earlier. After the planned purchase of the estate in the Ukraine fell through in December of the previous year, Chekhov became particularly anxious to acquire a permanent home away from Moscow. He learned from a newspaper advertisement that Melikhovo was for sale and sent his brother Mikhail to inspect it. Mikhail visited Melikhovo when the grounds and the buildings were covered with a thick layer of snow. Nevertheless, he advised his brother to purchase it. Chekhov bought it sight unseen, and when the snow began melting in March any number of additional structures and features—hothouses, sheds, an avenue of lindens—suddenly became visible. The purchase turned out to be an excellent move, providing Chekhov with an almost ideal home. But making the estate livable did require a considerable amount of work on the part of the entire Chekhov family, as some of the following letters testify.

2. "The Neighbors."

3. Mikhail Menshikov, the editor of *The Week*, was at one time a sailor.

4. Sergei Rachinsky, a professor of Moscow University, devised a system of elementary education based on religious instruction.

5. Dmitry Averkiev, a popular playwright of the time, now quite forgotten.

6. Both are Orthodox Lenten prayers.

7. Chekhov repeated and developed this passage in his letter to Suvorin of March 17, adding: "The so-called religious education cannot do without a little screen, invisible to the eye of the outsider. Behind that screen is torture, but in front of it people smile and are moved. No wonder so many atheists graduate from seminaries and divinity schools. It seems to me that Rachinsky sees only the façade of his own school, and has no idea of what goes on there during choir practice and Old Church Slavic instruction."

69. To Alexei Suvorin

Melikhovo,
March 11, 1892

A workingman's labor has been devalued to practically nothing, and this is why things are so easy for me. I'm beginning to understand the charms of capitalism. Demolishing the furnace in the servants' quarters and putting in a kitchen stove with all the trimmings, then demolishing the kitchen stove in the house and installing a tile stove costs only twenty rubles. Two shovels cost twenty-five kopecks. A day laborer gets thirty kopecks a day for keeping the ice cellar full. A young worker who knows how to read, neither drinks nor smokes, and whose duties include plowing the fields, shining boots and looking after seedbeds gets five rubles a month. Floors, partitions, wallpapering—everything is dirt cheap. And I have a feeling of utter freedom. But, if I had to pay for their work only a quarter of what I receive for my leisure, I'd go bankrupt within a month, because the number of stove setters, carpenters, and cabinetmakers, etc. that I need threatens to be as unending as a repeating decimal. The spacious life, unenclosed by four walls, requires a spacious pocketbook. I've already succeeded in boring you, I know, but let me say one more thing: clover seed costs a hundred rubles, and I need more than a hundred rubles' worth of oats for sowing. How am I to manage?[1] A good harvest and great riches have been predicted for me, but what the hell am I going to do with it? Five kopecks in the hand is worth a ruble in the future. I'll have to stick with it and work. I'll need to earn at least five hundred or so for all the little necessities. I've already earned half that amount. In the meantime the snow is melting, it's warm, the birds are singing, the sky is clear and it's a spring sky.

I'm getting loads of reading done. I read Leskov's "Legendary Characters" in the January issue of the *Russian Review*. It is both devout and piquant, a combination of virtue, piety, and lechery, but very interesting. Read it if you haven't yet. I've reread Pisarev's criticism of Pushkin.[2] It's terribly naïve. The fellow tries to debunk

Onegin and Tatyana, yet Pushkin remains intact. Pisarev is the grandpa and papa of all our present-day critics, including Burenin: the same petty kind of debunking; the same cold, self-enamored wit; the same crude, indelicate approach to people. It's not Pisarev's ideas that turn people into brutes (he doesn't have any ideas), it's his crude tone. His attitude toward Tatyana—and especially toward her sweet letter I love so dearly—strikes me as no less than sickening. His criticism reeks of the malicious, captious public prosecutor.[3] Anyway, the heck with him!

When are you going to pay me a visit? Before Annunciation by sleigh or after it by carriage? We're almost completely settled in; the only thing left is the shelves for my books. Once we take the winter windows off, we'll start painting everything all over again, and then the house will really start looking decent. In the summer we're going to install a flush toilet.

In the orchard we have linden-lined pathways, apples, cherries, peaches and raspberries.

You once wrote me to give you an idea for a comedy. I am so anxious for you to write a comedy that I'm willing to give you every single idea I have in my head. Come and we'll talk it over in the fresh air.

In the meantime stay well and happy. Regards to your family. It's a good thing that Alexei Alexeyevich has gone off to the country.

Yours,
A. Chekhov

1. The idiomatic phrase Chekhov uses (*Vot tut i vertis'!*) was given by him later to the schoolmaster Medvedenko in the first act of *The Seagull*, providing the translators of that play with a perennial stumbling block.

2. Constance Garnett for some reason decided that this was the title of the work in question and put "Criticism of Pushkin" in quotation marks. Chekhov is writing about "Pushkin and Belinsky," the famous 1865 essay by Dmitry Pisarev (1840–68), which is probably the wittiest and most honest piece of writing produced by the entire radical-utilitarian tradition of Russian criticism. Where Belinsky, Chernyshevsky and their present-day disciples in the Soviet Union read into Pushkin's work the didactic and subversive ideas their tradition requires, the young Pisarev sat down and read *Eugene Onegin* as it was actually written rather than as the inherited Belinskian tradition said it was. With admirable logic and with numerous parodistic citations of Pushkin's text (reminiscent in method of Tolstoy's subsequent parodistic debunking of Wagner's *Der Ring des Nibelungen*), Pisarev demonstrated that, viewed from Belinsky's own position, Pushkin himself was a frivolous, outmoded writer and the characters of his celebrated novel in verse were aristocratic drones and ninnies. Pushkin's reputation and Belinsky's distorted

reading of *Eugene Onegin* were too securely established to be debunked that easily; but Pisarev's position, persuasively argued in this article, that any writer, past or present, must possess demonstrable social relevance or be dismissed from any serious consideration casts its long shadow over Russian literature to this very day.

3. The critic as "public prosecutor" is not a polemical exaggeration, but a remarkably apt metaphor for the methods and style of literary criticism inherited by Russian literature from Pisarev's time and practiced in Chekhov's day with equal ruthlessness by both pro-government reactionaries such as Burenin and anti-government dissidents such as Mikhailovsky. In the twentieth century and especially after the 1930s, when literary critics demanded and obtained a labor-camp sentence for the poet Nikolai Zabolotsky because he used surrealistic imagery in a poem about collectivization, and in more recent times, when literary critics appeared as witnesses for the prosecution at the trials of Andrei Sinyavsky and Iosif Brodsky, and Mikhail Sholokhov complained in print that Sinyavsky's sentence was too light, Chekhov's metaphor of critic as prosecutor has become a hard reality.

70. To Alexei Suvorin

Melikhovo,
April 8, 1892

I'll be in Moscow on the Wednesday and Thursday of St. Thomas week[1] for sure. When you're ready to set off for Moscow, send a wire to Ivan's address: Chekhov, The Mius School, Tver Gate, Moscow. I'd have arrived even earlier, but the story is still not ready.[2] Ever since Good Friday I've been having guests, guests and more guests . . . and I haven't gotten a single line written.[3]

If Shapiro[4] were to present me with the gigantic photograph you wrote about, I wouldn't know what to do with it. It would be an unwieldy sort of gift. You say I was younger then. You're right, you know. Strange as it may seem, I turned thirty long ago and already feel close to forty. And I've aged in spirit as well as in body. In some silly way or other I've grown indifferent to everything around me, and for some reason the onset of this indifference coincided with my trip abroad. I get up and go to bed with the feeling that my interest in life has dried up. It's either the illness that newspapers call exhaustion or that hard-to-detect emotional process that novels call a fundamental emotional turning point. If it's the latter, then all's for the best.

Yesterday and today I've been plagued by a headache that began with an intermittent flashing in my eyes, a malady I've inherited from dear Mother.

Levitan the painter is staying with me. He and I went out to the woodcock mating area yesterday evening. He fired at a woodcock and the latter, wounded in the wing, fell into a puddle. I picked it up. It had a long beak, large black eyes, and a magnificent costume. It looked at us in wonder. What could we do with it? Levitan knit his brow, closed his eyes, and begged me with a tremor in his voice, "Please smash its head against the butt of the rifle." I said I couldn't. He kept shrugging his shoulders nervously, twitching his head and begging me. And the woodcock kept looking on in wonder. I had to obey Levitan and kill it. And while two idiots went home and sat down to dinner, there was one beautiful, enamored creature less in the world.

Jean Shcheglov, with whom you spent a boring evening, is a great opponent of all sorts of heresies, including female intellect. And yet if you compare him with, say, Kundasova, he's like a blushing nun. By the way, if you happen to see Kundasova, give her my regards and tell her we're expecting her. She's usually quite interesting in the open air and much more intelligent than in the city.

Gilyarovsky was here for a visit. The things he did, good Lord! He rode all my jades to exhaustion, climbed trees, scared the dogs and smashed logs to show off his strength. And he never stopped talking.

Keep well and happy. See you in Moscow!

Yours,
A. Chekhov

1. The week beginning with the first Sunday after Orthodox Easter, on which the story of Doubting Thomas is read in churches.

2. "Ward Number Six."

3. Chekhov's phenomenal hospitality could finally come into its own after the purchase of Melikhovo. Throughout his life on that estate house guests remained a constantly present feature. The first few pages of Kornei Chukovsky's book *On Chekhov* are a set of clever variations on the theme of Chekhov's hospitality and of his friends' inconsiderate acceptance of it even at the cost of Chekhov's own discomfort.

4. A prominent St. Petersburg photographer.

71. To Pyotr Bykov[1]

Melikhovo,
May 4, 1892

Dear Pyotr Vasilyevich,

Ieronim Ieronimovich[2] has written me that you are on close terms with the editors of *World-Wide Illustration*. Please let them know if you have a chance that the advertisement which touts me as "highly talented" and prints the title of my story in letters that are big enough for a signboard—that this advertisement has made an extremely unpleasant impression on me. It is like an advertisement for a dentist or masseuse and is at any rate in poor taste. I realize the value of advertising and have nothing against it, but a writer's best and most valid publicity comes from being modest and remaining within the bounds of literature when dealing with his readers and colleagues. All in all, I've had bad luck with *World-Wide Illustration*: I asked for an advance and got an advertisement. All right, so they didn't send the advance, so be it, but they should have spared my reputation. Forgive me for having to bore you with a first letter that is so grumpy.

I earnestly beg you to forgive me and to believe that I turned to you with a complaint only because I sincerely respect you.

A. Chekhov

1. Bykov was not merely "on close terms with the editors of *World-Wide Illustration*," as Chekhov writes—he was the acting chief editor of this popular magazine. The first page of the magazine's April issue was taken up by an announcement that "a new work by our highly talented writer Anton Pavlovich Chekhov," called "In Exile," was to appear in one of the magazine's next issues.

2. Ieronim Yasinsky.

72. To Alexei Kiselyov

Melikhovo,
May 11, 1892

My family described your stay at Melikhovo with great delight, and I was irritated I wasn't at home. Make sure you keep your word now, dear land captain: we'll be expecting you in June. If you don't come, I'll satirize you in the *Moscow Press*. I'll have some delicious sturgeon bellies ready, together with a large number of anecdotes about our agricultural experiences. We've been witnessing the damnedest homespun miracles: geldings turn into stallions, and mares impregnated by geldings in the evening turn into stallions by morning. I give you my word I'm not joking. Belonozhka [Whitefoot], one of our mares, was impregnated by a gelding in the presence of witnesses, after which she turned out to be a stallion.[1] Aren't you jealous? You never have miracles like that in Babkino.

We've planted ten dessiatines of oats and the same amount of clover and Timothy grass. We are planting three dessiatines of potatoes, which, if they yield a harvest, we'll sell to the monastery and to Serpukhov. We're planting lentils, peas and buckwheat, and we're continuing to sow the seeds of glory on Parnassus. We will of course take into account your advice on growing clover. I can't see any sense in raising rye and oats; it's so much trouble and the hopes of success are so pitifully small. Next year I'll plant ten more dessiatines of clover, etc., and when I put up a hut on the other plot, I'll plant about thirty dessiatines of clover there too.

You're right, life is hard without a river. But what can we do? Only comfort ourselves with the words of Voltaire, who said that Russia has nine months of winter and three months of bad weather. In the winter you can't see the river under the snow, and when the weather is bad its absence is a convenience. But don't despair, Your Excellency! When I set up a farm on my hundred fifty dessiatines of wooded land, we'll have spring water. I'll raise bees and two thousand chickens, I'll have a cherry orchard, and live like St. Serafim.[2] And it is essential to build a farm, because if we leave the hundred fifty dessiatines of woods untended, then ten years from now instead of the riches we're expecting it will yield nothing but grief.[3]

Yesterday we had our first rain after a dry spell. It rained again today. Things became cheerful. There will be lots of good grass.

So you've given your noble word of honor that you, Vasilisa Pantelevna, and the much-esteemed Bosko,[4] to wit Sergei, will be coming to see us in June. If Maria Vladimirovna were to consent to pay my wretched hut a visit, our joy would be ineffable. I could find a carriage with springs for her. In fact I ought to buy one, don't you think? I grew so tired of bouncing my sinful insides on tarantasses in Siberia that the drive from Melikhovo to Lopasnya feels like sheer torture each time.

It's raining.

My income exceeds my expenses, but wouldn't you know, I'm having as much trouble collecting my royalties as a beginning writer. First the notary-publisher[5] absconded, then they lost my address, then they sent the money to Serpukhov. There was a day when I was left without a kopeck and I felt like absconding after the notary. Incidentally, life in Melikhovo is cheaper than life in Moscow, but all sorts of trivia have gotten the best of me: first a room needs papering, then the well needs cleaning, then benches have to be built, and all these trifles add up to hundreds of rubles.

In June we'll have ninepins and croquet. You'll find many changes.

I couldn't have bought the neighboring estate (thirty-eight dessiatines), since it was sold for more than a hundred rubles a dessiatine. But our neighbors don't bother us. On the contrary. He and she, winsome lovebirds, are joined in illicit love. She is ten years older than he.

They've bought a number of agricultural machines, unusual plows, and are endlessly building. They have *nine* workers and four house servants. They plant clover separately from spring and winter crops. And you know we can't live anywhere that doesn't have a target in the neighborhood for our satirical arrows. We can't help gossiping. When our neighbors' criminal love cools off, so will their agricultural ardor. And then we'll buy it (if our estate hasn't been sold first).

I send you regards by the thousands. God grant you all the best.

Yours,
A. Chekhov

Yegorov will soon be in Voskresensk.

1. According to Maria Chekhova's recollections, the mare Whitefoot was stolen during the night and replaced with a dead gelding that had exactly the same markings, which caused understandable perplexity.

2. St. Serafim of Sarov, a hermit and mystic of the early nineteenth century, who lived in the woods together with a tame bear. Revered as a saint in Chekhov's time, he was officially canonized in 1903.

3. This letter is selected from a large group of similar letters Chekhov wrote to various friends during the spring and summer of 1892 describing his agrarian life at Melikhovo. His horticultural interests and talents came to the fore, he took up animal husbandry seriously and he constructed a pond, which he stocked with a wide variety of fish. These interests were not a transient whim, for they continued throughout Chekhov's Melikhovo period and were taken up again later, though on a smaller scale, when he had to move to the Crimea.

4. Chekhov's nicknames for Alexei and Maria Kiselyov's two children.

5. The publisher of the journal *Russian Review* had formerly been a notary public.

73. To Alexei Suvorin

Melikhovo,
May 28, 1892

Life is short, and Chekhov, whose answer you are awaiting, would like it to flash by with brilliance and verve. He would like to go to the Princes Islands and Constantinople and back to India and Sakhalin. But first, he's not free; he has a noble family that needs his protection. And second, he is endowed with a large dose of cowardice. Cowardice is the only word I can use to qualify my peeking into the future. I'm afraid of getting in over my head, and each trip considerably complicates my financial situation. No, tempt me not in vain.[1] Write me not of the sea.

I wish you would return from abroad in August or September; then I could go to Feodosia with you. Otherwise I won't get to the sea at all this summer. I yearn terribly for a steamship. I yearn terribly for any kind of freedom. I've had enough of this ordered, pious life.

We're having a hot spell with warm rain, but the evenings are delightful. A verst away there are good swimming and picnic sites, but there's no time to go swimming or picnicking. Either I gnash my teeth and write, or work out picayune financial problems with the carpenters and workers. Misha was given a harsh reprimandus by his superiors for spending weeks and weeks here with me instead of at home, so that now I am left alone to take care of running a farm I don't believe in because it brings in so little and is closer to a gentlemanly hobby than real work. I bought three mouse traps and catch twenty-five mice a day and take them off to the woods. I feel wonderful in the woods. It's terribly stupid of landowners to live among parks and fruit orchards rather than in the woods. There's a feeling of divine presence in the woods, to say nothing of the practical advantages: no one can steal your timber and you're right there when it comes to looking after the trees. If I were in your shoes, I would buy two to three hundred dessiatines of high-quality wooded land, put in roads and paths, and build a castle on it. Paths cut out of the woods are more majestic than tree-lined paths in parks.

What shall I do with Monte Cristo?[2] I've abridged him so much he looks like someone who's just gotten over typhus; he started out fat and ended up emaciated. The first part, while the count is still poor, is very interesting and well done, but the second part with very few exceptions is unbearable because everything Monte Cristo says and does in it is pompous and asinine. But in general the novel is striking. Shall I put it aside until fall?

Three young ladies have come for a visit all at once. One of them is a countess, and Misha is trying to *faire la carrière* with her. The second you know—Natasha Lintvaryova, who has brought along her gaiety and her fine laughter from the south.

Judging by the papers, life is dreary all over. They say that there's a cholera epidemic in the Transcaucasus and that Paris has had one too. Before you go to Constantinople, find out whether they are quarantining ships from Black Sea ports. Being quarantined is a surprise I wouldn't wish on anyone. It's worse than being arrested. It has now been tenderly dubbed "a three-day observation period."

Horses in central Russia are suffering and dying from influenza. If you believe there is a purpose for everything that happens in nature, it is obvious that nature is doing everything in her power to rid herself of all weaklings and organisms for which she has no use. Famines, cholera, influenza . . . Only the healthy and strong will be left. And it's impossible not to believe in purposefulness. One day our starlings, young and old, suddenly flew off. It puzzled us, because they aren't due to migrate for some time yet. But then we suddenly heard that clouds of southern dragonflies, which were mistaken for locusts, had flown over Moscow the other day. The problem is how our starlings found out that on such and such a day at so many versts from Melikhovo those insects would be in flight. Who told them? Verily this is a great mystery.[3] But it's a wise mystery too. I can only conclude that the same kind of wisdom underlies famines and epidemics. We and our horses are the dragonflies, and famine and cholera the starlings.

I bought a wonderful croquet set at your store. The merchandise is good and the price very reasonable.

Do write and tell me when you're leaving. God grant you win or inherit three hundred thousand so you can buy an estate near Lopasnya. Keep well.

Yours,
A. Chekhov

1. Citation of the first line from an art song by Mikhail Glinka, which is a setting of Yevgeny Baratynsky's poem "Disillusionment." There is a superb performance of it by Jennie Tourel in her album *None but the Lonely Heart*, where it is called "Vain Temptation."

2. Chekhov agreed to abridge *The Count of Monte-Cristo* by Alexandre Dumas for a popular edition Suvorin was planning.

3. A partial and slightly altered quotation of the Church Slavic text of Ephesians 5:32 ("This is a great mystery: but I speak concerning Christ and the church").

74. To Nikolai Leykin

Melikhovo,
June 8, 1892

I received your letter, my most kind Nikolai Alexandrovich. I can only assume that Mikhail Suvorin is presently at his estate in Pskov Province and that it is almost impossible to get the truth from him. I'll write to my brother Alexander today. If he were to pay me a visit, there couldn't be a better opportunity. If the dogs need leashes and collars, please buy them yourself and we'll settle it later. Alexander will know as little about what to buy as I do because neither of us has ever had occasion to transport dogs. But I'm hungering to have those dachshunds here.[1]

Yes, veterinary medicine is still in the most pitiful state in Russia. There are times when its prescriptions leave you open-mouthed.

People still prescribe belladonna, lead acetate, flowers of sulphur, and similar nonsense from old veterinary handbooks. The handbook published by *Mediator* for the peasants is of absolutely no use.[2] It's all terribly backward.

We haven't had any rain, and it's hot. We're languishing. The rye is doing fine, but the spring crops are weeping. Irrigating the vegetable garden has worn out both my family and the servants. It's strange that your apple trees have not blossomed yet, while our cherries are already turning red, our apples have grown as large as three-kopeck pieces, and the strawberries and gooseberries are ripening. There will be a bumper crop of berries this year. We'll probably get several poods of strawberries alone. What are we going to do with them?

We have all the books you wrote me about. I familiarized myself with Schroeder[3] back on Sakhalin while studying the local agriculture. The trouble is I don't have any time for gardening. I ought to be out examining every sprout, but I write instead. The workers are in the fields, my sister tends the vegetables, my mother does the housework. And, whenever I have a moment free, I'm needed either in the fields or by the carpenters or in the vegetable garden, or else all the shovels are in use and there's nothing I can dig around the trees with. I started pruning out the dead fruit-tree branches, but after puttering around for three days I gave up. The old trees are bending down to the ground, and before you know it they'll topple over. When the plum trees were in full bloom, they were literally lying on the ground. We had to axe them, since there was no way of saving them. We ought to prop up trees with prongs, but there's no one to go to the woods. By August things ought to be a little freer.

I've ordered a hundred lilac bushes and fifty Vladimir cherry trees for the fall. The area which I've now fenced in with a solid base trellis and which serves as a continuation of our orchard will have to be planted with no less than seven hundred trees. The result will be a superb orchard, and in eight or ten years my heirs will receive a good income from it. Next year I'm going to start an apiary.

I have excellent buckwheat, but no bees.

Did I ever thank you for the books? I received them long ago. Forgive me for being impolite enough not to send you my books. My one consolation is that I'll send them all together.

Alexander has astounded me. He's published a *History of Fire Fighting*. An excellent idea. He has appealed to me as well with the question about his little son. I promised to look into the matter, but there is such a mass of letters in my archives that I'm afraid to go near it.[4]

My humblest respects to your family. I wish you warm, dry weather.

Keep well and happy.

Yours,
A. Chekhov

1. Despite some unkind things Chekhov had to say about Leykin in some of his letters to Suvorin, he remained on cordial terms with him in later years and contributed an occasional story to his humor magazine. Leykin was one of the earliest Russian breeders of dachshunds, which were considered a rare and exotic breed. He offered Chekhov two dachshund puppies and Suvorin's second son, Mikhail, volunteered to transport them from St. Petersburg to Melikhovo. But he later backed out of his promise and Chekhov is suggesting that Leykin entrust the dogs to Alexander Chekhov, who was planning to visit his family at Melikhovo.

When the dachshunds arrived, they were named Brom and Khina (Bromine and Quinine). They became general favorites and potbellied Quinine in particular was Chekhov's inseparable companion throughout his stay at Melikhovo.

2. *Mediator* was a Tolstoyan publishing house whose aim was to be of service to the impoverished peasants.

3. A popular gardening manual.

4. Alexander Chekhov's family life was disorganized to such a degree that when his eldest son had to be registered at school it turned out that the boy's father had no idea of the date or year of his birth. Alexander therefore asked his brother Anton and various acquaintances to look through their correspondence to see if he had perhaps mentioned the birth of his son in any of his old letters.

75. To Alexei Suvorin

Melikhovo,
July 3, 1892

An important correction. I have been sent *Fin de siècle*.[1] I received it yesterday evening, after three days' delay because *Fin* lay around for three days in Serpukhov. For the time being all I can say is that the format is very nice. The book looks appealing. I'll start reading it tonight, and in a few days I'll let fly my criticism and profound comments.

Cholera has been creeping higher and higher, but lethargically and indecisively. No city has as many as two hundred cases a day. Most have only seven or eight. It is only in Astrakhan and Baku that they are counted in the tens and add up to a hundred. The papers have been writing a lot of nonsense, but in general they do get a great deal accomplished. In matters of cholera *New Times* has behaved excellently. Dr. Galanin's[2] articles are entirely satisfactory. The city population is alarmed, and even the countryside is beginning to talk despondently about the epidemic. The danger has been exaggerated; cholera is not as terrifying as it's made out to be, but there's something vile, depressing and fulsome about the word itself. If it had another name, people would be a lot less afraid of it.

Even so, it's upsetting. Last year famine, this year fear. Life has been taking so much from the people, but what has it been giving them? We are told to put up a fight, but is the game worth the candle?

I received plans for a new theater society that is being organized by Grigorovich, Vsevolozhsky, Savina and others. In my opinion, it's an utterly superfluous society. They'll get a hundred rubles from you, five from me, collect 2,137 rubles 42 kopecks altogether and wilt. The functions are very ill defined, the general tone of the constitution servile.

Let me know your address if you leave Franzensbad.

I have a piece of literary news. I've received a letter from *Russian Thought* proposing we forget our former misunderstanding. I responded with a touching letter and promised them a story.[3]

What else shall I write you? We have so many cherries we don't know what to do with them. There's no one to pick the gooseberries. I have never in my life been so rich. Standing under the cherry tree and eating cherries, I feel strange that no one boots me out. In my childhood I had my ears boxed daily for stealing berries.

A pre-cholera portent: birds are laying poorly and having trouble bringing up their young. Three geese hatched only three goslings, and the ducks had no luck at all. The hens have been leaving their nests. That's how it is everywhere. The flowers are coming up poorly, and everything is dwarflike. Zdekauer[4] was right when he called influenza the harbinger of cholera, but his article in *New Times* is a bit naïve. You'd think he was an old army doctor of the Bazarov-*père*[5] variety instead of a professor.

Misha keeps pushing me to write faster and faster because Frol[6] is about to drive to the station. So keep well. Come as soon as you can, and write and tell me where you're going to be living in the fall.

Yours,
A. Chekhov

1. A novel by Suvorin.

2. Dr. Modest Galanin published a series of articles on the cholera epidemic in *New Times*.

3. On June 23, 1892, Vukol Lavrov wrote Chekhov, apologizing for the misunderstanding that caused Chekhov to write an angry letter (Letter 43) and assuring him that *Russian Thought* was anxious to publish his work. The result was the publication of "Ward Number Six" and "An Unknown Man's Story" in Lavrov's journal, followed in the next few years by "A Woman's Kingdom" and "Three Years."

4. Professor Nikolai Zdekauer, the court physician of the imperial family, also published a few brief pieces on the cholera epidemic in *New Times*.

5. The father of the hero in Turgenev's *Fathers and Sons*.

6. The hired hand at Melikhovo.

76. To Nikolai Leykin

Melikhovo,
July 13, 1892

Forgive me, my most kind Nikolai Alexandrovich, for having waited so long to answer your letter. As a result of the cholera epidemic, which has not yet reached us, I've been invited to join the *zemstvo* force of sanitary inspectors and assigned my own region, and I am now traveling from village to village and from factory to factory gathering material for a conference of sanitary inspectors. I have no time even to think of literary work. My region was very heavily attacked by cholera in 1848, and we're expecting it won't be any weaker this time round, though, of course, it's all in God's hands. The regions are large, so most of the inspectors' time will be spent on exhausting field trips. There are no shelters, so the tragedies will take place in huts or out in the open. We have no assistants. We are promised unlimited quantities of disinfectants and medicine. The roads are foul, and my horses worse. As for my health, I begin feeling exhausted and wishing to collapse into bed by noontime. That's what it's like without cholera; we'll see what happens when cholera arrives.

There is an epidemic besides cholera that I am sure will visit my estate: penury. By cutting off my literary activities, I also cut off my income. Apart from the three rubles I received today for treating a case of the clap, my income is down to zero.

All fourteen dessiatines of rye are successful and are now being harvested. Thanks to the rains we've had lately the oats have recovered. The buckwheat is splendid. There are heaps of cherries.

It's now after seven in the evening. I have to go to the land captain's; he has called a meeting for me. This land captain, Prince Shakhovskoy, is my neighbor (three versts away). He is a young man of twenty-seven, gigantic build and stentorian voice. He and I both practice eloquence at the village meetings by trying to argue skeptics out of believing in the healing powers of pepper vodka, dill pickles, etc. Every single peasant child has diarrhea, often with blood.

Keep well, now. Send the fee to Serpukhov because Lopasnya has no post office. All you need is Melikhovo, Serpukhov District.

Once again, keep well. Send my regards to your family. Dr. Sirotinin[1] is living in a cottage nearby.

Yours,
A. Chekhov

1. A one-time colleague of Chekhov's from his Voskresensk *zemstvo* hospital days.

77. To Yevgraf Yegorov

Melikhovo,
July 15, 1892

My most kind Yevgraf Petrovich,

I can't give you any good news, because I don't know a single doctor who is free and I have no acquaintances among medical students. And even if I do encounter someone, my intervention has little chance of success, because no doctor is likely to be willing to go to your district for two hundred and fifty rubles.[1]

We too are working for all we're worth. There are so few doctors here in Serpukhov District that when cholera comes, the district will be practically without aid. They've even dragged up poor me, sinner that I am, and had me appointed a sanitary inspector. I've been traveling from village to village giving lectures. The day after tomorrow at the council of sanitary inspectors we are going to discuss how to find doctors and medical students. Most likely we won't come up with any solution.

So you're not getting a chance to rest after your famine efforts. It's a sad and irritating business.

I am now on my way to the monastery to ask them to put up a shelter. Stay well and under Heaven's protection. Regards to your family.

Yours,
A. Chekhov

1. Yegorov had written to Chekhov asking him to recommend a doctor for the *zemstvo* in which he was the land captain.

78. To Natalia Lintvaryova[1]

Melikhovo,
July 22, 1892

Dear Natalia Mikhailovna,

Tell Ivanenko I paid a ruble for his telegram. It was a waste of money, because Masha had been told that if Alexander Ignatyevich consented he should leave at once without going to the trouble of sending telegrams or scratching his head indecisively. He's been expected for a long time now. I myself am anxiously awaiting his arrival.[2]

Rumor has it that your sister Yelena Mikhailovna[3] passed nearby on her way to Khotun. The day before yesterday I heard she had been appointed to a position in Belopesotsk Rural District. Could we have imagined three years ago that we'd be fighting cholera together in Serpukhov District? The Khotun Medical Region borders on my Melikhovo Region, which was set up on July 17th. So fate herself meant us to be "esteemed colleagues." Yelena Mikhailovna will now have to organize her region. It's going to be hard on her nerves because our *zemstvo* is noted for its procrastination and has loaded all the difficult organizational work onto the backs of the doctors. I'm as frustrated as a dog on a chain. I'm in charge of twenty-three villages, and so far I haven't received a single cot. I'll probably never get the medical orderly that the Council of Sanitary Inspectors promised me. I travel from factory to factory begging for room for my future patients as if I were begging for alms. I'm on the road from morning till night. I'm already exhausted, and the epidemic hasn't even arrived here yet. Last night I got drenched in a downpour and slept away from home, and in the morning I walked home through the mud, cursing all the way. My lazy side is deeply offended. And I don't suppose Yelena Mikhailovna will have an easier time of it. But that's only temporary. In a week or two everything will fall into place and we'll be settled. We are assuming that the epidemic won't be especially intense. But, even if it is, it won't be that bad, because the *zemstvo* has given the doctors extremely broad powers. That is, I haven't received a kopeck, but I can rent as many huts and hire as many people as I need. In extreme cases I can import a sanitary detachment from Moscow. The *zemstvo* people here are intelligent, my colleagues efficient and knowledgeable. What's more, the peasants are sufficiently accustomed to being treated medically so that we will almost certainly not have to start convincing them that we, the doctors, did not cause the epidemic. We're not likely to be physically attacked.

When is Masha coming back? The vegetable garden is getting terribly run down without her. The heifer and the geese have eaten up half of it, and the chicks are helping them along. I have no time to keep an eye on it, since I'm away from home for days on end.

I've read that there's some cholera in Kharkov Province. Where? Has there been any on the Sumy stretch of the railroad? It will be a pity if it starts making its way to the western provinces. It could build itself a good solid nest there and return to Russia in the spring.

A highly important note: if anyone on your estate should get cholera, give him naphthalene at the very beginning. If a person has a strong constitution, you can give it to him with calomel or castor oil. It dissolves in the latter. Give them up to ten grains. Here is the treatment we've decided on: first naphthalene, then apply the Cantani method, that is, tannin enemas and hypodermic injections of a solution of table salt. In addition I will be keeping the patients warm in every possible way (hot coffee with cognac, hot pads, hot baths and so on), and in the early stages I will supplement the naphthalene with santonin, which has a direct effect on intestinal parasites. The santonin was my own idea. If there is no cholera, I won't use any of it.

I hope the thrice-accursed cholera will pass us by and that we'll see each other another 283 times in our lives. Of course I can't visit you this summer. But if you come visit us in August or September, it will be very, very magnanimous of you. According to the historical data I have compiled, Melikhovo had no cholera at all in 1871–72 and only two cases in 1848, both of which came from outside. There is never any diphtheria or typhus here. . . . Why not move here? I'd build you a house on my second lot and forbid our maid Katerina to set foot there; she's turned out to be a terrible thief and imbecile. Darya is wreaking havoc.[4]

Keep well now and under God's protection. My sincere greetings to everyone. If Masha and Klara Ivanovna[5] still haven't left, my regards to them too.

Yours with all my heart,
A. Chekhov

1. The third daughter of Chekhov's landlady at Luka, the loud-voiced Ukrainophile who once refused to meet Suvorin for ideological reasons. See Letters 21 and 22.

2. Maria Chekhova (Masha) and the flutist Alexander Ivanenko were both staying with the Lintvaryovs at Luka at the time this letter was written. Chekhov had arranged for Ivanenko a part-time job as a clerk on the estate of his neighbor the land captain Prince Sergei Shakhovskoy.

3. Dr. Yelena Lintvaryova, the second daughter of the Lintvaryov family,

described in Letter 21 as infinitely kind, loving and homely. The eldest sister, Dr. Zinaida Lintvaryova, whose stoical endurance of her brain tumor Chekhov described in Letter 21, died in November of 1891. Chekhov published a brief but warm and sympathetic obituary of her in the medical journal *The Physician.*

4. The family cook at Melikhovo, given to bouts of drunkenness, at which times she would go around breaking the eggs under brooding hens and geese.

5. Countess Klara Mamuna, later temporarily Mikhail Chekhov's fiancée.

79. To Natalia Lintvaryova

Melikhovo,
July 31, 1892

Dear Natalia Mikhailovna,

To begin with, many thanks for the *zubrovka.* I drank five shots of it one after the other and found it does wonders for cholera. Ivanenko is living with us and telling us stories about his uncle. Today he went off somewhere with his boss Prince Shakhovskoy, a young man who also likes to talk—but about his aunt. (His aunt, the Princess Shakhovskaya, works in General Baranov's medical shelter.) What a storm they'll talk up!

Masha was delighted with the Psyol and with all of you and your hospitality. If it weren't for my cholera duties and tight money situation, I would certainly have paid you a visit this year. Cholera will most likely occupy my entire autumn. It is presently in and around Moscow and is coming at us from the north and south and along the Oka from the east. It should be gracing us with its presence between the fifth and seventh of August and making hors d'oeuvres out of our local rustics. Each time there was an epidemic in my region between 1848 and 1872, it lasted about forty days, so I can expect the cholera epidemic to be over in September. Then we'll have the conference of sanitary inspectors and turn in our cholera equipment, so the whole rigmarole will drag on into October, and by October it will be too late to visit you. I'm up to my ears in work now and therefore won't be earning a kopeck until October; I don't have a thing to my name.[1] So after the epidemic I'll have to stay at home and scrawl and try to skin each publisher twice over. Consequently, I won't be able to come in the fall either.

I haven't seen your sister yet. I'd like to see her and talk things over with her. Cholera will strike any day now, and the *zemstvo* is just beginning to send to Berlin for Cantani syringes and even Esmarch dishes. I have one dish for twenty-five villages, not a single thermometer, and only half a pound of carbolic acid. Your sister is probably no better off. Blessed are the doctors who live at their hospitals—we clinic organizers always feel impoverished and alone. I have shelters at two factories; one is excellent, the other poor; there are some smaller shelters in the villages. All this I've managed to obtain by begging from the local residents; I haven't as yet spent a kopeck of *zemstvo* money. None of this is of any importance, of course, and I can only suppose that in a week's time the domains of the King of the Medes will be ready to welcome the Indian commas.[2] Our *zemstvo* is slow-moving, but intelligent and flexible, our neighbors good people, and in all likelihood the peasants will not resort to violence because they're accustomed to being treated medically and are afraid of cholera.

I just had some company in my study. The conversation was about you and your fall trip to Melikhovo. I've taken mental note of it. Please do come.

They're mowing the oats. A horse has fallen ill. Our neighbor has given us a small thoroughbred pig in gratitude for my having treated his wife. We have bought two Romanov sheep: an eligible bachelor and his young lady. The heifer has grown as potbellied as a *zubrovka* bottle from eating apples.

Keep well, now. God protect you from illnesses and fears. My sincere greetings to all your family and my thanks for looking after my sister. Come, so you can take another trip to the glove factory with

Your dashing soldier boy,
A. Chekhov

The glove manufacturer presented me with a half dozen pairs of gloves for Masha in payment for treating him.

1. An archaic Russian proverb is cited in medieval Russian in the original.
2. Natalia Lintvaryova liked to refer to Melikhovo as the domain of the King of the Medes. "Indian commas" is a euphemism for the cholera bacillus, *Vibrio cholerae*, which refers to its shape and to its supposed origin in India.

80. To Alexei Suvorin

Melikhovo,
August 1, 1892

My letters have been chasing you, but you are too elusive. I've written you often, to St. Moritz among other places. But, judging by your letters, you haven't received a thing from me. First of all, the cholera epidemic is in and around Moscow and will be in our area any day now. Second, I have been appointed a cholera doctor, and my district encompasses twenty-five villages, four factories and a monastery. I am organizing things, setting up shelters and so on, and I'm lonely, because everything that has to do with cholera is alien to me, and the work, which requires constant trips, talks and fuss and bustle, tires me out. There is no time to write. I abandoned literature long ago, and I'm poor and broke because I thought it desirable for myself and my independence to refuse the remuneration cholera doctors receive. I'm bored, although from a detached point of view cholera has its interesting sides. I'm sorry you're not in Russia. Material for your column is going to waste. There is more good than bad, and this makes the cholera epidemic strikingly different from the famine we observed last winter. Now everyone is working. Working fiercely. The wonders going on at the Nizhny Novgorod fair are enough to make even Tolstoy regard medicine with respect—medicine and the participation of the educated classes in the life of their country. It looks as if the cholera epidemic has been held at bay. Not only has the number of cases been lowered; the percentage of deaths has gone down as well. In all Moscow, immense as it is, the number of cases has been kept to fifty a week, while in the Don region it's polishing off a thousand people a day—an impressive difference. We district doctors are prepared; we have a definite plan of action, and there is every reason to believe that we will also decrease the percentage of cholera deaths in our regions. We are without assistants; we will have to be doctors and attendants at one and the same time. The peasants are crude, unsanitary and mistrustful, but the thought that our labors will not be in vain makes it all almost unnoticeable. Of all the Serpukhov doctors I am the most pitiful; my carriage and horses are mangy, I don't know the roads, I can't see anything at night, I have no money, I tire very quickly, and most of all—I can't forget that I ought to be writing. I have a great urge to drop this whole cholera thing and sit down and start to write. I also feel like having a talk with you. I am completely and utterly alone.

Our attempts at farming have been crowned with complete success. The harvest is quite respectable, and when we sell our grain Melikhovo will bring in more than a thousand rubles. The vegetable garden is dazzling. We have mountains of cucumbers, and the cabbage is amazing. If it weren't for the accursed cholera epidemic, I could say I've never spent as good a summer as this one.

I had a visit from the astronomer.[1] She is living at the hospital with the lady physician and is meddling in typical female fashion with cholera affairs. She exaggerates everything and sees intrigue everywhere. She's an odd sort of person. She accepts you and is fond of you, though she doesn't belong to the set that the censors would pass, as Chertkov[2] puts it. But Shcheglov[3] is definitely wrong. I don't like that kind of literature.

There's been no word yet about cholera uprisings, but there is talk of arrests, proclamations and so on. They say that Astyryov,[4] the writer, has been sentenced to fifteen years' hard labor. If our socialists do in fact exploit the epidemic for their own ends, I will feel utter contempt for them. Repulsive means for good ends make the ends themselves repulsive. Let them make dupes of the doctors and their assistants, but why lie to the people? Why assure them that they are right to be ignorant and that their crass prejudices are the holy truth? Can a beautiful future really expiate this base lie? If I were a politician, I'd resolve never to disgrace my present for the sake of my future even if I were promised tons of bliss for a pennyweight of base lies.[5]

Will we be seeing one another in the fall? Will we stay together in Feodosia? You after your trip abroad and I after the epidemic could have many interesting things to tell each other. Let's spend October in the Crimea. It won't be boring, honestly it won't. We'll write, talk, eat. . . . There's no more cholera in Feodosia.

In view of my exceptional situation please write me as often as you can. My present mood cannot possibly be good, and your letters distract me from my cholera interests and transport me temporarily to another world.

Keep well. Greetings to my school friend Alexei Petrovich.[6]

Yours,
A. Chekhov

I'll be using the Cantani method to treat cholera: sizable tannin enemas at forty degrees and hypodermic injection of table-salt solution. The former works superbly: it warms the patient up and checks his diarrhea. As for the injections, they sometimes produce miracles, but sometimes result in paralysis of the heart.

1. Olga Kundasova.
2. Vladimir Chertkov, Tolstoy's principal disciple and apostle.
3. Reference to a recently published story by Ivan Shcheglov.
4. The ethnographer Nikolai Astyryov. He published an exposé of inhuman conditions in the mining industry in the Transbaikalia region, for which it was rumored he might be put on trial.
5. The annotators of both Soviet editions of Chekov's letters become what can only be described as hysterical at this point, insisting that there were never any such things as cholera rebellions in nineteenth-century Russia, that peasant uprisings caused by political and economic conditions were

misrepresented by the tsarist government as cholera rebellions, and that, furthermore, had there been any such rebellions, they were sure to have been instigated by the kulaks and other reactionary elements. But cholera rebellions in the Russian countryside were in fact a recurrent and well-documented phenomenon throughout the century, with peasants repeatedly refusing to be treated by government-appointed doctors, accusing doctors and other medical personnel of deliberately spreading the cholera and, in some instances, lynching them. See Roderick E. McGrew, *Russia and the Cholera 1823–1832*, Madison and Milwaukee, 1965, for a study of this phenomenon during a particular decade.

Both sets of Soviet annotators seem to miss the point that Chekhov is not really accusing the socialists of exploiting the cholera for their own political ends, but is merely raising a hypothetical but highly significant point about political morality.

6. Alexei Kolomnin.

81. To Alexei Suvorin

Melikhovo,
August 16, 1892

Do whatever you like, I won't write another word. I've sent letters to Abbazia, to St. Moritz, I've written ten times at least. You haven't yet sent me one correct address, so not one of my letters has gotten to you, and my long descriptions of and lectures on cholera have gone to waste. What a shame. But even more shameful—after all the letters I sent you about my scrapes with cholera—was your letter from gay, turquoise-hued Biarritz, where you suddenly write that you envy my leisure. May Allah forgive you!

In any case, I'm alive and well. The summer was wonderful—dry, warm and abundant in the fruits of the earth. But starting in July all its charm was ruined by news of cholera. While your letters were inviting me to Vienna or Abbazia, I had become a district doctor for the Serpukhov *zemstvo* and was out chasing cholera by the tail and organizing a new district at top speed. My district consists of twenty-five villages, four factories and a monastery. I see patients in the morning and make the rounds for the rest of the day. I ride, lecture the local rustics, treat patients and fume, and since the *zemstvo* hasn't given me a penny for organizing clinics, I have to wheedle one thing after the other from the rich. I've turned out to be an excellent beggar, and thanks to my beggarly eloquence my district now has two excellent fully equipped shelters and about five that are not so excellent, in fact quite poor. I've even saved the *zemstvo* all expenses for disinfectants: I begged enough lime, vitriol and similar smelly junk from the factory owners for all my twenty-five villages. In short, Kolomnin should be proud to have studied at the same school as I did. My soul is weary. I'm bored. Not being your own master, thinking only of diarrhea, being startled at night by dogs barking and a knock at the gate (have they come for me?), riding abominable horses over uncharted roads, and reading only about cholera, and waiting only for cholera, and at the same time feeling perfect indifference to the disease and the people you're serving—let me tell you, those are the kind of cooks that could spoil any broth. The epidemic has already reached Moscow and the Moscow District. We must expect it any minute now. Judging by its progress in Moscow, we can reasonably believe that it has already passed its peak and that the comma is beginning to lose its virulence. We can also reasonably believe that the measures taken both in Moscow and here have considerably impeded its progress. The intelligentsia has been working hard, sparing neither effort nor money. I see them every day and I'm overcome with admiration, and when I think of how the Resident and Burenin poured their bilious acid over the heads of the intelligentsia, I start to gag. In Nizhny doctors and the entire educated sector of the population have done wonders. I was both horrified and delighted when I read about the epidemic. In the good old days when people fell ill and died by the thousands, no one would even have dreamed of the astounding victories taking place before our very eyes. It's a shame you're not a doctor and can't share my pleasure, that is, deeply sense and understand and appreciate everything that is happening. But I can't express it all in a few words.

Treating cholera requires first and foremost that the doctor take his time; that is, he must devote between five and ten hours to each patient, often more. Since I intend to use the Cantani method, tannin enemas and table-salt-solution injections, my position will be sillier than a fool's. While I'm fussing with one patient, ten others will fall ill and die. The thing is, I am all that those twenty-five villages have, except for my orderly, who calls me Your Excellency, is afraid to smoke in my presence and can't take a step without me. I'll be effective with single cases, but if even a five-case-a-day epidemic breaks out, all I'll do is get irritated and exhausted and feel guilty.

Of course I have no time to give even a thought to literature. I'm not writing a thing. I've refused all salary to retain a modicum of freedom of action. So I don't have a kopeck. Until the rye has been threshed and sold, I'll be living off *The Bear* and mushrooms, which grow everywhere you look. By the way, I've never lived as cheaply as now. Everything we have is our own; even our bread. I figure that two years from now my household expenses should not exceed a thousand rubles a year.

When you read in the papers that the epidemic is over, you'll know I've begun to write again. But as long as I'm working for the *zemstvo*, don't think of me as a writer. You can't run after two hares at once.

You write I've given up Sakhalin. No, I can't give up that particular brainchild. When fiction begins to bore or oppress me, I enjoy taking up something nonfictional. And I am not particularly concerned with when I'll finish Sakhalin or where I'll publish it. As long as Galkin-Vrasky sits on the prison throne, I don't really feel like releasing the book. Of course if I absolutely had to publish it or starve, that would be a different story.

In all my letters I kept importuning you with one question, though you don't have to answer it if you don't want to: where will you be living in the fall and wouldn't you like to spend a part of September and October with me in Feodosia and the Crimea? I am so unbearably looking forward to eating, drinking, sleeping and talking about literature, that is, doing nothing and at the same time feeling like a decent human being. Of course, if you find my idleness disgusting, I can promise to write a play or short novel with you or in your presence. How about it? You don't want to? Well, do as you like.

The astronomer has come by twice; I felt uneasy with her both times. Svobodin has also come. He's getting better and better. His grave illness has put him through a spiritual metamorphosis.[1]

Look at what a long letter I'm writing even though I'm unsure as to whether this letter is going to reach you. Picture my choleric boredom, my choleric loneliness and my forced literary idleness, and write me longer and more frequent letters. I share your squeamish feeling toward the French. The Germans stand high above them, though for some reason they're always called dullards. And I cherish Franco-Russian friendship about as much as I cherish Tatishchev.[2] There's something dissolute in that friendship. On the other hand, I was tremendously pleased with Virchow's[3] visit to Russia.

Our potato crop is delicious, our cabbage divine. How can you get along without cabbage soup? I don't envy you your sea or your freedom or the good mood you enjoy while you're abroad. Russian summer is better than anything. And incidentally, I don't particularly feel like going abroad. After Singapore, Ceylon and possibly our Amur, Italy and even the Vesuvius crater don't seem seductive. I've been to India and China, and I saw no great difference between foreign countries and Russia.

My neighbor Count Orlov-Davydov, owner of the famous Otrada,[4] is in Biarritz now to escape the cholera epidemic. All he gave his doctor to fight the cholera epidemic was five hundred rubles. His sister the

Countess lives in my region, and when I visited her to discuss putting up a shelter for her workers, she treated me as if I had come to apply for a job. That hurt me, and I lied to her and told her I was rich. I told the same lie to the archimandrite, who refused to allot me room for the cases that are likely to occur at the monastery. When I asked him what he would do with those who were stricken in his hostel, he answered, "They are well-to-do. They will pay you themselves." Can you grasp that? And I flared up and said I was interested not in the fee, because I'm rich, but in the monastery's safety. Some situations are extraordinarily stupid and humiliating. Before Count Orlov-Davydov left, I went to see his wife. She had gigantic diamonds in her ears and was wearing a bustle. She has no idea of how to behave. A millionairess. With people like her, you feel that stupid seminary feeling of wanting to tell them off for no reason.

The local priest often comes and stays with me for hours. He's a wonderful fellow, a widower with illegitimate children.

Please write. Things are bad enough as it is.

Yours,
A. Chekhov

1. Chekhov's actor friend Pavel Svobodin was to die less than two months later in the midst of a performance.

2. Sergei Tatishchev, diplomat, historian and contributor to *New Times*.

3. Rudolf Virchow, the famous German pathologist and political leader, had paid a recent visit to Russia.

4. The estate of the Counts Orlov, the favorites of Catherine the Great, which was later inherited by the Orlov-Davydov branch of the family.

82. To Alexei Suvorin

Melikhovo,
November 25, 1892

You're very easy to understand, and you're wrong to reproach yourself for not expressing yourself clearly. You're used to strong stuff, and I've offered you some sweet lemonade.[1] Then, though you give the lemonade its due, you cogently note it contains no alcohol. But that's precisely what our works lack: the alcohol capable of intoxicating and enslaving, and you make that very clear. Why is that? Putting "Ward Number Six" and myself aside, let's talk in general terms; that's more interesting. Let's talk about general causes if it doesn't bore you, and let's embrace an entire era. Tell me truthfully now, who among my contemporaries, that is, authors between thirty and forty-five, has given the world a single drop of alcohol? Aren't Korolenko, Nadson and all of today's playwrights lemonade? Have the paintings of Repin and Shishkin[2] turned your head? They're nice, they're talented, you're delighted by them, but at the same time you can't forget your desire for a smoke. Science and technology are now going through a period of greatness, but for us this is a precarious, sour, dreary period, and we ourselves are sour and dreary. All we can give birth to is gutta-percha boys,[3] and only Stasov, whom nature gave the rare talent of getting intoxicated on anything, even slops, cannot see this.[4] The causes do not lie in our stupidity, our insolence or our lack of talent, as Burenin thinks, but in a malady that for an artist is worse than syphilis or sexual impotence. We truly lack a certain something: if you lift up the skirts of our muse, all you see is a flat area. Keep in mind that the writers we call eternal or simply good, the writers who intoxicate us, have one highly important trait in common: they're moving toward something definite and beckon you to follow, and you feel with your entire being, not only with your mind, that they have a certain goal, like the ghost of Hamlet's father, which had a motive for coming and stirring Hamlet's imagination. Depending on their caliber, some have immediate goals—the abolition of serfdom, the liberation of one's country, politics, beauty or simply vodka, as in the case of Denis Davydov[5]—while the goals of others are more remote—God, life after death, the happiness of mankind, etc. The best of them are realistic and describe life as it is, but because each line is saturated with the consciousness of its goal, you feel life as it should be in addition to life as it is, and you are captivated by it. But what about us? Us! We describe life as it is and stop dead right there. We wouldn't lift a hoof if you lit into us with a whip. We have neither immediate nor remote goals, and there is an emptiness in our souls. We have no politics, we don't believe in revolution, there is no God, we're not afraid of ghosts, and I personally am not even afraid of death or blindness. No one who wants nothing, hopes for nothing and fears nothing can be an artist. It may be a malady and it may not; what you call it is not what counts, but we must admit that we're in a real fix. I don't know what will become of us in ten or twenty years; maybe things will have changed by then, but for the time being it would be rash to expect anything worthwhile of us, irrespective of whether we're talented or not. We write mechanically, giving in to the long-established order whereby some serve in the military or civil service, others trade and still others write. You and Grigorovich find me intelligent. Yes, I am intelligent enough at least to refuse to hide my malady from myself and lie to myself and cover up my emptiness with other people's rags like the ideas of the sixties, etc. I won't throw myself down a flight of stairs the way Garshin did, but neither will I flatter myself with thoughts of a better future. I am not responsible for my malady and I am not the one to treat it, because I can only assume that it has goals that are good, yet hidden from us and that there is a motive behind its being sent. . . . There is a method to this madness.[6]

And now a few words about intelligence. Grigorovich thinks that intelligence can overpower talent. Byron was as intelligent as a hundred devils, but still his talent survived.[7] If you tell me that X has taken to writing nonsense because his intelligence overpowered his talent or vice versa, then I would say that this means X had neither intelligence nor talent.

Amfiteatrov's[8] articles are much better than his stories, which read like translations from the Swedish.

Yezhov writes he's collected or rather selected some stories for a book he is intending to ask you to publish.[9] He's down with influenza and so is his daughter. The man's in a bad way.

I'm coming to Petersburg, and if you don't throw me out I'll stay about a month. I may make a jaunt to Finland. When will I be arriving? I don't know. It all depends on when I manage to write a seventy-page story in order not to have to apply for a loan in the spring.

May the heavens protect you.

How do you feel about going to Sweden and Denmark?

Yours,
A. Chekhov

1. Chronologically and textually, it would seem that Chekhov is answering Suvorin's letter that contained an appraisal of the just published "Ward Number Six." But, since the mind boggles at the idea that either Suvorin or Chekhov could refer to that grim work as "sweet lemonade," Chekhov could also be responding to some other point raised in the now lost Suvorin letter.

2. Ilya Repin and Ivan Shishkin were two highly admired academic painters of Chekhov's time. Their reputations dwindled during the artistic renaissance of the early twentieth century, but the aesthetics of socialist realism has reinstated them in more recent decades as giants of nineteenth-century painting, at least in the Soviet Union. In the Soviet film based on Chekhov's "The Grasshopper," the screen play emphasized the moral contrast between the virtuous doctor-husband (played by Sergei Bondarchuk) and the irresponsible painter-lover by making the husband (he was pointedly indifferent to the arts in Chekhov's original story) an admirer of Repin and the lover (an academic painter in Chekhov) a decadent, modernist denigrator of Repin.

3. Reference to Grigorovich's story "The Gutta-Percha Boy."

4. Vladimir Stasov (1824–1906) was an influential music critic, who also wrote on the visual arts. His writings supplied the official Soviet aesthetics with the one ingredient it did not get from Chernyshevsky and other radical utilitarians: its extreme and intolerant nationalism. Stasov did much to bring about a true appreciation of Russian composers, especially Glinka and the Mighty Five, but it is his ultra-nationalistic bias (praising a Russian opera or a Russian painting enhances the prestige of the Russian people and is therefore morally preferable to praising a foreign opera or painting) that makes him so popular with the present-day Soviet cultural establishment. Collections of his articles are regularly reissued in the Soviet Union, with official introductions that represent Stasov's academic and nationalistic attitudes as "democratic" and "revolutionary."

5. A poet and guerrilla leader during the Napoleonic wars, Davydov cultivated in his poetry the *persona* of a dashing, hard-drinking hussar.

6. Since *Hamlet* is mentioned in this letter, we have borrowed this formula to replace a Russian saying of similar import that Chekhov used in the original.

7. Several days earlier Chekhov had read a Russian prose translation of Byron's *Don Juan* and written to Suvorin: "*Don Juan* in prose is sheer magic. There's everything in that gigantic thing: Pushkin, Tolstoy and even Burenin, who's been stealing Byron's puns. *Manfred* is striking in its setting, but compared to Goethe's *Faust* it seems rather wishy-washy. I saw *Manfred* performed on the stage of the Bolshoi Theater when [Ernst] Possart was in Moscow and it produced a strong impression" (Letter of November 22, 1892).

8. Alexander Amfiteatrov, novelist and journalist.

9. The perfidious Yezhov not only used Chekhov to get this collection published, but put Chekhov in charge of approving the book's design and selecting the type face and the cover.

83. To Alexei Suvorin

Melikhovo,
December 3, 1892

The fact that the work of the recent generation of writers and artists has no goals is a perfectly legitimate, consequent and interesting phenomenon, and if Sazonova[1] suddenly chose to see fire and brimstone in it, that doesn't mean that I was being devious or insincere. You yourself didn't read any insincerity into the letter until after she'd written to you. If you had, you wouldn't have sent the letter to her in the first place. In my letters to you I'm often unfair and naïve, but I never write anything I don't feel.

If it's insincerity you're after, there are tons of it in Sazonova's letter. "The greatest wonder of all is man himself, and we shall never tire of studying him . . ." or "The aim of life is life itself . . ." or "I believe in life, for whose bright moments we not only can, but should live. I believe in man, in the good side of his soul," etc. Can all that really be sincere and mean anything? That's no view of life; that's a lollipop. She stresses "can" and "should" because she's afraid to talk about what does exist and must be taken into account. If she first states what exists, I'll be willing to listen to what can be and what should be. She believes "in life," but that means that she doesn't believe in anything if she's intelligent or else, if she's uneducated, that she actually believes in the peasant God and crosses herself in the dark.

Under the influence of her letter you write me of "life for life's sake." My humble thanks. Why, her cheerful letter is a thousand times more like a tomb than mine. I write that there are no goals, and you assume that I consider those goals necessary and would be only too happy to set out in search of them, while Sazonova writes that it is wrong to tantalize men with advantages they will never know. "Value what already exists"; in her opinion all our troubles boil down to the fact that we all seek lofty, remote goals. If that's not female logic, it certainly must be a philosophy of despair. Anyone who sincerely thinks that man has no more need of lofty, remote goals than do cows and that those goals cause "all our troubles" can do nothing more than eat, drink and sleep, or when he's had his fill, take a flying leap and bash his head against the corner of a trunk.

I'm not berating Sazonova; I only want to say that she is far from being a cheerful individual. She seems to be a good person, but you were still wrong to show her my letter. She and I are strangers, and now I feel embarrassed.

People here are driving single file[2] and eating meatless cabbage soup with smelts. We've had two bad snowstorms that played havoc with the roads, but now everything's quiet and it smells of Christmas.

Have you read Viktor Krylov's article on theaters abroad in *Russian Thought*? Krylov loves the theater, and I believe him, though I am not fond of his plays.

It seems I owe you an apology. I have tempted one of these little ones,[3] Yezhov the well-known writer, to be exact. I once spoke to him about having a book of his published and then corresponded with him about it, in very indefinite terms, and today I suddenly get a letter from him informing me he has already sent you the stories to be typeset. The title of the book is *Clouds and Other Stories*. Clouds! It sounds like apples.[4]

Rumor has it that twelve Moscow writers have sent you a protest against Amfiteatrov.[5] Is that true?

Keep well, and don't ever write me that you are more sincere than I am. I wish you all the best.

Yours,
A. Chekhov

1. Suvorin had sent Chekhov's previous letter (Letter 82) to Sofya Smirnova, who wrote for *New Times* under the pen name Sazonova and whom Chekhov did not know personally. She sent Suvorin her rebuttal to Chekhov's letter, which Suvorin conveyed to Chekhov and which Chekhov is here answering.

2. An untranslatable pun on the two meanings of the Russian word *gus'*, which means both "goose" and "single file."

3. Chekhov is quoting the beginning of Matthew 18:6 (almost identical with Mark 9:42 and Luke 17:2), which in the English version reads "But whoso shall offend one of these little ones. . . ." In the Russian Church Slavic Bible, however, the verb rendered into English as "offend" is traditionally translated as "tempt."

4. Clouds is *oblaka* in Russian and apples is *yabloki.*

5. The protest was caused by Amfiteatrov's high-handed ridicule of a journalist who was a defendant in a murder trial that Amfiteatrov was covering for *New Times.*

IX

SETTLED LIFE

After the cholera threat abated in the fall of 1892, Chekhov was again able to devote himself to his writing and to his personal life. But his involvement in the civic and *zemstvo* affairs of the Serpukhov District continued to occupy a considerable portion of his time for the rest of his stay at Melikhovo. He went on giving the local peasants free medical treatment at his private clinic. Urged by the local Melikhovo peasants, Chekhov took charge of planning and supervising the building of the local school and did it so successfully that he was asked to build two more schools in neighboring villages during the next three years. He persuaded the authorities to construct a needed local highway, which he helped plan and, not to forget the peasants' aesthetic sensibilities, he built them a beautiful bell tower for their church. There were numerous committees, jury duty at the local court, hospital matters, collecting books for libraries (including the library in Chekhov's native city of Taganrog, for which he was constantly purchasing and donating books), referrals of mental cases and alcoholics to Moscow colleagues for treatment and hospitalization, and innumerable other activities.

As a creative writer, Chekhov kept expanding his range and trying to explore new varieties of fictional narrative during the next three years. In "The Black Monk," he rather unexpectedly turned to the Romantic tradition of Vladimir Odoyevsky, the first Russian writer to investigate the literary possibilities of the subconscious and the irrational, a friend and a contemporary of Pushkin and Gogol and an important precursor of Dostoyevsky. (Odoyevsky's work was anathematized by the radical utilitarians, and Suvorin was the only publisher of the second half of the nineteenth century who dared reissue it.) Following the example of such typical Odoyevsky stories as "The Sylph," Chekhov's "The Black Monk" suggests that pathological conditions such as insanity or hallucination might provide us with valuable spiritual and psychological insights.

Some of Chekhov's most striking stories about women's response to the male-dominated environment in which they are caught were also written during this period: "Big Volodya and Little Volodya," "Ariadne," and "Anna on the Neck." Another theme that particularly preoccupied him at this time was that of social dislocation—the effect on a person of being brought up in one social stratum and then being transplanted to another. "A Woman's Kingdom" has a heroine brought up in poverty who ends up owning a large factory she inherits from a rich uncle. Not really able to function fully in either the proletarian world of her childhood or in the cultivated milieu into which her wealth and position have thrust her, the likable and appealing Anna Akimovna is trapped in a social no-man's land all her own, and the reader feels trapped with her. In terms of its elegantly organized narrative time span and its artful interplay of social and cultural contrasts, "A Woman's Kingdom" is probably the most carefully designed piece of fiction Chekhov ever wrote—a marvel of meticulously planned literary architecture. The almost novel-length "Three Years" deals with the similar predicament of an entire family of merchant-class origin and their difficulty in making the transition from the traditional patriarchal ways of Russian merchants to the Westernized culture of the educated intelligentsia.

Chekhov always pleaded that literary criticism was beyond his abilities. But the passages in his correspondence of this period dealing with Turgenev, Pisemsky, Zola, Sienkiewicz and his own relationship to Tolstoy show that there was in Chekhov an able literary critic, as was the case with almost all other important Russian writers. His letters dealing with Tolstoy are particularly significant. He disagreed repeatedly with Tolstoy's moral preachings and with his religious philosophy, but there was no literary artist, past or present, whom he admired as much and whom he considered as important. After several overtures on Tolstoy's part, Chekhov finally made a pilgrimage to Yasnaya Polyana in August of 1895 and met the great man in person. There were many things the two of them could have argued about, but their mutual respect and liking were so great that this did not even occur to them. His infrequent personal encounters with Tolstoy remained a source of pride and pleasure for Chekhov throughout the remaining years of his life.

Melikhovo was his permanent home now, but he loved to travel. He kept going to Moscow regularly—to see his friends, to attend plays, operas and art exhibits, to consort with lovely women such as Lydia Yavorskaya and Lydia Avilova. There was also time for brief trips to St. Petersburg, to the Crimea and even to Italy. Not as hectic as 1890–92, the years 1893–95 were a busy and rewarding period in Chekhov's life.

84. To Alexei Suvorin

Melikhovo,
February 24, 1893

I haven't seen *Russian Thought* yet, but I'm looking forward to it. I don't like Protopopov;[1] he is a rationalist, cerebrally and oppressively boring, sometimes just, but dry and heartless. I am not personally acquainted with him and have never seen him; he has written many things about me, but never once have I read them. I am not a journalist; I am physically repelled by abuse no matter at whom it is aimed. I say "physically," because reading Protopopov, the Resident, Burenin and all those other judges of mankind always leaves a rusty taste in my mouth and ruins my whole day. They actually cause me pain. Stasov called the Resident a bedbug, but why, why did the Resident abuse Antokolsky?[2] That's not criticism or a world view; it's hate, insatiable animal spite. Why is Skabichevsky so abusive? Why must they write in a tone fit for judging criminals rather than artists and writers? I just can't stand it, I simply can't.

Please don't reply to Protopopov. First, it's not worth it; second, Lavrov and Goltsev are as responsible for Protopopov's writings as you are for Burenin's; and third, the stand you have taken has been wrong from the very outset. You write indignantly about how your son is being abused, but no one is abusing your son; they are abusing A. A. Suvorin, the journalist who wrote *Palestine*, writes for *New Times* and himself once heaped abuse on Martens,[3] spoke in Paris in the name of the Russian press, and printed an article about his trip above his own signature. He is an independent entity and can look after himself. Your letter gives the impression that Alexei Alexeyevich stands apart from *New Times* and is being penalized for its sins, while having nothing to do with the press. No, don't reply to him, or else your answers and his questions and then your new answers will take you so deep in the woods that you'll have ten headaches before you find your way out. Protopopov's slanderous, or to put it more mildly, unscrupulous article neither adds nor subtracts a thing; you will still have the same number of friends and enemies. Yet I understand your mood, I understand it very well. . . . Why don't you forget about them!

Speaking of Alexei Alexeyevich, tell him I still have the manuscript he sent me. I don't know what to do with it, but I guess I will do something with it eventually.[4] Tell him not to be angry at the delay. May the heavens protect him.[5] He'd do best not to take up smoking. I get bronchitis from nothing more than cigars.

My story will come to an end in the March issue. "To be continued" instead of "To be concluded" is my error; while reading the last proofs, I carelessly jotted down one instead of the other.[6] You won't like the conclusion, I botched it. It should have been a bit longer, but writing something long would have been dangerous because there are so few protagonists, and when the same two characters keep coming back over a space of thirty to fifty pages, the whole thing becomes a bore and the two characters tend to blur. But what's the use of talking about experienced old hands like me? What about you? When are you going to send me your novel? I'm dying to get at it so I can write you a long critique.

Good Lord! How magnificent *Fathers and Sons* is![7] It makes you want to shout for joy. Bazarov's illness is so powerfully done that I went weak and had the feeling that I myself had caught the infection from him. And then Bazarov's end. And his old parents. And Kukshina. How did he ever do it? It's sheer genius. I dislike *On the Eve* in its entirety except for Yelena's father and the ending. The ending is full of tragic pathos. "The Dog" is very good; the language is amazing. Please read it if you've forgotten it. "Asya" is charming but "The Quiet Spot" is botched and unsatisfying. I don't like *Smoke* at all. *A Nest of Gentlefolk* is weaker than *Fathers and Sons,* but the ending also comes close to being a miracle. Not counting Bazarov's old mother and mothers in general—especially the society ladies, who incidentally are all one like the other (Liza's mother, Yelena's mother), and Lavretsky's mother, a former serf girl, and the peasant women too—all Turgenev's girls and women are unbearably affected and, forgive me, fake. Liza and Yelena are not Russian girls; they are Pythian priestesses[8] who utter profundities and overflow with a pretentiousness beyond their station. Irina in *Smoke,* Odintsova in *Fathers and Sons,* and all those lionesses, the torrid, appetizing, insatiable seekers, they are all so much nonsense. One thought of Tolstoy's Anna Karenina, and all Turgenev's ladies and their seductive shoulders collapse and disintegrate. The negative female types whom Turgenev caricatures slightly (Kukshina) or pokes fun at (in his ballroom scenes) are remarkably well delineated and are so successful you've got to take your hat off to him, as the saying goes. His nature descriptions are fine, but . . . I have the feeling that we're no longer accustomed to that type of description and need something different.

My sister is getting better. So is Father. We're expecting cholera, but we're not afraid, because we're prepared—not to die, no, but to spend the *zemstvo's* money. If cholera does come it will take up a good deal of my time.

Keep alive and well, and don't worry. My special respects to Anna Ivanovna.

Entirely yours,
A. Chekhov

We've been sent a large quantity of Ukrainian lard and sausage. What bliss!

Why haven't you described to me the writers' dinner? After all, it was I who thought up those dinners.

1. Mikhail Protopopov (1848–1915), a thoroughly unimaginative and insensitive literary critic, who was read and respected mainly because he was a self-proclaimed disciple of Chernyshevsky and an upholder of the ideals of the sixties. Chekhov later gave Protopopov's first and last name to Natasha's disagreeable offstage lover in *Three Sisters* (changing the patronymic for safety's sake).

This letter was written at the time of the Panama Canal scandal in France, as a result of which Ferdinand de Lesseps, the planner and builder of the Suez Canal, was sentenced to five years' imprisonment. The *New Times* found his sentence too lenient and Chekhov wrote to Suvorin on February 5, 1893: "Your news story was cruel indeed. Five years' imprisonment, deprivation of all civil rights, etc.—this was the highest possible penalty, which satisfied even the prosecutor; and in your story: 'We consider this too lenient.' Ye heavenly hosts, what is needed then? And by whom is it needed?" There were also insinuations in the French press that Suvorin's *New Times* was involved in the shareholding fraud for which de Lesseps had been tried. Suvorin's eldest son Alexei traveled to Paris to try and exonerate his father's newspaper. In the interviews he gave in Paris, Suvorin junior represented the insinuations against *New Times* as an attempt to slander the entire Russian press.

Protopopov's literary criticism column in Vukol Lavrov's *Russian Thought* took issue with Suvorin junior's claim that *New Times* was representative of the entire Russian press, arguing that it was a major concern of "every decent publication and every honest writer" in Russia not to have their names associated with this "conservative-liberal-progressive-reactionary newspaper."

2. Mark Antokolsky (1843–1902) was an academic sculptor whose work was hugely overrated in Russia and enjoyed a certain reputation in Western Europe as well. Chekhov was later instrumental in persuading Antokolsky to donate his equestrian statue of Peter the Great to the city of Taganrog. The exhibit of Antokolsky's work which opened early in February at the St. Petersburg Academy of Arts was reviewed in *New Times* by the Resident (Alexander Dyakov) on the very day of its opening. The nasty, abusive tone of the review was obviously motivated not by the quality of Antokolsky's work

but by his Jewish origins. Dyakov's review was answered by Vladimir Stasov, writing in, of all places, the *St. Petersburg Stock Exchange Gazette*. Exposing the anti-Semitic prejudice which motivated Dyakov's rejection of Antokolsky's sculptures, Stasov also proved that Dyakov could not have possibly seen the actual exhibit he was reviewing, since his article went to press at the time the public was first admitted to the premises of the exhibit. In abusiveness of tone, however, Stasov managed to outdo even Dyakov—the concluding sentence of his rebuttal, to which Chekhov is referring, read: "A bedbug's bite is not dangerous, but it leaves a revolting stench."

3. Professor Fyodor Martens, a specialist in international law.

4. Suvorin junior had sent Chekhov a story by Alexander Chekhov, asking him to abridge it.

5. After Suvorin followed Chekhov's advice not to reply to Protopopov's column, his son decided to take matters into his own hands. On March 11, Chekhov wrote to his sister: "Alexei Alexeyevich Suvorin has slapped Lavrov's face. He came [to Moscow] especially for the purpose. This means it's all over between Suvorin and me, even though he keeps writing me sniveling letters. That son of a bitch who scolds people daily has now become famous because he struck a man who scolded him. Fine justice, this. It's disgusting."

On March 4, Chekhov had been a guest of honor at one of Lavrov's famous dinners. They had reconciled their former differences and Chekhov was now *Russian Thought*'s most highly valued and highest-paid contributor. He was in the process of forming close and friendly relations with Lavrov and with his chief editor Goltsev. The action of Suvorin's son genuinely outraged him and so did the Resident's treatment of Antokolsky. From this point on, no further work by Chekhov was to appear in *New Times*. *Russian Thought* became his chief outlet for publication in periodicals. But there was no final break with Suvorin himself, despite what he wrote his sister; nor was there one later on, after Chekhov's violent disagreements with Suvorin over the Dreyfus case and the student disturbances. No matter how disgusted he sometimes was with Suvorin's newspaper, Chekhov could never bring himself to turn against the man to whom he owed his literary career.

6. Chekhov's "An Unknown Man's Story" was appearing in *Russian Thought* in two installments. The statement "To be continued" at the end of the first installment led some readers to expect it to be longer than it actually was.

7. The rest of this paragraph deals with Ivan Turgenev's novels and stories and characters who appear in them. Lavretsky and Liza are the hero and heroine of *A Nest of Gentlefolk*. On February 13, Chekhov wrote to Suvorin: "I am reading Turgenev. Delightful, but much weaker than Tolstoy. I don't believe Tolstoy will ever grow dated. His language might, but he himself will remain young forever." Turgenev's "The Dog," a story of the supernatural, was deplored by most critics of Chekhov's time as an unfortunate aberration of an otherwise admirably realistic writer (as were Turgenev's other visionary and metaphysical works, which are now seen as a key to an important aspect of his creative makeup).

8. Most Russian-English dictionaries translate the Russian *pifia* as pythoness. The translator of the truncated version of this letter in Lillian Hellman's collection read a herpetological meaning into this word and consequently rendered "Pythian priestesses" as "female pythons."

85. To Alexei Suvorin

Melikhovo,
April 26, 1893

Greetings and welcome back. I didn't write you while you were in Berlin because the flooded roads made it impossible to get to the station very often, and I received your letter from Venice at a time when I figured you must already have reached Berlin.

First of all, let me tell you about myself. I'll begin by saying I'm ill. It's a vile, disgusting illness, not syphilis, something worse—hemorrhoids,[1] [. . .], pain, itching, and nervous tension; I can't sit or walk, and my whole body is so irritated it makes me want to slip a noose around my neck. I feel that no one wants to understand me and that everyone is stupid and unfair, I'm always getting angry and saying stupid things, I think my relatives will breathe a sigh of relief when I leave. How do you like that! My illness can't be explained by my sedentary way of life, for I have always been lazy, or by any dissolute behavior or by heredity. I once had peritonitis though, and I can only conclude that it caused the lumen of my intestine to diminish in size and that the constriction has put pressure on a vessel somewhere along the way. In sum: I'll have to have an operation.

Everything else is fine. The cold spring seems to be over; I can take walks through the fields without my galoshes on and warm myself in the sun. I've been reading Pisemsky.[2] He's a major, a really major talent. His best work is "The Carpenters' Guild." His novels are exhausting in their detail. Everything that pertains to his own times, all those digs at the reigning critics and liberals of the period, all the critical remarks with pretensions of being apposite and up-to-date, and all those would-be profound reflections scattered here and there—how shallow and naïve they all are in this day and age! And therein lies the heart of the problem: the novelist interested in art should pass over everything that is of only temporary significance. Pisemsky's characters are alive, and his artistic temperament is powerful. Skabichevsky accuses him of obscurantism and betrayal of ideals in his *History*,[3] but good Lord, of all our contemporary writers there isn't one who is a more passionate and confirmed liberal than Pisemsky. Every single one of his priests, government officials and generals is a villain. No one has reviled the old judicial and conscript systems the way he has. By the way, I've also read Bourget's *Cosmopolis*. Bourget throws together Rome and the Pope and Correggio and Michelangelo and Titian and the Doges, and a fifty-year-old beauty and Russians and Poles—but how wishy-washy and forced and cloying and false it all is in comparison with our own—well, all right—with our own coarse and simple-minded Pisemsky.

And now a page right out of a novel. It's a secret. Misha's fallen in love with a little countess,[4] laid siege to her heart, and just before Easter was officially pronounced her fiancé. His love was fierce, his dreams wide-ranging. At Eastertime the countess wrote she was going to visit an aunt in Kostroma. Until recently, there were no letters from her. Hearing that she was in Moscow, lovelorn Misha went after her and—lo and behold—found people hanging out the windows and crowding the gate of her house. What was going on? It turned out to be a wedding: the countess was marrying a gold-mine proprietor. Now how do you like that! Misha came home in despair and shoved the countess's tender, loving letters under my nose, begging me to resolve his psychological problem. But who the devil can? A woman will lie five times before wearing out a pair of shoes. But Shakespeare has already said as much, if I'm not mistaken.

Another piece of news, from the realm of psychiatry this time instead of from a novel. Yezhov seems to be going out of his mind. I haven't seen him, I can only judge by his letters. He is upset and swears obscenely in his letters for no reason, something he never used to do; he used to be shy, meek and chaste to the point of philistinism. Now his cynicism is of the coarsest variety. He wrote me that he submitted a filthy story to a journal and asked me to read a copy of the story so as to ease his troubled conscience. The story is about two lady philanthropists who meet a bedraggled little boy as they are out walking. When they ask him where he lives, the boy answers, "In [. . .]." The business about his book has completely shattered his nerves. I ought to go to Moscow, refer him to the right doctors, and see that he gets medical attention, but I have hemorrhoids and can only walk. I am forbidden to ride.

I probably won't go to America; there's no money for it.[5] I didn't earn a thing all spring. I was ill all the time and fuming at the weather. It's a good thing I left the city! Tell all the Fofanovs, Chormnys[6] and *tutti quanti* who live off literature that life in the country is immeasurably cheaper than in the city. This is brought home to me every day. My family doesn't cost me anything any more because the room, bread, vegetables, milk, meat and horses are all our own and don't have to be paid for. But there's so much work I have no time for anything else. I alone of all the Chekhov family am free to lie down or sit at a desk;

the rest of them work from dawn till dusk. Drive all poets and novelists into the country! Why should they beg and starve? Life in the city can't provide the poor with rich poetic and artistic material. They live within their four walls; the only places they see people are editorial offices and beer halls.

I have many patients. For some reason there are many consumptives. But you keep well now.

A drought is setting in. . . .

Yours,
A. Chekhov

1. Chekhov was tortured by hemorrhoids intermittently for the rest of his life.

2. Alexei Pisemsky (1820–81) was, as Chekhov rightly points out, a genuinely major Russian novelist and dramatist of the nineteenth century. Among his works, which deserve to be far better known in the West than they actually are, at least one novel (*A Thousand Souls*) and one play (*A Bitter Fate*) belong in the front rank of Russian literature of all periods. There is a study of his life and work in English, *Pisemsky: A Provincial Realist* by Charles Moser (Cambridge, Mass., 1969).

3. Alexander Skabichevsky's *History of Modern Russian Literature*, published in 1891, judged all writers on the basis of their adherence to a narrowly understood realism and their continuing fidelity to the social and didactic principles postulated by Chernyshevsky and Dobrolyubov in the 1860s. Pisemsky did not come off too well in Skabichevsky's book, but then neither did Tolstoy.

4. Countess Klara Mamuna, whom Maria Chekhova introduced to the family after meeting her during a vacation in the Crimea. Maria's memoirs describe her as a dwarf who spoke in a basso voice.

5. Chekhov and Tolstoy's son Lev had made vague plans to attend the Chicago Exposition of 1893.

6. Apollon Chormny, whose real name was Cherman, a totally forgotten writer.

86. To Ivan Gorbunov-Posadov[1]

Moscow,
November 8 or 9, 1893[2]

In Shakespeare's play *As You Like It*, Act II, Scene I, one of the lords says to the Duke:

> To the which place a poor sequester'd stag,
> That from the hunter's aim had ta'en a hurt,

Did come to languish; and indeed, my lord,
The wretched animal heav'd forth such groans
That their discharge did stretch his leathern coat
Almost to bursting, and the big round tears
Cours'd one another down his innocent nose
In piteous chase. . . .[3]

I wish you all the best.

A. Chekhov

1. A close friend and follower of Tolstoy who corresponded with Chekhov on behalf of the Tolstoyan publishing house *Mediator* in connection with securing the rights to publish some of Chekhov's stories in the *Mediator*'s volumes intended for peasants and the proletariat.

2. This text is a message on a postcard, which was dated on the basis of a not entirely legible postmark.

3. In his letter to Suvorin of December 17, 1892, Chekhov wrote: "If you happen to see Leskov, tell him that Shakespeare in *As You Like It*, Act II, Scene I, has some good words concerning hunting. Shakespeare himself used to go hunting, but you can see from this scene what a poor opinion he had of hunting and of murdering animals in general."

Chekhov enjoyed bird hunting in his youth and he described this sport in excruciating detail in a very early story, "St. Peter's Day" (1881). But he lost his taste for it by the time he turned thirty. The episode involving Isaak Levitan and the wounded woodcock, which took place in April of the previous year (see Letter 70), must have consolidated his distaste.

87. To Alexei Suvorin

Melikhovo,
November 11, 1893

If my latest letter is dated August 24th, you apparently never received the ones I sent you while you were abroad. Or maybe you did receive them and then forgot them? Though what difference does it make?

Your talk of Pleshcheyev's co-heiress reminded me of a conversation I had with a lawyer, Plevako's assistant. This lawyer told me that there is still another heiress, but that she has been bought off. I somehow got the feeling at the time that the lawyers themselves had tried to produce this co-heiress to give Pleshcheyev a scare and fleece him for all he's worth.[1]

I'm alive and well. I'm coughing more than I used to, but I'm still a long way from consumption, I think. I've reduced my smoking to one cigar a day. I stayed in one place all summer, riding from patient to patient, treating them, waiting for cholera. I saw a thousand patients and wasted much time, but cholera never came. I didn't write a thing. Whenever I was free from medical work, I would go for walks, read or try to put my cumbersome *Sakhalin* in order. The day before yesterday I got back from two weeks in Moscow which I spent in a daze. Because my life in Moscow consisted exclusively of feasts and new acquaintances, I've been nicknamed Avelan.[2] Never before have I felt so free. First of all, I have no apartment, so I live wherever I please, and second of all, I still don't have a passport, and . . . girls, girls, girls. I was tormented all summer by a lack of funds and was constantly agonizing over it, but now that my expenses have gone down, my mind is at rest. I feel liberated from money, that is, I'm beginning to think that I no longer need any more than two thousand a year and that I can either write or not.

Pascal[3] is well done, but there's something intrinsically wrong in the character of Pascal himself. When I have diarrhea at night, I put a cat[4] on my stomach to serve as a hot pack and keep me warm. Clotilde is the same as Abishag, the "cat" that kept King David warm. Her earthly destiny consists of nothing but keeping the old man warm. What an enviable fate! I'm sorry for that Abishag. She may not have composed the psalms, but she was probably purer and more beautiful in the eyes of God than the abductor of Uriah's wife. She's a human being, an individual, she is young and naturally desires youth, and forgive me, but you'd have to be a Frenchman to turn her into a hot-water bottle for a gray-haired Cupid with stringy rooster legs in the name of some damned principle or other. It hurts me to read about Clotilde being screwed by Pascal instead of someone younger and stronger. Old King David straining himself in the embrace of a young girl is a melon that has already known the frost of a fall morning and is still hoping to ripen. But every fruit has its own season. And what nonsense! Is potency a sign of true life and health? Is screwing the only thing that makes one a real person? All thinkers are impotent at forty, while ninety-year-old savages keep ninety wives apiece. Serf owners retained their reproductive powers and went on fertilizing their Agashkas and Grushkas up to the very moment when a stroke would force them to give up the ghost in their venerable old age. I'm not moralizing, and my own old age probably won't be free of attempts to "pull my bowstring," as Apuleius puts it in *The Golden Ass*. There's nothing wrong in human terms with Pascal sleeping with the girl. That's his private business. What is wrong is that Zola praises Clotilde for sleeping with Pascal and that he calls this perversion love.[5]

The astronomer is destitute.[6] She's aged, grown thin and nervous, and has dark circles under her eyes. The poor thing is beginning to lose faith in herself and that's the worst thing that can happen. Blessed is he who is without faith and has always been without faith. All attempts to help her have foundered on her terrible pride.

I've been possessed lately by a certain frivolity, and at the same time I feel drawn to people as never before. Literature has become my Abishag, and I've grown so attached to it that I've come to disdain medicine. But what I love in literature is not the novels or stories you expect or have stopped expecting from me; it is what I can read stretched out on my couch for hours on end. I lack the passion for writing.

I have no plans for writing a drama. I have no desire for it. I see Potapenko often. The Odessa Potapenko and the Moscow Potapenko are as alike as a crow and an eagle. The difference is unbelievable. I like him more and more.[7]

Sakhalin is being sent to the Central Prison Administration in page proofs instead of proof sheets, although when they admitted me to Sakhalin they specified proof sheets as one of the conditions. I received a letter in an irritatingly official style from the Prison Administration that began "In correspondence to your letter . . ." The letter bears an official number. "In correspondence to" for "in response to." How stuffy.

I've been told you're writing a new play. Glad to hear it.

It's time I said good-bye now. We'll talk about the stories when we get together. You'll be in Moscow in November or December, won't you?

I wish you all the best. When you come, I'll stay at the Slavic Bazaar Hotel too. Yasinsky is in Moscow.

Hura-a-a-ah!

Yours,
A. Chekhov

1. The poor Pleshcheyev was allowed to enjoy his huge inheritance for only two years. An heiress turned up with apparently more valid claims than he and he was forced to relinquish to her most of his new fortune. He died a few months afterward, but as Zinaida Gippius tells us in her memoirs, his last two years were marvelously elegant and happy.

2. Admiral Avelan was in command of the Russian fleet that visited France when an alliance was concluded between the two countries. Russian newspapers published detailed reports of receptions and dinners given in France in Avelan's honor. Chekhov was nicknamed after him because of his own almost equally strenuous social life during this period.

3. The novel *Doctor Pascal* by Émile Zola.

4. This cat is a mere figure of speech. With all of Chekhov's tremendous

affection and sympathy for animals, cats were the only kind of animal he did not care for. Not long after marrying Olga Knipper, he wrote to her on August 30, 1901: "You wrote me about a female cat named Martin, but—ugh!—I'm scared of cats. I respect and value dogs. Why don't you get yourself a dog? We can't keep a cat, I'll remark in passing, because our Moscow apartment will have to stay unoccupied for six months out of almost every year. However, do as you like, darling; you may get yourself a crocodile if you like, I allow you everything and anything and for your sake I'd be even prepared to sleep with a cat."

This did not prevent the literary artist in Chekhov from seeing cats with an observant and sympathetic eye. Certainly, the dignified elderly tomcat Fyodor Timofeich in "Kashtanka," the hurt mother cat in "An Event" ("An Incident" in Constance Garnett's version) and the baffled kitten who is the hero of "Who Is to Blame?" are as warmly and appealingly presented feline characters as any that could be found anywhere in Russian literature.

5. We were able to reconstruct this passage in its entirety by combining the version in Maria Chekhova's edition with those of the two Soviet editions, since each chose to censor a different set of words and phrases. Through some miracle of oversight, the censors of the 1944–51 edition failed to realize (or perhaps chose not to notice) that the verb *upotreblyat'*, deleted by Maria Chekhova, is employed by Chekhov in its secondary, crudely sexual meaning, rather than in its primary one, which is quite inoffensive and means "to use." Their reinstatement of this verb and of several phrases Maria Chekhova omitted enabled us to fill out her deletions; the passages the Soviet censors cut, by contrast, all appear in the pre-revolutionary edition.

6. Olga Kundasova again.

7. Ignaty Potapenko (1856–1929) had published stories since 1881, but his meteoric rise to fame began about 1890 with the publication of his novel *On Active Duty*. For the next ten years or so, his literary fame rivaled that of Chekhov and Korolenko. His reputation abroad preceded that of Chekhov and we can read in American magazines of *ca.* 1900 serious debates about whether Gorky, Korolenko or Potapenko was more likely to "inherit the mantle of Tolstoy." By the first decade of the twentieth century no one any longer took Potapenko seriously as a writer, in Russia or abroad.

He and Chekhov came to be good friends and it was Potapenko who got Lika Mizinova off Chekhov's hands by seducing her and taking her to Paris. Potapenko's memoirs about his friendship with Chekhov are among the better ones we have; they are particularly good and authoritative about the true circumstances of the initial failure of *The Seagull* at its première in 1896. The reference to "the Odessa Potapenko and the Moscow Potapenko" has to do with the contrast between his early stories of Ukrainian life and the successful novels and stories about the Russian intelligentsia and clergy he began writing after 1890.

88. To Alexei Suvorin

Yalta,[1]
March 27, 1894

Greetings!! For almost a month now I've been living in Yalta, ever so boring Yalta, at the Hotel Russia, Room 39. Room 38 is occupied by Abarinova,[2] your favorite actress. We're having spring weather, it is warm and sunny, and the sea is as it should be, but the people are excruciatingly dull, dreary and lackluster. It was stupid of me to sacrifice all of March to the Crimea. I should have gone to Kiev and devoted myself to contemplating the holy shrines and Ukrainian spring.

My cough still hasn't died down, but I'm nevertheless setting off for the north and my penates on April 5th. I can't stay here any longer and besides, I'm out of money. All I took along is three hundred and fifty rubles. Subtract my travel expenses, and all that's left is two hundred and fifty. And you can't get fat on that. If I'd had a thousand or fifteen hundred, I would have gone to Paris, which for many reasons would have done me good.

Generally speaking I'm in good health; it's only in the particulars that I'm ill: my cough, for example, my palpitations and my hemorrhoids. Once the palpitations lasted six days straight and I felt foul the whole time. Now that I've completely given up smoking, I'm no longer overcome by moods of gloom or anxiety. Maybe it's because I've given up smoking, but Tolstoy's moral philosophy has ceased to move me; down deep I'm hostile to it, which is of course unfair. I have peasant blood flowing in my veins, and I'm not the one to be impressed with peasant virtues. I acquired my belief in progress when still a child; I couldn't help believing in it, because the difference between the period when they flogged me and the period when they stopped flogging me was enormous. I've always loved intelligent people, heightened sensibilities, courtesy and wit, and paid as little attention to whether people pick their corns or have suffocatingly smelly footcloths as to whether young ladies walk around in the morning with curlpapers on. But Tolstoy's philosophy moved me deeply and possessed me for six or seven years.[3] It was not so much his basic postulates that had an effect on me—I had been familiar with them before—it was his way of expressing himself, his common sense, and probably a sort of hypnotism as well. But now something in me protests. Prudence and justice tell me there is more love for mankind in electricity and steam than in chastity and abstention from meat. War is an evil and the court system is an evil, but it doesn't follow that I should wear bast shoes and sleep on a stove alongside the hired hand and his wife, and so on and so forth. But that's not the issue; it's not a matter of the pros and cons, the point is that in one way or another Tolstoy has departed from my life, he's no longer in my heart and he's left me, saying, "Behold, I leave your house empty."[4] He dwells in me no longer. I'm tired of listening to disquisitions, and reading phonies like Max Nordau[5] makes me sick. When people have a fever, they do not want to eat, but they do want something, and they express that undefinable desire by asking for "something slightly sour." Well, I too want something slightly sour. Nor am I alone in this sensation; I notice the very same mood all around me. It's as though everyone had been in love and gotten over it, and was looking around for new interests. It looks very likely that Russians will once again become absorbed in the natural sciences and that materialism will come back in style. The natural sciences are presently working miracles, and they can advance on the populace like Mamai[6] and subdue it by their sheer mass and grandeur. But of course all this lies in the hands of God. And if you start philosophizing, it's bound to make you dizzy.[7]

A German from Stuttgart has sent me fifty marks for a translation of a story of mine. How do you like that? I'm in favor of the copyright convention, and some swine publishes an article saying that I denounced the convention in an interview with him. He ascribes statements to me I couldn't even pronounce.[8]

Address your letters to Lopasnya,[9] and if you feel like wiring, a wire will still reach me in Yalta, since I'll be staying here until the fifth of April.

Keep well and don't worry. How's your head? Are your headaches more or less frequent than before? Mine are less frequent—from having given up smoking.

My humble regards to Anna Ivanovna and the children.

Yours,
A. Chekhov

1. In February of 1894 Chekhov's coughing became unbearable. He refused to recognize it as a symptom of tuberculosis, assuming that it was a bad case of bronchitis. Being a physician himself he did not seek outside medical help; instead he decided to spend a month in the warmer climate of the Crimea as a cure for his cough.

2. Antonina Abarinova, a well-known operatic contralto of the 1860s and '70s, who became a dramatic actress when her operatic career was finished. She later played the role of Polina in the original production of *The Seagull.*

3. The high point of the impact of Tolstoy's moral philosophy on Chekhov

occurred in 1887, when he wrote his two most overtly Tolstoyan stories, "An Encounter," with its typical preaching of nonviolent resistance to evil, and "The Beggar," which asserts the human and moral superiority of an unlettered Russian peasant over a university-educated intellectual. Apart from these two atypical stories, Tolstoyan ideas have been discerned by various scholars in "The Cossack," "The Name-Day Party," "My Life" and a few other stories. A detailed study of the literary, philosophical and personal interrelationship between these two writers was published in 1963 by the fine Soviet literary scholar Vladimir Lakshin. Called *Tolstoy and Chekhov,* this excellent and absorbing book should be placed somewhere at the very top of any list of Russian works that need to be translated into other languages.

4. Slightly incorrect quotation of Matthew 23:38.

5. Remembered today as an early advocate of Zionism, Nordau was known in Chekhov's time mainly as the leading exponent of the theory of the *fin de siècle* degeneration and decadence of Western man.

6. A fourteenth-century Mongol chieftain, defeated by Dmitry of the Don at the Battle of Kulikovo in 1380. His name is used here as a synonym for a brutal, barbaric conqueror.

7. Quotation from Griboyedov's *The Misfortune of Being Clever,* Act II, Scene 1.

8. Chekhov was interviewed by a reporter from *News of the Day* in February of 1894. Almost all of his replies and opinions were garbled or replaced by their very opposite when the interview was published in the March 1 edition of that newspaper.

9. The nearest railroad and postal station to Melikhovo, Lopasnya was used as the postal address for Chekhov's estate.

89. To Alexei Suvorin

Moscow,
October 15, 1894

With God's blessings let me begin by asking a favor of you. The writer Ertel[1] has sent me a letter asking me to write you the following. In a school in Voronezh Province of which he is an honorary superintendent (he is a superintendent of the school, not the province) there is a library being started for peasants, and in part for teachers too. He wants to know whether you will consent to donate the books you publish that are suitable for readers of the category mentioned above. Ertel is troubling you with this request because you are a native of Voronezh Province and because the honorary superintendent of the school is a writer: he feels that the latter circumstance cannot fail to have an impact on your sense of solidarity with fellow writers. But the main reason he decided to ask you this favor is that you are "a good man who is genuinely in sympathy with popular education." While fulfilling his request, let me take the opportunity to call your attention to Ertel's story "The Seers" (in *Russian Thought*, XI, 1893), a very good story. For my part I wrote Ertel that I was very happy to be of service to him, but that he would do better to choose the books he needs from your catalogue and send you a list of them. His address is Alexander Ivanovich Ertel, Voronezh.

I'm still in Moscow, writing, reading proof, settling my highly shaky financial affairs and dreaming of Wednesday, the day I'll finally go home. Masha says the constant rains have completely ruined the roads and that passage is possible only by the most roundabout routes, in daylight, and only by simple cart. I'll probably have to walk from the station.

My same sister, Masha, says the house has become as cozy and warm as paradise after repairs. In my absence Masha not only installed new stoves and painted everything; she even constructed a heated lavatory. In return I made her a present of a ring, and will present her with twenty-five rubles when I have the money.

Today I had dinner at Morozova's.[2] She is an extraordinarily wealthy and likable woman. We had crayfish soup with sterlet.

My humble regards to Anna Ivanovna, Nastya and Borya.

One more thing about Ertel: on his way back from abroad his suitcases and pockets were searched by the police.

Keep well.

Yours,
A. Chekhov

Send me the address of Father Alexei Maltsev.[3]

1. Alexander Ertel (1855–1908), a rather interesting novelist, whose *magnum opus*, the two-volume novel *The Gardenins, Their Retainers, Their Friends, and Their Enemies*, was so highly admired by Tolstoy that he wrote an introductory essay for its second edition. Until about 1890, as his correspondence with Korolenko makes clear, Ertel did not believe that Chekhov possessed real writing talent and was highly suspicious of Chekhov's political orientation. But, under the impact of Korolenko's arguments and especially after meeting Chekhov in person at Lavrov's in 1893, Ertel came to realize that Chekhov was a writer to whom the standard criteria of Russian criticism were not applicable. This led him to an unprejudiced rereading of the stories he had earlier rejected and to the discovery that he could genuinely admire Chekhov's work. In subsequent years, the two writers carried on a friendly correspondence and exchanged copies of their books and other publications.

2. The philanthropic millionairess mentioned in Letter 64.

3. The priest of the Russian embassy church in Berlin. He is mentioned several times in Chekhov's letters to Suvorin but their connection remains unclear.

90. To Alexei Suvorin

Melikhovo,
January 21, 1895

I will most definitely wire you. Please come, but don't bother to kiss "Kupernik's[1] feet." She's a talented little girl, but I doubt you'll find her appealing. I'm sorry for her; she makes me annoyed with myself because three days a week I find her repulsive. She's a devious little devil, but her motives are so petty that the end result is more rat than devil. Now Yavorskaya[2] is something else again. She's a very kind woman, and might even have turned out to be a good actress if she hadn't been ruined by her training. She's something of a hussy, but that doesn't matter. It never even occurred to me to use Kundasova in the story,[3] for heaven's sake! First, Kundasova's attitude toward money is completely different; second, she has never had any family life; and third, everything else aside, she is something of an invalid. Nor does the old merchant resemble my father, because to the end of his days my father will remain what he's been all his life: a man of average caliber unable to rise above his situation. As far as religion is concerned, young merchants have little patience with it.[4] If you had been whipped as a child on account of religion, you'd understand why. And what's so silly about their lack of patience? It may be expressed in a silly way, but in and of itself it's not as silly as you might think. It requires less justification than, say, an idyllic attitude toward religion, a gentlemanly, casual way of loving religion—like loving a snowstorm or a tempest from the comfort of your own study. I'll write the astronomer that you wish to see her. She will be touched and will probably try to come and see you.

I sent my book to Andreyevsky[5] because he sent me his speeches a year or two ago. And since you haven't sent me the bound copy of your *Love*[6] you promised, I was fully justified in not sending you my book. Besides, I knew you weren't any too fond of us "young writers" (and even saw fit to express uncertainty as to "whether they know anything or not"), I've lost interest in my books myself and so have no great desire to send them to anyone, and anyway Sytin[7] has allocated me only ten copies so far. What do you say? Have I succeeded in exonerating myself?

Phew! Women rob men of their youth, but not me. I don't run

my own life; I'm only the caretaker, and fate has done little to spoil me. I've had few affairs; I'm about as much like Catherine the Great as a hazelnut is like a battleship. And the only excuse I can see for silk underwear is that it's softer to the touch and therefore more comfortable. I have a penchant for comfort, but debauchery doesn't tempt me, and I would never have appreciated Maria Andreyevna,[8] for example.

I ought to take eight to ten months off and go somewhere far away for my health, Australia or the mouth of the Yenisei. Otherwise I'm going to kick the bucket. All right, I'll go to Petersburg, but will I have a room there where I can hide? It's a highly important question because I'll have to spend all February writing to earn enough for the journey. Oh, how badly I need to get away! My chest is one big wheeze, and my hemorrhoids are enough to turn the devil's stomach. I'll have to have an operation. No, to heck with literature, I should have concentrated on medicine. Though of course it's not for me to decide. I owe the happiest days of my life and my best impulses to literature.

My humble respects to Anna Ivanovna, Nastya and Borya.

Yours truly,
A. Chekhov

I'll be in Moscow on the twenty-sixth. The Grand Moscow Hotel.

1. Tatyana Shchepkina-Kupernik (1874–1952) was the literary prodigy of the early 1890s. Because of the low standards of taste in poetry at that time, her trite and facile doggerel, full of obvious pseudo-poetic clichés, was acclaimed by the critics and liked by the reading public. By the time she was twenty, three of her comedies had been produced at the Maly Theater and by Fyodor Korsh. With her actress friend Lydia Yavorskaya, Tatyana formed something like a two-woman sexual-freedom league, which numbered among its joint conquests both Chekhov and the old Suvorin. She remained on close and friendly terms with Chekhov's family after his fling with her was over (chronologically it overlapped with his affairs with Lydia Yavorskaya and Lydia Avilova). Her affectionate and factually interesting memoir about her friendship with Chekhov, written in Soviet times, carefully avoids all mention of their one-time intimacy.

2. Lydia Yavorskaya (1871–1921), an exquisitely beautiful blonde, was the kind of theatrical personality we've come to associate with Hollywood in its heyday. Possessed of only a modest acting talent, she had a genius for publicity and self-promotion, for the sake of which she was willing to do anything: associate with Suvorin, join an anti-government student demonstration, call Viktor Burenin the greatest Russian playwright (in a self-glorifying interview she gave while on a visit to Paris) or exploit her affair with Chekhov. As Suvorin's journal (which contains many memorable passages on her) and the memoir of Alexander Lazarev tell us and as Ivan Bunin

was to remember in his old age, Chekhov's affair with Yavorskaya was at its height during the period when he wrote *The Seagull* and was arranging its first performance. It was at her apartment that he read *The Seagull* to a group of friends and was surprised and shocked to hear that they believed it depicted Potapenko's affair with Lika Mizinova.

The period of Chekhov's involvement with Yavorskaya is the same one (1895, early 1896) that Lydia Avilova later identified in her patently spurious memoir *Chekhov in My Life,* written forty years after the events, as the period Chekhov was in love with *her*. That memoir seems to have fooled a total of two people: David Magarshack, who translated it into English and made it the basis of his biography of Chekhov; and Ivan Bunin, who read it in his old age and, remembering how attractive and desirable *he* had found Avilova in the 1890s, decided that Chekhov must have been in love with her too. As later Western biographers of Chekhov have pointed out, a careful reading of Chekhov's published letters to Avilova will convince anyone that there could never have been any serious or lasting emotional involvement with her on his part. His letters to Yavorskaya during the period in question were destroyed by her after she married a teen-aged and not very bright nobleman late in 1896 and, having become the Princess Baryatinskaya, resolved to obliterate the traces of her recent past.

After Chekhov's "Ariadne" was published in *Russian Thought* in December of 1895, Yavorskaya began spreading rumors, which managed to leak into the press, that she had served as the model for the heartless and predatory heroine of that story, acting apparently on the theory that bad publicity is better than no publicity at all. This may have been the cause of Chekhov's ending his affair with her; her engagement to Prince Baryatinsky came a few months after Chekhov's break with her. She was anxious in subsequent years to appear in *The Seagull* and in Chekhov's other plays, but he carefully prevented her from performing in any of them, rightly feeling that the showy, melodramatic acting style for which she was noted was ill suited for his plays. But he did recommend that Suvorin hire her when the latter started his own theatrical company, and it was with Suvorin's company that Yavorskaya was to score her most memorable successes, in Edmond Rostand's *La Princesse lointaine* and *L'Aiglon,* both of them translated into inflated and bombastic Russian verse by Tatyana Shchepkina-Kupernik.

3. Chekhov was repeatedly accused of depicting his personal friends and relations in his work. The painter Levitan broke off his friendship with Chekhov when he thought he recognized himself and his mistress in two of the characters in "The Grasshopper." The similarity of Lika Mizinova's affair with Potapenko to the Nina-Trigorin situation in *The Seagull* is one of the most recurrent themes in Chekhov criticism. In these two works, the resemblance was confined to the external situations: a painter having an affair with a doctor's wife in the story, a famous writer seducing and abandoning a girl in the play. The fictional characters themselves bore no resemblance to their alleged prototypes—as a personality, Nina is quite unlike Lika Mizinova;

there was no personal resemblance between Levitan and the painter Ryabovsky in "The Grasshopper"; and so on. The case is somewhat different with "Three Years." There, the personality, the physical appearance and the speech mannerisms of two of the characters had easily identifiable real-life models in Chekhov's life. The warehouse clerk Pochatkin had the physical appearance, the career and speech patterns of Chekhov's cousin Misha, while the character of Polina Rassudina looked, spoke and acted recognizably like Olga Kundasova. Chekhov's denial, therefore, is less convincing in this case than it was in other similar ones.

4. Suvorin's identification of Alexei Laptev's blind millionaire father in "Three Years" with Chekhov's own father seems off the mark, except for Laptev's attitude toward his father's cold and pharisaical religion. In this one aspect of the story, Chekhov must have drawn on his own conflict with his father. Laptev's discussion of his religious upbringing with his wife is strikingly similar to certain passages on this subject in Chekhov's own letters to Shcheglov and Suvorin (see Letter 68 and note 7 to that letter).

5. Sergei Andreyevsky (1847–1919), a noted criminologist, who was also a poet, essayist and literary critic. His critical study of *The Brothers Karamazov* (written in 1889) is one of the very few pieces of Dostoyevsky criticism written in Russian in the nineteenth century that can be read today without wincing. Andreyevsky's most durable accomplishment as a critic was his single-handed revival of the literary reputation of the poet Yevgeny Baratynsky, the greatest of Pushkin's contemporaries, who was banished from Russian literature in the 1840s by Belinsky for being too undesirably romantic and not sufficiently relevant socially. It is due to Andreyevsky's efforts in the 1890s that Baratynsky is today honored as a national classic in the Soviet Union and his works are published in large academic editions. Andreyevsky's own writings, on the other hand, have been banned since the Revolution because of his opposition to tendentiousness in literature; they have been out of print from 1924 to this day. His highly interesting posthumous philosophical work, *The Book of Death,* appeared in a German translation a few years ago.

6. Suvorin's novel, which is also called *Fin de siècle.*

7. The publisher of Chekhov's collection *Stories and Novellas,* 1894.

8. The lady whom Potapenko married after divorcing his first wife and abandoning Lika Mizinova.

91. To Yelena Shavrova

Melikhovo,
February 28, 1895

You're right: it's a risky topic. I can't tell you anything definite; I can only advise you to lock up the story in a trunk, keep it there for a year, and then read it over. By that time things will seem clearer to you. I am afraid to decide for you for fear of making a mistake.[1]

The story is a little wishy-washy, it exudes tendentiousness, the details all run together like spilled oil, and the characters are barely sketched out. Some of the characters are superfluous, the heroine's brother, for example, and the heroine's mother. Some of the episodes are superfluous, the events and conversations before the wedding and in fact everything that has to do with the wedding. But if these are faults, they are not important ones. What in my opinion is much more important is that you failed to cope with the formal aspects. To resolve problems of degeneracy, psychoses, etc., you must be scientifically acquainted with them. You have exaggerated the importance of the disease (out of modesty let us designate it with a capital Latin S).[2] First, S is curable, and second, if doctors find some serious disease in a patient, locomotor ataxia (tabes) or cirrhosis of the liver, for instance, and if this condition is due to S, then their prognosis will be comparatively favorable, because S can be treated. Degeneracy, general nervousness and flabbiness are not due to S alone, but to a combination of many factors: vodka, tobacco, the gluttony of the intellectual class, its appalling upbringing, its lack of physical labor, the conditions of urban life and so on and so forth. What is more, there are other diseases no less serious than S. Tuberculosis, for example. I also feel that it's not the duty of the artist to lash out at people for being ill. Am I to blame for having migraines? Is Sidor[3] to blame for having S just because he is more predisposed to it than Taras? Is Akulka to blame because her bones suffer from tuberculosis? No one is to blame, or if someone is, then it's a matter for the health authorities, not the artist.

The doctors in your story behave abominably. You make them break the Hippocratic Oath, and what's more, you have them force a gravely ill, paralyzed patient to travel to the city. Was that unfortunate victim of mysterious S bounced all the way into the city on a tarantass? The ladies in your story regard S as if it were hellfire and brimstone. Well, they're wrong. S isn't a vice, it isn't the product of ill will, but a disease, and the people who have it need warm, human care. It's wrong for a wife to desert her sick husband with the excuse that the disease is contagious or disgusting. She is free to react to S however she likes, of course, but the author must remain humane to the very end.

By the way, do you know that influenza also ravages the organism in ways that are far from insignificant? Oh, there's very little in nature that isn't harmful and isn't handed down by heredity. Even breathing is harmful. For myself, I stand by the following rule: I write about sickness only when it forms part of the characters or adds color to them.

I am afraid of frightening people with diseases. I can't accept the idea of "our nervous age," because people have been nervous in all ages. Anyone who is afraid of being nervous should turn himself into a sturgeon or a smelt. A sturgeon can make a fool or a blackguard of himself once and only once, by getting caught on a hook. After that he goes into soups and pies.

I'd like to see you write about something cheerful and bright green, a picnic, for example. Leave it to us medics to write about cripples and black monks. I'm soon going back to writing humorous stories, because my psychopathological repertory is exhausted.

I'm building a steam bath.

I wish you all sorts of heavenly and earthly bliss. Send me some more "business papers," I enjoy reading your stories. But please allow me to lay down one condition: no matter how harsh my criticism, you must not think the story unsuitable for publication. My carping is one thing, publishing and royalties quite another.

Yours,
A. Chekhov

1. When she sent her story to Chekhov, Shavrova wrote: "The subject of the story seems too audacious to me and perhaps unsuitable for publication; my attention is so exhausted that I can no longer judge its structure, form, details and other such things" (Shavrova's letter to Chekhov of February 16, 1895).

2. Chekhov's drawing on a foreign alphabet for the letter to designate syphilis seems to correspond to the modern medical practice in the West, where the Greek sigma is commonly used as a symbol for this disease.

3. Sidor, Taras and Akulka are used by Chekhov as typical Russian peasant names and do not designate any particular persons.

92. To Alexei Suvorin

Melikhovo,
March 16, 1895

You wrote you'd be in Moscow, and I waited and waited for a wire or a letter, counting on seeing you, but apparently you changed your Moscow plans. Instead of you the heavens sent me Leykin, who paid me a visit with Yezhov and Gruzinsky, two young lummoxes who didn't say a word and bored the whole estate to tears. Leykin has put on weight, gone physically downhill and looks a bit mangy, but he's grown kinder and more affable, which might mean that he hasn't long to live. When my mother was at the butcher's ordering meat, she told him she needed high-quality meat because Leykin from Petersburg was staying with us. "Which Leykin is that?" the butcher asked in amazement. "The one who writes books?" And he sent us excellent meat. So the butcher doesn't know I too write books, because all he ever sends me is gristle.

A very nice and very intelligent doctor, an admirer of Nietzsche, came from Moscow to visit me,[1] and we had a very pleasant two days together. The flutist Ivanenko, whom you've seen here, is down with consumption of the throat. That's all the news there is.

Well, we're releasing *Sakhalin* without waiting for permission.[2] It will be a thick book with endless footnotes, anecdotes and statistics. Who knows? We may get away with it. And if we don't, so be it, we all die in the end.

Have you read "The Mystery Correspondent" in February's *Historical Herald*?[3] Do you know who she is? What a story it would make! It's a pity I don't know any history or I'd write it myself. She's a remarkable individual, provided she isn't someone's invention.

Your short column on sports for university students will do a lot of good if you keep the idea alive.[4] Sports are absolutely essential. They are healthful and beautiful and liberal, liberal in the sense that nothing contributes more to breaking down class barriers, etc. than street games and public games. Sports would provide friends for our young people living on their own. Young men would fall in love more often. But sports should not be instituted as long as there are still Russian students going hungry. Neither croquet nor skates on an empty stomach will contribute to a student's well-being.

May the heavens visible from Earth and visible from Sirius protect you. Let my name be remembered in your orisons, and drop me two or three lines. Has the astronomer been to see you?

Yours,
A. Chekhov

1. Dr. Nikolai Korobov.

2. Chekhov worked on *The Island of Sakhalin* from 1890 to 1894. He was dissatisfied with an early draft, which he showed to Suvorin, and started a new version early in 1893. "Forget what I've shown you, for it is all false," he wrote to Suvorin on July 28, 1893. "I kept writing and kept feeling I was on the wrong track, until I finally discovered where the false note was. It was in my trying to teach something to someone with my *Sakhalin* and at the same time trying to conceal something and to hold myself back. But as soon as I started to admit what an oddball I felt like while I was on Sakhalin and what swine live there, things became easy and my work surged ahead, even though it is ending up a bit on the humorous side."

Most of the book was serialized in *Russian Thought* in 1893–94. But, for purposes of book publication, Chekhov had a verbal agreement with Galkin-Vrasky to submit the proof sheets for approval by the Prison and Penal Colony Administration. After waiting many long months for an authorization, Chekhov and the editors of *Russian Thought* decided to publish the book without any governmental authorization at all, despite the fact that the last few chapters were not cleared by the censors for publication in the journal and did not appear in it. Actually, all that could befall Chekhov at that historical juncture for an unauthorized publication was the confiscation of the entire edition. However, neither the censors nor any other branch of the government made any fuss when *The Island of Sakhalin* was published in this manner. (The essay that accompanies *The Island of Sakhalin* in the 1963–64 edition of Chekhov's collected works stresses at great length the censorship difficulties with the last chapters at the time of the magazine publication, but neglects to mention that the complete book was published with impunity in violation of both the official censorship regulations and Chekhov's verbal agreement with Galkin-Vrasky.)

The Island of Sakhalin was widely and favorably reviewed in the Russian press. A wealth of documentation proves that Chekhov's book was instrumental in bringing about much-needed reforms in the penal-colony administration and that it helped improve the conditions under which the convict-settlers lived. Chekhov was far less successful in accomplishing the other goal of his Sakhalin trip. When his friend Dr. Grigory Rossolimo approached the dean of the medical school of Moscow University at Chekhov's request, to inquire into the possibility of the book on Sakhalin being accepted in lieu of a dissertation, "the dean opened his eyes wide, glanced at me over his spectacles, turned around and walked out without saying a word" (Rossolimo's memoir of Chekhov).

3. A possibly spurious memoir, purportedly written by a woman who lived during the reign of Catherine the Great.

4. Suvorin advocated in his columns the establishment of physical-education departments at Russian universities.

93. To Alexei Suvorin

Melikhovo,
March 23, 1895

I told you Potapenko was a very lively person, but you didn't believe me. There are a great many treasures hidden deep down inside every Ukrainian. I have a feeling that when our generation grows old Potapenko will be the most cheerful and ebullient old man of us all.

Very well, then, I shall marry if you so desire. But under the following conditions: everything must continue as it was before, in other words, she must live in Moscow and I in the country, and I'll go visit her. I will never be able to stand the sort of happiness that lasts from one day to the next, from one morning to the next. Whenever someone talks to me day after day about the same thing in the same tone of voice, it brings out the ferocity in me. I turn ferocious in the company of Sergeyenko,[1] for example, because he's very much like a woman ("an intelligent and responsive woman") and because it occurs to me when I'm in his presence that my wife could be like him. I promise to be a splendid husband, but give me a wife who, like the moon, does not appear in my sky every day. I won't write any better for having gotten married.

So you're going to Italy, are you? Splendid, but if you're taking Mikhail Alexeyevich along for a cure, then climbing stairs twenty-five times an hour and running to fetch the *facchino*,[2] etc. certainly won't help improve his health. What he needs is to sit somewhere by the sea and take sea baths. And if that doesn't help, he might try hypnotism. Give my best to Italy. I love her passionately, even though you did tell Grigorovich that I lay down in the middle of St. Mark's Square and said, "How good it would be to stretch out for a while on the grass somewhere near Moscow."[3] Lombardy made such an impression on me that I seem to remember her every tree, and Venice, I can see Venice by closing my eyes.

Mamin-Sibiryak[4] is a very nice fellow and an excellent writer. *Bread,* his latest novel (in *Russian Thought*), has been generally praised; Leskov was especially taken with it. There are many excellent things to be found in his work, and the portrayal of peasants in his more successful stories is by no means worse than in "Master and Man."[5] I'm glad to hear you've gotten to know him somewhat.

This is the fourth year I've been living at Melikhovo. My calves have turned into cows, my forest grown an arshin or more. My heirs will make good money from the timber and call me an ass, because heirs are never satisfied.

Don't go abroad too early; it's cold. Wait until May. I may go too. We could meet somewhere. . . .

Write me again. Isn't there anything new in the realm of the nonsensical and well-intentioned daydreams?[6] Why did Wilhelm recall General W.?[7] Is it that we're about to fight the Germans? In that case I'll have to go to war and perform amputations, and then write it all up for the *Historical Herald.**

Yours,
A. Chekhov

* *Would it be possible to get an advance out of Shubinsky*[8] *for the articles?* [*Chekhov's own footnote*].

1. Chekhov first met Pyotr Sergeyenko (1854–1930) when they were both students at the same school in Taganrog. Sergeyenko later became a writer, journalist and a disciple of Tolstoy, publishing in 1898 a book about Tolstoy's day-to-day life at Yasnaya Polyana, which has retained some of its documentary value. Chekhov inevitably found Sergeyenko dull and depressing as a person, and there is no doubt that he turned down several invitations to meet Tolstoy and that their meeting was delayed for several years because he was unwilling to make Tolstoy's acquaintance in Sergeyenko's presence. Even more unfortunate was Sergeyenko's later role in helping to arrange the exploitative contract with the publisher Adolf Marx, in accordance with which, at the end of his life, Chekhov was done out of so much money that was rightfully his.

2. All Russian editions and the Koteliansky-Tomlinson translation into English reverently retain Chekhov's misspelling of the Italian word for porter as "fokino." The replacement of *a* with *o* results from the same extension of Moscow *akanie* dialect phonetics into a foreign language that Vladimir Mayakovsky was guilty of when he spelled Laredo as "Loredo" during his visit to America.

3. This joke of Suvorin's is gleefully quoted by Zinaida Gippius in her memoir *Living Portraits* as an actual statement of Chekhov's (although she probably got it from Maria Chekhova's edition of the letters, which she admittedly consulted before writing her memoir) as evidence of Chekhov's provinciality and lack of culture.

4. Dmitry Mamin (1852–1912), who published under the pen name Mamin-Sibiryak, was a novelist who specialized in describing life in the Urals and in Siberia.

5. A short story by Tolstoy.

6. Reference to the statement made by Nicholas II on January 17, 1895, when he received a delegation made up of representatives of the gentry, the *zemstvos* and the major cities, which came to him to plead for a more representative form of government. The tsar's reply was that some of the *zemstvo* conferences were carried away by "nonsensical daydreams" and that he intended to "support the principle of autocracy as firmly and unswervingly as his late lamented father did." After Chekhov read about this declaration, he wrote to Suvorin on January 19: "After the general jubilation caused by these great and joyous events subsides, write me. I'd be interested to know what the morning after is like, what kind of hangover he'll have, his condition at the moment when a person comes to feel like a wreck and at fault and to realize dimly that he had behaved offensively the day before."

Suvorin was in Moscow for the coronation of Nicholas II in May of 1896 and his journal contains one of the most vivid and indignant accounts we have of the infamous catastrophe of Khodynka, when a huge crowd was lured into an enclosed area by promises of gifts and souvenirs during the coronation and when thousands of people were trampled to death owing to the lack of even the most elementary precautions by the authorities.

A week after the catastrophe, Chekhov and Suvorin went to the Vagankovo Cemetery in Moscow to observe the interment of the victims, which was still going on. Suvorin was particularly struck by the number of children and adolescents who were killed.

7. General Werder, the titular head of the German colony in St. Petersburg, stated in a public speech, reported in *New Times*, that he was going to Germany at the request of the Kaiser.

8. The notes to the 1944–51 edition identify this man as Sergei Shubinsky, the editor of *Historical Herald* (owned by Suvorin), which makes sense. The 1963–64 edition insists that Chekhov meant Nikolai Shubinsky, a lawyer married to the actress Maria Yermolova, but gives no reason for this supposition.

94. To Alexei Suvorin

Melikhovo,
April 13, 1895

You ask me whether I received that letter. Yes, I did and I spoke to you about it in Petersburg. It shows you in a particularly suspect light, because you criticize both the present and the past. Remember what you wrote about Catherine the Great and silken underwear! While looking for that letter, I incidentally glanced through all your letters and put them into some semblance of order. How much good they contain! The period when your *Tatyana Repina* and my *Ivanov* were being produced is especially vivid. They bubble with life.

I am plowing my way through Sienkiewicz's *Polaniecki Family*.[1] It's a Polish cottage-cheese cake with saffron. Add a little Potapenko to Paul Bourget, sprinkle with Warsaw eau-de-cologne, divide in two, and there you have Sienkiewicz. *The Połaniecki Family* shows clear traces of Bourget's *Cosmopolis*, Rome and marriage (Sienkiewicz was recently married). It has catacombs and an old oddball professor who pines for idealism, and the heavenly countenance of Pope Leo XIII, who now resides among the saints, and an exhortation to return to the prayerbook, and a calumny on a modernist who dies of morphine addiction after confessing and taking communion, that is, repenting the errors of his ways in the name of the Church. It has an ungodly profusion of family happiness and disquisitions on love, and the hero's wife is so extremely true to her husband and her heart so subtly in tune with God and life that the result is cloying and uncomfortable, like a slobbery kiss. It is clear that Sienkiewicz has not read Tolstoy and is unfamiliar with Nietzsche, he talks about hypnotism like a philistine, but on the other hand every one of his pages is swarming with Rubenses, Villa Borgheses, Correggios, and Botticellis—the better to show off his culture to the bourgeois reader and covertly stick out his tongue at materialism. The novel's goal is to lull the bourgeoisie in its golden dreams. Be true to your wife, pray with her according to the prayerbook, make a fortune, enjoy sports—and you're all set in this world and the next. The bourgeoisie is very fond of what are commonly referred to as "positive heroes" and of novels with happy endings, because they make them feel at ease with the idea that you can hoard capital while maintaining your innocence, be a beast and yet be happy.[2]

We've been having a pitiful sort of spring. The fields are still covered with snow, you can't get anywhere either by sleigh or carriage and the cattle are pining for grass and freedom. Yesterday a drunken old peasant stripped and took a swim in the pond, while his ancient mother beat him with a stick and everyone else stood around and laughed. After his swim, the peasant walked home through the snow in his bare feet, followed by his mother. A while ago the old woman had come to me to be treated for black and blue marks; her son had beaten her. How base it is to keep putting off educating the illiterate masses!

Yavorskaya is not having an affair with Korsh, but it's true he's jealous.

How did the play at the Literary Artists Club go?

I wish you all the best. My congratulations on the Sino-Japanese peace,[3] on our good luck in grabbing an ice-free Feodosia on the Pacific and constructing a railroad line to it. As if we didn't have enough problems as it is. I have a feeling we're letting ourselves in for a whole lot of trouble with that ice-free port. It will end up costing us more than if we'd set out to conquer all of Japan. Of course, *futura sunt in manibus deorum.*[4]

Misha arrived with the announcement that he's received a Stanislav medal, third class.

Yours,
A. Chekhov

1. Henryk Sienkiewicz (1846–1916) is remembered today primarily as a writer of historical romances dealing with either ancient Rome (*Quo Vadis?*) or the history of his native Poland (*With Fire and Sword, The Deluge,* etc.). In Chekhov's time he was also admired for his two novels of contemporary Polish life, *The Polaniecki Family* (translated into English as *The Irony of Life* and also as *The Children of the Soil*) and *Without Dogma.* Vukol Lavrov, the publisher of *Russian Thought,* was Sienkiewicz's principal translator and popularizer in Russia.

2. Chekhov was somewhat kinder to Sienkiewicz's other contemporary novel, *Without Dogma,* of which he wrote to Vukol Lavrov on November 13,

1893: "I've enjoyed reading *Without Dogma*. It's an interesting and intelligent book, but it is so full of discussions, aphorisms, references to Hamlet and to Empedocles, repetitions and emphases that reading some stretches is as strenuous as reading a narrative poem in verse. Much coquetry and little simplicity. But nevertheless it is attractive, warm and vivid. . . ."

The word rendered as "innocence" can also mean "virginity" in Russian; Chekhov quotes a popular saying about a prostitute who plies her trade and manages to preserve her virginity at the same time.

3. The conclusion of the war of 1894–95, in which the newly modernized Japan defeated China.

4. Japan had acquired the rights to the ice-free port of Dalny (Dairen) on the Liaotung Peninsula by its peace treaty with China. Russia, backed by Britain and France, forced Japan to give up this port and started plans for constructing the Eastern China Railway from Siberia to Dalny. The resultant series of events culminated in Russian defeat in the Russo-Japanese War of 1904–1906.

95. To Alexei Suvorin

Melikhovo,
October 21, 1895

Thank you for your letter, warm words and invitation. I will come, but probably not before late November; I have a hell of a lot of things to do. First, in the spring I'm going to build a new school in the village[1] where I serve as honorary superintendent, and before I start I have to draw up the plans and estimates and make trips here and there, etc. Second, believe it or not, I'm writing a play that I probably won't finish until the end of November. I can't say I'm not enjoying writing it, though I'm flagrantly disregarding the basic tenets of the stage. The comedy has three female roles, six male roles, four acts, a landscape (a view of a lake), much conversation about literature, little action and five tons of love.[2]

Reading about Ozerova's[3] fiasco made me feel sorry for her because there's nothing more painful than failure. I can imagine how much that little Jewess wept and shivered when she read the *Petersburg Gazette*, where they call her acting downright ridiculous. I read about the success of *The Power of Darkness* at your theater. Of course Anyutka should be played by Domasheva and not by "little darling," whom (in your own words) you find so appealing. Little darling ought to play Matryona.[4] When I visited Tolstoy in August, he told me while washing and drying his hands that he would not alter the play. And, with that in mind, I now think he knew back then that his play would be passed *in toto* for the stage. My visit with the Tolstoys lasted a day and a half.

He made a marvelous impression on me. I felt as free and easy as if I had been at home. The talks I had with Lev Nikolayevich were equally free and easy. I'll tell you about them in detail when we get together.[5]

My "Murder" will appear in *Russian Thought* in November, and "Ariadne," another story, in December.

I am horrified, and here's why. There is a superb journal that is published in Moscow and known even abroad called *Surgical Chronicle*. It is edited by the well-known surgeon-scientists Sklifosovsky and Dyakonov. Every year there is an increase in the number of subscribers, but by the end of the year there is still a deficit. This deficit has always (until January of next year, 1896) been underwritten by Sklifosovsky, but because he has been transferred to Petersburg, Sklifosovsky has lost his practice and has no money to spare and now neither he nor anyone on earth knows who will underwrite the 1896 deficit, in case there is one, and, judging by previous years, we can expect a deficit of a thousand to fifteen hundred rubles. When I learned that the journal was in danger, I did something rash. The absurd thought that an absolutely indispensable journal which would be making a profit in three or four years was going to expire for such a paltry sum, the absurdity of it all struck me so hard that in the heat of the moment I promised to find them a publisher, being quite certain that I would. I did everything I could: I searched, I begged, I humiliated myself, I drove here and there, I had dinner with the damnedest people, but I found no one. Only Soldatenkov[6] is left, but he's abroad and won't be back before December, and our problem has to be solved by November. How I regret that your printing plant is not in Moscow. If it were, I wouldn't be forced into this ridiculous role of unsuccessful middleman. When we get together, I'll paint a true picture[7] of the perturbations I have gone through. If I weren't building the school, which will cost me about fifteen hundred, I would undertake the publication of the journal at my own expense, that's how painful and difficult it is for me to reconcile myself with this clear absurdity. On October 22nd I'm going to Moscow to suggest to the editors as a last resort that they ask for a subsidy of fifteen hundred to two thousand a year. If they agree, I'll rush straight to Petersburg and start pleading my case. How are these things done? Will you teach me? To save the journal I am willing to see anyone and wait in anyone's reception room, and if I succeed, I'll heave a sigh of relief and satisfaction, since saving a good surgery journal is as useful as performing twenty thousand successful operations. In any case advise me as to what I should do.[8]

After Sunday write to Moscow if you want to reach me. The Grand Moscow Hotel, Room 5.

How is Potapenko's play? What's Potapenko up to in general? Jean Shcheglov has sent me a despondent letter. The astronomer is destitute. Everything else is all right for the time being. I'm going to go to operettas in Moscow. During the day I'll putter around with the play, and in the evening I'll go to an operetta.

My humble respects. Write, I beg of you.

Yours,
A. Chekhov

1. The village of Talezh.

2. Chekhov began writing *The Seagull* in October, 1895. There was an early draft, which he reworked in the spring of 1896, and the final draft, submitted to the censorship for approval in July of 1896.

3. The actress Lyudmila Ozerova, who was Suvorin's particular favorite, had appeared in the role of Luise in Schiller's *Kabale und Liebe*. Her performance was panned by one of the leading critics. Her first name and her patronymic Ivanovna make it highly unlikely that she was actually Jewish.

4. Suvorin opened his private theater with a widely acclaimed production of Tolstoy's peasant tragedy *The Power of Darkness*. The role of the little girl Anyutka was played by Maria Domasheva, who was twenty in 1895. In 1915, when she was forty, Domasheva scored one of her greatest hits playing a fifteen-year-old girl in Meyerhold's production of *The Green Ring* by Zinaida Gippius. Chekhov felt that Domasheva was more suited for the young girl's role in Tolstoy's play than Lyudmila Ozerova ("the little darling"). The role of Matryona in *The Power of Darkness* is that of the hero's aged and evil mother.

5. Chekhov stayed with Tolstoy in Yasnaya Polyana on August 8 and 9, 1895. He was present at Tolstoy's reading of the recently completed portions of *Resurrection* and pointed out to Tolstoy the improbability of the sentence of two years' hard labor, which the heroine of the novel, Maslova, is given. From his experiences at Sakhalin, Chekhov knew that four years was the shortest possible hard-labor sentence. Tolstoy thereupon made the necessary correction in his manuscript.

6. Kuzma Soldatenkov, a prominent Moscow publisher.

7. Quotation from Pushkin's *Eugene Onegin*, Chapter One, Stanza XXXIII, line 1.

8. Suvorin wrote back, offering a loan of fifteen hundred rubles to help the journal. A suitable publisher was eventually found, but the journal ran into trouble getting its next editor approved by the authorities. Chekhov's correspondence for 1896 frequently mentions his involvement in trying to rescue this foundering medical journal. A considerable portion of the time he spent in St. Petersburg in connection with the première of *The Seagull* in October of 1896 was devoted to arranging various matters connected with the *Surgical Chronicle*.

X

"THE SEAGULL"

THERE EXISTS NO EXACT, incontrovertible evidence about just when Chekhov reworked *The Wood Demon* into *Uncle Vanya.* In her chronicle of Chekhov's life, Nina Gitovich amasses some impressive indirect evidence to show that he did it in the very early 1890s, only to put *Uncle Vanya* aside and to bring it out after the successful revival of *The Seagull* at the Moscow Art Theater. But most of the knowledgeable Soviet commentators insist that *Uncle Vanya* was in fact written after *The Seagull,* and the logic of the situation is on their side, for *Uncle Vanya* is surely the more authentically "Chekhovian" play of the two, more totally free from the conventions of Ostrovskian drama that had dominated the Russian stage since the 1850s and from the patterns and formulas of the Western well-made social play. It was in *The Seagull* that this liberation first occurred, the creative breakthrough which made Chekhov as much an innovator in the field of drama as he already was in the art of prose narrative. The characters in the plays of Ostrovsky's heirs had clear-cut motivations, always knew what they wanted and expressed their wishes and intentions in simple and direct terms. In Chekhov's mature plays, the characters do not necessarily fully understand what it is they want and an entirely new form of artfully oblique and seemingly irrelevant dialogue is devised to show the reality behind their overtly stated intentions and emotions. Where earlier drama depended on startling and dramatic events for its structure and its impact, Chekhov's plays show that something *not* happening can also be valid dramatically; when an overtly dramatic event does occur (Uncle Vanya's firing a pistol at the professor, Tusenbach's death in *Three Sisters*), it neither concludes the play's action, nor changes the basic situation of the other characters. Dramatic events are internalized—the implications of people's interrelations are just as important as their external manifestations. Except for Konstantin Treplyov's suicide at the end of *The Seagull* (a holdover from *Ivanov*, although far better motivated dramatically), the action of Chekhov's mature plays does not conclude at the final curtain—the future lives of Nina Zarechnaya, of Sonya and Uncle Vanya, of the three sisters, of Ranevskaya and Anya are all discernible because Chekhov has indicated or suggested their probable form. Above all, it is the dramatic possibilities of human noncommunication that Chekhov explores and demonstrates in his plays from *The Seagull* on.

He did not devise his new manner entirely by himself. The years that separate the writing of *The Wood Demon* from *The Seagull* (1889–95) were a time of exciting new developments in Western European drama. New dramatic forms and new subject matter were being discovered and developed by Henrik Ibsen, Bjørnstjerne Bjørnson, August Strindberg, Gerhart Hauptmann, and Maurice Maeterlinck. Tolstoy rejected these new playwrights with veritable fury. Younger Russian realists—Gorky and Bunin—did not deign to notice them. But Chekhov, like the younger writers who were later to form the Russian Symbolist movement, followed the development of the new drama in the West with avid and fascinated interest (Tatyana Shakh-Azizova's little book *Chekhov and Western European Drama of His Time*, Moscow, 1966, is a highly knowledgeable account of his relationship to his Western contemporaries). He did not care for some of the new playwrights, but Maeterlinck and Strindberg fascinated him and he found many interesting things in Ibsen, Bjørnson and Hauptmann. Reading these writers and seeing productions of their plays suggested to Chekhov that a totally new approach to writing drama was possible. *The Seagull* was the result.

It is the last of Chekhov's *pièces à thèse*. While it does not include social, political or ecological polemics, as *Ivanov* and *The Wood Demon* did, *The Seagull* is the most complicated play Chekhov ever wrote. In addition to its intricately plotted series of amorous triangles, and its variations on the Oedipal implications of Shakespeare's *Hamlet* (on this aspect of the play, see Thomas G. Winner, "Chekhov's *Seagull* and Shakespeare's *Hamlet*," in *The American Slavic and East European Review*, XV, February, 1956), it comprises, as its essential element, Chekhov's typology of the varieties of creative personality. The play contrasts two successful noninnovative artists, the writer Trigorin and the actress Arkadina, who owe their success to exploiting what is safe and accepted in their respective arts, with two young innovative artists, the writer Konstantin Treplyov and the actress Nina Zarechnaya, whose road to artistic integrity, originality and innovation brings them to personal tragedy. *What Is Art?*, the title of

Tolstoy's treatise, with which Chekhov was to disagree so strongly, would also make a suitable subtitle for *The Seagull.*

Chekhov's meditations on the nature of creative personality, which are such an integral part of *The Seagull,* can be read in part as a comment upon and response to the disquisitions on the same topic in Guy de Maupassant's travel sketch *Sur l'eau* (Maupassant was as overrated in the Russia of Chekhov's time as he later was in America; the more myopic French and American critics have repeatedly suggested that Maupassant is Chekhov's Western counterpart, even though his shallow despair and misanthropy are the very opposite of Chekhovian depth and compassion). Trigorin's second-act speech about his obsessive collecting of literary material, which Tolstoy believed was Chekhov's self-portrait and in which others saw a portrait of Potapenko, is actually almost a paraphrase of corresponding passages in Maupassant. But Chekhov also pointed out his disagreement with Maupassant by having Arkadina read a passage from *Sur l'eau* at the beginning of Act II and then close the book with the remark: "The rest is both uninteresting and wrong."

The opening night of *The Seagull* on October 17, 1896, has gone down in history as one of those celebrated occasions when the first-night audience failed to realize that they had witnessed a masterpiece destined to be admired by posterity, an opening night similar to those of Verdi's *La Traviata,* Bizet's *Carmen* and Stravinsky's *The Rite of Spring.* The Russian tradition blaming the fiasco on inept direction and poor performances by unimaginative actors is a legend created much later by the directors of the Moscow Art Theater, especially Stanislavsky, in their understandable desire to claim all the credit for rescuing the unappreciated masterpiece from oblivion. A study of eyewitness accounts—the journal of Nikolai Leykin, the memoirs of Potapenko and Koni, some of the contemporary press accounts—shows that the original production, while underrehearsed and by no means ideal, was not as bad as subsequent legend made it out to be. The key role of Nina was taken by Vera Kommissarzhevskaya, probably the most creative and sensitive actress in the entire history of Russian theater, then on the threshold of her brilliant career. The director was the playwright Yevtikhy Karpov, usually treated by Western commentators on Chekhov as an unimaginative hack who ruined the play with his direction. But Karpov was the man who discovered and developed Vera Kommissarzhevskaya's acting genius and who was later to direct her in some of her greatest triumphs. In later years he also staged some highly acclaimed productions of Gorky. A look at Karpov's own naturalistic plays, such as *The Workers' Quarter* or *The Community-Supported Widow,* shows that he was one of the more interesting minor playwrights of Chekhov's time, highly aware of new theatrical forms and open to original and innovative ideas. While Chekhov was to object to many things in Stanislavsky's subsequent production of *The Seagull,* he found little to criticize in Karpov's direction and was actually moved to tears at one of the rehearsals.

The fact of the matter is that the audience which gathered at the Empress Alexandra Theater in St. Petersburg on October 17 would have booed any production of *The Seagull,* even one directed by Stanislavsky himself. In an unbelievably ill-advised move, Chekhov allowed his fervent admirer, the actress Yelizaveta Levkeyeva, to use *The Seagull*'s opening night for her benefit performance. A one-time protégée of Alexander Ostrovsky, noted for playing the ingénue roles in his plays, she was now, in the nineties, a popular comic actress specializing in broad farces. The house was filled, in consequence, with Levkeyeva's admirers. For these people Chekhov was primarily the comic author of "A Horsy Name" and "The Malefactor" (he remains the favorite humorist of many Russians to this day), and they came, attracted by the combination of Chekhov's and Levkeyeva's names, expecting an evening of hilarious laughter.

Because the audience was packed with Levkeyeva's lowbrow fans on the opening night, many members of the St. Petersburg intellectual community were not able to see the play until its second and third performance. Repeated a few days later before a sold-out house and a more discerning audience, *The Seagull* became an artistic triumph. As Vera Kommissarzhevskaya wrote to Chekhov after the second performance:

> Petersburg,
> October 21, 1896
> Monday, 12 midnight
>
> I've just returned from the theater, dear Anton Pavlovich. Victory is ours.
>
> The play is a complete, unanimous success, just as it ought to be, just as it had to be. How I'd like to see you now, but what I'd like even more is for you to be present and hear the unanimous cry of "Author." Your—no—our *Seagull,* because I have merged with her forever heart and soul—is alive; her sufferings and faith are so ardent that she will compel many others to have faith. "Think of your vocation and have no fear of life." I clasp your hand.
>
> V. Kommissarzhevskaya

Had the management allowed the play to run for the rest of the season, it would have undoubtedly become a major hit, and there would have been no need for Stanislavsky's revival three years later. But the management read the press notices based on the first-night reaction and closed the play after a total of five performances. The whole experience was probably the most harrowing emotional ordeal of Chekhov's entire life.

96. To Anatoly Koni

Melikhovo,
November 11, 1896

Dear Anatoly Fyodorovich,

You can't imagine how happy your letter made me.[1] I saw only the first two acts of my play from out front. After that I went backstage, feeling all the while that *The Seagull* was failing. After the performance, that night and the following day, people kept assuring me that my characters were all idiots and that my play was dramatically unsound, ill-considered, incomprehensible, even nonsensical, and so on and so forth. You can see the situation I was in. It was a failure I couldn't have imagined in my worst dreams. I was embarrassed and chagrined, and left Petersburg filled with all sorts of doubts. I thought that if I had written and staged a play so obviously abounding in monstrous shortcomings, then I had lost all sensitivity and that consequently my mechanism had run down once and for all. When I got home, I had word from Petersburg that the second and third performances had been successful. I received several letters, both signed and anonymous, that praised the play and berated the critics. Reading the letters gave me pleasure, but I was still embarrassed and chagrined, and it unwittingly came to me that if kind people found it necessary to console me, then I was certainly in a bad way. But your letter had a very decisive effect on me. I've known you for a long time, I respect you highly, and I believe you more than all the critics put together. You felt as much while you wrote your letter, which is why it is so beautiful and convincing. I am reassured now and can think about the play and the production without revulsion.

Kommissarzhevskaya is a marvelous actress. At one of the rehearsals many people wept as they watched her, and they said she is the best actress in all Russia today. Yet on opening night even she succumbed to the general mood of hostility to my *Seagull* and seemed to grow frightened and was barely audible. Our journalists are undeservedly cold to her and I feel sorry for her.

Let me thank you for the letter from the bottom of my heart. Believe me, the feelings that prompted you to write it are more valuable to me than I can express in words, and I will never, never forget, no matter what may happen, the concern you call "unnecessary" at the end of the letter.

Your sincerely respectful and devoted,
A. Chekhov

1. Here is the complete text of Koni's letter which Chekhov is answering:

Petersburg,
November 7, 1896

Dear Anton Pavlovich,

My letter may surprise you, but even though I'm drowning in work, I cannot resist writing you about your *Seagull*, which I finally found time to see. I heard (from Savina) that the public's attitude to the play upset you greatly. Let one member of the audience—uninitiated as I may be in the secrets of literature and dramatic art, but acquainted with life as a result of my legal practice—tell you that he thanks you for the deep pleasure your play afforded him. *The Seagull* is a work whose conception, freshness of ideas and thoughtful observations of life situations raise it out of the ordinary. It is life itself on stage with all its tragic alliances, eloquent thoughtlessness and silent sufferings—the sort of everyday life that is accessible to everyone and understood in its cruel internal irony by almost no one, the sort of life that is so accessible and close to us that at times you forget you're in a theater and you feel capable of participating in the conversation taking place in front of you. And how good the ending is! How true to life it is that not she, the seagull, commits suicide (which a run-of-the-mill playwright, out for his audience's tears, would be sure to have done), but the young man who lives in an abstract future and "has no idea" of the why and wherefore of what goes on around him. I also very much like the device of cutting off the play abruptly, leaving the spectator to sketch in the dreary, listless, indefinite future for himself. That's the way epic works end, or rather turn out. I won't speak of the production, in which Kommissarzhevskaya is marvelous. But Sazonov and Pisarev, or so it seems to me, didn't understand their roles and don't play the characters you meant to portray.

Perhaps you are shrugging your shoulders in amazement. Of what concern is my opinion to you, and why am I writing all this? Here is why. I love you for the moments of stirring emotion your works have given and continue to give me, and I want to send you a random word of sympathy from a distance, a word which as far as I know may be quite unnecessary.

Sincerely,
A. Koni

In his memoirs, Koni recalled that he was moved to write this letter by the outrage he felt at the unruly behavior of the opening-night audience and by the gloating and slanderous reviews of the play he read in the next few days in St. Petersburg newspapers. The entire affair made him recall the story that the initial failure of *Carmen* helped aggravate Georges Bizet's heart disease and led to his untimely death and the accounts of Mikhail Glinka's pain and anguish at the hostile reception of his subsequently popular second opera *Ruslan and Lyudmila* by the musicians and by the general public.

97. To Lydia Veselitskaya (V. Mikulich)[1]

Melikhovo,
between November 11 and 13, 1896

Dear Lydia Ivanovna,

I left Petersburg the very day after my play's opening and didn't read the papers (they looked ominous). Then my kind friends kept assuring me in their letters that it was bad acting and not the play itself that was at fault and that the second and third performances had been successful. I was happy to take their word for it, and so my chagrin was very soon dispelled. Nonetheless your charming letter came just in time; it breathed concern and friendship, and I yielded to its spell and cheered up. Then I made a long series of inquiries to find out what your patronymic is. I wanted to send you my book with an inscription about how greatly I respect and thank you. Finally, after a long wait, the information came from Ivan Ivanovich Gorbunov,[2] and I am now sending you the book and asking you to accept it.

I haven't been to the Tolstoys. First the play prevented me from going; then it snowed and it was too late. Permit me to thank you once again from the bottom of my heart and clasp your hand.

Devotedly,
A. Chekhov

1. Lydia Veselitskaya (1857–1936) was a popular writer of books for juveniles, which she published under the pen name V. Mikulich. Her best-known nonjuvenile work was a trilogy of satirical novels about a giddy society girl named Mimochka. In the course of her life she had interesting encounters with Tolstoy, Dostoyevsky and Leskov and she wrote valuable memoirs about each of them. She and Chekhov were not acquainted personally. Chekhov's letter to her is one of about half a dozen similar ones he wrote to various literary figures (Viktor Bilibin and Yelena Shavrova were two of them) who had gotten in touch with him to tell him they considered *The Seagull* a remarkable achievement and to urge him to disregard the unjust verdict of the opening-night audience and the St. Petersburg press.

2. Ivan Gorbunov-Posadov.

98. To Alexei Suvorin

Melikhovo,
December 14, 1896

I got your two letters about *Uncle Vanya*, one in Moscow, the other at home. Not so long ago I got a letter from Koni, who was at *The Seagull*. You and Koni have given me many good moments with your letters, but nonetheless my heart has become metal-plated; I feel nothing for my plays but disgust, and I have to force myself to read the proofs. You may say again that this is not very intelligent, that I'm being silly, proud, egocentric and so on and so forth. Yes, I know that, but what can I do? I'd be glad to rid myself of this silly feeling, but I can't, I simply can't. The trouble is not that my play was a failure; after all, most of my earlier plays also failed, and each time it was like water off a duck's back. It isn't the play that was unsuccessful on October 17th; it was my own person.[1] One thing struck me as early as the first act, to wit: the people with whom I'd been open and friendly up to October 17th, the people with whom I had enjoyed carefree dinners, in whose defense I had broken lances (Yasinsky, for example)—they all wore peculiar expressions on their faces, extremely peculiar expressions. . . . In short, what happened was what justified Leykin's writing me a letter of condolence for having so few friends,[2] and enabled *The Week*[3] to query, "What did Chekhov ever do to them?" and *The Theatergoer*[4] to print a whole article (in issue ninety-five) claiming that my fellow writers had staged a demonstration against me at the theater. I am calm now; my mood is back to normal. But I still can't forget what happened, any more than I could forget it had they punched me in the face.

And now I have a favor to ask of you. Send me my usual yearly bribe—your yearbook—and do you think you could get hold of someone in close contact with the central administration to find out why we haven't received authorization yet for the journal *Surgery*?[5] Will it be authorized? I submitted the application back on October 15th in behalf of Professor Dyakonov. Time can't wait, and we're suffering terrible losses.

Sytin has bought an estate near Moscow for fifty thousand. It is fourteen versts from the station and near the highway.

You divide plays into those meant to be played and those meant to be read. Into which category, pray tell, would you put *A Bankrupt*,[6] particularly the act during the whole of which Dalmatov and Mikhailov talk all by themselves of nothing but bookkeeping and score a huge success? I think if a play meant to be read is acted by good actors, it becomes one meant to be played.

I'm gathering material for a book along the lines of *Sakhalin* in which I will treat all sixty *zemstvo* schools in our district exclusively from the vantage point of their day-to-day operational problems. It will be aimed at helping *zemstvo* officials.[7]

I wish you earthly and heavenly bliss, sound sleep and a good appetite.

Yours,
A. Chekhov

1. The fact that *The Seagull* first opened in St. Petersburg and not in Moscow was an additional reason for the play's failure. The giggles and hisses in the audience during the first act's play-within-the-play made a large number of St. Petersburg journalists and literary men realize that here was a heaven-sent opportunity to express in a quasi-legitimate manner their long-standing resentment of Chekhov and his ever-growing success. He had previously made himself unpopular in St. Petersburg literary circles by his lack of sociability when he was there to arrange his trip to Sakhalin (Letter 40). Upon his return from Sakhalin, the hostility of his St. Petersburg colleagues was openly expressed (Letter to Maria Chekhova, quoted on p. 183). Alexander Chekhov's letters to his brother testify that this hostility turned to actual hatred when Suvorin chose to serialize *The Duel* in *New Times* in ten lengthy installments, which usurped the space normally allocated to a number of the newspaper's columnists and other regular contributors.

Returning home from the opening night, Nikolai Leykin recorded in his private journal a vivid account of how various journalists and drama critics jumped out of their seats in the middle of the first act and rushed off to the bar, exclaiming happily to each other: "He's lost his talent" and "He's written himself out." After looking over the reviews in the morning papers the next day (October 18), Leykin wrote in his journal:

> Except for *New Times,* all the papers are solemnly announcing the failure of Chekhov's *Seagull,* with genuine solemnity and with a note of gloating. You'd think they've finally caught a wolf who prior to his capture had massacred a large number of cattle. How could *St. Petersburg Gazette* permit itself such a tone when writing of Chekhov? I'm simply astounded. Its drama critic all but hops with joy along the columns of his review and heaps abuse [on Chekhov] most authoritatively. And Chekhov wrote so many things for the *St. Petersburg Gazette* once, and published some of his finest stories there, including his very best story, "The Huntsman."

2. In his letter to Chekhov, Leykin wrote:

> Oh, how indignant we, your friends, were about the reviewers after the first performance of *The Seagull*! Right after the first act there they were, hissing, running along the corridors and the bar, exclaiming with self-assurance: "Where is there any action? Where are there any [recognizable] types? It's all so watery." They were actively organizing the failure of the opening night, since their words were addressed to the benefit-performance habitués. The opening of your play attracted all the journalists and all the fiction writers, and as I exchanged a few words with all of them, I had occasion to observe how very few true friends you have.

Ieronim Yasinky, whom Chekhov had considered a personal friend, wrote in his review that the play produced a "wild and incoherent impression." The only favorable notice that *The Seagull* received in the St. Petersburg press was Suvorin's article published in his own newspaper, in which he blamed the failure on lack of rehearsals, and Lydia Avilova's letter to the editor of *St. Petersburg Gazette* written in protest against their review.

3. The current-events column in *The Week* contained this query: "Whom could Chekhov have harmed, whom could he have offended, in whose way might he have stood to have deserved all that hatred suddenly advancing upon him from somewhere or other? Or is it simply enough to be talented, famous and loved?"

4. The St. Petersburg correspondent of *The Theatergoer,* a magazine published in Moscow, wrote that the opening of *The Seagull* was unparalleled in his experience in the overt hostility of a large part of the audience toward the playwright and the actors. He came to the disbelieving conclusion that one half of the audience consisted of Chekhov's personal enemies, who were using the occasion to settle personal grudges.

5. The medical journal that was formerly called *Surgical Chronicle* (see Letter 95).

6. A play by Bjørnstjerne Bjørnson.

7. Chekhov never accomplished this project.

XI

THE INESCAPABLE DIAGNOSIS

Chekhov returned to Melikhovo from the St. Petersburg opening of *The Seagull* in an embittered mood. Neither the steady flow of letters from various literary figures and anonymous admirers, who wrote that they had seen one of the five St. Petersburg performances and recognized the play's beauty and importance (these letters continued arriving until the end of 1896), nor the news that Nikolai Solovtsov had staged a Kiev production of *The Seagull* which was received with great enthusiasm by Kiev audiences and newspapers managed to dispel his bitterness and disappointment completely. He at first turned down Lavrov's and Goltsev's offer to publish the text of the play in *Russian Thought* and gave his permission only after their repeated and insistent pleas. In its printed form *The Seagull* brought Chekhov many new admirers, but it was also rejected and disliked by some intelligent and articulate people, among them Tolstoy, who thought it an inept imitation of Ibsen. After its magazine publication, Chekhov allowed Suvorin to include *The Seagull* in a volume of his collected plays. There it was unexpectedly joined by *Uncle Vanya,* which had not been published or performed anywhere previously, or even mentioned in Chekhov's correspondence.

Chekhov spent the last two months of 1896 correcting the proofs of "My Life," which was serialized in the monthly literary supplement to the popular magazine *The Cornfield* (*Niva*), and writing "The Peasants," first published in *Russian Thought* in April of 1897. These were two of the most significant works of his maturity. "My Life" is a short novel about a young nobleman who rejects the values of his father and of his social class. It is a description of what in today's America has come to be called dropping out, except that Chekhov's Misail Poloznev does his dropping out the hardest possible way. Instead of expressing his protest by joining the dissident revolutionary counterculture, as many of his contemporaries did, he decides to become a member of the proletariat. He does it openly and honestly, without self-dramatization and, above all, as a purely private, personal gesture. He is cursed by his uncomprehending father, harassed by provincial authorities, admired by a few intellectuals who understand his motivation, and mostly resented by the common laborers with whom he tries to live. At the end of the story, after losing the woman he loves and bringing tragedy into his sister's life, Misail attains integrity and moral stature, but his path is shown to have been a hard and lonely one. "The Peasants" was the result of Chekhov's close, first-hand observations of the conditions in which the peasants around Melikhovo lived. Similar in method to some of the recent American semi-fictionalized studies of urban poverty, "The Peasants" is an overwhelmingly vivid closeup of what living on the edge of starvation will do to human beings and to their relationships with each other. In no other work is Chekhov's biological training and adherence to scientific methods so telling: where another writer would try to shock or to involve the reader, Chekhov offers him sober and precise observations of peasant life, which make the harrowing conditions described all the more real and believable.

Both "My Life" and "The Peasants" had considerable trouble passing the official censorship. The sympathetic presentation of a young man's rejection of the ruling-class culture and the demonstration of how little the government and the Church did to alleviate the physical misery in which a large percentage of the population of the Russian Empire lived—this was strong stuff indeed. Numerous cuts were made by the censors in both these stories, but before the year was over, they were published by Suvorin in a volume in which not only were the censors' deletions restored, but some of the objectionable formulations reinforced and made more pointed. The fact that the pro-government Suvorin was the publisher apparently made it possible to print things that could not be allowed to appear in the liberal-dissenting *Russian Thought* of Lavrov.

"My Life" was largely overlooked by the critics at the time of its publication, but "The Peasants" created a greater sensation in the press than any of Chekhov's other published works. The peasant problem was of tremendous concern to everyone, and various political and economic factions tried to use Chekhov's story to support their own view of what needed to be done and to disprove their opponents' theories. The leader of the "legal" Marxists saw in "The Peasants" an indictment of Populist views; the followers of Tolstoy insisted that Chekhov neither knew nor understood the Russian peasants; while Nikolai Mikhailovsky characterized it as the weakest thing Chekhov ever wrote and cautioned against drawing any conclusions about peasant life on the basis of anything written by such an irresponsible writer. The success of these two works with the general reader was genuine and spectacular. Chekhov's older contemporaries could remember nothing comparable to the excitement generated by the publication of "The Peasants" since the first appearance of the major novels by Turgenev or Dostoyevsky. It was after "My Life" and "The Peasants" that most educated Russians realized that in Chekhov their country had a truly great living writer, second only to Tolstoy in importance.

Early in 1897, the Russian government was conducting a population census. Believing that the availability of precise demographic and economic information about the countryside might eventually lead to improved living conditions for the peasants, Chekhov became deeply involved in the strenuous census taking in the neighboring villages. But in March an event occurred which forced him to slow down his pace and eventually to change his entire mode of life. By 1897 Chekhov had had tuberculosis for at least ten years without realizing it. All the expected symptoms were there: racking cough, night sweat, palpitations, spitting blood. He still refused to see another doctor about any of these symptoms, and when the possibility of tuberculosis was mentioned by others, he'd reply that if he had it, he would have been dead years ago. On March 22, 1897, Chekhov met Suvorin for dinner at one of Moscow's most elegant restaurants, the Hermitage. During the first course, Chekhov opened his mouth to say something, a torrent of blood came out and he collapsed at the table. He had hemorrhages again the next day and the next. On March 25, his colleague Dr. Nikolai Obolonsky (the same one who had deprived him of rowboats by not sending them to Luka some nine years earlier), prevailed on Chekhov to allow himself to be hospitalized and to get a thorough medical examination, apparently his first one since his student days. At the clinic of Dr. Ostroumov, where he was taken, tuberculosis in an advanced stage, affecting both lungs, was diagnosed.

99. To Alexei Suvorin

Melikhovo,
January 17, 1897

Today is my saint's day!!

You can't stay in the Panayev Theater, of course. There's a crying need for a theater, and if you don't build one someone else will, and then you'll be angry at yourself for the rest of your life and heap abuse on the new theater in your newspaper. There's no risk whatsoever involved in building a new theater.[1]

You ask me when I'm coming. The problem is, I'm terribly busy.[2] I've never had as much work as I do now. It's hard for me to take the time off, but I'll have to spend some time in St. Petersburg before spring in any case, for something very important—important mainly for me.

Russian Thought is doing a brisk book business. There's a tremendous demand in the provinces for serious scientific literature. The bookstore is in a room adjoining the editorial offices, next door to the business office. There are educated people on the sales staff. Sytin's new gray-covered self-teaching manuals based on English models are also selling briskly.

As for whether the plague will strike us, nothing definite can be said at present. If it does, it probably won't raise much of a fright; both populace and doctors have long since grown used to the accelerated mortality rate caused by diphtheria, typhus, typhoid fever and the like. After all, even without the plague no more than four hundred out of a thousand reach the age of five here; in villages and in cities, at factories and on back streets you won't find a single healthy woman. The most frightening thing about the plague is that it will make its appearance two or three months after the census. The peasants will put their own interpretation on the census and start pouncing on the doctors, claiming they have been poisoning the excess population so there is more land left over for the landowners. Quarantine measures are not strong enough. Khavkin's inoculations do offer some hope, but unfortunately Khavkin is unpopular in Russia: "Christians have to be on their guard against him; he's a Jew."[3]

Write me something. I wish you all the best.

Yours,
A. Chekhov

The clock Alexei Petrovich sent has breathed its last. Pavel Bouré announced to me yesterday it cannot be repaired—and the clock has now gone for scrap.[4]

1. The private theatrical company organized by Suvorin was temporarily housed in the Panayev Theater in St. Petersburg. Suvorin had apparently asked Chekhov's advice as to whether he should build his own theater.

2. Chekhov was deeply involved in census taking at the time.

3. Dr. Vladimir Khavkin was a Russian bacteriologist and a disciple of Louis Pasteur. In 1897, he was testing a vaccine against the bubonic plague in Bombay.

4. Alexei Kolomnin had sent Chekhov an elegant clock in a leather case, and it had arrived smashed. Pavel Bouré was the best-known watchmaker in Moscow.

100. To Vladimir Yakovenko[1]

Melikhovo,
January 30, 1897

Dear Vladimir Ivanovich,

Having read your letter in *The Physician*, I wrote to Moscow to have my *Island of Sakhalin* sent to you. In it you will find some information on corporal punishment and, incidentally, a reference to Yadrintsev,[2] whom I recommend to you. If you contact Senator Anatoly Fyodorovich Koni by mail, he will probably agree to tell you which literary sources he used while writing the biography of the well-known philanthropist Dr. Haas (the prison doctor).[3] I also recommend Kistyakovsky's[4] study of capital punishment; it is an account of all the tortures that the punishers have ever inflicted on the punished.

By the way, lawyers and jailers understand corporal punishment (in the narrow, physical sense) to encompass more than birch rods, lashes or blows with the fist. They also include shackles, unheated cells, withholding of meals (as practiced on schoolboys), bread and water, prolonged kneeling, repeated bowing to the ground and being tied to a post.

The census has exhausted me. I've never before had so little time for anything.

I wish you all the best and clasp your hand.

Yours,
A. Chekhov

My humble regards to Nadezhda Fyodorovna and Drs. Heinicke and Vasilyev.

That corporal punishment affects physical health is evident from the doctors' statements you will find in the court proceedings involving charges of torture.

Koni's address is: Anatoly Fyodorovich Koni, Nevsky Prospect 100, Petersburg.

1. Dr. Vladimir Yakovenko (1857–1923) was a noted Russian psychiatrist. At the Sixth Congress of the Russian Medical Association he was elected to head a committee charged with collecting evidence in support of a petition to the government to abolish corporal punishment in prisons. Accordingly, Yakovenko and a colleague published a letter to the editor in the January issue of *The Physician* asking the readers of that journal to supply

them with case histories of patients whose health was demonstrably harmed by corporal punishment. Chekhov, who had met Yakovenko and his wife, Nadezhda, previously, is here writing in response to this request for information.

2. Yadrintsev was the author of a study dealing with the life of convicts in Siberia.

3. Dr. Fyodor Haas (1780–1858) was a much-admired humanitarian of the early nineteenth century. He brought about important reforms in the treatment of prison inmates and he spent all of his personal earnings on helping them. At the time this letter was written, Anatoly Koni was working on his biography of Dr. Haas, which was published in book form later in 1897.

4. A. F. Kistyakovsky's book on the death penalty was published in St. Petersburg one year earlier.

101. To Alexei Suvorin

Moscow,
February 8, 1897

The census is over.[1] I've had enough of the whole business; I had to count and write until my fingers ached and issue instructions to fifteen census takers. The census takers did an excellent job, though they were almost ridiculously pedantic. On the other hand the land captains who were in charge of the census in the districts behaved disgracefully. They did nothing, understood little and, when the going was at its roughest, pleaded illness. The best of them turned out to be a vodka-loving prevaricator à la Khlestakov,[2] who was a character suitable for a comedy if nothing else. The rest of them were as colorless as hell, and it was irritating to have to deal with them.

I am in Moscow at the Grand Moscow Hotel. I'll be staying here a while, about ten days, and then go home. All through Lent and all through April I'll be tied up with carpenters and caulkers and such. I'm building another school. A deputation of peasants came and begged me, and I didn't have the heart to say no. The *zemstvo* is putting up a thousand, the peasants have collected three hundred—no more, and the school can't possibly cost less than three thousand. Which means I'll be spending another summer thinking about money and scraping it together here and there. All in all, life in the country involves a lot of bother. In view of imminent expenses it is very much to the point to ask whether you've sent the contract to the theater administration.[3]

Guess who's been to see me! Who do you think? It's Ozerova, the famous Ozerova-Hannele. She arrives, sits with her feet on the couch, and never looks you in the face. When the time comes for her to leave, she puts on her jacket and worn-out galoshes with the awkwardness of a little girl ashamed of her poverty. She's a little queen in exile.[4]

The astronomer, on the other hand, has perked up. She is running all over Moscow giving lessons and is carrying on debates with Klyuchevsky.[5] She's almost recovered and is apparently beginning to regain her former pace. We collected two hundred fifty rubles for her, which are in my keeping, but it's been a year and a half now and she still has not touched them.

Chertkov, the well-known Tolstoy disciple, has had his apartment searched. Everything Tolstoy's followers had collected about the Dukhobors and all other sects was confiscated, and thus all the evidence against Mr. Pobedonostsev and his satanic hosts has disappeared in a flash, as if by magic. Goremykin went to see Chertkov's mother and told her, "Your son has a choice: either the Baltic provinces, where Prince Khilkov is already living in exile, or abroad." Chertkov chose London. He's leaving February 13th. Tolstoy has gone to Petersburg to see him off, and yesterday they sent Tolstoy his warm coat, which he had left behind. Many people are going to see him off, even Sytin, and I am sorry I cannot do the same. I cherish no tender feelings for Chertkov, but I am deeply, deeply outraged at what they have done to him.[6]

Why not stop in Moscow on your way to Paris? It would be nice if you did.

Yours,
A. Chekhov

1. Chekhov worked as census taker and supervisor continuously from January 10 to February 5, 1897.

2. The bragging young impostor in Gogol's *The Inspector General.*

3. Chekhov still had not received his royalties for the five performances of *The Seagull* in St. Petersburg because of a mix-up about his signature on the contract.

4. On February 22, 1897, Chekhov wrote in his notebook: "Went to Serpukhov to see the amateur theatricals for the benefit of the Novoselki school. Hannele Ozerova traveled with me as far as Tsaritsyno. She's a little queen in exile imagining herself to be a great actress; she's illiterate and rather vulgar." Chekhov seems to have seen quite a lot of Lyudmila Ozerova in the early months of 1897. The wording in the Russian original that connects Ozerova's name with the heroine of Gerhart Hauptmann's *Hanneles Himmelfahrt* (known simply as *Hannele* in both Russian and English) may be interpreted to mean that she was a famous performer of Hannele (i.e., "Ozerova of Hannele fame"). But Hauptmann's play was banned by ecclesiastic censorship in Russia as sacrilegious and except for a single performance in honor

of the coronation of Nicholas II, directed by Stanislavsky, it was not played. Therefore it seems more likely that Chekhov is using the name of Hauptmann's heroine as a nickname for Ozerova.

5. Vasily Klyuchevsky was a famous historian, the author of the standard history of Russia used in Chekhov's time. He was Olga Kundasova's (the "astronomer's") teacher at the Vladimir Guerrier courses, where she attended his classes together with Maria Chekhova.

6. The beginning of the reign of Nicholas II was marked by intensified government persecution of religious minorities. Tolstoy and his disciples collected evidence of such persecution, which was carried out at the instigation of the sinister Ober-Procurator of the Holy Synod, Konstantin Pobedonostsev. Among his prime victims at that time was the Dukhobor sect. The aim of the search operation Chekhov describes (it took place on February 2) was double: to destroy evidence of religious persecution which could be used abroad and to separate Tolstoy from his most intransigent apostle, Chertkov. Ivan Goremykin was the Minister of the Interior, and Prince Dmitry Khilkov was an aristocratic disciple of Tolstoy who was exiled by the government and had his children taken away from him for following Tolstoy's teachings. During Tolstoy's stay in St. Petersburg, where he went to say good-bye to Chertkov and two other disciples who were being exiled to remote provinces, he had a conversation with Suvorin in which he expressed his negative opinion of *The Seagull.* As Tolstoy was leaving to return to Moscow a tremendous public demonstration of support and sympathy took place at the railroad station. Two years after this incident, Tolstoy helped a large number of Dukhobors and members of other persecuted Russian sects to emigrate to Canada and the United States.

102. To Alexei Suvorin

Melikhovo,
March 1, 1897

I stayed in Moscow some twenty days, spent all my advances and now I'm at home, leading a chaste and sober life. If you go to Moscow during the third week of Lent, I will too. I am presently spending my time building[1] (for the *zemstvo*, not for myself), but I can get away provided you send me a wire to Lopasnya a couple of days ahead of time. At the actors' conference you'll probably see the plans for the huge people's theater we are planning. *We* means the representatives of the Moscow intelligentsia (the intelligentsia is meeting the capitalists halfway, and the capitalists are not averse to reciprocating). A theater, auditorium, library, reading room, buffets and so on and so forth will be gathered under one roof in a neat, attractive building. The blueprints are ready,[2] the constitution being drafted, and the only thing that is holding us up is a paltry half million. There will be stockholders, but it will not be a charitable organization. We are counting on the government's sanctioning us to issue one-hundred-ruble shares. I've become so caught up in the project I already believe in its success and can only wonder why you don't build a theater. In the first place, it's needed. And, in the second, it's fun and will take up two years of your life. If the theater building is not constructed nonsensically, if it doesn't resemble the Panayev Theater, it can't possibly operate at a loss.

I recently helped arrange a benefit performance in Serpukhov to raise funds for the school. The actors were amateurs from Moscow. Their acting was quite respectable, even restrained, and better than that of professionals. There were Paris gowns and genuine diamonds, but all we netted was a hundred and one rubles.[3]

There's no news, or rather there is, but it's uninteresting or sad. There is much talk about the plague and the war and about the Synod and the Ministry of Education merging into one body. Levitan, the landscape painter, seems close to death.[4] He has an aneurysm of the aorta.

I'm having bad luck. I've written a short novel based on peasant life, but people say it will never pass the censors and will have to be cut by half.[5] In other words, more losses.

If we have good spring weather in Moscow, let's go to Sparrow Hills and the monastery. From Moscow we'll go together to Petersburg, where I have a piece of business to attend to.[6]

I've written you and you haven't written back, so I've authorized my brother to pay you a visit and find out what the matter is. I've also asked him to find out the location of the contract the theater management sent me and is now demanding back.

Has Davydov left the Empress Alexandra Theater? What a capricious hippopotamus.

Well, I'll be seeing you soon. In the meantime drop me a line or two. My humble regards to Anna Ivanovna, Nastya and Borya.

Be happy.

Yours,
A. Chekhov

1. The village school at Novoselki, not far from Melikhovo.

2. The plans for this "popular theater," i.e., a theater with cheaply priced seats and with a repertoire designed for audiences with little or no education, were drawn up by Chekhov's architect friend Schechtel. For all the enthusiasm expressed in this letter, the project never got off the ground.

3. According to Mikhail Chekhov's *Around Chekhov*, the "Paris gowns and genuine diamonds" were worn by Yelena Shavrova and her sister Olga,

who on Chekhov's invitation agreed to come and help a group of amateurs put on a play for the benefit of the village school at Novoselki.

4. Chekhov's friend Levitan died in 1900. In accordance with his last wish, his brother destroyed all his correspondence after his death, which deprived the world of a large number of Chekhov's letters.

5. "The Peasants."

6. Apparently a reference to Chekhov's consent to pose for a portrait which the owner of the Tretyakov Gallery commissioned Iosif Braz to paint for that gallery's series of portraits of Russian writers.

103. To Rimma Vashchuk[1]

Moscow,
March 27, 1897

Dear Madam,

I read your story "In the Hospital" in the clinic, where I am now confined. I'm writing my reply from my bed. The story is very good, starting from the point I marked in red. But the beginning is banal and unnecessary. You ought to continue, provided, of course, that you enjoy writing, that's condition number one; condition number two is that you're young and can still learn how to punctuate properly.

As far as your "Fairy Tale" is concerned, I wouldn't call it a fairy tale. It seems to me more like a conglomeration of words like gnome, fairy, dew and knights—all of which are fake diamonds, at least on Russian soil, which has never known the tread of knights or gnomes and where you'll have trouble finding anyone who can picture a fairy dining on dew and moonbeams. Drop all that. You must be a sincere artist and depict only what exists or what in your opinion should be; you must paint coherent pictures.

To go back to the first story: you shouldn't write so much about yourself. You write about yourself, you yield to exaggeration, and you run the risk of ending up the loser. Either people won't believe you or they'll be cold to your effusions.

I wish you all the best.

A. Chekhov

1. Arriving at his hotel in Moscow on March 21, Chekhov found a note from Rimma Vashchuk, who described herself as an experienced writer who had been "writing for many years" and asked him to look at some of her manuscripts. She was in fact a schoolgirl of seventeen who had just begun her studies in the women's courses of Moscow University. Chekhov complied with her request, but was able to read her stories only after he was hospitalized at Dr. Ostroumov's clinic.

104. To Rimma Vashchuk

Moscow,
March 28, 1897

Instead of getting angry,[1] why don't you read my letter through a little more attentively. I clearly stated, did I not, that your story is *very good,* except the beginning, which feels like an arbitrarily added structure. It is not up to me to permit or prohibit you to write. I referred to your youth because at thirty or forty it is too late to start. I referred to the need for learning to punctuate properly because in a work of art punctuation often plays the part of musical notation and can't be learned from a textbook; it requires instinct and experience. Enjoying writing doesn't mean playing or having a good time. Experiencing enjoyment from an activity means loving that activity.

Forgive me, I'm having trouble writing; I'm still in bed.

Read my letter once more and stop being angry. I was totally sincere then, and I'm writing you again now because I sincerely wish you success.

A. Chekhov

1. After reading the preceding letter, Rimma Vashchuk sent Chekhov an angry reply in which she accused him of "pouring cold water on her ardent dreams" and said that she expected "more heart and more generosity" from Chekhov. Upon receiving the present letter, she sent Chekhov a note of apology for her rudeness. She published Chekhov's letters to her in the Soviet journal *The Young Guard* in 1957, one year before her own death.

105. To Alexei Suvorin

Moscow,
April 1, 1897

The doctors have diagnosed pulmonary apical lesions and have ordered me to change my way of life. I can understand the former but not the latter, because it is almost impossible. They order me to live in the country, but living permanently in the country presupposes constant fussing about with peasants, animals and the elements in all their forms, and it is as difficult to avoid cares and anxieties in the country as to avoid burns in hell. But I will still try to change my life as much as possible, and I've already sent word with Masha that I will no longer practice medicine in the country. It will be both a relief and a great deprivation for me. I am giving up all my district duties and buying a dressing gown, and I will bask in the sun and eat and eat. My doctors have ordered me to eat about six times daily, and they are indignant at finding I eat so little. I am forbidden to do much talking, to go swimming and so on and so forth.

All my organs besides the lungs were found to be healthy. [. . .] Until now I felt I had been drinking exactly as much as I could without doing any harm to myself, but it turns out I'd been drinking less than I was entitled to. What a shame!

The author of "Ward Number Six" has been transferred from ward number sixteen to ward number fourteen. It is spacious and has two windows, Potapenko-type lighting, and three tables. I am not losing much blood. After Tolstoy came to see me one evening (we talked at great length), I hemorrhaged violently at four in the morning.[1]

Melikhovo is a healthful spot. It's right on a watershed and at a good altitude, so it's free from fever and diphtheria. After taking counsel, we all decided I should continue living at Melikhovo and not go off anywhere. All I have to do is make the house a bit more comfortable. When I get tired of Melikhovo, I'll go to the neighboring estate I've rented for my brothers when they come to visit.

I have a constant stream of visitors. They bring me flowers and candy and things to eat. Heaven, in a word.[2]

I read about the performance at Pavlova Hall in the *Petersburg Gazette*.[3] Tell Nastya that had I been there I would definitely have presented her with a basket of flowers. My most humble respects and greetings to Anna Ivanovna.

By now I can write sitting up instead of lying on my back, but as soon as I finish writing, I go back to reclining on my sickbed.

Yours,
A. Chekhov

Please write, I beg of you.

1. Tolstoy visited Chekhov at Dr. Ostroumov's clinic on March 28. Visitors were restricted to ten minutes but Tolstoy stayed for more than thirty. The medical personnel at the clinic must have realized that Tolstoy's visit was exciting and exhausting their patient, but there was nothing they could do: one didn't ask Lev Tolstoy to leave. The two writers argued about the premises of Tolstoy's treatise *What Is Art?* (see next letter) and talked about immortality. On April 16, Chekhov wrote to Mikhail Menshikov: "Tolstoy came to see me while I was at the clinic and we had a most interesting conversation, interesting mainly for me because I listened more than I talked. We discussed immortality. He recognizes immortality in its Kantian form, assuming that all of us (men and animals) will live on in some principle (such as

reason or love), the essence of which is a mystery. But I can only imagine such a principle or force as a shapeless, gelatinous mass; my I, my individuality, my consciousness would merge with this mass—and I feel no need for this kind of immortality, I do not understand it, and Lev Nikolayevich was astonished that I don't."

In the course of this visit, Chekhov told Tolstoy of an article he had read about the folk theater of the Siberian tribe of Voguls. Tolstoy later used this account in the final version of *What Is Art?*, where he cited the Vogul theater as an example of simple, infectious and therefore good art.

2. In addition to Tolstoy, Chekhov was visited at the clinic by Lydia Avilova, Lyudmila Ozerova and Ivan Shcheglov. After the news of his illness spread, he had to suffer a steady stream of callers. On April 7, he wrote to Suvorin: "Yesterday I had visitors all day long, it was simply disastrous. They let them in two at a time, they would all ask me not to talk but at the same time they kept asking questions." There were also a large number of letters from well wishers, which Chekhov had to answer personally.

3. A charity soirée, at which Suvorin's daughter Anastasia (Nastya) made her acting debut, appearing in the company of Savina and Kommissarzhevskaya. According to the annotations in Suvorin's published journals, she was active as an actress in the United States in the 1920s.

106. To Alexander Ertel

Melikhovo,
April 17, 1897

My dear friend Alexander Ivanovich,

I'm at home now. Before Easter I spent two weeks in Ostroumov's clinic coughing blood. The doctor diagnosed apical lesions in my lungs. I feel splendid. I feel no pain whatsoever and nothing bothers me internally. But the doctors have forbidden me *vinum*,[1] motion and talk, ordered me to eat a lot and forbidden me to practice—and I am bored, as it were.

There is no news of the people's theater. It was discussed at the conference in a muted and uninteresting manner, and the group in charge of drafting the constitution and getting things started seems to have lost its enthusiasm.[2] It must be because of spring. The only member of the group I've seen is Goltsev, and I didn't have a chance to discuss the theater with him.

There's no news. Literature is at a standstill. A lot of tea and cheap wine is being consumed in editorial offices without much pleasure, for no other reason, apparently, than that there's nothing better to do. Tolstoy is writing a book on art. He visited me at the clinic and told me that he'd abandoned his *Resurrection* because he didn't like it and that he was now writing exclusively about art and had read sixty books on the subject. His idea is not new; it's been reiterated in various forms by clever old men in every century. Old men have always been inclined to think the end of the world is at hand and to assert that morals have fallen to the *nec plus ultra*, that art has grown shallow and threadbare, that people have grown weak, and so on and so forth. Lev Nikolayevich is out to convince everybody in his book that art has in our time entered upon its final phase, that it is stuck in a blind alley from which it has no way out (forward).[3]

I do nothing but feed the sparrows with hempseed and prune a rosebush a day. When I prune them, the rosebushes bloom luxuriantly.[4] I have no household duties.

Keep well, dear Alexander Ivanovich. Thank you for your letters and your friendly concern. Write me for my infirmity's sake, and don't reproach me too greatly for not keeping up my end of the correspondence. From now on I will try to answer your letters the moment I read them.

I clasp your hand warmly.

Yours,
A. Chekhov

1. Actually, all alcoholic beverages.
2. Cf. Letter 102.
3. Chekhov rejected *in toto* two of the basic premises of Tolstoy's *What Is Art?* even before reading it, namely the idea that in order to be good, moral and "infectious," a work of art has to be instantly comprehensible to an illiterate peasant or to a child (a premise that led Tolstoy to his violent rejection of Shakespeare, Baudelaire and Wagner as being inaccessible and immoral) and the concomitant notion that all the arts and especially painting and music were going through a period of utter decline throughout the Western world at the end of the nineteenth century. Chekhov's disagreement deepened after he read the published work.
4. Chekhov was widely admired by his neighbors around Melikhovo for his way with plants. His rosebushes were considered particularly remarkable, and some of his published letters to his neighbors contain advice on the care and treatment of roses.

107. To Prince Vladimir Argutinsky-Dolgorukov[1]

Melikhovo,
April 28, 1897

I envy you, dear Vladimir Nikolayevich. I envy your stay in England,[2] your knowledge of English, and your youth and health.

I like your story, but it's not your work, is it? It's a translation from English. There's not a single Russian sentence in it, not a one! I enjoyed it very much, and I hasten to do your bidding: I am returning it to you, on the condition, however, that you send me another story as soon as possible. I am interested in following your beginnings and in seeing where you finally arrive. Only, please do write more; writing so little will get you nowhere. You must hurry and develop a skilled hand so that by the time you're thirty your work will have a definite character and you can win yourself a place in the literary market.

I spent March and early April in a clinic. I was coughing blood. Things are better now. The spring is magnificent, but I'm so short of money that I'm at my wits' end.

Well then, I'll be looking forward to your story and letter. Keep well. I clasp your hand and wish you all the best.

Yours,
A. Chekhov

Give my regards to Balmont and his wife.[3]

1. Argutinsky-Dolgorukov was twenty when he briefly met Chekhov in Odessa in 1894. On December 29, 1894, he wrote Chekhov a letter in which he reminded him of their acquaintance and said: "Our brief encounter in Odessa made such an indelible impression on me that since then, in moments of sadness or dissatisfaction, the thought of you awakens within me with such power that I want to talk only of you and to share with others the spell that your personality casts over everyone." Chekhov replied with a friendly letter and offered to meet Argutinsky-Dolgorukov in Moscow. He came to believe that this young man might possess a literary talent and strongly encouraged him to write fiction. But, despite Chekhov's encouragement and his own half-hearted efforts, nothing worth publishing was ever produced by the young prince.

2. Argutinsky-Dolgorukov was studying at Oxford.

3. The poet Konstantin Balmont (see Letter 155) was giving a series of lectures on Russian poetry at Oxford at the invitation of the Taylor Institute.

XII

NICE. THE DREYFUS CASE

CHEKHOV'S CONVALESCENCE after he returned to Melikhovo proceeded slowly, handicapped by his inability to curtail his numerous activities and involvements as the doctors had ordered him to do. The same stream of visitors and well wishers of which he had complained at the Ostroumov clinic continued at Melikhovo, with people who had come to inquire about the state of his health staying overnight, then staying for a few days, and requiring to be fed and housed. Both Chekhov and his family received such visitors with unfailing hospitality, and only occasionally do we detect a note of irritation in his reaction, as in the letter to Leykin of July 4, 1897: "I have enough house guests to fill a pond. I'm out of space, out of bedding and out of patience conversing with them." As soon as he was able to move about, his time was claimed by the *zemstvo*, by the school where he was honorary superintendent, by the library affairs in Taganrog and by a special clinic for alcoholics which he was helping to organize. There were trips to surrounding villages, to Serpukhov and to Moscow. Chekhov probably would not have lasted for more than two years had his doctors not insisted categorically that he not spend his winters in the harsh climate of Central Russia. They urged him to move either to the Crimea or to the French Riviera. He accordingly decided to spend the winter of 1897–98 in Nice, the city whose status as the Mecca for tubercular patients from all over the world was so grimly described by Maupassant in *Sur l'eau*.

Chekhov left Russia on September 1, 1897, and stayed in France until early May of 1898. He settled in Nice at the Pension Russe, a boardinghouse for visiting Russians on Rue Gounod, where Mikhail Saltykov-

Shchedrin had also once resided. It was owned by a Russian lady and was especially celebrated for its elegant Russian-style cuisine (a typical dinner menu: borscht, *poisson glacé*, squab, veal, salad greens, ice cream and fruit). Chekhov's most frequent companion in Nice was Maxim Kovalevsky, a professor of sociology who had been dismissed from Moscow University in 1887 on political grounds (as Chekhov put it in a letter to his sister, "for being a freethinker"). There were also visitors from Russia: Potapenko, the artist Alexandra Khotyaintseva, the actor-playwright Alexander Sumbatov and others. The stories Chekhov wrote in Nice deal for the most part with people trapped in remote Russian provinces: "In the Cart," about a selfless young village schoolmistress who finds some satisfaction in her work despite the atrocious working conditions; "The Homecoming" (V *rodnom uglu*), in which a young girl prefers a loveless marriage to provincial stagnation and idleness; and "Ionych," a portrait of a pleasant young doctor who gradually degenerates into a selfish, obese miser in an environment of provincial inactivity. It was also in Nice that Chekhov began writing his 1898 trilogy of stories about human self-domestication, consisting of "The Man in a Shell," his great study of deliberate conformity; "Gooseberries," which dissects self-enslavement in response to the acquisitive instinct; and "About Love," which shows a case of the suppression of the natural desire to love under the weight of custom and convention. The common framework shared by these three stories underlines the unity of their themes and outlook.

Chekhov's stay in Nice coincided with the reopening of the Dreyfus case, which had been racking France since 1894. Chekhov followed the most recent developments in the case—the acquittal of Major Esterhazy, the true perpetrator of the crime for which Dreyfus had been convicted, at a patently rigged court-martial; the publication of Émile Zola's celebrated article "J'accuse," denouncing that acquittal; and Zola's own trial on charges of libel—both in the Russian press and in various French newspapers (it was in Nice that he finally learned to read French fluently). After reading the transcripts of the original trial, Chekhov became convinced of the falsity of the charges against Dreyfus. It came as something of a shock to Chekhov to realize to what extent the case and its new developments were distorted in much of the Russian press. He was particularly revolted by the stance taken by Suvorin's *New Times*, which represented the reopening of the case and the trial of Esterhazy as a shady conspiracy cooked up by an international Jewish syndicate. Chekhov made resolute efforts to convince Suvorin of the injustice of his paper's position, but Suvorin, although in his talks with Chekhov he agreed with his arguments, was either unwilling or unable to change the anti-Semitic policy of his editors and staff. Chekhov's involvement with the Dreyfus affair reached its peak during his visit to Paris in April, 1898, when, after making the personal acquaintance of Mathieu Dreyfus (the brother of the defendant) and Bernard Lazare, the journalist whose disclosures had led to the reopening of the case, he agreed to be interviewed by Lazare and to lend the prestige of his name to the Dreyfusard cause. But Lazare let someone else write up the notes of his interview with Chekhov, with the result that when Chekhov was sent the text for approval he found his own statements and opinions distorted. The trend of the entire piece was to present Chekhov not as defending Dreyfus but as denouncing Russian public opinion and the Russian government (Chekhov's letter to Ivan Pavlovsky of April 28, 1898). This left Chekhov with no choice but to veto the publication of the interview.

108. To Alexandra Khotyaintseva[1]

Biarritz,[2]
September 17, 1897

You ask me, most esteemed artist, if the weather is warm here. In the first few days after I arrived, it was cold and damp, but now I'm as hot as if I were in a baker's oven. It is especially hot after lunch, which consists of six greasy courses and a whole bottle of white wine. The single most interesting thing here is the ocean: it roars even in quiet weather. From morning till night I sit in the *Grande Plage* and swallow newspapers, while a motley crowd of cabinet ministers, wealthy Jews, Adelaides,[3] Spaniards and poodles passes before me. The ladies' dresses, varicolored parasols, the bright sunshine, lots of water, cliffs, harps, guitars, singing—all this combined carries me a hundred thousand versts away from Melikhovo.

When are you coming to Paris? It's nice there now.

A few days ago there was a cowfight in Bayonne. Spanish picadors engaged in combat with cows. Spunky little cows, evil-tempered and quite agile, ran about the arena like dogs, chasing the picadors. The spectators were in a frenzy.[4]

Makovsky[5] is here. He is painting portraits of the ladies.

Keep well. Give my regards to your mama and your brother and remember me in your orisons. Thanks for your letter.

Yours,
A. Chekhov

1. Alexandra Khotyaintseva (1865–1942) was an artist of some talent. Her drawings and sketches of Chekhov, made during his stay in Nice, com-

bine the method of a newspaper cartoon with some Toulouse-Lautrec-like features. She was another attractive woman brought into Chekhov's life by his sister, who met her at an evening art course in which they were both enrolled. Khotyaintseva became a frequent visitor at Melikhovo, and when Chekhov went to Nice, she suddenly appeared there, too. Although she was clearly smitten with Chekhov and although he wrote to his sister that he found her more pleasant and intelligent than the other ladies he met at the Pension Russe, he insisted they remain merely good friends, and Khotyaintseva accepted the situation with much better grace than had Lika Mizinova when she was in a similar position a few years earlier. Alexandra Khotyaintseva wrote an amusing little memoir about Chekhov's life in Nice.

2. Chekhov went to Biarritz at the invitation of the wealthy Varvara Morozova and her editor-husband Sobolevsky (who wore a bathing suit on the Biarritz beach which, in Chekhov's opinion, made him look like Petronius Arbiter). He spent two weeks there, staying at the Victoria and passing leisurely days on the same beach where ten years later the eight-year-old Vladimir Nabokov would be playing with a little girl named Zina, also aged eight. Chekhov, for his part, acquired while in Biarritz, a nineteen-year-old teacher of French named Margot, of whom he wrote to Anna Suvorina and Lika Mizinova. Margot supposedly followed him to Nice at his suggestion, but for some reason was not able to locate him once she got there.

3. "Adelaide" was Chekhov's nickname for a certain lady, the wife of a military-school director, who was never without a lorgnette. It is used here, by extension, as a generic term to describe all lorgnette-carrying ladies.

4. Chekhov's reaction to this cowfight stands in amusing contrast to Vladimir Mayakovsky's account of the bullfight he witnessed in Mexico in 1925. Mayakovsky immediately identified with the bulls, and applauded a bull's goring of a spectator, feeling quite certain that the bull was doing it to avenge his fallen fellow bulls.

5. Konstantin Makovsky, an academic painter of opulent pseudo-historical pageants. His huge canvas depicting a rather operatic wedding ceremony in a boyar's family today graces the De Young Museum in San Francisco's Golden Gate Park.

109. To Alexei Suvorin

Nice,
October 1, 1897

You're not quite right about Gorev.[1] One time out of five he gives a good, even remarkable, performance. He has a bad way of raising his shoulders and firing out his lines, but sometimes, in some plays, he is capable of reaching a pitch of intensity which no other Russian actor can duplicate. He's particularly good when backed up by a good ensemble, when those around him are also giving good performances.

I am staying at the Russian boardinghouse here. My room is rather spacious and has a southern exposure, carpeting, a couch like Cleopatra's and a lavatory. The lunches and dinners are prepared by a Russian cook (borscht and meat pies), and the food is plentiful, as plentiful as at the Hôtel Vendôme and every bit as delicious. I pay eleven francs a day. The weather here is warm; even in the evening it doesn't feel like fall. The sea is touchingly affectionate. The Promenade des Anglais is all covered with verdure and looks radiant in the sun. Every morning I sit in the shade and read the paper. I do a lot of walking. I've made the acquaintance of Maxim Kovalevsky, a former Moscow professor who was dismissed under the provisions of Article 3.[2] He is a tall, fat, lively, utterly good-natured man. He eats a lot, jokes a lot, and works an awful lot, and I feel cheerful and lighthearted with him. He has a contagious, resonant sort of laugh. He lives in Beaulieu in his own pretty little villa. Yakobi[3] the artist is also here; he calls Grigorovich a blackguard and a swindler, Aivazovsky[4] a son of a bitch, Stasov an idiot, etc. Kovalevsky, Yakobi and I had dinner together the day before yesterday, and we laughed so much during the meal that our sides ached, much to the amazement of our waiters. I have oysters all the time.

Morozova writes it's cold in Biarritz: it's even gone below freezing. Paris is having beautiful weather judging by *Figaro*. If you go to Paris, I'll go too. But the way I see it you ought to come to Nice first to take in some sun, and then we could go on to Paris together. The weather in Nice, I repeat, is warm and very pleasant. Sitting on the embankment, basking in the sun and looking out to sea is sheer delight.

My regards and heartfelt greetings to Anna Ivanovna, Nastya and Borya. I wish you all the best. Don't pay any attention to that odd sensation in your legs. You have a very sound constitution.

Nice, Pension Russe.

Yours,
A. Chekhov

I miss Russian newspapers and get no letters.

1. The actor Fyodor Gorev, who back in 1888 played the male lead in the Moscow production of Suvorin's *Tatyana Repina* (cf. Letter 14, note 2). Gorev was an adherent of the emotional, underrehearsed school of acting and scored some of his greatest successes in intuitive and improvisational performances, introducing sudden pauses and bits of pantomime that came as total surprises to the other actors in the play.

2. After his dismissal from Moscow University for holding and advocating opinions that were considered subversive, Kovalevsky voluntarily chose to

emigrate and live abroad. In his memoir about his friendship with Chekhov, he quoted a sort of political credo he claimed to have pieced together from various lengthy conversations, despite Chekhov's aversion to political discussions. Here are two of that credo's most salient passages: "He wished particularly that the peasants be allowed to own their land, not as a group, but each as his personal property; that the peasants live in freedom, sobriety and material affluence and have at their disposal numerous schools and have proper medical facilities."

"Chekhov was not particularly concerned with the relative advantages of republic or monarchy, federalism or parliamentarism. But he wanted Russia to be free, purged of all national animosities, its peasantry given the same rights as all the other classes, allowed to participate in the *zemstvo* system and represented in the legislative assembly. A broad tolerance of various religious denominations, a press allowed to evaluate current affairs without hindrance from anyone or anything, freedom of assembly, association and political rallies, total equality of everyone before the law and in the courts—such were the indispensable conditions of that better future for which he consciously yearned and the advent of which he expected" (Maxim Kovalevsky, "On A. P. Chekhov," first published in 1915 in *Stock Exchange News*, St. Petersburg, and reprinted in Moscow in 1960 in the collection *Chekhov as Remembered by His Contemporaries*.

3. Valerian Yakobi, painter and illustrator, whose illustrations for *The Cornfield* were oleographically reproduced and sent to that journal's subscribers as bonuses. Chekhov enjoyed his humor but did not think much of his art.

4. Ivan Aivazovsky (1817–1900) was a painter of marine subjects whose very name became a synonym for art and beauty in nineteenth-century Russia. "A sight worthy of Aivazovsky's brush" was the standard way of describing something ineffably lovely (Chekhov quoted this phrase in *Uncle Vanya*). Aivazovsky's seascapes (remarkably similar to the pictures of waves and sea spray that one sees today in galleries specializing in commercial non-art) were a rare instance of noncivic, non-storytelling painting that nineteenth-century critics liked and praised.

Chekhov met Aivazovsky in person during his visit with the Suvorins in the Crimea in 1888. He described the encounter in his letter to Maria Chekhova of July 22, 1888:

> Yesterday I visited Shakh-Mamai, Aivazovsky's estate, situated some twenty-five versts from Feodosia. The estate is as opulent as something out of a magic tale, the sort of estate that one may probably still see in Persia. Aivazovsky himself is a hale and hearty old man of about seventy-five, looking like a mixture of an insignificant Armenian and an overfed bishop; he is full of a sense of his own importance, has soft hands and shakes your hand like a general. He's not very bright, but he is a complex personality, worthy of further study. In him alone there are combined a general, a bishop, an artist, an Armenian, a

naïve grandpa and an Othello. He is married to a very lovely young woman, whom he controls with an iron hand. Among his friends are sultans, shahs and emirs. He helped Glinka compose *Ruslan and Lyudmila* [it is a matter of historical record that Aivazovsky supplied Glinka with three Tatar folk melodies, which were all utilized in that opera]. He was a friend of Pushkin's but he has never read Pushkin. He has not read a single book in his life. When he is offered something to read, he says: "Why should I read it? I have my own opinions." I spent the whole day with him and stayed for dinner.

At that dinner Chekhov met Dr. Praskovya Tarnovskaya, née Kozlova, the wife of a famous venereal-disease specialist and a prominent writer of medical texts and a civic leader in her own right. She was also the sister of Vladimir Nabokov's maternal grandmother. Chekhov described his encounter with her in the already quoted letter to Maria: "She's an obese, bloated chunk of flesh. If she were stripped naked and painted green, she'd be a swamp frog. After a chat with her, I mentally crossed her off my list of physicians." For a more sympathetic and attractive view of Dr. Tarnovskaya, see Vladimir Nabokov, *Speak, Memory*, pp. 67–68.

110. To Alexei Suvorin

Nice,
January 4, 1898

Here is my schedule. At the end of January (old style),[1] or more probably at the beginning of February, I'm going to Algiers, Tunis, *et caetera*. I'll then come back to Nice to wait for you (you wrote you'd be coming to Nice), and after spending some time here we'll go to Paris together if you like, and from there take the express train to Russia in time to celebrate Easter. Your last letter arrived here unsealed.

I go to Monte Carlo very rarely, once every three or four weeks. When I first arrived and Sobolevsky and Nemirovich[2] were here, I gambled very moderately and at low stakes (*rouge et noir*) and would occasionally bring home fifty or a hundred francs. But then I had to give up gambling because it exhausts me—physically.

The Dreyfus case has gotten up steam and is on its way, but it's still not going full power ahead. Zola is a noble soul, and I (I belong to the syndicate and have already received a hundred francs from the Jews)[3] am delighted by his outburst.[4] France is a wonderful country and has wonderful writers.

On New Year's Eve I sent you a New Year's telegram. I'm afraid it may not have reached you in time because there was a large backlog of telegrams at the post office. So, just in case, I wish you a Happy New Year again, this time in writing.

Write and tell me whether I should expect you in Nice. I hope you haven't changed your mind.

Koni's friend Hirschmann,[5] the Kharkov eye doctor, a well-known philanthropist, has come to Nice to visit his tubercular son. He is a saintly man. We get together and talk from time to time, but his wife gets in the way. She is a fussy woman, not particularly bright, and more boring than forty thousand wives.[6] There is a Russian artist here, a woman, who draws ten to fifteen caricatures of me a day.[7]

Judging from the excerpt printed in *New Times*, Lev Nikolayevich's article on art is of no particular interest.[8] It's all so old hat. Saying that art has grown decrepit and entered a blind alley, that it isn't what it ought to be, and so on and so forth is like saying that the desire to eat and drink has gone out of date, outlived its usefulness, and is no longer necessary. Of course hunger is old hat and the desire to eat has led us into a blind alley, but eating is necessary all the same, and we will go on eating no matter what fortunes our philosophers and angry old men dream up for us in their clouded crystal balls.[9]

Keep well.

Yours,
A. Chekhov

1. Russians traveling abroad referred to the Julian calendar still in use in their country as "old style" and to the Western Gregorian calendar as "new style." Because Chekhov mentions the publication of Zola's article (see note 4 below), this letter must have been dated according to the Gregorian calendar.

2. Vladimir Nemirovich-Danchenko, the future founder of the Moscow Art Theater.

3. A sarcastic reference to the repeated assertions of *New Times* that anyone offering proof of the innocence of Dreyfus was in the pay of an international Jewish syndicate.

4. Émile Zola's "J'accuse," which outlined the conspiracy that led to the conviction of Dreyfus and the acquittal of Esterhazy, was published in *L'Aurore* on January 1, 1898.

5. Leonard Hirschmann, professor of medicine at the University of Kharkov.

6. There are numerous variations in Chekhov's stories and letters on a humorous formula that can be expressed schematically as: more (something) than forty thousand (some kind of relatives). The formula has its origin in Hamlet's lines (Act V, scene 1):

> I lov'd Ophelia; forty thousand brothers
> Could not (with all their quantity of love)
> Make up my sum.

7. Alexandra Khotyaintseva, some of whose drawings of Chekhov, Kovalevsky and various denizens of Pension Russe are reproduced in Volume 68 of *Literary Heritage*.

8. Tolstoy's *What Is Art?*, a portion of which was printed in *New Times* as a separate article.

9. "Clouded crystal balls" replaces an untranslatable reference to a Russian peasant saying about the use of beans for fortunetelling.

111. To Fyodor Batyushkov[1]

Nice,
January 23, 1898

Dear Fyodor Dmitrievich,

I am returning the proofs to you.[2] The printers didn't leave any margins, so I had to paste in my corrections.

Please send the reprints of your article, the one you wrote me about, to Nice.[3] I'll most likely be staying here until April, so I'll be bored, and your article will do me a double service.

All we talk about here is Zola and Dreyfus. The overwhelming majority of the intelligentsia is on Zola's side and believes that Dreyfus is innocent. Zola has been growing by leaps and bounds. His letters of protest are like a breath of fresh air, and every Frenchman now has the feeling that, thank God, there is still justice on this earth and that if an innocent man is convicted, there is someone to defend him.[4] French newspapers are extremely interesting, whereas Russian newspapers are hopeless. *New Times* is simply disgusting.

I hope you will send some copies of my story to my sister. Her address is: Maria Pavlovna Chekhova, Lopasnya, Moscow Province.

The weather here is wonderful and summery. I haven't once put on my galoshes or fall coat all winter, and in all that time I've had to carry an umbrella only twice.

Allow me to wish you all the best and to thank you for your concern, which I value highly. I clasp your hand, and looking forward to your article, I remain,

Sincerely and respectfully yours,
A. Chekhov

1. Fyodor Batyushkov (1857–1920) was a literary scholar and one of the founders of comparative-literature studies in Russia. He corresponded with Chekhov in his capacity as the editor of the Russian portion of *Cosmopolis*, an international journal published in Paris and St. Petersburg in four languages.

2. "A Visit with Friends," which Chekhov wrote at Batyushkov's request especially for *Cosmopolis.*

3. A published version of the lecture Batyushkov delivered at the Shakespeare Circle of St. Petersburg on the subject of "Peasants in Balzac, Chekhov and Korolenko."

4. The innocence of Dreyfus and the justice of Zola's position are repeatedly asserted in Chekhov's letters dating from this period. Here are two of the more eloquent passages:

To Alexandra Khotyaintseva, February 2, 1898:

> You ask me whether I still think that Zola is right. And I ask you: could you have such a poor opinion of me that you could doubt even for a moment that I am on Zola's side? One of his fingernails is more important than all those who now sit and judge him in the assizes, all those generals and noble witnesses. I've been reading the stenographic transcript and I cannot see where Zola was wrong and what other *preuves* are needed.

To Mikhail Chekhov and Mikhail's wife Olga, February 22, 1898:

> You ask what my opinion is about Zola and his trial. First of all, I take into account what is self-evident: all of Europe's intelligentsia is on Zola's side, and against him is everyone who is questionable and disgusting. Here is the way things stand: imagine the university administration dismissing one student instead of another due to an error. You start objecting and they shout at you: "You are insulting science!" although the only thing science and the university administration have in common is that both the administrators and the professors wear dark blue frock coats. You give them your word, you assure them, you expose the culprits and they shout at you: "Where's your proof?" "Very well," you say, "let's go to the registrar's office and have a look at the records." "You can't! That is classified information!" So what can you do? The motives of the French government are clear. Just as a respectable woman who was one single time unfaithful to her husband will then permit herself a series of flagrant indiscretions, fall victim to insolent blackmail and finally commit suicide, all in order to hide her first misdeed, so is the French government forging blindly ahead, stumbling left and right to avoid admitting its mistake.
>
> *New Times* is conducting an absurd campaign, but the majority of Russian newspapers, if not exactly on Zola's side, are opposed to prosecuting him. Appealing the sentence won't do any good, even if the outcome is favorable. The whole issue will be settled of its own accord, in some accidental way, as a result of the explosion of all those gases that are accumulating in Frenchmen's heads. It will all come out all right in the end.

112. To Alexei Suvorin

Nice,
February 6, 1898

The other day I was struck by the conspicuous advertisement on the first page of *New Times* announcing the publication of *Cosmopolis* with my story "On a Visit" in it. In the first place, my story is called "A Visit with Friends," not "On a Visit." In the second, that kind of publicity turns my stomach. Besides, the story itself is far from conspicuous; it's the kind that can be turned out one a day.

You write that you are irritated by Zola, while everyone here has the feeling a new and better Zola has been born. His trial has been as effective as turpentine in cleansing him of his incidental grease spots, and the French now see him shining in all his true radiance. There is a purity and moral intergrity in him that no one suspected. Try to follow the entire scandal from its very beginnings. Just or unjust, Dreyfus's demotion made a gloomy, disheartening impression on everyone (including you, now that I think of it). Everyone noticed that during the degradation ceremony Dreyfus behaved like a decent, well-disciplined officer, while those attending—the journalists, for example—shouted, "Shut up, you Judas" at him, that is, they behaved badly, indecently. Everyone left the ceremony dissatisfied and with a disturbed conscience. Dissatisfaction was especially great on the part of Dreyfus's defense attorney, Démange, an honest man who had felt there was something suspicious going on behind the scenes as far back as the hearing. Then there were the experts who, to convince themselves they hadn't made a mistake, spoke only of Dreyfus and his guilt, and kept wandering and wandering all over Paris. As it turned out, one of the experts was insane, the author of a monstrously absurd scheme, and two were crackpots. Inevitably the Ministry of War's Information Bureau—that military consistory that goes after spies and reads other people's letters—had to be brought into the discussion. It had to be brought in because Sandherr, the Bureau's head, turned out to be stricken with progressive paralysis, Paty de Clam proved to be a sort of Berlin Tausch, and Picquart suddenly resigned under mysterious and scandalous circumstances.[1] And wouldn't you just know it, a large number of juridical errors came to light. Little by little people became convinced that Dreyfus had in fact been condemned on the basis of a secret document which had been shown neither to the defendant nor his attorney, and law-abiding people saw in this a fundamental violation of the law. Even if the letter had been written by the sun itself and not merely Wilhelm, it ought to have been shown to Démange. All sorts of guesses were proffered as to the contents of the letter. Cock-and-bull stories started making the rounds. Dreyfus is an officer, so the military became defensive. Dreyfus is a Jew, so the Jews became defensive. . . . There was talk of militarism, of Yids. Such utterly disreputable people as Drumont[2] held their heads high. Little by little, a messy kettle of fish began stewing; it was fueled by anti-Semitism, a fuel that reeks of the slaughterhouse. When something is wrong within us, we seek the cause from without and before long we find it: it was the French who messed things up, it was the Yids, it was Wilhelm. . . . Capitalism, the bogeyman, the Masons, the syndicate and the Jesuits are all phantoms, but how they ease our anxieties![3] They are a bad sign, of course. Once the French began talking about the Yids and the syndicate, it meant they had begun to feel something was wrong, that a worm had begun to grow within, that they needed the phantoms to ease their stirred-up consciences. Then there's that Esterhazy, that duelist straight out of Turgenev, a bounder, a man who has long been an object of suspicion, not respected by his colleagues, and the striking similarity between his handwriting and that of the document, the uhlan's letters, the threats he somehow never carried out, and finally a trial that was shrouded in mystery and that came to the odd conclusion that the document was written in Esterhazy's handwriting, but not by Esterhazy's hand. And the gas kept accumulating, pressure began to build up, and the atmosphere became depressingly stifling. The free-for-all in the Chamber of Deputies was purely and simply a phenomenon of nerves, a hysterical result of this tension.[4] Zola's letter and his trial are both phenomena of the same order. What do you expect? The first to sound the alarm are bound to be the nation's best people, its vanguard, and that is exactly what happened. The first to speak up was Scheurer-Kestner.[5] Frenchmen who know him well (according to Kovalevsky) say he's a "dagger blade," he's so clear and above reproach. The second was Zola. And now he's being tried.

Yes, Zola's no Voltaire.[6] None of us are Voltaires, but there comes a time in our lives when the reproach of not being a Voltaire is as irrelevant as can be. Think of Korolenko, who stood up for the Multan pagans and saved them from forced labor.[7] Nor was Doctor Haas a Voltaire, yet his wonderful life ran its course quite happily.[8]

I know the trial from the stenographic transcripts, which are utterly different from the newspaper accounts, and I have a clear understanding of Zola. The main thing is that he is sincere, that is, he bases his judgments only on what he can see, not on phantoms the way the others do. Even sincere people can err, that goes without saying, but their errors cause less harm than sober-minded insincerity, prejudices or political motivations. Let us assume that Dreyfus is guilty—even so Zola is right, because the writer's job is not to accuse or persecute, but to stand up even for the guilty once they have been condemned and are undergoing punishment. "What about politics and the interests of the state?" people may ask. But major writers and artists should engage in politics only enough to protect themselves from it. There are enough accusers, prosecutors and secret police without them, and in any case the role of Paul becomes them more than that of Saul. No matter what his sentence, Zola will still experience vital joy at the end of the trial, his old age will be serene, and he will die with a clear, or in any case assuaged, conscience. The French have suffered much pain and they grasp at every word of consolation and every healthy reproach that comes from without. That's why Bjørnstjerne Bjørnson's letter[9] and the article by our own Zakrevsky (which was read here in *The News*)[10] were so popular here and why the abuse heaped on Zola—which the tabloids they despise offer them every day—is so disgusting. No matter how nervous Zola may act,[11] in court he still represents French common sense, and the French love him for it; they are proud of him, even though they also applaud the generals who in their simple-minded way try to scare them first with military honor, then with war.[12]

Look at what a long letter I've written. It's spring here. The mood is similar to that of the Ukraine at Eastertime. The weather is warm and sunny, the bells are ringing, the past keeps coming to mind. Come! Duse is going to appear here, by the way.

You write that my letters haven't been reaching you. Really? I'll send them registered.

I wish you health and all the best. My most respectful regards and greetings to Anna Ivanovna, Nastya and Borya.

This paper comes from the offices of *Le petit Niçois.*

Yours,
A. Chekhov

1. Colonel Jean-Conrad Sandherr was actually the head of the so-called Statistical Section, a cover name for the counter-intelligence branch of the French army; Major du Paty de Clam was the principal manipulator of the rigged-up evidence that was used to convict Dreyfus; Major Tausch of the German secret police was put on trial in Berlin in 1897 for engaging in blackmail with the aid of confidential information to which he had access in his work; Lieutenant Colonel Georges Picquart was forced to resign from the French General Staff after he discovered documents establishing the guilt of Esterhazy and tried to use them to clear Dreyfus.

2. Édouard Drumont, the author of a two-volume anti-Semitic tract *La*

France Juive and publisher of the ultra-reactionary newspaper *Libre Parole,* which led the anti-Dreyfus press campaign.

3. This sentence is printed in full in both Soviet editions of Chekhov's letters. But when the passage is quoted in various other Soviet sources (e.g., Ilya Ehrenburg's essay on Chekhov), the word "capitalism" is usually deleted.

4. During the session of the Chamber of Deputies on January 22, 1898, Jean Jaurès verbally assaulted the anti-Dreyfusard Prime Minister Jules Méline, and the rightist deputy Comte de Bernis was slugged physically by some Socialists, whereupon he ran after the departing Jaurès and hit him on the back of the head.

5. Auguste Scheurer-Kestner, the vice-president of the French Senate, led the fight for reopening the Dreyfus case in 1897.

6. In his regular column in *New Times,* Suvorin had accused Zola of publicity seeking and remarked that Zola must be envious of Voltaire's laurels. Suvorin's column and Chekhov's letter both refer to Voltaire's frequent defense of victims of religious persecution and his fight for the abolition of cruel and unjust laws. Among Voltaire's numerous humanitarian activities in the sixties and seventies of the eighteenth century were his successful intercession on behalf of the Calas family, Protestants who were falsely accused of having murdered their son for wanting to convert to Catholicism; his futile efforts to save the life of the nineteen-year-old Chevalier de la Barre, condemned to torture and death for having blasphemed and mutilated a crucifix; and his struggle to save from decapitation the governor of the French West Indies, convicted without proper trial for having been taken prisoner by the British.

7. In Chekhov's lifetime and during the first two decades of the twentieth century, Vladimir Korolenko amassed a record as a one-man Civil Liberties Union that could stand comparison to that of Voltaire. The Multan case Chekhov refers to is the best-known instance where Korolenko's intercession led to a reversal of an unjust legal verdict. In December of 1894, seven Udmurts (members of a Finnic tribe also known as Votyaks) from the village of Old Multan were put on trial and convicted in Vyatka Province for having allegedly murdered a Russian beggar for purposes of ritual sacrifice to their pagan gods. Korolenko became involved in the case after the first appeal of the sentence failed, although the appeal proceedings revealed that the accused and some of the witnesses had been subjected to torture to extract the evidence against them. In 1896, Korolenko appeared as one of the defenders and also as a witness at the third trial of the Old Multan villagers. He succeeded in proving that human sacrifice was never a part of the Udmurt religion and that the whole case had been fabricated by the local Russian authorities in order to smear the entire Udmurt nation, to compel them to abandon their native gods, and to bring about their conversion to Christianity. Despite governmental meddling in the selection of the jury and the introduction of supposedly scholarly witnesses willing to testify that the religion of the Udmurts required blood sacrifices, the second appeal resulted in full acquittal of the Udmurts.

In 1913, Korolenko was involved in a case that was far more famous than the Multan one, but that was in fact almost its literal repetition—that of Mendel Beilis, the Jew who was put on trial in Kiev on similar charges of human sacrifice, supposedly required by his religion. Beilis had a far more adequate defense than the obscure Udmurts, but nevertheless Korolenko volunteered to help with the preparation of the defense. Because of his heart condition, he was not allowed to do so by his doctors, but he nevertheless organized writers' protests, wrote a series of articles and insisted on being present at the trial as the correspondent of several liberal newspapers.

Volume 9 of the ten-volume edition of Korolenko's collected works, published in Moscow in 1955, contains more than seven hundred pages of his articles on humanitarian issues and civil-liberty causes. There are studies of conditions in prisons, re-examinations of unjust verdicts of courts-martial, accounts of brutal dispersals of strikers and infringements on the freedom of the press, articles urging famine relief and a summary of the Dreyfus affair. The volume also documents Korolenko's campaign of several decades to abolish the death penalty. These articles range chronologically from 1890 until World War I. Not included are Korolenko's humanitarian and publicistic writings and his letters to Maxim Gorky from the period after the October Revolution. These are among the most eloquent writings in Russian on human rights, championing the freedom of thought, decrying the death penalties imposed by Lenin's government for the illegal sale of bread and pleading for mercy toward the old-time liberals and revolutionaries who were being killed in the name of the very revolution to which they had devoted their lives. (Lenin's reaction to Korolenko's post-revolutionary writings was: "They are all the same. They call themselves revolutionaries, socialists, even 'of the people,' but they have no notion of what the people need.") Two years after the October Revolution, Korolenko no longer had any forum in which he could object to injustice and defend the oppressed.

Because of the considerable prestige of his name both in Russia and abroad, Lenin made a determined effort to win Korolenko to his side, and in 1920 he sent the People's Commissar of Education, the intellectual Anatoly Lunacharsky, to Korolenko's home in the Ukraine to try to enlist his support. Lunacharsky invited Korolenko to express his objections to Leninist practices in writing, promising to publish them with his own commentary and, if necessary, rebuttal. Korolenko wrote a set of six essays in which he developed the idea that a socialism which speaks in the name of the proletariat while disregarding the proletariat's wishes and depriving it of all freedom and of basic human rights is neither revolutionary nor democratic. Korolenko's *Letters to Lunacharsky* were never printed in the Soviet Union and his Soviet biographers pretend that this work does not exist; but shortly before his death in 1921, Korolenko sent these essays to be published abroad, thus becoming the first in a long list of important twentieth-century Russian writers to resort to this stratagem.

8. On Dr. Fyodor Haas, see Letter 100, note 3.

9. Bjørnstjerne Bjørnson wrote Zola an open letter, in which he called

Zola's fight for justice a service to the whole of humanity.

10. The Russian journalist Ignaty Zakrevsky published a glowing eulogy of Zola in the *St. Petersburg Stock Exchange Gazette* on January 27, 1898.

11. While the Russian text speaks unequivocally of Zola's nervousness, both Constance Garnett and Sidonie Lederer in Lillian Hellman's edition of the letters have Chekhov accuse him of being "neurotic." In general, while Lederer cannot begin to match many of Garnett's excellent renditions, she has a great knack for repeating some of her predecessor's worst misreadings.

12. In a number of Chekhov biographies, both Soviet and Western, and in the respective memoirs of Maria and Mikhail Chekhov, this letter is represented as signaling Chekhov's final and definite breaking-off of his relations with Suvorin. When this is asserted, it has become customary to quote Chekhov's letter to his brother Alexander of February 23, 1898, where he wrote: "*New Times* has been behaving revoltingly about the Zola case. The old man and I have exchanged letters on this subject (in a rather moderate tone, however) and have both lapsed into silence. I don't want to write him and I don't want his letters, in which he tries to justify his newspaper's tactlessness by his love for the military. I don't want them because they became a bore a long time ago." The passage in the letter to Alexander goes on to criticize *New Times* for conducting a campaign of vilification against Zola while at the same time serializing his new novel without paying him royalties and concludes: "And in any case, berating Zola while he is on trial is unworthy of literature."

There was indeed a lapse in Chekhov's correspondence with Suvorin, but it lasted for only a few months. On April 20, 1898, Suvorin was in Paris and, as his journal tells us, Chekhov came there and spent a week with him. After that, their correspondence and personal encounters went on as before. Chekhov's Russian biographers and his younger siblings wanted him to drop Suvorin so badly that they invented a break that in fact never happened. As a close reading of Suvorin's journal and of some passages in the journal of Ivan Shcheglov suggests, the cooling-off in their relationship that took place during the last few years of Chekhov's life came from Suvorin's side rather than from Chekhov's. Like many writers of the older generation, Suvorin considered all Chekhov's plays after *The Seagull* failures and believed that they were a sign that Chekhov's talent was declining. In the early years of the twentieth century, Suvorin was far more interested in the literary career of his second literary discovery and protégé, Vasily Rozanov, who shared Suvorin's reactionary beliefs, his anti-Semitism and anti-materialism as Chekhov never could.

XIII

YALTA

When chekhov returned to russia from France in May of 1898, he brought two gifts for his native city of Taganrog: Mark Antokolsky's statue of Peter the Great, which he had talked the sculptor into donating to the city when he met him in Paris, and over three hundred volumes of classical French writers for the Taganrog municipal library, for which he paid out of his own pocket. Once Chekhov was back in Melikhovo, the same round of school building, medical and literary projects, and endless stream of visitors was resumed. But the stay on the French Riviera did not seem to have done his health much good. It is from this period on that the image of Chekhov as an invalid—the emaciated look, the graying beard, the long black overcoat buttoned to the top, all so familiar to modern readers—becomes a reality, attested in photographs and in memoirs. As the fall of 1898 approached, he left for the Crimea, expecting to spend the fall and part of the winter in Yalta. But what was intended as a visit of a few months turned out to be a permanent stay.

In October, Chekhov's father died quite unexpectedly. With the father dead, Mikhail married and living independently, and Chekhov himself forced to reside in the south the greater part of every year, it no longer made sense to maintain Melikhovo for his mother and sister only. The estate in which so much work had been invested by the entire family and where Chekhov had lived some of his happiest years was put up for sale. Chekhov purchased a plot of land in Autka, a Tatar village situated within twenty minutes' walk of Yalta, on which he began building his new permanent home. By now there was a steady demand for his writing of all periods and Chekhov began making plans for an edition of his complete collected works. There were plans to have this edition brought out by Suvorin, but Suvorin's publishing house handled things in such a haphazard and unsatisfactory way that in January of 1899 Chekhov allowed Pyotr Sergeyenko to talk him into signing the ill-advised, exploitative contract with the publisher Adolf Marx (see Letter 118 and the notes to it). It enabled Chekhov to finish building his Autka home but involved him in endless busywork and in financial problems that were to plague him for the rest of his life.

Among the letters Chekhov wrote during his first two years of residence in Yalta we find several of his more important and personal statements about life, literature, justice and the relationship between the individual and the state. Chekhov's self-appraisal as a writer in the postscript of his letter to Grigory Rossolimo (Letter 130) is an indispensable companion piece to his other credo, the 1888 letter to Pleshcheyev (Letter 23). It is the lack of familiarity with these two basic Chekhovian documents or the failure to realize their paramount importance that is responsible for so much of the misunderstanding of Chekhov's person and his work by foreign critics. Chekhov's letters about the student riots that occurred in the spring of 1899 show his deepening concern about control of the press by the government and the absence in Russia of adequate channels for expression of popular sentiments, such as he could observe in France during the trial of Zola. Chekhov's letter to Suvorin about the "court of honor" to which Suvorin was subjected as a result of his published opinions of the student disturbances is an eloquent plea against putting any writer on trial for the content of his writings (Letter 123).

Of special interest is Chekhov's correspondence with Maxim Gorky, whose literary star began its dazzling ascent at about that time and whose enormous fame and popularity eclipsed within a few short years the reputations of all Russian writers except Tolstoy, both at home and abroad. Chekhov's letters of literary advice to Gorky stand out in the ocean of words published in Russian since Chekhov's time about this celebrated but uneven writer as the most astute literary critique of Gorky's work ever written. For all his personal fondness for Gorky, Chekhov was able not only to see the interesting and attractive sides of the younger man's talent, but also to point out and to warn Gorky against the maudlin, affected and bombastic aspects of his writing, which were indeed to come to the fore in Gorky's work written roughly between Chekhov's death and World War I and which make so much of his output from that period such an unreadable bore today.

Because of his worsening physical condition, Chekhov was obliged to curtail drastically the volume of his creative writing after he settled in Yalta. But, as if in compensation, almost everything he wrote in his final period is a major or a minor masterpiece. Back in 1895, Chekhov extended his recurrent theme of the lack of mutual comprehension, and the inability of living creatures to communicate fully with each other, to the world of animals, when he wrote his children's story "Whitebrow," about the encounter of a domestic puppy with a she-wolf and her cubs. All the animals in the story as well as the puppy's peasant owner misunderstand and continually misinterpret each other's intentions and motives. Late in 1898, Chekhov wrote a profound little story about a similar situation among humans, "The New Villa," in which a well-meaning liberal engineer and his wife fail to bridge the cultural gap that separates them from the peasants in a nearby village; they are ultimately forced to move away by a hostility that no amount of good will or effort on both sides can overcome. "The Lady with the Dog" of 1899 is one of the great love stories in Russian literature. The overwhelmingly attractive heroine of this story, trapped in an unfortunate marriage, can stand comparison to the similarly trapped Tatyana in Pushkin's *Eugene Onegin* and to Tolstoy's Anna Karenina, but Chekhov manages to avoid both Pushkin's neo-classical and rationalistic choice of duty over love and Tolstoy's moralistically motivated condemnation of his heroine's adultery. The shattering "In the Ravine" of 1900, arguably Chekhov's highest achievement in prose fiction, confronts the theme that in a more subdued form and in a totally different social milieu is also basic to the play *Three Sisters*, written at about the same time: the inability of the good but weak to defend themselves from those who are armed with the strength of selfishness.

The move to the Crimea coincided with the beginning of Chekhov's greatest period as playwright. This period is connected with the Moscow Art Theater, whose involvement with Chekhov dates from the production of *The Seagull* in their very first season in the winter of 1898–99, which marked the beginning of the most brilliant age in the history of Russian theater, extending from the last two years of the nineteenth century till the forcible standardization of theaters by the Stalinist regime in the 1930s. Chekhov's two last and greatest plays were written for this company, and its productions of his major plays brought them their world-wide fame and set the pattern for subsequent productions in Russia and abroad. Yet the circumstances of Chekhov's association with this company, particularly in its initial stages, have been so distorted by the mythologizing proclivities of the theater's founders, whose version of the events has become internationally accepted, that it would not be out of order to outline some of the actual facts.

The accepted version goes something like this: After the St. Petersburg failure of *The Seagull* in 1896, Chekhov lost faith in his own powers as a playwright. His plays were not performed anywhere, and when Vladimir

Nemirovich-Danchenko asked for permission to produce *The Seagull* during his company's first season, Chekhov refused, saying, as Nemirovich-Danchenko's memoirs have it, that he would never be able to survive the emotional ordeal of having this play performed and that his plays were worthless. There followed, according to the memoirs of both Nemirovich-Danchenko and Stanislavsky, prolonged negotiations, after which Chekhov yielded to their powers of persuasion. After the rehearsals began, Maria Chekhova supposedly made a dramatic visit to the theater, begging them to cancel their plans as being too dangerous for her brother's health. The production itself was a triumph, bringing *The Seagull* out of oblivion and setting the scene for the company's subsequent triumphs with Chekhov's other plays. This is the account we find in most Soviet sources on Chekhov to this day and this is roughly what Western scholars tell us, including such knowledgeable ones as Maurice Valency, who outlines this version of events in his thorough study of Chekhov's plays, *The Breaking String.*

As a matter of historical record, the St. Petersburg première of *The Seagull* was followed, as we have seen, by a highly successful Kiev production in November of 1896. During the next year, the play was produced in Astrakhan, Taganrog, Kharkov and other provincial cities. By the fall of 1898, it had its first foreign production, when it was presented in Prague in Czech translation. After the publication of Chekhov's collected plays by Suvorin in 1897, *Uncle Vanya* was produced in rapid succession in Odessa, Kiev, Nizhny Novgorod, Saratov and Tiflis in Georgia. All these productions were received with acclaim, they were written about in the press, and, by the end of 1898, royalties from these two plays represented a sizable portion of Chekhov's income. Therefore, it made no sense for him to lose faith in his plays or dread a Moscow production of *The Seagull.*

Vladimir Nemirovich-Danchenko was a stage director and author of popular Ostrovskian social melodramas that indicted the wealthy plutocracy and the merchant class. His friendship and correspondence with Chekhov dated from 1888. Despite the rather shoddy quality of his own plays, Nemirovich had good taste in literature and saw the originality and importance of Chekhov's plays. He had a hard time persuading his cofounder of the Moscow Art Theater, Konstantin Alexeyev, the wealthy heir to a textile fortune, who later became famous as actor and director under the name Stanislavsky, to include *The Seagull* in the repertory of their revolutionary new theater. In this theater, for the first time in the history of the Russian stage, the director was to have total control over all the elements of the production, and the production itself was thought of as a coherent artistic whole rather than the sum of its diverse parts.

On April 25, 1898, Nemirovich wrote to Chekhov asking for his permission to produce *The Seagull* in Moscow (his letters to Chekhov were published in the *Moscow Art Theater Yearbook* for 1944). Chekhov was traveling from France to Russia when the letter was mailed and he did not receive it until May 6 (as stated in his letter of that date to Alexander Sumbatov). Chekhov's initial reply to Nemirovich was lost (or possibly destroyed), but it must have been negative, for on May 12 Nemirovich complained in his letter to Chekhov: "Why won't you authorize our production? After all, *The Seagull* is playing all over the country. Why can't we do it in Moscow? The play has numerous admirers, I know [some of] them. The enthusiastic reviews in Kharkov and Odessa newspapers are quite unprecedented." On May 16, i.e., *ten* days after receiving the original request, Chekhov wrote to Nemirovich authorizing him to produce any Chekhov play he liked. So much for the protracted negotiations, Chekhov's stubborn refusals, the danger to his life, and the rescue of the forgotten *Seagull.* As for Maria Chekhova's dramatic intervention, she denied it ever happened after the first publication of Stanislavsky's *My Life in Art* and of Nemirovich's memoirs; in her own memoirs she cited documentary evidence to prove that she could not have made the visit they both described, because she did not know of the production until the very last moment, when she received an invitation to attend the opening night. But theatrical legends are resilient and the fantasies of the Moscow Art Theater's founders will probably go on being cited as fact for some time to come.

Chekhov was gratified by the new success of *The Seagull* in Moscow, but he was not particularly happy about the scenario of stage effects which Stanislavsky devised for it and he strongly disliked some of the performances. When Nemirovich wanted to do the Moscow première of *Uncle Vanya,* Chekhov's answer was to offer that play to the Maly Theater, a tradition-bound, government-owned company, which was the very opposite of the Moscow Art Theater in its artistic methods and principles. But since the Maly was an official theater, the play had to pass a government-appointed committee of literary experts. There ensued the unique little comedy, already described in the introductory essay, of three liberal literary scholars finding *Uncle Vanya* dramatically unsound and socially irrelevant and therefore unfit to be played in the Imperial Theaters unless Chekhov revised it according to their specifications. After reading their recommendations, Chekhov handed the play over to Nemirovich, who produced it in October of 1899. The success of this play in Moscow was hampered by the character of Professor Serebryakov, which was correctly seen by some of the public and some of the press as a caricature of the Russian liberal academic intelligentsia. This caused widespread resentment in Moscow's academic and university circles (Nemirovich's letter to Chekhov of October 27, 1899, shows that he, Chekhov and the actor who played the role were all aware of this interpretation and wanted it that way). Yet gradually, after some uncertain months, *Uncle Vanya* became accepted as the important play it was both in Moscow and in St. Petersburg. But while the satirical aspects of Professor Serebryakov's role were either resented or acclaimed, the equally important ecological message the play contains seems to have escaped general notice entirely.

By the time Chekhov came to write his next play, *Three Sisters,* his fortunes as a playwright were firmly linked with the Moscow Art Theater, both through its successful presentations of *The Seagull* and *Uncle Vanya* and through his love affair with the company's leading actress, Olga Knipper.

113. To Alexei Suvorin

Melikhovo,
August 24, 1898

Sytin tried to buy my humorous stories for five, not three thousand. The temptation was great, but I still decided not to sell; I have no particular desire for a collection with a new title. I've grown tired of turning out collections every year and constantly giving them new titles; it's so dreary and disorganized. No matter what Kolyosov says, sooner or later I'll have to publish the stories in numbered volumes and call them just that: Volume One, Two, Three . . . , in other words publish an edition of my collected works. It would solve a number of my problems, and it's what Tolstoy advises me to do. The humorous stories I've collected now would make up the first volume. And if you have no objections, I could start work editing the future volumes sometime in the late fall and winter when I won't have anything else to do. Another consideration in favor of my plan is that it's better if I myself take care of the editing and publishing rather than my heirs.[1] The new volumes won't do the old, unsold ones any harm because the latter will dwindle away at railroad stands, though for some reason they refuse to stock my books. The last time I took the Nikolayev line I didn't see any of my books on the stands.[2]

I'm building another new school, the third to be exact.[3] My schools have the reputation of being model schools. The reason I'm telling you this is I don't want you to think I spent the two hundred rubles you donated on some nonsense or other. I won't be at Tolstoy's on August 28th[4] because first, the trip there is cold and damp, and second, what's the point of going? Tolstoy's life is one long celebration; there's no reason to set aside a special day. And third, Menshikov[5] dropped by on his way from Yasnaya Polyana and said Lev Nikolayevich was grumbling and making faces at the very thought of having visitors come to wish him a happy birthday on August 28th. And fourth, I won't go to Yasnaya Polyana because Sergeyenko will be there. Sergeyenko and I were at school together in Taganrog. He used to be a joker, a clown, a wit, but as soon as he began thinking of himself as a great writer and friend to Tolstoy (whom, by the way, he wears out terribly), he became the most tiresome man on earth. I'm afraid of him. He's a hearse stood up on end.

Menshikov said that Tolstoy and his family had made a special point of inviting me to Yasnaya Polyana and that they would be offended if I didn't go. ("But not on the 28th, please," added Menshikov.) But I repeat: it's grown damp and very cold, and I've begun coughing again. I'm told my health has improved greatly, and at the same time they're chasing me away from here. I'll have to go south. I'm in a rush finishing off all sorts of things I've started and there are certain things I must do before I leave. I have no time to think about Yasnaya Polyana, though I ought to go there for a day or two. And I really want to go there.

My route: first the Crimea and Sochi, then, when it gets cold in Russia, I'll go abroad. The only place I want to go is Paris; I'm not at all attracted to warm regions. I fear this trip as if it were exile.

I've received a letter from Vladimir Nemirovich-Danchenko in Moscow.[6] His project is in full swing. They've had nearly a hundred rehearsals, and the actors are attending lectures.

If we decide to publish my stories in volumes, we ought to get together before I leave, talk it over, and, incidentally, raid your finance bureau for a bit of cash.

Where is Kolomnin now? If he's in Petersburg, would you do me a favor and tell him to send me as quickly as possible the photographs he promised me?

Keep well and happy. I wish you all the best.

Yours,
A. Chekhov

Send me a telegram about something or other. I love getting telegrams.

1. The publisher Ivan Sytin wanted to bring out a collected edition of Chekhov's humorous stories only, but Chekhov was more attracted by the prospect of a multivolume, chronologically arranged edition of all of his prose fiction. This letter is a part of his negotiations with Suvorin on this subject. Fyodor Kolyosov was the manager of Suvorin's bookstores.

2. As already mentioned, Suvorin held a monopoly on bookstands in all the railroad stations in Russia.

3. The peasant school at Melikhovo.
4. August 28, 1898, was Tolstoy's seventieth birthday.
5. On Mikhail Menshikov, see Letter 134.
6. Possibly the letter of August 21, 1898, outlining the preparations for rehearsals of *The Seagull* (Nemirovich-Danchenko's letter to Chekhov of that date in the *Moscow Art Theater Yearbook* for 1944).

114. To Mikhail Chekhov

Yalta,
October 26, 1898

Dear Michel,

No sooner had I mailed you my postcard than I received your letter. I knew what all of you had to go through at Father's funeral, and I felt vile inside. I didn't hear of Father's death until the evening of the thirteenth, when Sinani told me.[1] For some reason nobody wired me, and if I hadn't happened to stop by Sinani's shop I would have remained in the dark a good deal longer.

I'm buying a plot of land in Yalta so I can build a place to spend my winters. Constantly wandering around, moving from hotel to hotel, with their doormen and undependable food and so on and so forth is a frightening prospect. Mother could spend the winters with me. There is no winter here; it is late October and the roses and other flowers are outdoing one another with blossoms, the trees are green and the weather warm. There's water everywhere you look. Nothing more than a house itself is needed here, no outbuildings, because everything is located under one roof. Coal, firewood, janitor's quarters and everything else is in the basement. Hens lay all year round, and they don't even need any special housing; a few partitions are enough. There is a bakery and a market place nearby. So it will be very warm and very comfortable for Mother. Incidentally, everyone gathers saffron milk caps and chanterelles in the State Forest all autumn long. That will keep Mother entertained.[2] I won't do the building myself; everything will be done by an architect. The house will be ready by April. By city standards the lot is large. There will be room for an orchard, flowerbeds and a vegetable garden. Starting next year Yalta will have its own railroad line.[3]

Kuchukoy[4] is unsuitable for a permanent residence. It's a very charming summer cottage and worth buying only because it's so charming and—reasonably priced.

As for your insistence on marriage, what can I say? Marriage for love is the only kind of marriage that's interesting. Marrying a girl only because she's nice is like buying something you don't need at a market merely because it is pretty. The point around which family life revolves is love, sexual attraction, one flesh. Everything else is dreary and unreliable, no matter how cleverly it is calculated. Therefore, the point is one of finding a girl you love, not one you think is nice. As you see, a mere bagatelle is all that's holding us back.[5]

There's nothing but sad news from Serpukhov District: Witte has had a stroke, Kovreyn has had a stroke, Sidorov has died and Vasily Ivanovich (the bookkeeper) has consumption.[6]

Masha's coming tomorrow. We'll hold counsel and discuss everything thoroughly. I'll let you know what we decide.

Prince Urusov, the lawyer, is here.[7] He is an able raconteur. He too wants to buy a plot of land. Soon there won't be a single patch left in Yalta; everyone is in such a hurry to buy. My literature helped me to buy the lot. The only reason they sold it to me so cheaply and on credit is that I'm a writer.

Keep well, and give Olga Germanovna and Zhenya[8] my regards. Guarding against typhus is not so hard; it's not contagious. All you have to do is refrain from drinking unboiled water.

My *Uncle Vanya* is making the rounds of the provinces and has been successful everywhere. You never know when you're going to win and when you're going to lose. I'd placed no hopes whatsoever on that play. Keep well and write.

Yours,
A. Chekhov

I'm glad to hear that Father was buried in the New Virgin Cemetery. I wanted to wire and tell you to bury him there, but I thought it was too late. You guessed what I had in mind.

Doctor Borodulin[9] is here and sends his regards. A nice little official at the State Bank asked after you and also wished to have his regards forwarded.

1. Isaak Sinani owned a bookstore in Yalta. Subsequently, he and Chekhov became good friends. Chekhov's father died on October 12 as a result of an unsuccessful minor operation. On October 20, Chekhov wrote to Mikhail Menshikov: "My father died. The main cog in our Melikhovo mechanism is gone. I expect that life at Melikhovo will now lose all its charm for my mother and my sister and that I'll have to build a new nest for them elsewhere. This is all the more likely since I'll no longer be in Melikhovo in the winter and the two of them won't be able to manage without male help."

2. A mother who was a passionate mushroom collector is another thing that Anton Chekhov and Vladimir Nabokov have in common (see *Speak, Memory*, pp. 43–44). How very much alive the traditional Russian mushroom-

gathering mystique is in the Soviet Union today was made evident a few years ago by Vladimir Soloukhin in his delightful book *The Third Sport* (*Tretya okhota,* Moscow, 1968)—the first two sports being hunting and fishing, respectively.

3. This was only a rumor; no railroad to Yalta was built in Chekhov's lifetime.

4. An almost inaccessible little estate on the seacoast, situated in Gurzuf, some thirty versts from Yalta, which Chekhov bought hoping to use it as an excursion and picnic site in the summer, after he visited it with Isaak Sinani and became captivated by its scenic beauty.

5. Of the previous translators of Chekhov's letters, only Koteliansky understood this sentence.

6. Dr. Ivan Witte, Dr. Ivan Kovreyn and the bookkeeper Vasily Fyodorov were Chekhov's associates during his voluntary work at the Serpukhov *zemstvo* and its hospital. It is not known who Sidorov was.

7. Prince Alexander Urusov (1843–1900) was a practicing lawyer, drama critic and historian of Russian theater. He published one of the earliest critical articles on Chekhov in the West (a study of "The Duel," which appeared in *La Plume*, Paris, No. 67, 1892). He was the only critic who had a high opinion of *The Wood Demon* in the early nineties and he tried to convince Chekhov to arrange a staging of that play after the success of *The Seagull* at the Moscow Art Theater. Urusov's critical article about the latter gave Chekhov much pleasure, which was expressed in two letters of appreciation he wrote to Urusov.

8. Mikhail Chekhov's wife and daughter.

9. Dr. Vasily Borodulin, a Yalta physician. Chekhov was to inquire about the state of Dr. Borodulin's health in a letter he wrote to Maria from Badenweiler a few days before his own death.

115. To Jacques Merpert[1]

Yalta,
October 29, 1898

Dear Yakov Semyonovich,

So far it's very good. But throw out the word I've underlined in green. And I have a feeling the biographical detail is a bit excessive. I wouldn't name all his brothers and teachers; it only clutters things up. I would use another device for indicating dates. "In 1839" means very little to a Frenchman; it might be better to say instead: "When Dostoyevsky was twenty years old." Nor would it be out of place to give a very short and uncomplicated historical and literary summary of the period during which Dostoyevsky made his debut and lived. You should point out that he made his debut under such and such circumstances during the reign of Nicholas I and the reign of Belinsky and Pushkin (remember that the latter had an enormous, an overwhelming influence on him).[2] And names like Belinsky, Pushkin and Nekrasov are to my mind more effective for purposes of dating than figures, which listeners don't absorb and which say nothing to them.

The general tone of your article is even, pleasant and convincing. I'm looking forward to the next part.

If you see Ivan Yakovlevich,[3] give him my regards.

Yours,
A. Chekhov

I sent you the Pushkin by parcel post. I hope you've received it by now.

1. Merpert was a Russian-speaking Frenchman whom Chekhov met in Paris in the spring of 1898. He was planning to give a series of public lectures on Dostoyevsky in Paris and he asked for Chekhov's permission to send him the texts of these lectures for approval and suggestions. The present letter is Chekhov's reaction to the first installment. He must have agreed to look at the lectures as an act of kindness toward Merpert. Of the important Russian writers of the nineteenth century, Dostoyevsky interested Chekhov least of all.

Chekhov waited until he was twenty-nine years old before he got around to reading Dostoyevsky's major novels. On March 5, 1889, he wrote to Suvorin: "I've purchased Dostoyevsky in your store and now I'm reading him. It's all right, but much too long and lacking in modesty. Too pretentious." In Chekhov's early story "An Enigmatic Character" (1883), the heroine, a self-dramatizing fortune huntress, keeps justifying her preying on rich old men by saying that she is "a sufferer in the Dostoyevskian manner." In other Chekhov stories and letters, the name of Dostoyevsky occurs only when Chekhov is ridiculing someone's posturings or hysterical behavior.

This lack of affinity for Dostoyevsky is only natural if we remember Chekhov's gentle humanity, relativistic moral outlook and scrupulous reliance on precise and unbiased observations of everyday life—all the basic Chekhovian essentials that make him the very antipode of Dostoyevsky in the Russian literary tradition. But there is also a historical dimension involved. We must remember that Tolstoy found all Dostoyevsky's novels with the exception of *Notes from the House of the Dead* artistically unbearable and that Chekhov's younger contemporary Bunin refused to recognize that Dostoyevsky possessed any literary talent at all. It was only in the Symbolist age—in the early twentieth century—that Dostoyevsky was given his full measure of recognition and became a living literary influence in Russian literature.

2. Even if we take into account Chekhov's lack of enthusiasm for

Dostoyevsky's work, the astoundingly ill-informed statement that Dostoyevsky made his debut "in the reign of Pushkin" (and the fact that Chekhov did not know it was Gogol rather than Pushkin who had had "an enormous, an overwhelming influence" on the young Dostoyevsky) must be blamed on the generally embryonic state of Russian Dostoyevsky studies and criticism at the end of the nineteenth century.

3. Ivan Pavlovsky, the Paris correspondent of *New Times,* whom Chekhov had known since childhood and through whom he met Merpert.

116. To Alexei Peshkov (Maxim Gorky)[1]

Yalta,
December 3, 1898

Dear Alexei Maximovich,

I very much enjoyed your last letter. Thank you from the bottom of my heart. I wrote *Uncle Vanya* a very long time ago.[2] I have never seen it staged. In the last few years it has often been produced in provincial theaters, perhaps because I included it in my volume of collected plays. I feel indifferent toward all my plays and have long since ceased following the theater. I have no desire to write for the theater any more.[3]

You ask what I think of your stories. What do I think? Your talent is not to be doubted, and it is a genuine major talent to boot. It manifested itself with extraordinary power, for instance, in your story "In the Steppe." I actually felt envious at not having written it myself. You are an artist and an intelligent man. You have an admirable ability to feel. You are three-dimensional, i.e., when you describe a thing, it becomes visible and palpable. That is genuine art. There you have what I think, and I'm very glad to be able to tell it to you. I'm very glad, I repeat, and if we were to get to know one another and chat for an hour or two, you would become convinced of how highly I esteem you and what hopes I place on your talent.

Shall I talk about your shortcomings now? That's not quite so easy. Talking about a talent's shortcomings is like talking about the shortcomings of a tall tree growing in the garden; the issue at hand is not the tree itself, but rather the tastes of the person looking at the tree. Isn't that so?

I'll start by saying that, in my opinion, you lack restraint. You are like a spectator in the theater who expresses his delight with so little restraint that he prevents himself and others from listening. This lack of restraint is especially evident in the nature descriptions you use to break up your dialogues. When I read them—these descriptions—I feel I'd like them to be shorter, more compact, only about two or three lines long. Frequent reference to languor, murmuring, plushness and the like give your descriptions a rhetorical quality and make them monotonous; they discourage the reader and become almost tiresome. The same lack of restraint is evident in your descriptions of women ("Malva," "On the Rafts") and love scenes. It is neither a majestic sweep nor bold strokes of the brush; it is simply lack of restraint. Then the frequent use of words that do not belong in the type of stories you write —such words as musical accompaniment, discus, harmony—is annoying. You often speak of waves. In your descriptions of intellectuals I feel a tenseness somewhat akin to caution. That doesn't come from not having observed intellectuals enough. You know them, but you don't know exactly from what angle to approach them.

How old are you? I don't know you, I don't know where you come from or who you are. But I feel you ought to leave Nizhny for two or three years while you're still young and rub shoulders with literature and the literary world—not to learn the ropes from us and become a real pro,[4] but to submerge yourself in literature totally and grow to love it. Besides, people age faster in the provinces. Korolenko, Potapenko, Mamin, Ertel are all wonderful people. They may bore you a bit at first, but you'll get used to them in a year or two and come to value them as they deserve, and their company will more than make up for the discomforts and inconveniences of life in the capital.

I'm off to the post office. Keep well and happy. I clasp your hand. Thank you once again for your letter.

Yours,
A. Chekhov

1. Alexei Peshkov (1868–1936), whose last name suggests the Russian word for "pawn," chose Maxim Gorky ("Max the Bitter") as his pen name when he became a writer. *The Concise Literary Encyclopedia* (Moscow, 1964) tells us that he is "the founder of the literature of socialist realism and the progenitor of Soviet literature." He traveled a long and convoluted road before he attained that eminence. Of middle-class origin, self-educated, Gorky worked as a stevedore and baker and tramped all over Russia before he made his debut as a journalist and short-story writer at the age of twenty-four. He became a protégé of Vladimir Korolenko, whose friendship gained him entry into important literary journals. Gorky's early stories about vagabonds and romantic outsiders, who are rejected by a society they despise, brought to Russian literature a dimension that neither Tolstoy nor Chekhov had: genuine flamboyance. These stories combined social criticism with a Nietzschean note of contempt for the common herd (the young Gorky's Nietzscheanism has been declared a bourgeois invention and a heresy by

Soviet literary historians, but it is obvious and well documented). As Gorky wrote to a Ukrainian worker who aspired to become a poet: "The public is a herd of cattle and it is our enemy. Smash it in the face, in the heart, on its noggin! Smash it with strong, hard words! Let it feel pain, let it feel discomfort!" (Gorky's letter to A. Shablenko, written at the end of 1900.)

Such sentiments found a warm response in the hearts of the Russian liberal intelligentsia and the educated members of the merchant class, whose guilty and masochistic frame of mind can be very easily imagined in the America of the 1970s. Alexander Solzhenitsyn caught the very essence of the Gorky cult in pre-revolutionary Russia when he made Gorky the favorite writer of the educated peasant-born millionaire Roman Tomchak in *August 1914*: "Roman loudly praised his books and plays everywhere. He found in him his own trait: never fawn on those who favor you. Roman was thrilled by the insolence with which Gorky lashed out at and poured bilious acid over the kingpins of commerce and industry, who applauded him delightedly—so full-flavored, so biting, so new." The still-powerful Nikolai Mikhailovsky threw all his prestige into asserting Gorky's reputation and succeeded better than in his attempts to wreck Chekhov's. By 1899, Gorky was a friend and correspondent of Tolstoy and Chekhov and a living legend throughout Russia. A carefully projected personal image of an uneducated laborer, expressed in clothes, demeanor and speech mannerisms, lent Gorky an aura of "the man of the people"; the tsarist government cooperated in making him a celebrity and a martyr by subjecting him periodically to brief but well-publicized arrests, expelling him from various cities on trivial pretexts and keeping him under constant all-too-visible police surveillance.

It was during his friendship with Chekhov that Gorky wrote his best early works: the novel *Foma Gordeyev* and the plays *The Philistines* and *Lower Depths*. The production of the latter by Stanislavsky in Moscow and by Max Reinhardt in Berlin made Gorky as famous as Tolstoy in the West. In the first few years of the twentieth century his work was translated into many languages. By 1902 there was a book in English about his life and work; by 1905 there was one in French (there were only a handful of Chekhov's stories available in English and in French at the time and not a single play; surveys of the Russian literary scene in American, British and French magazines were likely to assign Chekhov fourth place in their list of Tolstoy's younger successors, after Gorky, Korolenko and Potapenko). This enormous and not fully deserved celebrity of Gorky in the West (comparable to Yevgeny Yevtushenko's fame in our own day, which is likewise not based on literary significance or excellence) delayed the realization of Chekhov's importance in other countries for several decades and it entirely screened from Western view the genuine literary brilliance of the exciting Symbolist period in Russian literature, which took place in the early years of the twentieth century.

By the time of Chekhov's death, Gorky was deeply involved in politics and in revolutionary activities. He became a member of the Bolshevik party in 1905, raised funds for it, but frequently dissented from its aims and policies in pre-revolutionary years. His propagandistic novels and plays that date from that period enjoyed a great popular success, but they are inferior to his earlier and later work—not because of their political or revolutionary content, but because their melodramatic plots, cardboard exploiters and saintly factory workers who spout pseudo-philosophical pseudo-profundities are so obviously shoddy when compared to what Gorky could do when he was at his best. These are the very works, however (e.g., the novel *The Mother* and the play *The Enemies*) that are extolled in Soviet criticism as the fountainhead of the Socialist-Realist method in literature. Gorky's novel *The Confession* (1908), which suggested that there might be a religious and mystical dimension in the coming Revolution, resulted in a serious ideological clash with Lenin.

In the years immediately preceding the Revolution, Gorky was the center of an artistic coterie that included the composer Sergei Rachmaninov, the basso Fyodor Chaliapin and the writer Ivan Bunin, which was dedicated to the preservation of nineteenth-century forms and traditions and was opposed to the innovative trends represented by Symbolism and Futurism in literature and Cubism in the visual arts. Genuinely revolutionary innovators, such as Vladimir Mayakovsky and Velimir Khlebnikov, no longer took Gorky seriously as a literary artist. In 1916, with the writing of the first part of his autobiographical trilogy, Gorky's literary output took a retrospective turn, which resulted in some of the finest things he ever wrote—the autobiographical trilogy and his series of literary portraits of various writers.

Gorky was still a Bolshevik party member at the time of the October Revolution, but he was as outraged as Korolenko by its betrayal of all the professed aims of the Russian revolutionary movement and by its crushing of what civil liberties did exist. He remained in Russia for some three years after the Revolution, using his political influence and connections to protect various writers from government persecution and to fight for the preservation of the Russian classical literary heritage, which post-revolutionary proletarian literary groups were eager to discard altogether. In 1921, Gorky went into voluntary exile with the encouragement of Lenin, who came to regard as an acute embarrassment Gorky's presence and his constant criticism of government practices (expressed in a series of newspaper essays that were collected later in the book *Untimely Thoughts* and in other similar writings, all of which are today banned in the Soviet Union). An interesting and revealing portrait of Gorky in exile is to be found in Nina Berberova's recent book *The Italics Are Mine* (New York, 1969).

The death of Lenin, to whom he had been personally attached, put Gorky through an emotional crisis and reconciled him to Soviet realities. After a few exploratory visits in the late 1920s, he returned to Russia permanently in 1931. The same Gorky who as a young man declared freedom to be the highest value in human life, whose very name symbolized liberation to countless young Russians at the turn of the century, now lent the prestige of his name to consolidating Stalin's regime and helped formulate the restrictive, oppressive and entirely artificial doctrine of Socialist Realism, which is still officially the only possible mode of expression any Soviet writer may use. For all this Stalin rewarded Gorky in a way that no other government ever rewarded a writer. He was deified.

While Gorky was still alive, the major and ancient Russian city of Nizhny Novgorod was renamed Gorky. So were countless schools, universities, research institutes and theaters. The Moscow Art Theater, which owed its first success and its international reputation to its productions of Chekhov's plays, is known today as the Gorky Moscow Art Theater. Gorky's profile appears on the masthead of the *Literary Gazette,* next to Pushkin's and below Lenin's, the three presumably representing the greatest literary figures Russia ever produced. "Gorky is the founder of Socialist Realism" a young government official reminds a literary lady in Chapter 56 of Solzhenitsyn's *The First Circle*, which takes place in December of 1949. "To cast doubt on Gorky is as criminal, you know, as to doubt . . ." The name that the young man dares not pronounce is of course that of Stalin. Solzhenitsyn's brief evocation of Gorky's name in this novel and similar references to him in Solzhenitsyn's other novels and stories invariably cut to the very heart of the matter and reflect what must have been decades of meditation over the causes and results of the Gorky cult both before and after the Revolution.

It has been possible to doubt the wisdom of Stalin in the Soviet Union during the last few decades, but anyone who dared question the artistic value of Gorky's work today would be in major trouble with the authorities. A government-decreed campaign of critical acclaim, begun in the thirties and continuing to this day, assigns to Gorky a wide-ranging influence on other writers and other literatures which he in fact never exercised and an innovative originality he never possessed. It is partly as a result of this campaign that the true and dazzling innovators of twentieth-century Russian literature, such as Alexei Remizov, Fyodor Sologub and Andrei Belyi are forgotten in Russia and unknown abroad.

Gorky died in 1936 under mysterious and still unexplained circumstances. The persistent avoidance of the subject of his death by his Soviet biographers lends credence to the supposition that he was poisoned on Stalin's orders to make sure he did not cause any embarrassment during the show trials of the old Bolsheviks which Stalin was then preparing.

The correspondence between Chekhov and Gorky was initiated by the latter, when he sent Chekhov an adoring letter in October or November of 1898, couched in that same "aw-shucks-I'm-just-a-simple-boy" tone and diction that he affected in his letters to Tolstoy and Anatoly Koni (but not in his letters to his wife or personal friends). Chekhov's reply began an exchange that went on intermittently until his death. The most fascinating thing about their correspondence is the way each of the two recasts the other in his own mold. Chekhov keeps seeing a subtle and poetic Gorky that never existed and Gorky keeps telling Chekhov how brutal his writing manner is and what a powerful indictment of society he has managed to write. Gorky loved and admired *Uncle Vanya* and *The Cherry Orchard,* but it would be hard to misunderstand and to misinterpret these two plays more than he did.

This is why the Chekhov we meet in Gorky's oft-translated and oft-quoted memoir of him lacks the verisimilitude of the Chekhov memoirs by such lesser writers as Ignaty Potapenko and Alexander Serebrov. Gorky's other literary portraits are masterful. His memoir of Lev Tolstoy is probably the finest single literary portrait of this complex, towering writer that we have. Gorky's memoir of Alexander Blok testifies to his ability to get into a mind totally alien to his own and take his readers along with him. But Gorky's portrait of Chekhov is refracted through the prism of his wishful thinking. The Chekhov we meet there is the kind of Chekhov Gorky wanted to exist and the kind he could have loved, rather than the Chekhov who actually lived and whom we know from his stories, plays and letters.

2. Most scholars assume that *Uncle Vanya* was written at the end of 1896. Chekhov's statement that he wrote it "a very long time ago" gives some support to Nina Gitovich's theory that it was written shortly after *The Wood Demon*. But the statement may also represent Chekhov's excuse for refusing to discuss this play with Gorky or to answer his questions about it, since he so clearly failed to understand it (see note 3 below).

3. Chekhov is replying to the ecstatically enthusiastic letter Gorky wrote him after seeing the Nizhny Novgorod production of *Uncle Vanya.* Gorky wrote that "*Uncle Vanya* is a completely new species of dramatic art, it is a hammer with which you pound on the public's empty heads." Gorky went on to compare the powerful effect produced by *Uncle Vanya* to a pig that he once saw destroy a flowerbed; he doubted that such brutal attacks on public sensibilities could lead to practical results, such as awakening the Russian public from its torpor. Gorky also praised Chekhov for what he thought was his indifference to human suffering: "You know, I feel that in this play you are colder than the devil to human beings. You are as indifferent toward them as snow, as a blizzard." This was precisely the point about Chekhov that Nikolai Mikhailovsky had been making repeatedly for the past twelve years, much to Chekhov's disgust; but where Mikhailovsky thought it a shortcoming, Gorky is offering praise. Small wonder that Chekhov preferred to thank Gorky curtly for liking his play and to change the subject by passing on to a discussion of Gorky's own stories.

4. In the original, this is a quotation from Ivan Krylov's fable "The Jackass and the Nightingale," in which the jackass advises a singing nightingale to take some lessons from the barnyard rooster in order to get professional polish.

117. To Alexei Peshkov (Maxim Gorky)

Yalta,
January 3, 1899

Dear Alexei Maximovich,

This is a reply to both your letters.[1] First of all, Happy New Year. From the bottom of my heart I wish you happiness—new happiness or old, as you like.

Apparently you didn't quite understand me. I said nothing about crudity.[2] I only said that certain foreign words—words without Russian roots—or rarely used words seemed out of place. With other authors words like "fatalistically" go by unnoticed, but your stories are musical and well proportioned and every little rough spot cries bloody murder. All this, of course, is a matter of taste, and maybe it's merely excessive irritability on my part, the conservatism of a man who has long since formed certain set habits. I can reconcile myself to "collegiate assessor" and "captain second class" in descriptions, but "flirtation" and "champion"[3] (when used in descriptions) repel me.

So you're an autodidact.[4] In your stories you're an artist through and through and a genuinely intellectual one at that. The crudity you spoke of is what characterizes you the least. You are intelligent and extremely sensitive. Your best works are "In the Steppe" and "On the Rafts," or have I already written you that? They are excellent stories, exemplary stories. They show an artist who has gone through a very good school. I don't think I'm mistaken. Your only fault is your lack of restraint and lack of grace. When someone expends the least amount of motion on a given action, that's grace. You tend to expend too much.

Your nature descriptions are artistic; you are a true landscape painter. But your frequent personifications (anthropomorphism), when the sea breathes, the sky looks on, the steppe basks, nature whispers, talks, grieves, etc.—these personifications make your descriptions a bit monotonous, sometimes cloying and sometimes unclear. Color and expressivity in nature descriptions are achieved through simplicity alone, through simple phrases like "the sun set," "it grew dark," "it began to rain," etc., and this simplicity is more characteristic of you than of most any writer.

I didn't like the first volume of the recently renovated *Life*.[5] It can't be taken seriously. Chirikov's story is naïve and dishonest. Veresayev's story is a crude imitation of something or other, possibly of the husband in your "Orlov and His Wife." It is crude and naïve as well. That type of story won't get him very far. Your "Kirilka" is ruined by the figure of the land captain; the general tone is well sustained throughout. Don't ever write about land captains. There's nothing easier than writing about disagreeable men in power, readers love it, but only the most unpleasant, untalented sort of readers.[6] I have the same aversion to characters of the latest vintage (such as land captains) that I have for "flirtation" and therefore I may be wrong. But I live in the country, I know all the land captains of my own and the neighboring districts, I've known them for years and I find that they and their activities are completely atypical, entirely uninteresting, and I think I'm right about that.

And now a word about vagabondage.[7] Vagabondage is all well and good and quite alluring, but as the years go by, you lose mobility and become attached to one spot. And the literary profession has a way of sucking you in. Failures and disappointments make time go by so fast that you fail to notice your real life, and the past when I was so free seems to belong to someone else, not myself.

The mail has come. I have to read my letters and newspapers. Keep well and happy. Thank you for your letters and for seeing that our correspondence is now on a firm footing.

I clasp your hand.

Yours,
A. Chekhov

1. Gorky's letters to Chekhov of *ca.* December 6 and December 29 (or 30), 1898.

2. In the first of his two letters, Gorky thanked Chekhov for advising him against using pretentious words and said that he was led to use them by his fear of appearing crude.

3. Both here and in his previous letter, Chekhov is objecting to Gorky's use of foreign loan words, which were acceptable Russian words at the time but clashed stylistically with the speech of Gorky's characters. A modern equivalent would be to use such words as "Zeitgeist" and "discothèque" in a story that described the life of sharecroppers.

4. In the first of his two letters, Gorky wrote: "I am a thirty-year-old autodidact. I don't expect to become better than I am; may God help me stay on the rung I have attained—it is not a high one but it is good enough for me. In general, I'm not a very interesting figure."

5. The journal *Life* was taken over by Vladimir Posse (see Letter 132) at the end of 1898 and turned by him into the literary organ of the Russian "legal" Marxists (i.e., those Marxists who had hoped to bring about a Marxist form of government in Russia by nonviolent means). Gorky became a leading contributor to that journal; he and its other contributors later formed the nucleus of Gorky's literary group "Knowledge" (*Znanie*), which opposed the innovative and experimental trends in Russian literature in the first decade of the twentieth century. Yevgeny Chirikov and Vikenty Veresayev, mentioned in this letter, were later associated with the "Knowledge" group.

6. If there ever was a wasted piece of literary advice, this is it. Gorky's greatest successes and some of his most admired works were portrayals of "unpleasant men in power." His role as the progenitor of Socialist Realism is derived from his demonstration of class origins and of the biologically determined inevitability of the villainy of such men under the conditions of capitalism.

7. Gorky rejected Chekhov's suggestion that he move to one of the capitals. He wrote: "I do not like big cities and before I got into literature, I was a vagabond."

118. To Ivan Orlov[1]

Yalta,
February 22, 1899

Greetings, dear Ivan Ivanovich,

Your friend Krutovsky[2] came to see me, and we talked about the French and about Panama, but I didn't get to introduce him to my circle of Yalta friends because when he'd finished talking about politics he went off to see the Hurdy-Gurdies.[3] That was yesterday, and today he's in Gurzuf.

I've sold Marx everything—my past and future—and I've become a Marxist for the rest of my life.[4] For every three hundred twenty pages of prose already published I will receive five thousand from him. In five years I'll get seven thousand, etc., and every five years I'll be getting a raise, so when I'm ninety-five I'll be earning barrels of money. I'm getting seventy-five thousand for my past. I managed to haggle out of him the income from the plays for myself and my heirs. But nonetheless, alas, I still have a long way to go to catch up with Vanderbilt. Twenty-five thousand is already down the drain,[5] and the other fifty thousand will be spread out over a period of two years, so I can really live it up.

There's no news in particular. I'm writing very little. Next season my play will be staged at the Maly Theater,[6] its first performance in either Petersburg or Moscow, so I'll obviously be getting a few extra pennies. My house in Autka has failed to get under way as yet because of the damp weather we've been having throughout most of January and February. I'll have to leave before it's completely built. My Kuchukoy vanilla (as Pastukhov, editor of the *Moscow Press*, calls the villa)[7] is enchanting, but nearly inaccessible. I'm dreaming of building an inexpensive cottage there, European style, so I can spend time there in the winter too. The present two-story cottage is suitable for summer living only.

My telegram about Devil's Island was not meant to be published; it was a completely private telegram. It has caused a great deal of indignant grumbling here in Yalta.[8] Kondakov,[9] who is a member of the Academy and one of the local oldtimers, said to me, "I'm hurt and annoyed."

"What do you mean?" I asked in amazement.

"I'm hurt and annoyed that I wasn't the one who had that telegram put in the papers."

And, in fact, Yalta in the winter is a pill not everyone can swallow: the boredom of it all, and the gossip, intrigues, and most shameless slander. Altschuller[10] is having a tough time getting adjusted. Our dear Yalta residents are gossiping about him something ferocious.

You cite the Scriptures in your letter. Let me likewise cite a passage from the Scriptures in reply to your complaints about the governor[11] and your various setbacks: place not your hope in princes nor the sons of man. . . .[12] And let me remind you of another expression that has to do with the sons of man, the very ones who are so holding you back: the sons of our age. The governor is not at fault, no sir, it's the whole intelligentsia, all of it. As long as our boys and girls are still students, they're honest and good, they're our hope, they're Russia's future; but as soon as those students have to stand on their own and grow up, our hope and Russia's future goes up in smoke, and all that's left on the filter is cottage-owning doctors, rapacious public officials, and thieving engineers. Keep in mind that Katkov, Pobedonostsev and Vyshnegradsky[13] are all university graduates, they are our professors, they are not old fogies, but professors and guiding lights. . . . I have no faith in our intelligentsia; it is hypocritical, dishonest, hysterical, ill-bred and lazy. I have no faith in it even when it suffers and complains, for its oppressors emerge from its own midst. I have faith in individuals, I see salvation in individuals scattered here and there, all over Russia, be they intellectuals or peasants, for they're the ones who really matter, though they are few. No man is a prophet in his own country,[14] and the individuals I've been talking about play an inconspicuous role in society. They do not dominate, yet their work is visible.[15] Think what you will, but science is inexorably moving forward, social consciousness is on the increase, moral issues are beginning to take on a more disturbing character, etc., etc., and all this is going on independently of the intelligentsia *en masse*, in spite of everything.

How is Witte? Kovreyn is here. He is comfortably settled. Koltsov is feeling a bit better.[16] I clasp your hand. Keep well, happy and cheerful. Write!!

Yours,
A. Chekhov

1. Dr. Ivan Orlov was a *zemstvo* physician in a district that adjoined the Serpukhov *zemstvo* where Chekhov had been active throughout his stay at Melikhovo. He and Chekhov began a lively correspondence after Chekhov moved to Yalta.

2. The horticulturist Vsevolod Krutovsky came to Yalta with a letter of introduction from Dr. Orlov, addressed to Chekhov. In his letter, Orlov asked Chekhov to introduce Krutovsky into the circle of his Yalta friends.

3. This was Chekhov's nickname for the wife and sister-in-law of the

writer Sergei Yelpatyevsky, who were Chekhov's Yalta neighbors. The nickname is a pun on the Russian word for hurdy-gurdy (*sharmanka*) and the French adjective *charmante*.

4. Suvorin's failure to take a serious interest in Chekhov's project to publish a complete collected edition of his works made Chekhov receptive to the offer he received at the beginning of 1899 from the German-Russian publisher Adolf Marx to purchase the rights to his already published writings and to bring them out in one multivolume edition. Marx owned the most popular illustrated magazine in Russia, *The Cornfield,* and his publishing house rivaled Suvorin's in bringing out reasonably priced editions of major Russian writers. The negotiations between Marx and Chekhov were carried out by Pyotr Sergeyenko, Chekhov's one-time acquaintance from his Taganrog school days and now a disciple and factotum of Tolstoy; but the initiative for the entire transaction came from Tolstoy himself. Tolstoy considered Chekhov a moral, edifying writer, and he believed that Marx's inexpensive editions would make Chekhov's stories easily available to large masses of Russian people. Tolstoy was not concerned with the financial aspects of the arrangement, and when he urged Chekhov to accept Marx's terms it apparently never occurred to him what this would do to Chekhov's financial situation.

For seventy-five thousand rubles Chekhov sold Marx all rights in perpetuity to everything he had written up to 1899—both the widely popular early humorous stories and the great stories of his maturity, which were read and discussed with ever greater avidity throughout Russia. The future profits, which Chekhov enumerates in such sanguine tone in this letter, were to apply only to Chekhov's *future* fiction, works which Marx was to include in later editions after Chekhov had published them for a fee in periodicals. But, as Chekhov was to write only eight more stories between the time the contract was signed and the time of his death, this part of the contract turned out to be meaningless. By selling his lifetime's work to Marx, Chekhov in effect cut himself off from his most important source of earnings. Marx had originally insisted on getting all the rights to Chekhov's plays as well, but fortunately Chekhov held out and reserved the rights to the plays for himself and for his heirs after his death and thus saved himself and his family from certain penury.

The seventy-five thousand which Marx agreed to pay Chekhov came in three installments spread over a two-year period. The first installment was spent immediately to pay the debts that Chekhov had incurred in connection with his illness and the need to live abroad. The other two installments barely covered the expenses of building Chekhov's Autka home and relocating his mother and sister to the Crimea. The terms of the contract also required Chekhov to provide Marx with copies of all his early humorous stories. This necessitated many months of research in order to find the hundreds of little stories and sketches that Chekhov had published in his youth in dozens of ephemeral humor magazines that had become bibliographical rarities. Chekhov did a part of this work himself, and he was also obliged to hire researchers in Moscow and St. Petersburg, among them Lydia Avilova. Because Chekhov was dissatisfied with the stylistic aspects of some of his early work, he embarked on an extensive project of editing much of his early output. The research and editing that Chekhov had to do without any extra pay as a result of his deal with Marx can be said to have robbed him of something like two years of creative writing. As for Marx, he recouped more than twice his initial investment after the very first printing of his edition of Chekhov's collected works. During the next five years (by an irony of fate Chekhov and Marx both died the same year), numerous subsequent printings kept increasing Marx's already considerable fortune by hundreds of thousands of rubles without bringing Chekhov a penny.

Even before the contract was signed, people close to Chekhov advised him against it. Maria Chekhova, who usually bowed to her brother's judgment, strongly urged him not to sign and so did Alexei Suvorin, who wired Chekhov an offer of a twenty-thousand-ruble loan in an effort to save him from selling Marx "his past and future." But Tolstoy's intervention and urging were decisive and Chekhov signed the contract despite the warnings of others and his own misgivings. In the next two years, Maxim Gorky repeatedly urged him to break the contract or to change its terms. In 1903 a large group of writers and lawyers, including Bunin, Gorky and Leonid Andreyev, drafted a petition addressed to Marx that urged him to release Chekhov from his contract and to restore to him the rights to his own life's work; but Chekhov found out about the petition and asked that it not be submitted to Marx since he could see no valid reason for backing out of an agreement into which he had entered of his own free will and in full awareness of its consequences.

5. Chekhov uses a bit of Russian baby talk at this point to describe the quick disappearance of the money. The expression, *tyu-tyu,* means "vanished" or "quickly disappeared" in baby talk (and not "already on hand" as the translator of the Lillian Hellman edition wrongly guessed).

6. Chekhov had still hoped to get *Uncle Vanya* staged at the Maly, rather than at the Moscow Art Theater.

7. This pun involving gastronomy and realty replaces an analogous one in the original (*mayonez* and *mayorat*).

8. In response to Nemirovich-Danchenko's telegram about the triumphant opening of *The Seagull* at the Moscow Art Theater on December 17, 1898, Chekhov wired back: "Convey to everyone my heartfelt gratitude. Am stuck in Yalta like Dreyfus on Devil's Island. Regret I'm not with you. Your telegram made me healthy and happy." Nemirovich published this telegram two days later in the newspaper *News of the Day.*

9. On Nikodim Kondakov, see Letter 119.

10. Dr. Isaak Altschuller, Chekhov's doctor in Yalta and his close personal friend. Altschuller's two memoirs of Chekhov are important sources for understanding the depth of Chekhov's commitment to medicine and to the biological sciences.

11. Orlov's letter, which Chekhov is here answering, described an attempt by a group of physicians from Orlov's *zemstvo* to organize a society dedicated to improving the sanitary and economic conditions of the local populace. The project was submitted to the local governor, who passed it on to the Ministry of the Interior, where the entire undertaking was prohibited. Orlov suspected that the veto was the governor's idea and wrote: "Oh, how much we could get done, if we only had a little bit of freedom."

12. The citation of Psalm 146 that we already saw in Chekhov's letter to Korolenko (see Letter 16, note 4) is again garbled.

13. A trio of repressive and reactionary political thinkers. On Mikhail Katkov, see Letter 14, note 5. Konstantin Pobedonostsev, the Ober-Procurator of the Holy Synod, was mentioned in Letter 101, in connection with his persecution of Tolstoy's followers. Ivan Vyshnegradsky was at that time the Minister of Finance.

14. Quoted by Chekhov in the Russianized Church Slavic of the Russian Bible; the wording used is closer to Matthew 13:57 and Mark 6:4 than to the analogous passages in Luke 4:24 and John 4:44.

15. This idea about the civilizing role of cultivated individuals was later to be expressed with greater eloquence in Vershinin's speech on the same subject in the first act of *Three Sisters*.

16. On Witte and Kovreyn, see Letter 114, note 6. Koltsov was a Yalta physician.

119. To Alexei Suvorin

Yalta,
March 4, 1899

Professor Kondakov[1] and I are staging the monastery scene from *Boris Godunov* as a benefit for the Pushkin School. Pimen will be played by Kondakov himself. Could you do me a great favor and for the holy cause of art write to Feodosia and have them send me the gong you have hanging there, the Chinese gong? We need it for the church bells. I'll return it to you safely. If you can't, write me quickly. In that case we'll have to bang a washbasin.

That's not all. I have favors, favors and more favors to ask of you. If photographs or any kind of reproductions of Vasnetsov's[2] latest paintings are available, please have them sent to me C.O.D. Here as everywhere there is much talk about the student disturbances and much clamor over the newspapers' lack of coverage.[3] According to the letters people have been receiving from Petersburg, general sentiment is in the students' favor. Your columns on the disturbances were unsatisfactory, and could not be otherwise, because no one can pass judgment in print on the disturbances when all mention of the facts is prohibited.[4] The state forbade you to write, it forbids the truth to be told, that is arbitrary rule, and you talk lightheartedly about the rights and prerogatives of the state in connection with this arbitrary rule. The mind refuses to accept this combination as logical. You talk about the rights of the state, but you're disregarding what is legal. Rights and justice are the same for the state as for any juridical person. If the state wrongfully alienates a piece of my land, I can bring an action against it and the court will re-establish my right to that land. Shouldn't the same rules apply when the state beats me with a riding crop? Shouldn't I raise a hue and cry over my violated rights if it commits violence upon me? The concept of the state should be founded on definite legal relationships. If it is not, it is a bogeyman, an empty sound that produces an imaginary fright.

Sluchevsky has written me about the Pushkin miscellany, and I have answered. I don't know why, but I somehow feel sorry for him at times.[5] Have you read Michel Deline's open letter? I saw him several times in Nice; he used to come visit me. He is a Déroulède despite his Judaism.[6]

I've been invited to go to Paris, but we're starting to have good weather here as well. Are you coming? Come toward the end of Lent and we'll go back together. If there's no way of my getting the gong, send me a telegram. Our performance is the week after next. Greetings to Anna Ivanovna, Nastya and Borya. Keep well and happy.

Yours,
A. Chekhov

1. Professor Nikodim Kondakov (1844–1925) was a famous and highly influential scholar of remarkable versatility. Historian, archeologist and theologian, he left his mark primarily on the study of Russian icon painting, the artistic value of which he was one of the first to assert (see Letter 142). Of serf origin, he had risen very high in the Russian academic hierarchy by the time he and Chekhov became friends in Yalta. A selection of Kondakov's letters to Chekhov, dealing for the most part with the crisis at the Imperial Academy caused by the annulment of Gorky's election (see Letters 153, 154 and 158), was published in the *Bulletin of the Language and Literature Section* of the *U.S.S.R. Academy of Sciences Publications*, Volume 19, Number 1, Moscow, 1960. After the Revolution, Kondakov moved to Prague, where he taught at Charles University and was the founder of an important institute devoted to Byzantine studies (Seminarium Kondakovianum); there he trained a whole generation of eminent Byzantine historians, who were subsequently active in various Western countries.

Chekhov took the amateur performance of Pushkin's tragedy, in which Professor Kondakov was to play the old chronicler Pimen, quite seriously and tried to invite several professional actor friends to come from Moscow and participate in it.

2. The painter Viktor Vasnetsov was having a particularly successful exhibit at the Art Academy in St. Petersburg at the time.

3. Student disturbances at Russian universities were a more or less constant occurrence throughout Chekhov's adult life. He ignored them during his own university years and he showed no particular sympathy toward the student strike he described in the letter he wrote to Suvorin on the eve of his departure for Sakhalin (Letter 41). However, the wave of student unrest that swept the entire country in February and March of 1899 attracted Chekhov's interest and engaged his sympathy both because of the government's brutality in putting it down and because a number of sons and daughters of his personal friends were among the striking students.

It all began at the University of St. Petersburg on February 8, when a group of students who were celebrating the university anniversary was dispersed by mounted police, who attacked them with riding crops. A protest strike was called by the students and suppressed by the police so brutally that sympathy strikes were called in numerous other Russian universities, including such traditionally nonradicalized establishments as teachers' colleges, religious seminaries and the Naval Academy. Chekhov was informed of the progress of the student strike in St. Petersburg through a series of detailed letters from his brother Alexander. Like the majority of the Russian intelligentsia, Alexander Chekhov sympathized with the students' situation, and he had a hard time reconciling his feelings with the anti-strike position taken, predictably enough, by his employer, *New Times*. Early in March, a total news blackout on the events connected with the strike was imposed on the Russian press by the government. On March 17, both the Moscow and St. Petersburg universities were temporarily closed and the buildings were occupied by the police. To resume their studies, students were required to supply evidence of their political reliability, and those who refused were dismissed.

4. In his widely read column, Suvorin praised the government for its handling of the strike and complimented Nicholas II for his wisdom in appointing a commission to investigate the causes of the student unrest.

5. The poet Konstantin Sluchevsky (1837–1904), a sort of Russian Swinburne, was indeed one of the most pitiable casualties of the radical-utilitarian dictatorship in Russian criticism. As an aristocratic young army officer, he published a few fantastic and mystical poems in one of the leading journals in 1859. A war of literary annihilation was declared against Sluchevsky by the Chernyshevsky circle for daring to treat such irrelevant themes, and during the next year the press campaign against him was conducted in such a slanderous manner that he was forced to resign his army commission and go into exile abroad. Turgenev, who was a friend and admirer of Sluchevsky, did not dare to speak in his defense. A poet of genuine talent and imagination, greatly admired by Dostoyevsky, Sluchevsky was not able to get a single

poem published anywhere in Russia for the next two decades. He resumed publication in the eighties and he lived long enough to see Symbolist poets such as Valery Bryusov and Konstantin Balmont publish and receive praise for the kind of poems for which he had once been crucified. The Symbolists recognized him as their precursor, but he never really matured as a poet and never became the important writer he could have been had the leading literary critics in his homeland not rejected him with such brutality.

6. Michel Deline was the pen name of a Russian Jew named Mikhail Ashkenazi, who lived in France and Switzerland, where he worked as a journalist and published novels and books on Russian literature in French. He was repeatedly attacked by *New Times*, which accused him of hating the Russian people and of having been bribed by the sinister Jewish syndicate to whitewash Dreyfus. Deline defended himself in an open letter addressed to Suvorin, which *New Times* refused to print but which appeared in two other Russian newspapers and in the literary journal *Life*, where it was accompanied by an open letter to Suvorin by Maxim Gorky, who compared Suvorin's pro-reform position in the sixties with his present siding with the government against the striking students. The last two of the numbered paragraphs of Deline's letter, quoted below, were of personal concern to Chekhov:

> 5. It is not my attitude toward the Dreyfus case that is disgraceful, but yours. I would like to refer you to a man you love and respect, if indeed you are capable of love and respect. I would like to refer you to that sensitive literary artist Anton Pavlovich Chekhov. He was in France during Zola's trial. Ask him what he thinks of the culpability of Dreyfus and about the vile tricks to which Esterhazy's defenders resorted. Ask him what he thinks about your attitude toward this case and about the Jewish problem in general. Neither you nor *New Times* will look very good after you learn his opinion.
>
> 6. In conclusion, I will make you an offer, Mr. Suvorin: let us ask the great writer of the Russian land Lev Nikolayevich Tolstoy to be our judge. You will tell him the story of your life and I'll tell him mine and he will then say which of us loves the Russian people more—you, the publisher of a major newspaper which never ceases sowing racial hatred, anti-Semitism, Anglophobia, hatred for the Finns, the Armenians, and contempt for the good—or I, a contributor to French and Russian newspapers, who never wrote a single line directed against the truly Christian principle of brotherly love, truth and peacemaking.

Chekhov had met Deline in Nice through Alexandra Khotyaintseva the previous year. He must have expressed some opinions in Deline's presence which were not meant for publication. When he read the open letter in the newspaper *The Courier*, he became quite angry and wrote to his sister: "They've printed the letter of that charlatan Deline, a vile letter, in which Deline tries to prove what a scoundrel and bastard Suvorin is and quotes my opinion as evidence. Damn it all, this is an unprecedented piece of tactlessness" (Letter of March 2, 1899). The same anger made Chekhov compare Deline to the French rightist leader Paul Déroulède in the present letter. At a time when Suvorin was going through the worst crisis of his life and was being attacked by everyone and from all sides, Chekhov felt he simply could not add his voice to the general chorus, no matter how much he came to despise Suvorin's paper and to disagree with his views (see Letters 122 and 123).

120. To Ivan Orlov

Yalta,
March 18, 1899

Dear Ivan Ivanovich,

Altschuller has probably written you by now—Koltsov[1] died, and we buried him on a warm, clear day in the Autka cemetery.

Spring has already come to Yalta. Everything is verdant and in bloom, and there are new faces along the embankment. Mirolyubov[2] and Gorky are coming today, the season is about to begin, and in two or two and a half weeks I'll be merrily on my way north to be closer to you. My house is all set, but my muse is upset:[3] I'm not doing any writing and I have no desire to work. I need to breathe another sort of air; I feel so indolent here in the south! I'm in bad spirits most of the time; it's the letters my friends and acquaintances send me. My letters keep having to console people or lecture them or snarl like fighting dogs. I get many letters about the student events—from students and adults.[4] I even got three letters from Suvorin. What's more, I have visits from students who have been expelled. The way I see it, the adults, that is the fathers and men in power, have made an awful blunder; they've acted the way the Turkish pashas acted with the Young Turks and Sufis, and for once public opinion has very eloquently proven that Russia, thank God, is no longer Turkey. I'll show you some of the letters when we get together.[5] But now let's talk about you. How have you been? Are you thinking of coming to Yalta? When? Will I find you in Podsolnechnoe this summer if I go there?

In my opinion Koltsov died of embolism. Shortly before his death he had a pulmonary infarction. He probably had endocarditis, but what could have caused it? I didn't ask the doctors who treated him. I heard in passing that they'd found a large quantity of albumen. Apparently the man was utterly exhausted from his numerous troubles and died as a result.

Altschuller is well, but moping. The Most Reverent Elpatius[6] is erecting a building and strutting around energetically. He is cheerful, indefatigable and witty. I've been spending less time at the girls' school.[7] Everything is fine there; they are as hospitable and nice as ever. Sinani is the same as always.

I firmly clasp your hand. Keep well and cheerful, and have a good appetite, don't be ill or bored, and most important of all—come visit us every year.

Yours,
A. Chekhov

1. Dr. A. I. Koltsov, a friend and associate of Dr. Orlov, who was mentioned in Chekhov's previous letter to him.

2. Viktor Mirolyubov was an opera singer and a journalist. Because of incipient tuberculosis, he had to abandon his musical career and move to Yalta. He became the publisher of the monthly *Everyone's Magazine*, in which some of Chekhov's last stories were published. Mirolyubov frequently accompanied Chekhov on his strolls around Yalta, where he was known, because of his gigantic build, as the "pyramidal water buffalo."

3. This reproduces the equally feeble pun in the original.

4. The letters that Alexander Chekhov wrote from St. Petersburg to his brother in Yalta in February and March of 1899 contain detailed, specific and highly knowledgeable accounts of the student strike's progress. Alexander had contacts in the press and at the university and he also had a reliable informant at the imperial court, thanks to whom he relayed to Anton the reactions and attitudes of Nicholas II, of his ministers and of the Dowager Empress. The letters that Chekhov received about this event from various other quarters are described, analyzed and quoted at length in A. N. Dubovnikov's article "Letters Written to Chekhov About the Student Movement of 1899–1902," which appeared in *Literary Heritage*, Volume 68, 1960. The following excerpt from a student's letter to Chekhov is quoted at length from Dubovnikov's article both because it helps us understand Chekhov's frame of mind and because its tone and content are so unmistakably recognizable in our present-day America. The letter was written by Vukol Lavrov's student son Mikhail (who also preserved for posterity Chekhov's description of Mikhailovsky as a sociologist who was deaf to literature). The letter was written one day after the universities were closed and occupied by the police in both Moscow and St. Petersburg.

> Moscow, March 18, 1899
>
> The strike at Moscow University began on Saturday the 13th. Everyone was expelled and is now signing statements of repentance. As soon as the university is reopened, the strike will resume, and this will keep up until the students' demands have been satisfied. Dis-

> turbances have also resumed in Petersburg. The students are happy: the authorities are in total confusion, a new form of struggle has been introduced, a new weapon has become available, and the Marxists are hailing the triumph of the implementation of a practical Marxist program. The facts are not yet known; the police break into student meetings and take down everybody's name, but an imperial edict proscribing intervention in academic affairs puts them in the position of a cat looking longingly at a sparrow. The general result is an unholy mess. With the appearance of comic, trumped-up appeals from the rector, a spirit of mockery has been invading the university. Everyone is laughing heartily and without the slightest malice at the *Moscow News*. The general mood is gay and cheerful. Of course, the fathers are gloomy and, as always, judicious. There is no sign of sympathy on the part of society at large, nor is there any need for it; no one is asking for any. It's time to abandon the crutches of benevolent guardianship! It is time to set up a boundary between practical wisdom and faith in broad theories of the future. It is time to recognize the necessity of human sacrifice, for only by so doing can we live for the distant future, glorifying and idealizing those who sacrifice themselves. There are very few students with a clear understanding of the full import of the present events, and you will find even fewer people outside the university who understand them. But that only serves to bolster our confidence, enthusiasm and sense of invincibility. This is a time when life is on its way to becoming pure pleasure. This is what the new age is like.

5. Orlov's reply to this letter expressed sympathy for the students' position and compared the spreading of student unrest to provincial schools and universities to a tidal wave. Orlov was especially concerned because his daughter was a student at the Bestuzhev courses in Moscow and had been expelled because of her participation in the strike.

6. The writer Yelpatyevsky.

7. Very soon after he settled in Yalta, Chekhov was nominated honorary superintendent of the local girls' school. He spent much time in the next few years helping out with school affairs and getting support for its projects.

121. To Georgy Chekhov[1]

Yalta,
March 26, 1899

Dear Georges,

I was all set to go to the ship to see you off when along came three numbskulls to invite me to a literary soirée. They sat around for a half hour, and by the time I got to the pier, your ship was gone.

How was your trip? Please write me all the details. After you left yesterday, I had guests who stayed all evening. Tonight I have to go to a meeting of the commission, and so I'm kept constantly on the run, like a squirrel on a treadmill.[2]

Let me know as soon as Iordanov[3] gets back. I have some business with him.

Give my best to your mother, Sanya, Lyolya and Volodya.[4] I clasp your hand. Keep well.

Yours,
A. Chekhov

1. Chekhov's Taganrog cousin, the son of his Uncle Mitrofan. Cousin "Georges" had just departed after a three-day visit to Yalta.

2. This message on a postcard testifies to Chekhov's inability, despite his worsening physical condition, to curtail his civic and social activities. In the first three months of 1899, he was not only appointed honorary superintendent of the local girls' school, but he initiated a campaign to raise funds to help the victims of the recent famine in Samara Province, and was nominated by the municipal administration to a commission for organizing the commemoration of the centenary of Pushkin's birth.

3. Pavel Iordanov was the mayor of Taganrog. Chekhov carried on an extensive correspondence with him that dealt mainly with the endowment of the Taganrog municipal library and other matters of a similar nature.

4. Sanya and Lyolya are Georgy Chekhov's sisters Alexandra and Yelena; Volodya is his brother Vladimir.

122. To Anna Suvorina[1]

Yalta,
March 29, 1899

Dear Anna Ivanovna,

If Petersburg weren't so far away and so cold, I'd go there and attempt to abduct Alexei Sergeyevich. I receive many letters and listen morning, noon and night to people talking, and I have some idea of what's happening to you both.[2] You accuse me of perfidy, you write that Alexei Sergeyevich is goodhearted and altruistic and that I am not responding in kind. But as a person who sincerely wishes him well, what else could I have done? Tell me. Today's mood did not materialize all of a sudden; it took shape over a period of many years. The things being said now were said long ago, everywhere, and you and Alexei Sergeyevich have been kept in ignorance of the truth much the way royalty is. I am not speculating; I am telling you what I know. *New Times* is going through a difficult period, but it has remained a force and will continue to remain a force. After some time has gone by, everything will go back to normal, and nothing will have changed; everything will be as it was.

I am more interested in whether Alexei Sergeyevich should stay in Petersburg or leave; and I'd be very glad to hear that he'd drop everything for at least a week and leave. I've written him to that effect and asked him to wire me, but he hasn't sent me a word, and I don't know what to do with myself now—stay in Yalta and wait for him or go north. Come what may, I'll be off for Moscow by April 10th or 15th, and it seems to me that the best thing for Alexei Sergeyevich to do would be to go to Moscow for the holidays too. Spring can be beautiful in Moscow. The surrounding countryside is interesting, and there are many places to visit. I'll be writing Alexei Sergeyevich, but you have a talk with him too, and have him send me a wire.

Where will you be this summer? Where are you going? It's spring here, and my health is tolerable, but I'm bored, I'm tired of all this rigmarole.

How is Nastya? And Borya? Please give them my regards. I often think of them and superpraise them to everyone.

My sincere thanks for thinking of me and sending me a letter. Keep well and happy. I kiss your hand and wish you the very, very best.

Yours,
A. Chekhov

1. Anna Suvorina was the second wife of Alexei Suvorin, the mother of his two youngest children, Anastasia and Boris (the Nastya and Borya to whom Chekhov so frequently sends his regards in his letters to Suvorin). There is an interesting portrait of her in Chekhov's letter to his sister of July 22, 1888, from the Crimea, in which he described his visit to Aivazovsky's estate:

> There are a lot of women here; Suvorina is the best among them. She is every bit as original as her husband; her way of thinking is not feminine. She talks a great deal of nonsense, but when she wants to speak seriously, she says intelligent and independent things. She is enamored of Tolstoy and therefore cordially detests contemporary literature. When you discuss literature with her, you get the feeling that Korolenko, Bezhetsky, myself and all the rest of us are her personal enemies. She has an extraordinary talent for chattering nonsense for hours on end, chattering with so much talent and inspiration that you can listen to her all day long without being bored, as you would to a canary. All in all, she is an interesting, intelligent and good person. . . .

This letter to Anna Suvorina appears in only one of the three Russian editions of Chekhov's letters, that of 1944–51. It was not available for publication at the time of Maria Chekhova's edition and it was omitted from the 1963–64 one, clearly because the warm solicitude for Suvorin that Chekhov expresses in it is too much at odds with the annotators' picture of Chekhov's angry final break with Suvorin in 1898.

2. After the government imposed a total ban on all the news pertaining to the student strike, it was generally assumed throughout Russia that this had been done at Suvorin's request. We know now from Suvorin's published journals and from Alexander Chekhov's letters to his brother that this was not true. Nevertheless, the practical result was that while the rest of the Russian press could write nothing about the situation, *New Times* kept printing Suvorin's column, in which he went on complimenting the government for its handling of the developments which neither he nor anyone else was allowed to state and describe. The outcome was a wave of public indignation and revulsion against *New Times* and against Suvorin that took on unprecedented dimensions. Subscriptions were canceled by the thousands, students kept breaking the windows of the editorial office, private banks and other firms canceled their advertisements, two of the paper's most popular contributors, Ignaty Potapenko and Alexander Amfiteatrov, withdrew demonstratively, and dozens of editorials all over Russia screamed, as Alexander Chekhov put it, "Crucify him!" (after which Alexander added: "And they just might").

Suvorin appealed to the government, desperately pleading for it to announce that he had not been responsible for the news blackout, but to no avail. On March 26, he wrote in his journal: "This month I've lived through has been like years. Never in my life was I so anxious. It seemed to me that everyone had turned against me and that it was the end."

123. To Alexei Suvorin

Moscow,[1]
April 24, 1899

The first thing I did after arriving in Moscow was change apartments. My address is The Sheshkov House, Malaya Dmitrovka, Moscow. I've rented this apartment for the whole year with the vague hope I may be allowed to live here a month or two next winter.

Your last letter (with the Court of Honor[2] correspondence) was forwarded to me from Lopasnya; it arrived yesterday. I can't for the life of me understand why and for whom this Court of Honor was considered necessary or why you felt it necessary to appear before a court you don't recognize (as you have stated in print more than once). A Court of Honor for writers and critics, who do not form a separate corporation as do officers or attorneys, for example, is nonsensical, absurd. In a backward country where there is no freedom of the press or of conscience, where the government and nine-tenths of society considers journalists their enemies, where life is so oppressive and foul and there is so little hope for better days ahead, pastimes like slinging mud at one another, courts of honor, etc. put writers in the ludicrous and pitiful position of helpless little animals biting off one another's tails when locked together in a cage. Even if you agree with the position of the Alliance, which recognizes the Court, can you tell me what the Alliance wants? What is it after? Putting you on trial for openly expressing your own opinion (whatever it may be) is a risky business; it's an attempt to jeopardize freedom of speech, it's a step toward making the position of the journalist intolerable, because after your trial not a single journalist could be certain that sooner or later he wouldn't stand trial in that strange court. I'm not talking about student disturbances or about your column. Your column may serve as a pretext for pointed polemics, hostile demonstrations against you and letters of abuse, but never for court action. The charges seem to be formulated almost deliberately for the purpose of covering up the principal cause of the scandal; they deliberately blame everything on the disturbances and your column so as to avoid the main issue. And what the point of all this business is I simply cannot understand, I'm at a loss. If some people feel the need or desire to wage war on you unto death, then why don't they come right out and say so? Our society (not the intelligentsia alone, Russian society as a whole) has felt hostile toward *New Times* for the past few years. People have come to believe that *New Times* receives a subsidy from the government and from the French general staff. And *New Times* did everything in its power to maintain this undeserved reputation; and it was hard to understand why, in the name of what god. No one, for instance, understands your exaggerated attitude toward Finland[3] lately. No one understands your denunciation of the newspapers that were banned and supposedly started reappearing under different names; perhaps it can be justified by the goals of "national policy," but it has no place in literature. No one understands why *New Times* ascribed to Deschanel and General Bilderling words they never said,[4] etc., etc. In most people's opinion you are a man who has great influence on the government, a cruel and implacable man. And once again *New Times* has done everything in its power to preserve that misapprehension in our society as long as possible. The public puts *New Times* in the same category as other government organs it finds objectionable, and while it complained and waxed indignant, misapprehension increased, legends materialized, and soon the snowball had grown into an avalanche that has started to roll and will keep rolling and getting larger and larger. But there's not a word in the charges about this "avalanche," even though the avalanche is the real reason they want to bring you to court. Such lack of sincerity upsets me violently.

I'm leaving for Melikhovo some time after the first of May, and until then I'll be in Moscow receiving visitors, of whom there is no end. I'm exhausted. Yesterday I went to see Lev Tolstoy. He and Tatyana[5] talked about you warmly; they very much liked your reaction to *Resurrection.* Yesterday I had supper at Fedotova's.[6] She's a real actress, an authentic actress. I am well. Are you coming to Moscow?

Yours,
A. Chekhov

1. Chekhov was in Moscow to discuss the plans for the production of *Uncle Vanya* at the Maly Theater. It was during this visit that he was informed of the recommendation of the government-appointed committee of scholars that he rewrite the play.

2. As the public indignation against Suvorin began to assume quasi-hysterical proportions, the Alliance of Russian Writers for Mutual Assistance, of which Suvorin was a founding member, arranged a Court of Honor, at which it directed that he appear and justify the contents of his column on student disturbances. Chekhov totally disagreed with these columns (cf. Letter 119), but the idea of putting a writer on any kind of trial for the mere expression of his opinion was abhorrent to him.

3. Finland had been an autonomous grand duchy within the Russian Empire, with its own laws and customs, since 1809. In line with the ultra-nationalistic policy that Nicholas II embarked on at the beginning of his reign, it was decided in 1898 to extend Russian laws and customs to Finland by force. This generated considerable resentment and hostility on the part of the Finns. *New Times* ran a series of chauvinistic, anti-Finnish articles in 1899, accusing the Finns of ingratitude for refusing to become Russians.

4. *New Times* published an article that quoted verbatim a conversation that supposedly took place between the President of the Chamber of Deputies Paul Deschanel and General Bilderling at the funeral of President Félix Faure of France. General Bilderling sent a letter to *New Times* denying that any such conversation ever occurred.

5. Tolstoy visited Chekhov on April 22, and on April 23 Chekhov had dinner at Tolstoy's. Tatyana was Tolstoy's eldest daughter, with whom Chekhov corresponded.

6. Glykeria Fedotova was, like Maria Savina and Maria Yermolova, one of Russia's most celebrated actresses of the period.

124. To Alexei Peshkov (Maxim Gorky)

Moscow,
April 25, 1899

You've vanished without a trace, my dearest Alexei Maximovich. Where are you? What have you been up to? Do you have any travel plans?

The day before yesterday I went to see Lev Tolstoy. He praised you highly and called you "a remarkable writer." He likes your "Fair" and "In the Steppe" and doesn't like "Malva." He said: "A writer can invent whatever he pleases, but he can't invent psychology, and Gorky occasionally goes in for psychological inventions. He describes things he's never felt." So there. I told him that when you come to Moscow the two of us would pay him a visit.

When will you be in Moscow? There is going to be a private performance of *Seagull* especially for me on Thursday. If you come, I'll get you in. My address is The Sheshkov House, Apt. 14, Malaya Dmitrovka (you enter from Degtyarny Lane), Moscow. Some time after the first of May I'm going to the country (Lopasnya, Moscow Province).

I've been receiving depressing, almost penitent letters from Petersburg, and it's hard on me because I don't know how to reply or what attitude to take.[1] Yes, when it's not a psychological invention, life's a tricky business.

Drop me a line or two. Tolstoy questioned me about you at great length. You have aroused his curiosity. He seems to be moved.

Keep well now. I clasp your hand. Regards to your Maximka.[2]

Yours,
A. Chekhov

1. Lillian Hellman's edition appends this note: "From Suvorin. Chekhov very probably meant that Suvorin was repentant over his anti-Zola attitude in the Dreyfus Affair." Suvorin's journal shows that he sincerely believed until the end of his life that Dreyfus was guilty. Unbeknownst to Miss Hellman, Suvorin had many other things to be repentant about by April of 1899.

Gorky replied to this portion of Chekhov's letter with a long sympathetic letter of his own that showed his concern for Chekhov's position in connection with Suvorin's plight. With greater clarity and compassion than many of Chekhov's later biographers, Gorky realized the full difficulty of Chekhov's situation. The man to whom he had been enormously obligated and who for many years had been his closest friend was currently the most-hated man in Russia. It was unthinkable for Chekhov to join the general attack, but he also could not defend Suvorin, since he totally disagreed with him on all the issues involved. Gorky wrote: "I would very much like to say something to you that would ease your situation in his regard. I would have paid dearly to be able to say it,—but I don't know what to say. What can one say? You see more in him than anyone else can. He is probably precious to you. I can imagine that you might feel his pain—but forgive me. . . . This may be cruel, but leave him. Leave him to himself. You have to look after your own self. He is after all, a rotten tree, so how could you help him? Such people as he can be helped only by a word of kindness, but if you have to force yourself to say it, it is better to remain silent" (Gorky's letter to Chekhov of April 29, 1899). In the remainder of that letter, Gorky told Chekhov about the climactic event of the student strike wave, the self-immolation in the Nizhny Novgorod jail of a student named Hermann Lieven, who poured kerosene over himself and set himself on fire to protest the suppression of the student strike.

2. Gorky's little son Maxim.

125. To Alexei Peshkov (Maxim Gorky)

Melikhovo,
May 9, 1899

My dearest Alexei Maximovich,

I'm sending you Strindberg's play *Miss Julie*. Read it and return it when you're finished to Yelena Mikhailovna Just, Panteleimonovskaya 13/15, Peterbsurg.[1]

I used to enjoy hunting small game, but it doesn't attract me any more.[2] I saw *Seagull* without any sets. I can't judge the play with equanimity, because the seagull herself gave such an abominable performance—she blubbered loudly throughout—and the Trigorin (the writer) walked around the stage and spoke like a paralytic. He is not supposed to have "a will of his own," but the way the actor conveyed it was nauseating to behold.[3] It wasn't bad on the whole, though, quite gripping in fact. There were moments when I found it hard to believe I had written it.

I'll be very happy to meet Father Petrov.[4] I've already read about him. If he's in Alushta in early July, it won't be hard to arrange for us to get together. I haven't seen his book.

I'm living on my estate in Melikhovo. It's hot, the rooks are cawing, and the peasants keep coming. For the time being things aren't too boring.

I've bought myself a watch. It's gold, but commonplace.

When are you coming to Lopasnya?

Keep well, happy and cheerful. And don't forget to write every once in a while.

If you decide to write a play, go ahead and write it and then send it to me. Don't let anyone know you're working on a play until you finish. Otherwise they'll disrupt your train of thought and break your mood.

I firmly clasp your hand.

Yours,
A. Chekhov

1. Yelena Just was the married name of Yelena Shavrova. She had done a new translation into Russian of August Strindberg's famous play. Gorky read *Miss Julie* with great enthusiasm. On May 12 or 13, he wrote Chekhov: "That is some audacious Swede! Never in my life have I seen the aristocracy of flunkeys depicted so vividly. I see some shortcomings in the dramatic technique; I believe that Julie's and the butler's accounts of their families are superfluous—but this is a trifling matter. The essence of the play struck me and the author's power aroused my envy and admiration and also pity for myself and many sad thoughts about our own literature."

Chekhov himself had read *Miss Julie* in another translation some ten years earlier and had liked it very much even then, as he informed Yelena Shavrova in his letter to her written on the same day as the present letter to Gorky. "If you would only translate Strindberg's short stories and publish a little volume of them!" he wrote Shavrova. "He is a remarkable writer. His power is quite out of the ordinary." But Chekhov had little sympathy for what he took to be Strindberg's misogyny. In Chapter XI of *The Island of Sakhalin*, after describing the many attractive qualities he found in the Gilyak people—their absence of warlike traits, their painfully scrupulous honesty—Chekhov admitted that he was disgusted by the Gilyak treatment of their women, whom they had reduced almost to the level of domestic animals. Chekhov cited several examples of inhuman treatment of Gilyak women by their menfolk that he had witnessed and then added: "The Swedish writer Strindberg, well known for his misogyny, who would like to see women enslaved and made to serve men's whims, is actually a spiritual ally of the Gilyaks; should he ever visit the north of Sakhalin, they would squeeze him in their arms for hours."

2. This is a reply to Gorky's offer to give Chekhov a hunting rifle.

3. Chekhov saw some of the early rehearsals of *The Seagull* at the Moscow Art Theater in the fall of 1898, but he was in Yalta when the play opened in December and he had not seen the finished production. During his April visit to Moscow, Nemirovich arranged a private performance so that Chekhov could see the production that was the greatest theatrical event of the year and that had been playing to full houses throughout the season. Gorky was unable to accept the invitation Chekhov had extended to him in his previous letter to attend that private performance, since he was barred from Moscow by order of the police. Chekhov is sharing his impressions of the performance with Gorky at Gorky's request.

While generally satisfied, Chekhov thought Stanislavsky's elaborate scenario of sound effects and group scenes gimmicky and distracting. He felt that the slow tempo of the last act distorted the play and suggested jokingly that the play be ended with Act Three. But above all he disliked the interpretations of the two key roles: Nina's by Maria Roxanova and Trigorin's by Stanislavsky.

By 1899, the old Mikhailovskian cliché of a cold and indifferent Chekhov had been largely superseded in the popular mind by the image of Chekhov as the poet of spineless and frustrated intellectuals. Chekhov always thought that it was absurd to reduce the entire meaning of his work to this one dimension. But Stanislavsky, who in comparison with his partner Nemirovich-Danchenko and his disciples Meyerhold and Vakhtangov, was always somewhat deficient in literary understanding and judgment and who inevitably took the simplifications of Russian criticism at face value (his discussions of *Hamlet* with Edward Gordon Craig, published in the *Moscow Art Theater Yearbook* for 1944, in which he tries to convince Craig that their production of *Hamlet* must not deviate from Vissarion Belinsky's understanding of this play, are quite telling in this respect), saw in the new critical cliché the key to his interpretation of Trigorin. Roxanova's weepy and neurotic Nina also fit this popular stereotype, again to Chekhov's displeasure. At a later date, Chekhov lost patience with her excesses and demanded that Nemirovich replace her with another actress. This presented Nemirovich with a hard dilemma—Roxanova gave exactly the kind of tearful performance that the turn-of-the-century critics had led the public to expect in a work by Chekhov; changing her characterization could conceivably jeopardize the company's newly won success.

4. Father Grigory Petrov, the author of the popular book *The Gospel as the Foundation of Life*, was a unique example of a revolutionary-minded Orthodox priest in nineteenth-century Russia. His appeal to return to the original teachings of the New Testament in their social as well as religious aspects brought him many radical young followers. The government became alarmed and insisted that he be defrocked by the Church. Gorky was a great admirer of Father Petrov and his teachings, and Chekhov wrote Suvorin of Father Petrov's book with excitement and enthusiasm.

126. To Olga Knipper[1]

Yalta,
September 3, 1899

Dear Actress,

Let me answer all your questions. I arrived safely.[2] My traveling companions let me have a lower berth, and then the way things worked out there were only two of us left in the compartment: a young Armenian and I. I drank tea several times a day and had three glasses each time, with lemon, sedately, taking my time. I ate up everything that was in the basket. But the way I look at it, fussing around with a basket and running to the station for boiling water is undignified and undermines the prestige of the Art Theater. It was cold until we got to Kursk, then it began to warm up, and by the time we got to Sevastopol it was quite hot. I had my own house to go to in Yalta, and this is where I'm now living, guarded by my faithful Mustafa.[3] I don't have dinner every day because it's too far to walk to town, and fussing around with a kerosene burner is also very bad for prestige. In the evening I eat cheese. I see Sinani now and then. I've been to the Sredins'[4] twice. They examined your photograph with obvious emotion and ate up all the candy. Leonid Valentinovich is feeling tolerably well. Im not drinking any Narzan[5] water. What else? I spend almost no time in the garden; I stay inside and think of you. Riding past Bakhchisarai[6] I thought of you and recalled our trip. Dear, extraordinary actress, wonderful woman, if only you knew how happy your letter made me. I send you my humble regards and bow so low that my forehead touches the bottom of my well, which is already eight sazhens deep. I've grown used to you, I miss you, and I can in no way reconcile myself to the idea that I won't be seeing you until spring. In other words, I'm upset. If Nadenka[7] knew what was going on in my heart, we'd never hear the end of it.

The weather in Yalta is marvelous, but for no reason at all it's been raining these last two days; everything is muddy, and I have to put on my galoshes. There are centipedes creeping all over the walls as a result of the dampness, and in my garden toads and young crocodiles are leaping about. Your gift, the green reptile in the flower pot, is now sitting in the garden soaking up the sun.[8] It took the journey quite well.

The fleet has arrived. I'm watching it through my binoculars.

They are doing an operetta in the theater. Trained fleas are continuing to serve sacred art. I have no money. I have frequent visitors. All in all, I'm bored, and my boredom is idle and meaningless.

Well, I firmly clasp and kiss your hand. Keep well, cheerful, happy, work, leap, let yourself be carried away, sing and, if possible, don't forget a provincial writer, your zealous admirer,

A. Chekhov

1. Olga Leonardovna Knipper (1868–1959) came from a cultivated German-Russian family. She studied drama with Alexander Fedotov and Vladimir Nemirovich-Danchenko, who entrusted her with leading roles in the first season of the Moscow Art Theater even though she lacked any previous stage experience. Chekhov first saw her on September 14, 1898, when he attended a rehearsal of Alexei Tolstoy's verse drama *Tsar Fyodor Ioannovich*, in which she played the tsar's wife Irina. He wrote to Suvorin: "I was agreeably touched by the intelligence of their tone; there was a breath of true art wafting from the stage, although none of them have great talents. I thought Irina magnificent. Her voice, her nobility, her sincerity—it's all so fine it brings a spasm to your throat [. . .]. Were I to stay in Moscow, I would fall in love with this Irina" (Letter of October 8, 1898). During his visit to Moscow in April of 1899, Chekhov quite unexpectedly paid an Easter Sunday call on Olga Knipper's family and invited her to attend an exhibit of Isaak Levitan's paintings with him. On May 1, he saw her play Arkadina in the private performance of *The Seagull* that he describes to Gorky in Letter 125.

Early in May she came to Melikhovo for a three-day visit and met his mother. In July she stayed for several weeks with mutual friends in Yalta while Chekhov was also there. By the fall of 1899 they were in love.

This letter is the first authentic love letter by Chekhov that we have. Its tender, affectionate tone is light years away from the chatty, humorous and defensive letters he once wrote (and went on writing even after his marriage) to Lika Mizinova or Lydia Avilova, which his gullible biographers in their desperate search for romance managed to see as some kind of amorous epistles. Nor is there any reason to suppose that had Chekhov's letters to Olga Kundasova and Lydia Yavorskaya been preserved we would have found in them this kind of lyrical tenderness. We know of a number of affairs that Chekhov had had before this time with various women, but this is the first affair of his life that is also a love affair.

2. Chekhov returned to Yalta from Moscow on August 27.

3. On February 10, 1899, Chekhov wrote to his sister from Yalta: "I've hired a Turk named Mustafa. He's trying very hard. Sleeps in the little shed. A kindly face; tremendously strong; penury, sobriety, noble principles. I've bought for him a shovel, a pick and an axe. We'll dig up the ground and then plant trees."

4. Dr. Leonid Valentinovich Sredin and his wife Sofya were Yalta acquaintances of Chekhov's; they were also friends of Olga Knipper's family and of Maxim Gorky. She stayed with them in July when she came to see Chekhov in Yalta.

5. To this day the most popular brand of mineral water in the Soviet Union. Thus far, the letter answers, point by point, a set of detailed questions in Olga Knipper's letter of August 29, 1899.

6. The palace of the former rulers of the Crimea, made famous in Russian literature by Pushkin's verse tale "The Fountain of Bakhchisarai."

7. This imaginary person kept popping up in Chekhov's correspondence with Olga Knipper. She was supposedly Chekhov's jealous wife or fiancée, who resented Olga's presence in his life.

8. It was a cactus and its name (and species) was Queen of the Night.

127. To Alexei Peshkov (Maxim Gorky)

Yalta,
September 3, 1899

Greetings again, dearest Alexei Maximovich! Here is my answer to your letter.

In the first place, I am generally opposed to dedicating anything whatsoever to people who are still alive. A long time ago I used to dedicate things, and now I feel that perhaps I shouldn't have. Such is my general sentiment. In particular, however, I will be only too happy and honored to accept your dedication of *Foma Gordeyev*.[1] But what have I done to deserve it? Of course, that is for you to judge; all I can do is bow and offer my thanks. Make the dedication with as few surplus words as possible, I mean, write no more than "This is dedicated to . . ." and let it go at that. Only Volynsky[2] likes long dedications. Here's another piece of practical advice if you want it: arrange for larger printings, no less than five or six thousand copies. The book is sure to sell fast. You can have the second printing done simultaneously with the first. Another piece of advice: when you read proof, cross out as many modifiers of nouns and verbs as you can. You have so many modifiers that the reader has a hard time figuring out what deserves his attention, and it tires him out. If I write, "A man sat down on the grass," it is understandable because it is clear and doesn't require a second reading. But it would be hard to follow and brain-taxing were I to write, "A tall, narrow-chested, red-bearded man of medium height sat down noiselessly, looking around timidly and in fright, on a patch of green grass that had been trampled by pedestrians." The brain can't grasp all of this at once, and the art of fiction ought to be immediately, instantaneously graspable. Here is something else: You are lyrical by nature, the timbre of your soul is gentle. If you had been a composer, you'd have avoided writing marches. Deliberately offensive language, loudness, causticity and frenzied denunciations are not characteristic of your talent. Therefore you should understand why I advise you not to spare, as you proofread, the sons of bitches and other assorted curs and mutts that keep reappearing here and there in the pages of *Life*.

Shall I expect you at the end of September? Why so late? Winter's going to start early this year; fall's going to be short. You'll have to hurry.

Keep well now. Stay nicely alive and healthy.

Yours,
A. Chekhov

Performances begin at the Art Theater on September 30th. *Uncle Vanya* is scheduled for October 14th.

Your best story is "In the Steppe."

1. Gorky had asked for Chekhov's permission to dedicate to him his novel *Foma Gordeyev*, a story of a young merchant who revolts against the values of his class and is crushed by it. *Foma Gordeyev* enjoyed an enormous international success at the time of its publication and was quickly translated into many languages. On December 3, 1901, Chekhov received the American edition of the book and quoted the English text of the dedication in his letter of that date to his wife. It was from Gorky's dedication that many foreign literary critics and readers first learned of Chekhov's existence. When in 1902 the two pioneers of American Chekhov criticism, Abraham Cahan writing in

The Bookman and R. E. C. Long in *The Living Age*, tried to get American readers interested in Chekhov, they had to introduce him as "the man to whom Gorky dedicated *Foma Gordeyev*" (Cahan). Both Long and Cahan were perfectly aware that the reason "Western critics have tumbled over one another to acclaim Gorky" (Long) was that he was "of the people" and "a bitter enemy of the present *régime*," and that the lack of interest in Chekhov abroad was due to the assumption (believed even by the generally well-informed Cahan) that he was "a nobleman by birth and education" (Cahan). In actual fact, of course, Gorky's father was a cabinetmaker and his maternal grandfather the prosperous owner of a dyer's shop, while both of Chekhov's grandfathers were serfs.

2. Akim Volynsky, the literary critic who at the end of the nineteenth century was one of the first to challenge the monopoly of utilitarian criticism and to question its ethics.

128. To Anastasy Govallo[1]

Yalta,
September 26, 1899

Dear Sir,

May I express my sincere gratitude to the Autka community for the water I used while building.[2] Please accept a contribution of twenty-five rubles for the Autka mosque.[3]

I respectfully remain

Yours,
A. Chekhov

1. Govallo was a member of the Yalta municipal administration.

2. There was no water outlet on the lot which Chekhov had purchased at the time he built his home; water was connected only after the construction was completed.

3. The building of his home brought Chekhov into close contact with the Crimean Tatar community in Autka. The contractor who built the house, a Tatar named Babakai Kalfa, remained Chekhov's factotum and personal friend for the rest of his life. On March 12, 1900, Chekhov wrote to his brother Ivan, describing the visit he had received from the Autka mullah, who came to discuss the situation of the local Moslem school. Chekhov sent Ivan an extensive list of school supplies which he asked him to purchase in Moscow for the school. The letter to Govallo and the cited letter to Ivan Chekhov appeared in the 1944–51 edition, but were both excluded from the 1963–64 one, since this evidence of Chekhov's sympathy for the Crimean Tatars was not a convenient subject to bring up during their post-Stalinist ordeal.

The Crimean Tatars are descendants of the Mongols who invaded Russia repeatedly in the Middle Ages. They were the indigenous population of the

Crimean peninsula prior to its conquest by the Russians in 1783. After the Revolution, they made an attempt to form an independent Crimean nation, which was quickly put down. In 1944, after the German occupation of the Crimea, the entire Crimean Tatar people were declared guilty of treason by Stalin's fiat and something like a quarter of a million men, women and children were deported to the arid regions of Central Asia, where almost half of them died of privation in the next two years. In the post-Stalin years, there began a desperate effort by the Tatars, helped by a few Russian sympathizers, to get the accusation of treason, which extended by Soviet law to persons who were not even born at the time of the German occupation, rescinded. This was done officially in 1967, but the government order that canceled the original charges also barred the Crimean Tatars from residence in their ancestral homeland. Two of the most courageous Soviet dissenters of the older generation, the old Communist writer Alexei Kosterin and General Pyotr Grigorenko, acting in the great traditions of Tolstoy's and Korolenko's aid to persecuted minorities, have tried to bring the plight of the Crimean Tatars to the attention of the Soviet and world press in recent years. But Kosterin died and Grigorenko ended in a mental institution. The Tatars, as a collection of documents on their situation published in New York in 1969 shows, are still barred from living in the Crimea, and the ban on expressions of sympathy for them in the press is still so tight that it extends even to the pre-revolutionary writings of Anton Chekhov.

129. To Olga Knipper

Yalta,
October 4, 1899

My dear actress,

It's clear you greatly exaggerated everything in your gloomy letter, because the papers were most civil about your opening-night performance.[1] Be that as it may, one or two unsuccessful performances are insufficient cause for being crestfallen and spending a sleepless night. Art, and especially the stage, is an endeavor in which stumbling is unavoidable. There will be many unsuccessful days ahead, many entirely unsuccessful seasons, there will be great misunderstandings and deep disappointments and you have to be ready for all that, you have to expect it, and despite it all you must stubbornly, fanatically do what you think is right.

And of course you're right: Alexeyev had no business playing Ivan the Terrible. That's not his job. When he directs, he's an artist, but when he acts he's a rich young merchant who has taken it into his head to dabble a bit in art.[2]

I was sick for three or four days, and I've been staying at home. The number of visitors is unbearable. I'm so bored by the chatter of those idle provincial tongues that I seethe with anger and I envy the rat that lives under the floor of your theater.

You wrote your last letter at four in the morning. If you should feel that *Uncle Vanya* isn't as successful as you want it to be, please go to bed and have a good night's sleep. Success has very much spoiled you; you can no longer tolerate everyday existence.

It looks as if Davydov is going to play *Uncle Vanya* in Petersburg. He'll do a good job of it too, but the play will most likely flop.

How have you been? Write more. As you see, I write you nearly every day. An author writing an actress that often—before you know it my pride will begin to suffer. Actresses should be kept under strict supervision and not written to. I keep forgetting I'm the inspector of the actresses.[3]

Keep well, little angel.

Yours,
A. Chekhov

1. In addition to *The Seagull*, the biggest other hit of the Moscow Art Theater's first season was *Tsar Fyodor Ioannovich*, the second play of Alexei Tolstoy's trilogy of verse plays about the troubled period that followed the death of Ivan the Terrible. Encouraged by that play's success, Nemirovich-Danchenko and Stanislavsky staged the first play of the trilogy, *The Death of Ivan the Terrible*, in their next season. Olga Knipper thought this production a failure and wrote Chekhov a despondent letter about it.

2. In the 1944–51 edition, this sentence reads: "When he directs, he's an artist [. . .]." In the late 1930s, Stanislavsky's style of directing and the method of acting he had devised were proclaimed the only ones compatible with Socialist Realism and all other styles of directing and acting were condemned as "formalist." To criticize Stanislavsky for anything whatsoever became unthinkable. Chekhov's reference to Stanislavsky's merchant-class origin and to his personal wealth (both perfectly true) was even more shocking to the Stalinist censor than the disrespectful gibe at his dabbling in art. The deleted portion of the sentence was restored in the 1963–64 edition.

3. "Inspector of the actresses" was a nickname given to Chekhov by some of the company's actors because of his close relationship with Olga Knipper.

130. To Grigory Rossolimo[1]

Yalta,
October 11, 1899

Dear Grigory Ivanovich,

I sent Dr. Raltsevich eight rubles fifty for the photograph and five rubles for dues today.[2] I'm sending a photograph of myself (a pretty poor one, taken when my *enteritis* was at its worst) to your address, registered mail. My autobiography? I have a malady called autobiographophobia. It is real torture for me to read any details whatsoever about myself, to say nothing of writing them up for the press. I am enclosing several dates entirely unadorned on a separate sheet of paper. That's the best I can do. If you like, you may add that on my application to the rector for admission to the university I wrote: The School of Med*a*cine.

You ask when we're going to see one another. Not before spring, probably. I'm in Yalta, in exile, a beautiful exile perhaps, but exile just the same. Life goes by drearily. My health is tolerable, but I'm well only on certain days. In addition to everything else I have hemorrhoidal piles and catarrh *recti*, and there are days when frequent bowel movements leave me utterly exhausted. I'll have to have an operation.

I'm very sorry to have missed the dinner and the chance to see all my old friends. An Alumnal Aid Society for members of our graduating class is a fine idea, but it would be more practical and more practicable to have a "mutual aid fund," something like our writers' fund. Whenever a member died, his family would receive the benefits; new payments would be collected only when a member died.

Why don't you come to the Crimea in the summer or fall? It's a pleasant place to relax. By the way, the southern coast has become the favorite vacation spot for Moscow Province *zemstvo* doctors. They find the accommodations here cheap and good and always leave delighted.

If something interesting comes up, please write me about it. I'm really bored here, and if I don't get any letters, I may hang myself, learn to drink bad Crimean wine, or start an affair with a plain and stupid woman.

Keep well. I firmly clasp your hand and send my most cordial regards to you and your family.

Yours,
A. Chekhov

I, A. P. Chekhov, was born on January 17, 1860, in Taganrog. I was educated first at the Greek school of the Church of the Emperor Constantine and then at the Taganrog gymnasium. In 1879 I entered the Medical School of Moscow University. I had a very dim idea of the university at the time, and I do not remember exactly what prompted me to choose medical school, but I have had no reason to regret the choice. During my first year of studies, I began publishing in weekly magazines and newspapers, and by the early eighties these literary activities had taken on a permanent, professional character. In 1888 I was awarded the Pushkin Prize. In 1890 I traveled to the Island of Sakhalin and wrote a book about our penal colony and hard labor. Not counting trial reporting, reviews, miscellaneous articles, short news items and the columns I wrote from day to day for the press and which would be difficult to locate and collect, during the twenty years I have been active in literature I have written and published more than forty-eight hundred pages of novellas and stories. I have written plays as well.

There is no doubt in my mind that my study of medicine has had a serious impact on my literary activities. It significantly broadened the scope of my observations and enriched me with knowledge whose value for me as a writer only a doctor can appreciate. It also served as a guiding influence; my intimacy with medicine probably helped me to avoid many mistakes. My familiarity with the natural sciences and the scientific method has always kept me on my guard; I have tried where-ever possible to take scientific data into account, and where it has not been possible I have preferred not writing at all. Let me note in this connection that the principles of creative art do not always admit of full accord with scientific data; death by poison cannot be represented on stage as it actually happens. But some accord with scientific data should be felt even within the boundaries of artistic convention, that is, the reader or spectator should be made to realize that convention is involved but that the author is also well versed in the reality of the situation. I am not one of those writers who negate the value of science and would not wish to be one of those who believe they can figure out everything for themselves.

As for my medical practice, I worked as a student in the Voskresensk Zemstvo Hospital (near the New Jerusalem Monastery) with the well-known *zemstvo* doctor Pavel Arkhangelsky and spent a brief period as a doctor in the Zvenigorod Hospital. During the years of the cholera epidemic (1892 and 1893) I headed the Melikhovo Region of the Serpukhov District.

1. Dr. Grigory Rossolimo was Chekhov's fellow student at the Medical School of Moscow University and he eventually returned there as a professor of medicine. At the class reunion held in 1899 which Chekhov attended, it was decided to publish an album containing the photographs and autobiographies of all the alumni of the 1884 class. Rossolimo and Dr. Raltsevich were put in charge of editing the volume and collecting the materials for it.

Chekhov and Rossolimo became particularly friendly during Chekhov's Yalta years. Rossolimo's memoir of Chekhov is another nonliterary memoir that, like Altschuller's, shows us Chekhov the physician and scientist.

2. The money was in payment for alumni association dues and for the photograph of the class reunion.

131. To Vsevolod Meyerhold[1]

Yalta,
October, 1899

Dear Vsevolod Emilyevich,

I don't have the text handy and can therefore talk about the role of Johannes only in the most general terms. If you send me the role, I'll read it to freshen my memory and then write you in more detail.[2] For the time being all I will say is what may be of the most direct, practical interest to you. To begin with, Johannes is an intellectual through and through. He is a young scholar who has grown up in a university town. He lacks all bourgeois characteristics and has the manners of a well-bred young man who is accustomed to the society of decent people (such as Anna). His movements and appearance are gentle and full of youth, like those of a man who has been brought up in a family and pampered by that family and is still living under mamma's wing. Johannes is a German scholar and is therefore dignified in dealing with men. When left alone with women, on the other hand, he becomes tender in a feminine manner. The scene where he cannot keep from caressing his wife even though he already loves or is beginning to love Anna illustrates this point nicely. Now about his nerves. Don't stress his nervousness to the point of allowing his neuropathological nature to obstruct or subjugate what is more important: his loneliness, the sort of loneliness that only lofty, yet healthy (in the highest sense) personalities experience. Project a lonely man, and show his nervousness only insofar as the script indicates. Don't interpret his nervousness as an individual phenomenon. Keep in mind that nowadays almost every civilized person, no matter how healthy he may be, never feels so irritated as when he is at home among his own family because the discord between past and present is felt primarily within the family. The irritation is chronic; it has no pathos, no convulsive outbursts. It is an irritation that guests fail to notice, because its entire burden falls primarily on the people he is closest to—his mother or wife. It is an intimate, family irritation, so to speak. Don't dwell on it, show it as only *one* of his typical traits, and don't overdo it, or you'll make him an irritable young man rather than a lonely one. I know, Konstantin Sergeyevich[3] will insist on playing up his excessive nervousness; he'll take an exaggerated view of it. But don't give in, don't sacrifice the beauty and power of your voice and delivery for something as trivial as a highlight. Don't sacrifice them, because the irritation is in fact only a detail, a triviality.[4]

Many thanks for having thought about me. Please write again. It will be very magnanimous on your part because I'm bored. The weather here is magnificent and warm, but that's only gravy, and what good is gravy without the meat?

Keep well. I firmly clasp your hand and wish you all the best.

Yours,
A. Chekhov

My regards to Olga Leonardovna, Alexander Leonidovich, Burdzhalov and Luzhsky.[5] Thank you once again for the telegram.

1. If Stanislavsky and Nemirovich-Danchenko were the original pioneers of the great flowering of Russian theater at the beginning of our century, Vsevolod Meyerhold (1874–1940) was the most creative and innovative theatrical genius that age produced. He began as an actor with the original Moscow Art Theater company after studying drama with Nemirovich-Danchenko. Chekhov was highly pleased with Meyerhold's tense and sensitive interpretation of Treplyov in *The Seagull* and he later wrote the role of Tusenbach in *Three Sisters* with him in mind. After the first few seasons, Meyerhold left the Moscow Art Theater, since it no longer satisfied his urge for theatrical innovation and his growing political radicalism. He worked in the provinces as a director, staging some memorable productions of Chekhov's plays, until in 1906 he was invited to join Vera Kommissarzhevskaya's company, where for a while he was given a free hand to be as inventive and experimental as he liked. In the years preceding the Revolution, Meyerhold became the leading director at the Imperial Theaters, where he was allowed to do some highly innovative productions of drama at the previously convention-bound Empress Alexandra Theater and of opera at the Empress Maria (Mariinsky) Theater in St. Petersburg.

Unlike Stanislavsky, who mistrusted too much modernism, Meyerhold had a Diaghilev-like knack for sensing new and interesting developments in the arts. In his Kommissarzhevskaya and Imperial Theater period, he did memorable productions of poetic dramas by Alexander Blok, Fyodor Sologub, Zinaida Gippius and Alexei Remizov (whom he encouraged to write for the theater and in whose prose he had tried earlier to interest Chekhov), plays that were far more original and profound as literature than the plays by Gorky and Andreyev, in which Stanislavsky specialized after Chekhov's death.

The October Revolution opened a dazzlingly creative new period in Meyerhold's career. Once more he made common cause with the finest new playwright of the age, Mayakovsky. The specifically theatrical and highly imaginative concept of the theater that Meyerhold had devised before the Revolution now underwent a series of spectacular transformations, with the result that, as another important director of the period remarked, each new production of Meyerhold could become a source for a whole new school of stagecraft. In addition to his productions of Mayakovsky, the highlights of

Meyerhold's post-revolutionary achievement were his drastically modernistic reinterpretations of nineteenth-century Russian playwrights: Griboyedov, Ostrovsky, Sukhovo-Kobylin and especially Gogol. It was Meyerhold's production of *The Inspector General* that returned to this play its true surrealistic, dreamlike essence after a century of simplistically reducing it to mere photographic realism. In the 1920s and '30s, Meyerhold's company was one of the Soviet Union's principal cultural exports; its influence on theaters in other countries had an impact that is still with us today.

In 1938, during the witch hunt on "formalism" and the imposition of ever-greater standardization in the arts, Meyerhold's theater was closed after a brief, government-inspired campaign of vilification in the press. Only one man in the whole of the Soviet Union dared come to Meyerhold's defense: Stanislavsky, who gave him a minor appointment on his staff. In 1939, at a congress of stage directors in Moscow, Meyerhold got up and instead of repenting for his past mistakes, as everyone had expected, accused the authorities of murdering the Russian theater by their forced standardization and their total ban on all creativity and originality. He was arrested as he was leaving the auditorium and sent to a labor camp, where he died a year later under still unexplained circumstances. His wife, the actress Zinaida Raikh, was brutally murdered in their apartment. A legend of his retirement to the provinces was concocted for dissemination abroad, and one can still read in American and British theater journals of the 1940s that Meyerhold's theater lost its one-time popularity and that he was transferred at his own request to some remote town, where he was alive and working happily.

There followed one of the most amazing exercises in revising history that was ever undertaken. In 1937, Soviet papers wrote that Meyerhold was a bourgeois formalist; from 1939 on, the line was that he had never existed. Not only was his name no longer mentionable anywhere, it also had to be removed from works written before he was purged. For the next fifteen years, his name was systematically deleted from all publications devoted to three of the most popular and highly honored figures in the entire field of the Russian arts, who were all intimately connected with Meyerhold: Chekhov, Stanislavsky and Mayakovsky. The entire voluminous documentation on the origins of the Moscow Art Theater that was published in the forties is full of holes and deletions due to the frequent appearance of Meyerhold's name in the original documents. Key passages had to be removed from the new editions of Stanslavsky's ever-popular *My Life in Art.* The 1944–51 edition of Chekhov's letters omitted the present letter to Meyerhold and deleted his name from most of the letters to other persons where it occurred, but through either oversight (which is unlikely) or deliberate sabotage, a few references to him in Chekhov's letters to his wife were allowed to remain. To avoid trouble, the editors have not listed Meyerhold's name in the detailed alphabetical indexes with which each volume of that edition is provided—the only such instance of a non-indexed name in the entire twenty volumes.

Meyerhold has been rehabilitated in the post-Stalinist period. Collections of his articles have appeared in the late sixties and a fine, detailed biography (which, however, totally avoids discussing the last three years of Meyerhold's life) by Konstantin Rudnitsky was published in Moscow in 1969. A set of letters from Meyerhold to Chekhov was included in the Chekhov volume of *Literary Heritage*. The present letter from Chekhov to Meyerhold is the only one that survived from about a dozen letters Chekhov is known to have written him. It was originally published in the *Imperial Theater Yearbook* for 1909 and reprinted in the 1963–64 edition of Chekhov's letters.

2. On September 29, 1889, Meyerhold wrote to Chekhov: "I am addressing to you a small request, apologizing in advance if you think it insolent. Here is what it is. I have been given the role of Johannes in *Lonely Lives* by Hauptmann. Please help me in my work on preparing for this role. Write me what you would expect from a performer of Johannes. How do you see him? Write me, even if only in very general terms, if doing this will not fatigue you. Rehearsals begin next week."

3. Stanislavsky.

4. After receiving this letter, Meyerhold wrote back on October 23: "Thank you for your characterization of Johannes. Although you touched upon it only very generally, you did it so masterfully that the personality of Johannes was quite clearly outlined. [. . .] And anyway, everything you sketched out about Johannes in your letter, even in its generality, suggests of itself a whole series of details which thoroughly harmonize with the image of a lonely intellectual, who is elegant, healthy and nevertheless profoundly melancholy."

Meyerhold's admiration for Chekhov kept growing, as his subsequent letters reveal; it found a culmination of sorts when Meyerhold sent Chekhov his photograph, inscribed: "From the pale-faced Meyerhold to his God."

5. Olga Knipper and the Moscow Art Theater actors Alexander Vishnevsky, Georgy Burdzhalov and Vasily Luzhsky.

132. To Vladimir Posse[1]

Yalta,
November 19, 1899

Dear Vladimir Alexandrovich,

Your letter is still lying on my desk waiting for an answer. It has been like a severe reproach all this time, but now that I've sent you an answer to your telegram, I have finally taken up my pen to write. You see, I've been writing a short novel for *Life*, and it will be ready soon, by the second half of December, most likely. It is only about fifty pages long, but it has a multitude of characters milling about, and things are very crowded; it takes quite a bit of fuss and bother to keep the milling about from getting too noticeable. At any rate, it will have taken shape completely around the 10th of December and will be ready then to be typeset. But here's the problem: I'm haunted by the fear that the censors are going to pluck it bare. I won't be able to endure the censors' cuts, at least I don't think I will. The reason why I couldn't make up my mind to write you anything definite or give you a final answer is that the censors might not like the way certain passages have turned out. Now, of course, I am giving you a definite answer, provided that you return my story to me if you too find that certain passages will be unacceptable to the censors, that is, if you too foresee the danger of its being cut here and there by the censors.[2]

And now a favor: please don't print my name in such tall characters in your advertisements. Really, that's not the way to do things. Print it in the same line as the rest, in alphabetical order.

Where is Maxim Gorky?

Keep well, now. I wish you many subscribers and as many readers as possible—a hundred thousand or so. I clasp your hand.

Devotedly,
A. Chekhov

1. The publisher of the "legal" Marxist journal *Life*.
2. "In the Ravine," which was published in the January 1900 issue of *Life* and which had no difficulty with the censorship whatsoever.

133. To Grigory Rossolimo

Yalta,
January 21, 1900

Dear Grigory Ivanovich,

You may add the appropriate P.S. to my autobiography, but it would be best to wait for the general meeting of the Academy when the election results will be made final.[1]

I am sending you by registered mail the pieces I have written that would seem most suitable for children, my two dog stories.[2] I don't think I've done anything else along those lines. I lack the ability to write for children; I write for them once every ten years. I don't like what is known as children's literature; I don't recognize its validity. Children should be given only what is suitable for adults as well. Children enjoy reading Andersen, *The Frigate Pallada*, and Gogol, and so do adults. One shouldn't write for children; one should learn to choose works suitable for children from among those already written for adults—in other words, from genuine works of art. It is better and more to the point to learn to choose the correct medicine and to prescribe the correct dosage than to try to dream up some special medicine just because the patient is a child. Forgive me for this medical comparison, but it happens to be quite timely; I've been practicing medicine for four days now, treating myself and my mother. It looks like influenza: headaches and temperature.

If I write anything, I'll let you know in time, but one man and one man only may publish what I write—Marx! For everything published by someone other than Marx, I have to pay a five-thousand-ruble fine for every sixteen pages of print.

My brother Ivan Pavlovich is a teacher and has been involved with small children for over twenty years. He has an excellent knowledge of what does and does not appeal to children. He would be of no help to you in putting the collection together because he's a poor editor, but if you ever take it into your head to put out a bibliography of fiction and nonfiction suitable for children my brother could give you quite a lot of good advice. He teaches in Moscow. His address is: Novaya Basmannaya, Moscow. He has a good nose for practical matters.

Your letter made me very happy and mixed a bit of soda into my acid mood. Thank you for thinking of me. My story will be coming out soon in *Life*; it's the latest one dealing with the peasant life.[3]

I firmly clasp your hand.

Yours,
A. Chekhov

1. In commemoration of the Pushkin centennial, the Imperial Academy of Sciences instituted a literary section. Nominated as honorary members of the new section of the Academy were Tolstoy, Chekhov, Korolenko, Koni, the very important and influential philosopher and poet Vladimir Solovyov, the playwright Alexei Potekhin, minor poets Arseny Golenishchev-Kutuzov and Alexei Zhemchuzhnikov, literary historian Konstantin Arsenyev and the Grand Duke Konstantin, who published verse under the initials K.R. (for Romanov). Rossolimo wanted to add the election to the Academy to the autobiography Chekhov had sent him for the class album.

2. Rossolimo was active in the Family Section of the Russian Pedagogical Society and was preparing an anthology of literary works suitable for children. Chekhov's two dog stories are "Kashtanka" of 1887 and "Whitebrow" of 1895.

3. "In the Ravine."

134. To Mikhail Menshikov[1]

Yalta,
January 28, 1900

Dear Mikhail Osipovich,

Tolstoy's illness is beyond me.[2] Cherinov[3] hasn't answered my letter, and it's impossible to draw any conclusions from what the newspapers say or from what you have now written. Intestinal or stomach ulcers would involve different symptoms. So he doesn't have any, or he may have had several bleeding lacerations caused by gallstones which passed and wounded the intestinal wall. Nor does he have cancer, because cancer would have shown itself in a loss of appetite and in his general condition, but above all, his face would have betrayed it, if he had cancer. No, Lev Nikolayevich is most probably well (except for the gallstones) and has another twenty years ahead of him. His illness frightened me and made me very tense. I fear Tolstoy's death. His death would leave a large empty space in my life. First, I have loved no man the way I have loved him. I am not a believer, but of all beliefs I consider his the closest to mine and most suitable for me. Second, when literature has a Tolstoy, it is easy and gratifying to be a writer. Even if you are aware that you have never accomplished anything and are still not accomplishing anything, you don't feel so bad, because Tolstoy accomplishes enough for everyone. His activities provide justification for the hopes and aspirations that are usually placed on literature. Third, Tolstoy stands firm, his authority is enormous, and as long as he is alive bad taste in literature, all vulgarity in its brazen-faced or lachrymose varieties, all bristly or resentful vanity will remain far in the background. His moral authority alone is enough to maintain what we think of as literary trends and schools at a certain minimal level. If not for him, literature would be a flock without a shepherd or an unfathomable jumble.

To finish with Tolstoy, let me say a word about *Resurrection*, which I read in one sitting, and not in bits and snatches. It is a remarkable work of art. The least interesting aspect is everything pertaining to Nekhlyudov's relationship with Maslova;[4] the most interesting—the princes, generals, Nekhlyudov's aunts, the peasants, prisoners and prison wardens. I could barely breathe as I read the scenes with the general who is both the commandant of the Peter and Paul Fortress and a spiritualist—it was so good! And Madame Korchagina carried around in her chair and Fedosya's peasant husband! The peasant says his wife can handle anything.[5] That's just what Tolstoy's pen is like—it can handle anything. The novel has no ending; what it does have can't be called an ending. To write so much and then suddenly make a Gospel text responsible for it all smacks a bit too much of the seminary. Resolving everything by a Gospel text is as arbitrary as dividing prisoners into five categories. Why five and not ten? Why a Gospel text and not a text from the Koran? First he has to force his readers to believe in the Gospel, to believe that it alone is the truth, and only then can he resolve everything by the text.

Have I bored you? When you come to the Crimea, I'm going to

do an interview with you and print it in *News of the Day*. What reporters write about Tolstoy is like what old women say about holy idiots—unctuous nonsense. He shouldn't waste his time talking with those Yids.[6]

I was unwell for about two weeks, but I managed to get along. Now I have a plaster under my left clavicle, which makes me feel quite well. Actually it's not even the plaster that makes me feel well; it's the red spot left over from it.

I'll be sure to send you my photograph. I am happy to be elected a member of the Academy because it's gratifying to know that Sigma[7] is envious of me now. I'll be even happier, though, when I lose the title after some misunderstanding. And there is sure to be a misunderstanding, because the scholars of the Academy are always afraid we're going to shock them.[8] They elected Tolstoy only grudgingly. In their eyes he's a nihilist. At least that's what a certain lady—the wife of a privy councilor—has called him, which I think is cause for giving him my heartfelt congratulations.

I haven't been receiving *The Week*. Why not? The editorial offices have in their possession a manuscript I sent them called "Ivan Ivanovich Makes a Fool of Himself" by S. Voskresensky.[9] If it isn't accepted, send it back to me.

Stay well. I firmly clasp your hand. Greetings to Yasha and to Lydia Ivanovna.[10]

Yours,
A. Chekhov

Write!

1. Mikhail Menshikov was a well-known journalist and magazine editor.

2. Chekhov was alarmed by press reports about Tolstoy's recovery from an "attack of colic." Actually, Tolstoy was reasonably well at the time and leading an active life in Moscow. While Chekhov was worrying about the state of Tolstoy's health, Tolstoy was becoming alarmed at the moral turn he thought Chekhov's work was taking. Early in January of 1900, he read "The Lady with the Dog" and commented: "All that comes from Nietzsche. People who had never formed a clear-cut world view to help them distinguish good from evil." On January 24, Tolstoy suddenly appeared at the Moscow Art Theater during a performance of *Uncle Vanya*. Numerous memoirs have recorded that historical evening and all of them agree that Tolstoy found the play inept dramatically and repellent morally. It was in connection with *Uncle Vanya* that Tolstoy was to remark to Chekhov subsequently: "You know I can't stand Shakespeare, but your plays are even worse than his."

3. Professor Mikhail Cherinov of the Medical School of Moscow University.

4. What Chekhov finds least interesting is the central relationship of the entire novel: a nobleman's moral resurrection after he recognizes in a

prostitute being tried for murder an innocent young girl he had once seduced and abandoned.

5. In Tolstoy's *Resurrection,* Fedosya is a teen-aged peasant girl, married against her will into a family where she at first feels so lost and terrified that she tries to poison her young husband. Arrested by the police, Fedosya is then released on bail to her husband's family and after a few days realizes that she likes all of them very much once she has gotten to know them. To show her repentance, she works very hard during the gathering of the harvest, eliciting by her dexterity her husband's admiring adjective *ukhvatistaya,* translated here contextually as "can handle anything." Constance Garnett, a great expert in Russian literature, does not seem to have read *Resurrection,* for she translated that last sentence as: "The peasant calls his grandmother 'an artful one.'" (The poor Fedosya is only sixteen years old.) In Lillian Hellman's collection the passage appears as "This peasant calls his old lady a crafty character. So it is with Tolstoy; he has a crafty pen."

6. A possible reference to Michel Deline, to whom Chekhov took a strong dislike after his open letter to Suvorin and whose unctuous manner of writing about Tolstoy irritated Chekhov.

7. Sigma was the pen name of a *New Times* reporter whose real name was Sergei Syromyatnikov.

8. In view of Chekhov's subsequent resignation from the Academy, this turned out to be a prophetic statement.

9. This was a story written by Father Sergius Shchukin, the Yalta priest whose literary ambitions Chekhov encouraged. See also Letter 183.

10. Lydia Veselitskaya (V. Mikulich), who, judging from Chekhov's other letters, was living with Menshikov at the time and taking care of his little son Yasha.

135. To Ivan Leontyev (Shcheglov)

Yalta,
February 2, 1900

Dear Jean,

Here is my answer to your last letter.[1] Stanislavsky's full name is Konstantin Sergeyevich Alexeyev, The Alexeyev House near Red Gate, Moscow. Plays are also read by Vladimir Nemirovich-Danchenko (The Art Theater, Carriage Row). To date they don't seem to have put on any one-act plays. If they like the play, they'll put it on. "Liking it" in their language means it suits them and is interesting from the director's point of view and generally theatrical. For such an out-of-the-ordinary theater you'd do best to write a play in four acts that is authentically Shcheglovian and artistic, something like *The Gordian Knot,* without any reporters or noble old writers. Dear Jean, you aren't suited for exposés, bile, anger or what you call "independence," i.e., criticism directed against liberals and the new generation. The Lord gave you a kind and tender heart, so why not put it to good use? Write with a gentle pen and a carefree spirit. Don't think about the wrongs that have been done you. You say you're my admirer. Well, I'm your admirer too, and a very steadfast one, because I know you and I know the stuff your talent is made of, and no one can shake me loose from my firm conviction that you possess a genuine divine spark. But because of the way things have turned out you're irritated, you're knee deep in trivialities, you're worn out by trivialities, you always expect the worst, you lack faith in yourself. That's what makes you think constantly of illnesses and poverty, of a pension and of Weinberg.[2] You're too young to think about a pension, and if Weinberg has begun to treat you coldly, he has a basis or a right for doing so. You published a protest exposing the Literary and Theatrical Committee which at the time made a painful impression on everyone, probably because that sort of thing is not normally done. Be objective, take a look at everything with the eye of a good, kind man, with your own eye, I mean, and sit down and write a story or play about life in Russia—not a criticism of Russian life, simply a joyous song, the song of the Goldfinch,[3] about Russian life and life in general. Our life comes only once, and there is no point, honestly there isn't, in wasting it on exposing Yids, venomous wives and the Committee. Dear Jean, be fair for once to yourself and your talent. Set your ship upon the open seas; don't confine it to the Fontanka.[4] Forgive everyone who has offended you, forget about them, and, I repeat, sit down and write.

Forgive me for lapsing into the singsong tones of a prayerful woman. But my feelings for you are sincere and comradely, and this is not the time to try to get by with a brief, businesslike answer.

I would be very glad should fate bring us together this spring. I haven't seen Laur[5] for a long time, nor have I heard any gossip from him.

I have not entirely regained my health, but I'm getting along. I'm doing better this year than last. Mother sends many thanks for your regards and asks me to send you hers.

Give my best to your wife and keep well, dear Jean. I firmly clasp your hand.

Yours,
A. Chekhov

1. Ivan Shcheglov's literary and playwriting career had been steadily going to seed throughout the 1890s. He had apparently written Chekhov asking him if he could offer a play to the Moscow Art Theater.

2. Pyotr Weinberg, a satirical poet, popular in the 1860s and a translator of Heine into Russian. He was the chairman of the Literary and Theatrical Committee.

3. The name Shcheglov is derived from the Russian word for goldfinch.

4. A small river in St. Petersburg.

5. Dr. Alexander Laur, a now-forgotten physician-playwright.

136. To Alexei Suvorin

Yalta,
February 12, 1900

I've been racking my brains over the fourth act, and the only thing I've come up with is that you can't end with the nihilists. It's too stormy and strident. What your play needs is a quiet, lyrical, touching ending. If your heroine grows old without getting anywhere or coming to terms with herself and sees that everyone has abandoned her and that she is uninteresting and useless, if she comes to realize that the people around her are idle, useless and wicked people (her own father included) and that she's let life pass her by—isn't that more frightening than nihilists?[1]

Your columns about Korsh and "The Water Nymph" were very good.[2] The tone is brilliant, and they're marvelously written. But in my opinion you shouldn't have written about Konovalova and the jurors, no matter how tempting a topic it may have been.[3] Let A-t[4] write as much as he pleases, not you; it's not your specialty. Only a narrow person can treat issues like those with boldness and self-assurance; but you, halfway through the column you are sure to stumble, the way you did when you suddenly began going on about how everyone wishes to commit a murder at one time or other and everyone wishes the death of his neighbor. When a daughter-in-law is fed up with a cranky, ailing old mother-in-law, she may breathe easier at the thought that the old woman will soon be dead, but that doesn't mean she wishes her to die. It is merely exhaustion, spiritual infirmity, irritation and a yearning for peace and quiet. If the daughter-in-law were ordered to murder the old woman, she would rather kill herself, no matter what desires had stirred within her.

Yes, of course jurors are only human and can make mistakes, but what does that prove? It sometimes happens that alms are mistakenly given to the well fed rather than the hungry, but no matter how much you write about it you won't get anywhere, and if anything you'll harm the hungry. Whether, from our vantage point, jurors make mistakes or not, we must admit that they judge each individual case conscientiously and follow to the utmost the dictates of their consciences. If a ship's captain navigates his ship conscientiously, keeping a constant eye on the map and compass, and if there is a shipwreck nonetheless, isn't it more correct to seek the cause for the shipwreck in something other than the captain, an out-of-date map, perhaps, or a change in the ocean floor? After all, jurors have to take three things into account: (1) Besides official law, besides codes and juridical decisions, there is moral law, which always precedes official law and determines our actions whenever we wish to act in accordance with our conscience. Thus, according to law your daughter is entitled to one-seventh of your estate, but you, prompted by demands of a purely moral nature, go beyond the law and in spite of it leave her as much as you leave your sons because you know that, had you acted in any other way, you'd have been acting contrary to your conscience. Jurors also sometimes find themselves in the position of knowing and feeling that official law does not satisfy their conscience, that the case they are deciding contains nuances and niceties not encompassed by the Penal Code, that to arrive at the correct decision something else is needed, and that the lack of that "something else" will lead them to deliver a sentence in which, whether they like it or not, something will be lacking. (2) Jurors are aware that acquittal is not the same as absolution and that acquittal does not free the defendant from the Day of Judgment in the other world, from the court of his own conscience or the court of public opinion. They resolve an issue only in its legal aspects and leave it up to A-t to decide whether murdering children is good or bad. (3) The defendant comes to court already exhausted by prison and inquest and remains in a state of torment during the trial, so that even if acquitted he does not leave the court unpunished.

But whether I'm right or wrong, it looks as if my letter is almost finished, and I have written essentially nothing.

It is spring here in Yalta. There's nothing new or interesting. I bought the last volume of Tolstoy's collected works in the local bookshop, the volume that includes *Resurrection*, but it turned out to be a clear and simple forgery of Tolstoy's edition—Klyukin's fine handiwork.[5] When I asked where they had ordered it, they told me it was from Suvorin's outlet in Odessa.

Who is the Doubting Thomas?[6] Greetings and humble regards to Anna Ivanovna, Nastya and Borya. Won't you come to the Crimea in the spring? We could take a carriage from Yalta to Feodosia and the monastery. Keep well. I send you my regards.

Yours,
A. Chekhov

Resurrection is a remarkable novel. I enjoyed it very much, but it has to be read all at once, in one sitting. The ending is uninteresting and false, false in a technical sense.

1. When Suvorin was undergoing his ordeal during the student strike, Maria Savina performed his melodrama *Tatyana Repina* during her guest appearance in Berlin, where the play enjoyed a considerable success. This gave Suvorin the encouragement to write a new play in a similar manner. He decided to base it in part on his earlier novel *Fin de siècle*. In January of 1900, he sent Chekhov the draft of the first three acts of the new play, asking for his suggestions. Chekhov's conception of drama had undergone a considerable evolution since 1888, when he had thought highly of *Tatyana Repina* and had helped arrange its Moscow production. On January 23, Chekhov wrote Suvorin, offering him a detailed critique of his new play, which he thought in many ways old-fashioned and conventional.

The first paragraph of the present letter represents Chekhov's reaction to the fourth act of Suvorin's new play, which was sent to him separately. Chekhov is here advising Suvorin to abandon the traditional melodramatic dénouement, so typical of Suvorin's other plays, and to end the play with a quiet, lyrical scene—the sort of ending that Chekhov himself had devised for *Uncle Vanya* and was to use again in *Three Sisters* and *The Cherry Orchard.* The solution was patently alien to the school of dramatic writing that Suvorin represented, as he himself demonstrated by the derogatory comments we find in his journal about the supposedly ineffectual ending of *Three Sisters*.

The play, called *The Question,* was eventually finished by Suvorin in 1902. It was presented at the end of that year in Maria Savina's benefit performance, and during the next two years or so it was played by such leading actresses as Vera Kommissarzhevskaya throughout Russia.

2. After having to disagree violently with the contents of Suvorin's column for such a long time, it must have been a relief for Chekhov to find a group of columns he could approve. This set of six columns contained Suvorin's point by point refutation of a supposedly scholarly study by the philologist Fyodor Korsh (not to be confused with the theatrical impresario of the same name), in which Korsh had tried to prove that a patently spurious and forged ending of Pushkin's unfinished play *The Water Nymph* (also known in English as *Rusalka*) published by the journal *Russian Archive* in 1897 was in fact Pushkin's own work.

3. The publication and success of Tolstoy's *Resurrection* in 1899 had an unexpected and rather unfortunate side effect. The early chapters of the novel, which depict a miscarriage of justice during a trial by jury, served to revive the criticism of the whole jury system in the more conservative segment of the press. The jury system had been a repeated target of Russian conservatives ever since its introduction in the 1860s and especially after the trial of Vera Zasulich, who was accused of shooting the mayor of St. Petersburg and acquitted at a trial by jury presided over by Anatoly Koni in 1879. Never one to miss a conservative trend, Suvorin published a column

on February 3, 1900, in which he attacked the jury's acquittal of a woman who was on trial on charges of infanticide. Her acquittal led Suvorin to express doubts about the efficacy of the jury system in general. Chekhov, drawing on his own experience as a jury member in his Melikhovo days, is here gently reminding Suvorin of the human dimensions of that institution.

4. A-t was the pen name of *New Times*'s court reporter, Vladimir Peterson, who in his article about the same trial to which Suvorin had devoted his column openly demanded the conviction of the defendant.

5. The publisher Maxim Klyukin came out in 1900 with an unauthorized edition of *Resurrection,* which was disfigured by a large number of arbitrary cuts and abridgments.

6. "Doubting Thomas" was the pen name used by the historian Grigory Nemirov to sign an article about a Mardi Gras celebration in Moscow, which he published in *New Times*.

137. To Alexei Peshkov (Maxim Gorky)

Yalta,
February 15, 1900

Dear Alexei Maximovich,

Your article in the Nizhny Novgorod *Press* was balsam to my soul.[1] How talented you are! All I can write is fiction, while you have full command of the journalist's pen as well. At first I thought I liked the article merely because you were praising me, but then it turned out that Sredin and his family and Yartsev[2] are all delighted with it. Well, go ahead and take your chances with journalism too, and the Lord will bless you.

Why hasn't anyone sent me *Foma Gordeyev*? I've only read it in bits and snatches, and I ought to read it all the way through in one sitting, as I recently read *Resurrection*. Everything in that novel—except for the rather vague and contrived relationship of Nekhlyudov to Maslova—everything contributed to my amazement at the power and wealth and breadth and insincerity of a man who fears death, but refuses to admit it, and therefore grasps at texts from the Scriptures.

Write and tell them to send me *Foma*.

"Twenty-Six Men and a Girl" is a good story, the best of anything yet published in that dilettante journal *Life*. It very strongly evokes its setting. You can smell the rolls.[3]

Life printed my story with some blatant misprints despite the fact that I had read proof.[4] There are other things I find irritating about *Life*: Chirikov's provincial vignettes, that "Happy New Year" picture, and Gurevich's story.[5]

Your letter has just been brought to me. So you don't want to go to India? Too bad. Once you've got an India and a long ocean voyage in your past, you're never at a loss for something to think back on when you have insomnia. A trip abroad doesn't take that much time, and it won't stop you from taking that walking tour around Russia.[6]

I'm bored, but not in the *Weltschmerz* sense, not in the sense of metaphysical yearning;[7] I am merely bored because I miss company, I miss music—which I love, and I miss women—of which Yalta has none. I also miss caviar and sauerkraut.

I'm very sorry that you seem to have changed your mind about coming to Yalta. The Art Theater will be here from Moscow in May. It will give five performances and then stay on to rehearse. Why don't you come? You can study staging methods and possibilities during the rehearsals, and then you'll be able to write a play within five to eight days, which I would welcome gladly, from the bottom of my heart.

Yes, I now have the right to stress that I'm forty and no longer a young man. I used to be our youngest writer, but then you came along—and all at once I grew sedate, and now no one calls me the youngest any more.[8] I clasp your hand. Be well.

Yours,
A. Chekhov

I've just received Zhukovsky's article.[9]

1. On January 30, 1900, Gorky published in that provincial newspaper a remarkably bland little essay on Chekhov's story "In the Ravine," in which he praised the story but said almost nothing concrete about it. The annotators of this letter in the 1944–51 edition of Chekhov call that article "a profound characterization of Chekhov's *oeuvre*" but are at a loss to quote or paraphrase anything to support this statement.

2. The painter Grigory Yartsev, who was a friend of Dr. Sredin's family in Yalta.

3. The kind of roll that Chekhov mentions is the hard one with the hole in the middle which is now called "bagel" in the United States. But a translation of *bubliki* as "bagels" would have moved the setting of Gorky's story from a bakery in Russia to a New York Jewish delicatessen for most American readers.

4. The publication of "In the Ravine" in Posse's *Life* caused Chekhov considerable worry because of the unprecedented number of typographical errors the proofs contained and the printers' failure to correct them in the second set of proofs that was sent to Chekhov at his request.

5. In addition to Chekhov's story and Gorky's "Twenty-Six Men and a Girl," the January 1900 edition of *Life* contained Yevgeny Chirikov's "Provincial Vignettes," a front-page photograph of an unidentified hobo with the inscription "Happy New Year!" and a story by the woman writer, critic and editor Lyubov Gurevich called "The Fare."

6. In his letter of *ca.* February 11, Gorky thanked Chekhov for "writing me sermons like an archpriest" and informed him that he had given up his plans to travel to India and had decided to go on a walking tour of Russia instead.

7. In the same letter, Gorky wrote: "You know, it's very unpleasant to read in your letters that you are bored. It is utterly unbecoming to you, you see, and entirely unnecessary."

8. Gorky had written, in the letter cited in the last two notes: "You write: I am already forty. You are still only forty! And in the meantime, what a lot you've written and how you've written it! That's the whole point. It is tragic that all Russians value themselves for less than they are worth and you seem to be guilty of it too."

9. An article on Chekhov by the journalist D. E. Zhukovsky. It bore a title that was typical of Chekhov criticism at the turn of the century: "The Poet of Decadence." For some reason, Gorky thought the article quite wonderful.

138. To Vladimir Posse

Yalta,
February 29, 1900

Dear Vladimir Alexandrovich,

Gorky has informed me that you two are planning a trip to Yalta. When will you be coming? There's never any telling what Gorky will do; he keeps constantly changing his mind.[1] Could you please write and tell me if you're actually coming and when, etc., etc. I won't set foot out of Yalta until Easter. At Eastertime I may take a short trip to Kharkov, but then I'll hole up in Yalta.

Rumor has it that the Moscow Art Theater is going to perform in Sevastopol and Yalta at Eastertime. If it does, you won't be bored.

Foma Gordeyev is written as monotonously as a dissertation. All the characters speak the same way; they all have the same way of thinking. They never speak plainly; they are always so deliberate. They all have something in the back of their minds; they always leave something unsaid, as if they knew something special. But in point of fact they don't know a thing. Talking and leaving something unsaid is simply their *façon de parler*.[2]

Foma does have some excellent passages.[3] Gorky will make a tremendous whopper of a writer, provided he doesn't weary of it all, lose interest, and grow lazy.

Keep well and happy now. I am looking forward to hearing when you plan to arrive.

Devotedly,
A. Chekhov

1. For all Chekhov's doubts, Gorky did keep his promise. On March 16, he and Posse came to Yalta for a visit.

2. *Façon de parler,* which usually means "a figure of speech," is not, contextually, appropriate for what Chekhov is trying so say. *Façon de s'exprimer* would probably be closer. Chekhov puts his finger here on a constant mannerism of Gorky's which became a basic device in his work written after *ca.* 1905. Anyone who witnessed a performance of a Gorky play of the middle period in one of the East European capitals in the years after World War II, when Gorky plays became the basic theater fare in the people's democracies, will instantly recognize what Chekhov means. The speeches of ideologically correct characters, e.g., the girl revolutionary Rachel in *Vassa Zheleznova,* have an oblique, elliptic quality that implies not only the condemnation of social inequities or the inevitability of proletarian revolution (which is the overt message of these speeches) but also something profound and mysterious that the other characters in the play or perhaps even the audience cannot hope to understand. This manner of writing bred a corresponding manner of acting. Thus, the young actress who played Rachel in the East Berlin *Kammerspiele* 1949 production of *Vassa Zheleznova* that starred the excellent Therese Giehse conveyed her revolutionary awareness by speaking to other characters in a tone of pitying condescension that would have sounded haughty and aristocratic in any other context.

3. When Gorky visited Tolstoy's home on January 13, 1900, Tolstoy expressed his criticism of *Foma Gordeyev* in the following terms: "It is all concocted. Nothing like it ever happened nor could have happened." For Chekhov's opinion of this novel two years later, see Letter 168.

XIV

"THREE SISTERS." MARRIAGE

IN APRIL OF 1900 the Moscow Art Theater was giving guest performances in the Crimean cities of Sevastopol and Yalta. Crowds of people streamed from Moscow to the Crimea and the occasion was dubbed by the participants "The Migration of the Peoples." Everyone connected with the company seemed to bring along his family, children or friends. The presence of both the company and of Chekhov in the Crimea attracted a large number of younger writers, artists and musicians, among them Bunin, Gorky, Kuprin and Rachmaninov. It was all meant as a combination of spring vacation and a huge homage to Chekhov.

Chekhov was suffering at the time from a bad case of hemorrhoids that caused a great loss of blood. He had a racking cough and his temperature was high most of the time. He went to Sevastopol, saw the company's productions of Ibsen's *Hedda Gabler* and Hauptmann's *Fuhrmann Henschel,* but cut his visit short and returned to Yalta in a state of near-collapse before he could see a performance of *The Seagull.* The Moscow Art Theater followed him to Yalta. By the time of their arrival he had recovered enough to entertain the members of the company and a large group of younger writers at his home. Two weeks later he wrote to Mayor Pavel Iordanov of Taganrog: "The week before Easter I had a hemorrhoidal hemorrhage from which I don't seem to be able to recover. During Easter week, the Art Theater was in Yalta and I can't recover from that either. After a long, quiet and boring winter, I had to stay up every night until three or four in the morning and have a large group in for dinner every day. I am now resting from it all" (Letter of April 27, 1900).

Doctors from all over Russia took to referring their tubercular patients to Chekhov. People would arrive with letters of introduction from total strangers, requesting help with housing or hospitalization. Friends of friends made a point of stopping by for a visit if they happened to be in the Crimea. To get away from some of this Chekhov joined Gorky, Dr. Sredin and a few other friends to take a tour of Georgia in June. At the end of the summer, he was back in Yalta reading proofs for Adolf Marx and writing a new play. It had seemed to Chekhov at first that he could complete *Three Sisters* in about a month, but he had not reckoned with his dwindling strength and with the endless stream of callers. With no other work was his lack of privacy such a handicap. "I am being constantly interrupted—cruelly, nastily, meanly," Chekhov wrote to Olga Knipper on August 18. "I have the play in my mind, it has taken shape and form, it begs to be put on paper, but the moment I touch the paper, the door opens and some swine comes crawling in." To her admonitions not to let his visitors in, he replied: "I cannot turn people away, it is beyond me."

Despite the interruptions, despite bouts of influenza and a severe throat infection he suffered early in October, Chekhov kept working on *Three Sisters*. At the end of October he went to Moscow and read the new play to the Moscow Art Theater company. They found it rather perplexing, more like an outline for a play than a finished work. He himself felt that it needed additional revisions, so he stayed in Moscow for a while, hoping to rework the play to his satisfaction. But the social demands were more than he could cope with. "I am hardly ever at home," wrote Chekhov in a note to a masseur with whom he was arranging an appointment, "as I am usually out by eight or nine in the morning and then I am all over town until three in the morning." Chekhov suggested that the masseur might catch him at his sister's at five in the afternoon (Letter to Pavel Stefanovsky of November 17, 1900). Partly in order to get a modicum of privacy (there is, incidentally, no word in Russian to convey the concept of privacy) necessary to finish *Three Sisters*, Chekhov went to Nice in December and settled again at the Pension Russe. Within less than a week he finished the revisions.

Three Sisters seems such an organic whole, so perfect in its conception and construction, that it is hard to believe it was written with so many interruptions. And yet Chekhov kept sending additional bits of dialogue to Moscow even after it went into rehearsals in the middle of December. The play is Chekhov's dramatic masterpiece and it is one of the three conceivable contenders for the title of the greatest play ever written in Russian. It is more accessible than its two principal rivals, Griboyedov's *The Misfortune of Being Clever* (which is practically untranslatable) and Gogol's *The Inspector General*, and it travels better. There is no polemical or typological superstructure in this play. What we have instead is a miraculous unity between the plot line, the developing characterizations and the overall time structure. The special art of Chekhovian dialogue reaches its summit in this play, with its varied and subtle rhythms, unmatched anywhere in prose drama.

One of the most difficult feats that Chekhov had brought off in *Three Sisters* was to individualize each of the three heroines so thoroughly, and yet to show that the fate of each of the three is just another aspect of the same predicament. Olga is forced to accept the career she does not want, Masha is caught up in her loveless marriage, and Irina can find no outlet for her idealism and desire to serve others because they are all trapped in a provincial environment where the options available to cultivated and intelligent young women are so wretchedly few. This aspect of the play is the culmination of the long line of portrayals of sensitive young women in Chekhov's stories (Kisochka in "Lights," Vera in "The Homecoming" and at least half a dozen others) and plays (Masha in *The Seagull* and Sonya in *Uncle Vanya*) who are caught in drab provincial existences and either seek solace in productive work or drift into loveless marriages.

Tom Prideaux once called the story of Chekhov's three sisters a great three-voiced fugue; to develop his musical imagery further, one might add that the downward progression of the three principal voices in this fugue is opposed in contrary motion by an implacable *cantus firmus* in the person of their sister-in-law Natasha. Natasha's selfishness and vulgarity enable her to thrive in the environment that stifles the three heroines and to take over first their brother, then their father's home and finally their way of life. The Andrei-Natasha marriage, based in part on Chekhov's earlier story "The Teacher of Literature," can also be read as Chekhov's commentary on the two earlier sweet and innocent Natashas of Russian literary tradition, who underwent metamorphoses after exposure to matrimony: Tolstoy's heroine in *War and Peace*, who lost her charm but found fulfillment through marriage, and Griboyedov's Natalia Dmitrievna (in *The Misfortune of Being Clever*), who reduced her young husband to total subjugation and, vampirelike, became beautiful and happy in the process. The figure of Captain Solyony is the final unmasking of the brawling and dueling hero of Russian Romantic fiction (Pushkin's Silvio from "The Shot," the heroes of Alexander Bestuzhev-Marlinsky's high-society tales, Lermontov's Pechorin), who had already been partially unmasked by Tolstoy in his Dolokhov from *War and Peace*. In Solyony, Chekhov strips away the veneer of idealization that accompanied this type in the Romantic age and shows the pathologically painful insecurity that underlies his hostility to other men and his disregard for the feelings of the woman he professes to love.

The setting and the milieu of *Three Sisters* had been treated by Chekhov in his earlier stories (this is his only full-length play that is not set in a landed estate). We have met provincial schoolteachers who could have been colleagues of Olga and of Kulygin in "The Man in a Shell" and "The Teacher of Literature." The cultivated army officers, such as Yevgraf Yegorov, whom Chekhov had known in his Voskresensk days in 1883–84, provided him with material for "The Kiss" (1887), but they really come into their own in this play. The situation of the provincial doctor, Chebutykin, is not unlike that of Dr. Ragin in "Ward Number Six." All these seemingly disparate elements have been woven together by Chekhov into an apparently seamless dramatic fabric of matchless transparency and awesome strength. It is to *Three Sisters,* more than to any other work by Chekhov, that we can apply the observation of Charles Du Bos that Chekhov shows us life's depths at the very moment when he seems to reflect its shimmering surface.

Olga Knipper visited Chekhov in Yalta in July of 1900 and the two of them spent some time together at Chekhov's Kuchukoy cottage in Gurzuf. It is after that visit that the affectionate tone of their previous "Dear Writer—Dear Actress" letters gives way to the utter intimacy of two lovers. From that point on they write each other daily, often passionately. The nature of their relationship was generally known to others (as early as January of 1900 Gorky wrote to Chekhov from Nizhny Novgorod: "Everyone says you are marrying some woman who is an actress and has a foreign name. I don't believe it. But if it's true, I'm glad. It's a good thing to be married provided the woman is not made of wood and is not a radical"). Chekhov was quite willing to continue things as they were, but the conventions of the day were making things uncomfortable for Olga, as she made pointedly clear to him in several of her letters of March and April, 1901. On April 26, Chekhov wrote to Olga: "If you give me your word that not a soul in Moscow will know about our wedding until after it happens I will be willing to marry you on the very day of my arrival, if you like. For some reason I'm terrified of the wedding ceremony, the congratulations and the champagne which you have to hold in your hand with a vague smile." They were married very quietly in a suburban church in Moscow on May 25, 1901, in the presence of four witnesses required by law. These were Olga's uncle, one of her brothers and two of this brother's fellow students. The only announcement sent out was Chekhov's telegram to his mother: "Dear Mama, give me your blessings, I'm getting married. Everything will remain as before. I'm off to the koumiss cure." Their strange honeymoon took them first to Nizhny Novgorod, where they visited Gorky and then to a remote koumiss resort in the province of Ufa, where tubercular patients drank the calorie-rich beverage made from fermented mare's milk.

Chekhov got exactly the kind of wife and marriage he wanted, the kind he described in advance in his letter to Suvorin about the wife who appears and disappears like the moon (Letter 93). A number of people ranging from Ivan Bunin to some uninformed Western commentators have written unkindly about Olga Knipper-Chekhova because she did not abandon her stage career to settle down as a nurse to her sick husband. The censure is clearly based on the assumption that every marriage should be like every other one and that Chekhov had the same set of standards and expectations as the commentator. The marriage of Anton Chekhov and Olga Knipper was a partnership of equals and they arranged it to provide themselves with the independence they both wanted to be a part of that marriage. In the short time they had together, with all the occasional misunderstandings, with his deteriorating physical condition and her severe illnesses, with all the separations, they managed to give each other more real happiness than many other couples achieve in a long lifetime together.

Two of the more significant events in Chekhov's life of this period were his quiet resignation from the Imperial Academy over the annulment of Gorky's election (see Letters 153, 154 and 158) and his trip to a mining complex in the Ural Mountains in June of 1902 at the invitation of the millionaire Savva Morozov (Morozov was a financial backer of the Moscow Art Theater, who later donated large sums of money to the revolutionary movement and committed suicide after the débacle of the 1905 revolution). During his visit to Morozov's mines and foundries, Chekhov prevailed on him to cut the working day of his miners and workers from twelve to eight hours. An additional dividend of that visit was Chekhov's encounter with the twenty-two-year-old student of mining engineering named Alexander Tikhonov, who took excellent notes of his conversations with Chekhov and many years later, after he had become the Soviet writer Alexander Serebrov, described Chekhov's visit to the Urals in a chapter of his book *Time and People* (Moscow, 1955), which is probably the single most vivid, appealing and believable literary portrait that we have of Chekhov at the end of his life.

139. To Leonid Sredin[1]

Nice,
December 26, 1900[2]

Dear Leonid Valentinovich,

My best wishes for a healthy, happy and prosperous new year. This is the second week I've been in and around Nice, and—what can I say? Living all winter in Yalta is useful, very useful, because after

Yalta this area seems like heaven! Yalta is Siberia. The first two days after my arrival, when I was out strolling in my summer coat or in my room, sitting in front of the door that opens onto the balcony, I was so unaccustomed to it that it all looked funny. And the people on the streets are cheerful and boisterous; they are always laughing. There's not a police officer in sight, nor any Marxists with their self-important faces.[3] But suddenly and unexpectedly two days ago the temperature dropped below freezing, and everything wilted. They never have freezing weather here, and where it came from is perfectly incomprehensible. Do you happen to know where my mother and sister are presently staying? If they're in Yalta, write and tell me whether they are well and how they are feeling. I've written them, but haven't received any answer.[4]

Give my regards and respects to Sofya Petrovna, Nadezhda Ivanovna[5] and the children. Write and tell me how Nadezhda Ivanovna is doing in Yalta and whether she misses the theater. Write in detail about everything if you can. No matter how wonderful the Riviera is, it is a bore not getting any letters. My house hasn't caved in, has it?

I clasp your hand firmly and embrace you. Keep well and happy.

Yours,
A. Chekhov

Regards to the Yartsevs.[6]

1. On Sredin, see Letter 126, note 4.

2. Although his doctors forbade Chekhov to remain in Central Russia in winter, he tarried in Moscow until December 11 and left for Nice mainly because he found it impossible to complete *Three Sisters* in the midst of his busy Moscow social life. Isaak Altschuller, Chekhov's friend and personal physician, wrote in his memoir that he considered Chekhov's involvement with Olga Knipper and the Moscow Art Theater to have been his death warrant. According to Dr. Altschuller, the frequent trips to Moscow and the activities they entailed shortened Chekhov's life more than any other factor.

3. The 1944–51 edition printed this passage with the cautionary comment that Chekhov had met only "legal" Marxists. The implication of the comment is that Chekhov must have been fed up with his non-Leninist Marxist friends and that therefore this remark could not possibly apply to anyone connected with the founding of the Soviet state or have any current relevance. The 1963–64 edition played things safe by omitting the entire letter.

The continuous fear of the Soviet annotators that the reader might apply any statement of Chekhov's to present rather than to pre-revolutionary times is most amusingly manifested in their comment to his letter to Suvorin of February 6, 1899. In it, Chekhov informed Suvorin that he had been reading *The Book of My Life* by Bishop Porfiry Uspensky, a Russian nineteenth-century churchman-archeologist, and quoted an anti-militaristic passage that struck him: "Standing armies in peacetime are locusts who devour people's bread and leave a stench in society, while in wartime they are artificial military machines and if they are allowed to develop—then it's good-bye to freedom, safety and the national reputation! They are the lawless defenders of unjust and unfair laws, of privilege and of tyranny." The note appended to this passage in the 1944–51 edition points out that Bishop Porfiry wrote this in 1848 and that he meant the statement to apply only to the armies of capitalist countries.

4. Engaging in a bit of whimsical censorship of her own, Maria Chekhova deleted the preceding three sentences in her edition of the letters.

5. Dr. Sredin's wife and mother, respectively.

6. On Yartsev, see Letter 137, note 2.

140. To Konstantin Alexeyev (Stanislavsky)[1]

Nice,
January 2, 1901

Dear Konstantin Sergeyevich,

Not until yesterday did I receive the letter you sent me before December 23rd. There was no address on the envelope, and according to the postmark the letter left Moscow December 25th, so there must have been reasons for it to take so long.

Happy New Year, and, I hope, happy new theater, the theater you will soon be starting to build.[2] And here's wishing you five wonderful new plays. As for that old play *Three Sisters*, it is not to be read at the countess's soirée under any circumstances or in any form.[3] If you do, you will cause me great chagrin.

I sent off Act Four long ago, before Christmas. I addressed it to Vladimir Ivanovich.[4] I've introduced many changes. You write that when Natasha is making the rounds of the house at night in Act Three she puts out the lights and looks under the furniture for burglars. It seems to me, though, that it would be better to have her walk across the stage in a straight line without a glance at anyone or anything à la Lady Macbeth, with a candle—that way it would be much briefer and more frightening.

Happy New Year to Maria Petrovna.[5] I send her my cordial greetings and sincere wishes for all the best, especially good health.

I thank you from the bottom of my heart for your letter; it has made me very happy.[6] I clasp your hand.

Yours,
A. Chekhov

1. That Konstantin Stanislavsky (1863–1938) should have gone down in history as the definitive director of Chekhov's plays is only one of the ironies

and paradoxes in which the career and the popular image of this remarkable reformer of Russian theater abound. Bearer of the very ordinary Russian name Alexeyev, he is known to the world by the Polish surname (properly spelled Stanisławski) which he assumed by sheer accident and kept for good. Son of a millionaire manufacturer of merchant-class origin, he created a theater that was to become the only acceptable model for all theaters in a state supposedly founded for the benefit of workers and peasants. An eclectic director, who scored some of his most memorable successes in historical costume drama reconstructed with archeological precision (Alexei Tolstoy's *Tsar Fyodor Ioannovich*), grimly naturalistic productions complete with real peasants on the stage and costumes bought from a flophouse (Tolstoy's *Power of Darkness*, Gorky's *Lower Depths*), fairy tales (the fantasy plays of Hauptmann, Maeterlinck's *Bluebird*), and such stylized fancies as the production of *Hamlet* done entirely in gold and of Andreyev's *The Life of Man* with only black sets—Stanislavsky is honored in his country as the originator of Socialist Realism in the theater. If Stanislavsky is assigned an exalted place in the official pantheon of the Soviet arts that is second only to that of Gorky among twentieth-century figures, it is not for his genuinely innovative reforms of *ca.* 1898–1905 (if that were the case, there would have been parallel cults of Meyerhold and Alexander Tairov), but, on the contrary, because of the increasingly conservative artistic position that the Moscow Art Theater began assuming in the first decade of our century, which eventually led to its congealing into the inert theatrical museum it has remained throughout most of the Soviet period.

After 1906, the younger disciples and followers of Stanislavsky (such men as Meyerhold, Fyodor Kommissarzhevsky, Nikolai Yevreinov and Alexander Tairov) were staging the masterpieces of Russian poetic drama of the twentieth century that were then being written by Alexander Blok, Fyodor Sologub, Innokenty Annensky and Alexei Remizov, plays of tremendous verbal beauty and genuine metaphysical depth. Stanislavsky, however, lent the prestige of his company and his name to popularizing the facile, shallow, pseudo-Symbolist plays of Leonid Andreyev, helping this superficial playwright to acquire a national and international fame that is out of all proportion to his true significance. While enthusiastically staging plays by Andreyev and such third-rate imitators of Chekhov and Gorky as Yevgeny Chirikov and Ilya Surguchov, Stanislavsky could not bring himself to produce the beautiful and poetic play *The Rose and the Cross* written especially for him by the great poet Alexander Blok. Having turned it down in 1913 as supposedly incomprehensible, Stanislavsky yielded two years later to the entreaties of Nemirovich-Danchenko and Leonid Andreyev, both of whom recognized the unique value of this play, and *The Rose and the Cross* went into rehearsals in March of 1916. By 1918, after some two hundred rehearsals, Stanislavsky decided to abandon the production, having lost faith in both the play and his ability to convey its meaning to the audience (two earlier, less perfect, but even more complex plays by Blok were successfully staged by Meyerhold in 1906 and 1913 and were received with acclaim). This entire episode is a vivid illustration of Stanislavsky's built-in aversion to genuine literary quality and originality. It helps explain why, for all of his genius as a director, Stanislavsky so frequently missed the meaning of the Chekhov plays he directed, causing Chekhov so much irritation, anger and despair, in spite of the outward success of these productions.

Stanislavsky's book of theatrical reminiscences *My Life in Art* is a highly important account of the origins and results of the reform which he and Nemirovich-Danchenko effected in Russian theater at the turn of the century. It also happens to be the source of more distortions, misconceptions and historical inaccuracies about Chekhov's person and his plays than any other work ever published. Some of the more glaring errors were corrected by Stanislavsky after the first edition of his book, but numerous others were allowed to stand. Having been quoted uncritically in numerous subsequent works on Chekhov, Stanislavsky's mistakes and fantasies have by now attained the status of indisputable fact. The whole melodramatic story of the revival of *The Seagull,* supposedly brought out of total obscurity by the Moscow Art Theater and staged by it at the cost of endangering Chekhov's life and health, is entirely disproved by the published correspondence between Chekhov and Nemirovich-Danchenko, yet such is the prestige of Stanislavsky's name that the story goes on being cited even by people who have read the pertinent letters. The statement that Chekhov was angered after he read the first version of *Three Sisters* to Stanislavsky's actors and they failed to understand that the play was a merry comedy or even a farce has found its way into almost every English-language work on Chekhov and has given rise to a great deal of perplexity in Western scholarship about the meaning of the play. None of the authors who quote this statement ever tell their readers that it appears only in *My Life in Art* (written several decades after the events in question) and that its interpretation of the play is flatly contradicted by Chekhov's own letters at the time he was writing *Three Sisters* and by all the other contemporary documentation we have, in which *Three Sisters* is invariably referred to as a drama.

The same Chekhov who could explain dramatic characters eloquently and in detail (cf. Letters 14 and 131) suddenly loses this ability and can only mumble "He whistles" or "He wears white pants" when pressed by Stanislavsky to explain a character in *The Seagull* or *Uncle Vanya.* Or else he prefers to shrug the whole thing off by saying "It's all in the text." Since Chekhov went on to analyze his characters effectively in his letters to his wife and even to a stranger (cf. Letter 167) during the same period, the inescapable conclusion is that he simply did not believe Stanislavsky capable of understanding any subtleties. Meyerhold's essay "Naturalistic Theater and Theater of Mood," originally written in 1906, and his letters to Chekhov, as well as Alexander Blok's diaries for 1913, all contain devastating examples of Stanislavsky's inability to deal with literary complexity or to perceive the value of literary novelty and originality; Stanislavsky's own brief and out-of-focus account of *Uncle Vanya*'s meaning in *My Life in Art,* especially when compared to his lengthy eulogies of such simple-minded plays as Ostrovsky's *The*

Snow Maiden and Hauptmann's *The Sunken Bell,* should drive this point home for anyone. A great deal of what is puzzling, paradoxical and nonsensical in the entire body of Chekhovian studies becomes clear and understandable the moment *My Life in Art* is removed from the scene as a basic source.

Another regrettable legacy with which Stanislavsky's book and his separate memoirs on Chekhov have saddled the Russian tradition is the peculiar dialect which he invented and ascribed to Chekhov in his writings about him. Stanislavsky's Chekhov speaks in stammering phrases, punctuated with endless *Poslushaite* ("See here, now") and saturated with the reinforcing particle *zhe* which turns him into an owlish crackpot. None of the numerous diaries or personal journals that have recorded Chekhov's speech for us contains anything remotely like it. Writers who knew Chekhov personally, such as Ivan Bunin and Alexander Serebrov, have protested that they never heard Chekhov speak the way Stanislavsky quotes him for pages and pages. The real Chekhov probably didn't; but the imaginary melancholy bard of the Russian critics—yes, this would be the right diction for him. This was the Chekhov Stanislavsky remembered.

2. Construction of the permanent building for the Moscow Art Theater, which was designed by Chekhov's friend Franz Schechtel, was not begun until 1902.

3. In a letter he wrote to Chekhov in December of 1900, Stanislavsky informed him that Countess Sofya Tolstaya, the wife of Lev Tolstoy, was planning a charity soirée at which she wanted the actors of Stanislavsky's company to perform selections from *Three Sisters,* then being rehearsed by the company. Stanislavsky expressed the hope that Chekhov might veto such a reading. Chekhov complied all the more willingly because he did not consider the play completed at the time.

4. Nemirovich-Danchenko.

5. The actress Maria Lilina, Stanislavsky's wife, who gave memorable performances at the Moscow Art Theater as Masha in *The Seagull,* Sonya in *Uncle Vanya* and Natasha in *Three Sisters.*

6. Stanislavsky's letter, mentioned in note 3 above, gave Chekhov a detailed progress report about the forthcoming production of *Three Sisters.*

141. To Mikhail Chekhov

Yalta,
February 22, 1901

Dear Michel,

I'm back from my trip abroad and can now answer your letter.[1] Your plan to live in Petersburg is of course all very fine and good for your soul, but as for taking a job with Suvorin, I can't tell you anything definite though I've thought long and hard about it.[2] Of course, if I were you, I'd prefer to work at the printing plant; I'd stay away from the newspaper. *New Times* has a very bad reputation these days. The staff is made up entirely of smug, well-fed people (not counting Alexander, who is blind to it all).[3] Suvorin is deceitful, terribly deceitful, especially in his so-called moments of frankness. What I mean is he may talk sincerely enough, but there's no guarantee that half an hour later he won't turn around and do just the opposite. Any way you look at it, it's a tough decision to make. Heaven help you; I don't see how my advice can be of much help to you. If you do go to work for Suvorin, keep in mind every day that he is very easy to cross, so you'd better have a government job or a law practice ready.[4]

Suvorin does have one good man, at least he used to be a good man—Tychinkin.[5] Suvorin's sons are nonentities in every sense of the word[6] and even Anna Ivanovna has started acting petty. Nastya and Borya, however, seem to be decent people. Kolomnin was a good man, but he died recently.

Keep well and happy. Write me how things turn out. Olga Germanovna[7] and the children will be better off in Petersburg than in Yaroslavl.

Write me all the details as soon as there are any. Mother is well.

Yours,
A. Chekhov

1. Chekhov had returned to Russia in the middle of February, after completing *Three Sisters* in Nice and then going on an extended tour of Italy with Maxim Kovalevsky.

2. Mikhail was bored with his low-paid civil service job in the provincial town of Yaroslavl. He received a job offer from Suvorin and wrote to his brother asking if he should accept it. The attractive aspect of the offer was that it would enable Mikhail and his family to move to St. Petersburg. But by then, anyone working for Suvorin was treated with open contempt by the majority of educated Russians. This made Mikhail's choice a hard one.

3. As Alexander Chekhov's letters of that period to Anton show, he was keenly aware of the general disrepute into which *New Times* had fallen after the student-strike affair. On January 17, 1902, Alexander wrote to Anton: "Once we had a newspaper, but there's no newspaper now. It used to be a hole in the ground, now it's an outhouse. This is how the public sees us. Only state councilors on active service would shake the hand of a *New Times* man; anyone younger or lower in rank recoils from us as if we were carrion."

4. In April, Alexander wrote to Anton that their brother Mikhail had begun to work for Suvorin.

5. Konstantin Tychinkin worked evenings managing the *New Times* printing plant, while holding a morning job as a schoolteacher.

6. Suvorin's older sons Alexei and Mikhail used their father's generosity to start a rival newspaper, even more reactionary than *New Times,* with which they tried to lure away their father's subscribers and advertisers. They were not successful.

7. Mikhail Chekhov's wife.

142. To Nikodim Kondakov

Yalta,
March 2, 1901

Dear Nikodim Pavlovich,

I thank you cordially for the book.[1] I found it very interesting and enjoyable. You see, my mother is a native of the Shuya District, and fifty years ago she used to visit her icon-painter relatives in Palekh and Sergeyevo (which is three versts from Palekh), who at the time were very prosperous. The ones in Sergeyevo lived in a two-story house with a mansard, an enormous house. When I told Mother about the contents of your book, she became very excited and started telling me about Palekh and Sergeyevo and that house, which even then was very old. According to the impressions that have remained with her, they had a good, prosperous life. While she was there, they received orders for big churches in Moscow and Petersburg.

Yes, the peasants have infinitely great and varied strength, but this strength cannot resurrect what is no more. You call icon painting a craft, and like any craft it gives rise to cottage industry. Then it is gradually taken over by the Jacquot and Bonacoeur factory,[2] and if you close down the latter, new manufacturers will spring up. They'll make icons on boards the way they're supposed to be made, but Kholuy and Palekh will not rise again.[3] Icon painting lived and thrived as long as it was an art, not a craft, as long as talented people were in charge. But when easel painting appeared in Russia and artists started taking lessons and being made into noblemen, painters like Vasnetsov and Ivanov[4] began to appear. The only painters left in Kholuy and Palekh were craftsmen, and icon painting became a craft.

By the way, there are almost no icons left in peasant huts. The ancient ones have all been lost in fires, and the new ones are entirely makeshift, some are on paper, others on tinfoil.[5]

I haven't seen or read *Henschel*, so I have no idea what it's like. But I like Hauptmann, and I consider him a major playwright. And, in any case, it's impossible to judge it on the strength of seeing only one act, particularly if Roxanova was doing the acting.[6]

I haven't been well these days. I had a coughing attack the likes of which I haven't had in a long time.

Your book on icon painting is written with fervor, in places with passion. That is why it is so lively and interesting to read. There is no doubt that icon painting (Palekh and Kholuy) is dying or becoming extinct. If only someone could be found to write the history of Russian icon painting! It's the sort of work to which a man could devote his entire life.[7]

But my heart tells me I've begun to bore you. The public has greeted Tolstoy's excommunication with laughter. The Church Slavic text which the bishops stuck in the middle of their proclamation did not help a bit. It's either very insincere or has the ring of insincerity.[8]

Keep well and under God's protection, and try not to forget your sincerely devoted and respectful

A. Chekhov

1. Nikodim Kondakov's book *The Present Situation of Russian Folk Icon Painting*, St. Petersburg, 1901. The book was an account of the expedition which Kondakov undertook together with the art historian Sergei Sheremetyev to the three traditional centers of old Russian icon painting, the villages of Mstera, Kholuy and Palekh in the Vladimir Province. Although illustrious foreigners ranging from Goethe to Henri Matisse have repeatedly expressed great admiration for traditional Russian icons, the educated class of nineteenth-century Russia, with its taste for academic realism in painting and its frequently anticlerical orientation, regarded icon painting as something backward, superstitious and devoid of artistic merit. Until the 1890s, the icon-painting centers survived through the patronage of the peasants and the merchants, but the advent of industrialization (see next note) posed a serious threat to their further existence. Kondakov's book, which outlined the economic background of icon painting and asserted its artistic importance, was the first step in the series of developments that led to the reassessment of folk icon painting in the Russian art journals of the early twentieth century, such as Sergei Diaghilev's *The World of Art*, and resulted in universal appreciation of this native Russian art form.

2. Jacquot and Bonacoeur was a French-owned firm that manufactured tin boxes for shoe polish and floor wax. In 1900, the Holy Synod, the governing body of the Russian Orthodox Church, awarded this firm a monopoly on manufacturing cheap, mass-produced icons printed on tin plates. This decision threatened to wipe out economically the traditional peasant icon painters. Kondakov's book argued eloquently against this sabotage of a native art form by the ecclesiastical authorities.

3. The day before Chekhov wrote this letter, Kondakov was received by Nicholas II at the Winter Palace. He talked to the tsar for forty-five minutes about the plight of the Mstera, Kholuy and Palekh artists. "He stated that he

will take them under his personal protection," Kondakov wrote Chekhov on March 1, "and requested me to draft a full report. There is no telling what will happen next, but we have hopes of squashing that reptile Pobedonostsev" (the Ober-Procurator of the Holy Synod, who was responsible for the Jacquot and Bonacoeur decision).

What happened next to the icon-painting villages showed what a poor prophet Chekhov was. Special funds were allocated by the tsar, Kondakov organized a Committee for the Encouragement of Russian Icon Painting, and schools were started in the three villages to ensure the continuation of their tradition. With the new interest in icon painting promoted by the periodical press of the Symbolist period, there came a demand for icons not only as religious objects but as artistic ones as well.

During the anti-religious and anti-icon campaigns of the first post-revolutionary decade it looked at first as if the days of Russian icon painting were over. The market dwindled and most of the peasant artists had to take up farming. However, owing largely to the intercession of Maxim Gorky with the Soviet authorities, the village of Palekh has retained its role as a center of folk art to this day. Christian and hagiographic subjects, traditional in icon painting, were banned by the government, but there seemed to be no objection to subjects taken from earlier Russian pagan mythology, folk tales and classical Russian literature. A new Soviet myth that might be termed "The Great Writer Is the Voice of the People" is basic to Palekh painting of recent decades: Pushkin is shown surrounded by the creatures of traditional Russian mythology, who dictate his *Ruslan and Lyudmila* to him (in actual fact, that verse tale owed far more to Voltaire's *La Pucelle d'Orléans,* Evariste Parny's erotic poems and *The Castle of Otranto* by Horace Walpole than to any native Russian goblin or mermaid); a Ukrainian beekeeper dictates to Gogol Gogol's own stories; and the young Maxim Gorky is told his revolutionary poem about the falcon and the snake by a wise old peasant. Production of iconlike portraits of Lenin, Stalin, Gorky and various Red Army generals was another price that Palekh artists had to pay for the survival of their art form under Soviet conditions. Today, their black-lacquered wooden boxes and plaques, depicting the traditional tale of Prince Ivan, his faithful gray wolf and his capture of the Firebird are great favorites with the American tourists who visit Moscow souvenir shops. A typical Palekh plaque even made the cover of a Jefferson Airplane rock album in recent years.

4. The painter Viktor Vasnetsov was a contemporary and acquaintance of Chekhov; some of his illustrations of folk tales influenced the more recent work of the peasant painters of Palekh. Alexander Ivanov (1806–58) was a Russian painter of the Romantic Age, who lived in Rome and was a close friend of Gogol.

5. Chekhov was quite wrong about the absence of wooden icons in the Russian villages. During the anti-religious campaigns of the 1920s, large numbers of icons were confiscated from the peasants and either destroyed or sold abroad for hard currency. Vladimir Soloukhin's two recent books, *Letters from a Russian Museum* and *The Blackened Boards* (Moscow, 1968 and 1969,

respectively), tell of the careful and systematic work that was begun in the Soviet Union in the 1960s to salvage, clean and restore wooden icons that were used as construction materials or dumped in barns and cellars in the twenties and rediscovered in post-Stalinist years when liking icons and having them around again became permitted and even fashionable.

6. Kondakov had written to Chekhov that he left the theater after seeing only one act of the Moscow Art Theater's production of *Fuhrmann Henschel* by Gerhart Hauptmann. Chekhov had taken a strong dislike to the actress Maria Roxanova after her lachrymose performance as Nina in *The Seagull.*

7. Chekhov did not live long enough to see the many excellent histories of Russian icon painting that came to be written in the early decades of the twentieth century. A recent beautifully illustrated history of the Palekh school of painting by one of the oldest practicing painters of that tradition (Nikolai Zinovyev, *The Art of Palekh*, Leningrad, 1968) gives Gorky the entire credit for saving Palekh. It mentions Kondakov's role only obliquely and in passing, without explaining what he actually did. As could be expected, the book omits all mention of the benevolent intercession of Nicholas II.

8. By the decision of the Holy Synod of February 22, 1901, Lev Tolstoy was excommunicated from the Russian Orthodox Church. His excommunication caused a great number of public demonstrations of sympathy and solidarity throughout Russia and much indignation abroad. After it was announced in the newspapers, the Minister of the Interior Dmitry Sipyagin imposed a ban on all editorial discussion of this event in the Russian press. When even more petty restrictions were imposed in the following months, such as prohibiting the mention of Tolstoy's name in private telegrams and the ban on public display of his portraits, Alexei Suvorin wrote in his private journal:

> Apparently these fellows think they are immortal! And indeed, they will survive as immortal idiots, since it is hard to imagine even worse idiots in the future. When Gogol died fifty years ago, Turgenev was placed under arrest for publishing an article in which he called Gogol a writer of genius. Now Gogol is being taught in all the schools and his monuments are everywhere. Tolstoy will not have to wait fifty years for his monument, nor will Sipyagin to be branded with disgrace on his idiotic forehead.

Within two years, Sipyagin was assassinated by revolutionary terrorists.

143. To Boris Zaitsev[1]

Yalta,
March 9, 1901.

Cold, dry, long, not youthful, though talented.

Chekhov

1. The writer Boris Zaitsev (1881–1972) sent Chekhov the manuscript of his story "An Uninteresting Story" with a request for an urgent evaluation. This is the telegram Chekhov sent him in reply. As a very young man, Zaitsev met Chekhov briefly in June of 1899 when he was sent by his father to inspect Melikhovo, which Chekhov had put up for sale, and was invited to stay for lunch.

In post-revolutionary years, Boris Zaitsev became one of the leading writers of the Russian emigration. In addition to novels and stories he also wrote literary biographies. His books on Turgenev and on the poet Vasily Zhukovsky are quite attractive in many ways. His biography of Chekhov (New York, 1954), however, is probably the least satisfactory book on Chekhov ever written. Zaitsev's book has the same basic thesis as the other émigré biography of Chekhov (M. Kurdyumov, *A Heart in Alarm*, Paris, 1934)—namely, that Chekhov, whether he knew it or not, was a believing member of the Russian Orthodox Church—not metaphysically or in terms of his ethics (for which a good case has been made in the unpublished diaries of Boris Poplavsky), or even through his undeniable empathy for everything Russian Orthodox, but as a matter of plain fact. This led Zaitsev into constant arguments with statements from Chekhov's own letters (as an Orthodox Christian, Chekhov could not possibly have liked reading Darwin or have been a friend of Maxim Gorky, even if he says he did and was). Where Soviet commentators stress "The Bride" as Chekhov's ultimate statement on life and politics, Zaitsev dismisses it as pallid and insignificant and instead writes a whole chapter on "The Bishop," in which he sees proof of Chekhov's continuous journey toward God ("The Steppe," the trip to Sakhalin and the famine fighting were supposedly earlier stages of that journey). Combined with an overall image of sweet, saintly and ethereal Chekhov, seemingly made of equal parts of treacle, holy water and cotton candy, the book adds up to a literary portrait of Chekhov that is as badly distorted as the worst of Stalinist falsifications.

144. To Maria Chekhova[1]

Axyonovo,[2]
June 4, 1901

Dear Masha,

The letter in which you advise me not to get married was forwarded to me from Moscow, and I received it here yesterday.[3] I don't know if I've made a mistake or not, but I got married mainly because, first, I'm over forty; second, Olga comes from a highly moral family; and, third, if we have to separate, I'll do so without the least hesitation, as if I had never gotten married. After all, she is an independent person and self-supporting. Another important consideration is that my marriage has not in the least changed either my way of life or the way of life of those who lived and are living around me. Everything, absolutely everything will remain just as it was, and I'll go on living alone in Yalta as before.

Your desire to come here to Ufa Province has made me very happy.[4] It would be wonderful if you do in fact make up your mind to come. Come in early July and we'll stay here a while and have some koumiss, and then we'll all follow the Volga as far as Novorossiysk and from there return to Yalta. The best route here goes through Moscow, Nizhny Novgorod and Samara. It may look farther, but in the long run it takes two or even three days less. When I told Knippschütz[5] you were coming, it made her very happy. She went to Ufa today to do some shopping. It's rather boring here, but the koumiss is delicious, the weather is hot and the food not bad at all. In a day or two we'll go off fishing.

I'm sending you a check for five hundred rubles. If it seems like too much and you don't feel like keeping it all at home, deposit some of it in the state bank in your own name. Sinani will show you how to do it. Take along about a hundred rubles plus ticket money when you come. I have money; I'll pay your way back.

The telegraph address is Chekhov, Axyonovo. If you decide to come, wire one word only: Coming.

A seventeen-year-old girl, the daughter of the late Liza, is living with Anna Chekhova[6] here. She seems to be a fine girl.

When you send a telegram to "Chekhov, Axyonovo," draw a line at the bottom of the blank and write Samaro-Zlatoustovskoy underneath it like this:

Samaro-Zlatoustovskoy

Put it at the bottom of the page.

The koumiss doesn't upset my stomach. It looks as if I'll be able to tolerate it.

My humble respects and greetings to Mama. Tell Varvara Konstantinovna[7] that I thank her for her telegram. Keep well and don't worry. And please write more often.

Yours,
Anton

1. To avoid hurting the feelings of Olga Knipper, with whom she was close friends before Chekhov's marriage, and to whom she became very attached again after his death, Maria excluded this letter from her edition of her brother's letters and vetoed its publication in the 1944–51 edition. The letter was finally published in the Chekhov volume of *Literary Heritage* in 1960 after the death of both Maria and Olga.

2. Axyonovo was a resort in Ufa Province where tubercular patients were sent for the koumiss cure. This is where Chekhov and Olga Knipper went for their honeymoon.

3. Although Maria was very fond of Olga and regarded Chekhov's intimacy with her with favor, their marriage came to her as a great shock. Chekhov is replying here to her letter of May 24, 1901 (first published in the volume of her letters to her brother in 1954), in which she wrote:

> I will now permit myself to state my opinion about your marriage. For me personally, a wedding ceremony is odious! And you would be much better off without all this additional excitement. If a certain person loves you, she would not leave you and there is no sacrifice entailed on her part. Nor were you being selfish. How could you ever think such a thing? Where is there selfishness? There's always time to get hitched. Tell this to your Knippschütz from me. [. . .] I want you to be healthy and happy—that's all I want. In any case, do what you think right; it might well be that I am being partial in this particular case. You yourself have brought me up not to have any prejudices.

4. In the same letter Maria also wrote: "My God, to be parted from you for two entire months and to live in Yalta to boot! If only you would permit me to come see you at that koumiss place even for only one week!"

5. An affectionate and humorous nickname Chekhov and Maria used for Olga. Throughout their relationship Chekhov was given to ribbing Olga good-naturedly about her German origins. The nickname is patterned on the Russian transcription of the names of such German operas as Karl Maria von Weber's *Der Freischütz* and Albert Lortzing's *Der Wildschütz.*

6. Anna Chekhova, who happened to be at Axyonovo at the same time as Chekhov and Knipper, was the wife of Chekhov's cousin Mikhail Mikhailovich Chekhov (see Letter 1), to whom Chekhov wrote affectionate letters in his youth, but from whom he was totally estranged by this time. The young girl staying with Anna Chekhova was the daughter of cousin Mikhail's sister Yelizaveta, who died of tuberculosis in the early nineties.

7. Varvara Kharkeyevich, the headmistress of the girls' school in Yalta where Chekhov was active as honorary superintendent.

145. To Olga Vasilyeva[1]

Axyonovo,
June 12, 1901

Dear Olga Rodionovna,

Don't sell for a hundred twenty-five thousand rubles; after all, there's no hurry. If something is evaluated at five rubles at first sight, that means it can be sold for seven and a half. Wait a while, for at least a year, or even six months, and in the meantime have someone reliable go to Odessa and see how much your house is actually worth and whether you can't sell it at a higher price. Since the proceeds of the house will be used for a hospital, have a doctor go to Odessa, a man with a vested interest and consequently all the more reliable. I recommend Mikhail Alexandrovich Chlenov, M.D. You couldn't find a more honest man. If you write me that you have nothing against his taking the trip, I'll write him, he'll go, and then write you.

Building a hospital is an excellent project. But here's a piece of advice: don't build it without getting the *zemstvo* involved, in other words, make it a *zemstvo* hospital. The *zemstvo* will provide the blueprints for the hospital, it will provide you with a doctor, and you will end up spending considerably less if the *zemstvo* takes a hand in the project. A contribution of ten to fifteen thousand, in my opinion, should more than suffice for the early stages; it's better to increase the amount later when the project is firmly on its feet and under way and when you can see everything clearly. Write to Doctor Dmitry Nikolaevich Zhbankov (a *zemstvo* doctor) in Smolensk. Ask him what you ought to do and whom you ought to see, and describe how great the need for medical facilities is, and he will write you back immediately and refer you to the right place; but don't write how much you want to contribute. You yourself won't know until later.

Then be sure to write me all the details of how things shape up. The main thing is not to hurry.

My health is better; my coughing has abated. Keep well and under God's protection for many long years. My humble regards to charming Masha.[2]

Yours,
A. Chekhov

1. Olga Vasilyeva was one of the earliest translators of Chekhov's stories into English. She was an orphan, adopted by a wealthy lady from Odessa, who had her educated in France and England. She wrote to Chekhov from Cannes while he was staying in Nice in 1898 and asked for permission to translate some of his work into English. Chekhov was rather skeptical that his stories could be of interest to anyone in England, but he gave his consent and helped her with some passages she had found difficult. Chekhov met the young woman personally and found her quite charming and Westernized to the point where she was forgetting her Russian. In 1900, Olga Vasilyeva's benefactress died and left her considerable real-estate holdings in Odessa. With Chekhov's encouragement, Vasilyeva returned to Russia in order to sell some of this property and use the proceeds for endowing a hospital. Chekhov put his medical connections and his *zemstvo* experience at her disposal and conducted an extensive correspondence with her about this project.

2. Masha was a five-year-old girl whom Olga Vasilyeva was raising as her foster child. A rather touching friendship developed between Chekhov and Masha, and Chekhov's correspondence with Olga Vasilyeva contains a number of adult-sounding messages between Chekhov and Masha. Alexander Kuprin's memoir of Chekhov contains a description of an encounter between Chekhov and the little girl.

146. To Vasily Sobolevsky[1]

Axyonovo,
June 23, 1901

Dear Vasily Mikhailovich,

Many, many thanks for your letter and telegram, your friendly attitude toward me, and the joyful news.[2] I will definitely become a contributor to *Russian Bulletin*. As far as I'm concerned, it is the best newspaper around, and if I haven't contributed to it for some time, it is because I've been failing to keep up with things in general and doing nothing because of my illness. I've been forbidden to work, and I've obeyed and written practically nothing.

During my koumiss cure here I've gained ten pounds and my cough has grown much weaker, but all the same I'll be returning home with exactly what I brought here: dull sound beneath the clavicle.[3] Be that as it may, I'll settle down in the Crimea, and if it isn't too hot there, I may get something done.

Your degeneration of the arteries, or what is known as atheromatosis, is as natural at your age as hair turning gray. The reason you're taking it so badly is probably that you have always been very healthy and are unaccustomed to being ill. You should do a lot of walking but not exhaust yourself; avoid beef and eat fowl, veal, fish and ham; don't drink any alcohol, not even a drop; if you must, drink only beer, but make sure it's a high-quality beer (Imperial beer, for instance, the kind in the white cone-shaped bottles); avoid hot meals; take baths and have rubdowns, but stay away from showers; avoid constipation, and if you take enemas, don't use more than five glasses at thirty degrees centigrade. And, if I were treating you, I'd prescribe only one medicine: potassium iodide. It's a harmless but wonderful medicine. It has an excellent effect on the vascular system. There now, you see? I couldn't refrain from giving you a medical lecture without your even asking for it.

I've been drinking koumiss, but I haven't been able to drink more than four bottles a day; otherwise I get sick at my stomach. I'm terribly tired of the place. My life is like life in a military stockade. I'm so enormously bored I feel like breaking out. I most likely will break out of here and I'm already writing everyone to send all letters to my Yalta address starting the first of July. I'll probably leave here on the first of July. Incidentally, nature here is marvelous; there are large quantities of wildflowers, a hilly landscape, and many streams. But the people here are uninteresting, sluggish, homely, and devoid of song. They are mostly Bashkir.[4] You can feel the grasses growing quickly and avidly, because their summer is over in August and they still want to live and grow. There are no orchards. The hunting is apparently excellent, and you can catch grayling and trout in the stream.

I've received a letter from Korotnev.[5] He is on Lake Baikal. Baikal is one of the most picturesque places I've ever seen. Korotnev will probably write something semifictional; that's the sort of mood he's in now.

In all probability I'll be in Moscow by late August. My wife and my sister will rent an apartment in Moscow which will have a room for me. I'll live in that room until the first snow, and then it's back to Yalta without my wife.

I clasp your hand firmly and embrace you. I wish you good health and all the best.

Yours,
A. Chekhov

1. Chekhov first got to know Vasily Sobolevsky, lawyer, journalist and editor of *Russian Bulletin*, and Sobolevsky's wife Varvara Morozova during his famine relief work in 1891 (see Letter 64). In 1897, Chekhov stayed with Sobolevsky and Morozova in Biarritz (see Letter 108, note 2). In the decade after Chekhov's death Morozova became the hostess of a literary salon that played a significant role in the Russian Symbolist movement.

2. Sobolevsky's liberal newspaper had been in trouble with the government censors for the past three years. The letter and telegram he sent Chekhov contained the news that all earlier charges against *Russian Bulletin* had been dropped and that the newspaper would be henceforth free from preliminary censorship.

3. Before the discovery of x-rays by Wilhelm Roentgen the standard method of examining tubercular patients was by percussion. The quality of sound obtained and its location informed the doctor of the extent of damage to the lung.

4. Axyonovo was located in what is now the Bashkir Autonomous Soviet Socialist Republic.

5. Alexei Korotnev was a professor of zoology, whom Chekhov had encountered in Nice and whose indignant letters about the cancellation of Gorky's election to the Imperial Academy were instrumental in influencing Chekhov to tender his resignation (see Letter 153, note 1).

147. To Maria Chekhova[1]

Yalta,
August 3, 1901

Dear Masha,

I bequeath to you my house in Yalta for as long as you live, my money and the income from my dramatic works; and to my wife, Olga Leonardovna, my house in Gurzuf and five thousand rubles. You may sell my house if you so desire.[2] Give my brother Alexander three thousand, Ivan five thousand, and Mikhail three thousand, Alexei Dolzhenko one thousand and Yelena Chekhova (Lyolya)—when she marries—one thousand rubles.[3] After you and Mother die, all that remains except the income from the plays is to be put at the disposal of the Taganrog municipal administration for the purpose of aiding public education, while the income from the plays is to go to my brother Ivan and after his—Ivan's—death to the Taganrog municipal administration for the same educational purpose. I have promised one hundred rubles to the peasants of the village of Melikhovo to help pay for the highway. I have also promised Gavriil Alexeyevich Kharchenko[4] (The Kharchenko House, Moskalevka, Kharkov) that I would pay for his older daughter's gymnasium education until she is released from tuition. Help the poor. Take care of Mother. Live in peace among yourselves.

Anton Chekhov

1. This letter is Chekhov's last will and testament. After writing it, he simply gave it to his wife for safekeeping and after his death Olga handed it over to Maria. Because the document was not notarized, its legality was not recognized by the authorities. On February 11, 1905, a probate court in Moscow ruled that Chekhov's estate was to be divided among his surviving brothers, Alexander, Ivan and Mikhail, and his widow. The four designated heirs accepted the court's decision, but one month later they made a legal deed of gift of everything awarded to them by the court to Maria and empowered her to carry out the provisions of the present letter at her discretion.

2. Far from selling the house in Yalta, Maria made it into a Chekhov Museum and devoted the remainder of her long life to maintaining it. With single-minded determination, she defended it from looters during the civil war that followed the October Revolution, saved it from nationalization by getting it assigned to the Lenin Library in Moscow in the mid-1920s, rebuilt it after it was damaged by an earthquake in 1927 and stayed in it during the German occupation of the Crimea in 1941.

In 1921, during a visit to Moscow to arrange for the safekeeping of the

Chekhov archives and to try to place the Chekhov Museum under the protection of the Soviet authorities, Maria Chekhova had a memorable encounter with Tolstoy's youngest daughter, Alexandra, who was trying to do the same thing for her father's house at Yasnaya Polyana (the encounter is recorded in the memoir of Maria's long-time assistant Sergei Bragin, included in the collection of her correspondence and of testimonials by people who knew her, published in Simferopol, Crimea, in 1969). Tolstoy's daughter was handicapped in her role as a museum keeper by her lack of patience with the distortion of her father's ideas and principles by Soviet ideologues, by her inability to overlook the curtailment of civil liberties and by her refusal to remain silent about the persecution of Russian writers by the Soviet government. This brought her first to a labor camp and then led to her emigration to America.

Chekhov's sister could not understand that kind of involvement. She saw as her task in life the preservation of her brother's house for future generations and the encouragement of those future generations to read his writings. To achieve these basic objectives, she was prepared to make considerable concessions and adjustments: to remove all evidence of Chekhov's one-time friendship with Bunin, when Bunin angered the Soviet authorities by becoming an émigré and denouncing their literary policies in foreign publications; to place collected works of Lenin on Chekhov's bookshelf, so that the visitors might think Lenin was among his favorite authors; to plaster the house with numerous portraits of Gorky when Gorky became the central phenomenon of Soviet culture in the thirties and to exaggerate Chekhov's admiration for him beyond all plausibility; and to remove all these Gorky portraits during the German occupation and replace them with a portrait of Gerhart Hauptmann in order to impress the invaders. In Maria Chekhova's published correspondence we find equally gracious letters addressed to genuine literary scholars and to party-lining hacks, who were distorting every view Chekhov ever held in their tendentious Stalinist studies and turning him into a narrow and intolerant fanatic in their own image. It must be admitted that, within the limited scope of her aims, Maria Chekhova succeeded admirably in accomplishing the task she had set for herself.

3. Alexei Dolzhenko was the son of Chekhov's maternal aunt Fedosya; Yelena Chekhova was the daughter of his Taganrog uncle Mitrofan and the sister of Georgy Chekhov.

4. As a very small boy, Gavriil Kharchenko worked in Pavel Chekhov's grocery store in Taganrog, where he was mistreated and unfairly accused of theft. Although Kharchenko did quite well for himself in later years, Chekhov harbored a kind of guilt toward this man whom his father had once mistreated. This provision in his will seems a way of making partial amends. Kharchenko resumed contact with Chekhov by writing him in 1899 and reminding him of their childhood experiences.

148. To Alexei Peshkov (Maxim Gorky)

Moscow,[1]
September 24, 1901

Dear Alexei Maximovich,

I am in Moscow and I received your letter here in Moscow. My address is: The Boitsov House, Spiridonovka Street. Before I left Yalta I went to see Lev Nikolayevich.[2] He is extremely fond of the Crimea; it makes him as joyous as a child, but I'm not happy with the state of his health. He's aged a lot; his main illness is age, and it has completely taken hold of him. I'll be living in Yalta again in October, and if they give you permission to go, it would be wonderful.[3] There are very few people in Yalta during the winter, so no one pesters you or keeps you from working—that's number one, and number two, Lev Nikolayevich clearly misses having people around, and we could go and visit him.

Do finish your play.[4] You may feel it's not turning out as you'd planned, but don't put any faith in that feeling; it's deceptive. It is usual not to like a play while you are writing it, and it is usual not to like it afterward either; let other people judge and decide. But make sure you don't give it to anybody to read. Send it straight to Moscow—to Nemirovich or to me so I can pass it on to the Art Theater. Then, if something isn't right, it can be changed during rehearsals or even the day before the première.

Do you have the ending of "The Three"?[5]

I'm forwarding you an entirely useless letter. I received one too.[6]

Well, may the good Lord keep you. Stay well and, if such a thing be possible in your condition as Arzamas resident, happy.[7] My regards and greetings to Yekaterina Pavlovna and the children.

Yours,
A. Chekhov

Please write.

1. Chekhov came to Moscow from Yalta on September 17 and stayed until the end of October. He attended rehearsals and performances of *Three Sisters* at the Moscow Art Theater and was allowed by Stanislavsky to revise and change some of the *mise en scène*, which according to some of the press reports improved the already successful production. He also spent some time helping Olga Vasilyeva with the legal formalities connected with her recent inheritance.

2. Tolstoy was staying at Gaspra, the estate of Countess Panina, situated

not far from Yalta. Chekhov spent a day with him there on September 12. He was most graciously received, but Tolstoy strongly advised him to stop writing plays, and to dedicate himself instead to "writing what he writes best," citing "In the Ravine" as an example of what he meant.

3. Police authorities barred Gorky from residence in his home town of Nizhny Novgorod, and he was wavering between moving to some small town in the Nizhny Novgorod Province and petitioning the authorities to allow him to settle in Yalta.

4. Throughout the summer, Gorky was working on his first play, *The Philistines*, commissioned by Nemirovich-Danchenko and Stanislavsky. Because of his enormous popularity, the progress of his writing was widely reported in the press.

5. Gorky's short novel *The Three* was serialized in Vladimir Posse's journal *Life*. In May of 1901, the journal was closed by the police, so that the ending of *The Three* did not have a chance to appear in it. The work was published in its entirety as a separate book in the latter part of 1901.

6. The letter was from a translator in Germany who wanted exclusive rights for translating the work of Chekhov and Gorky.

7. Pending the decision of the authorities about Gorky's new place of residence, he was officially registered as a resident of the provincial town of Arzamas.

149. To Alexei Peshkov (Maxim Gorky)

Moscow,
October 22, 1901

Dear Alexei Maximovich,

About five days have passed since I read your play,[1] and the reason I haven't written you all this time is that I never received the fourth act. I was waiting for it, but it did not arrive. So I read only three acts, but that should be enough, I think, for me to be able to form a judgment about the play. As I expected, it is very good. It is written in an authentically Gorkian manner; it is original, very interesting, and to start off by talking about its faults, I have so far found only one, a fault as irreparable as red hair on a redhead—its conservatism of form. You have new, original people singing new songs from a score that has a second-hand appearance. You have four acts, your characters deliver moral sermons; your fear of long speeches shows through, and so on and so forth. But all this is unimportant, for it all dissolves, as it were, in the play's merits. How alive Perchikhin is! His daughter is charming, and so are Tatyana and Pyotr.[2] Their mother is a magnificent old woman. Nil, the play's central figure, is powerfully done and extremely interesting![3] In short, the play is sure to be gripping right from the first act.

But, for heaven's sake, make sure that no one but Artyom[4] plays Perchikhin and that no one else but Alexeyev-Stanislavsky plays Nil. These two will do exactly what needs to be done. Have Meyerhold play Pyotr. Only make Nil's part—it's a wonderful part—two or three times longer. It should end the play and be made into the leading role. Only don't try to pit him against Pyotr and Tatyana; let him stand on his own and let them stand on their own, and then show that they are all wonderful, excellent people independently of one another.[5] When Nil tries to appear superior to Pyotr and Tatyana and keeps patting himself on the back, he loses an element that is so characteristic of our decent workingman, the element of modesty. He boasts and argues, but even without all that it is plain enough what kind of a man he is. Let him be cheerful, let him clown his way through all four acts, let him eat a lot after work, and that is quite enough to captivate the audience. Pyotr, I repeat, is well done. You probably have no idea how well done he is. Tatyana is also a well-rounded character except (1) she ought to be a real teacher, she ought to be teaching children and coming home from school and fussing with textbooks and homework, and (2) a hint to the effect that she has already tried to poison herself should come out in the first or second act; then the poisoning in the third act won't seem so unexpected and will be appropriate. Teterev talks too much; people like him should be presented a little at a time, almost in passing, because no matter how you look at it, they are only episodic both in life and on the stage.[6] Have Yelena eat dinner in the first act with all the rest, have her sit there and make jokes, because otherwise there is so little of her that she seems unclear. Her love scene with Pyotr is somewhat abrupt; it will stand out too much on stage. Make her a passionate woman—if not loving, then amorous.

There's still plenty of time before the play goes on stage, and you'll have time to revise it ten times over. What a shame I'm leaving! I'd sit in on the rehearsals of the play and write you everything that had to be done.

I'm leaving for Yalta on Friday. Keep well and under God's protection. My most humble respects and greetings to Yekaterina Pavlovna and the children. I firmly clasp your hand and embrace you.

Yours,
A. Chekhov

1. *The Philistines*, also known in English as *The Petty Bourgeois* and as *Smug Citizens*, may lack the stagecraft and the exotic appeal of his more famous *Lower Depths*, but it is arguably the single most interesting play by Gorky. It is, as Alexander Blok once pointed out, his most carefully and

thoughtfully written play. Its individualized, full-blooded characters are strikingly unlike the flattened stereotypes we encounter in the plays of Gorky's middle period. The play is a vivid examination of generational and intellectual conflicts within a family of the Russian urban bourgeoisie. An elderly middle-class couple named Bessemenov have struggled all their lives to give good educations to their two children, Pyotr and Tatyana, and their adopted son Nil. The exposure to university life and to the social and cultural currents of turn-of-the-century Russia have turned Pyotr and Tatyana into intellectuals, incomprehensible to their parents. Nil has become a railroad mechanic, active in the labor movement and alienated from both his adopted parents and their university-educated children. There is thus a three-way communication gap within the family, which leads to a number of dramatic explosions. *The Philistines* is full of situations and emotional attitudes which American university students of *ca.* 1970 find startlingly familiar and recognizable. This play has also been rediscovered in the Soviet Union in recent years, where its picture of intellectual and generational polarization has given it an unexpected new relevance.

2. By finding the kitchen maid Polya Perchikhina, the play's most attractive female character from Gorky's point of view, as charming as Pyotr and Tatyana, Chekhov betrays his basic misconception of Gorky's intentions in writing *The Philistines*. As the letter Gorky wrote to Stanislavsky during the rehearsals of *The Philistines* in January 1902 confirms, the characters of Pyotr and Tatyana were meant to be an indictment of spineless liberal intellectuals, who might be better educated than their semiliterate parents, but who are equally philistine and equally supportive of the existing social structure.

3. Nil is the earliest of Gorky's single-minded revolutionary heroes. He is described as follows in the already-cited letter to Stanislavsky: "Nil is a man who is serenely confident of his own strength and of his right to transform life and all of its institutions in accordance with his own understanding. And his understanding is based on his wholesome, optimistic love of life, whose shortcomings arouse in him only one feeling: the passionate desire to destroy them. He is a workingman and he knows that life is hard and tragic; but it is the best thing that exists and it must and can be improved and rebuilt by his will and in accordance with his wishes." The name of Nil, incidentally, is derived from Latin Nilus and is identical in form with the Russian name of the river Nile. American commentators on Gorky are quite wrong to derive it from the Latin *nil*, "nothing," and to assign to the name a corresponding symbolism. Because the Russian transcription of Latin *nil* would require a palatalized *l*, neither Gorky nor any other speaker of Russian could possibly connect that word with Nil's name, with its hard *l*.

4. Alexander Artyom, the actor who was the first performer of Chebutykin in *Three Sisters* and of Firs in *The Cherry Orchard*.

5. It was possible and normal for Chekhov to see the self-assured, strong-willed Nil and the wavering, high-strung intellectuals Tatyana and Pyotr as equally valuable human beings. But this idea was quite foreign to Gorky, as

his letter to Stanislavsky eloquently shows. Discussing the play's dramatic climax, Tatyana's suicide attempt because of her unrequited love for Nil, Gorky wrote that her unhappiness must not arouse pity or sympathy, but "something else, much less attractive." Gorky's anti-intellectualism became more pronounced in subsequent years. One of its ugliest manifestations is described in Nadezhda Mandelstam's *Hope Against Hope*, in which we find Gorky using his august position in the post-revolutionary literary life to deprive the freezing and starving poet Osip Mandelstam of the pair of trousers he needed to survive through the winter. "The trousers themselves were a small matter," wrote Mandelstam's widow, "but they spoke eloquently of Gorky's hostility to a literary trend that was foreign to him. Here too was a question of 'spineless intellectuals' who were worth preserving only if they were well equipped with solid learning. Like many people of similar background, Gorky prized learning, but had a quantitative view of it: the more the better."

6. Stanislavsky's *My Life in Art* contains a rather sentimental account of how the role of the church chorister Teterev ruined the life of the man who played it in the original production of *The Philistines*. In their striving for authenticity, Nemirovich and Stanislavsky decided to cast a real chorister in this role. The man gave a highly acclaimed, believable performance, but he identified with the character in the play to such an extent that it affected his mind, causing him to become an alcoholic and to end his days on skid row.

150. To Olga Knipper

Yalta,
November 17, 1901

My dearest helpmate,

The rumors you have heard about Tolstoy's illness and even death are completely unfounded.[1] There neither are nor have been any particular changes in his health, and his death is still apparently a long way off. It's true that he's weak and looks frail, but he doesn't have a single threatening symptom, not a one, except old age. . . . Don't believe any of it. If, God forbid, something should happen, I'll let you know by telegram. I'll call him "grandpa" in the telegram, or else it may never reach you.[2]

Alexei Maximovich is here and in good health. He is staying at my place and is officially registered here. A policeman came by today.[3]

I am writing and working, but it's impossible to work in Yalta, darling, totally impossible. It's far from the world, uninteresting, and worst of all—cold. I've received a letter from Vishnevsky.[4] Tell him I will write a play, but not before spring.

The desk lamp is burning in my study now. As long as it doesn't stink of kerosene it works fine.

Alexei Maximovich hasn't changed; he's the same decent, cultivated, kind man. There's only one thing about him—or rather on him—I find incongruous: his peasant shirt. It's as hard for me to get used to as the uniform of the Gentleman of the Chamber.[5]

We're having autumn weather; it's not very pleasant.

Stay alive and well now, light of my eyes. Thank you for the letters. Don't fall ill, and be a good girl. Give my best to your family. I kiss you hard and embrace you.

Your husband,
Antonio

I am well. Moscow had an amazingly good effect on me. I don't know if it's you or Moscow that's to blame, but I've been coughing very little.

If you see Kundasova or anyone who will be seeing her soon, let her know that Dr. Vasilyev[6] the psychiatrist is in Yalta and is very seriously ill.

1. Tolstoy's stay in the Crimea gave rise to persistent rumors about his imminent death. Because of the news blackout that had been imposed at the time of his excommunication, the newspapers could not inform the public of his condition and there was considerable anxiety about the state of his health.

2. The ban on mentioning Tolstoy's name in telegrams was also still in force.

3. Gorky had been permitted to travel to the Crimea, but was barred from residing in any of its larger cities. The village of Autka, where Chekhov's home was located, had not yet been officially incorporated into the Yalta municipality as one of its suburbs at the time this letter was written. Because of this technicality, Gorky was able to stay with Chekhov as his house guest. A further technical requirement was that while Gorky could visit the city of Yalta freely he was not allowed to stay in it overnight.

4. Alexander Vishnevsky, the Moscow Art Theater actor, and a native of Taganrog, whom Chekhov had known since his childhood.

5. There had been other Russian writers before Gorky who had affected a peasant costume for one reason or another (e.g., Tolstoy, who wore bast shoes and peasant clothes to show his sympathy for the peasants and his protest against their oppression), but Gorky was the first to make it a part of a consciously projected public image. His costume contributed in a very tangible way to the image of "the man of the people" on which Gorky's instant popularity at home and abroad was largely based. Chekhov is making a subtle and striking comparison between Gorky's peasant shirt and the uniform of

the Gentleman of the Chamber which Nicholas I had forced Alexander Pushkin to wear in the last years of his life, much to the poet's resentment. Both Pushkin's forced masquerade and Gorky's voluntary one were equally wrong from Chekhov's point of view because they both represented the writer to the public as something he was not.

6. Dr. Vasily Vasilyev, whom Chekhov had known since his Melikhovo days.

151. To Viktor Mirolyubov

Yalta,
December 17, 1901

Dear Viktor Sergeyevich,

I am unwell or not entirely well—that's more accurate—and can't write. I've been spitting blood and now feel weak and cross. I've got a hot compress on my side, and I'm taking creosote and all sorts of nonsense. Be that as it may, I won't let you down: you'll get "The Bishop" sooner or later.[1]

I read the article of that cop Rozanov[2] in the *New Times*. It informed me, among other things, of your new activities.[3] If you only knew, dear Viktor Sergeyevich, how saddened I was! It seems to me you definitely ought to leave Petersburg immediately. Go to Nervi or come to Yalta, but leave. What do you—a fine, direct person—have in common with Rozanov or that most lofty and cunning Sergius, or supersmug Merezhkovsky?[4] I feel like writing much, much more, but I had better restrain myself, especially since letters are these days read mostly by people to whom they are not addressed. I will say, though, that for the problems that interest you, it's not forgotten words or idealism that matters; it is a consciousness of your own purity, that is, the perfect freedom of your soul from all forgotten and unforgotten words, idealisms and all the rest of those incomprehensible words. One should either believe in God, or if faith is lacking, one should do something other than fill the void with sensationalism, one must seek, seek on one's own, all alone with one's conscience. . . .

Anyway, keep well! If you intend to come, drop me a line. Tolstoy is here and Gorky is here, so you won't be bored, I hope.

There's no news. I firmly clasp your hand.

Yours,
A. Chekhov

1. "The Bishop" had been promised by Chekhov for the journal Mirolyubov was editing.

2. Chekhov's attitude toward Vasily Rozanov, who replaced him as Suvorin's principal protégé and whose highly popular articles and essays saved the *New Times* from total intellectual eclipse (Igor Stravinsky recalled once that as a young man he subscribed to that newspaper only because of Rozanov), was somewhat ambiguous. Like everyone in Russia, Chekhov admired the brilliance of his style, but like most of the Russian intelligentsia, he deplored Rozanov's reactionary political views. Chekhov seems not to have noticed that Rozanov, almost single-handedly, made the sphere of sexuality again a respectable intellectual subject for the first time since the 1820s. Following his example, the poets and novelists of the Symbolist period could deal with sexual topics, which were previously regarded with equal horror by the official censors and by the Russian radical tradition. While berating Rozanov in this and several other letters of this period, Chekhov wrote to Mirolyubov on December 30, 1902, urging him to read Rozanov's essay on the poetry of Nikolai Nekrasov. About that essay Chekhov wrote: "It has been a long, long time since I've read anything like it, anything as talented, sweeping, affirmative and intelligent."

3. The article by Rozanov mentioned above informed the Russian public of the existence of the Religious-Philosophical Society, organized by Rozanov, Merezhkovsky, Zinaida Gippius, Archbishop Sergius and Mirolyubov for the purpose of establishing a dialogue between the Orthodox Church and Russian intellectuals. The estrangement between the two had become almost total by the end of the nineteenth century. Apart from compulsory instruction in catechism, no subject remotely connected with religion was taught at any Russian university (when Vladimir Solovyov needed to learn the history of Russian Orthodoxy for his master's thesis at Moscow University, he shocked the university community by enrolling for a course at the religious seminary, the only place where this subject was taught). Most Russian intellectuals considered the Church to be a servant of the tsarist government, ready to carry out whatever policies it decreed. Persecutions of dissidents and minority sects, a missionary branch that effected conversions by force and intimidation, and the recent excommunication of Tolstoy all combined to bring the prestige of the ecclesiastic authorities down to a very low point. Under these circumstances an attempt at a rapprochement with them was regarded by much of the liberal intelligentsia as a sellout. This was how Gorky saw Mirolyubov's participation (see next note). Chekhov's objections, however, were not politically motivated. He simply did not agree that a search for religious or mystical experience should be a public occasion.

As can now be seen in retrospect, the encounters between the intellectuals and the clergy at the Religious-Philosophical Society constituted a significant step forward in the temporary liberation of Russian culture from the strait-jacket of dogmatic and doctrinaire utilitarianism. The religious revival in Russian culture, triggered by the newly found appreciation of Dostoyevsky and by the influence of Vladimir Solovyov, was as important an aspect of this many-sided liberation as the philosophy of Nietzsche, the Symbolist, Cubist and Futurist forms in the arts and Sergei Diaghilev's path-breaking journal. It gave Russia a constellation of important religious thinkers, such as Nikolai Berdyayev and Lev Shestov, and informed the poetry of Alexander Blok, Andrei Belyi and Boris Pasternak with its essential mystical strain; its influence is still felt in such important Russian novels of recent decades as Bulgakov's *The Master and Margarita* and Solzhenitsyn's *August 1914*.

4. After Maxim Gorky found out about Mirolyubov's participation in the Religious-Philosophical Society encounters with the clergy, he wrote him a furious letter that heaped abuse on Merezhkovsky and asserted that the entire undertaking could only serve the cause of oppression. As Zinaida Gippius described it in the chapter on Rozanov in her book of memoirs, *Living Portraits,* the immediate effect of the encounters was to broaden the outlook of some of the younger participating priests, with the result that some of them either left the Church or joined various dissident sects. The alarmed ecclesiastic authorities banned the encounters after the first year.

152. To Ivan Bunin[1]

Yalta,
January 15, 1902

Dear Ivan Alexeyevich,

Greetings and Happy New Year! May you become world famous, start a liaison with the prettiest of all women, and win twenty thousand rubles in each of the three state lotteries.[2] I was ill for a month and a half, but I now consider myself well, though I still cough off and on, do almost nothing, and keep waiting for something—spring, apparently.

Have I written you anything about your "Pines"? First, many thanks for the offprint. Second, "The Pines" is very innovative, very fresh and very good, but it is a little too compact, something like bouillon concentrate.[3]

Well then, we'll be expecting you!! Come as soon as you can. I'll be happy to see you. I clasp your hand very, very firmly and wish you good health.

Yours,
A. Chekhov

My reply to the *Southern Review*'s invitation was that I had no objections, but that I wasn't writing anything at present. I begged to be excused and told them I would send them something once I got something written.[4] That's how I answer them all.

1. After corresponding with Chekhov for a number of years, Ivan Bunin (1870–1953) became a good friend of the entire Chekhov family in 1899.

Because of their personal closeness, which lasted until Chekhov's death, some short-sighted critics decided that Bunin was a literary disciple of Chekhov. But, apart from a few technical devices he may have learned from Chekhov, it would be hard to imagine two writers who are more disparate in their outlook, themes and range of interest. Although younger, Bunin was stylistically a far more conservative writer than Chekhov. With the exception of Marcel Proust and Vladimir Nabokov, whose work he came to value very highly, Bunin was unable to appreciate or even to understand any literary forms or trends that came into existence later than the 1890s (he shared this inability with Sergei Rachmaninov and Fyodor Chaliapin, his close friends and, later, fellow émigrés). This explains why Bunin thought that the last play of any consequence that Chekhov wrote was *The Seagull. Three Sisters* and *The Cherry Orchard* were steps into the kind of twentieth-century sensibility where Bunin could no longer follow Chekhov. Thematically, Bunin's ever-growing fascination with the triad of sex, pain and death, and his conviction that these three elements are inseparable in any human life, could not be further from everything that attracted and interested Chekhov.

After Chekhov's death, Maria Chekhova, who became close friends with Bunin, repeatedly urged him to write her brother's biography, considering him the most suited of all Russian writers for this task. In 1904, Bunin wrote a brief memoir about his encounters with Chekhov but he kept postponing his planned longer work. He finally got around to it shortly before his death and did not live to finish it. His fragmentary sketches for the book were published by his widow in New York in 1955. At the end of his life, Bunin's view of Chekhov and his recollections of their association were strongly colored by his enthusiasm for two of the least reliable texts on Chekhov ever published: Lydia Avilova's spurious memoir and Lev Shestov's essay "Creation Out of the Void" (Shestov's view of Chekhov as the cruel destroyer of all hope and optimism actually fits some of Bunin's own later work far better than it does anything by Chekhov). Because of this, despite its many interesting and believable glimpses of Chekhov, Bunin's fragmentary study lacks the depth and immediacy it might have had if it had been written shortly after Chekhov's death.

2. Three decades later, Chekhov's good wishes were realized in ways he could not have imagined. By 1933, Bunin had been awarded the Nobel Prize for literature and was living in a magnificent villa on the French Riviera with a devoted and understanding wife and a beautiful young mistress.

3. Chekhov's "bouillon concentrate" simile refers to the same aspect of Bunin's style that Vladimir Nabokov was to describe later as his "brocaded prose." In Bunin's *magnum opus*, his autobiographical novel *The Life of Arsenyev*, written during his emigration, his Russian attains a density and a perfection that should drive to total despair any translator who attempts to convey it in another language.

4. *Southern Review* was an Odessa newspaper which took Chekhov's polite and noncommittal answer at face value and displayed posters all over town, announcing that Chekhov had become a contributor.

153. To Vladimir Korolenko

Yalta,
April 19, 1902

Dear Vladimir Galaktionovich,

My wife arrived from Petersburg with a high fever. She is extremely weak and in terrible pain. She cannot walk and had to be carried here from the steamer. . . . She seems to be a little better now. . . .

I will not pass the protest letter on to Tolstoy.[1] In a conversation we had about Gorky and the Academy he came out with the following statement: "I do not consider myself a member of the Academy" and stuck his nose in a book. I gave Gorky a copy and read him your letter. I somehow have a feeling that there won't be any Academy meeting on May 25th, because by early May all the members will have left for the summer. I also have the feeling that they won't elect Gorky the second time round and that he'll be blackballed.[2] I'd so much like to see you and have a talk with you. Is there any chance of your coming to Yalta? I'll be here until the fifteenth of May. I'd go and visit you in Poltava, but my wife has fallen ill and will probably be in bed for another three weeks. Or will we get together after May 15th in Moscow, on the Volga, or abroad? Write.

I firmly clasp your hand and wish you all the best. Keep well.

Yours,
A. Chekhov

My wife sends her regards.

1. This is a reply to Korolenko's letter of April 10, 1902. At the end of February Gorky was elected an honorary member of the literary section of the Imperial Academy of Sciences. The election occurred at the height of a new wave of student disturbances, which led to temporary closing of the St. Petersburg and Kiev universities and to deportation of a number of student strike leaders to Siberia. Chekhov was fully informed of the university situation and of the circumstances of Gorky's election by a series of detailed letters he received from Nikodim Kondakov in March and April of 1902. Early in March, the Minister of the Interior submitted to Nicholas II a report about Gorky's election accompanied by a copy of Gorky's police record. On March 9, the president of the Academy was informed of the tsar's "profound chagrin" occasioned by the election of a person who was under police surveillance. The next day, the government ordered the Academy to announce the annulment of its election of Gorky. The Academy was also ordered to revise its

election rules to make sure that no undesirables were elected in the future.

Korolenko sent a carefully argued protest against the annulment to the head of the literary section of the Academy and forwarded a copy to Chekhov, urging him to join him in the protest. (This letter renewed their contact for the first time since the late 1880s.) Korolenko also enclosed an additional copy of his protest, which he requested Chekhov to pass on to Tolstoy, who was still at Gaspra.

In his capacity as an honorary member of the Academy, Chekhov received a number of other letters asking him what action he proposed to take. The zoologist Alexei Korotnev's letter described the government-imposed annulment as a slap in the face of the Russian people and concluded: "I can't believe that the other honorary members will not resign. A tacit acquiescence on their part can only be taken for approval of this revolting act that has been perpetrated."

2. Korolenko's letter proposed that the Academy request the government to free Gorky from police surveillance and then re-elect him again. But from Kondakov's letters of March 10 and April 8, Chekhov knew something that neither the government nor the general public realized. Gorky's election was an extremely close one and many members voted for him only to break a tie between him and several other candidates (among them Mikhailovsky and Lydia Veselitskaya). Kondakov's letter also makes clear that neither he nor any other member expected any governmental objections when they voted for Gorky. It is because of this inside information that Chekhov expressed a doubt that Gorky would be elected for the second time.

154. To Vladimir Korolenko

Yalta,
April 20, 1902

Dear Vladimir Galaktionovich,

My wife is still ill, and I can't seem to collect my thoughts enough to write a decent letter. In the letter I wrote you yesterday I asked whether we would be getting together in April or early May. I think we would do best to take joint action, so we'll have to settle on a plan. I share completely the opinion you state in your letter to Veselovsky,[1] and I wish you would say a few words on my behalf as well at the May 15th meeting—if it takes place. If we don't get together before the fifteenth, we'll have to settle things by mail.

My wife has a high temperature and is flat on her back. She's lost weight. What did you talk to her about in Petersburg? She's complaining bitterly that she can't remember.[2]

I firmly clasp your hand. Be well and happy.

Yours,
A. Chekhov

1. The literary historian Alexander Veselovsky headed the literary section of the Academy.

2. In his capacity as the defender of civil liberties, Korolenko left his home in the Ukraine and traveled to St. Petersburg for a few days early in March to observe the events at the university. Olga Knipper was there with the Moscow Art Theater and Korolenko informed her of his findings, which he wanted conveyed to Chekhov.

155. To Konstantin Balmont[1]

Yalta,
May 7, 1902

Dear Konstantin Dmitrievich,

May the heavens bless you for your charming letter! I am alive and almost well, but I'm still stuck in Yalta and will be staying on here for quite some time because my wife is ill. I received the *Buildings on Fire* and the second volume of Calderón, and thank you infinitely.[2] You know that your talent is precious to me and that every one of your books affords me great pleasure and excitement. Maybe it's because I'm a conservative.[3]

I also received the play your wife translated—I received it long ago—and forwarded it to the Art Theater. I liked the play; it's modern, but unnecessarily, forcedly grim. And there's a good chance the censors won't pass it.[4]

I envy you. Stay as long as you can in lovely Oxford.[5] Work, enjoy one another, and every once in a while think of us living out our gray, sluggish, dreary lives.

Keep well and under the protection of the cherubim and seraphim. Write me again, if only a line or two.

Yours,
A. Chekhov

1. Konstantin Balmont (1867–1942) was one of the leading figures in the revival of Russian poetry that began at the very end of the nineteenth century. Although Chekhov showed little interest in or understanding of the poetry of other early Symbolists, such as Fyodor Sologub and Zinaida Gippius (primarily because of their mysticism and their Dostoyevskian orientation), he was captivated by Balmont's festive and life-affirming poems. They met in 1898 and after that Balmont and his wife were frequent visitors of Chekhov's in Yalta.

Balmont's poetry enjoyed a considerable popularity in Russia in the first two decades of our century. His poems were set to music by both Stravinsky (the cantata "Zvezdoliki," also known as "Le Roi des étoiles" for chorus and orchestra and "Two Poems of Balmont" for voice and piano) and Prokofiev (the cantata "They Are Seven," a set of Balmont songs and the cycle of piano pieces usually called "Visions fugitives," which was inspired by a Balmont poem). After the Revolution, Balmont emigrated and his name was deleted from literary history in the Soviet Union. After Stalin's death, Ilya Ehrenburg and other surviving admirers of Balmont repeatedly attempted to use this letter of Chekhov's as a testimonial in their efforts to convince the Soviet literary authorities to authorize a new publication of Balmont's poetry. But Balmont's modernism, something that the Soviet literary establishment tolerates only in certifiably revolutionary writers, such as Mayakovsky or Brecht, proved a stumbling block. A carefully selected volume of Balmont's lyrics was finally published in 1969.

2. In addition to being a gifted poet, Balmont was a prolific translator (but not a very good one), especially from the English and the Spanish. *Buildings on Fire* was the title of one of his finest and most successful verse collections.

3. The vividly colorful, imaginative and joyous poetry of Balmont was seen by many critics of his time as a betrayal of the mournful, civic-minded traditions of Nekrasov and Nadson (present-day American university students have been known to describe Balmont's poems as "psychedelic"). Chekhov ironically calls himself a conservative for daring to like Balmont's poetry despite the absence in it of the social themes that utilitarian critics required Russian poets to treat.

Actually, Balmont was genuinely radical in his personal politics. His volume *Songs of the Avenger* (1905), which explicitly called for the overthrow of the Romanov family, was seized by the authorities and Balmont had to emigrate for a few years. He was amnestied in 1913 and allowed to return to Russia. In the 1920s, after the October Revolution forced him to emigrate for the second time, Balmont published an article in a French journal in which he documented the suppression of all literary freedom in the Soviet Union. His disclosures were answered by Romain Rolland, who chided Balmont in print for being a tsarist reactionary trying to block humanity's progress toward freedom and equality.

4. Balmont's wife Yekaterina had translated an unpublished play by an obscure German playwright.

5. Balmont was frequently invited to Oxford, where he lectured on modern Russian literature. His numerous translations from the English included the complete poetry of Percy Bysshe Shelley and Edgar Allan Poe (His version of "The Bells" was set to music by Sergei Rachmaninov) and the first Russian translation of Walt Whitman's *Leaves of Grass*.

156. To Olga Solovyova[1]

Yalta,
May 24, 1902

Dear Olga Mikhailovna,

I am leaving for Moscow tomorrow. Enclosed you will find a draft of the letter. If you accept it, make a copy and send it to me at the following address: The Gonetskaya House, Neglinny Lane, Moscow, and I'll pass it on to Umov. I'll let you know immediately what the president tells me.

Keep well and cheerful. I wish you a wonderful summer, health and a good disposition.

Devotedly,
A. Chekhov

I am coming back in July.

To His Excellency the President of the Moscow Imperial Society of Earth Sciences, Nikolai Alexeyevich Umov.[2]

Your Excellency:

I hereby address to you the following proposal, which I wish to submit to the Moscow Imperial Society of Earth Sciences. Desiring to commemorate the name of the engineer and State Councilor Vladimir Ilyich Berezin with an institution which will serve the cause of science, I have settled upon the idea of establishing a biological research center on my estate near Gurzuf on the Black Sea. This center would offer living space and research facilities for from twenty to thirty university graduates who have chosen a career in science.

I would like the Berezin Biological Research Center to be open to all those who have devoted their lives to science. I would like the Center's fellows not only to dispose of all the necessary scientific equipment, but to have their own private apartments at the Center as well.

It is to this end that I intend to build the Center and adjoining living quarters for fellows and to provide the Center with all necessary equipment and propose to the Moscow Imperial Society of Earth Sciences, the oldest Russian naturalist society, that they draw up a plan for the construction of the Center, draft its constitution, intercede with the government for permission to open the Center and name it after V. I. Berezin, and then undertake complete administration of the Center's activities.

In addition to the money necessary for constructing and equipping the Center, I will set aside three hundred thousand rubles for its maintenance.

Olga Solovyova

My address is: Gurzuf, Crimea.

1. Olga Solovyova was an extremely wealthy lady who owned a magnificent estate near Chekhov's cottage at Kuchukoy (Gurzuf). After the death of her common-law husband Vladimir Berezin, she was casting about for a

way to commemorate his name. Chekhov suggested that she endow a marine-biology research center on the Black Sea and have it named after Berezin.

2. Nikolai Umov, in addition to being the president of the Imperial Society of Earth Sciences, was a professor of physics at Moscow University. The poet and novelist Andrei Belyi studied physics with Professor Umov in 1900 and in his later narrative poem "The First Rendez-Vous," written in 1921, placed Professor Umov in the center of a dazzling verbal fantasy about atomic physics, which not only described a nuclear holocaust, but mentioned the atomic bomb by name several decades before it was actually invented.

157. To Alexei Peshkov (Maxim Gorky)

Lyubimovka,[1]
July 29, 1902

Dear Alexei Maximovich,

I've read your play.[2] It is original and undoubtedly good. The second act is very good, it's the best and most powerful, and when I read it, and in particular its ending, I almost jumped for joy. The mood is grim and oppressive; the public isn't used to this, and some people may walk out before the end, and at any rate you can say good-bye to your reputation of being an optimist. My wife will play Vasilisa, the dissolute, ill-tempered female. Vishnevsky is walking around the house impersonating the Tatar; he is certain that that is his role. Artyom, alas, cannot be entrusted with the role of Luka; he'll merely repeat what he has done before and tire himself out. On the other hand he'll make a perfect policeman, and Samarova can be his mistress. The Actor, whom you've brought off so successfully, is a magnificent role; it must be entrusted to an experienced actor, Stanislavsky, for instance. Kachalov can play the Baron.[3]

You've excluded the most interesting characters (except for the Actor) from Act Four, so you'd better watch out. This act may sound boring and unnecessary, especially if only mediocre actors are left on stage after the more powerful and interesting actors have made their exits. The Actor's death is terrible. It's like giving the spectator a box on the ear and it happens for no reason at all, with no preparation. What brought the Baron to the flophouse and why he has to be a Baron are also insufficiently clear.

I'm leaving for Yalta around the tenth of August (my wife will remain in Moscow). Then, before the end of August, I'll go back to Moscow and live here, unless something out of the ordinary happens, until December. I'll see your *Philistines* and attend the rehearsals of your new play. Is there any chance of your escaping from Arzamas and coming to Moscow even if for no more than a week? I've heard that you're going to be permitted to take a trip to Moscow, that there are people interceding for you. The Lianozov Theater in Moscow is being turned into the Art Theater. Work is in full swing, and they have been promised that it will be ready by October 15th. But there is little prospect of holding performances there before the end of November or even December. The rains, the violent rains we've been having, seem to me to be holding up construction.

I'm living in Lyubimovka in Alexeyev's cottage, and I fish all day from morning till night. The river here is wonderful; it is deep and filled with fish. And I've grown so lazy it's disgusting.

Olga's health appears to be improving. She sends her cordial regards. Give my regards to Yekaterina Pavlovna, Maximka and your daughter.

Leonid Andreyev's *Thought* is a pretentious kind of thing, hard to understand and—as far as I can tell—unnecessary, but it is brought off with talent. Andreyev lacks simplicity, and his talent resembles the song of an artificial nightingale.[4] Now Skitalets is a sparrow, but a sparrow that is at least alive and real.[5]

We'll get together somehow or other at the end of August.

Keep well and happy, and don't be bored. Alexin[6] came to see me and had nice things to say about you.

Yours,
A. Chekhov

Drop me a line to tell me you've gotten the play back. My address is: The Gonetskaya House, Neglinny Lane.

Don't rush with the title. There's time enough to think one up.

1. After returning from a trip to the Ural Mountains, where he inspected Savva Morozov's mines, Chekhov joined his wife in Moscow, and they went to the summer cottage in the village of Lyubimovka which Stanislavsky lent them for the month of July.

2. *The Lower Depths*, which Gorky began writing even before he had finished *The Philistines*.

3. Alexander Vishnevsky, Alexander Artyom, Maria Samarova and Vasily Kachalov were all leading actors with the Moscow Art Theater.

4. If the enormous prestige of Maxim Gorky at the beginning of the twentieth century can be explained in terms of the social and political pressures of that age, the almost equally spectacular ascent to fame of Gorky's friend and literary associate Leonid Andreyev seems in retrospect an inexplicable case of mistaken literary identity. A minor writer of respectable but not overwhelming talent in his more realistic pieces, such as his short

novel *The Seven That Were Hanged* and the play *Savva*, Andreyev became tremendously celebrated both in Russia and abroad for his murky, pretentious, pseudo-Symbolist productions, such as *Anathema*, *The Life of Man* and *He Who Gets Slapped*.

Not only were the critics and the public won over by Andreyev, but he was taken very seriously by almost all the leading figures of Russian Symbolism as well. In all of Russia, only Tolstoy and Chekhov seemed to be able to resist the Andreyev craze. Tolstoy's comment was: "He's doing his best to frighten me, but I'm not a bit scared." Chekhov's other most pointed comment on Andreyev (with whom he was to exchange a few polite letters) is found in Alexander Serebrov's *Time and People*: "What makes you think Leonid Andreyev is a writer? He is simply a lawyer's clerk, the kind that loves talking prettily."

5. Stepan Petrov, who published his writings under the quasi-poetic pen name Skitalets ("The Wanderer") was another member of the Gorky-Andreyev-Bunin circle of younger realists.

6. Yalta physician Dr. Alexander Alexin, who personally delivered the manuscript of Gorky's *Lower Depths* to Chekhov in Lyubimovka.

158. To Vladimir Korolenko

Yalta,
August 25, 1902

Dear Vladimir Galaktionovich,

Where are you? At home? In any case, I'm sending this letter to you in Poltava. Here is what I wrote to the Academy.[1]

> Your Imperial Highness.[2]
>
> In December of last year I received notification of the election of A. M. Peshkov to the rank of honorary member of the Academy. I was quick to visit Peshkov, who was then in the Crimea; I was the first to notify him of his election and the first to congratulate him on it. Shortly thereafter the newspapers reported that in view of the charges brought against Peshkov under Paragraph 1035 his election had been declared null and void. Furthermore, it was made very clear that this new notification proceeded from the Academy of Sciences, and since I am an honorary member, the notification proceeded in part from my person as well. I offered Peshkov my heartfelt congratulations, and yet I declared his election null and void—I could not reconcile myself to this contradiction, my conscience refused to accept it. Looking up Paragraph 1035 explained nothing to me.[3] After long deliberation I could come to but one decision, a painful, regrettable decision, namely respectfully to request that Your Imperial Highness divest me of my membership in the Academy.[4]

Well, there it is. It took me a long time to write it; the weather was very hot, and I was unable to write anything better. I probably wouldn't have been able to in any case.

I couldn't come. I wanted to take a trip along the Volga and Don with my wife, but in Moscow she fell seriously ill again, and we were both so exhausted that we no longer felt up to the trip. But it doesn't matter; if we're still alive next year, perhaps I'll make the trip to Gelendzhik, about which, incidentally, I read an article in the *Historical Herald* the other day.

I wish you all the best and firmly clasp your hand. Keep well and cheerful.

Yours,
A. Chekhov

1. After it became clear that no re-election of Gorky to the Academy would be possible, Korolenko tendered his formal resignation. Because of Chekhov's natural aversion to any demonstrative action, he could not at first bring himself to follow Korolenko's example. However, there was considerable pressure from a number of his friends and correspondents, including Olga Kundasova, who saw him in Moscow early in July and strongly urged him to resign. On August 4, Korolenko sent Chekhov a copy of his own letter of resignation, in which he outlined the parallels between the forced cancellation of Gorky's election and the harassments of famous Russian writers by the government in earlier, supposedly less enlightened periods. This letter finally tipped Chekhov's decision in favor of resigning.

2. Chekhov addressed this letter to the Grand Duke Konstantin, erroneously believing him to be the head of the literary section of the Academy. The next day he was informed of his mistake by Nikodim Kondakov and readdressed his letter of resignation to Professor Alexander Veselovsky. The Grand Duke was simply another honorary member, like Chekhov and Korolenko.

3. Under Paragraph 1035 of the existing penal code, Gorky had been charged with writing and distributing appeals urging factory workers to engage in disturbances against the government. However, since the authorities did not have sufficient evidence to bring him to trial, they allowed the charges to stand, expelled him from Nizhny Novgorod and placed him under constant surveillance.

4. Chekhov received no response from the Academy to his letter of resignation. No reprisal of any kind was taken by the government. He meant the resignation to be a purely private gesture, as can be seen from the letter to his wife, instructing her to inform Gorky of his action, but otherwise keep the matter a secret. But Chekhov's and Korolenko's letters of resignation were published in an underground Russian newspaper in Berlin and in this manner became known in literary circles.

159. To Olga Knipper

Yalta,
August 27, 1902

My darling, my river perch,

After a long wait I've finally received a letter from you. I'm leading a quiet life; I don't go into town, I chat with my visitors, and every once in a while do a bit of writing. I won't be writing a play this year; my heart isn't in it. But if I do write something playlike, it will be a one-act farce.

Masha didn't give me your letter. I found it in Mother's room, on the table. When I picked it up mechanically and read it, I realized why Masha had been so upset.[1] The letter is terribly rude and, what is more important, unfair. Of course I can sense the mood you were in when you wrote it, and I understand. But your last letter is rather strange, and I don't know what the matter is or what's going on in your head, my darling. You write: "Isn't it odd of them to expect you in the south when they knew I was sick in bed. Someone evidently resented your staying with me while I was sick."[2] Who resented it? When was I expected in the south? Didn't I give you my word of honor in my letter that no one had ever asked me to go south alone, without you? You mustn't be so unfair, darling, you really mustn't. One must be pure, perfectly pure, in matters of fairness and unfairness, particularly so because you are kind, very kind and understanding. Forgive me for sermonizing, darling, I won't do it again. That sort of thing frightens me.

When Yegor[3] submits the bill, you pay for me and I'll pay you back in September. Here are my plans: I'll be staying in Moscow until the beginning of December and then go to Nervi. I'll stay there and in Pisa until Lent, and then I'll come back. I've been coughing more in Yalta than I did in dear Lyubimovka. It's not a bad cough, but it's still there. I haven't been drinking. Today Orlenev[4] came to see me. So did Nazimova.[5] Doroshevich has arrived.[6] I saw Karabchevsky[7] the other day.

Have I written you about *The Seagull*? I sent Gnedich in Petersburg a tearful letter begging him not to produce *The Seagull*. Today I got a letter from him saying they had to go through with it because new sets had been painted, and so on and so forth. So I'm in for some more abuse.[8]

Don't tell Masha I read your letter to her. Oh well, do what you like.

Even though your letters have been cool, I keep pestering you with my affections and think about you endlessly. I kiss you a billion times, I hug you. Darling, write me more often than once every five days. I am after all your husband. Don't leave me so soon, before we've had a chance to live together the way we should and before you've borne me a little boy or girl. Once you do give me a child, you can do what you like. I kiss you again.

Yours,

A.

1. Chekhov's marriage to Olga Knipper occasioned an emotional crisis in the life of his sister. The correspondence of Olga Knipper and Maria Chekhova, published in 1969 in the collection of Maria Chekhova memorabilia entitled *The Hostess of the Chekhov House*, shows that before the wedding ceremony there was a gushingly affectionate friendship between the two women; after Chekhov's death there were many years of long, uninterrupted intimacy and many happy reunions in Moscow and in Yalta, reflected in letters that extend to 1957 and include discussions of Sviatoslav Richter recitals and plays by Lillian Hellman. But in the first year after Chekhov's marriage Maria often felt that her role in his life had been unfairly usurped and her resentment brought about reciprocal resentment on the part of Olga.

2. This is a quotation from Knipper's letter to Chekhov of August 22. She felt that the time they had spent together at Stanislavsky's cottage in Lyubimovka in July was among the happiest and most memorable in their marriage and she believed that Chekhov had cut his stay at Lyubimovka short because of the urgent pleas of his sister and mother that he return to Yalta.

3. Yegor was Stanislavsky's manservant. The expected bill was for the meals the Chekhovs were served at the cottage in Lyubimovka. However, Stanislavsky's wife later refused all payment and insisted that the Chekhovs were her guests.

4. Pavel Orlenev was a celebrated actor of the period, noted for his portrayals of tortured, neurasthenic characters in the plays of Ibsen and in dramatizations of Dostoyevsky's novels.

5. Alla Nazimova (1879–1945) did a brief stint in minor roles at the Moscow Art Theater before she was discovered by Pavel Orlenev, whose partner she became both on the stage and in private life. She eventually made her way to Western Europe and to the United States, where she was to appear in the silent film classic *Salome*, to play Christine in the world première of Eugene O'Neill's *Mourning Becomes Electra* and to make a string of Hollywood films. In the summer of 1902, she and Orlenev frequently visited Chekhov.

6. Vlas Doroshevich was a well-known muckraking journalist.

7. Nikolai Karabchevsky was a Yalta lawyer.

8. Pyotor Gnedich, journalist and playwright, was in charge of the repertory at the Empress Alexandra Theater. Chekhov did not wish to have *The Seagull* played in the same theater where it had suffered its initial failure.

In a subsequent letter, Gnedich assured Chekhov that every possible care would be taken with the production of this by now widely popular play. And, in fact, the new production was highly successful, making the actors and the press forget the resounding opening-night failure of only six years earlier.

160. To Olga Knipper

Yalta,
September 1, 1902

My dear one, my own,

Once again I have had an odd letter from you.[1] Once again you blame my poor head for anything and everything. Who told you that I don't want to return to Moscow, that I've left for good and won't be going back this fall? Didn't I write you in plain and simple language that I would definitely be coming in September and would live with you until December? Well, didn't I? You accuse me of not being frank, yet you forget everything I write or say to you. I am at a loss as to what I should do with my wife or how I should write her. You write that you tremble when you read my letters, that it's time for us to part, that there's something you fail to understand in all this. . . . It seems to me, darling, the guilty party in all this mess is neither you nor I, but someone else, someone you've had a talk with. Someone has instilled in you a mistrust of my words and feelings; everything seems suspicious to you—and there's nothing I can do about it, nothing at all. I won't try to dissuade you or convince you I'm right, for that's useless. You write that I am capable of living with you in complete silence, that I need only the amiable woman in you and that as a human being you are alien to me and isolated. Dearest darling, you are my wife, when are you finally going to understand that? You are the person who is closest and dearest to me; I loved you infinitely, I still love you, and you describe yourself as an "amiable" woman who is alien and isolated. . . . Well then, have it your way, if you must.

My health is better, but I've been coughing violently. There hasn't been any rain, and it's hot. Masha is leaving on the fourth and will be in Moscow on the sixth. You write that I will show Masha your letter. Thanks for the confidence. By the way, Masha is in no way to blame. You'll see that for yourself sooner or later.

I've begun reading Naidenov's play.[2] I don't like it. I have no desire to read it through to the end. Send me a wire when you move to Moscow. I'm tired of writing to other people's addresses. Don't forget my fishing rod; wrap it up in paper. Be cheerful and don't mope, or at least try to look cheerful. Sofya Sredina came to see me; she had a lot of things to say, none of which were interesting. She knew all about your illness and about who stayed by your side and who didn't. The elder Madame Sredina is already in Moscow.

If you plan on drinking wine, let me know and I'll bring you some. Write and tell me if you have any money or if you can make do until my arrival. Chaleyeva[3] is living in Alupka; she's doing very poorly.

We've been catching mice.

Write and tell me what you're doing, which roles you're playing again and which new ones you're rehearsing. You're not as lazy as your husband, are you?

Darling, be my wife, be my friend, write good letters, stop spreading melancholera, don't torture me. Be a kind, gentle wife, the kind you really are anyway. I love you more strongly than ever before, and as a husband I am blameless. Why can't you finally understand that, my joy, my little scribble?

Good-bye. Keep well and cheerful. Be sure to write me every day. I kiss you, kewpie, I hug you.

Yours,

A.

1. During the last week of August, in a state of depression and in obvious need of reassurance, Olga wrote Chekhov several despondent letters, asking whether he truly needed her and was not perhaps tired of being married to her.

2. Sergei Naidenov was a playwright of the Gorky circle. His first play, *Vanyushin's Children*, similar in theme and treatment to Gorky's *The Philistines*, but not devoid of interest in its own right, was widely played all over Russia in the first decade of the century and is still occasionally revived in the Soviet Union.

3. Varvara Chaleyeva was an actress of the Moscow Art Theater who had to leave the stage and settle in the Crimea because of her tuberculosis.

161. To Lev Bertenson[1]

Yalta,
October 10, 1902

Dear Lev Berngardovich,

I have seen *Angelophyllum ursinum* only on Sakhalin. None of the local residents could tell me what the plant was called, and the agricultural inspector, a botanist and agronomist, said it was a local plant and had no Russian name. I had to wait until I came back from Sakhalin to find out even its Latin name. I learned it from a professor who studied the eastern coast during the sixties. "Bear root" is in fact a very fitting name. Sakhalin has many bears. They are shy and don't attack *Mammalia*; instead, they feed on fish and probably plants of the *Angelophyllum* type, which, it may be assumed, have a sweet-tasting root. Please accept my profound gratitude. I will definitely make use of your information (provided there is a second edition, of course) and make reference to Annenkov's dictionary. I will also ask you to accept from me a copy of *The Island of Sakhalin.*

It is through no fault of my own that I have taken so long to answer your letter. The letter was addressed to Feodosia, and I live in Yalta. I have stayed with the Suvorins in Feodosia, but that was twelve or fourteen years ago.

Allow me to thank you once again from the bottom of my heart and wish you all the best. I remain your sincerely devoted and respectful

A. Chekhov

1. Dr. Bertenson, a prominent St. Petersburg physician, was Alexei Suvorin's personal doctor. While reading *The Island of Sakhalin,* he was struck with Chekhov's description of a beautiful plant that grew on the island. Chekhov cited only its Latin name, adding that there was no popular Russian name for it. Dr. Bertenson looked the plant up in a botanical dictionary and discovered that it did, after all, have a Russian name. He wrote Chekhov to inform him of this discovery. *Angelophyllum ursinum* is the largest member of the angelica family, and the closest thing it has to a popular name in English is "giant angelica."

162. To Ivan Bunin

Moscow,
October 26, 1902

Dear Jean,

Put something over your pale legs![1]

1. This one-line letter to Bunin is a parody of the one-line poem by the Symbolist poet Valery Bryusov. At the beginning of his literary career, Bryusov deliberately sought notoriety by shocking the reading public. Neither the erotic content of some of his early poetry nor his startlingly surrealistic imagery brought him the celebrity he finally achieved with the one-line "narrative poem" that went: "O cover up your pale legs." Wittily parodied by Vladimir Solovyov and ridiculed in an article by Vasily Rozanov, this one line made Bryusov's name famous throughout Russia. Once fame was achieved, Bryusov was able to settle down and develop into the important and influential poet he subsequently became.

Chekhov's amusement over this poem can also be seen in the statement recorded by Alexander Serebrov in which Chekhov expressed his disapproval of the so-called "decadent" writers (at that time in Russia this meant primarily Sologub, Bryusov and Zinaida Gippius): "They are swindlers, not decadents! They try to sell rotten goods—religion, mysticism and all sorts of devilry. Russian peasants were never religious, and as for the devil, the peasants hid him under the steam-bath shelf a long time ago. They've thought it all up to delude the public. Don't you believe them! And their legs are not pale at all, but hairy like everyone else's."

163. To Alexander Kuprin[1]

Moscow,
November 1, 1902

Dear Alexander Ivanovich,

I've received and read your "In Retirement," and I thank you very much for it. It's a good story; I read it, like "At the Circus," in one sitting, and truly enjoyed it. You want me to talk about its shortcomings only and that puts me in an awkward position.[2] The story has no shortcomings, and if there's anything I disagree with, it is several of its own special traits. Your treatment of your heroes, for instance, the actors, is old-fashioned. You write about them the way everyone has been writing about them for the past hundred years; you add nothing new. In the second place, your first chapter is taken up with descriptions of people's appearances—again an old-fashioned device; you could easily do without those descriptions. Describing in detail how five people look overburdens the reader's span of attention, and ultimately loses all value. Clean-shaven actors resemble one another like Catholic priests, and they'll go on resembling one another no matter how much effort you put into describing them. In the third place, your general tone is crude and you overdo your descriptions of drunks.

That's all I can say in response to your question about shortcomings; I can't come up with anything else.

Tell your wife not to worry; everything will turn out all right.[3] Delivery will take about twenty hours and will be followed by a most blissful state when she will smile and you'll be so moved you'll feel like weeping. Twenty hours is the usual maximum for the first baby.

Keep well, now. I firmly clasp your hand. I have so many visitors it makes my head spin and keeps me from writing. The new Art Theater building really is good. It isn't particularly luxurious, but it is comfortable.

Yours,
A. Chekhov

1. Alexander Kuprin (1870–1938) was another important younger writer of the traditionalist realistic school to form a close association with Chekhov in the last years of his life. Unlike Bunin and Gorky, on both of whom Chekhov's influence was minimal, Kuprin was a writer who learned a great deal from Chekhov not only in his literary manner but in his general outlook. Many of his stories and novels develop Chekhovian themes and the ethical points that Kuprin likes to make are also frequently Chekhovian. With all that, Kuprin was not a mere imitator, but a writer who built a manner and a personality of his own on what he took from Chekhov. Kuprin's memoir about his association with Chekhov is not only warm and affectionate, but also remarkably objective. Kuprin does not attempt to transpose Chekhov to some other level where he could deal with him more comfortably (as was the case, for example, with everything Stanislavsky wrote about Chekhov), but simply tells what struck him and what he remembered, allowing the reader to decide what kind of person Chekhov was—an eminently Chekhovian approach.

2. In the middle of October Kuprin had sent Chekhov a copy of the printer's proof of his story "In Retirement" and asked for some negative criticism. The basic criticism Chekhov had to offer here is quite similar to the one he voiced repeatedly about Gorky's plays and Bunin's short stories. He could not understand why these three writers, so much younger than himself, continued to restrict themselves to the traditional forms and conventions of nineteenth-century realism, from which he himself had moved away long since.

3. Kuprin and his wife were expecting their first child. In his letter to Chekhov, Kuprin had described some of his wife's anxieties.

164. To Olga Knipper

Yalta,
December 17, 1902

Greetings, my actressicle,

Your last two letters were cheerless: one of them had a bad case of melancholera, the other was about a headache. You shouldn't have gone to Ignatov's lecture. After all, Ignatov is an untalented, conservative man even though he fancies himself a critic and a liberal. So the theater encourages passivity, does it? Well, what about painting? And poetry? After all, a spectator looking at a picture or reading a novel is also deprived of the opportunity to express sympathy or lack of sympathy with whatever happens to be in the picture or book. "Long live enlightenment and down with darkness" is the sanctimonious hypocrisy of everyone who is backward, tin-eared, and impotent. Bazhenov is a charlatan; I've known him for a long time. Boborykin has grown old and bitter.[1]

If you don't feel like going to the club or to the Teleshovs', then don't, darling. Teleshov is a nice person, but down deep he's a merchant and a conservative; he'll bore you, for all people tangential to literature are boring, with very few exceptions.[2] You'll come to see how old-fashioned and backward all our Moscow literature is—both old and new—when in two or three years you begin to understand more clearly the attitude these gentlemen take to the Art Theater's heresies.

There's a frenzied wind blowing. I can't work. The weather has worn me out. I'm ready to lie down and bite my pillow.

Some pipes in the water main have broken, and there's no water. They're being fixed. It's raining. It's cold. It's not even warm inside. I miss you violently. I've turned into an old man; I can't sleep alone, I keep waking up.[3] I read a review of *Uncle Vanya* in *Perm Territory* that says that Astrov is extremely drunk; he must have swayed his way through all four acts.[4] Tell Nemirovich I haven't answered his wire because I still haven't decided what plays should be put on next year. There will be plays enough, I think. It wouldn't hurt to put on three Maeterlinck plays with music, as I told him.[5] Nemirovich promised to write me every Wednesday, and he even noted down his promise, but to date he hasn't written me a single letter, not a thing.

If you see Leonid Andreyev, tell him to have *The Courier* sent to me in 1903. Please! And tell Èfros[6] about *News of the Day*.

Good girl, my love, my joy and my dog, keep well and cheerful. May God bless you and keep you. Don't worry about me. I am in good health and well fed. I hug and kiss you.

Yours,

A.

I'll be receiving *The Citizen*. I received a book of poetry from Alexander Fyodorov.[7] The poems are all bad (or so they seem to me), shallow, but there is one I liked very much. Here it is.

[An eight-line sentimental poem by Alexander Fyodorov about a man yearning for his distant beloved is appended to the original.]

1. On December 11, Olga Knipper wrote to Chekhov that she had attended a public lecture by the literary critic Ilya Ignatov on "The Stage and the Spectator" at which the prominent psychiatrist Nikolai Bazhenov and the writer Pyotr Boborykin appeared as commentators. All three berated the lack of social involvement and ideological commitment of the more recent school of drama. The conclusion of Ignatov's lecture was that new drama generates a sense of passivity in the spectator. The main speaker and the two com-

mentators all ended their statements by exclaiming: "Long live enlightenment and down with darkness!" Olga wrote that she had found the entire experience extremely depressing.

2. Nikolai Teleshov (1867–1957) was a writer who belonged to Gorky's "Knowledge" group. By the 1940s, he was an orthodox Soviet writer laden with medals and honors for the conservative, traditionalist form of his writings and for his loyal support of Stalinist policies. In the 1944–51 edition of Chekhov, the first phrase of this sentence reads: "Teleshov is a nice person [. . .]." The prominent position of Teleshov in the official Soviet literary hierarchy of that time made calling him a conservative and mentioning his merchant-class origin highly awkward. The censored passage was restored in the 1963–64 edition, which appeared after Teleshov's death.

3. This sentence was deleted by the puritanical censors of the 1944–51 edition and restored in 1963–64.

4. This was a review of the production of *Uncle Vanya* at the Municipal Theater of Perm.

5. It was Chekhov who originally urged the Moscow Art Theater to include the Symbolist plays of Maurice Maeterlinck in its repertoire. His suggestion was heeded a year after his death, when Stanislavsky staged a triple bill of one-act plays by Maeterlinck (*Les aveugles, L'Intruse* and *Intérieur*). The success of this production led Maeterlinck to give Stanislavsky the rights to the first production of his popular *Bluebird*, which became the company's single biggest success and its biggest moneymaker.

6. On Nikolai Èfros, see Letter 175.

7. Chekhov himself considered the plays of Alexander Fyodorov (1868–1949) inept, his stories dull and his poems, as we see here, shallow. Nevertheless, he sent this mediocre writer long and detailed critiques of his work, offering numerous suggestions in the vain hope that he might help Fyodorov improve his art.

165. To Sergei Diaghilev[1]

December 30, 1902

Dear Sergei Pavlovich,

I have received *The World of Art* with the *Seagull* article and read the article.[2] Thank you very much. When I finished the article, I felt like writing a play, and I probably will after January.

You write that we spoke about a serious religious movement in Russia. We were speaking about a movement in the intelligentsia, not in Russia. I can't say anything about Russia as a whole, but as for the intelligentsia it is so far only playing at religion, mostly because it has nothing better to do.[3] It is safe to say that the educated segment of our society has moved away from religion and is moving farther and farther away from it, whatever people may say or whatever philosophical and religious societies may be formed. I won't venture to say whether this is good or bad, but I will say that the religious movement you write about is one thing and all contemporary culture something quite different, and there's no point in trying to derive the latter from the former. Present-day culture is the beginning of work in the name of a great future, work which will perhaps continue for tens of thousands of years with the result that finally, if only in the distant future, mankind will perceive the truth of the real God, that is, not make conjectures or search for Him in Dostoyevsky, but perceive Him as clearly as they perceive that two times two is four. Present-day culture is the beginning of work, while the religious movement we talked about is a vestige, the end or nearly the end of something that has had its day or is on its way out. But it's a long story, something that can't be put in a letter. When you see Mr. Filosofov, please convey to him my deep gratitude. Happy New Year, and all the best.

Your devoted,
A. Chekhov

1. The accepted Western view of the significance of Sergei Diaghilev was well expressed in 1951 by a young essayist named Jacqueline Lee Bouvier in her prize-winning *Vogue* essay:

> Sergei Diaghilev dealt not with the interaction of the senses but with an interaction of the arts, an interaction of the cultures of East and West. Though not an artist himself, he possessed what is rarer than artistic genius in any one field, the sensitivity to take the best of each man and incorporate it into a masterpiece all the more precious because it lives only in the minds of those who have seen it and disintegrates as soon as he [sic] is gone. What he did with the music of Rimsky-Korsakov, the settings of a Bakst or a Benois, the choreography of a Fokine, the dancing of a Nijinsky, makes him for me an alchemist unique in art history.

The view, which its author was to repeat in a somewhat modified form to Igor Stravinsky when she and her first husband entertained him at the White House some years later, is not erroneous. It is, however, incomplete, for it states only one part of Diaghilev's accomplishment. Ten years before he ever took his ballet company to Western Europe—and, in the process, completely changed the art of the ballet, brought the finest twentieth-century painters to the attention of the general public by commissioning them to do sets and caused some of the towering musical masterpieces of the century to be composed—Diaghilev spearheaded the greatest liberation that Russian art and literature had known in modern times. The artistic group he organized in 1898 and its journal, both bearing the name *The World of Art,* came right out and stated publicly and in print the very things that Chekhov had asserted so passionately in his private letters of the late 1880s: that the simplistic utilitarian theories of Belinsky, Chernyshevsky and Stasov were not a foolproof, eternally valid aesthetic gospel, obligatory for all literature and art; that there were aspects of human existence other than sociological which the arts could legitimately explore; and that photographic realism was not necessarily the only possible and desirable artistic method. Chekhov's revolt against this code fifteen years earlier was a private and isolated phenomenon; Diaghilev's open defiance was an act of public sacrilege, met with ridicule by the reactionary pro-government press and with outrage by the majority of entrenched literary and art critics. But *The World of Art* served as a catalyst and a rallying point for the forces of the nascent Russian Symbolism and other modernist trends. With the liberation of Russian literature and art from the narrow and stifling aesthetic which might have been revolutionary forty years earlier but by then had become provincial and oppressive, all the miracles of the Russian artistic revival of the next quarter century came pouring out as if from a cornucopia: the greatest age Russian painting ever saw, ranging from Vrubel to Russian Cubists and Suprematists; the unbelievably rich period in Russian poetry, called the Silver Age today, although its total brilliance, ranging from Balmont and Bryusov to Mandelstam and Pasternak, can easily outshine anything that went on in any other age; the great experimental novels of Andrei Belyi and Alexei Remizov, which were the basis for the later accomplishments of Isaak Babel, Mikhail Zoshchenko and Andrei Platonov; the music of Skriabin, Stravinsky and Prokofiev; the path-breaking theatrical directors who continued Stanislavsky's reform along modernist lines; and the ballets with which Diaghilev so dazzled the Western world ten years after he founded *The World of Art.*

Above all, there were the literary and artistic journals that followed and developed the format of Diaghilev's journal in the next decade—*Balance, Apollo, Golden Fleece* and a few others—which are among the finest, freest and culturally richest journals ever published anywhere. It is to them that we owe our appreciation of traditional Russian church architecture and icon painting and our present-day views of earlier literary figures distorted or underestimated by utilitarian criticism, especially Pushkin, Gogol and Dostoyevsky. Lesser poets and writers, expelled from Russian literature by the utilitarians—Baratynsky, Leskov, Fet, Apollon Grigoryev, Karolina Pavlova, among a number of others—were brought back from obscurity, re-examined and made a permanent part of Russian literature. The debt that present-day Soviet culture owes to *The World of Art* and everything it started is incalculable. But, because of its aversion to all modern art, its commitment to Chernyshevskian aesthetics and its general desire to depict the time that preceded the Revolution as one of unrelieved oppression and drabness, the Soviet cultural establishment did everything in its power to minimize the significance of the cultural revival that Diaghilev helped initiate, to slander it and even to suppress the evidence of its existence.

The reasons for this suppression and its frightening success are vividly outlined in the crucial Chapter 55 of Solzhenitsyn's novel *The First Circle*, where a young Soviet diplomat goes through his late mother's papers and discovers the newspapers and the journals of her youth (*The World of Art*, *Balance* and *Apollo* are specifically named). The realization of the full range and scope of pre-revolutionary art and literature and the intellectual freedom that had been possible in the decades just before the Revolution, which Soviet policies had concealed from succeeding generations, triggers a subtle ethical evolution in Solzhenitsyn's hero, leads him to form a moral code that differs from the prevailing one, and eventually delivers him into the hands of the secret police.

"Historically speaking, there is something immensely tragic in this recoil of art from its social matrix," wrote critic Hilton Kramer in his otherwise handsome tribute to *The World of Art* (*New York Times*, May 3, 1970), obviously not realizing that within the Russian cultural context of the time Diaghilev's emphasis on the supremacy of aesthetics and craftsmanship was the only way to liberate the arts from the insistence of the utilitarian critical tradition that all art be topical and political at all times and that its other dimensions were irrelevant if not actually harmful. "Indifferent," "aristocratic," "anti-social," "apolitical"—the very charges that had been leveled against Chekhov some two decades earlier, were also made against Diaghilev's group and his journal. It was therefore only fitting that Diaghilev believed Chekhov to be his natural ally in his deliberate campaign to free Russian art from its ideological captivity.

Diaghilev's letters to Chekhov were published in the collection of materials bearing the title *From A. P. Chekhov's Archive*, Moscow, 1960. Annotations to these letters inform the Soviet reader that Diaghilev was an important propagandizer of Russian ballet abroad and that he edited a decadent journal called *The World of Art*, which "insistently opposed the realistic traditions of Russian painting and the foundations of the materialistic aesthetics that had been developed by Russian revolutionary democrats."

2. An article on the revival of *The Seagull* at the Empress Alexandra Theater, written by the literary critic Dmitry Filosofov, appeared in *The World of Art*, No. 11, 1902. Filosofov was Diaghilev's closest friend at the time this letter was written. He later deserted Diaghilev to become a partner in a (mostly mystical) *ménage à trois* with Zinaida Gippius and Dmitry Merezhkovsky. It was under the impact of losing Filosofov's friendship that Diaghilev shifted his interests from literature and painting to music and ballet.

3. Diaghilev had written: "At the art exhibit we were interrupted at the most interesting point: whether a serious religious movement is possible in Russia today. The question is, in other words, a 'to be or not to be' of the whole of contemporary culture. I hope to see you again and continue where we left off" (Diaghilev's letter to Chekhov of December 23, 1902). Diaghilev participated in the encounters of the Religious-Philosophical Society and followed the religious revival among the intelligentsia with interest, seeing

in it one of the possible ways out of the cultural impasse of dogmatic utilitarianism. However, as his letters to Chekhov of 1903 show, he quickly became alarmed at the possibility of a religious dogmatism superseding the utilitarian one. During the next two years, Diaghilev tried to steer *The World of Art* away from any kind of sectarian ideological commitment, including the religious kind.

XV

"THE CHERRY ORCHARD"

VLADIMIR NEMIROVICH-DANCHENKO'S BOOK of memoirs *Out of the Past* begins with three portraits of Chekhov drawn from the eighteen-year period during which Nemirovich knew him. The first portrait is from the mid-1880s. Chekhov is known as the prolific author of innumerable humorous stories. "He is very sociable and prefers listening to talking. Not even a touch of self-importance. Everyone considers him talented, but no one could have ever imagined that his name would one day be among the classics of Russian literature."

The second portrait is of Chekhov in the early 1890s. His book of stories has been awarded an academic prize, he is courted by editors, Tolstoy and Grigorovich speak of him in glowing terms, and every new story he writes is a literary event. "But the oracle of all the young people, Mikhailovsky, never tires of pointing out that Chekhov is a non-ideological writer and this has its influence, putting the brakes on the possibility of open and unanimous acclaim." "During this period Chekhov is to be found at the very center of the social whirl of both capitals. He belongs to writers', actors' and artists' circles. He's now in Moscow, now in St. Petersburg. He loves large gatherings and spirited conversation, loves being invited backstage. He travels a great deal, both in Russia and abroad; he's as modest as ever and as fond of listening and observing. His fame is steadily growing."

The final portrait in Nemirovich's triptych is the Chekhov of Yalta and of the Moscow Art Theater. There is little talk now about his lack of ideology. The two or three stories he publishes every year are eagerly awaited by everyone. He is now known principally as "Chekhov the playwright,

Chekhov the creator of the new form of drama." The reading public is aware that his days are numbered, and every new work is received "with a sort of tender gratitude, with the realization that it was written with the remainder of his dwindling strength."

Not only his personal, social and philanthropic involvements interfered with Chekhov's writing in the last two years of his life. The very act of writing became an uphill physical climb. There was a time when he could turn out a long story or a one-act play in one day. By the end of 1902, he had to take to his bed after writing half a page. But he still had three major works to give the world. His last two important stories are something of a final testament. "The Bride," which shows its young heroine's escape from traps of family structure, class limitations, provincial backwardness and doctrinaire rigidity, comes as a startling reversal of a long series of stories and plays in which similarly bright and appealing young women were hopelessly caught in a dull world they had never made. "The Bishop" is an entirely plotless and scrupulously realistic account of the last few days in the life of a high-ranking Orthodox Church dignitary of humble social origins. But, for all his matter-of-fact tone, Chekhov's Russian prose in this story reaches such lyrical power, throbs with such resignation before life's inevitabilities and glows with so much love for this world's radiant beauty that literary comparisons seem for once inadequate. Only in the slow movement of Mozart's Piano Concerto in A major, K. 488, do we find the same kind of transfigured resignation, and it is conveyed by Mozart in equally simple terms, with the same total control of craftsmanship which makes the technique invisible and which only the highest mastery can achieve.

Chekhov's last full-length play, *The Cherry Orchard*, is, even more than *Three Sisters*, a focal point for many of the themes and characters he had treated in his earlier work. The loss of a family's homestead is a theme that appeared in Chekhov's very first play, the unwieldy *Platonov* of 1881, one of whose four heroines is a recognizable prototype for Lyubov Ranevskaya of *The Cherry Orchard*. To point out that one of the strongest impressions of Chekhov's own childhood was the usurpation of his parents' home by a stranger as a result of his father's poor management of the family resources is to belabor the obvious. Be that as it may, the situation of a family about to be evicted from its home reappears in a number of Chekhov's stories from "The Late-Blooming Flowers" of 1882 and "Other People's Misfortune" of 1886 to "A Visit with Friends" of 1898. The character of Yermolai Lopakhin continues the line of socially dislocated wealthy merchants and manufacturers of peasant origin whom we have already met in "Three Years" and "A Woman's Kingdom." The smug and insolent butler Yasha is the culmination of Chekhov's long line of semi-educated hicks whose contact with Western ways has added nothing to their culture but taught them instead to treat their native traditions with contempt and to despise any woman who loves them as immoral and inferior.

We know that after completing *The Cherry Orchard* Chekhov conceived an idea for still another play, which was to deal with arctic explorers and was to show the ghost of the hero's beloved and a ship crushed by the polar ice onstage. Even the fragmentary information we possess about this unwritten play shows that at the end of his life Chekhov was drifting toward the Symbolist conception of drama, which had become the dominant dramatic mode by that time. If this is the case, *The Cherry Orchard* can be seen as the very beginning of that drift away from the combination of theatrical realism and impressionism brought by Chekhov to such perfection in *Uncle Vanya* and *Three Sisters*. The open-ended structure that worked so effectively in the last two plays is abandoned for a more symmetrical and formal arrangement of events. The use of symbols (present, of course, in both *The Seagull* and *Three Sisters*) is more subtle and more integrated. Where *Uncle Vanya* and *Three Sisters* ended in nonrealistic lyrical soliloquies, *The Cherry Orchard* ends in the poignant and deeply symbolic silent scene of the forgotten old family retainer, locked in the house while the orchard is being chopped down. Chekhov had come a long way since the time when he complained while writing *The Wood Demon* that the only two effective ways he knew of ending a play were to get the hero married or to kill him at the final curtain.

The characters of *Uncle Vanya* and *Three Sisters* all belong in the same Chekhovian world, the literary allusions evoked by Natasha and Solyony notwithstanding. But the *dramatis personae* of *The Cherry Orchard* is invaded by three non-Chekhovian interlopers: the landowner Simeonov-Pishchik, who, as Ivan Bunin correctly pointed out, really belongs in a play by Gogol, and the two time travelers from the future, the clerk Yepikhodov, straight out of Mikhail Zoshchenko's stories of the 1920s, and the governess Charlotte, a Nabokovian artist-in-disguise. All these features indicate that *The Cherry Orchard* represents some new departure in Chekhov's evolution as a playwright which his death prevented him from developing. They also deprive this play of the organic unity and overall perfection that mark *Three Sisters*—which does not mean for a moment that *The Cherry Orchard* is not an important and fascinating play.

While depicting the characters of this play in his own Chekhovian way, Chekhov came close in three of them to a deliberate debunking of the stereotypes of the conventional Russian drama of his time. The female character of a Decadent Aristocratic Hedonist and the male one of a Greedy Capitalist On-the-Make were standard fare in melodramas by Nemirovich-Danchenko, Suvorin and Sumbatov; an Idealistic, Revolutionary-Minded Student had also been present on the Russian stage ever since

Turgenev's *A Month in the Country*. Many critics and writers saw Ranevskaya, Lopakhin and Petya Trofimov in *The Cherry Orchard* as a kind of turning upside down of these three cherished stereotypes and they resented it. Some of the earliest reviews of this play accused Chekhov of slandering young activists, of justifying capitalist exploitation and of idealizing the decadent aristocrats. This is more or less how Vladimir Korolenko understood the play and he said so in a critical article he published under a pen name in 1903. A year later he wrote to Fyodor Batyushkov: "To my mind, the main defect of the play is its lack of a clear-cut artistic design or perhaps of a keynote. You are quite wrong about it: Ranevskaya is an aristocratic slut, of no use to anyone, who departs with impunity to join her Parisian gigolo. And yet Chekhov has whitewashed her and surrounded her with a sort of sentimental halo. Similarly, that moldy 'better future' [i.e., Petya Trofimov] is something incomprehensible and unnatural" (Letter of September 2, 1904).

Korolenko's disagreement with Chekhov's play is at least honest. Maxim Gorky, however, who could neither imagine disliking anything by Chekhov nor accept the play as it was actually written, fell back upon the time-honored device of the Belinsky-Chernyshevsky tradition in Russian criticism: he simply read *The Cherry Orchard* as the kind of play he would have liked it to be. In Gorky's memoir of Chekhov, first published in 1905, we read: "There's that weepy Ranevskaya and the other former masters of *The Cherry Orchard*, as egotistical as children and as flabby as senile old men. They missed their chance to die in time and now they are moaning, seeing and understanding nothing,—parasites who lack the strength to latch onto life again. The miserable student Trofimov talks prettily about the need to work and spends his time in idleness, entertaining himself with stupid ribbing of Varya, who works tirelessly for the benefit of these drones." One would have thought that Chekhov had written a brutal social satire, a powerful indictment of an entire class, with Varya (whom Chekhov himself saw as a "kind-hearted idiot") as its sole attractive, sympathetically depicted character. Elsewhere in the same memoir, Gorky indicated that he considered Ivanov, Treplyov from *The Seagull* and almost the entire cast of *Three Sisters* equally useless survivals of an earlier epoch whom one would do best to exterminate, and he praised Chekhov for exposing them in all of their revolting weakness and inefficiency. As the mistrust which had accompanied the first decade of Chekhov's rise to fame gave way to awe and admiration, it became clear that many of his new admirers, among them some people personally close to him, were as little prepared to understand what he was trying, with wisdom and compassion, to tell his fellow countrymen as were his earlier disparagers.

Chekhov finished "The Bride" at the end of February of 1903. The greater part of the rest of that year he spent writing *The Cherry Orchard.* He worked on it longer than on any other play. While *Three Sisters* was designated by Chekhov as a drama, *The Cherry Orchard* was styled by him a comedy, as had been the case with *The Seagull* earlier. This term has caused considerable perplexity and confusion in non-Russian works on Chekhov. What Chekhov clearly had in mind was a high, serious comedy—in the same sense that Shakespeare's *Measure for Measure,* Molière's *The Misanthrope* and Turgenev's *A Month in the Country* were all designated comedies, which did not prevent their authors from treating serious themes and tragic situations in them. The tragic element of the *The Cherry Orchard* is its inalienable and self-evident component, but its comedic aspect has to be brought out in any stage production if the play is to have the rhythm and balance that Chekhov intended. This was admirably conveyed in the Eva Le Gallienne Broadway production of the mid-1940s, which puzzled the critics accustomed to Stanislavskian traditions, but delighted and pleased the unprejudiced audiences. Chekhov had strong misgivings about what Stanislavsky would do to this play—he feared that Lopakhin would be turned into a standard kulak, that the revolutionary background of Trofimov would be toned down and, above all, he feared the slow and mournful tempo he knew Stanislavsky would try to achieve.

His anxiety about this and his ever-worsening physical condition led to the uncharacteristic angry peevishness of his letters to Olga Knipper and to Nemirovich when the advance press notices distorted the subject and the setting of the new play. On January 17, 1904, Chekhov was in Moscow for the opening of *The Cherry Orchard.* After the third act, a huge public ceremony was held on the stage, commemorating the twenty-fifth anniversary of Chekhov's literary debut. Chekhov had not been warned. Surprised and abashed, he heard himself eulogized by important scholars, journalists and actors (among them the fabled Glykeria Fedotova) and hailed as a great and beloved writer, the living successor of Pushkin, Gogol and Turgenev. It was an overwhelming, almost frightening experience.

By now one of Chekhov's lungs was almost gone, his digestive tract was ruined and he had emphysema. He gradually succumbed to that euphoria which frequently affects people in advanced stages of tuberculosis, and we read in his letters of his last few months that he believed himself to be on the road to complete recovery. In June of 1904, he and his wife left for Germany, where he hoped to have his emphysema treated. Olga Kundasova came to see him on the eve of his departure. "I saw Anton just before his departure," she wrote to Alexei Suvorin a few months later in one of her rare letters that have been preserved in the archives. "It was one of the most depressing encounters that any mortal ever had, but I cannot bear to write about it."

166. To Vera Kommissarzhevskaya

Yalta,
January 27, 1903

Dear Vera Fyodorovna,

Many thanks for your letter.[1] Not many thanks, multitudinous thanks—there you are. I'm very glad you're getting on so well. Let me tell you the following about the play: (1) It's true I've got an idea for a play and a title for it (*The Cherry Orchard*,[2] but that's still a secret), and I'll most likely settle down to writing no later than the end of February, provided of course I'm well; (2) the central role in the play is that of an old woman, to the author's great regret; and (3) if I let the Art Theater have it, then in accordance with the theater's rules and regulations the Art Theater gains exclusive production rights of the play for Petersburg as well as Moscow, and there's nothing that can be done about it.[3] If the Art Theater doesn't go to Petersburg in 1904 (which is highly possible—it isn't going this year, is it?), then there is no problem at all, and if the play seems suitable for your theater I will be only too glad to let you have it. Or what about this: why don't I write a play *for you.* Not for this or that theater, but simply for you. It's an old dream of mine. Well, it's all in God's hands. If my health were what it used to be, I wouldn't waste time talking; I'd sit right down and start writing the play on the spot. I've had pleurisy since December—can you imagine?—and I'm leaving the house tomorrow for the first time since being confined for so long.

Anyway, I've written to Moscow asking for exact information whether the Art Theater is going to Petersburg. I'll have an answer in eight to ten days and will write you then.

You've seen my wife, and I won't see her until spring. First she's sick, then I have to leave, so that nothing ever turns out the way it should for us.

You write, "I am proceeding on the strength of my faith which, if it breaks, will kill within me . . ."[4] That's entirely as it should be. You're quite right, but for heaven's sake, don't stake it all on the new theater. After all, you're an actress, and being an actress is like being a good sailor: no matter what ship he sails, be it government- or private-owned, in all places, under all conditions he always remains a good sailor.

Once more let me thank you for your letter. I send you my humble respects and firmly clasp and kiss your hand.

Yours,
A. Chekhov

1. Early in January, Kommissarzhevskaya wrote to Chekhov that she had resigned from the government-owned Imperial Theaters and was starting a private theatrical company of her own. In her letter, she wrote: "The point is that you must help me, Anton Pavlovich. Yes, you, and yes, you must. Promise to let me have your new play for my Petersburg company. Surely you can understand how badly I need it and what you will be doing for me."

2. Stanislavsky's *My Life in Art* contains a detailed account of Chekhov's long search for a title for *The Cherry Orchard* after he wrote the play and his consulting Stanislavsky about the two possible versions of the title after he decided what he wanted to call it.

3. As we know from Chekhov's letter to Olga Knipper written one day before this letter, he was highly dubious about the success of Kommissarzhevskaya's private company and expected her to lose all interest in the venture after one month. It actually turned out to be an important and innovative company which continued to exist until Kommissarzhevskaya's untimely death in 1910.

4. The complete sentence in Kommissarzhevskaya's letter reads: "I am proceeding on the strength of my faith, which, if it breaks, will kill within me everything that gives my life meaning."

167. To Marianna Pobedimskaya[1]

Yalta,
February 5, 1903

Dear Madam:

Your opinion of Yelena Andreyevna is completely justified. But I'm afraid you won't receive this letter until after the ninth of February. I didn't receive your letter, which was mailed January 30th, until today. Yelena Andreyevna may produce the impression of being incapable of thinking or even loving, but while I was writing *Uncle Vanya* I had something completely different in mind.

I wish you all the best.

Respectfully yours,
A. Chekhov

1. The addressee was the wife of a provincial doctor and the letter is a reply to an inquiry she sent Chekhov about the character of Yelena in *Uncle Vanya,* which she was to play in an amateur production. In her letter, Pobedimskaya wrote: "Is Yelena Andreyevna, the professor's wife, an average intelligent woman, who is a thinking and decent person, or is she an apathetic, idle woman, incapable of thinking or even loving? I cannot reconcile myself to this second interpretation and I dare to hope that my understanding of her as a reasoning, thinking person who is made unhappy by her dissatisfaction with her present life is the correct one."

168. To Prince Alexander Sumbatov (Alexander Yuzhin)[1]

Yalta,
February 26, 1903

Dear Alexander Ivanovich,

Many thanks for your letter.[2] I agree with you that it's hard to form an opinion of Gorky: one has to wade through the mass of things written and said about him. I haven't seen his play *Lower Depths* and I don't know it all that well, but stories like "My Traveling Companion" or "Chelkash" are enough for me to class him as a far from minor writer. *Foma Gordeyev* and *The Three* are unreadable; they're very bad. And *The Philistines* is, in my opinion, the work of a schoolboy. But Gorky's importance does not lie in the fact that he's popular; he is important because he is the first in Russia and the world at large to write about philistinism with contempt and disgust and at the very time when society is ready for this protest. From the Christian point of view, from the economic point of view, from any point of view you choose, philistinism is a great evil. Like a dam in a river it has always led only to stagnation. And though Gorky's tramps may be drunk and far from elegant, they are still an effective means—or at least they've turned out that way—if not of completely breaking down the dam, then at least of springing a powerful and dangerous leak in it. I don't know if I'm making myself clear. In my opinion there will come a time when Gorky's works will be forgotten, but he himself is not likely to be forgotten even a thousand years from now. That's what I think or that's the way it seems to me, but then again I may be wrong.[3]

Are you in Moscow? Or have you gone off to Nice and Monte Carlo? I often think back on the years of our youth when we sat next to one another playing roulette. Potapenko too.[4] Speaking of Potapenko, I got a letter from him today. The clown is thinking of publishing a journal.

I firmly clasp your hand. Keep well and prosperous.

Yours,
A. Chekhov

1. Alexander Sumbatov (1857–1927), who wrote and acted on the stage as Alexander Yuzhin, was an authentic Georgian prince who made a considerable name for himself in Russian theater of the turn of the century as playwright, actor and stage director. As an actor, he was a typical nineteenth-century matinee idol, given to a great deal of melodramatic excess that was much appreciated by his audiences. As a playwright, he wrote

enormously successful social melodramas with evil capitalist villains, decadent aristocrats, innocent wives and startling, showy dénouements. One of the best ways of understanding what Chekhov tried to accomplish in his plays is to read a play or two by Sumbatov, for they were the plays considered in Chekhov's time to be the very model of soundly constructed, socially involved drama. Every important Russian actor and actress of the period appeared in Sumbatov's plays; Sarah Bernhardt herself performed in one of them in Paris. Although Chekhov did not think much of Sumbatov's plays and in fact wrote *Ivanov* partly as a rejoinder to one of them (see Letter 14, note 12), he and Sumbatov were quite friendly personally. Sumbatov, for his part, had enough theatrical sense and taste to appreciate Chekhov's last plays and to realize their importance.

2. Sumbatov had written to Chekhov expressing his liking for Gorky's *Lower Depths* and his disapproval of *The Philistines*. He asked Chekhov for his opinion of Gorky.

3. Chekhov's idea that Gorky's work might soon be forgotten is also reflected in Suvorin's journal, where in the entry for September 4, 1902, we read:

> I've spent two days with Chekhov, at his home; we were together almost continuously. We conversed in a friendly way all the time, mostly about literature. He is astounded that abroad they consider Gorky a socialist leader. "Not socialist, but revolutionary," I pointed out. Chekhov could not understand this. I, on the contrary, do. His stories are filled with protest and optimism. His tramps seem to say: "We feel within ourselves a tremendous strength and we will prevail." Gorky's popularity bothers Chekhov's self-esteem. "Earlier they used to say Chekhov and Potapenko and I survived it. Now it's Chekhov and Gorky." What he meant to say was that he will survive this also. According to him, Gorky will lose his significance in two or three years, because there will be nothing for him to write about. I don't agree.

4. Sumbatov and Potapenko both spent some time with Chekhov in Nice in 1898. All three of them, occasionally joined by Nemirovich-Danchenko, paid frequent visits to the gambling casinos at Monte Carlo.

169. To Olga Knipper

Yalta,
March 23, 1903

Dearest Gramsie,

You're angry at me because of the address, you keep assuring me you've written several more times. Wait, I'll bring you your letters and you'll be able to see for yourself, and until then let's forget about it and talk no more about the address. I've already calmed down. Then you write that I'm asking you about Turgenev's plays all over again and that you've already told me about them and that I forget the contents of your letters. I don't forget them at all, darling, I read them all several times over; the trouble is that no less than ten days pass each time between my letter and your answer. I've read almost all Turgenev's plays. *A Month in the Country*, as I've already written you, was not at all to my taste, but *The Sponger*, which you will be performing, isn't all that bad or all that badly put together, and if Artyom doesn't drag things out and sound monotonous, the play won't come off too badly. *The Provincial Lady* needs to be shortened, don't you think? The roles are good.[1]

I haven't had hemorrhoids all summer, and today I feel like a regular titular councilor. The weather is magnificent. Everything is in bloom, and it's warm and quiet, but there has been no rain, and I fear for the plants. You write you'll hold me in your arms for exactly three days and nights. But what about dinner or tea?

I've received a letter from Nemirovich. Give him my thanks. I won't write him now because I sent him a letter not long ago.

Keep well now, mongrel pup. I've already written you about Gorky: he visited me and I visited him. His health is all right. I can't send you my story "The Bride," because I don't have a copy. You'll be able to read it soon in *Everyone's Magazine*. I've written many stories like it before, so you won't get anything new out of it.

May I turn you upside down, then give you a shake or two, then hug you, and bite your ear? May I, darling? Write, or I'll call you a tramp.

Yours,

A.

1. Casting about for suitable plays for their company, Nemirovich-Danchenko and Olga Knipper both hit upon the idea of reviving some play by Ivan Turgenev. Turgenev's plays were pronounced undramatic and unsuited for the stage by the critics of his time, all of whom considered Ostrovsky's well-structured and socially critical plays superior to those of Turgenev. Turgenev bowed to their superior judgment and wrote no more works for the Russian stage after 1852. His plays had some performances in Germany and Italy in the second half of the nineteenth century, but in Russia, despite his tremendous prestige as a novelist, there were only two or three scattered revivals of *A Month in the Country*, put on by Maria Savina for her benefit performances. Otherwise his plays were generally believed to be unplayable.

Chekhov's mature plays are of course a vindication of Turgenev's dramatic method, a proof that drama which internalizes the outward events and concentrates on conveying the finer psychological nuances can be convincing and theatrically effective. Nothing would be easier than to postulate Chekhov's derivation of his dramatic method from Turgenev, especially because we know Turgenev was his favorite writer at the beginning of his literary career. But this letter and two others, which Chekhov wrote after he read Turgenev's plays at his wife's request, demonstrate beyond any doubt that he simply did not know Turgenev as a dramatist until this point. Particularly unexpected is his preference for the conventionally structured *The Sponger* and his dislike for the Chekhovian *A Month in the Country.* About Turgenev's subtle masterpiece of delicate psychological characterization, *It Breaks Where It Is Thinnest,* Chekhov wrote to Olga Knipper on March 24, 1903: "It was written at the time when the best writers were still under the influence of Byron and of Lermontov with his Pechorin. Gorsky is after all the same as Pechorin. A bit watery and a bit trite, but Pechorin nonetheless. This play may turn out to lack all interest when performed; it's a little too long and its main interest is as a document of earlier times. But I might be mistaken, which is entirely possible. Look at how pessimistic I was last summer about *Lower Depths* and look at the success it's having! So I'm no judge."

But, if Chekhov failed to perceive the similarity of Turgenev's plays to his own, others saw it soon enough. In 1909, Stanislavsky produced a memorable revival of *A Month in the Country* with Olga Knipper in the leading role, and three years later his company presented an evening of Turgenev's one-act plays. These two revivals demonstrated how effective the acting methods devised for Chekhov's plays were for performing the plays of his illustrious predecessor. Paradoxical though it may seem, it was the success of Chekhov the playwright that had made possible a true appreciation of Turgenev's important contribution to Russian drama, which his contemporaries underestimated so short-sightedly. Only after Chekhov had made his mark was it possible for Turgenev's plays to enter permanently the repertoire of Russian and foreign theaters.

170. To Alexei Suvorin

Naro-Fominskoye,[1]
June 17, 1903

Angels and ministers of grace, defend us![2] A letter addressed twenty times over and speckled with twenty postmarks arrived for me yesterday. It looked as if it had come from Australia. What did I find when I opened it? It turned out to be a letter you had sent to New Jerusalem on May 23rd! I haven't even gone to New Jerusalem. I went to Zvenigorod District to spend a day with Maklakov and told Vasya and Misha too, I think, that I was going to New Jerusalem because New Jerusalem is generally considered the closest address to Maklakov's.[3] So if you've had to wait a long time for an answer, don't blame me.

I spent only a few hours in Petersburg. I saw Marx. We didn't have anything special to say to one another. He offered me in German five thousand for medical expenses, and I declined. Then he made me a gift of two or three poods of his editions, which I took, and we parted with the firm resolve to meet and talk things over in August and to think them over until then.[4]

I haven't told Misha anything about Marx, and the things he's told you are nothing more than his own conjectures. There's been a sort of turnabout in my personal life again. I went to see Professor Ostroumov, and after a thorough examination he gave me a bad scolding, told me my health was in very bad shape, that I had emphysema, pleurisy, and so on and so forth, and ordered me to spend the winter in the north, near Moscow, and not in the Crimea. I'm happy, of course, but what a chore it's going to be to find a cottage for the winter. Where in the Moscow area will I find a place whose cold and lack of comfort won't send me to my grave? At any rate, I'm looking, and when I find something, I'll let you know.

Send me the next issues of the newspaper. I've sealed up the previous issues in a package and given it to Vasya to hand over to you.[5] My address is: Naro-Fominskoye, Moscow Province. Should there be any change in address, I'll let you know in plenty of time.

We have a fine river here at the cottage, but there's no one to go fishing with.

Lavrov, the publisher of *Russian Thought*, is very ill (nephritis, angina pectoris) and is anxious to arrange it so that his journal doesn't fall into the hands of his heirs. Apparently the affair has already been settled; the journal has been sold and is now safe. Goltsev has remained at the helm, and they've even invited me to be fiction editor.[6]

And so I'll be staying in the Moscow area for the winter; Ostroumov won't let me go abroad. ("You're an invalid," he says.) I've grown so unused to the cold I'll be freezing all the time. Keep well and happy. I wish you and yours all the best. If I receive the next issues of the newspaper from you, I'll return them just as you sent them, in a package delivered by Vasya.

Yours,
A. Chekhov

The abolition of lashing and head shaving is a major reform.[7]

1. This was a country estate not far from Moscow where Chekhov settled for a part of the summer, after traveling extensively throughout Russia in May and early June, in violation of the orders of his personal physician, Dr. Isaak Altschuller.

2. Quoted in Nikolai Polevoy's somewhat distorted translation.

3. Chekhov was in St. Petersburg from May 13 to May 15, at which time he informed his brother Mikhail (Misha) and Suvorin's valet Vasily (Vasya) of his future travel plans. At that time he considered renting a cottage on the estate of the lawyer Vasily Maklakov (Maklakov became an important parliamentary leader when the Duma was established after the 1905 Revolution; after the October Revolution, he was one of the principal leaders of the anti-Soviet Russian émigrés in Paris). However, Chekhov changed his plans and chose to settle at Naro-Fominskoye, which occasioned a mixup in his correspondence with Suvorin.

4. Like all of Chekhov's friends, Suvorin kept urging him to do something about the unfair contract with Adolf Marx. But Chekhov insisted that any change in the contract had to be suggested by Marx himself.

5. With the abolition of censorship restrictions after 1905, Maria Chekhova felt free to admit in the note to her edition of her brother's letters that the newspaper mentioned here was the underground anti-government biweekly *Liberation,* published in Stuttgart by Russian émigrés, which was illegal in Russia. This was one of several such publications with which Suvorin regularly supplied Chekhov.

6. Actually, Vukol Lavrov recovered and the journal did not have to be sold.

7. The government administrative order of June 15, 1903, abolished the following penalties in all hard-labor compounds and Siberian and Sakhalin penal colonies: shaving of the head, lashing and being manacled to wheelbarrows. The last-named penalty, which existed only on Sakhalin and which was vividly described by Chekhov in his book, suggests that the reform was carried out under the impact of *The Island of Sakhalin.*

171. To Solomon Rabinovich (Sholom Aleichem)[1]

Naro-Fominskoye,
June 19, 1903

Dear Solomon Naumovich,

I'm writing nothing or very little these days, so I can make you only a conditional promise: I'll be glad to write the story if my illness doesn't prevent it. As for stories of mine that have already been published, they are entirely at your disposal, and I will be nothing if not deeply gratified to see them translated into Yiddish and printed in a miscellany for the benefit of the Jewish victims in Kishinyov.

With my sincere respect and devotion,
A. Chekhov

I received your letter yesterday, June 18th.[2]

1. The great Yiddish storyteller wrote to Chekhov asking him to contribute a story to a collection he was editing and which was to be published in Warsaw for the benefit of the victims of the recent atrocious pogrom in Kishinyov. Since Chekhov was not able to supply a new story, Sholom Aleichem selected his earlier piece, "Difficult People," which was translated into Yiddish and included in the collection.

2. On August 6, 1903, Chekhov wrote to Sholom Aleichem again, offering to help place a Russian translation of one of Sholom Aleichem's stories in any journal of his choice.

172. To Sergei Diaghilev

Yalta,
July 12, 1903

Dear Sergei Pavlovich,

I've been a little slow in answering your letter because I received it not in Naro-Fominskoye, but in Yalta, where I have recently arrived and where I will probably stay until fall. I've given your letter much thought, and even though your proposal or invitation is very tempting, I'm afraid that in the last analysis I won't be able to respond the way you and I would have liked.[1]

I cannot be an editor of *The World of Art* because it is impossible for me to live in Petersburg; the journal won't move to Moscow for my sake, editing by mail and wire is impossible, and the journal will gain nothing by having me as a nominal editor only. That's point number one. Point number two is that just as only one artist can paint a picture and only one orator can make a speech, so only one person can edit a journal. I'm no critic, of course, and would probably do a poor job of editing the criticism section. What is more, how could I work under the same roof as Dmitry Merezhkovsky? He is a resolute believer, a proselytizing believer, whereas I squandered away my faith long ago and never fail to be puzzled by an intellectual who is also a believer. I respect Merezhkovsky and value him as a person and writer, but if we ever do get the cart moving, we will end up pulling it in opposite directions.[2] Be that as it may, whether my attitude is mistaken or not, I've always thought and am certain that there should be only one editor, and that *The World of Art* in particular should be edited by you alone. That is my opinion, and I don't expect to change it.

Don't be angry with me, dear Sergei Pavlovich, but it seems to me that if you continue editing the journal for another five years you'll come to agree with me. A journal, like a painting or a poem, must have a single personality and represent a single will. That is the way *The*

World of Art has been until now, and it has worked well. And that is the way it should continue.[3]

I wish you all the best and firmly clasp your hand. The weather in Yalta is cool, or at least not hot, and I am flourishing.

I send you my humble regards.

Yours,
A. Chekhov

1. While Diaghilev initially welcomed the new religious interests of his closest literary associates, by the summer of 1903 the new ascendancy of religion over art and aesthetics began to alarm him. Some of the leading contributors to *The World of Art*—the Merezhkovskys, Vasily Rozanov and even Diaghilev's handsome personal friend Filosofov—were all deeply involved in a new religious journal, *The New Way,* which was an outgrowth of the meetings of the Religious-Philosophical Society. It now seemed to Diaghilev that the influence of *The New Way* was invading *The World of Art* and that the literary section of his journal was becoming too theological to suit his taste. He consulted Chekhov personally about his misgivings at the end of June and on July 3 sent him a plan for an editorial reform of his journal. What Diaghilev proposed to do was divide the editorial chores among four principal editors, putting Chekhov in charge of poetry and fiction, Merezhkovsky in charge of literary criticism, and entrusting the theater section and the visual-arts section to Dmitry Filosofov and Alexander Benois, respectively. The entire plan was contingent on Chekhov's consent.

2. Reference to Krylov's fable "The Swan, the Pike and the Crayfish," in which these three creatures are harnessed to a cart and end up pulling it in three different directions. In his letter of July 26, Diaghilev replied to Chekhov's objections with an offer to put him in charge of all the editorial decisions and to retain Merezhkovsky only as a regular contributor.

3. Despite Chekhov's firm refusal, Diaghilev continued coaxing him to agree in two more letters, assuring him that he saw no way of continuing his journal without Chekhov's help.

173. To Konstantin Balmont

Yalta,
August 5, 1903

Dear Konstantin Dmitrievich,

I am leading the life of an idle, well-fed, world-weary tramp. I am now in Yalta, which is why your "Hymn to the Sun" took exactly ten days to reach me. I find it one of your most beautiful poems, but it still has to pass through the hands of Viktor Alexandrovich.[1] For the time being I'm an editor *in spe* only. I'm not reading manuscripts and probably won't be reading them and determining their fate before next year. I've heard you're coming to Yalta in late August. If so, we'll soon be getting together for a chat, and I'll explain it all to you.

"Hymn to the Sun" is presently in Moscow. I sent it there with a covering letter.

I have received your *Let Us Be Like the Sun*.[2] I have read it and passed it on for others to read. I didn't thank you when I should have because first I didn't know your address, and second, I assumed that it was one of my friends who had sent it to me (it doesn't have your usual autograph).

Well, never mind, it's never too late to say thank you. Please accept my three low bows.

You ask whether I'm going to be in Moscow in September. My answer is I will.

I clasp your hand.

Your Autka burgher,
A. Chekhov

1. While Chekhov rejected Diaghilev's offer to edit *The World of Art*, he accepted a similar request from his friends Vukol Lavrov and Viktor Goltsev to help edit the literary section of *Russian Thought* during the difficult period the journal was undergoing because of Lavrov's illness. In actual fact, Chekhov was probably in no condition by now to handle any editorial chores for anyone. But his editorship was announced by *Russian Thought*, and Balmont saw in this announcement an opportunity to get his poetry on the pages of a traditional liberal journal, which would normally be leery of publishing anything as modernistic as his work. He accordingly sent Chekhov his "Hymn to the Sun," a long set of variations on the poem of the same name by St. Francis of Assisi. Chekhov forwarded the poem to Goltsev, who found it too long and too pretentious (one is tempted to agree with him in this case—as Balmont's poems go, "Hymn to the Sun" is astoundingly long and even more astoundingly dull). The following year the poem was published in Balmont's usual outlet, *The World of Art*, and he also included it as the opening poem in his collection *Love Alone*.

2. *Let Us Be Like the Sun*, subtitled "Tetraphony of the Elements," was Balmont's single most successful collection of verse. It was published at the end of 1902.

174. To Olga Knipper

Yalta,
October 19, 1903

Greetings, sweet horsy, my darling,

I didn't write you yesterday because I was waiting with trepidation for a telegram all day. Late last night your telegram came, and early this morning I got a hundred-eighty-word telegram from Vladimir Ivanovich.[1] Many thanks. I was so worried, so afraid. The things that worried me most of all were the second act's lack of movement and a certain sketchy quality in the role of Trofimov, the student. After all, Trofimov is constantly being sent into exile, he is constantly being expelled from the university. How can you put all those things across?

Tell them to send me a copy of the repertoire, darling, I haven't received it. If somebody's coming this way, don't bother about sending my cap; send me a package of high-quality paper, some tooth powder, and a package of stationery (the cheapest) and some other exciting things. I am living well. The kitchen is functioning satisfactorily, though last night they did serve sturgeon and roast beef again, neither of which are on Masha's list.[2] Speaking of Masha, tell her that my digestion is improving daily and that Mother is feeling fine. The weather is excellent, even better than it was.

Is my play going to be performed? If so, when?

I have received a very nice letter from Konstantin Sergeyevich;[3] it was cordial and sincere. Will *The Pillars of Society*[4] be performed this season? I still haven't seen it, you know. I'll be arriving in early November. I'll probably publish the play in Gorky's miscellany, only I don't know how I'm going to get around that German, Marx.[5]

The Odessa newspapers have reported the plot of my play. It doesn't resemble it a bit.[6]

Darling horsy, a thousand rubles for a steam bath! I long for a steam bath. Mushrooms and ferns are sprouting all over my body.

Meanwhile, be on the lookout for a very good tailor to make me a winter coat. And be on the lookout for some lightweight fur. Make me a detailed list on a separate sheet of paper of the things I should take to Moscow with me. And write me who is going to play Charlotte. It it really Rayevskaya? If so, instead of Charlotte you'll have an unfunny, pretentious Eudoxia.[7]

I've just finished reading an article by Rossov the actor on *Julius Caesar*.[8] It's in *New Times* (Wednesday). His warm praise for Kachalov and Vishnevsky is odd, because last year Rossov wrote about the Art Theater with hatred and majestic revulsion.

Mikhailovsky and Kostya are here.[9] They've just dropped by.

Yours,

A.

1. Chekhov had sent the completed manuscript of *The Cherry Orchard* to the Moscow Art Theater. His wife's telegram informed him that the manuscript had been received and the long, enthusiastic telegram from Nemirovich-Danchenko told Chekhov that the play was the finest thing he'd ever written

and went on to compare its characters to those of Chekhov's earlier plays.

2. In view of Chekhov's digestive difficulties, his sister had prepared a detailed list for the family cook of the things Chekhov was and was not allowed to eat.

3. Stanislavsky.

4. *The Pillars of Society* by Ibsen and Shakespeare's *Julius Caesar* were among the successful new productions of the Moscow Art Theater.

5. Chekhov had planned to publish the text of *The Cherry Orchard* in *Knowledge,* a miscellany which was being prepared by Gorky's literary group. But his contract with Adolf Marx permitted him to publish his new works only in periodicals or in nonprofit publications "issued for purposes of charity." To get around this restriction, *Knowledge* agreed to donate a percentage of its profits to endow a medical school for women and for other worthy causes.

6. An article in *Odessa News* outlined the plot of *The Cherry Orchard* on the basis of some third-hand account of the play. According to the article, the first act showed a cherry orchard in full bloom and a group of young people in it, who then gradually age as the play progresses. This was one of the several garbled accounts of the play's content that appeared in the Russian press prior to its opening. Chekhov reacted to these distortions with an untypical angry irritability, which testified to his deteriorating physical condition.

7. In several of his letters Chekhov expressed anxiety lest the actress Yevgenia Rayevskaya might be allowed to play Charlotte. The reference to Eudoxia (the Byzantine-Greek version of the name is cited rather than its standard Russian form) is not clear.

8. Nikolai Rossov was one of the Moscow correspondents of *New Times.*

9. This Mikhailovsky is not the powerful literary critic but the novelist Nikolai Garin, the author of the Russian juvenile classic *Tyoma's Childhood.* His real name happened to be Nikolai Mikhailovsky, and he took the pen name of Garin in order not to be confused with the critic. Kostya is Olga's brother Konstantin Knipper, who was a friend of Garin's. Both Garin and Konstantin Knipper were railroad engineers by profession and they were in the Crimea looking over prospective sites for a projected railroad branch.

175. To Olga Knipper

Yalta,
October 23, 1903

You write that Èfros can't do anyone any damage with his lies, horsy. But all the newspapers—literally all the provincial newspapers—are reprinting him, and today I saw it in the *Moscow Courier.* What a harmful animal he is![1]

You write that Vishnevsky can't play Gayev. Well, who then?

Stanislavsky? Then who'll play Lopakhin? Lopakhin is not to be given to Luzhsky under any circumstances. He'll either make him very pallid or clown his way through the part. His job is to play Yepikhodov. No, please don't deprive Vishnevsky of his role.

It's getting colder; there's winter in the air. That tall Olga Mikhailovna[2] came to see us yesterday. She discussed love and promised to send some herring.

There's absolutely nothing new. I get up in the morning, muddle through the day in one way or another, lie down in the evening and fall quickly asleep, and that's all. Almost no one comes to see me.

Nemirovich writes that my play has a lot of tears and a certain amount of coarseness. Write and tell me what you think is wrong, darling, and what they say, and I'll correct it. It's not too late, you know; I could still rework an entire act.

So the actors like Pishchik? I'm glad to hear it. I think Gribunin will do a splendid job playing him.[3]

I bow very low before you, darling. I kiss you and hug you. Be cheerful and content. So far everything's going fine in the kitchen, that is, they've been cooking me the things on the list Masha left. I can't wait to get to Moscow and dig into some corned beef and veal cutlets. Especially the corned beef. And I want to pet my horsy too.

Yours,

A.

1. Chekhov's mounting irritation with mistakes and distortions in the advance publicity for *The Cherry Orchard* reached an explosive climax with the publication of an unsigned announcement of the play's production in the newspaper *News of the Day* on October 19. Chekhov happened to know that the announcement was written by the drama critic Nikolai Èfros, one of Moscow Art Theater's most enthusiastic boosters, later on its historian and, until this incident, an acquaintance and a correspondent of Chekhov's. The seemingly insignificant errors about the play's setting and the more serious ones about its characters (see next letter) first enraged Chekhov and then put him into a state of prolonged depression that seems out of all proportion to the provocation. There were bitter complaints in letters to his wife, an exchange of angry telegrams with Nemirovich-Danchenko and a request to the local Yalta newspaper to print a retraction of Èfros's announcement. Even less characteristically, Chekhov conceived a hatred for Èfros and in subsequent months forbade his correspondents to mention the man's name in their letters.

The depth of Chekhov's emotional reaction to this trivial incident can be seen in his letter to Olga Knipper of October 25: "My dearest horsy, today *The Crimean Courier* and *Odessa News* have reprinted that thing from *News of the Day.* It is sure to be reprinted in all the newspapers. Had I known that this stunt of Èfros's would have such a bad effect on me, I would never have let the Art Theater have my play. I feel as if I had been splashed with slops which I am now forced to drink."

2. Olga Solovyova. The ironic tone might have been occasioned by her backing out of financing the marine-biology laboratory which Chekhov had helped her plan (cf. Letter 156).

3. After several changes in casting plans, it was indeed Vladimir Gribunin who played Pishchik in the first performance of *The Cherry Orchard.*

176. To Vladimir Nemirovich-Danchenko

Yalta,
October 23, 1903

Dear Vladimir Ivanovich,

When I let your theater have *Three Sisters* and an announcement about it appeared in *News of the Day, both you and I* were indignant. I talked with Èfros, and he gave me his word it would never happen again.[1] Now I suddenly read that Ranevskaya is living abroad with Anya, that she is living with a Frenchman, that Act Three takes place somewhere in a hotel,[2] that Lopakhin is a kulak, a son of a bitch, and so on and so forth. What could I think? How could I suspect you had a hand in it? In my telegram I had only Èfros in mind, I accused only Èfros, and I felt so strange, I couldn't believe my eyes as I read the telegram in which you tried to shift all the blame onto yourself.[3] It makes me sad that that's how you understood me and even sadder that it resulted in this misunderstanding. But let's forget the whole affair as quickly as possible. Tell Èfros I never want to have anything to do with him again, and then forgive me if I overdid things in my telegram. And *basta*!

Today I had a letter from my wife, the first one dealing with the play. I will so much be looking forward to your letters. It takes four to five days for a letter to get here—how awful!

I've had an upset stomach and a cough for a long time now. My bowels seem to be on the mend, but that cough keeps on as before, and I don't know what to do, whether to go to Moscow or not. I'd very much like to sit in on some rehearsals and have a look at things. I'm afraid Anya will speak in a tearful tone of voice (for some reason you find her similar to Irina), I'm afraid she won't be played by a young actress. Anya never once cries in the play and nowhere does she even have tears in her voice. She may have tears in her eyes during the second act, but her tone of voice is gay and lively. Why do you say in your telegram that there are many weepy people in my play? Where are they? Varya's the only one, and that's because she's a crybaby by nature. Her tears are not meant to make the spectator feel despondent. I often use "through her tears" in my stage directions, but that indicates only a character's mood, not actual tears.[4] There's no cemetery in the second act.

I lead a lonely life, keeping to a diet, coughing, and losing my temper from time to time. I'm tired of reading. There you have my life.

I haven't seen *The Pillars of Society* yet, I haven't seen *Lower Depths* or *Julius Caesar*. If I could go to Moscow now, I'd be in a state of bliss for a whole week.

It's growing cold here too. Keep well and calm, now. Don't be angry. I'm looking forward to your letters. Not letter, letters.

Yours,
A. Chekhov

In all probability the play will be published in Gorky's miscellany.

1. At the time of the first performance of *Three Sisters*, Èfros published an announcement that *Three Sisters* was only the working title of the play and that Chekhov intended to change it to another, more suitable one.

2. This misunderstanding arose from the close similarity of the Russian words for hotel and living room. In his extreme irritation, Chekhov seems to have actually feared that Stanislavsky might move the setting of Act Three to a hotel, merely because of the mistake in the Èfros announcement.

3. In an effort to placate Chekhov, Nemirovich sent him a telegram in which he tried to take the blame for the mixup, explaining that he had told Èfros the content of *The Cherry Orchard* orally, instead of showing him the text and therefore was partly responsible for the garbled announcement.

4. This remark is an extremely important guide for any production of *Three Sisters* and *The Cherry Orchard*. All too often, Chekhov's frequent stage direction "through her tears" is taken all too literally by directors and actresses.

177. To Konstantin Alexeyev (Stanislavsky)

Yalta,
October 30, 1903

Dear Konstantin Sergeyevich,

Many thanks for the letter and thank you for the telegram too.[1] Letters are very precious to me because in the first place I'm all alone here and in the second I sent the play off three weeks ago and didn't receive your letter until yesterday, and if it hadn't been for my wife I'd have known nothing and could have imagined any number of things. As I worked on Lopakhin, I thought of him as your role. If for any reason he doesn't appeal to you, take Gayev. Lopakhin may be a merchant, but he is a decent person in every sense; his behavior must be entirely proper, cultivated and free of pettiness or clowning. I had the feeling you could do a brilliant job of this role, the central role in the play. If you take Gayev, give Lopakhin to Vishnevsky. He won't be an artistic Lopakhin, but he won't be a petty one either. Luzhsky would make an unfeeling foreigner of the role, Leonidov would turn it into a cute little kulak.[2] When you're selecting an actor for the role, don't forget that Varya, a serious and religious young lady, is in love with Lopakhin; she could never have loved a cute little kulak.

I very much want to go to Moscow, but I don't see how I can break away from here. It's growing cold, and I almost never leave the house, I'm not used to being out of doors and keep coughing. It's not Moscow or the trip I'm afraid of; it's the layover in Sevastopol that lasts from two o'clock until eight—and in the most boring company imaginable.

Write and tell me what role you take. My wife has written that Moskvin wants to play Yepikhodov. Well, that's fine; the play will only gain from it.

My most humble regards and greetings to Maria Petrovna.[3] I wish you and her all the very best. Keep well and cheerful.

I haven't yet seen *Lower Depths*, *The Pillars of Society* or *Julius Caesar* and am very anxious to see them.

Yours,
A. Chekhov

The reason I'm sending this to the theater is that I don't know where you live.

1. While Stanislavsky had originally disliked *The Seagull* and had strong doubts about the possible success of *Uncle Vanya* and *Three Sisters*, he fell in love with *The Cherry Orchard* at first sight. On October 20, he sent Chekhov a telegram and a letter expressing his wildly enthusiastic reaction. In his letter he wrote: "I hereby proclaim this play to be outside of all competition and not subject to any criticism whatsoever. Anyone who does not understand it is an idiot. This is my sincere conviction. I will play in it with delight, and if such a thing were possible, I would like to try playing all of the roles, not excluding the charming Charlotte." In his letter, Stanislavsky also informed Chekhov

that he was wrong to have called his play a comedy, for it was a tragedy "regardless of what escape into a better life you might indicate in the last act."

2. For the final distribution of the roles, see the commentary to the next letter.

3. Stanislavsky's wife, the actress Maria Lilina, was by now also carrying on an active correspondence with Chekhov.

178. To Vladimir Nemirovich-Danchenko

Yalta,
November 2, 1903

Dear Vladimir Ivanovich,

Two letters from you in one day! Thank you very much. I'm not drinking any beer; the last time I had any was in July. And I'm not allowed to eat honey; it gives people stomach aches.[1] And now to the play.

1. Anya can be played by anyone at all, even a complete unknown, as long as she is young and looks like a little girl and speaks in a youthful, vibrant voice. It's not a particularly important role.[2]

2. Varya is a much more important role. What about having Maria Petrovna play her? Without Maria Petrovna the role will seem flat and crude, and I'll have to rework it, tone it down. Maria Petrovna doesn't have to worry about being typecast, because in the first place she is a talented person, and in the second, Varya isn't at all like Sonya or Natasha; she wears black, she's a nun, she's slightly simple-minded, a crybaby, and so on and so forth.[3]

3. Gayev and Lopakhin are roles for Konstantin Sergeyevich to try out and choose from. If he were to take Lopakhin and do well in the role, the play would be a success. Because if Lopakhin is pallid, portrayed by a pallid actor, then both the role and the play are ruined.[4]

4. Pishchik is for Gribunin. For heaven's sake, don't give the role to Vishnevsky.

5. Charlotte is an important role. You can't give it to Pomyalova, of course. Muratova might be good, but she's not funny. This is Miss Knipper's role.[5]

6. Yepikhodov—if Moskvin wants it, so be it. He'll make an excellent Yepikhodov. I had assumed that Luzhsky would play him.[6]

7. Firs is for Artyom.

8. Dunyasha is for Khalyutina.[7]

9. Yasha. If the Alexandrov you wrote me about is the one who is your assistant director, then let him have Yasha. Moskvin would make a wonderful Yasha. Nor do I have anything against Leonidov.

10. The Passerby is for Gromov.

11. The stationmaster who recites "The Peccatrix"[8] in the third act is for an actor with a bass voice.

Charlotte speaks correct, not broken Russian, but every once in a while she hardens a final soft consonant and uses a masculine adjective with a feminine noun or vice versa.[9] Pishchik is a true Russian, an old man afflicted by the gout, old age and too much to eat; he is stout and wears a long coat (à la Simov)[10] and boots without heels. Lopakhin wears a white vest and yellow shoes; he takes big steps and waves his arms as he walks. He thinks while he walks and walks in a straight line. Since his hair is rather long, he often tosses his head back. When lost in thought, he strokes his beard from back to front, that is, from neck to mouth. Trofimov is clear, I think. Varya wears a black dress with a wide belt.

For three years I've been planning to write *The Cherry Orchard,* and for three years I've been telling you to engage an actress to play the role of Lyubov Andreyevna. And now you're stuck with a game of solitaire that is not working out.[11]

I'm in the most idiotic situation imaginable: I'm trapped here all alone with no idea why. And you are wrong to say that, despite all your work, it is "Stanislavsky's theater." It is only you they talk about, only you they write about, while Stanislavsky is being criticized for his Brutus.[12] If you leave, I leave. Gorky is younger than we are, and he has his own life to live. . . . As for the theater in Nizhny Novgorod, that's a passing fancy; Gorky will give it a try, have a taste of it and drop it. By the way, both theaters for the people and literature for the people are ridiculous; they're all merely lollipops for the people. What needs to be done is not lower Gogol to the people's level, but raise the people to Gogol's level.[13]

I'd so very much like to go to the Hermitage[14] and have some sterlet and a bottle of wine there. There was a time when I could drink a bottle of champagne *solo* without its affecting me and then have some cognac and still not be affected by it.

I'll be writing you again, and until then I send you my humble regards and thanks. Is it true that Luzhsky's father has died? I read about it today in the papers.

Why is Maria Petrovna so determined to play Anya? And why does Maria Fyodorovna think she's too aristocratic for Varya?[15] After all, she plays in *Lower Depths*, doesn't she? Oh, let them do what they want. I embrace you. Keep well.

Yours,
A. Chekhov

it never occurred to me to give *Cherry Orchard* to the Empress Alexandra Theater. The play belongs to the Art Theater. I let Nemirovich-Danchenko have it for both Moscow and Petersburg. This year it doesn't seem as if the Art Theater is going to Petersburg, but even so there would be no use in talking to the management about the play.

The reason I can tell you this so light-heartedly is that I am firmly convinced that my *Cherry Orchard* is not at all suitable for you. The central female role in the play is an old woman who lives entirely in the past and has nothing in the present. The other parts, at least the other female parts, are more or less minor and lacking in subtlety, and are of no interest to you. My play will soon be published in the miscellany *Knowledge*, and if you read it you'll see for yourself that there is nothing in it to interest you, no matter how indulgent you feel toward it.

How is your health? Did traveling from Baku to Tiflis tire you out? Happy New Year. I wish you health, strength, success, and—at least one day a week—complete and utter happiness. I kiss and clasp your hand.

Devotedly,
A. Chekhov

1. Kommissarzhevskaya's telegram, sent on December 21, 1903, from Rostov-on-the-Don, read: "Insistently beg you not to give *Orchard* to anyone in Petersburg prior to my letter. Writing, mailing it at once. Kommissarzhevskaya."

In her letter, she wrote:

> Dear Anton Pavlovich,
>
> I am opening my own theater in St. Petersburg. I want its inauguration to be connected with your name and am therefore asking you to let me have *The Cherry Orchard* for my opening. I know that you would like to give it to the Empress Alexandra Theater and to have Savina play it. Judging by the few bits of information I have about this play, the role is just right for her and she would play it very well. But you, of all people, cannot possibly refuse to help me with my insanely difficult undertaking. Need I tell you how many enemies I have? But there are also, I believe, people who will help me realize what the best that is in me wants to do. I want you to be the first among them, I must have it this way. I will not say another thing. You can't fail to sense how anxious I am, how I need your word and your consent. Send me a telegram to the Orient in Tiflis. Happy New Year. Write me something—anything.
>
> V. Kommissarzhevskaya

180. To Olga Knipper

Yalta,
February 27, 1904

My fine spouse,

Even though you have no faith in me as a doctor, let me tell you that Korsakov has a marked tendency toward pessimism; he always assumes the very worst. Once, when I had been treating a little girl for some two or three months, I called him in for a consultation. He sentenced her to death, yet she's alive to this day and has long since married. If tuberculosis is in a vertebra, it still has a long way to go before reaching the brain or the spinal chord. Just make sure the boy isn't dragged from place to place on visits or allowed to jump around too much.[1] And may I ask you once again why they chose Yevpatoria?[2]

The sun hasn't come out once the whole time I've been in Yalta, i.e., since February 17th. It's terribly damp, the sky is gray, and I've been keeping to my room.

My luggage has arrived, but it looks rather despondent. First, there are fewer pieces than I had thought, and second, both of the ancient trunks developed cracks en route. My life here is boring, uninteresting. The people around me are annoyingly uninteresting; they have no interests, they are indifferent to everything.

Meanwhile, *The Cherry Orchard* is having three or four performances in every city; it's a success, can you imagine? I've just been reading about Rostov-on-the-Don, where it is having its third performance.[3] Oh, if it were only not Muratova and Leonidov[4] and Artyom playing in it in Moscow! I've been keeping it to myself, but that Artyom is giving an abominable performance.[5]

You write you haven't received any letters from me, but I've been writing every day. Yesterday was the first day I didn't write. Even though there isn't anything to write about, I still write. Schnapp,[6] that son of a bitch, has made himself at home, he has already taken to lying in my study with his hind legs stretched out. He sleeps in Mother's room. He plays outside with other dogs, so he's always dirty.

You have an awful lot of uncles, and you're constantly seeing them off. Watch out you don't catch cold. Stay at home, at least during the fourth week of Lent when the theater has no performances.

Have you come up with anything for the summer? Where are we going to live? I'd like it to be near Moscow, near a railroad station, so we could do without a carriage and without benefactors and admirers. Think about a place to live, darling, think hard and maybe you'll come up with something. After all, you're so clever, so judicious, so reliable—when you're not angry, that is. I remember with such pleasure our trip to Tsaritsyno and back.

Well, God be with you, darling, my kind, affable little puppy. I miss you, I have no choice but to miss you; you've become a part of me. I kiss my wife, I embrace her.

Yours,

A.

1. Olga was worried about the health of her little nephew Lev Knipper (b. 1898), the son of her brother Konstantin. The boy had been examined by the renowned pediatrician Dr. Nikolai Korsakov, who found tuberculosis in a vertebra. Lev Knipper recovered and lived on to become a much-honored Soviet composer, who in addition to large quantities of derivative, academic music also wrote the lilting song "Meadowland," known in English as "The Red Cavalry Song," which enjoyed a great international popularity during World War II and has remained a perennial favorite ever since.

2. A resort in the Crimea.

3. A Rostov newspaper, which Chekhov received, announced that an additional performance of *The Cherry Orchard* had been scheduled at the local municipal theater "by tumultuous popular demand."

4. Stanislavsky and Nemirovich-Danchenko had cast Yelena Muratova as Charlotte and Leonid Leonidov as Lopakhin against Chekhov's wishes and he was extremely unhappy with their performances.

5. Artyom had been Chekhov's own choice for the role of Firs.

6. A new dog.

181. To Olga Knipper

Yalta,
March 6, 1904

You ought to be ashamed of yourself writing with such awful ink, my little baby cachalot, my darling. You may not believe it, but I give you my word, I had to peel the envelope away from the letter, as if they'd been glued together on purpose. Masha has sent me the same sort of sticky letter. It's downright revolting. Not only are the letters sticky, but you use them to frighten me with your premonitions: "There's something horrible hanging over my head," etc. Our vile cold weather makes me feel bad enough as it is. There's snow in the mountains and a thin layer of snow on the roofs, and the air is colder than in Moscow.

Go ahead and take the apartment on Leontyev Lane, it's a good location, close to everything. I'll come two or three days before your arrival from Petersburg. Got it? I received a letter from Vishnevsky. He writes about the splendid full houses you've been having in Petersburg, praises the apartment on Leontyev Lane, and so on. Mikhailovsky[1] came to see me. He's going to the Far East and says that your brother Kostya is also planning to go—for an enormous salary, of course. And you can't deny that when a woman never stops talking about ovaries, kidneys and bladders, and when she talks of nothing else, it makes you want to throw yourself out the window. Lyova[2] will recover, barring any unforeseen developments, of course.

What a revolting dream I had! I dreamed I was sleeping in bed with someone other than you; with some lady, very repulsive, a bragging brunette, and the dream went on for more than an hour. Now what do you make of that!

I want to see you, my darling. I want to talk with my wife, with my only woman. There's nothing new. All anyone talks about is the Japanese.[3]

Well, may the Lord bless you and keep you; don't mope, don't overwork, and be cheerful. Where did you get the idea that I had caught cold on the way from Tsaritsyno to Moscow? Please excuse my crudity, but what utter nonsense! It's only in Yalta that people catch colds. What I have is the most abominable case of sniffles.

I embrace my little cockroach and send her a million kisses.

A.

1. The novelist Nikolai Garin (see Letter 174, note 9). He wrote a memorial piece describing his last encounter with Chekhov before his departure for the Far East, which was published on July 22, 1904, in the army newspaper *The Manchurian Army Herald* and reprinted in the collection of memoirs about Chekhov (*Chekhov as Remembered by His Contemporaries*, Moscow, 1960).

2. Lev Knipper. The woman mentioned in the previous sentence is his mother.

3. The Russo-Japanese War had just begun.

182. To Boris Lazarevsky[1]

Yalta,
April 13, 1904

Dear Boris Alexandrovich,

Your long, sad letter reached me yesterday.[2] After reading it, I sympathized with you with all my heart. I can only suppose you are no longer in need of my sympathy because spring has come, the weather is warm, and the famous harbor has been cleared of ice. When I was in Vladivostok, the weather was wonderfully warm even though it was October and there was a real live whale crossing the harbor and splashing with its huge tail. In short, my impression was a glorious one—perhaps because I was on my way back home. When the war is over (and it soon will be), you'll begin to take trips to surrounding areas; you'll go to Khabarovsk, to the Amur, to Sakhalin, and up and down the coast, you'll see a host of things that you've never before experienced and that you'll remember to the end of your days, you'll meet with so much joy and suffering that you won't even notice that the three years which now so frighten you have flashed by. In peacetime, at least, life in Vladivostok is not all that boring; it's quite European in fact, and I don't think your wife will be making a mistake if she joins you after the war. If you're a hunter, I've heard endless stories about hunting and tigers![3] And what delicious fish! There are enormous, delicious oysters all along the coast. The state of my health permitting, I am going to go to the Far East as a doctor in July or August.[4] I may even spend some time in Vladivostok. I'll soon be off to Moscow, but keep writing to Yalta nonetheless; my letters are always punctually forwarded from here no matter where I am.

I firmly clasp your hand and wish you good health and an excellent frame of mind. You write there isn't anything to read in Vladivostok. What about the libraries? What about journals?

If there's a bombardment or something of the sort, write a description of it and send it as quickly as possible either to a newspaper or to *Russian Thought*, depending on how long it is.

Yours,
A. Chekhov

1. Boris Lazarevsky was a lawyer attached to the legal branch of the Imperial Russian Navy, who was stationed in Sevastopol when Chekhov met him. Lazarevsky was also a very minor writer who openly imitated Chekhov in his work. The two of them carried on an extensive correspondence in the last four years of Chekhov's life, dealing mostly with Lazarevsky's literary output and Chekhov's help in getting his writings placed with various publications.

2. In connection with the Russo-Japanese War, Lazarevsky was transferred to Vladivostok. He wrote a bitterly complaining letter to Chekhov in which he expressed his dismay at the prospect of staying in Siberia for another three years.

3. The Siberian tiger was still being widely hunted in Eastern Siberia and Manchuria as late as the 1930s.

4. Believing himself to be on the way to recovery, Chekhov expressed his intention of volunteering as a military doctor with the Far Eastern army in several letters written in the last months of his life.

183. To Father Sergius Shchukin[1]

Moscow,
May 27th, 1904

Dear Father Sergius,

Yesterday I discussed the case you are interested in with a well-known lawyer, and now let me tell you his opinion.[2] Have Mr. N. and his fiancée put together *all* the necessary documents and go to another province, Kherson, for instance, and get married there. Once they've been married, tell them to return home and go on living as if nothing had happened. It's no crime (it is not incest, after all); it is merely the violation of a long-established custom. If in two or three years someone denounces them or finds out or starts meddling and the case is taken to court, the children will still be recognized as legitimate, no matter what. Even if someone bothers to initiate a case against them (and it will be a flimsy case), they can petition the Emperor. Imperial authority will not condone what is forbidden by law (which is why there is no use petitioning for permission to get married), but it does have a wide latitude for granting pardon and will usually pardon what is inevitable.

I can't tell if I'm making myself clear. Forgive me, I'm in bed, I'm ill. I've been ill since May 2nd, and I haven't gotten dressed once since then. I can't carry out your other requests.

I'm going abroad on the third. You can find out my foreign address from my sister. Write me what you decide to do and how Mr. N. decides to act.

I firmly clasp your hand and wish you all the best.

Yours,
A. Chekhov

1. Father Shchukin was a Yalta priest who taught religion at the local girls' school (his first name is rendered as Sergius to convey the Church Slavic form Sergy, which clergymen used in preference to the standard Russian form Sergei). He was another literary protégé of Chekhov's. In 1911, Father Shchukin published a memoir in *Russian Thought* in which he reproduced some of his literary discussions with Chekhov and told the little-known story of Chekhov's intercession on behalf of the Greek community at Autka. After Autka was incorporated into the city of Yalta, the local Greek population found itself evicted from the Autka Orthodox Church when the ecclesiastical authorities decided to have its Greek rite replaced with the Slavic one. At the request of the local Greeks, Chekhov appealed to the local authorities to allow the Greeks to keep their native rite. Some of the members

of the municipal administration, irritated at what they thought was Chekhov's meddling in administrative affairs, tried to discredit him by spreading the rumor that he was actually a Greek.

2. Father Shchukin had written to Chekhov asking for advice about the plight of Grigory Neklyukov, a teacher at the Yalta Municipal School. Neklyukov, a widower, desired to marry his late wife's sister. It turned out that there was a law prohibiting such marriages as supposedly incestuous.

184. To Maria Chekhova

Berlin,
June 6, 1904

Dear Masha,

I am writing you from Berlin. I've been here a whole day now. It turned very cold in Moscow and even snowed after you left; the bad weather must have given me a cold, I began having rheumatic pains in my arms and legs, I couldn't sleep at night, lost a great deal of weight, had morphine injections, took thousands of different kinds of medicine, and recall with gratitude only the heroin Altschuller once prescribed for me.[1] Nonetheless, toward departure time I began to recover my strength. My appetite returned, I began giving myself arsenic injections, and so on and so forth, and finally on Thursday I left the country very thin, with very thin, emaciated legs. I had a fine, pleasant trip. Here in Berlin we've taken a comfortable room in the best hotel, I am very much enjoying the life here and haven't eaten so well and with such an appetite in a long time. The bread here is amazing, I've been stuffing myself with it, the coffee is excellent, and the dinners are beyond words. People who have never been abroad don't know how good bread can be. There's no decent tea (we have our own kind) and none of our hors d'oeuvres, but everything else is superb, even though it's cheaper here than in Russia.[2] I've already put on weight, and today, despite the chill in the air, I even took the long ride to the Tiergarten. And so you can tell Mother and anyone else who's interested that I'm on my way to recovery or even that I've already recovered.[3] My legs no longer ache, I don't have diarrhea, I'm beginning to fill out, and I now spend the entire day on my feet, out of bed. Tomorrow I will be visited by a local celebrity, Professor Ewald, an intestinal specialist. Dr. Taube wrote him about me.

Yesterday I drank some marvelous beer.

Is Vanya[4] in Yalta? Two days before I left he came to see me in Moscow, but then he disappeared; I saw no more of him. And I must confess that the thought of him, where he is and why he suddenly disappeared, troubled me throughout my trip. Please write and tell me what is happening.

The day after tomorrow we're leaving for Badenweiler. I'll send you the address. Write me whether you need money and when to send a check. I like Berlin very much, even though it is cool here today. I am reading German newspapers. The rumors about Russians coming in for a lot of abuse in the German press are exaggerated.

Keep well and cheerful now, and may the heavenly hosts protect you. Give my regards to Mother, and tell her that everything is coming along fine.

I'll arrive in Yalta in August. Regards to Grandma, Arseny and Nastya.[5] To Varvara Konstantinovna too.[6] I kiss you.

Yours,
A. Chekhov

We forgot to take along the dressing gown.

1. Both morphine and heroin were available on prescription at the time as sedatives.

2. Apparently because of the four preceding sentences, this letter was omitted from the 1963–64 edition, which otherwise included almost all the other letters from Chekhov's last weeks.

3. Most of the letters to family and friends that Chekhov wrote from Berlin and Badenweiler assert that his tuberculosis had been miraculously cured and that he was recovering by leaps and bounds.

4. Ivan Chekhov.

5. The cook, the handyman and the maid at Chekhov's home in Yalta, respectively.

6. The headmistress of the girls' school in Yalta.

185. To Maria Chekhova[1]

Badenweiler,
June 28, 1904

Dear Masha,

We're having a fierce heat wave. It caught me unawares, and since all I have with me is winter clothes, I'm suffocating and dream of getting out of here. But where can I go? I thought of going to Italy, to Como, but everyone there has left because of the heat. All southern Europe is hot. I thought of taking a boat from Trieste to Odessa, but I don't know how feasible it is now in June-July. Can Georges[2] find out what sort of boats are available, whether they're comfortable, whether they make long and drawn-out stops, whether the food is good, and so on and so forth? It would be an irreplaceable excursion for me, provided the boat is good and not bad. Georges would be doing me a great favor were he to wire me *collect*. The wire should read as follows: "Badenweiler Tschechow. Bien. 16. Vendredi." This would mean: *bien*—the boat is good, *16*—the number of days the voyage takes, *vendredi*—the day the boat leaves Trieste. Of course, all I'm giving is the form the wire is to take, and if the boat leaves on Thursday, it would be unbecoming to write *vendredi*.

It won't matter if the weather is a bit hot; I'll have my flannel suit. And to tell the truth, I'm afraid to take the train. I'd suffocate in one of those cars, especially now that I'm so short-winded and become even more so at the slightest provocation. Besides, there are no sleeping cars available all the way from Vienna to Odessa so it would be uncomfortable. And anyway the train would get me home earlier than required, and I still haven't had my fill of vacationing.

It's so hot that you feel like taking all your clothes off. I don't know what to do. Olga has gone to Freiburg to order a flannel suit for me. Here in Badenweiler there are no tailors or shoemakers. As a model she took along the suit Duchard made for me.

The food here is very tasty, but it does not do me much good. My stomach keeps getting upset. I can't eat the kind of butter they have here. Apparently my stomach is ruined beyond all hope. About the only remedy for it is to fast, in other words, to refrain entirely from eating, and that's that. And the only medicine for being short-winded is to keep perfectly still.

There's not a single well-dressed German woman; their lack of taste is depressing.[3]

Keep well and cheerful now. My regards to Mother, Vanya, Georges, Grandma and all the rest. Write. I kiss you, I clasp your hand.

Yours,

A.

1. This is the last letter Chekhov ever wrote.
2. Chekhov's cousin Georgy.
3. Alexander Blok thought it both highly appropriate and utterly heartbreaking that this was the last comment we have from Chekhov on any subject.

EPILOGUE

CHEKHOV DIED IN BADENWEILER in the early-morning hours of July 2, 1904. His last moments were described by his wife. He awoke her shortly after midnight and asked that she send for a doctor. His pulse was extremely weak. The doctor gave him camphor injections, had an oxygen pillow brought in and, to ease Chekhov's breathing, ordered a bottle of champagne. "Chekhov sat up," Olga Knipper wrote, "and in a loud, emphatic voice said to the doctor in German (of which he knew very little): 'Ich sterbe . . .' Then he picked up the glass, turned to me, smiled his wonderful smile and said: 'It's been such a long time since I've had champagne.' He drank it all to the last drop, quietly lay on his left side and was soon silent forever. The awful stillness of the night was broken only by a huge nocturnal moth which kept crashing painfully into the light bulbs and darting about the room. The doctor left and in the stillness and heat of the night the cork flew out of the half-empty champagne bottle with a tremendous noise." Even if Olga Knipper had invented all this (and she would have to be a literary artist of considerable imagination to have done so), there could hardly be a more appropriate death scene for Chekhov, with its apt symbols for life, affirmation and stoic acceptance of the inevitable.

Chekhov was brought back to Russia in a refrigerated railroad car bearing the inscription "For Oysters" and buried at the New Virgin Cemetery in Moscow, between the grave of his father and that of a Cossack widow named Olga Kukaretkina. Maxim Gorky and his friend Fyodor Chaliapin attended the funeral, along with thousands of other admirers. Gorky described the funeral in a hysterical letter he wrote to his wife on the same day and again, in more subdued tones, in his Chekhov memoir. He hated the crowd, which instead of mourning for Chekhov kept ogling him and Chaliapin. He qualified the funeral as "a thick, greasy cloud of triumphant vulgarity." The car for oysters and the name of Kukaretkina (something like "Cock-a-Doodle-Carriage") were for Gorky the final revenge that Russian vulgarity (*poshlost'*) had wreaked against Chekhov. But this was Gorky's way—to hate the human herd, and to indict for the sake of thundering indictment. Chekhov, one can safely assume, would have been only wryly amused by the incongruous details that so pained Gorky.

Chekhov's impact on the literatures of the world began while he was still alive, even though he himself could not imagine that anyone in England would ever want to read one of his stories or that it would be possible to play *The Cherry Orchard* in Paris. That influence surges and ebbs periodically, and it has not yet reached anything resembling a stable level. Too many people see too many things in him. Could Katherine Mansfield, who once compared "The Steppe" to *The Iliad,* have seen the same things in Chekhov as did Mayakovsky? Could François Mauriac have loved the same Chekhov as does Vladimir Nabokov, whose view of Russian literary history in his novel *The Gift* so startlingly resembles that of Chekhov's letters and who recently confessed that "it is *his* works which I would take on a trip to another planet"? Did the Living Theater activists who, as Robert Brustein told us in "A Night at the Symposium," shouted obscenities at the mention of Chekhov's name truly hate him? Did they even know who he was? Could the judge who presided over the trial of Andrei Sinyavsky in 1966 and who admitted as evidence of Sinyavsky's anti-Soviet attitude a disrespectful mention of Chekhov in one of his essays really have read and understood Chekhov?

The multiplicity of views and reactions is to be expected. One of the most startling responses to Chekhov comes from a writer who was Chekhov's diametrical opposite on almost any artistic, emotional and human level. After seeing the Moscow Art Theater perform *Three Sisters,* Alexander Blok wrote an ecstatic and penitent letter to his mother in which he swore that the play made him revise many of his views and attitudes: "We are all unfortunate that our native land prepared for us this soil, fertile in anger and mutual quarrels. All of us live behind Chinese walls, half despising each other, while our sole mutual enemy—Russian state institutions, church institutions, gin mills, fiscal and government officials—do not show their face but sic us on each other.

"I shall strive with all my strength to forget all Russian politics, all Russian amateurishness, all this morass, in order to become a human being and not a machine for manufacturing anger and hatred."

No, Blok was not promising to become apolitical and uninvolved. He was merely reminding himself, under the impact of seeing Chekhov's play, of the essence of his own humanity, which the political passions of a polarized society tend to obscure and obliterate. This reaction to *Three Sisters* would have pleased Chekhov; but until about ten years ago it would have seemed incomprehensible to any Western reader or admirer of Chekhov. Now, however, those who have lived through these past ten years in the West should have no trouble understanding what Blok was talking about. This is significant. With his unbelievably sensitive antennae Blok caught the very gist of Chekhov's message. Most of his countrymen, of whatever persuasion, did not. It is now our turn. We are aware of Chekhov's miraculous art. It would be a tragedy if we too failed to become attuned to the lucid humanity and reasoned compassion which this art embodies.

BIBLIOGRAPHY OF PRINCIPAL SOURCES USED IN THE COMMENTARY

I. LETTERS TO CHEKHOV

Alexander Chekhov. *Letters to A. P. Chekhov from His Brother Alexander Chekhov*. I. K. Luppol, ed. Moscow, 1939.

Maria Chekhova. *Letters to My Brother A. P. Chekhov*. Moscow, 1954.

The Correspondence of Anton Chekhov and Olga Knipper. 2 volumes published out of projected 3. A. B. Derman, ed. Moscow, 1936.

The correspondence of Maria Chekhova and Olga Knipper in *The Hostess of the Chekhov House*. S. N. Bragin, ed. Simferopol, 1969.

Sergei Diaghilev. Letters to Chekhov in *From A. P. Chekhov's Archive*. Moscow, 1960.

Maxim Gorky. Letters to Chekhov in Volume 28 of his *Collected Works*. Moscow, 1954.

Vera Kommissarzhevskaya. Letters to Chekhov in *Vera Kommissarzhevskaya. Letters, Memoirs About Her, Biographical Materials*. A. Altschuller and Yu. Rybakova, eds. Leningrad and Moscow, 1964.

Nikodim Kondakov. Letters to Chekhov in *Bulletin of the Language and Literature Section* of the *U.S.S.R. Academy of Sciences Publications*, Volume 19, Number 1, Moscow, 1960.

Vladimir Korolenko. Letters to Chekhov in Volume 10 of his *Collected Works*. Moscow, 1956.

Literary Heritage. Volume 68. Moscow, 1960. This contains letters to Chekhov from Alexei Pleshcheyev, Alexander Kuprin, Ivan Bunin, and Vsevolod Meyerhold, and the articles "Letters to Chekhov About the Student Movement of 1899–1902" by A. N. Dubovnikov and "Chekhov in the Letters of His Brother Mikhail" by E. Z. Balabanovich.

Vladimir Nemirovich-Danchenko, Konstantin Stanislavsky and Maria Lilina.

Letters to Chekhov in *Moscow Art Theater Yearbook*, 1944 (published in 1946), Volume 1.

II. PERSONAL JOURNALS AND DIARIES

Literary Heritage, Volume 68, which contains excerpts from the journals and diaries of Ivan Shcheglov, Vladimir Tikhonov, Nikolai Leykin, Vladimir Telyakovsky, Viktor Mirolyubov and Vladimir Korolenko.

Alexei Suvorin. *Journals*. Moscow-Petrograd, 1923.

III. MEMOIRS

Mikhail Chekhov. *Around Chekhov. Encounters and Impressions*. Moscow, 1960.

Maria Chekhova. *Out of the Distant Past* (in collaboration with N. A. Sysoyev). Moscow, 1960.

Chekhov as Remembered by His Contemporaries. Moscow, 1960, which contains the memoirs of Alexander Chekhov, Mikhail Chekhov, Viktor Simov, Vladimir Gilyarovsky, Vladimir Korolenko, Ilya Repin, Alexander Lazarev-Gruzinsky, Vyacheslav Fausek, Lydia Avilova, Vladimir Ladyzhensky, Ignaty Potapenko, Sergei Semyonov, Konstantin Stanislavsky, Vladimir Nemirovich-Danchenko, Vasily Luzhsky, Vasily Kachalov, Maxim Kovalevsky, Father Sergius Shchukin, Lev Shapovalov, Nikolai Teleshov, Maxim Gorky, Ivan Bunin, Alexander Kuprin, Sergei Yelpatyevsky, Ivan Novikov, Isaak Altschuller, Mikhail Pervukhin, Mikhail Chlenov, Alexander Serebrov, Nikolai Garin, Grigory Rossolimo, Vikenty Veresayev, Nikolai Panov and Olga Knipper.

Zinaida Gippius. *Living Portraits*. Munich, 1971 (reprint of Prague, 1925, edition).

Olga Knipper. "Memoirs," in *Moscow Art Theater Yearbook*, 1949–50 (published in 1952).

Anatoly Koni. *Memoirs About Writers*. Leningrad, 1954.

Literary Heritage, Volume 68, which contains a number of additional memoirs, among them those of Nikolai Chekhov, Konstantin Korovin, Maria Zankovetskaya, Alexandra Khotyaintseva, Yekaterina Peshkova (Gorky's first wife), Alexei Sergeyenko (Pyotr Sergeyenko's son), Lydia Fyodorova (Alexander Fyodorov's wife), Ivan Bunin and Isaak Altschuller.

Vladimir Nemirovich-Danchenko. *Out of the Past*. [n.p.], 1936.

Alexander Serebrov. *Time and People*. Moscow, 1960.

Tatyana Shchepkina-Kupernik. "About Chekhov," in *Selected Works*. Moscow, 1954.

Konstantin Stanislavsky. *My Life in Art*. Moscow, 1962.

IV. BIOGRAPHICAL SOURCES

Mikhail Chekhov. The six biographical essays in Maria Chekhova's six-volume edition of Chekhov's letters. Moscow, 1912–16.

A *Chronicle of Maxim Gorky's Life and Work,* Volume 1 (1868–1907). Klavdia Muratova, ed. Moscow, 1958.

Nina Gitovich. A *Chronicle of Chekhov's Life and Work* (a compilation of biographical materials arranged chronologically, day by day). Moscow, 1955.

Nikolai Gusev. A *Chronicle of Lev Tolstoy's Life and Work, 1891–1910.* Moscow, 1960.

INDEX

(Page numbers in *italics* indicate detailed identification or discussion in the text or the commentary)

Simon Karlinsky has taught courses on Pushkin, Gogol, Chekhov, Russian poetry and Russian drama at Berkeley and Harvard. He is the author of a critical biography of the poet Marina Cvetaeva (or Tsvetaeva); his essays, articles and reviews have appeared in, among others, *California Slavic Studies, The New Yorker, The Nation, The New Review, TriQuarterly, Slavic Review, Studies in Romanticism,* and *The New York Times Book Review*. He is currently preparing a new course on Tolstoy, completing the first volume of a history of Russian drama as literature and gathering materials for a study of the Russian émigré poet Boris Poplavsky.

Michael Henry Heim has lectured on Russian drama, Russian intellectual history, and eighteenth-century Russian literature at the University of Wisconsin in Madison, and has recently begun teaching Czech language and literature at UCLA. He is at present translating a collection of stories by Bohumil Hrabal, one of the foremost contemporary Czech writers, and working on a study of an important mid-nineteenth-century Czech poet and thinker, Karel Havlíček Borovsky.

73 74 75 10 9 8 7 6 5 4 3 2 1